Islanders in the Stream

Islanders in the Stream

A History of the Bahamian People

VOLUME ONE

From Aboriginal Times to
the End of Slavery

MICHAEL CRATON AND

GAIL SAUNDERS

The University of Georgia Press
Athens and London

University of Georgia Press paperback edition, 1999
© 1992 by The University of Georgia Press
Athens, Georgia 30602
All rights reserved

Set in Palatino by Tseng Information Systems
Printed and bound by Maple-Vail

The paper in this book meets the guidelines for
permanence and durability of the Committee on
Production Guidelines for Book Longevity of
the Council on Library Resources.

Printed in the United States of America

08   09   10   11   12   13   P   7   6   5   4   3

The Library of Congress has cataloged the hardcover
edition of this book as follows:

Library of Congress Cataloging-in-Publication Data

Craton, Michael.
Islanders in the stream : a history of the Bahamian
people / Michael Craton and Gail Saunders.
2 v. : ill., maps ; 25 cm.
Includes bibliographical references and index.
Contents: v. 1. From aboriginal times to the end
of slavery — v. 2. From the ending of slavery to
the twenty-first century.
ISBN 0-8203-1382-3 (v. 1 : alk. paper) —
ISBN 0-8203-1926-0 (v. 2 : alk paper)
1. Bahamas—History. 2. National characteristics,
Bahamian. I. Saunders, Gail. II. Title.
F1656 .C72 1992
972.96—dc20   91-21737

Paperback ISBN-13: 978-0-8203-2122-6
ISBN-10: 0-8203-2122-2

British Library Cataloging-in-Publication Data available

Contents

Maps and Figures

Tables

Preface

THIS BOOK, with its sequel volume, is the culmination of both authors' involvement in the Bahamas and its history over nearly thirty-five years. Since the mid-1950s, when Michael Craton came from England to teach at the Government High School in Nassau and Gail Saunders was a student at nearby Queen's College, much radical change has occurred. Most important, the Bahamas has been transformed from a British colony under the control of an oligarchic white minority to a proudly independent nation led by a party representing the black majority. As a result of coincidental sociopolitical processes throughout the globe, the study of history too has fundamentally altered, with a far greater emphasis now placed on social history and the lives of ordinary people than on economic trends, political events, and the role of elites. Third, as a result of their commitment to the Bahamas and its people and in response to the transformation of the profession of history—as well as the mere process of maturation—the authors too have changed.

Most relevant to the present work, though, is the fact that it is only over the last thirty-five years that the Bahamas and its people have moved toward having a proper history of their own—a process in which both collaborators have been more closely involved than other historians. In the 1950s virtually all the history taught in Bahamian high schools was that of Britain and the British Empire, on the principles (expressed by the first black director of education as late as 1965) that not only was the British culture dominant, but Britain's political system was an ideal that the Bahamas should be encouraged to emulate, along the evolutionary lines followed by the more "advanced" and "enlightened" components of the British Empire. Bahamian history in the schools was consigned to the same limbo as that occupied by Caribbean and African history, or indeed all history outside the British orbit. Nor was there an adequate comprehensive history of the islands available for intelligent adults eager to repair the deficiencies of their schooling. Accounts of Bahamian history were nonscholarly, skimpy, and slanted, with the few more ambitious attempts seemingly jinxed.[1]

To some degree, the gap was filled by Michael Craton's *A History of the Bahamas*, first published by Collins in 1962, during the hiatus between the author's six years of high school teaching in Nassau and graduate studies leading to a Canadian university career. This book has been often reprinted over the years and was substantially revised and expanded for a third edition in 1986. But it remains essentially an old-fashioned narrative account, concentrating on political history, events, and the activities of the elite. It did, however, have an important influence on Gail Saunders, who, as a first-year student at Newcastle-upon-Tyne University eager to study both Caribbean and Bahamian history, remembers reading the book in the second-floor research room of the Southern Public Library in Nassau and having a long conversation with the author about Bahamian history. In particular, she was struck by Craton's comment that the Bahamas suffered from having no archives department, and by a feeling that much more needed to be known about Bahamian slavery—the latter idea being reinforced in talks with Gillian Bain, Craton's successor at GHS, whose own writing of a more socially oriented history was cruelly cut short by a stroke.

As a result, in her final year at Newcastle, Gail Saunders chose to write a short dissertation entitled "The Abolition and Amelioration of Slavery in the Bahamas" under the direction of the distinguished historian of the West Indies, Professor W. L. Burn. Subsequently, after a year as Gillian Bain's replacement at GHS, Saunders was recruited by the new Bahamian Ministry of Education to assist in the establishment of an archives section, later to become the Department of Archives, of which she has been in charge since 1971, two years before Bahamian independence. During this period she followed her interest in Bahamian slavery to complete a Master of Philosophy dissertation for the University of the West Indies under the direction of Professor Barry Higman. Out of this 1978 dissertation in due course came the book *Slavery in the Bahamas, 1648–1838*, privately published in 1985.

Michael Craton, meanwhile, after nearly twenty years researching and writing on Jamaica, the general history of the Caribbean, and the history of slavery, had come full circle back to the Bahamas. While pursuing more detailed scholarly research there, he became convinced of the need for a new, social history, not only to take advantage of the many advances in the approaches and techniques generally termed the New Social History, but also to place the archipelago and its people more clearly in their regional contexts, to provide a much-needed sense of identity for the new nation, and, if possible, to serve as a model for histories of similar small former British colonies in the region.

The interests of the Canadian academic and the Bahamian archivist quite literally converged in the period 1981–85, during which Gail Saunders obtained leave from the Bahamas government for an academic year in order to undertake the course work for a doctorate at Waterloo under the supervision of Michael Craton. Craton obtained a generous three-year research grant from the Social Science and Humanities Research Council of Canada, and the two scholars made a formal agreement to collaborate in writing a social history of the Bahamas. The subject chosen for Saunders's dissertation, completed in 1985, was "The Social History of the Bahamas, 1890–1953," a study running to almost six hundred pages and destined to provide the basis for the middle section of the authors' history of the Bahamas after slavery, which is in progress.

The working title for the entire joint enterprise was the Afro-Bahamian proverb "Time Longer dan Rope." This name (eventually rejected as much for its obscurity as because it had been used before) was intended to evoke the long struggle of the ordinary Bahamian people for identity and equality in the face of the chafing bonds of oppression. But it might have stood also for the protracted hardships of bringing the project itself to fruition. As often happens, it was the earliest stages of planning and discovery that were the most exciting; the subsequent writing and editing have been mainly slog.

For four months in the spring and summer of 1983, Craton's young family and three members of his senior seminar—Jim Martens, Christopher Egoff, and Godwin Friday—took over the large house belonging to Anatol Rodgers (another former teacher at GHS) in Dean's Lane, Nassau, close to historic Fort Charlotte and that sublime view over the western reaches of Nassau's harbor which inspired the greatest of all American watercolorists, Winslow Homer.

> Bliss was it in that dawn to be alive,
> But to be young was very heaven!

Each weekday morning, in Anatol's somewhat temperamental Toyota, the three- or four-man task force would descend upon the Bahamian Archives on Mackey Street for a seven-hour assault on the microfilms, ledgers, and files—the governors' correspondence, newspapers, assembly and council minutes, manuscript laws, deeds, and wills—broken only by a half hour snatched for a sandwich and Coke at the Health

Food and Deli at the foot of the Paradise Island Bridge. Each evening over Pat Craton's West Indian dinners the day's discoveries were shared and evaluated in an informal seminar, and each week at a more formal session on Anatol's upstairs porch, shared by Gail Saunders, progress was charted and research strategies planned, while Nassau's flamboyant sunset flared and faded in the west.

We will always be grateful for the unstinting work of our three graduate researchers of 1983, the sense they conveyed of a shared adventure, and the fact that there was never a hint of mutiny even when their supervisor left them at the Archives and took off by plane or boat to the Family Islands, sometimes with his own family, sometimes alone. But over a far longer period—many more trips to the Bahamian and other archives, and more than five years of writing—we have accumulated debts to a host of other individuals and institutions, without whom this book would never have been completed. Top of the list must come the staff of the Bahamas Department of Archives, especially Paulene Bastian Smith, Sherriley Strachan, Patrice Williams, Jolton Johnson, David Wood, and Tony Aarons, to whom must be added the staff and trustees of the Nassau Public Library and the staffs of the Bahamas Department of Lands and Surveys, Public Registry, House of Assembly, Senate, Supreme Court, and all other Bahamas government departments whose records we have used. Besides this we gratefully acknowledge the facilities provided in London by the Public Record Office, British Library, Royal Commonwealth Society, Commonwealth Institute, and West India Committee, and by the Institutes of Commonwealth Studies and Historical Research and the Senate House Library of London University.

Innumerable Bahamians, from all walks of life and most of the islands, have given us interviews, information, advice, and support, and though it may be invidious to single out some from the many, the following particularly come to mind: Cecil V. Bethel, Sr., Keva Bethel, Ruth Bowe-Darville, Holly Brown, Howland Bottomley, Edwina Burrows, Jenny Cancino, Delmore Cartwright, James Deveaux, the late Gurth Duncombe, Rowena Eldon, Arthur Fernandez, Ileana Esfakis, Kendal and Patsy Isaacs, Geoffrey Johnstone, Percy Hanna, the late Alphonso Blake Higgs, Henry Lee, Lorraine Lightbourn, Fr. Irwin McSweeney, Brent Malone, Leila Mitchell-Greene, Keith and Sara Parker, Kermit Rolle, Oris Russell, George and Alison Shilling, Luther E. Smith, Sir Henry M. Taylor, Margaret Thomas, Jeanne Thompson, Maxwell J. Thompson, and Penny Turtle.

An even longer list could be made of academic mentors and colleagues who have provided inspiration, interpretations, or advice, either for the present work or for earlier efforts which have become components of it. Some of them are acknowledged in appropriate endnotes, but others are part of that long-suffering angelic host (almost all the scholars we have encountered or read) whose contribution has been subliminal and cumulative, and remains unnoted. We would, however, like to thank in particular the growing number of fellow toilers in the vineyard of Bahamian studies—all of whom have been admirably professional in sharing their work and thoughts: Haziel Albury, the late Paul Albury, Peter J. Barratt, the late E. Clement Bethel, David Campbell, Antonio Canzoneri, Phillip Cash, J. Barry Coleman, Dean Collinwood, Peter Dalleo, Sandra Dean-Patterson, Steve Dodge, D. Reber Dunkel, Geoffrey Dunlop, Ruth Durlacher-Wolper, Cleveland Eneas, Godwin Friday, Donald and Kathy Gerace, Julian Granberry, Ruth S. Hamilton, Mrs. Leslie Higgs, Charles Hoffman Jr. and Nancy W. Hoffman, John Holm, Colin A. Hughes, William Keegan, Howard Johnson, Alan LaFlamme, Alton Lowe, John McCartney, Timothy McCartney, Dawn Marshall, Stephen W. Mitchell, Sandra Riley, Richard Rose, Sieghbert Russell, Joel Savashinsky, William H. Sears, Shaun Sullivan, Michael Symonette, John Trainor, Colbert Williams, Patrice Williams, John Winter.

Besides these, we gratefully acknowledge the help of colleagues in the Association of Caribbean Historians or the Universities of the West Indies and Waterloo, and academic friends, fellow conferees, and friendly commentators, particularly Bridget Brereton, Nigel Bolland, Hilary Beckles, Edward Cox, Richard S. Dunn, Stanley Engerman, Woodville Marshall, Philip Morgan, Robert Paquette, Arnold Sio, Mary Turner, James Walker, and James Walvin, as well as the several other anonymous scholars who read and usefully commented on the manuscript at different stages. For their contribution to the often unsung work of preparing the manuscript for the press, we specially thank Gail Heideman for her exemplary typing, David Wood, Lorenzo Lockhart, and Peter Ramsay for many of the photographs, Tim Farrell for help with the tables and figures, and Barry Leverly of the Cartograph Centre, University of Waterloo, for the maps.

Chief among supporting institutions that must be thanked are the collaborators' employers, the Bahamas government and the University of Waterloo, both of which provided paid leave at critical junctures. Besides the original three-year grant, the Canadian Social Sciences and Humanities Research Council has awarded several smaller travel and research subsidies, and the Rockefeller Foundation granted a memorable month at the Villa Serbelloni on the shores of Lake Como in 1987 for the completion of the manuscript of this volume and the start of a projected second volume. The organizers of several conferences and the editors of various journals (formally acknowledged in the endnotes) are to be thanked in general for valuable opportunities to air and give a foretaste of sections of the work while in progress.

Last because not least, we wish to thank the family members and close friends who have given us the support and encouragement without which no such work as this could ever come to fruition. Most directly, these include Gail Saunders's parents, E. Basil North and the late Audrey V. North; her mother-in-law, Keddie Saunders; both authors' brothers and sisters and their spouses, Terry and Bunny North, Barbara Craton-Toll, Margaret and René Cobb, David and Sherry Craton; and their own spouses, Winston V. Saunders and Patricia H. Craton. It is properly to these persons—the authors' essential begetters and sustainers—even more than to the admirable Islanders in the Stream who are the subjects of our study, that the work should ultimately be dedicated.

Introduction

A COMMON ENVIRONMENT, a common culture, and a common history are what give a people a sense of their national identity. Yet distancing is often necessary to lend perspective, especially to those living on small islands or an archipelago like the Bahamas. Divided internally, subtly by insular variations, or more severely through racial differences and class divisions, such a people recognizes its distinct identity best when it comes into contact with other peoples or is able to look back on its homeland, with a catalytic nostalgia, from a foreign country. This has often been noted by Bahamians abroad. At the level of a jest it is said that one has to go to London, New York, or Toronto to hear the most intimate secrets of what's happening in Nassau. But the joke illustrates a deeper reality. For example, black and white Bahamian student lawyers meeting by chance in London's Inns of Court and rejoicing in a familiar accent, are soon swapping news and reminiscences of home, admitting a longing for the more congenial climate, the incomparable seas, sands, and skies of their native land, a craving for conch salad, peas-and-rice, and guava duff, and a yearning for the shared experiences of Family Island Regatta, Junkanoo, and Goombay music. Only after parting does it suddenly occur to both that an identity and intimacy had been demonstrated on a foreign soil that would have been impossible in the artificially tighter social conditions actually found at home.

All persons born and bred in the Bahamas have an instinctive feeling that they share a unique heritage with all other Bahamians, though few can articulate this identity, and, sadly, its very nature is in danger of distortion or dilution through divisive politics, the invasive cultures of more dominant neighbors, and the dull homogenization of the shrinking modern world. It is not just our avocation as historians that makes us believe that what Bahamians need is an authentic social history, one that will search, feel, and declare the true bedrock, roots, and groundswell of their special identity, and thus help to protect it for the future.

Naturally, the political party that organized the black majority and led it proudly into independence feels that it has earned the right to rewrite a history largely distorted in the past. It is not easy to recognize the larger extraneous forces that have been in play, any more than it is to acknowledge the danger of substituting one official mythology for another. In the largest context, the recent history of the Bahamas and its people has been the product of global changes that have included almost universal decolonization, a surge in political power for the nonwhite peoples of the world, and many features conveniently bagged together as Modernization, not many of them altogether advantageous. Too narrow a viewpoint on the part of Bahamian actors in the process may lead them to ignore manifest dangers: that the ending of British imperialism may be followed by the more swamping cultural hegemony of the United States; that the triumph of Black Power may lead to writing the former white master-class and their descendants quite out of Bahamian history; and that the delusive promises of progress and unrecognized facts of dependency (most notably, involving the monoeconomy of tourism) will intensify the tendencies that have, for example, concentrated 60 percent of the Bahamian population in the twelfth largest of fifty sizable islands and made a country with perhaps five cultivable acres for every member of its population actually import over 90 percent of the foodstuffs consumed.

The rapidity and complexity of recent political and social change have led to further contradictions and confusions. Even the most educated Bahamians, of whatever color, remain ambivalent about the relative roles of Europe and Africa (not to mention Amerindia) in their social history, and are not quite sure how the Bahamas and its people fit in the regional Caribbean context. Just as some Bahamians deny, or at least decry, the lasting British influences on culture and institutions, others can still be found who downplay the importance of the African heritage and deplore any attempt to add more information about Africa and its history to school curricula. Many Bahamians now accept the undeniable parallels and direct connections between the Bahamas and the Caribbean proper, but this does not prevent at least as many continuing to resent the intrusion of Caribbean cultural influences and the migration into their country of persons from the British Commonwealth Caribbean, who are regarded as both arrogant and opportunistic. The cultural, demographic, and economic gulf between the Bahamas and Spanish-speaking, predominantly "Caucasian," and now Communist Cuba has a long history and a realistic modern political rationale. But the open antagonism and crude contempt

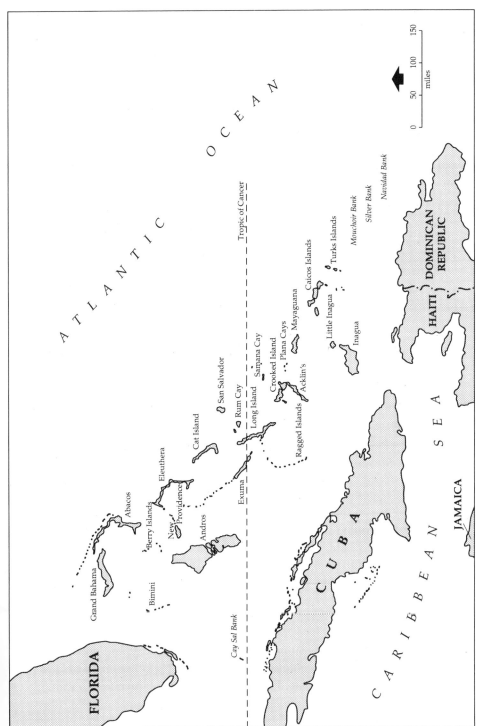

Map 1. Bahamas archipelago

of nearly all Bahamians for Haiti and its people—though explicable on the grounds of the fear of uncontrolled illegal migration—is scarcely a seemly attitude from one of the youngest purportedly "black" nations toward the oldest independent black republic in the world.

The problems of consciousness mentioned above concern mainly the second volume of this work, which covers the nineteenth century after the ending of formal slavery and all but that fragment that is still left of the twentieth century. The present volume, telling the story of all the people who lived in the Bahamas down to 1838, has quite enough concerns and problems of its own. The first of these is the question of continuity—or rather, discontinuities—particularly concerning the aboriginal Lucayans, who had disappeared from the Bahamas almost a century and a half before the English established a permanent settlement. To what extent can these people be regarded as similarly Bahamian when not lineally related to later inhabitants? As is shown in the first of the three parts of this volume, this problem is solved by stressing the common environmental and ecological factors that encouraged migrants from South America by way of the Antilles and from Europe, partly by way of Bermuda and the American mainland, to forge distinctively Bahamian creole variants of their original cultures.

A similar if lesser problem faces the interpretation of the flooding into the Bahamas of the American Loyalists and their slaves after 1783, an event which essentially forms the break between part 2 and part 3. It was in many respects a vital qualitative as well as quantitative change but has perhaps been exaggerated by those who trace their genealogy and cultural roots to the Loyalists rather than to the earlier settlers. The present work stresses the continuities, in the institution of slavery and the importance of the maritime lifestyle, and concludes that the Loyalists were as much transformed by the Bahamas as vice versa. By entitling part 3 "Loyalist Slavery" and concentrating on the lives of the black majority in due proportion, we also hope to convey the overall purpose of the book: to give recognition to ordinary Bahamians and to tell the story of their long struggle for self-realization against those same elites to whom history has hitherto belonged.

Such an ascription to the New Social History, which also involves as a matter of course a dedication to the multidisciplinary and cliometric techniques which have revolutionized the discipline of history over the last half century, has presented innumerable further difficulties in translating source materials into finished text. Each of the three parts of this volume necessarily relies on such different sources that a perfect continuity of method has proved impossible. When treating the Lucayans the sources are basically three: the evidence of archeology, of early European commentators, and of modern ethnologists. When dealing with the early settlers, one has to rely very largely on documentary sources emanating from the governing elite, provided for, and mainly stored in, the imperial metropole—most notably the materials down to 1738 listed and excerpted in the Calendar of State Papers Colonial, and the magnificent run of governors' correspondence found in the C.O. 23 series at the Public Record Office in London (which last, fortunately, are also to be found on microfilm in the Bahamas Archives). Only for the third part, examining the Loyalists and their slaves, can one also call upon voluminous local records, letters, journals, and sensitive travelers' accounts, as well as those types of meticulous census materials indispensable for revealing the lives and lifestyles of ordinary persons previously invisible. Accordingly, though we have striven for continuity of method as well as theme and have made many speculative extrapolations, we must beg indulgence for those sections of our work that inescapably fall short of our own ideals.

Having made this apology, however, we would also like to state that we find it impossible to divorce social history absolutely from the history of events or the operation of politics and economics, and to make it clear that we are writing a chronological narrative rather than strictly topical history. In principle, we have rejected the history of successive governors and other prominent individuals, partisan squabbles, wars, and laws, in favor of general social themes, a description of the lives and social interrelationships of all the people living in the Bahamas, and a study of social continuities. But it is impossible, for example, totally to ignore a governor who may have cleared out the pirates or the Spaniards, or forced through certain laws, and by so doing fundamentally altered the people's lives, just as it would be wrong completely to ignore wars that brought foreign invasion, slaughter, deportation, temporary fortune in the form of privateering, or more lasting social change through a doubling of the population and a trebling of the number of slaves. Likewise, it would be reprehensible to neglect political conflicts that illuminate fundamental social divisions, or the details of laws aimed at social control and having important social consequences; or to ignore any individuals who might have had an important general influence or who illustrated general social types.

Besides this, it is for the very reason that we believe in the delineation of themes and continuities that we are dedicated to the principle that our history should be essentially chronological. The history of a people, whether or not strictly genealogical, depends on both demographic and cultural evolution and on the steady accretion of both abstract tradition and material remains. Its depiction loses a vital dimension—is no more than a jumble of snapshots—unless firmly placed in sequence and dated. Put another way, the whole cloth of history is both synchronic weft and diachronic warp. The continuous themes, the warps, which we recognize in Bahamian social history would make no sense unless measured against the shuttling weft of passing time.

The major themes that we have traced in the following pages include the following: the adaptation of migrant peoples (first from South America and the Antilles, then from Europe, Africa, and North America) to a difficult marine environment; the ubiquity of the sea and its hugely greater determining importance when compared with the land and its meager resources; the tribulations and benefits of existence on the margins of a larger world; the ability to endure hard times, naturally coupled with an eagerness to seize fleeting chances of profit; the evolution of harsh racial and social divisions despite interdependence, shared fortunes, and a largely common culture; the long-drawn struggle of the oppressed majority to find freedom and a life of their own; and finally, what well may be taken as the prevailing theme and main justification for the entire project, the search for a national identity.

Overall, as the book's title is intended to indicate, what we tell is the story of a special people (or sequence of peoples) who have been shaped by the struggle for existence in a particular scatter of not very fertile islands, situated, as it were, on a fold in the map of the world. Located on the fringes both of the Caribbean and the North American mainland, islands and inhabitants have nonetheless been influenced by the ocean currents and related winds that flow steadily through and over the Bahamian archipelago—the fierce ocean river called the Gulf Stream which debouches from the Caribbean through the Florida Strait, the far wider and gentler drift flowing westward throughout the archipelago, and its associated almost constant current of air called the northeast trades. Over the period covered by this volume, these elemental flows brought to the Bahamian islands their original Amerindian inhabitants and European invaders, white settlers and black African slaves, as well as the trade which, if mainly destined for others, provided tenuous links with the larger world, and occasional plunder. In senses both figurative and literal, the Bahamian people of whom we write—ancient Lucayans, early settlers, American Loyalists, Afro-Bahamian slaves, and modern Bahamians alike—have always been, and remain, quintessential Islanders in (or athwart) the Stream.

I

Bahamian Genesis: The Lucayan Arawaks, A.D. 500–1525

Preceding page: Arawak women preparing flour, griddle cakes, and cassareep
(from Benzoni's *Historia del Mundo Nuovo,* 1563)

~ *1* ~

The Broken Water-Gourd: The Original People and Their Environment

A PEOPLE DEFINES ITSELF as much by its myths as by its material relics and recorded doings. The Lucayans, the first Bahamians of whom we have a record, shared in the general fund of mythic lore of the Arawak people from whom they sprang.[1] According to the account that the Tainan Arawaks of Hispaniola gave to the Spaniards, the entire universe originally existed in darkness, locked in the solid earth. Over all brooded a mighty spirit with a portentous name, Jocchu Vague Maorocon, sometimes called, more simply, Yocahú. Immortal and invisible like the Christian God, Yocahú was not quite as omnipotent, for he shared his power with his mother, usually known as Atabeyra, but also called Mamona, Iella, Guicarapita, or Guimoza. He also had a maternal uncle, called Guaca.[2]

These deities held the whole world in thrall, but one day while the guardians slept, sun, moon, and stars escaped from one cave, mankind from another. For the first mortals the sight of the sun was taboo, and those who gazed upon it were turned into animals, birds, and trees, thus filling the land with living things. The leaders of the survivors were legendary giants, either Ulysses-like travelers or sedentary kings. One hero, called Guaguiona, carried off the women and children to distant lands. The men left behind, needing a substitute for the women, found sexless creatures hidden in a tree and had woodpeckers provide them with female genitalia. Meanwhile, at Guanain the abducted children shriveled into frogs and lizards for want of food, while at Matinino, Guaguiona paid for his sexual adventures by inventing venereal disease. Some time later, another traveler called Caracaracol (the Scaly One) was credited with bringing back both manioc and tobacco, the staple food and holy herb.

Thus a hierarchy of gods, hero-leaders, and ordinary mortals existed from the beginning. The sequence of events described is also interesting, perhaps significant. That mankind was coeval with the celestial bodies was not all that remarkable, for how could sun, moon, and stars exist without men to observe them? But men were created before all living things, a reversal of the Darwinian theory of evolution. Most curious of all—and completely reversing the sequence of the Judaeo-Christian Genesis—the creation of the sea and its denizens came very late in the process (though presumably before the travels of Guaguiona and Caracaracol). As Peter Martyr, the Spanish court chronicler, recounted the story,

> There formerly lived in the island a powerful chief named Jaia who buried his only son in a gourd. Several months later, distracted by the loss of his son, Jaia revisited the gourd. He prised it open and out of it he beheld great whales and marine monsters of gigantic size come forth. Thus he reported to some of his neighbours that the sea was contained in that gourd. Upon hearing this story, four brothers born at a birth and who had lost their mother when they were born sought to obtain possession of the gourd for the sake of the fish. But Jaia, who often visited the mortal remains of his son, arrived when the brothers held the gourd in their hands. Frightened at being thus taken in the act both of sacrilege and robbery, they dropped the gourd, which broke, and took flight. From the broken gourd the sea rushed forth; the valley was filled, the immense plain which formed the universe was flooded, and only the mountains raised their heads above the water, forming the islands, several of which still exist today.[3]

IN DESCRIBING THE ORIGINS of the Bahamas and its people we can share none of the certainty and little of the poetry of the aboriginals who told (or sang) their genesis myths to the Spanish friars. Yet scientific explanations of geological origins do suggest curious, and surely coincidental, parallels with Arawak legends. Two hundred million years ago, in the Age of Reptiles, all modern landmasses were united in one supercontinent which geologists have called Pangaea. Volcanic activity inexorably split Pangaea apart to form the four modern continents—the "four brothers born at a birth . . . who had lost their mother when they were born"—and the sea flowed through the rifts to redistribute the oceans, with their fringing shoals and chains of islands once mountain peaks.[4]

The Bahamian archipelago is basically a fretted platform of oolitic limestone on the northern fringe of the islands of the Greater Antilles, forming the western third of the immense arc of outer islands connecting South with North America. The platform itself was formed over the millions of years during which the continents were stretched apart, enlarging the Atlantic Ocean to its present size. Untold trillions of marine organisms lived and died in the warm shallow waters, their shells and skeletons building up a deposit of almost pure calcium carbonate. This mass gradually sank under its own weight, until today it has been measured (at Cay Sal Bank) to be at least nineteen thousand feet thick. This accounts for the almost continuous bank of barely submerged limestone extending from north of Grand Bahama to the Crooked Island Passage. The smaller discontinuous banks and islands to eastward are thought to have been formed rather differently. Crooked Island and Acklin's, Mayaguana, Inagua, the Turks and Caicos Islands, and the Silver, Mouchoir, and Navidad banks may be only superficially similar to the rest of the archipelago, with layers of oolitic limestone capping the igneous rocks of former volcanoes.

Despite being predominantly shallow (one explanation of the islands' modern name, from the Spanish *baja mar*), the waters of the Bahamas are split by several ocean canyons, such as that which divides the Great from the Little Bahama Bank, and the Tongue of the Ocean which branches from it, curling round New Providence Island and licking the eastern reefs of Andros. Some geologists explain these as the remnants of huge river valleys gouged on the surface of the original continent, while others see them as tectonic fissures formed during the stretching and splitting process—the rifts and cracks in the gourd thrown down by the four brothers at the approach of Jaia in the Arawak myth.

For an archipelago totaling less than six thousand square miles of land set in an ocean shelf at least one hundred thousand square miles in extent, the sea, naturally, is the enveloping element. There are few spots in the Bahamas more than a couple of miles from the open ocean or saltwater creeks, and nearly all locations suitable for settlement are within sight, sound, and smell of the sea. The islands themselves scarcely rise above the waters, the areas of tidal flats and mangrove "swash" making it sometimes difficult to determine quite where land ends and sea begins. The sea, moreover, is more fertile and far more spectacular than the land. Besides a plenitude of fishes, mollusks, seals, and turtles, and the sea grasses, algae, and plankton on which they feed, the warm and shallow waters encourage a rich and continuous growth of every kind of coral. Today a skindiver's paradise, Bahamian waters are a living laboratory of coral formation, with classic examples of atolls and barrier reefs, and some of the most spectacular ocean holes and subterranean caves in the world.[5] Seen from above the surface, the waters are equally splendid:

a riotous palette, shading from the cobalt of ocean deeps through skeins of turquoise and emerald over banks, splotched with the purple of coral outcrops, to the yellow, white, and even pink of sands under the thinner panes of crystal water.

The grays, greens, and muddy reds of rock, scrub, and ponds are no match for the sea as spectacle, though they are shaped by and of it. Except where waves have broken through offshore reefs to carve low cliffs of jagged limestone, island shores are normally fringed by banks of coralline sand, behind which are narrow lagoons or troughs of a sandy white soil. This is ideal for growing root crops because of its porosity and the presence of "lenses" of fresh water on top of the underlying salt. Further inland, along the islands' axes, are the ridges of low hills— scarcely anywhere rising over 150 feet—which are the weathered and honeycombed relics of windblown dunes of the Pleistocene era, up to a million years ago. In between these bony ridges can be found valleys of potholed rock with meager pockets of three types of soil: the Bahama black loam which when found in sufficient quantity is called "provision soil," the red loam commonly called "pineapple soil," and the thin Bahamian marl formed from the direct breakdown of limestone in areas of permanent wetness.[6] Just as frequently, the low limestone ridges are interspersed with shallow, irregular lakes of brackish water, some almost choked with an odorous red mud and most rising or falling a foot or so with the ocean tide.

The present Bahama Islands can be described as the creation of long-, short-, and medium-term maritime forces, in geomorphological counterpoint. The colossal base on which the islands rest was laid down by the sea over almost unimaginable stretches of time, while day by day the ocean was constantly at work reshaping the land, through erosion and deposition, by wave and tide and occasional violent storms. Yet an even more important and dramatic shaping force has been the intermediate cycle of successive ice ages—a geographical *moyen durée*. These macroclimatic changes, causing the polar ice caps to wax and wane, have led to drastic if gradual changes in ocean levels throughout the world, and thus on the Bahama banks to a widely fluctuating ratio between land and sea. The present topography, ecological regions, indigenous flora and fauna, even man and his way of life, are essentially a product of the most recent of these fluctuations, over the last hundred thousand years.

During the interglacial thaw after the Sangamon Ice Age, which peaked some seventy thousand years ago, water levels rose by at least one hundred feet, almost entirely inundating the Bahamas. This was followed by the gradual cooling toward the most recent ice age, called the Wisconsin, which reached its climax no more than sixteen thousand years ago, when man was already established throughout the American continent. Sea levels fell by as much as three hundred feet, hugely increasing the land area of the Bahamas and narrowing the gaps between the islands and the main. The two chief and myriad small islands of the present Little Bahama Bank were joined in a single mass as large as Jamaica (though, of course, not so mountainous), while modern New Providence, Andros, Bimini, Berry Islands, Exumas, Long Island, and Ragged Island together formed a landmass as large as Hispaniola. The islands closely surrounded by deep water were never much larger than today, but the Cay Sal Bank and the Crooked Island–Acklin's complex, as well as the five most easterly present island groups and banks, formed islands almost as large as any in the present Bahamas. Because the islands were larger and stood higher, unlike later there were none out of sight of all others, while the huge central island, recently christened Paleoprovidence, was separated from Cuba by only the narrowest of channels.

That the Bahamas has a relatively small range of indigenous flora and fauna is as much due to the successive inundations over geological time as to a meager natural habitat. But the present range clearly includes the survivors of the Wisconsin Ice Age, when the Bahamas was one great mainland, Paleoprovidence, surrounded by satellite islands far larger than those traced on modern maps. Migratory birds, marine creatures, and even wind-, sea-, or bird-borne plants found in the Bahamas include a predictable mixture of those established in and around adjacent parts of North America and the Caribbean basin. But trees, plants, and less easily migrating animals show much closer affinities to Cuba and Hispaniola than to Florida or more distant parts of the Caribbean, even where modern habitats are similar. As in the islands of the Greater Antilles, there are no large indigenous mammals, the single colony of agouti still found on the Plana Cays, and the scattered pockets of iguana, being relics of much larger colonies of migrants, in the case of the iguana of much larger size—up to six feet long.[7]

Once-common large animals such as the alligator, monk seal, or manatee could easily have crossed from Cuba, Hispaniola, or even Florida to found Bahamian colonies but were last reported in 1804, the 1930s, and 1975 respectively. But more fascinating denizens of Paleoprovidence were those which could have come only by land or across very narrow stretches of sea. These include the once-numerous but long-extinct redfoot tortoise, whose closest relatives are now found only in South

America, or the tiny freshwater turtles still surviving tenuously in a few ponds on Cat Island and Inagua, separate subspecies to those found in Jamaica and Hispaniola respectively. But perhaps the most tantalizing survival of the Ice Age Paleoprovidence, though now extinct, was a barn owl, *Tyto pollens,* so huge that it could barely fly. Bones of this giant bird, a yard in height, have been found in New Providence, Exuma, Cuba, and Haiti alike. It may have survived in Andros—largest and most remote of Bahamian islands—into historic times, for it seems to have been the original of the three-toed, red-eyed, tree-living creature called the chickcharnie in modern local folklore. If not, its survival in legend is as puzzling in its way as the plausible account of the origin of Bahamian land forms given in Arawak mythology.[8]

One factor that would have conditioned the spread of plants and animals, even the migration of the Amerindian subspecies of *Homo sapiens,* was the much harsher temperature regime that prevailed during the Wisconsin period. In this era, when glaciers were found as far south as the present New England, the climate of the Bahamas would have been much like that of modern Britain (which itself was as cold as northern Norway is today). Preferable as this would have been for North American Indians, it would not have attracted those already long established in Central and South America, adapted to the high temperatures and limited seasonal variation of the tropics and without the means to withstand winter frosts and snow—quite apart from the paucity of land resources in the Bahamas compared with islands farther south. These factors were counteracted, though, by the generally limited, if varied, seagoing capabilities of the mainland Arawaks, which seem to have made the Straits of Florida a far more effective ethnic barrier than any channel between more southerly islands—which became stepping stones across the Caribbean from South and Central America.

Climatic, ecological, and technological factors thus conditioned the migration of the first people into the Bahama Islands, and their settlement patterns once there. Doubt still remains, though, as to who precisely they were, when they came, and by what routes. The usual explanation, based upon all archeological sites so far explored, is that the first Bahamian Amerindians were also the last: those people whom Columbus found in the islands in 1492. Calling themselves Lucayans ("small-island people"), these were an outlying branch of the Arawak-speaking Neo-Indians who, under pressure from the more aggressive Caribs, had migrated from South America into the Greater Antilles, forming a culture called Taino by archeologists, in the process pushing before them or forcibly assimilating earlier populations of Meso-Indians since called either Ciboney ("cave people") or Guanajatabey. By most chronologies, Neo-Indians had left Venezuela around the time of Christ, became established in Hispaniola within two hundred years, and reached the Bahamas no earlier than A.D. 600.

Tantalizing hints remain, however, based upon random stone and conch-shell artifacts, that parts of the central Bahamas may have been settled earlier, or at least visited, by the Ciboney Meso-Indians, who first inhabited the Greater Antilles about 500 B.C. and continued to maintain a precarious existence in western Cuba until around 1500. An even more intriguing possibility arises from the discoveries made since the 1960s in Cuba, Haiti, and the Dominican Republic of the remains of far older peoples: Paleo-Indians who arrived in the Greater Antilles as early as 5000 B.C. and almost certainly came from Central not South America. Contrary to earlier assertions that Paleo-Indians lacked the capability to navigate open waters, these people seem to have migrated by way of a chain of flat islands since submerged by rising ocean levels, either from the Yucatan Peninsula into Cuba or from the area of the Miskito Coast into Hispaniola by way of Jamaica.[9] That these Stone Age migrants may have passed on beyond the Greater Antilles into the Bahamian archipelago during the later stages of the Wisconsin era may be established by the rumored discovery of Amerindian bones in a cave far below the present ocean level in the Caicos Islands.[10] Certainly, in a macroclimatological scenario in which global temperatures, and thus ocean levels, were steadily rising, most if not all of the less recent archeological sites would be expected to have been washed away, or found below the present ocean level—where, of course, most would have been encrusted out of recognition by subsequent coral formations.

For the time being, then, we must regard the Neo-Indian Lucayans as the aboriginal Bahamians, relying on the most recent archeological surveys, digs, and speculations, as well as the ethnohistorical descriptions given by the first European explorers, to establish the Lucayans' arrival routes, settlement patterns, characteristics, and ways of life and thought.[11]

THE EARLIEST VENTURES in Bahamian archeology, perhaps naturally, concentrated on the most obvious and productive sites, mainly caves. Besides occasional petroglyphs, these disclosed an eclectic array of carved wood, stone, and pottery artifacts, and a range of Amerindian bones, often disturbed by later settlers and now shamefully scattered. More re-

cently, research has focused on open-air habitation sites—usually identified by their distinctive "kitchen middens" or surface pottery scatters—
of which over 360 had been located by 1990. While only a handful have
been systematically excavated and even the survey of sites is far from
complete—new ones come to light all the time[12]—patterns of Lucayan
settlement and life are already fairly clear.

The Lucayans were short-range mariners, living in small coastal villages and subsisting from a type of agriculture based upon manioc cultivation in combination with the harvesting of the natural resources of
the sea. As Keegan has recently argued, the pattern of Lucayan settlement at the time of the arrival of the Europeans was shaped by physical
constraints such as the separation and size of the islands in relation to
winds and currents, and the natural processes of colonization, taking
into account the point (or points) of origin of the migrants, their initial numbers and rate of demographic increase, and the length of time
involved in their migration and distribution. But the pattern of distribution (as Sears and Sullivan first suggested in 1978) was even more
critically determined by the considerable climatic and ecological variations found in the eight-hundred-mile archipelago, which extends from
twenty degrees north and sixty-nine degrees west to twenty-seven north
and eighty west, that is, almost equally north and south of the Tropic of
Cancer.[13]

Geographers identify three main zones in the Bahamas, all of which
are affected by prevailing northeastern winds and a west-to-north-setting
drift of ocean water. All too are in the median belt of Atlantic hurricanes, with a 30 percent average likelihood of a visitation in any given
year. Northwest of a line drawn through the center of the Northeast
Providence Channel is a "moist subtropical" zone of flat pine islands.
Rainfall averages above forty-seven inches a year, and between December and March temperatures fall below the agriculturally significant level
of fifty degrees Fahrenheit ten to twenty days a year, with occasional
southward shifts of cold northern air bringing temperatures below the
critical level of forty-five degrees at least once each year in most islands.
The predominant natural vegetation is Caribbean pine (the discontinuous remnant of a much wider distribution during the last ice age) and
savanna, interspersed with small stands of hardwood trees.

At the other end of the archipelago, southeast of a line through the
Mayaguana Passage, is a "dry tropical" zone of equally flat islands with
very few trees. Here the rainfall varies from thirty-one inches in a wet
year on North Caicos, down to sixteen inches in a dry year on Great

Table 1

Bahamian Archipelago: Lucayan Sites and Artifact
Collections by Islands, As Located August 1990

Island	Land Area (sq. m., approx.)	Open-Air Living Sites	Cave Sites	Collections
Grand Turk	10	1	0	0
East Caicos	37	2	4	0
Middle Caicos	50	36	8	1
North Caicos	36	9	4	2
Providenciales	15	9	2	1
West Caicos	8	0	0	1
Other Caicos[a]	—	10	2	1
Inaguas	645	17	6	2
Mayaguana	110	11		2
Acklin's Island	150	29	2	1
Crooked Island	92	19	5	1
Plana Cays	6	0	0	1
Samana Cay	15	11	0	0
Long Island	173	44	15	4
Rum Cay	30	19	9	4
Conception Island	4	5	0	0
San Salvador	63	32	13	3
Ragged Island	9	0	0	1
Exumas	72	17	0	0
Cat Island	150	31	1	1
Eleuthera	200	17	6	4
New Providence	80	11	9	4
Andros	2,300	5	8	8
Berry Islands	12	1	0	1
Abacos	649	31	14	5
Grand Bahama	530	4	3	1
Biminis	9	1	0	1
Cay Sal	2	1	0	0
Total		373	111	50

Source: Compiled by G. A. Aarons, Bahamas Archives.

[a] "Other" includes unspecified Caicos.

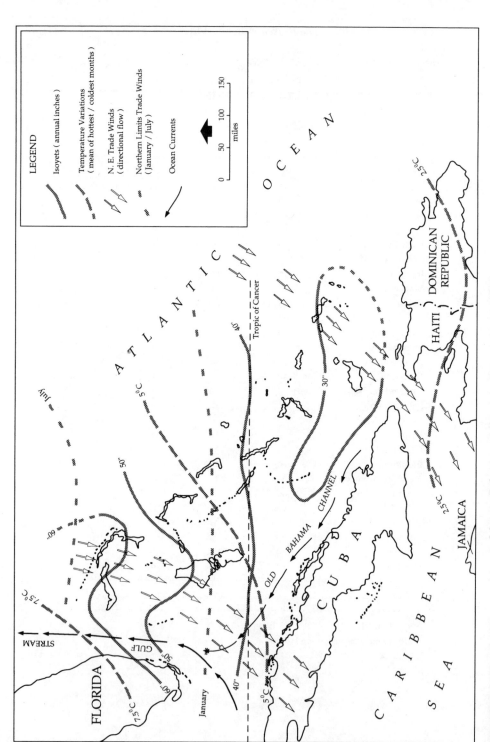

LEGEND

Isoyets (annual inches)

Temperature Variations
(mean of hottest / coldest months)

N. E. Trade Winds
(directional flow)

Northern Limits Trade Winds
(January / July)

Ocean Currents

miles
0   50   100   150

ATLANTIC

OCEAN

Tropic of Cancer

40°

30°

5°C

50"

60"

July

FLORIDA

7.5°C

January

GULF

STREAM

50"

60"

75°C

40"

5°C

OLD

BAHAMA

CHANNEL

CUBA

CARIBBEAN

SEA

JAMAICA

2.5°C

HAITI

DOMINICAN
REPUBLIC

2.5°C

Map 2   Bahamas archipelago geographical determinants

Inagua. This aridity, accentuated by two very dry seasons in winter and summer, by the absence of cloud cover, and by a very high rate of evaporation from the land, leads to the existence of natural salinas and produces a type of vegetation called "garrique scrub," consisting of stunted hardwood trees mixed with low thorn forest and cactus.

The central "moist tropical" zone is in many ways the optimal Bahamian habitat, since it also contains the islands with greatest relief and least infertile soils. Though the islands in the south and east of this zone—Long Island, Crooked Island, and Acklin's—are perceptibly drier than the rest, lacking the buildup of rain-bearing clouds that occurs over the Great Bahama Bank (especially Andros), all islands within the zone receive between thirty-one and forty-three inches of rain a year. In none of them does the temperature ever fall below forty-five degrees Fahrenheit. Today the prevalent natural vegetation is of the "coppice" type, with dense stands of low tropical hardwoods up to twelve feet tall, though before colonial settlement introduced slash-and-burn and plantation agriculture it was of the far more luxuriant type glowingly described by Christopher Columbus.[14]

Not surprisingly, the largest and most numerous Lucayan settlements already surveyed were found in this central zone. The moist subtropical islands of the northern zone, along with Andros and New Providence—today regarded as enjoying the best climate of all and containing some 90 percent of the Bahamian population—have so far disclosed few Lucayan sites, and even those are comparatively small and meager in material remains. On the contrary, a surprising number of sites have been discovered in the southeastern zone, though concentrated in the Caicos Islands, which provide the least inimical climate and growing conditions in the zone.

Carbon dating, the analysis of pottery styles, and speculative mathematical models have been used to explain this pattern of distribution, and three rival accounts of Arawak migration into the Bahamas have resulted. Sears and Sullivan have plausibly argued an initial wave of migration from Hispaniola by way of the Caicos Islands, during which the pure Tainan culture was transmuted into its Lucayan variant. Winter, on the other hand, arguing from close similarities in pottery styles and greater accessibility, has proposed a rather earlier initial migration into the central Bahamas by "Sub-Taino" peoples from northeastern Cuba. Most recently, Keegan has argued that Inagua was the most likely first landfall of the earliest settlers, who came from northwestern Hispaniola around A.D. 600 and spread successively to adjacent islands—including the Caicos Islands to eastward as well as those to the north and north-west—while quite quickly adapting to the new environment and developing the Lucayan subculture.[15] These different explanations, however, are by no means incompatible, merely suggesting a rather more complex migratory pattern, with overlapping waves, the mingling of Taino and Sub-Taino influences, and the creation of a rather less than totally homogeneous subculture.

As Sears and Sullivan point out, the earliest sites or lowest archeological levels uncovered in the Caicos Islands (which they date from about A.D. 800) contain only the Ostionoid, Chicoid, or Meillacoid pottery made in Hispaniola or Cuba. The very first Arawaks in the southeastern Bahamas, it seems, were only seasonal visitors, attracted by the sea salt from natural salinas and the dried shellfish demanded by the burgeoning population of neighboring Hispaniola. Within a century, however, permanent settlements were established as the visitors grew more numerous and learned to adapt their manioc agriculture to the drier and sparser island soils. They also begin to fashion an indigenous pottery from the local red marl, tempered first with limestone and then with crushed seashells. However, the continued presence of Antillean pottery in the later sites and levels, along with other artifacts of non-Bahamian provenance such as petaloid celts, stone axe heads, beads, and spirit fetishes (zemis), suggests that these islands remained important for trade and strongly under the influence of the Tainan heartland of Hispaniola. This is seemingly borne out by the patterns of settlements in double rows around a central batey or ceremonial ball court, which is the Antillean mode and uncommon in the rest of the Bahamas, and by the alleged discovery of a line of standing stones pointing out the optimum route between Middle Caicos and Hispaniola—much like the stone maps for maritime navigation discovered in Polynesia.

Sears and Sullivan hypothesize that the southeastern colonists exchanged salt and dried fish, especially conch, for the higher-grade pottery, stone implements, ceremonial objects, and ornaments which remain in their sites, as well, perhaps, as cotton, tobacco, and other agricultural products more easily grown in Hispaniola. Though the Caicos settlements were nearly all located in the limited areas where slash-and-burn agriculture is still practiced, their incomplete dependence upon farming, or the balanced mix of farming and fishing found elsewhere in the Bahamas, can be deduced from the location of settlements inland or on hilltops, rather than at the back of coastal dunes as in the rest of the archipelago. Other reasons for this, however, suggest themselves: differences in the incidence of fresh water, a greater need for protection against mosquitoes and sandflies (which still plague those islands), or even the need for lookouts and defense against human predators from farther east, such as the Caribs and Ciguayo, for whom these would be the nearest inhabited islands in the archipelago.

Such factors would help to explain an onward migration of Caicos Island Arawaks toward the northwest. Sears and Sullivan, however, suggest that the further diffusion throughout the Bahamas was mainly due to population pressure from Hispaniola, from about A.D. 1000. According to this theory, a growing number of migrants from Hispaniola used the Turks and Caicos Islands as stepping stones toward islands ecologically more suitable for settlements dependent upon agriculture and fishing rather than on trade, with the consequent speeding of the evolution of a separate Lucayan subculture. This wave of migration along the axis of the archipelago quite quickly populated the central islands, where conditions were optimal for farming, but long before 1492 stopped short of the less suitable islands of the northwestern zone.

The Sears and Sullivan scenario is seriously modified if not upset by that of Winter. Arguing from a much earlier dating of the lowest levels of Lucayan sites in the central Bahamas, and close parallels between the pottery sherds found there and those of the Cuban Baní culture, he has suggested that the central Bahamas was already colonized by Cuban Sub-Taino before the Caicos Islands were settled. This predicates an initial migration as early as A.D. 500 into Long Island by way of Cay St. Domingo and the Ragged Island chain, followed by the colonization of Crooked Island–Acklin's and islands as far north and northwest as San Salvador and Eleuthera by A.D. 600. Rather later, there was a counterflow of settlement and cultural influence toward the southeast, which included the introduction of pottery styles developed in the central Bahamas from Cuban models and reached as far as the already settled Caicos Islands by A.D. 900. From a dating point of view this seems much more consistent with the evidence than an initial migration of peoples from the Caicos Islands in the other direction. It also helps to explain why the Caicos sites differ in several key features from those so far found elsewhere in the archipelago.

Keegan's 1985 scenario of Lucayan diffusion throughout the islands after an initial settlement in Great Inagua around A.D. 600, like Winter's proposal, removes the dating problem inherent in the Sears-Sullivan theory. But it is much more dependent upon linear models of colonization and diffusion than it is upon the dating of artifacts or carbon deposits (which, he claims, are uncertain) or upon theories of ecological and climatic constraints. This helps to explain, in particular, why there are seemingly more Lucayan sites on such relatively unattractive islands as Mayaguana than on more distant but ecologically more suitable islands—with such attractive islands as New Providence and Andros having received comparatively few Lucayan settlers before the arrival of Columbus.

By Keegan's theory, further islands were colonized only after the initial population had grown to a size that critically pressed on available resources. This predicates either a very slow, steady diffusion lasting nearly a millennium or an accelerating diffusion after successful adaptation to the new environment led to a vigorously expanding population. In either case, the directions of colonization were, according to Keegan, determined mainly by physical factors such as the distances between suitable islands, winds, currents, and waves. This would suggest the successive settlement of Inagua, Acklin's–Crooked Island, Long Island, Cat Island, Eleuthera, and Abaco, with deviations from this axis to Rum Cay and San Salvador, Exuma, and New Providence, and (as also suggested by Winter) a delayed counterflow migration toward Mayaguana and the Caicos Islands—which, if not already settled from Hispaniola, would inevitably retain closer links to Hispaniola than any Lucayan island except Inagua.

While Keegan's theories are elegantly argued, they need testing by further research, particularly the dating of sites. Moreover, his mathematical models, while plausible within the available evidence, like all such suffer from having to make certain assumptions and ignore such factors as chance, accident, and irrational human behavior. One crucial assumption is that the whole process of colonization was initiated by a single band of migrants (some fifty strong) arriving at a single point, and that all successive Lucayans were descended from that founding band. A much more likely scenario is that initial settlements came at different places at different times and that there were successive waves of migration. Some earlier settlers would move on under the pressure of newcomers, while others might resist or even assimilate them. For their part, later settlers would displace the earlier, settle in alongside them, or leapfrog them to form settlements in farther islands. In any case, there would ·have been more continuous movement in different directions, more mingling of people and influences, and perhaps more tensions than Keegan's theories suggest. At the very least, this modified inter-

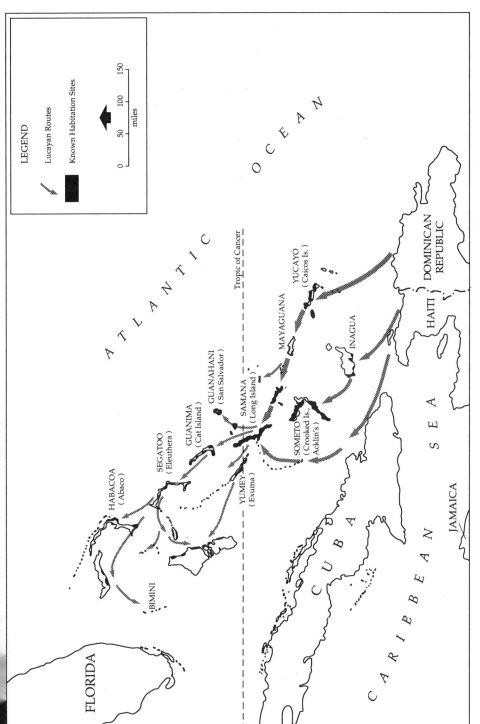

Map 3. Bahamas archipelago, projected Lucayan routes and known habitation sites

pretation is not inconsistent with the archeological and ethnohistorical evidence.

In sum, the most likely sequence of events is that the earliest Arawak penetration into the Bahamas occurred between A.D. 500 and 600. Coast-dwelling Taino, or rather Sub-Taino, some of whom had already bypassed Hispaniola to settle in northeastern Cuba and Jamaica (much farther by sea than to the nearest Bahamian islands), first visited or even settled the Turks and Caicos Islands and Inagua. But the most numerous, adventurous, and successful groups entered the Bahamas from Cuba by way of the Ragged Island chain. Since these people had always lived by the sea and had been forced in Cuba to develop a pottery made from inferior clay, they adapted easily to Bahamian conditions, developing a culture quite distinct from that of the Taino of Hispaniola (who were fast colonizing the island's interior) but not very different from the Sub-Taino Baní culture of the northeastern Cuban coast and islands.

Thus the Lucayan subculture developed mainly in the central Bahamas between A.D. 600 and 800, thinly spreading its people, their lifestyle, and their comparatively crude "Palmetto ware" along the axes of the archipelago, as far as Eleuthera in one direction, the Caicos Islands in the other. These early Lucayans, though, came under increasing pressure from about A.D. 1000 as the success of the Taino culture—based, as Sauer has argued, upon the development of *conuco* agriculture, primitive irrigation, and the introduction of maize[16]—led to a rapid increase in population and further waves of migration. This would account for the increased importance of the Caicos Islands as a trading center—almost a Tainan colony—while further migrations by way of the Cuban coast, as well as the natural increase in the Lucayan population, accounted for the gradual filling up of the central islands, the first settlements in the northern islands, and the final development of the Lucayan subculture before the Spaniards came.

Certainly the evidence of Columbus's journal suggests that the Lucayans of the central Bahamas had at least as close a contact with Cuba as Hispaniola, if not quite the close linkages claimed by Sears and Sullivan between the Caicos Islands and Hispaniola. The Lucayans told Columbus of great cities in Cuba as well as Hispaniola. They also complained of people who threatened them from the southeast, and this may have referred as much to would-be Tainan migrants as to the more warlike traditional enemies, the Caribs, who had pursued the original Arawaks along the Antilles as far as Puerto Rico and still harried the eastern and northeastern coasts of that island.[17]

The existence of "import wares" in virtually all Lucayan sites indicates continuing contacts and trade, if not migrations and conflict. Yet the predominance of the indigenous Palmetto ware (so called from a site at Palmetto Grove, San Salvador, excavated by Hoffman in the 1960s)[18] in the majority of Lucayan sites—increasing toward 100 percent according to the distance from Hispaniola—shows that if the Lucayans could not always resist the newcomers, their culture quickly changed them. In fact, it was the Bahamian ecology that was determinant. Language, customs, and beliefs did not greatly change, but lifestyles did. Above all, as Keegan conclusively shows, fishing soon took over from farming as the principal source of food. Manioc, however, remained crucial to the Lucayans, as to all Arawaks, and Sears and Sullivan are probably right in contending that it was the constraints on its cultivation, as much as the time factor stressed by Keegan, which prevented the complete colonization of the Bahamas by the Lucayans before 1492.

The central Bahamas proved highly suitable, if not ideal, for manioc and other root cultigens, and this alone might have accounted for their colonization, even without the development of fishing techniques. Later, the balance between manioc farming and fishing might well have led to the full population of all suitable islands by natural increase, without further migrations. Yet despite growing pressure on the resources of the central Bahamas through natural increase and migration over nine hundred years, the Lucayans had not penetrated in large numbers, or permanently, into all the northern islands before the European incursion catastrophically curtailed their development as a whole.

The few northern sites so far uncovered suggest only seasonal visits or, at most, longer-term settlements by a mere handful of families. The inability of Lucayans to adapt housing and clothing to the northern winter may have been one important cause. But the critical factor was more likely the Lucayans' dependence on manioc as their staple starch food. Bitter manioc, the form most easily processed and stored, withers where annual rainfall is less than twenty inches or where the soil is not moisture-retentive and lacks essential nutrients. Ideal growth is achieved with as much as eighty inches of rain a year with a marked dry season, and these conditions are found in some northwestern islands. But the aboriginal type of manioc is damaged by temperatures below fifty degrees Fahrenheit and the leaves and stems are killed at forty-five degrees, so the northwestern islands were almost barred to people dependent upon the plant. The cultivation of Indian corn—which flourishes where winter temperatures are far lower than ever experienced in the Bahamas—

would greatly have extended the settlement range of the Lucayans. But it is not certain that the Lucayans knew how to grow or process Indian corn, though its cultivation had already spread from Central America into Cuba and Hispaniola before the coming of the Europeans.[19]

~ 2 ~

Fragile Adaptation: The Lucayan Way of Life and Material Culture

THE LARGEST and most completely explored Lucayan site covers twelve acres at the head of Pigeon Creek, on the eastern side of San Salvador. First identified by Theodoor de Booy as early as 1912, raked over by Ruth Wolper in 1964, surveyed by M. K. Pratt in 1974, and scientifically excavated by Richard Rose after 1978, it can tell us much about Lucayan patterns of settlement, lifestyle, and culture in general.[1]

San Salvador, which the Lucayans called Guanahaní (the Place of the Iguana), is an oblong island some twelve miles by six at the outer, Atlantic Ocean, edge of the central moist tropical zone, enjoying an average annual rainfall of thirty-five inches, with monthly mean temperatures ranging only between seventy and eighty degrees Fahrenheit. Columbus's description of a numerous population and the archeological discovery of some thirty-two habitation sites show that the island was at the northeastern limit of the area fully settled by Arawakan peoples. Yet its isolated location and limited agricultural and material resources compelled an adaptation even more rapid and complete than elsewhere in the archipelago, toward the creation of what is now termed the Lucayan subculture.

Above all, the Lucayans of Guanahaní were bound to be capable mariners who lived very largely off the products of the sea. San Salvador is twenty-two miles beyond the next inhabitable island (Rum Cay) and forty-five miles from larger and more fertile islands (Cat Island and Long Island). The absence of hard indigenous rocks (let alone metals) compelled some long-distance trade, but the impracticality of carrying provisions over such long distances forced the islanders to rely on indigenous food resources. They grew manioc for cassava bread, but the fact that almost half of their island's fifty-nine square miles was made up of brackish lakes and the remainder was largely bare limestone determined that the Guanahanis, even more than other Lucayans, had to live more off the sea than the land.

Pigeon Creek, though, was the optimum site available on Guanahaní/San Salvador, and for this reason was the location of the major Lucayan settlement on the island (Richard Rose says perhaps the largest in the archipelago). Situated on a flat area of good soil behind the coastal dune ridge, at the head of a tidal lagoon connecting to the sea through a narrow inlet three and a half miles south, it stood in a strategic but sheltered position at the conjuncture of land and sea resources. With fresh water available from shallow wells, the settlement was close enough to the ocean to enjoy the onshore breezes which on most days kept away sandflies and mosquitoes. The offshore reef and ocean beaches provided many large fishes and occasional seals and turtles, but the lagoon was also rich in fish and mollusks, while offering shelter for the comparatively flimsy Lucayan canoes. In an excellent position to receive early warning of unwelcome human visitors, Pigeon Creek was within easy reach of refuges in the interior and of the other Guanahaní settlements, through the intricate network of waterways that crisscross the island.

Lucayan houses were too insubstantial to leave more than a few postholes and hearth spots to study, though careful sifting can uncover charcoal fragments suitable for carbon dating and a range of pottery, as well as ceremonial objects, ornaments, and other artifacts. Archeologists, however, learn at least as much from the refuse middens built up to the lee of the houses, which besides a compacted mass of fish and animal bones and shells, contain a wide variety of potsherds and other discarded artifacts. The extent and composition of the middens therefore allow for many deductions about the age, size, and history of the settlements and the lives of their inhabitants.

From its size and configuration, the main Pigeon Creek settlement seems to have consisted at its peak of twenty-five to thirty houses, each containing a whole extended family and thus suggesting a population as high as three hundred. Most houses stretched out in a line behind the dunes at thirty-yard intervals, but there was probably a cluster at the center around a central space or plaza. Some half a dozen satellite settlements, each consisting of a short row of houses, were found at intervals on both sides of Pigeon Creek as far as the sea inlet, among them probably housing as many persons as lived in the main settlement. Thus at least five hundred persons, and perhaps as many as one thousand, were concentrated around the creek—probably half the island's total population.

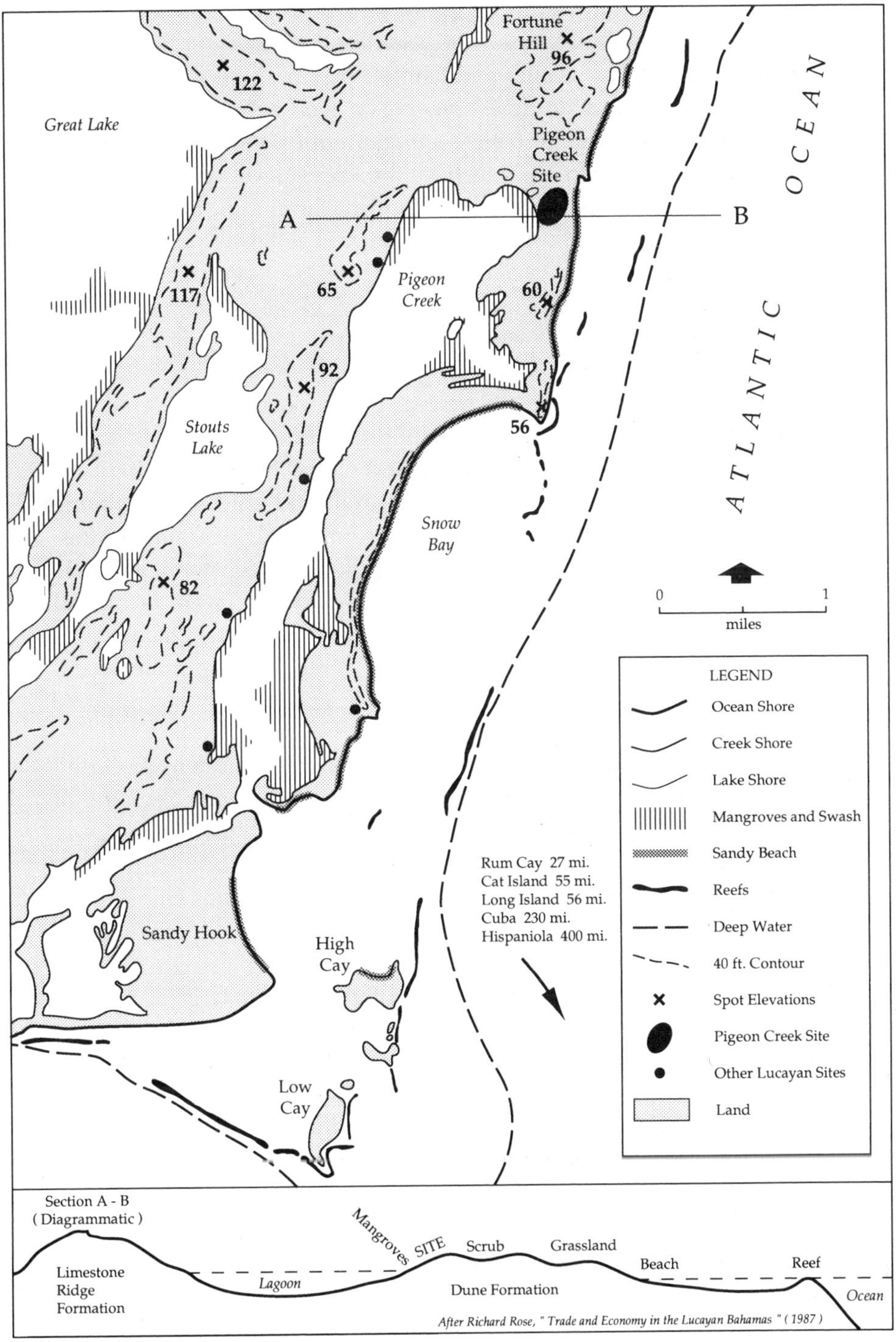
Great Lake
122
Fortune Hill
96
Pigeon Creek Site
A
B
OCEAN
ATLANTIC
117
65
Pigeon Creek
60
92
Stouts Lake
56
Snow Bay
82
0
1
miles
LEGEND
Ocean Shore
Creek Shore
Lake Shore
Mangroves and Swash
Sandy Beach
Reefs
Deep Water
40 ft. Contour
Spot Elevations
Pigeon Creek Site
Other Lucayan Sites
Land
Rum Cay 27 mi.
Cat Island 55 mi.
Long Island 56 mi.
Cuba 230 mi.
Hispaniola 400 mi.
Sandy Hook
High Cay
Low Cay
Section A - B
(Diagrammatic)
Mangroves
SITE
Scrub
Grassland
Beach
Reef
Limestone Ridge Formation
Lagoon
Dune Formation
Ocean
After Richard Rose, " Trade and Economy in the Lucayan Bahamas " (1987)

Map 4. Lucayan site, Pigeon Creek, San Salvador

Though the satellite villages and hamlets may have been the result of the final stage of Lucayan development, or even ephemeral, the main Pigeon Creek site seems to have been continuously occupied for hundreds of years. A carbon analysis from the lowest levels gave a surprisingly early date, around A.D. 600, which may argue for a Cuban Sub-Taino rather than Tainan origin for the original settlers—though this is by no means certain. The earthenware fragments of hemispheric bowls and manioc-baking griddles disclosed the full range of Palmetto types, including "mat-marked," "incised," and "appliquéd," though a simple plain style predominated (83 percent). These pottery artifacts were all made locally. However, some 2 percent of the pottery uncovered was "trade wares"—a thinner quartz-tempered earthenware of the Meillacoid and Ostionoid types from Hispaniola and Cuba. Nonceramic artifacts included objects fashioned from stone, coral, and shell—wood being absent or perished. Of these a very few were imported, including pestles, fragments of celts, and beads of aragonite, quartz, greenstone, and jade from as far away as Guatemala. The majority, though, were fashioned from indigenous materials: limestone bowls, troughs and slabs, shell scrapers, burins, beads and pendants, and coral grinders, graters, and rasps. This predominance of local materials suggests an ingenious (if constrained) degree of adaptation.

Analysis of the animal remains in the Pigeon Creek middens disclosed a predictable dependence upon the sea for protein food. Remains of grouper, parrot fish, and clams (*Codakia obicularis*) were particularly plentiful. If the inhabitants ate birds such as pigeon and duck, their bones have not survived in the refuse middens. The same holds true of land crabs and crawfish, which were surely as plentiful and as esteemed as food in Lucayan times as in the islands today. Also, though Arawaks elsewhere were known to have relished iguana and agouti (both of which were native to Guanahaní and its cays), bones of land animals were almost absent at Pigeon Creek, as were recognizable remains of seals and turtles. Equally surprising was the comparative rarity of conch shells—though this was probably because the Lucayans normally extracted the conch from their shells at the fishing grounds. Likewise, the bones, shells, and carcasses of larger prey such as turtles, seals, and manatees may have been discarded at a distance for hygienic reasons. Nonanimal foods, grown or collected, would not be expected to have left traces in the middens. But as to the starch food without which the Lucayans' diet would have been disastrously unbalanced, the dependence of cassava made from bitter manioc roots is attested by the prevalence of fragments of mat-marked griddles and various distinctive grinding and scraping implements among the man-made remains.

ARCHEOLOGY, by stressing adaptations to the Bahamian ecosystem, has proved invaluable in correcting impressions of the Lucayans too heavily derived from what is known of other Arawaks, particularly the much more sophisticated Taino of the Greater Antilles. Archeology can also corroborate other sources. Yet, at best, it provides a strictly limited view. A far more complete, if still not quite full-dimensional, picture of the Lucayans emerges when to the archeological evidence is added the testimony of Columbus, Las Casas, Peter Martyr, Oviedo, and others from first and second hand, along with cautious extrapolations from modern anthropologists' studies of Arawaks still living in traditional ways.[2]

The Lucayans were a copper-skinned people of handsome physique. The Spanish described them as above medium height, which suggests men about five feet six inches tall and women some four inches shorter. The women were graceful and sexually attractive to the Europeans, the men lithe and athletic, excellent swimmers and canoers, who enjoyed running, wrestling, and other competitive sports. Brown-eyed and thin-lipped, their broad faces and high cheekbones gave the Lucayans an almost oriental look, modified by the flattened forehead that resulted from binding a board to the front of the skull in infancy. Their hair was black, straight, and coarse, the men and women alike wearing it in tufts, between which the head was shaved. Their language, though strange, did not grate on the Spaniards' ears, being described by Peter Martyr as being "soft and not less liquid than Latin."[3] Except on ceremonial occasions, Lucayan men and children went completely unclothed, though grown men protected their genitalia in a small gourd worn on a belt. Females wore a cache-sexe of cotton once they reached puberty, and married women wore aprons of different lengths according to their rank. The Lucayans were a cleanly people who washed frequently, using an aromatic berry to lather the water. Other plants were used to produce red, white, black, and yellow dyes, with which the Lucayans painted their bodies, especially for festivals and in preparing for war. Women were said to favor the color white, and men red. The patterns of body paint clearly had symbolic significance and included representations of personal fetishes, called zemis. Such designs were sometimes tattooed into the skin with pointed reeds.

The Lucayans' ears and noses were pierced for ornaments of stone,

bone, shell, or, occasionally, gold—often again in the form of tiny zemis
—which were hung from cotton cords. Many Lucayans wore armlets or
leg bandages of cotton or strings of tiny beads, which pressed into the
flesh in a way that the Europeans found unsightly. Ornate necklaces
of pottery, stone, shell, or gold beads, usually disk-shaped but sometimes cylindrical and pierced with transverse holes for inserting colored
feathers, were commonly worn as a sign of rank. On special occasions
Lucayans wore ornate masks of wood or shell, and girdles fashioned
from cotton interwoven with feathers, strings of beads, and sometimes
pieces of gold.

Gold, imported from Hispaniola or Cuba, was highly regarded for its
rarity and beauty, and generally worn only by the chiefly class. The Lucayans knew of no other metal save an alloy of gold and copper called
guanin, so rare that it was worn only by the most potent chiefs, in the
form of a central necklace pendant. Guanin, none of which has survived,
seems to have originated from South America and may even have accompanied the Lucayans' ancestors on their original migration. This in
itself would account for the mystic power with which the metal was im-
bued. In general, though theirs was a cashless culture, comparatively
poor in material possessions, the Lucayans attributed value to all objects
according to their scarcity and exotic origin, especially if from places
associated with tribal origins, handed down through generations. Such
objects formed the centerpieces of all personal ornaments or furniture
and were accordingly treasured and handed on to the next generation at
the time of marriage or death.

Compared with the Tainos of Hispaniola, the Lucayans were a scattered population, living in small villages and hamlets, with a comparative
lack of social stratification and political organization. The thin ecology of
the Bahama Islands, particularly the shortage of fresh water and good
soil, could not support any permanent population on islands smaller
than about thirty square miles in extent, and even small settlements
required the exclusive use of an area several miles in radius for their
subsistence.[4] Las Casas claimed that there were half a million Lucayans
at the time of Columbus, but this was a wild guess. Peter Martyr more
realistically calculated that there were forty thousand, but even this was
probably an exaggeration. Columbus saw no villages with more than fifteen houses, and even if he missed many larger settlements and there
were as many as 150 villages occupied at any one time throughout the
archipelago, this suggests a total population no greater than twenty thousand. This, in fact, is quite plausible, for at no time in the subsequent

history of the Bahamas were there more than twenty thousand persons subsisting entirely on the islands' natural resources.[5]

The Lucayans lived in family units, and villages probably consisted largely of kin groupings without the almost absolute social divisions between aristocratic *nitainos*, commoners (sometimes called *guajiros*), and slaves (*naborías*) found among the Hispaniola Taino. Each sizeable village, though, had its chief, or *cacique*, whose family were the remnants of a traditional ruling class, descended matrilineally.

Lucayan society, like that of all Arawaks, was male-headed but with powerful women behind the scenes—a situation reflecting (or reflected in) the mythological status, respectively, of Jocahú, Atabeyra, and the maternal uncle Guaca. The continuance of a ruling class rather than a simple line of hereditary caciques was ensured by the tradition that sons rarely inherited from their fathers. The first choice was the eldest son of the eldest sister, followed by other sons of that sister, or sons of other sisters, in a descending order of choice. Failing sisters' sons, the chief-tainship passed to a brother, and only in the absence of all the above did a cacique's son inherit. On the even rarer occasions when a dead cacique had no relatives at all, the people chose as his successor the most worthy and powerful man available—a quasi-democratic solution which must have been rather more frequent among the attenuated Lucayan population than among the demographically teeming Taino.

The Lucayans were easygoing concerning private property, but the caciques and their families clearly owned more than the commoners. Such property was also transmitted matrilineally, being passed on either when the owner died, or at the time of marriage in reciprocal payments of bride-wealth and dowry. All Lucayan men were allowed to practice polygyny according to their means, but this meant in effect that it was more or less limited to the chiefly class. This privileged group controlled the allocation of land for agriculture and the storing of harvested food, determined fishing and hunting strategies, acted as judges, and decided on war and peace. Its power was manifested and reinforced by the fact that the caciques and their male relatives were also priestly shamans, practicing divination, intercession, and medical magic.

The caciques and their families lived in the largest houses, called *bohios*. Rectangular and gabled, these in Hispaniola were up to sixty feet long and fifteen feet wide, and stood fifteen feet high at the ridge. Adjacent to the cacique's bohio were normally a communal storehouse for dried cassava and a kind of temple for the village zemis, while in front was an open space called a *batey*, sometimes walled, used for public occasions, religious ceremonies, and community games, notably the ballgame with three or more men on a side called *batos*. Lucayan bateys have so far been located for certain only on the Caicos Islands, but they were probably a feature of at least the largest Lucayan villages.

The commoners lived in a different type of circular house with a conical roof called a *caney*, laid out at first in a single row, but in the larger villages scattered without streets on one side of the cacique's compound and the communal batey. All Lucayans' houses used similar building methods and materials. The bohio was erected by setting parallel lines of posts at twelve-foot intervals, joined by horizontal poles attached by vines or cotton rope. At the center of each end a taller post held up a long ridgepole, which might be supported by one or more intermediate posts with Y-shaped tops. The caney had a single central roof post some twelve feet high, surrounded by much slimmer wall posts about half as tall. All houses had rafters of straight slim boughs, and an almost rain-proof roof was made of palmetto thatch. Walls were made of canes or rattan stems woven with leaves, which kept out driving rain but provided ample ventilation. All houses were proof against normal winds, and even if stripped by hurricanes could quite easily be reconstructed from the standing posts.

However large, bohios and caneys alike consisted of a single room. All buildings had earthen floors, low doorways, tiny windows or none at all, and only rough exit holes for smoke, though fires were often lit inside the houses to keep flying insects at bay. Furniture varied with the rank of the householder but was never lavish. Most Lucayans slept in cotton mesh *hamacas* slung between the house posts, though some caciques had beds on raised platforms. Ordinary Lucayans squatted on the earthen floor or palmetto mats, but caciques possessed the elaborately carved wooden stools called *duhos* used on ceremonial or religious occasions. Bohios too might contain a more imposing range of pots and a more impressive array of ceremonial wear than the ordinary caneys. Yet in all houses food would be stored in gourds and baskets hung from the roof or, in the case of cassava cakes, on wooden platforms raised on legs, to protect against marauding insects and other creatures. Around the walls stood water pots, cooking utensils, hunting and fishing gear, weapons, and (in caneys at least) farming implements. And all houses contained household zemis, for protection against the elements, disease, or human predators.

Caves appear to have played an important part in Lucayan life, mainly as ritual centers and burial sites but also, surely, as refuges from tempestuous weather and predatory enemies. Caves abound in the oolitic limestone of the Bahamas, small openings in the sides of low hills often opening up into large caverns. It is in excavating such caves for bat guano, a much-prized fertilizer, that modern Bahamians have unearthed most of the wooden ceremonial duhos and large zemis so far found, as well as a considerable number of skeletal remains—one of the most remarkable recent discoveries being that of no less than three duhos in a cave near Mortimer's, Long Island, by Carlton Cartwright, a local fisherman out hunting for land crabs, in May 1988. Though the chance nature of most of these discoveries, and the almost inevitable disturbance of the evidence by the discoverers, is the bane of professional archeologists, the almost complete absence of food remains and normal domestic artifacts from the few sites carefully examined firmly suggests the ritual and ceremonial functions of such caves—all of them close to known Lucayan habitation sites. The fact that a very high proportion of the twenty-five or so duhos so far found in the Bahamas come from Long Island not only bears out the density of Lucayan settlement in the central Bahamas, but suggests to some that Long Island—particularly the area of central Long Island between Mortimer's and Deadman's Cay—may have been an area of ritual and ceremonial focus for the Lucayans as a whole.[6]

Traditionally, nitainos did not labor, yet it is unlikely that Lucayan society could afford a truly leisured class. Besides performing their leadership functions, even the caciques joined the other men in hunting and fishing. All able-bodied persons had their useful duties, and most of their work—indeed, a large proportion of all daylight hours—was devoted to the means of subsistence, as in all such semimarginal societies. Fishing and hunting were almost exclusively male activities, and men dominated the crafts of woodworking and pottery. Farming, however, was shared by males and females alike, including the older children. Women (the nearest to a Lucayan underclass) in fact had the widest range and most onerous of tasks, being responsible for food preparation, cooking, and other domestic chores, as well as much of the planting and reaping. They also seem to have been responsible for the plaiting and weaving of cotton and palmetto. As was a feature of Out Island life throughout later Bahamian history, children almost as soon as they could walk were employed in carrying water and scaring birds and land crabs from the crops. Like later generations they may also have been taught, almost from infancy, to plait palmetto and to make and net cotton thread—as almost a natural function of the hands.

THE WORD *Arawak* (more strictly, *aruac*) actually means "meal eater," and the cultivation of bitter manioc and the preparation of cassava meal and bread from it remained a predominant feature of Lucayan culture. Of necessity, Lucayan agriculture was rotational, using each patch for two or three years before allowing it to revert to bush. For a people without hard metals, using only stone or shell wood-shafted axes or adzes and a kind of hardwood cutlass called a *macana*, clearing the ground was a difficult task, involving more burn than slash. Making fire itself was difficult enough, kindling dry grass by chafing two kinds of wood. At a new site, or when choosing poles and posts for houses and trees suitable for canoes from the deeper woods, trees were felled by burning around their bases, using damp moss or seaweed to prevent total ignition, then chipping away the charcoal. Stumps and roots were left in the ground even where planting was planned, giving Lucayan farming plots a haphazard appearance much denigrated by European writers. Removing very large trees could take a day or more, but secondary growth was cleared more quickly by a general firing, the ash—along with urine and, perhaps, human feces—being used to enrich the soil. In addition, the Lucayans may have used bat guano from caves, as have all later Out Island farmers.

After the soil was broken with adzelike hoes or, where too thin, piled into suitable mounds, slips of manioc were planted in dampened holes made with a dibbing stick called a *coa*. This occurred twice a year in the rainier seasons, the plant needing moisture to start its growth but a drier period to come to maturity. Manioc is a tuber, with up to a dozen swollen roots weighing about a pound apiece, at the base of a five-foot plant with a distinctive spotted stalk (the spots marking fallen leaf stems) and dark green leaves with seven radiating leaflets. In ideal conditions, manioc is said to produce more starch per acre than any other plant, including potatoes and maize, though Bahamian conditions nowhere reached the optimum. Nor did the Bahamas permit that type of *conuco* agriculture with irrigation channels—with acres of close-set fertile mounds producing a rich and balanced variety of crops—to which Carl Ortwin Sauer attributed the remarkable population growth and social development of the Hispaniola Taino.[7] Lucayans, though, likely grew a variety of other food plants on an irregular basis: the tuber called *yahutía*, arrowroot, peanuts, various types of potatoes, beans, and squashes, and the forerunner of the fiery Bahama bird pepper—said to be the hottest in the world. Some authorities believe that the Lucayans also grew some corn, of the softer variety unsuitable for flour, in the most suitable locations, in the last phase of their development.[8]

Bitter manioc, which is more easily stored than the sweet variety when processed, remained the Lucayan staple, despite the problems involved in removing the hydrocyanic (prussic) acid in the tubers' juice. Once harvested, the reddish-brown tubers were first peeled with sharpened conch shells, then the white flesh was grated into shallow pottery bowls with coral rasps. After the excess fluid was drawn off, the pulpy residue was placed in an ingenious contraption called a *matapi*, a six-foot tube of woven palmetto open at the top, suspended from a beam. The remaining juice was squeezed out when the matapi was stretched by a long lever attached to its base. The product was a cylinder of starchy white cassava, impressed with the palmetto weave. Strangely enough, the poisonous juice was not thrown out, but boiled down into *cassareep*, the basis for the tangy stew still made throughout the West Indies and called "pepper-pot"—the prussic acid seemingly being evaporated in the boiling.

The cassava cylinders were grated and sieved through a palmetto mesh to form a crumbly flour, which was baked in flat round cakes on a distinctive pottery griddle over an open fire—five or six minutes a side—until golden brown. The finished disks were then placed on a platform or the sloping thatched house-roofs for several hours to dry, after which they were either eaten or stored in a dry and shady place, remaining in good condition for up to six months. The absence of the special corn-grinding pestles and mortars (*metapes*) on Bahamian sites indicates that the Lucayans did not make corn flour—any soft corn they grew being probably added to the pepper-pot stews.

Compared with the Greater Antilles, the Lucayans were not fortunate in the array of indigenous wild plants and fruits. Many items familiar today (including sugarcane and all citrus fruits) were not imported until the colonial period. But the Lucayans seem also to have lacked fruits found indigenously in the Antilles and even cultivated there, such as the avocado, banana, guava, guenip, papaya, and pineapple. However, they almost certainly gathered and ate the wild sea grape, cocoplum, pigeon plum, tamarind, prickly pear, pond apple, milk berry, and golden fig, and when desperate may even have eaten the bitter fruit of the mangrove tree. Besides, several other indigenous plants offered them wild greens: sea purslane, sawgrass, cattail, and the local wild onion. Though inedible, the fruit of the native calabash tree (*crescentia*) was also invaluable, providing gourds in a variety of useful sizes.[9]

Lucayans ate at least three times a day, at daybreak, noon, and sundown, and on special occasions such as festivals and marriages, at night as well. All meals included cassava bread, but not all were cooked—

conch, clams, and some fish, for example, being eaten raw. The pepper-pot bowl, though, was probably ever ready as is the modern West Indian custom, with the meat of turtle, fish, fowl, and other animals added to the base of cassareep and vegetables as they became available. Land crabs were hunted and eaten as by all later Bahamians. The flesh of the iguana and agouti were probably highly esteemed (as by later islanders) but must have been a rare treat, even reserved for caciques, as in Hispaniola. Lucayan meals may have included green vegetables and fruits, but more likely this was a deficiency made up more casually on foraging expeditions in the bush.[10]

At its best, the Lucayan diet was a healthy balance of carbohydrates, protein, and essential minerals and vitamins, differing from most modern diets by the almost total absence of animal fats (no bad feature at all). However, the diet was probably quite seriously deficient in the least favored islands, on long voyages of exploration, or in newly established settlements, and in all islands during periods of prolonged drought or in the wake of hurricanes. As the first Spaniards noted, the Lucayans were, in general, an active and healthy people who never starved; but none were fat.

Authorities differ as to whether the Lucayans cultivated any nonfood crops. Clearly they used and valued both cotton and tobacco. Columbus listed large balls of spun cotton and tobacco among the items that were initially offered as gifts or in trade. One Lucayan was prepared to exchange sixteen balls, an *arroba* in weight (twenty-five pounds), for three small copper coins. Two days later, Columbus reported that the single canoer found going ahead of the expedition in the open ocean between Rum Cay and Long Island carried—besides Spanish glass beads and copper coins, a lump of cassava, and a gourd of water—"some dried leaves, which must be highly prized among them since already at San Salvador they presented me with some of them." This evidence and the fact that in the eighteenth century the black loam soils of the central Bahamas were regarded as ideal for the growing of sea-island cotton—and perhaps tobacco too—has led some writers to speculate that the Lucayans not only produced cotton and tobacco for their own use but grew a surplus for trade. Richard Rose has gone so far as to suggest that the cultivation and trading of cotton (like the production of salt and dried conch in the Turks and Caicos Islands in the hypothesis of Sears and Sullivan) was sufficient reason for the colonization of the central Bahamas in the first place.[11]

Several facts, though, militate against this theory. The Bahama black

loam soils were not all that common and not always found in close
association with known Lucayan sites. The central Bahamas was not necessarily more suitable for cotton growing than many other locations in
the Antilles; and finally, so far absolutely no cotton-processing artifacts,
such as the spinning whorls which are commonly found, for example,
in Puerto Rico and Antigua, have been recovered from Lucayan sites.
Some cotton and tobacco were almost certainly grown by the Lucayans,
however, and this clearly required a fundamentally different type of agriculture from manioc and other food crops. Cotton bushes take years to
mature, and produce for many more years, and thus could not have been
farmed rotationally. Tobacco is an annual plant, cultivated in a style more
akin to manioc, but it has a different cultivation cycle, requiring moisture
for a much longer period and continual shade, as well as much more attention than either cotton or manioc—quite apart from the skill and care
needed for the curing of the leaf. In sum, the Lucayans probably had an
abundance of cotton and traded some, because it grew with comparative
facility on soils not required for growing food. But by the same token,
tobacco was thus "highly prized" not just because its use as a narcotic
was an essential part of the Arawak/Lucayan culture but because of its
relative scarcity.

There is no evidence one way or the other whether the Lucayans cultivated the *cahoba* bean, from which a narcotic snuff could be ground,
or the *bixio* (annatto) tree, of which the crushed beans produced a fast
red dye—both of which were reported in Hispaniola. More likely the
Lucayans found most of their dyes and medicines in the woods, building up a pharmacopeia by trial and error that can only be guessed at by
reference to later Out Island practice. Such indigenous plants, infused
as "teas," eaten or applied to the skin, probably included fever grass and
bay vine for fever and colds, catnip for constipation and worms, soldier
vine against skin eruptions, madeira or cascarilla bark (still used as the
basis for Campari liqueur) as tonics, and sundry plants as reputed aphro-
disiacs. As a counter to the effects of excessive venery, the Lucayans also
had a decoction of lignum vitae, which had a genuine effect in killing
the spirochetes of syphilis and was, indeed, the most effective specific
known until arsenical compounds were employed in the early twentieth
century. Probably the most useful and versatile of all medicinal plants,
though, was the aloe or agave plant, to which almost magical properties
have been ascribed by recent enthusiasts. Not only is the yellow sap a
wonderful ointment for burns and cuts, but the leaves when chewed are
said to aid digestion, and a bitter tea made from them to be a cure for

colds and constipation. Aloe sap can even be used as a form of shampoo, giving the hair a lustrous sheen.[12]

The knowledge of less benign bush medicines has mostly been lost, as have the aboriginal skills of making body paints from leaves, barks, and berries fixed with tree resins—and in any case Lucayans were probably far less adept in these mysteries than their Antillean cousins and enemies. For example, manchioneel wood was known to produce a potent poison, even drops of sap raising painful rashes on the skin; but it seems that the Lucayans did not use the boiled-down juice as a lethal poison for arrow and spear tips, as the Caribs did.

It is not known how far Lucayan bush medicine was a specialized craft or mystery, but it is likely that its fullest skills were developed and handed on by a very few practitioners, as in later times. The skills of hunting and fishing, however, were shared by all Lucayan men and learned by boys at an early age. Catching the scuttling land crabs was easy enough—child's play—but other game was scarcer and more elusive. Agouti and iguana, being timorous creatures, were soon chased from the peopled areas and required expeditions deep into the bush or to uninhabited cays. The Hispaniola method of catching agouti was for large numbers of men to drive them into corrals with the help of dogs and rings of fire, keeping them alive for later eating. The Lucayans, it seems, had far fewer dogs than the Tainos and insufficient numbers of persons to make circles of beaters and were forced therefore to hunt and kill for more immediate consumption. Iguana too were more commonly taken by guile than force of numbers, allegedly by chasing them up trees, persuading them to open their mouths in answer to an imitated call, thrusting in a stick and yanking them to the ground, to be beaten to death with clubs. Decoys were also used, as well as nets, to catch the native green parrots and flamingoes, and migrating ducks and geese. Parrots (much valued for their feathers if not their flesh) were entrapped with live birds already tamed, while flamingoes, ducks, and geese were stalked through shallow lake water by men under the cover of roughly shaped calabashes.[13]

By the Spaniards' accounts, fishing methods were even more varied and ingenious. Fishing—the Lucayans' mainstay—was of three distinct types, reef, tidal flats, and lagoon, with a nice balance between them according to weather and season. The richest but most dangerous grounds were the offshore reefs. Here the Lucayans sought grouper, snapper, parrot fish, porgies, and grunts, using stone-weighted nets made of cotton mesh or baited lines with bone or shell hooks. They may also have hooked the great spiny lobster (crawfish) from under the rocks with long crooked spears as do modern Out Islanders. Navigating the small Lucayan canoes between surge and rock while handling paddles, nets, lines, and spears, was delicate at the best of times, and impossible in stormy conditions.

The same fish species were found, in smaller numbers, on the tidal flats found between or in the lee of most Bahamian islands, along with the swift and wily bonefish, which the Lucayans seem to have eaten in greater numbers than any other. This was probably the preferred Lucayan fishing location, spears and fish traps being employed as well as nets and lines. The use of poison vines to stun fish in shallow waters (described in Hispaniola) is unlikely to have been a common Lucayan practice, though it is not so far-fetched as the use of a captive suckerfish (remora) to catch others, which is also described by early writers. Catching bonefish was as much a skill—maybe as much a sport—then as now, more akin to hunting than fishing. These nervous creatures have to be stalked without the slightest splashing, speared from behind, or caught in nets cast ahead of their sudden flight.

Lagoon or creek fishing was comparatively sedate, and may have involved women and children as well as men. Besides crabs, conchs, and other mollusks, most fishes, including small sharks, ventured with the tides into creeks or sea-connected lagoons. Again, nets, lines, and spears were used, but the most effective method was the use of weirs made of close-set stakes, converging on an enclosure which could be used to store the fish alive. Rather more substantial corrals were made for green and hawksbill turtles, which were caught either in the open sea or when they ventured ashore to lay their eggs, between April and July. Lucayans pursued the largest and most sluggish denizen of Bahamian creeks and lagoons, the manatee, with harpoons and spears, and this may explain its virtual extinction before the colonial period. The crocodile probably survived rather longer because it was too fierce for the Lucayans, or its flesh was not highly esteemed as food. Similarly, the mercurial monk seals which flocked on the reefs, as well as the great whales, sharks, and game fish which abounded in the deeper waters, were almost proof against Lucayan fishing techniques and survived until much later predators came, with their guns, power harpoons, and motorboats.[14]

As we have seen, Lucayan artifacts were sparser, cruder, more strictly functional than those of other Arawaks. This suggests that essential craft skills were shared by most adult Lucayans, rather than being the preserve of specialist craftsmen. This was certainly true of the making of houses and the plaiting of palmetto and cotton, and probably held for the manufacture of most utensils, tools, and weapons. In the absence of suitable materials, stone shaping and flint knapping were skills almost totally undeveloped, and the lack of distinctive styles, shapes or sizes for the tools and weapons of shell, bone or coral, testifies mainly to the chance occurrence of the available materials. Only in the making of very small objects, such as fishhooks and beads, in pottery, basket-weaving and the building of canoes, did the Lucayans exhibit real artisanal skills, and even here their products were noticeably inferior to those of Antillean craftsmen. Apparently neither the Lucayans or any other Arawaks knew the art of weaving cotton cloth, merely netting the cotton thread into meshes suitable for hammocks, nets and the types of flimsy clothing made by women to hide their private parts. The failure to develop cotton weaving is, perhaps, surprising considering the considerable skills developed in basket-weaving.

No samples of Lucayan basketwork survive, but the descriptions by early writers and the products of modern Arawak weavers suggest a variety of styles and uses, including fish pots, food containers, or even an urn-shaped basket with a weave so tight that it could be used for carrying water. Not much more is known about the making of Lucayan pottery, though it does seem likely that each household—certainly each settlement—fashioned and fired its own. No true clays exist in the Bahamas, and modern potters are at a loss to know quite how the Lucayans managed to make pottery from the Bahama red loam at all, especially without wheels or kilns. The flat griddles were apparently mass-molded, but all bowl shapes were fashioned by the coiling method. The mixed red loam paste, with its 10–25 percent temper of crushed *lucina* shell, was first kneaded into ropes and then coiled into the shape of platters, hemispherical or even deeper bowls, before being fired in open hearths.

The bases of Lucayan bowls were never flat, but rounded. The shoulders were straight or incurving, never out-flared. The rims were usually thickened and flat, with a sharper angle at the inner edge, though rounded and even beveled forms were known. The insides of bowls were moderately polished, the outsides rough, perhaps to facilitate handling, for few if any of them had handles or lugs. The great majority of Lucayan earthenware was completely undecorated, and even the palmetto-weave pattern found on some 10 percent of sherds may have been accidental. It occurs mostly on the outer surfaces of griddle sherds or the curved lower parts of the bowls, which suggests that the wet shaped paste was placed either on palmetto mats to dry or, in the case of bowls, into roughly made palmetto baskets to keep the rounded shape, before firing.

Just as essential as pottery to the Lucayan way of life was the building of canoes, with the Bahamian habitat imposing equal constraints. The huge soft-centered silk cotton tree (*ceiba*), out of which the Tainans fashioned *canoas* up to seventy-five feet long, carrying seventy to eighty men, were not indigenous to the Bahamas. The native cedar (*Juniperis lucayana*) and horseflesh tree (*Lysilonia sabicu*) never attained the height of similar trees in Hispaniola and Cuba. Lucayan canoes were therefore smaller and less seaworthy than those of the Greater Antilles. Plain square-ended dugouts, rarely more than twenty feet long or capable of carrying more than five men, they yet were each the result of many hundreds of man-hours of labor.[15] After the tallest straight tree available had been felled and even more laboriously trimmed, the trunk was hollowed where it lay, with fire and conch-shell adze. Once roughly shaped, the canoe, weighing perhaps a ton, would have to be manhandled down to the water, where it would be finished and its trim finally adjusted.

With no keel and little freeboard, Lucayan canoes must have been tricky to manage at the best of times. Swimming expertise was vital, for the canoes often capsized, being bailed once righted with the gourds invariably carried as a precaution. Navigation was very dependent upon the skill of the men handling the paddles, which were long and spade-shaped, with cross-bar handles. Indeed, paddles (an example of which was found in a cave as far north as More's Island, Abaco, in 1912) were vital implements which themselves took long hours and considerable skill to fashion.

Within the limits of materials and tools, the Lucayans were considerable woodworkers. Besides canoes and their fittings, they fashioned axe handles and wooden cutlasses, and perhaps some simple stools and platters, from the Bahamian hardwoods such as mahogany (*Sweitenia mahogani*, later called madeira). However, the more elaborate woodwork for which Hispaniola was famed was beyond the Lucayans' resources. Unlike those of the Greater Antilles, Lucayan canoes were not normally decorated with carving, and the rare carved wooden artifacts found in the Bahamas—such as the turtle-shaped duhos or large wooden zemis— were probably, like gold, guanin, and hardstone celts, imports or heirlooms, perhaps even relics of the original migration, possessing special, numinous value.

3

Yocahú and Atabeyra:
Life, Death, and the Lucayan Mentalité

WHAT WE HAVE LEARNED OR INFERRED from Lucayan artifacts and early writers about Lucayan behavior and beliefs allows us to proceed with some confidence from a relatively complete understanding of their way of life and the difficulties which they faced into the realm of their *mentalité*.[1]

By all accounts the Lucayans were the least warlike of all Amerindians, but this may have been as much due to their lack of formal integration and resources, and a realistic calculation of their chances in combat, as to an intrinsic pacifism. In fact, Lucayans were probably more politically sophisticated, and enjoyed better communications with their nearer neighbors, than the Spaniards realized, without having close political ties. Obviously, the word of the arrival of Columbus's ships was almost immediately disseminated throughout Guanahaní, and the Lucayan taken from his canoe near Rum Cay was clearly on his way to pass the news and prepare the settlements on Long Island for the Spaniards' coming. The people of each island, and those of adjacent islands such as San Salvador, Rum Cay, and Long Island, were likely to have had informal political ties based upon fairly close kinship; but the people of more distant islands, especially to the southeast, may have been regarded with much more reserve. The Lucayans of Long Island, for example, seemed to regard Crooked Island and Acklin's, across a mere thirty-mile channel to windward, as almost a foreign country or kingdom. For their part, the Lucayans of Crooked Island, though they suggested ties with Cuba—said to be only one and a half hours by canoe from the nearest Bahamian islet—appeared to regard Hispaniola as a semimythical land, full of people, cities, and rival kings.[2]

Even if Lucayans did not normally fight among themselves as some Taino chiefdoms did, they were, of necessity, prepared to defend themselves against attack. They had no bows and arrows but practiced spear and stone throwing and the dodging of missiles as a kind of game and prepared themselves as for battle by painting their bodies with fearsome designs and wearing protective zemis—particularly a type in the form of a dog with an out-thrust penis. At the same time they would steel their spirits by taking narcotic snuff and by dancing and chanting. The fact that these activities had become more or less ritualized suggests that they reflected earlier conflicts against the Caribs during the great migration rather than present realities. However, Columbus did note war wounds among the Lucayans of Guanahaní, who indicated that they were caused in defending themselves against predators "from other islands," who may have been Tainos as well as Caribs or Ciguayos, or even Indians from Florida.[3]

To most visitors the Lucayans, and most other Arawaks, seemed extravagantly hospitable—though this may well have been a defensive tactic. As the Spaniards noted, they were free with almost all of their meager possessions, though at the same time eager to obtain novelties in exchange, even by stealing. When male strangers arrived in Hispaniola they were offered the cacique's stool, and the elders even squatted before them. Visitors were feasted and quite casually invited to enjoy the sexual favors of the women—or at least some of them—a custom that filled long-distance mariners from less promiscuous cultures with grateful excitement. Though all Arawaks had rigid incest taboos and class divisions that kept upper-class women from lower-class men, they did not greatly value chastity. Males and females were initiated into sex at puberty, and females were expected to have considerable sexual experience before they were married. One unfortunate consequence was that venereal disease (syphilis) was endemic—as the first Spaniards and pretty soon most other Europeans found to their cost. After centuries of immunization, the form of syphilis was not nearly as serious to the Lucayans as to the unimmunized newcomers, but the disease very likely was a major factor in controlling the population, causing low fertility rates, increasing infant mortality, and contributing to adult disability and early deaths.[4]

Other factors which damaged the Lucayan population included endemic diseases such as forms of yellow and blackwater fever, amoebic dysentery and intestinal worms, infected wounds, accidental poisoning, and other accidents, especially drowning—not to mention the debility and death from starvation or near-starvation in times of drought or after hurricanes. However, compared with most other tropical parts of the world it was not an unhealthy environment, and by and large, the Luca-

yans who survived infancy were a healthy people, though their expectation of life was not high by modern standards. Extrapolations from other
similar populations studied suggest live birthrates for the Lucayans before the Europeans arrived no higher than twenty per thousand per year,
infant mortality rates around 20 percent of live births, an average life
expectancy at the age of five of some thirty further years, and a notable
paucity of persons over fifty years of age.[5]

Such demographic conditions, and perhaps a deeper trait in the
Lucayan psyche, induced a sense of fatalism, almost callousness toward
death, though this was perhaps mitigated (as in countless other cultures)
by an optimistic view of the afterlife. To the horror of Europeans, sick
persons were often carried into the bush and left in their hammocks with
a gourd of water and cassava, to die or, less commonly, recover on their
own. In Hispaniola terminally ill caciques were said to be strangled as
a mark of respect, along with their wives and slaves, whom they would
need in the other world (coyaba)—though for numerical reasons alone
this is unlikely to have been the Lucayan custom. For the Arawaks at
large there seem to have been no standard funerary customs. Rouse reports that those who died in their house might be cremated by setting the
house afire. The bones of those who died in the bush might be collected
later for burial, but often their skulls were kept by their surviving relatives in baskets in their houses. This was particularly true of caciques,
whose corpses might be disembowelled, dried over a fire, and kept as
human zemis. In other cases, says Rouse, the corpse was flexed, wound
with cotton, and placed either in a grave linked with sticks or in a special
cave—along with personal possessions (ornaments, zemis, and duho in
the case of a cacique) and a bowl of water and some bread for its last journey.[6] This last seems to have been the usual Lucayan custom. Human
bones have not yet been found on Lucayan habitation sites, or any signs
of cremation. The only Lucayans' remains found have been discovered
separate from settlements in caves, usually by farmers digging out bat
guano for fertilizer. The consequent disturbance of the soil has made it
difficult to reconstruct Lucayan funerary customs, but the frequent conjunction of valuable material relics with Lucayan bones, and the fact that
many of the caves show traces of petroglyphs, confirm that these were
regular and sacred burial sites.

From Spanish accounts we know rather more about Lucayan ceremonies and festivals at which the caciques presided, and about the
operations of the caciques—or the specially chosen members of their
class—in their role as priests or shamans. One of the most important

functions of such *bohuti* was that of medicine man, or ultimate doctor in the community. Ordinary bush medicine was in the common domain, though usually the preserve of certain older women, who administered their remedies over a period of up to twenty days, accompanied with a caution to abstain from meat and fish. Sick persons were also frequently bathed, both to clean and cool the skin. The shaman was called in only if the patient continued sick or declined further. His method then was mainly magical: intercessionary and symbiotic. Before the shaman's visit, shaman and patient both fasted, while the shaman took narcotic snuff in order to ascertain from his zemi the cause of the disease. He then blackened his face with soot, swallowed a purgative juice called *goia,* and proceeded for the first time to the patient's hut. There the shaman lighted a torch, took another type of drink, and performed a songlike incantation. Approaching the patient, he pretended to suck out the evil, in the form of a piece of flesh, bone or stone, specially secreted. Thrown outside the hut, these foreign objects were explained as something the patient had swallowed or which had been placed inside him by his zemi as a punishment for neglect. If the patient recovered, the discarded object was placed in a small basket and kept as a special form of zemi against a recurrence—a permanent memento of the shaman and his own particular zemi's power.

If, though, the patient died and his relatives were sufficiently powerful, there might be a formal inquest to see whether the shaman should be held responsible. The chief witness was the dead man himself, who was expected to answer by making certain signs, either after an infusion made with goia and powdered nail clippings and hair was forced down his throat, or when his body was placed on live coals under a blanket of earth. One of the incriminating signs was for the shaman himself to break out in sores, said to be caused by the accusing spirit of the deceased or by the smoke from his cremated body. If the shaman was found culpable he was beaten, though never killed for fear of retribution from his zemi in the form of snakes.[7]

To a skeptical person, all this suggests that the Lucayans were virtually powerless against the gravest diseases and that recovery was very much a matter of chance. The punishment of a shaman who both failed to save his patient and became ill himself suggests an instinctive recognition that certain diseases were communicable, though holding the shaman accountable (in itself, surely an admirable principle) was unlikely in those times to have improved his later performance. On the other hand, there were several positive aspects of Lucayan medicine. The isolation of the sick, the concern for cleanliness, the use of cooling lotions, the preference for simple well-tried specifics before more "heroic" medicine, the abstinence from meat and fish, and the period of more prolonged fasting (on the later folk-medicine principle of "starve a fever") may have saved some Lucayans who would have died under the ministrations of contemporary European doctors.

Except for occasional informal dances and contests, all Lucayan group activities revolved around the caciques and their class of leader-priests. Ball games and other contests sometimes took place between villages, when they were accompanied by dances of a semicompetitive kind and songs extolling the virtues of each group and its leaders. It is unlikely that the quasi-gladiatorial contests described in Hispaniola, in which the losers were killed—a form of ritualized and limited interclan warfare— ever occurred in Lucayan society. Most festivities, indeed, were held at the village level, with feasting followed by dances, involving the men and women separately and together, and songs narrating in mythical form the clan and tribal history and the lives of caciques and their ancestors.

The happiest occasions were marriage feasts and the ceremonies in honor of the cacique's and village zemis at the time of the main harvest, in autumn. More solemn formalities were held at the funerals of promi- nent men, and the most serious rituals of all were performed on those rare and drastic occasions when the Lucayans prepared for war. Songs and dances when combined were called an *ariéto*. Music was provided by wooden gongs made from hollowed logs, *maracas* made by seeds within small gourds or the dried pods of the tamarind tree, and castanets made out of plates of hardwood or guanin. Though the commoners danced with tinkling rattles made of small shells attached to their limbs, it was the caciques and other leading men who provided the main music—a rhythmic dominance that was more than symbolic. Similarly, it was the leaders who composed and handed down the songs from generation to generation, calling them out as they led the ariéto, for the commoners to repeat in a higher tone. The repertoire of such songs was the official myth-history of the group. New songs were composed mainly for the funerals of caciques, providing an idealized biography of the deceased to add to the cumulative, and self-perpetuating, oral history of the people and its ruling class.

Ariétos were almost invariably held at night when it was cool, at times when the moon was full. In preparation, the Lucayans bathed, painted themselves, and also, it was said, took an emetic drink, to empty their stomachs before dancing and perhaps to facilitate intoxication. Though the Hispaniola Taino concocted a potent beer from corn, the Lucayans seem to have lacked an alcoholic drink. Tobacco or some other narcotic snuff, however, was inhaled to achieve a degree of intoxication. In any case, dancing usually went on to the point of exhaustion and collapse, with insensible caciques carried to their houses, while stupified commoners were left where they lay.[8] Such behavior, which greatly intensified after the Spanish conquest, may well have been an expression of mass grief or despair—at the loss of a valued leader, the onset of a hopeless war—or through a desire to escape from the bitter and irreversible realities of mundane life, into the more roseate environment of the spirit world.

Needless to say, the Lucayans, like all Arawaks (and most Africans too), were classic animists. Theirs was a philosophy that related the spirits of all living things not only to each other, but to those of the dead and as yet unborn, and also to the spirits immanent in sun, moon, and stars, sea, rocks, and trees, and natural phenomena; and a religion that involved communication and intercession with the spirit world through various kinds of sorcery, especially the use of zemis. Many Lucayan ceremonies were basically religious, and all had religious undertones, with the cacique class combining its priestly with its leadership role. Dancing to the limits of exhaustion under the narcotic effect of drugs and rhythmic music was very much part of the process of communication, just as the myths incorporated in the accompanying songs can tell us much of the world from which the Lucayans believed they had sprung, and which they wished to rejoin.

Very much can also be learned from Lucayan iconography, as displayed in ceremonial objects such as duhos, in the form of zemis, and in the petroglyphs which have survived in several sacred caves. Some of the duhos found in the Bahamas and adjacent islands are simple stools, carved from hardwood with geometrical incised designs, indentations at each end for the insertion of poles to convert the seat into a palanquin for carrying the cacique owner from place to place. But the most elaborate duhos are made in the forms of four-legged animals, either an iguana or a turtle. Such forms Olsen regards as more than stools, and suggests they were altars for votive offerings.[9] Perhaps they were both, with the cacique/priest symbolically supported on the back of a sacred creature during ceremonies, and the duho used as the centerpiece of a votive shrine at other times, or after the death of its cacique owner. Certainly, the Lucayans revered the land-borne iguana and even more its amphibious equivalent, the turtle, as the original denizens of the islands and seas in which they lived. Both creatures have a primeval aspect, but the turtle really *is* primeval. It, or its ancestor species, has inhabited the Caribbean and Bahamas region for millions of years—a relic of the age of reptiles—living in balance between sea and land. As David Campbell has written,

> Although sea turtles are superbly adapted to life in the sea, they are, like all reptiles, tied by ancient bonds of physiology to the land. For the sea turtles must lay their eggs on the shore, buried in the sand above the reach of high tides. . . . The green turtle is highly specific in choosing her nesting site; by means of chemical cues or more subtle means of navigation, she returns to the same beaches on which she was born. These homeward exoduses often entail thousands of miles of swimming over a period of many weeks. Some researchers have hypothesized that in its quest for its natal nesting beaches, the green turtle has, over the millennia, followed the spreading continents and islands as they went scraping over the Earth's magma on tectonic plates.[10]

Clearly, the sea turtles were ideally suited to be sacred creatures for such island peoples as the Lucayans, providing them with an ideal of ocean navigation, and a dream of connection with the other peoples of the archipelago and basin, and with the places from which their own people sprang. It is a fascinating thought to imagine a Lucayan shaman with his magic communing with the turtles' spirit, even entering the dim common subconscious memory of the age when the islands were formed—and thus making at least an intuitive connection through the Lucayans' myths of their world's beginnings.

Less fanciful, though brilliantly imaginative, have been Fred Olsen's speculations on the origins and nature of Arawak religion and its relationship to the people's migration and dispersal, and changing ways of life.[11] For Olsen, the original and dominant cult was that of Yocahú. His was the image intended by the distinctive triangular zemis with incised facial features found in the Lesser Antilles, the progressively mutant and debased variants of which were found dispersed over the Greater Antilles and the Bahamas. To Olsen, whose work centered on Antigua, the triangular shape evoked both the volcanoes found in Guadeloupe, Martinique, and St. Vincent, and the hand-held mealing stones or pestles essential for the preparation of manioc and narcotic snuff. Yocahú was thus not just the fiery creative force within the universe but the father-provider of manioc, the staff of life, and of the holy herb which permitted communication with the spirit world.

Yocahú was unequivocally male, a reflection of and justification for the dominance of caciques and their class over the majority of Arawak womankind. Yet Arawak myths, as we have seen, also gave great power to a female figure, Atabeyra, with four alternative names, whose importance may well reflect the role of matrilineality and the consequent importance of queen mothers—indeed, all mothers—in the society. For Olsen, each of the names of Atabeyra represented one of her different functions, thus differentiating her cult: "mother of moving waters—the sea, the tides, and the springs—goddess of the moon, and the fertility goddess of childbirth." The images of Atabeyra are, understandably, much more varied than those of Yocahú. They include straightforward representations of the human female form in various degrees of abstraction, including almost monumental stone figures found in Puerto Rico. Female animal forms are also found, such as those of frogs. But the predominant image—found two-dimensionally in petroglyphs as well as in three-dimensional figurines—is that of a crouching female figure in the process of childbirth.[12]

Besides the direct representation of Yocahú and Atabeyra there are also found in the Antilles representations of a Cerberus-like dog-deity sometimes called Opiyel-Guaobiran, the most finished example of which (from Trois-Rivières, Haiti) depicts an upright figure with paws placed beneath its chin, as are the hands of Atabeyra in the childbirth figurines, though in place of the emerging fetus is a rampant penis. This type of canine image—like those of iguana and turtle with quasi-human heads—may well represent the basic male force inherent in Jocahú, though it may also be related to the somewhat obscurer maternal uncle figure in Arawak myth, Guaca.[13]

Because the early Spaniards were fascinated by Amerindian "idolatry" (using it to build up a case for their suitability as slaves to Christians), and because petroglyphs, zemis, and votive objectives stand out among the archeological remains, much is known about and can be inferred from the trappings of Arawak religion. Despite brilliant reconstructions by such as Olsen, though, much less is known about the actual ceremonies and rituals involved—which were, of course, of their nature well-guarded mysteries even then. Probably for that very reason they varied more from place to place, and changed more quickly, than did the visible iconography. Each household, each individual, had its own protective zemi, in the form of a sizeable image or much smaller amulet. The most important and potent sacred objects in each community, however, were kept in a shrine or shrines, under the control of the cacique-shaman and his acolytes. Such shrines would be the focus of ceremonies on regular occasions, such as the phases of the moon and tides, planting, reaping, and fishing seasons, but also in emergencies such as before wars, during drought or epidemics, or after hurricanes. Then, after the shaman had prepared himself with ritual bathing, goia, and narcotic snuff, the assembled clan would be led in rituals aimed to consult, implore, and propitiate the gods through their common zemis. Propitiation, it seems, rarely if ever took the form of blood sacrifices as elsewhere in the Americas but normally involved votive offerings of small stones or small carvings, representing specific animals (dogs, agoutis, birds, turtles, or manatee), different fishes (angel fish, grouper, sharks, or whales) and even persons.

Olsen's reconstructions of Arawak rituals are probably too specific. He does, however, make one very convincing conclusion about the distribution of cult figurines throughout the Arawak world. The representations of Atabeyra (and of the dog-deity Opiyet-Guaobiran) were much more common in the Greater than in the Lesser Antilles, where straightforward images of Yocahú predominated. For Olsen this signified not only the migration of the people from the homeland of volcanic fires, earthquakes, the most destructive hurricanes, and the constant threat of Carib attacks, into a gentler environment, with the consequent transmutation of the culture into one that was softer and more subtle, complex, and diverse.

What then of the Lucayan branch of the Arawak family, and its religion?[14] The zemis found in the Bahamas, though sparser than in other Arawakan areas, include examples of most Antillean types—"trade wares"—and also local variants. Recognizable images of Yocahú and Atabeyra occur, along with animal forms such as those of frogs, iguanas, and turtles (no dogs, it seems)—but there is no predominant form. The cult of Yocahú had, predictably, faded, and the zemis suggest a maritime and small-island variant of the propitiatory cult of Atabeyra and her female minions. The Lucayan petroglyphs, notably those found in the Hartford Cave on Rum Cay, however, suggest an even more basic form of religion—reduced to a simple fertility cult involving the male and female principles. Petroglyphs include stylized representations of iguanas and turtles as well as anthropomorphic forms. Other incisions appear to be simple geometric patterns. The predominant motifs, though, are clearly sexual in form. One type appears to be a variant of one intermittently found in the Antilles: a phallic pillar surmounted by a representation of the sun. This would seem to be a recognition of the sources of life and regeneration in the sun and semen alike—a very distant derivative of the worship of the male god Yocahú, source of fire and manioc. Another common motif is a pattern of concentric rings clearly representing the female genitalia. This would seem to be a recognition of the essential role of women in procreation, as symbolized elsewhere by the worship of Atabeyra—or rather, since the pattern of concentric circles is often pierced by phallic uprights, a representation of the necessary conjunction of male and female in the procreative process.

In sum, as befitted a population at the far oceanic edge of a large culture, Lucayan religion appears to have been a simpler, more basic form of communication and intercession with, and propitiation of, the forces that determined human survival, continuation, and increase. However, much more than protection against the elements and human enemies, and even more than rewards from the bounty of the sea, Lucayan religion craved of its gods a general fertility: for the fields through salutary regulation of the seasons, and for the people themselves through freedom from the effects of epidemic disease. Lucayan religion also included poignant echoes of an idealized world, situated somewhere to the south and east, from which the Lucayans had been expelled and to which they hoped to return—in death if not in life. The Lucayan heaven, coyaba, was a paradise in which there would be plenteous food and drink and sexual license; where there would be no disease and human enemies; where, indeed, the Caribs would be servants, not cruel and cannibalistic masters.

A fragile and peace-loving people in a meager environment, at the northwestern fringe of the Arawak world, the Lucayans were clearly disposed to regard any persons who came from farther north and east as very potent aliens, if not akin to gods. Of an entirely different color and aspect (not to mention smell), wearing clothes, riding in huge boats with wings, and bringing with them unimaginable wonders of technology, such beings would be as much beyond the scope of the Lucayans' imagination as the visitors from outer space created by modern science fiction. In all senses, the Lucayans were certain to be enthralled. Against such potent beings resistance would be futile. The best that the Lucayans could hope for was that the newcomers could be placated or were naturally benign and generous. In material terms the visitors from Europe had infinitely more to offer than the Hispaniola Tainos, who were technologically the most advanced people whom the Lucayans knew. But the ultimate bait which the Europeans could (and very soon did) offer was the chance of repatriation; to be carried in the wondrous winged boats under the protection of European swords and guns, back to the semimythical ancestral heartland to the south and east.

~ *4* ~

Unequal Exchange: The Spanish Fate of the Lucayan People, 1492–1525

IT IS FORTUNATE that this book deals only indirectly with the history of events, for the Lucayans entered the pages of *histoire événementuelle* only to be almost instantly (within twenty-five years) destroyed. The fatal first contact occurred at about 7 A.M. on Friday, October 12, 1492, when, having sighted land two hours after midnight and jogging till dawn, the *Pinta, Niña,* and *Santa Maria* came off what is now called Long Bay, San Salvador Island, Bahamas.[1]

Theodore de Bry in his 1594 engraving of Columbus's landing 102 years earlier, got it all right except the details. Some naked Indians flee in terror at the sight of ships and men, while others, more intrepid and curious, bring gifts to the Great Discoverer, who is standing with his armed captains in their Sunday (or new-continent-claiming) best suits and armor. "Soon many people of the island gathered there," wrote Columbus.

> I, in order that they might feel great amity towards us, because I knew they were a people to be delivered and converted to our holy faith rather by love than by force, gave to some among them red caps and some glass beads, which they hung round their necks, and many other things, of little value. . . . Afterwards they came swimming to the ships' boats where we were, and brought parrots and cotton thread in balls, and spears and many other things, and we exchanged for them other things, such as small glass beads and hawks' bells. . . . In fact, they took all and gave all, such as they had, with good will, but they seemed to me that they were a people very deficient in everything. They all go about naked as their mothers bore them, and the women also, although I saw only one very young girl. And all those whom I did see were youths, so that I did not see one who was over thirty years of age. . . . They should be good servants and of good intelligence,

since I see that they very soon say all that is said to them, and I believe that they would easily be made Christians, for it appeared to me that they had no creed.[2]

Though only an adopted Spaniard, Columbus inherited the harsh ethos of the long reconquest of peninsular Spain from the Moors, which coincidentally ended the year he reached San Salvador: that the expansion of Spain was a divinely inspired crusade, which ordained to the victors the souls and bodies of the conquered people, as well as their land and treasure. To this he added a new ingredient, based on a polarized view of man in the State of Nature. For Columbus, the Lucayans were the prototype Good Indians, impotent and ignorant but friendly and willing to learn, and thus suitable to be made into good Christians and good servants. The antithetical Bad Indians whom Columbus was predisposed to find were not very far away. These were clearly the people of whom the men of Guanahaní spoke, who "came from other islands which are near, and wished to capture them . . . to take them for slaves," from whom they had received wounds in defending themselves. Such men were the Caribs and Ciguayo, whom the Spaniards encountered soon enough, who by their resistance to God's mandate and their beastly behavior were themselves natural candidates for enslavement, once subdued. Not that subservience would necessarily save even the "good" Lucayans from involuntary servitude, for as Columbus wrote as early as Day Three of his fifteen-day tour of the central Bahamas: "I went this morning, that I might be able to give an account . . . where a fort could be built . . . although I do not see that it is necessary to do so, for these people are very unskilled in arms, as your Highnesses will see from the seven whom I caused to be taken in order to carry them off that they may learn our language and return. However, when your Highnesses so command, they can all be carried off to Castile or held captive in the island itself, since with fifty men they would all be kept in subjection and forced to do whatever may be wished."[3]

Having given the Lucayans some credit for intelligence, it is surprising that Columbus fell so easily into the notion that they were simple people fit only to be duped. Reading between the lines of Columbus's euphoric (perhaps ingenuous) journal we can, in fact, deduce that the Lucayans' behavior was much more equivocal and rational than simply to regard the Spaniards as godlike saviors—even that it was Columbus, not they, who was most misled.

Some of the inhabitants of Guanahaní appeared to ask the Spaniards if they came from heaven (in a sense, of course, Columbus, the Catholic zealot, thought they had). Columbus even quoted the thronging Lucayans as calling out to the rest to "come and see the men who have come from heaven; bring them food and drink," though quite how he could understand their words so soon is not made clear. Much more likely is that the Lucayans were fearfully offering propitiatory gifts to strange and potent creatures. At first only young men came forth to meet the Spaniards, probably sent with gifts by the elders, who prudently stayed back in the villages with the women. Columbus was clearly not invited into the villages themselves.[4]

The gifts of food, drink, cotton, parrots, and spears seemed to work the trick. The newcomers appeared to threaten no immediate harm, and offered in return glittering novelties. As Columbus candidly explained in his journal, his whole program of gift giving and treating the Indians well was aimed at reassuring them. But nervousness remained among the Lucayans, with adequate reason. The Spaniards clearly lusted for gold and were apt to seize it from the Lucayans even if in the form of valued personal ornaments. Even more disturbing was the quite casual way in which the Spaniards took Lucayan men to accompany them on their onward voyage. Seven were taken from Guanahaní to carry back to Spain, though Columbus gave them the idea that they were simply guides to help him find gold.[5]

All Lucayans seemed at pains to point the Spaniards on their way, and the captives always threatened to escape. As the Spaniards neared their second island (Rum Cay or Santa Maria de la Concepción) the Guanahanians told them that the inhabitants wore large gold ornaments. Though suspecting a ruse, Columbus ordered a landing party, which came back disappointed. Meanwhile, two of the captives absconded in a canoe that was moored alongside the *Niña*. Chased to the land, they abandoned the canoe and went off into the bush "like chickens." Shortly afterward, another Lucayan came in a canoe to barter some cotton, and when he would not come aboard two Spaniards jumped in the sea and secured him. Columbus ordered him released and sent ashore with gifts, and was relieved to see that he seemed to give a more favorable report of the Spaniards to his fellow islanders than might have been rendered by the two escapees.[6]

Likewise, the man overtaken between Rum Cay and Long Island was secured but well treated, being released once the Spaniards reached Long Island to give a favorable account of the newcomers' intentions. The people of Long Island (Fernandina) Columbus found marginally "more domesticated and tractable and more intelligent" than those of the first two islands, with rather more material goods and more skill in bargaining. However, they fell far short of the inhabitants of the island called Samoet, which the earlier islanders had described as a kind of El Dorado—let alone of the kingdoms of Cipangu and Cathay, which from his readings of Marco Polo and his "mappemonde" Columbus expected to find somewhere in those parts.

The Long Island Lucayans showed their intelligence by pointing out that the fabled Samoet was the next island to the south-southwest (Crooked Island and Acklin's) and freely giving the Spaniards the water they needed for their onward voyage. When he reached Samoet, Columbus was equally disappointed, having to go to even greater lengths to reassure the inhabitants and finding them no richer in gold than the inhabitants of Fernandina, Santa Maria, or San Salvador. For twenty-four hours he waited in vain at Cabo del Isleo (Landrail Point, Crooked Island) for delegates from the king of the golden city of which his Guanahaní captives spoke. Again he met a band of similar poor Indians, mainly men, trading cotton and spears for scraps of glass and pottery, and a few tiny gold ornaments for glass beads and brass hawks' bells.

Obviously, there was no gold mine or King Croesus in Samoet. So Columbus decided to sail onward to the land of "Colba" (Cuba) to the west-southwest, of which the Crooked Islanders gave him such exaggerated accounts that he believed it might verily be Cipangu, or Cathay, the land of Kubla Khan. After carefully navigating the Ragged Island chain, the Spanish flotilla set sail from the Bahamas at sunrise on October 27, 1492, leaving the stunned Lucayans to digest the significance of their coming—and of the equally sudden disappearance of some of their own men. Almost certainly, the Lucayans' feelings were a mixture of relief, excitement, and trepidation; a sense, perhaps, that their world was changed forever, but no inkling, surely, that it was so shortly to end.[7]

THE LARGEST AND RICHEST of the Greater Antilles, Hispaniola was far more attractive than the Bahamas to the Spanish *conquistadores*. Yet the Spanish preoccupation with Hispaniola provided only a short respite for the Lucayans, who were totally eradicated even before the Spaniards' interest shifted from the Antilles to the infinitely greater riches of Mexico and Peru.[8]

Beautiful, fertile, and well watered, Hispaniola in 1492 had perhaps a million inhabitants, organized into five great kingdoms or confederacies, with dozens of subordinate but still substantial *caciquazcos*. As the heartland of the Tainan culture of the island Arawaks, it was the natural focus of Spanish attention, quite apart from its strategic location at the center of the northern rim of the Caribbean Sea. Even more important, it was the source of the gold which the Spaniards sought above all else.

Christopher Columbus began the process of "pacification" and exploitation, warring against uncooperative caciques and enslaving the captives, exacting an annual tribute of four hawksbells of gold dust or one hundred pounds of cotton per adult, and not hesitating to make up his cargoes to Spain with Arawak slaves. But the process was completed by Governor Ovando and his underlings between 1502 and 1509. Ovando personally tricked and had slaughtered fifty-six caciques in Xaragua in 1503, Velasquez subdued southwestern Haiti before subjugating Cuba, and Esquivel and Ponce de León put down the last Hispaniolan revolt in Higuey, before going on to conquer Jamaica and Puerto Rico respectively. Once the chief goldfields had been located, the labor of slaves was augmented by the quite callous relocation of whole free villages to work at panning and digging for gold, in eight-month shifts.

The people, indeed, were the most exploitable resource. By the system of *repartimiento*, individual Spaniards were granted not a specific area of land but the control of native communities, identified by their caciques. As Sauer summarizes the system, "the assigned communities were at the disposal of the beneficiary, to plant conucos, have personal services, provide labor at the mines, or for anything else, without limit of benefit or tenure."[9]

The result of the wars of pacification, of the dislocation of the established communities and ways of life, and, above all, of the introduction of European diseases was demographic disaster. As Kenneth Kiple explains,[10] malaria, smallpox, measles, and influenza struck the unimmunized Arawaks with quadruple force, concentrating on the most active and fertile segments of the population. Apart from the immediate effect on the birthrate, the deathrate was accelerated by malnutrition and lack of hygiene as those available to farm and fish, to cook and clean the villages were depleted. Lethal forms of dysentery were added to the short-term killers, while over a rather longer period, tuberculosis and European forms of venereal disease, as well as diseases picked up in Africa and transmitted to the Americas by the Europeans, took additional toll. By the time Ovando left there were no more than 50,000 natives of working age in Hispaniola, and before the gold petered out around 1520, Zuazo computed that of 1,130,000 natives enumerated in 1496 there remained only 11,000.[11] Even this pitiful remnant included the survivors of the Arawaks rounded up from the offshore islands of Mona, Saona, Gonaive, and Tortuga, and from the entire Bahamian archipelago.

Enslaving the Caribs proved impossible for the Spaniards. Yet even compared with the Tainos of Puerto Rico and Cuba, whose labor was needed by their conquerors, and those of Jamaica, who were difficult to round up from the mountainous and forested interior, the Lucayans were pathetically vulnerable. Though only one of the Lucayans abducted by Columbus seems to have survived the journey to Spain, this did not prevent Alonso de Hojeda and Amerigo Vespucci from quite casually carrying off 232 Lucayans as slaves to augment a cargo of braziletto wood on their return voyage to Spain in 1499. As Vespucci explained in his letter to Lorenzo de Medici, his patron, "We agreed together to go in a northern direction, where we discovered more than a thousand islands and found many naked inhabitants. They were all timid people of small intellect; we did what we liked with them. . . . Since the men were worn out from having been nearly a year at sea and were rationed down to six ounces of bread a day to eat and three small measures of water to drink, and the ships were becoming dangerously unseaworthy, the crew cried out that they wished to return to Castile to their homes and that they no longer desired to tempt fortune. Therefore we agreed to seize shiploads of the inhabitants as slaves and to load the ships with them and turn towards Spain."[12]

Other small slaving raids may have followed, but the real "harvest" of Lucayans was begun at the instance of Ovando just ten years later. In May 1509 King Ferdinand, having been told that very few Indians remained in Hispaniola and having taken advice from learned clerics that there was no conscientious objection, authorized the importation of all the Indians who could be found from the other islands, "in the manner in which they have been brought on other occasions, so that those needed shall be placed in our enterprises and the others given in allotments, in the manner that has been used until now."[13] A few months later, the Crown empowered a consortium of a dozen Spanish settlers of Concepción de la Vega and Santiago (Spanish *villas*, or townships, close to the Cibao goldfield) to outfit ships to sail from Puerto de Plata and Puerto Real for the capture of Lucayans—the first of several such *asientos*. The share of the *asientistas* was to be a quarter, that of the Crown, three-quarters, though this was later reduced to a half, then a fifth, as recruitment grew more difficult. If the Lucayans came without resistance they were to be treated as *naborías* (the actual Arawak word was used, though defined as life-long servitude); but if they resisted they were to be regarded as outright slaves.[14]

Because of their dispersion and the comparatively low population density within settlements, the Lucayans at first were not quite as susceptible to new contagious diseases as were the Antillean Arawaks. Inroads, though, had certainly been made by infections intermittently introduced since the first contact with the Spaniards, quite apart from the depredations made by the first slavers. Many Lucayan populations were already suffering demographic and social crisis by 1509, especially those closest to the usual sailing routes between Hispaniola and Spain, and this made them totally incapable of resisting Spanish force or guile.

Some settlements were so depleted that the migration of the survivors was inevitable. Others, in which the leaders had died or been deported, were rudderless. Yet even elsewhere, the cacique-priests must have been concerned about the viability of settlements in the face of declining numbers, and inclined to suggest a migration toward a more populous and favored land, where viable communities might be reconstituted.

Overt resistance was certainly impossible, and effective flight almost equally difficult. Some Lucayans may initially have fled to the more northern islands or even to Cuba. But a far greater number, convinced of the ill will of the zemis and the superior force of the Europeans, were predisposed to accept the Spaniards' promises that transportation into the Tainan heartland offered them safety if not salvation, and meekly followed their leaders to their fate. As Peter Martyr explained it, their own priests had already paved the way by instilling the belief "regarding their souls, which, after expiating their sins must leave the cold lands of the north for the south." In this way the slavers had an easy task to convince them "that they would thus reach the country where they would find their dead parents, their children, relatives and friends, and where they would enjoy every delight in the embraces of their loved ones."[15]

The first asientistas in 1509 reported that the nearer Lucayan islands were already depopulated, but within the following three years all the other inhabited islands were systematically scoured and cleared. By this time there may have been as many as fifteen thousand Lucayans left to be transported, though Peter Martyr gave the figure of forty thousand and Las Casas half a million. Las Casas probably exaggerated the toll of the transportation as much as the numbers carried when he wrote that the route of the slave ships was marked by floating corpses. Yet the transported Lucayans undoubtedly succumbed in Hispaniola even more rapidly than their Tainan predecessors. They were also quickly disabused of any notion that they were being resettled in an earthly paradise, or even allowed to keep any semblance of their social structure and way of life.[16]

To the loss of their familiar habitat and the break-up of families was added the calculated demotion of the cacique class by their harsh new masters. Despite their lack of resistance and any promises made by their captors, the Lucayans were uniformly treated as slaves. Even the caciques were reduced to the level of naborías, and all the transported Lucayans, like the Tainan naborías before them, were formed into gangs without respect to family or clan, and marched off to work at the goldfields. That they were regarded simply as slaves is borne out by the fact that from the beginning they were bought and sold, the price for an able-bodied Lucayan being said to have risen from 5 pesos to 150 within a couple of years because of the awful decline in their numbers.[17]

Peter Martyr competed with Las Casas to describe and deplore the Lucayans' plight in Hispaniola. Many perished on the march or at work; others fled to die in the bush. Epidemics of typhoid, malaria, smallpox, and pneumonia carried off those already weakened by unaccustomed work or insufficient and unfamiliar food. Others, it was said, simply lay down and willed themselves to die. Peter Martyr wrote poignantly of some Lucayans who escaped into the northern mountains, "where they might breathe the air wafted from their native country; with extended arms and open mouths they seemed to drink in their native air, and when misery reduced them to exhaustion, they dropped dead upon the ground." He also described three heroic Lucayans who fashioned a dug-out from a *jaruma* (silk cotton) tree and set out for their native islands, only to be recaptured two hundred miles out to sea.[18]

Had these maritime runaways succeeded, theirs would have been an experience similar to that of survivors returning to a homeland blasted by a nuclear winter. They would have found no living inhabitants, the villages tumbledown, and fields reverting to bush. Las Casas mentioned that when some "pious persons" followed in the wake of the asientistas they could find but eleven Lucayans in the whole archipelago, while Ponce de León as early as 1513 came to the conclusion that the islands were completely empty of people. Ponce de León's famous first voyage to Bimini and Florida was, indeed, a search as much for slaves as for new lands to develop, and while the newly discovered peninsula of Florida held much promise, the Bahamas disappointed him in both respects.

Sailing first along the outer islands—probably by way of the Caicos,

Mayaguana, Acklin's, Rum Cay, San Salvador, and the eastern tip of Abaco—Ponce de León redoubled into the Bahamas after exploring the coasts of Florida and northern Cuba, apparently stopping at Bimini, Grand Bahama, Abaco, northern Eleuthera, the Berry Islands, and Andros on his way back to Puerto Rico. On the whole of his voyage through the Bahamas, Ponce de León encountered a single Amerindian, an aged woman on Bimini or Grand Bahama, which he therefore named La Vieja. It is thus ironic that Peter Martyr associated this voyage with the search for a fountain of youth, which later writers confidently said was located on the island now called Bimini.[19]

By 1513, then, all surviving Lucayans were in Hispaniola, except for a few carried onward to Cuba and Puerto Rico. But not all those transported were destined to die in the Greater Antilles. Alonso de Hojeda, the first major enslaver of Lucayans, had also, by a cruel coincidence, discovered the rich pearling grounds of Cubagua and Margarita, off the Carib coast of Venezuela. Christopher Columbus was able to send pearls to Spain from this region, and Ovando far more, but it was Diego Columbus and his successors who ensured that Margarita, Cubagua, and the adjacent coast remained under the direct authority of Hispaniola, and really exploited the pearl fisheries, between 1512 and 1520. Since Cubagua was a desert island, and the Spaniards needed to maintain friendly relations with the inhabitants of Margarita in order to ensure food supplies, they had to search elsewhere for labor. It was considered unwise if not impossible to coerce the neighboring Caribs, so the authorities looked to the Lucayans already enslaved in the Antilles, who were known to be excellent swimmers, accustomed to diving for conch.[20]

All the surviving Lucayans who could be rounded up—now numbered in hundreds rather than thousands—were reshipped across the Caribbean to Cubagua. These survivors were presumably the hardiest of their race, who had built up at least some immunity to European diseases. But neither their strength nor their seasoning could save them from what was in store. Bartolomé de Las Casas, who vainly attempted to establish a model colony on the nearby coast, witnessed the fate of the Lucayans at first hand and condemned it indelibly. "The tyranny which the Spanish exercise against the Indians in the gathering or fishing for pearls is one of the most cruel and condemnable things which there would have been on earth," he wrote.

> There is no more infernal or insane life in this century with which it could
> be compared, although that of mining gold is of its nature very arduous

and wretched. They put them into the sea in three, four or five fathoms depth, from morning until sundown; they are always underwater, swimming without being able to catch their breath, tearing off the oysters in which the pearls grow. They come back to the surface for air with a small net bag filled with them, where a cruel Spaniard waits in a canoe or small boat, and if they take long in resting he gives them blows and shoves them under the water by the hair to dive again. Their meals are fish, oysters, cassava, and some corn . . . with which they are never filled to excess. The bed they give them at night is to secure them in stocks on the ground, so they will not escape. Many times they dive into the sea . . . and never return to the surface, because the sharks, which can devour an entire man, kill and eat them.[21]

In its own self-interest, the Crown passed an ordinance in 1512 to regulate conditions at the pearl beds, but in the face of the operators' greed this was as ineffectual as the decree that no peaceable Spanish subjects should be enslaved. The effects of undernourishment and overwork were horrific. De la Pena described symptoms of over-diving better understood today: ruptured eardrums and lungs, and the build-up of nitrogen in the blood called "the bends," which produces short-term agonies and long-term brain damage. From being a people whom Peter Martyr described as living "in that golden world of which the old writers speak so much, wherein men lived simply and innocently without enforcement of laws, without quarrelling, judges and libels, content only to satisfy nature," the Lucayans had become completely brutalized by their toil. "Their hair also, which is by nature black," wrote Las Casas, "is hereby changed and made of the same colour as that of the sea wolves; their bodies are also so besprinkled with the froth of the sea, that they appear rather like monsters than men."[22]

In effect, the Lucayan pearl divers were worked to death, and the fact that they were corralled like beasts without any regard for family life (quite apart from any unwillingness to bring children into such a world) determined that they could have no descendants. By the 1520s, long before the riches of the Spanish Pearl Coast had been exhausted, the last of all Lucayans had perished in Cubagua. By a tragic irony they had died within sight of the promised land—the South American coast from which their ancestors had left some fifteen hundred years earlier. It was true that these particular shores were still held by the Lucayans' traditional enemies, the Caribs (though Arawaks were to be found not far to windward). But this was, perhaps, both ironic and just. For it was the Caribs who at least partially avenged their traditional foes, by setting up what Troy S. Floyd has called a "poisoned arrow curtain" and killing very many Spaniards—including the missionaries and settlers of Las Casas's model colony.[23] By their resistance the Caribs also pointed up the fact that indigenous conflicts, even the imagined dichotomy between Good and Bad Indians, had been subsumed in the far greater dialectic between all native Amerindians and the invading European economy, polity, and culture.

THERE ARE STILL about fifty thousand Arawaks to be found on the northern shores of South America—perhaps half of them living something like the traditional life.[24] A few thousand persons scattered among the modern populations of the Greater Antilles may be at least partially descended from the Tainos. Yet the Lucayans were a people eradicated without genetic trace, in the islands of their exile as in their native archipelago. With such a discontinuity between the first certain inhabitants of the Bahamas and all later Bahamians, we may well ask what justification there is in considering the Lucayans so fully in a history of the Bahamian people.

Probably no people ever carried less in the way of material goods or technical expertise to colonize a deserted region than did the original Arawak migrants into the Bahama Islands. Fugitives from more aggressive peoples, including those who were at least symbolically cannibalistic, they were almost completely lacking in aggression themselves. Even their attitude toward the new environment was nonexploitative. Bringing a limited range of farming and fishing skills, they merely sought subsistence. Thus they modified the environment less, and were more rapidly and completely reshaped by it, than were any later migrants.

In other words, the Lucayan aboriginals were, in every sense, the purest Bahamians. Their achievements and their experience—including their tragic demise—provided a model, and a moral, for all those who in the subsequent five hundred years have tried to make the Bahamas their home. Above all, the Lucayans adapted their economy to achieve a subtle but effective balance between the resources of the meager land and the richer sea. No subsequent Bahamians—however much constrained by poverty and isolation—have been able to achieve such a level of self-sufficiency or balance of resources, and modern Bahamians have rejected the attempt altogether—whether at a level of individual families or communities, or as a strategy for the nation as a whole.

The Lucayans effectively modified their political and social structures to suit the greater dispersion of settlements and lower population density which Bahamian conditions determined. This was in contrast both to the Antillean Taino, among whom a population explosion and the emergence of a leisured class led to social and political tensions even before the coming of the Europeans, and to the modern Bahamas, where grossly uneven patterns of settlement and development have led to tensions between rich and poor sections and islands. Similarly, the Lucayans modified their culture into the simpler forms which the islands' resources allowed, though it seems to have been an effective, even impressive, culture nonetheless. Without metals from the beginning, and now without native hardstones or a proper clay, the Lucayans crafted a simple local pottery and fashioned the local limestone, hardwoods, shell, and bones into a simple range of useful artifacts.

It has been not only believers in the myth of the Noble Savage like Peter Martyr, or equally romantic anthropologists in flight from the complex modern world, who have found an admirable dignity in the simple Lucayan lifestyle. Only in the structure of the Lucayans' beliefs and in their ultimate behavior does one discover a sense of dislocation, anomie, and failure. This was displayed in the pervading nostalgia for a forsaken world toward the south and east, in the passive acceptance of whatever fate held in store, and in the wish-fulfilling belief that death would be followed by a return to the paradise lost through the people's original migration. Such characteristics made them pliant victims for newcomers even more powerful and exploitative, if more subtle, than any Amerindian enemies.

In the last analysis, the Lucayans seem a people doomed from the beginning, and thus, despite their many admirable qualities, hardly an absolute ideal for any later Bahamians. They were a too-fragile people in a too-fragile environment. What their melancholy history also surely demonstrates is that later Bahamians would survive only if they more effectively tamed the land, identified with it, and more resolutely defended it; and beyond this, would only flourish if they became involved in the larger world and its economy on terms favorable to themselves.

II

A-Coasting in Shallops:
The Early Settlers
of the Bahamas, 1647–1783

Preceding page: Hogarth's allegory portrait of the assumption of Crown Colony rule in the Bahamas. Captain Woodes Rogers somewhat smugly scans what is either a set of new laws or the plan of a redesigned Nassau held by his son. His daughter-housekeeper and her white servant and elegant spaniel epitomize the introduction of cultured English society.

～ 5 ～

Motherlands:
The British and Bermudian Background
of Bahamian Settlement

WITH THE OLYMPIAN PERSPECTIVE AND CONFIDENCE which informs his most ambitious work, the historical geographer Daniel Meinig visualizes the great movements of peoples and cultures shaping North America between 1500 and 1750 as twin thrusts emanating from northwestern Europe and west Africa, aimed respectively at the mainland and islands of the Caribbean, before converging on what became the plantation colonies of the United States.[1] Yet even Meinig, when considering in more detail the ways in which the northern European powers competed with Spain over the sugar-rich Antilles, and taking into account such marginal imperial properties as the Bahama Islands, is forced to accept a modified and far more complex pattern of settlement and cultural development. Viewed diagrammatically, the Bahamas presents a particularly awkward and atypical picture: playing no part in the general process before the mid-seventeenth century, first peopled by a thin trickle of settlers from Bermuda—as it were, at right angles to the major streams—gradually reinforced by heterogeneous recruits from all points of the compass, and seeking a livelihood without plantations that when not actually parasitic (during the age of piracy), was peripheral to Antilles and mainland alike. From the beginning of English settlement, therefore, the Bahamian people were a people apart.

A scattering of desert islands to the north of a far richer archipelago and on the eastern fringes of a continent of fabulous potential had little to offer incoming settlers in the first century and a half of European expansion. Once the Lucayan natives had been destroyed by deportation and disease, the Bahamas were spurned for their lack of obvious mineral resources, foodstuffs, or even fresh water, and threaded with fear and caution by those mariners who, through accident or the threat of enemies, could not use the easier routes to and from the Caribbean.

Such islands were unlikely to be settled until the second or third stage of Europe's expansion, and even then the nation destined to provide permanent settlers and a colonial system—shaped by its distinctive metropolitan culture transmuted in the new environment—was by no means certain until the first decades of the eighteenth century. Naturally, Spain had the earliest chance to develop the Bahamas as a colony and might have made the islands a frontier extension of Cuba or Santo Domingo. Standing on the Eurocentric version of international law, Spain claimed the islands by right of first discovery and formal claim, as well as by papal grant. Though never backed up by the key principle of effective settlement once Spain discovered the potential of the mainland and bypassed all but the islands of the Greater Antilles, this claim was not formally relinquished until 1783, when a Spanish occupying force was evicted by the Treaty of Versailles.[2]

In the non-Iberians' challenge to Spain's primacy in the New World, the French might well have been the first effectively to settle the Bahama Islands, establishing in the process a colonial system intermediate in every respect between the centralized (but inefficient) church-state autocracy of Spain and the Protestant bourgeois individualism which characterized both the short-lived Dutch American Empire and the late-coming British Empire. France was essentially a Catholic country, with a monarchy almost as tied to feudal survivals as Spain's. But France's earliest colonial ventures were inspired by Huguenot Protestants linked to the types of expansionist merchant capital that elsewhere led to the creation of the Dutch Republic and shaped the late Tudor and Stuart regimes in England.

Officially tolerated by the Edict of Nantes (1598), the French Huguenots had already proved natural colonists, harnessing a desire for greater religious, social, and economic freedom to a crusading motive directed against Catholic Spain. As with the English Seadogs and Dutch Sea Beggars, some of these enterprises were semipiratical, but colonial bases were also sought strategically close to Spanish settlements and trading routes. Chief of these was the colony founded near the later St. Augustine by Laudonnière. A twin settlement was attempted in Abaco (called by the French Lucayoneque) as early as 1565—more than a dozen years before Queen Elizabeth I granted Sir Humphrey Gilbert the right to establish an English colony anywhere in North America beyond the line of permanent Spanish settlements. Abaco commanded the Providence

Channels often used by Spanish galleons and was almost as adjacent to the Florida Straits, but was far less vulnerable to Spanish attacks than Laudonnière's settlement, in an island chain known to possess excellent harbors, adequate fresh water, salt pans, and even supplies of wild boar in the woods. Nothing came of this enterprise, though: a second vessel sent from France found no trace of the first adventurers.[3]

But the French interest in the Bahamas did not evaporate with the failure in Abaco and the extinction of Laudonnière's settlement by Aviles in 1567. During the seventeenth century the French Crown and state-sponsored companies took over more of the responsibility for colonial enterprises, while conditions for Huguenots tightened down to the formal revocation of the Edict of Nantes in 1685. As part of this process, Cardinal Richelieu in 1633 made a quasi-feudal grant of four Bahamian islands, namely "Abaco, Inaugua, Mariguana and Gilatur," to one Guillaume de Caen, who was given the grand title of baron des Bahames. A colony did not materialize largely because the Protestant baron was forbidden to settle any but Catholic Frenchmen in his new propriety. The French state, however, showed increasing interest in the Turks and Caicos Islands, with their valuable salt pans and strategic location guarding the Windward Passage between Cuba and Hispaniola, attempting to capture and hold them on several occasions during the eighteenth century.[4]

French attentions naturally concentrated on the far greater potential of the Antilles, first the small islands of Martinique and Guadeloupe, and then the western third of Hispaniola, where their settlements were formally recognized by Spain in 1697 and became within the following century, as Saint Domingue, the richest plantation colony in the world. By this time, though, the British had established themselves in the Bahamas, as well as far more powerfully in the Caribbean, and resisted any French attempts to develop their earlier claims and make the islands a strategic dependency of Saint Domingue, ruled from the colonial capital of Cap François on the northern coast.

Geographical factors, chiefly the prevailing winds and currents, have determined that Hispaniola has always had rather more influence upon the Bahamas than Cuba, from the time of the Lucayans down to the modern Haitian migration. A greater affinity might also have been presumed between French and British than between British and Spanish colonial systems because of the propinquity of France to England, the familiarity of French language and culture to educated English persons, and the very similarity of French and British commercial and imperial enterprises. On the contrary, however, the pursuit of similar ends by similar means determined that the imperial wars against Spain were succeeded by bitter rivalry with France, so that Anglo-French wars took up more than a third of the years between 1660 and 1815. Such competition and conflicts—involving the Dutch and Danes as well as the Spanish, French, and British—ensured that the rival colonies established throughout the New World developed an almost artificial disparity, deriving more from the distinctive features of European systems and cultures than they partook of the common impulses that led the different European nations to explore and exploit the outside world, or of the common environment which they shared in tropical America.

SPECULATING what Spain or France might have done in the Bahamas may help an understanding of the common and divergent features of European colonialism, and their modern legacies. But such speculation is counterfactual history, and thus of dubious validity in particular cases. For it was in fact the English who first backed up a claim to the Bahama Islands with effective settlement, with some difficulty sustained their occupation, and in due course stamped their imperial character upon them—a process beginning with the grant to Sir Robert Heath in 1629, through the settlement of the Eleutherian Adventurers after 1647, the grant to the Proprietors of Carolina in 1670, and the gradual assumption of full control by the Crown between 1718 and 1787.

However, the form which English colonization was to take in the New World in general and the Bahamas in particular was by no means fixed or certain from the beginning, not just because of the varied and unexpected conditions found, the variety and dubious quality of settlers available, and (as often claimed) the peculiar pragmatism of the English character, but because England itself was in a process of rapid political, social, and economic change throughout the period of early expansion.

English—later British—expansionism was a natural overflow of those energies which helped the Tudor monarchy to stamp out the smoldering embers of feudal anarchy, reform the administration, and challenge the authority and dominance of Rome and the Catholic powers. But it was also made possible by new sources and forms of venture capital, by a renaissance spirit of inquiry and self-expression, and, above all, by the availability of enough people to lead, to follow and to provide the necessary sinews of empire. The first English ventures overseas during the late Tudor period were promoted by a new breed of capitalist, bourgeois as well as aristocratic. These, with the monarch's support and increasing power in Parliament, combined political, religious, and economic motivation to challenge the preeminence of Spain and Portugal (which were politically united from 1580 to 1640), employing a motley personnel of mariners, squires, and lesser landsmen, eager for booty, land, and sheer adventure.

Many of the activities of the Elizabethan adventurers were mere buccaneering, often in alliance with Huguenot French and Calvinist Dutch. But at the same time, English colonies, styled "plantations," were begun in Ireland, which served in many respects as models for later transatlantic enterprises. As part of the Protestant English conquest of the Catholic Irish fringe of the British Isles, lands were granted by the Crown to favored courtiers or investors somberly called Undertakers, and "planted" with English settlers. English institutions were introduced, including the shire, the Anglican parish, and English-style tenures, both freehold and leasehold. The natives were either expelled or reduced to the level of mere tenants-at-will or landless laborers, denigrated because of their alien language and customs, and denied civil rights because of their Catholic religion. This process began in Leix and Offaly as early as the 1550s, spread into Munster in the 1570s and 1580s, and accelerated once more as a result of the rebellions led by the Catholic Irish nobility under Spanish instigation in the 1590s.[5]

Toward the end of this period, many of those involved in (and often disenchanted with) the Elizabethan plantation of Ireland were looking farther overseas. Sir Humphrey Gilbert was given a vague but grandiose grant, presumably including the Bahamas, in 1578, and this was taken up by his half-brother Sir Walter Raleigh after Gilbert's failure to found a colony in Newfoundland or Nova Scotia and his death by drowning in 1583. Raleigh commissioned Richard Hakluyt to write *A Discourse of Western Planting*, outlining the ideal type of American colony and colonist, and sent Philip Amadas and Arthur Barlow out to discover the ideal site. These explorers skirted but shunned the Bahamas before fixing on the even less suitable Outer Banks of what is now North Carolina, while the first colonizing expedition of three ships under Sir Richard Grenville in 1585 included few of the sturdy yeomen, husbandmen, and artisans recommended by Hakluyt, and very few women. Grenville's flotilla, after pauses in Puerto Rico and Hispaniola (where they collected tropical plants before being seen off by the Spaniards) also sailed through the Bahamas on the way to Roanoke Island, stopping only long enough to explore the natural salt pans of the Turks and Caicos Islands, for the artist John White to admire the native flamingo and iguana, and for the commander narrowly to escape drowning while hunting for turtles.[6]

The sugarcane, pineapples, mammee apples, and cotton plants taken from Isabela might have had more chance of surviving in the Bahamas than on Roanoke Island, but it is unlikely that a colony there would have fared any better than Raleigh's ill-starred Roanoke ventures, given the unsuitability of the colonists and their poor provisioning, the absence of natives to teach them the skills necessary to live off the land and sea, and the opposition of the Spaniards, which became implacable after Sir Francis Drake's great West Indian raid of 1585–86, which included the sacking of St. Augustine and Santa Elena.[7]

The Anglo-Spanish war initiated by Drake, which lasted until 1604, distracted the Seadogs from colonial ventures, but a new phase of colonialism began with the death of Elizabeth I and the accession of King James of Scotland as the first of the English Stuart dynasty. The combination of the crowns of England and Scotland had only an indirect and delayed effect upon the British Empire, since the two countries were not politically united until 1707. Far more important in the short run were the trend away from open confrontation with Spain and the changes in royal style which aimed to emulate the quasi-feudal absolutism of Philip II and Charles V. Such pretensions, paralleled by an increasingly rigorous orthodoxy in the established church, aroused growing political and religious opposition, centered in Parliament. Thus, to the bourgeois and aristocratic elements interested in overseas ventures were added those seeking religious and political freedom. For its part, the Crown actively encouraged all such enterprises, both for the prestige and revenue they would bring and also (as Richard Hakluyt had suggested in 1584) as a means of disposing of troublesome persons: political and religious dissidents, and the growing surplus of "valiant youths rusting and hurtful by lack of employment."[8] Even such refugees valued the benefits of state support and were quite prepared to accept the royal requirements that all English colonies express loyalty to the Crown and faithful ascription to English laws and institutions, and be organized through royally chartered companies or (a Stuart invention) under the authority of proprietors appointed like feudal tenants-in-chief.

Under James I were established not only the Anglo-Scots Protestants of Ulster but the first effective English colonies in the Americas, in Virginia, Bermuda, and New England, while in the reign of his son Charles I areas more casually settled were placed under favored Lord Proprietors, the Carib-dominated no-man's land of the Lesser Antilles being granted to Lord Carlisle in 1627 and the entire area between Virginia and the Spanish settlements to Sir Robert Heath in 1629.[9] This last grant for the first time specifically included the Bahamas as well as "Carolana" and is therefore of great theoretical interest in Bahamian history, though no actual settlement was undertaken by Heath because of the conflict between Crown and Parliament which deteriorated into civil war by 1642. Of far more practical significance to the Bahamas was the colony of Bermuda, founded almost by accident in 1609 on a similarly uninhabited but far smaller coral archipelago eight hundred miles to the northeast. For not only did Bermuda provide an experimental model for Bahamian settlement, but the original settlers in the Bahamas came from the earlier colony. Bermuda and Bermudians retained very strong links with the Bahamas for a quarter century, and some connections, if less friendship, lasted over a far longer period.

BERMUDA, like the Bahamas, had long been known to the Spaniards but was settled only after Sir George Somers's flagship *Sea Venture* was wrecked there on its way to the infant Jamestown settlement in Virginia. Accounts of Somers's involuntary sojourn provided Shakespeare with inspiration for *The Tempest*, though the play transcended the incident to symbolize European colonization in general—or at least the first magical reciprocation between Old and New Worlds, and the subsequent problems of adapting European institutions and cultures to new conditions and native peoples.[10]

Found to be healthy and fertile, with splendid fishing grounds and plentiful stands of cedar and palmetto suitable for houses and ships, Bermuda seemed an ideal way-station between Europe, North America, and the West Indies—preferable even to Virginia as a plantation colony in its manageable size and lack of threat from Indian attacks. First placed under the authority of the Virginia Company, Bermuda was assigned to a distinct Company of Adventurers from 1615 to 1684, though most of the controlling shareholders held interest in both companies, as well as in many other English overseas enterprises. These investors included the whole spectrum of England's new ruling class; great landed nobles such as the earls of Warwick, Pembroke, and Southampton, prominent entrepreneur politicians like Sir Thomas Smith and Sir Edwin Sandys, and a whole range of lesser gentry and businessmen. But few ever ventured out in person, and from the beginning there were tensions and disparities, not just between the idea that Bermuda was simply a fragment of England translated overseas and the pragmatic requirements of setting up a colonial economy and society in such a different environment, but also between the London-based company with its concern for order, discipline, and profit, and the actual settlers, aiming to make a life of their own while faced with the realities of daily life and even subsistence.

The 1615 charter fulsomely acknowledged the English Crown as the fount of all authority and specified that all Englishmen were eligible to be colonists as long as they were not Catholics or jailbirds. Even foreigners might settle as long as they were naturalized and took the oaths of allegiance and supremacy. Once settled, the colonists and their descendants were promised all the "liberties, franchises and immunities of free denizens and natural subjects . . . as if they had been abiding and born within the Kingdom of England."[11] One must not exaggerate, though, what this meant in the context of 1615.

As in England, land was to be the basis of wealth and standing, and the framers of the charter of 1615 presumed to replicate in tiny Bermuda the whole panoply of English institutions, including (in Wilkinson's words) "counsellors, bailiffs, sheriffs, marshals, courts of law, grand juries, petty juries, justices of the peace, inquests, the militia system, trained bands, churchwardens, sidesmen, glebe, common land."[12] As early as 1620 there was also to be an elective general assembly or parliament, though this, naturally, was assumed not to be any more democratic than its English model, and the validity of local statutes was further circumscribed by the authority of the general court of the company sitting in London and by the principle of nonrepugnance to English laws in general.

A careful survey begun by Richard Norwood in 1616 implemented the original charter in dividing the twenty-two square miles of Bermuda into nine units. The area first settled, the group of islets at the eastern end where the capital, St. George's, was built, was designed general land, not to be alienated but worked in common to bring in revenue to support the administration. The remaining three-quarters of the land was divided into eight segments uniquely styled "tribes" (only later, parishes), each subdivided into fifty plots averaging twenty-five acres, with as much sea frontage as possible, for allotment to the shareholders according to their rank and investment. No individual was to hold more than fifteen allotments, though the family of the earl of Warwick held twenty-six altogether.[13]

What the initial system predicated was a graduated landed gentry monopolizing all the official posts in the colony, from governor and council to magistrates and militia officers, with a small intermediate class of yeoman tenants, townsfolk, and craftsmen to be vestrymen, jurors, and the noncommissioned officers in the militia, and the majority of landless settlers providing the labor and mass of the militia just as in the rural parts of England. Even the assembly would be dominated by the landed gentry, with the electorate restricted to those with landed property. Yet local conditions, and the fact that most of the initial landowners were absentees, considerably modified the English-based model.

At the top of local society were the few resident gentlemen who lived on their own lands or, like Robert Rich, the nephew of the earl of Warwick, were factors or managers for their absentee kinsmen. Below these were the lesser freeholders, overseers, and a few professionals, and a whole spectrum of smallholders with leasehold tenures, from yeomen or "goodmen" paying rent, down to "tenants-by-halves," that is, mere sharecroppers. Initially at the bottom of the social scale were landless men serving under a variety of contracts or "indentures." These ranged from those with short-term contracts, who might be working off their passage money or sharing crops with their employers, down to deportees whose service was virtually for life, cruelly maltreated and with obligations that were bought and sold almost as if they were slaves.

Formal slavery was not foreseen in the original charter, on the presumption that all settlers would be Englishmen and the principle that slavery had long been outlawed in England. But slavery did evolve quite rapidly, first in custom and then in law, once the number of white "servants" proved insufficient for the labor needs of the larger landowners and increasing numbers of Africans and Indians arrived in the islands. At first, as in Virginia, no one sought to enslave the Indians (maidens of chiefly caste, indeed, being regarded as fit wives for white settlers), and the very first Africans in Bermuda were a couple of "Spanish negroes" and their families brought in to teach the skills of planting and curing tobacco, given their own provision land, and treated much like white sharecroppers. From 1620, however, buccaneers began to import "parcels" of slaves seized from the Spaniards, who were shared out between the chief magnates or set to work on the general land. Likewise, a trickle of Indians were brought in to be used as slaves after the great "massacre" of 1622 in Virginia and the later Indian wars in New England. This latter trade died out not so much because it was regarded as improper to enslave Indian subjects, or that Indians proved unsuitable laborers (though both arguments were used), but because the supply of Africans became more than enough once the English were directly involved in the African trade and the blacks in Bermuda proved more fertile than the whites. By the third quarter of the seventeenth century blacks made up a third of Bermuda's population, and as a consequence not only was chattel slavery incorporated into the colonial code, but an absolute concurrence was presumed between nonwhite phenotype and unfree status—to the degree that Bermudian laws used phrases such as "any Negroes, Indians, Mulattoes or other Slaves."[14]

Bermuda, in sum, developed as a colony with rigid social stratification on the English model, complicated by a large slave underclass and growing pressure on the available land. The intention of the Adventurers was to create a true plantation colony, obtaining for the tiny islands a share with Virginia in the monopoly of English tobacco production and exportation in 1622. For a few years Bermuda had as many settlers as Virginia and almost kept pace in the amount of tobacco grown. But the expansion of the mainland colony (where some estates were almost as large as the entire colony of Bermuda) not only caused the collapse of Bermudian tobacco production but left the island colony relatively overpopulated. Agriculture remained important, if mainly for subsistence and supplying passing ships, but gradually Bermuda developed the maritime economy for which it was far more suited. Year by year more Bermudians and their black slaves took to the sea in Bermudian ships. At first these vessels were stumpy pinnaces or undecked double-ended "shallops," designed for inshore fishing, sealing, and turtling, or scouring small islands and shallow waters for dyewoods, ambergris, and wrecks. But in due course the distinctive Bermuda sloop evolved, sleek and swift, with a longer range and ideal for the coastal trade of the North American seaboard and the Antilles.[15]

As well as providing a base (along with ships and crews) for privateers, Bermudians became involved in the legitimate trade between the English and foreign settlements on the American mainland and in the Caribbean, in the New England and Newfoundland fisheries, and in the related salt industry of the Turks and Caicos Islands. The sea breeds its own freemasonry, but the restless energy of Bermudian mariners was also fueled by declining opportunities and increasing social, political, and religious tensions in their island base.

In the earliest years Bermuda enjoyed considerable social mobility, with fortunate time-expired indentured servants becoming smallholding tenants and tenants becoming freeholders and factors, acquiring a few slaves and perhaps a share in a ship, and aspiring to local office and militia rank. Some assemblymen and even councilors were former bondsmen, chosen by their peers or accepted, if reluctantly, by the distant company. The tendency toward democracy among the whites was aided, moreover, by the increase in the numbers of blacks "and other slaves." As Bermuda filled up, however, the social matrix hardened, for whites as well as blacks. Those who had preempted the land became increasingly conservative, closing up the ranks of office and passing more, and more severe, social legislation, while at the same time conserving the stocks of cedar and, as far as possible, monopolizing the shipbuilding, shipping, provisioning, and retail industries. As tribes became parishes in the English style, the established Church of England became more centrally important. Thus, in consonance with the growing conflict in the metropolis between backward-looking Stuart monarchy and progressive Parliament, the emergent ruling class in Bermuda tended to be royalist and Anglican, and as intolerant of political radicalism and religious dissidence as of the social pretensions of landless men.

It was in this atmosphere that an increasing number of Bermudians sought their fortune, or greater freedom, in other island colonies. Bermudians, besides retaining their close connection with Virginia and forging ever stronger links with Puritan New England, were involved in all English colonial ventures in the Caribbean after 1625, not just the successful colonies in Barbados, the Leewards, and Jamaica, but also the failed attempts such as in St. Lucia, Trinidad, Tobago, and Tortola. Most notably, Bermudians collaborated with the New England Puritans and their radical parliamentarian allies in England in the short-lived colony on Catalina, alias Providence Island, founded in 1630. This settlement, being located on a fertile if tiny island on the direct galleon route from Nombre de Dios to Havana, allowed the godly Calvinist settlers to combine privateering against Catholic targets with slave plantations, and it was consequently eradicated by a Spanish expedition in 1641.[16] Subsequently, and of most direct concern to the present book, it was similar Bermudian emigrés who first settled the poorer but much closer and safer Bahamas, significantly renaming the island of their choice (called by the Lucayans and Spaniards Segatoo) Eleutheria—soon shortened to Eleuthera— after the Greek word for freedom.

— 6 —

The Eleutherian Adventurers, 1647–1670

WILLIAM SAYLE, the leader of the Eleutherian Adventurers, was a prominent Bermudian sea captain and trader who, though often at sea between Bermuda, England, and the West Indies, had already served as colonial governor from 1640 to 1642 and 1643 to 1645. Identified with the religious Independents who had set up a separate congregationalist church in Bermuda in 1643, he was also close to the radical and republican faction among the Bermuda Company's shareholders in London, led, somewhat strangely, by its chief nobleman, the earl of Warwick. Sayle's two terms as governor were therefore marred by the religious and political (though not social) discord in Bermuda which gradually intensified as the English Parliament, with the help of the Presbyterian Scots, defeated and imprisoned the king and moved remorselessly toward a radical Puritan republic.[1]

In 1644 Bermudian dissidents had sent two vessels to explore the Bahamas for a suitable site for an Independent colony, though one was wrecked with the loss of all hands and the other returned without an enthusiastic report.[2] Over the following three years, however, William Sayle was often in England, at first begging for freedom of conscience and free trade for Bermuda, but then, having failed to win over a quorum of the company council, actively promoting a separate radical colony in the Bahamas. In this he was more successful, tapping much the same wellsprings as had watered the Providence Island venture some fifteen years before. Early in 1647 an optimistic (if studiously vague) *Broadside Advertising Eleutheria and the Bahama Islands* was circulated, which attracted the twenty-five shareholders who, with William Sayle, signed the Articles and Orders of the Company of Eleutherian Adventurers on July 9, 1647.[3]

The proposed constitution of the Eleutherian colony was idealistic and impractical but is profoundly interesting because it was one of the few colonial projects drawn up under the parliamentary regime. It was designed to throw off the shackles of Crown and established church, reduce the authority of governor and absentee company, and provide freedom of conscience and opportunity for ordinary settlers. But it stopped far short of the sociopolitical radicalism of the English Levelers as well as the practical theocracy of Puritan New England. It was closest in fact to the "aristocratic republicanism" advocated by James Harrington's *Oceana* (1656), with the initial investor-settlers having the largest share of land and power but all freemen enjoying access to land and natural resources, freedom of conscience, and a vote in the choice of political leadership.

The Eleutherian colony was visualized (quite realistically as it happened) as having a nucleus much the same size as Bermuda, with a far larger hinterland. All land was to be worked in common for the first three years, but thereafter each Adventurer investing one hundred pounds up to one hundred in number, was entitled to three hundred acres in the main settlement plus thirty-five acres for each dependent, but also up to two thousand acres outside the main settlement. These fortunate founding fathers were to form a sovereign unicameral legislature called a senate, its numbers kept up to one hundred by co-optation, and with absolute power to appoint justices, distribute public lands, assign tasks on public works, and manage the public finances, as well as pass laws. There was to be a governor, appointed for the first three years and thereafter elected by all freemen, along with an advisory council of twelve. But the governor's function was simply that of president of the senate, and only senators were eligible for the governor's council.

Theoretically, all free settlers could aspire to become Adventurers, senators, councilors, or even governor, through investment, co-optation, and popular approval, though in practice such upward mobility would be far from easy. Though not bound to an established church or required to pay tithes, all men between fifteen and fifty were liable to military service in defense of the main settlement and were required to labor on the public works. Ordinary settlers could presumably rent, lease, or buy land, and even indentured laborers were entitled to twenty-five acres once their contracts were up. On the other hand, colonists who preferred to roam the unadopted islands for the "wracks, ambergreise, metalles, salts and woods" which were (not inaccurately) listed as their chief resources, were to receive only a fraction of their finds. All such produce was to be sold by the company, and, once costs were deducted, one third was to go to the colonial treasury, one third to the original Adventurers, and only the remaining third to the actual finder.

Although William Sayle and other Adventurers were already slave-owners, slavery was not specified in the Eleutherian constitution. Indeed, the articles highmindedly decreed that no natives found in the Bahamas should be made into slaves, and that efforts should be made by the colonists to redeem any Amerindians enslaved by the Spaniards. Such provisions, though, merely indicate that the framers of the articles (including Sayle himself), while not entirely ignorant of the Bahamas, were more interested in Eleutherian ideals than in Bahamian realities.

The actual colony founded by the Eleutherian Adventurers fell far short of the articles of July 1647, and, indeed, the original proposals themselves were never formally established. The twenty-five signatories with William Sayle were of more solid bourgeois character and political commitment than the Adventurers of Bermuda, but like them they preferred to remain in London, where those with the best political connections negotiated for an act of incorporation and a charter. The *Journal of the House of Commons* records that a bill for the settling of a colony between twenty-four degrees north and twenty-nine degrees north (that is, in all the Bahama Islands north of a line through San Salvador, Great Guana Cay in the Exumas, and southern Andros) was read three times in August 1649 and passed, though no copy of the actual act has come to light.[4] Similarly, if a charter was ever drafted, it too has disappeared. This is especially unfortunate, for other evidence suggests that the original twenty-six shareholders had gone far beyond the original proposal and claimed a shared proprietorship. In any case, such a claim was made redundant by events in England. Obscure as the legal authority for a proprietary charter would have been under the Cromwellian Commonwealth, any such were automatically canceled by the Restoration of Charles II in 1660—so that by 1666 even the Sayles had given up hope that their interests in the Bahamas would be legally recognized by the Crown.[5]

This, though, is to jump far ahead of events. Newly commissioned governor of Eleutheria by his fellow Adventurers, Captain William Sayle had arrived back in Bermuda in October 1647 with a few English volunteers, provisions, and supplies, including, it was rumored, four hundred muskets.[6] Governor Turner feared insurrection at home and was relieved to find Sayle eager merely to recruit those who sought refuge and a new start in Eleutheria. Within a few months some seventy persons were gathered together, perhaps a dozen families, including as minister the aged Patrick Copeland. These persons were led aboard a fifty-ton ship—probably the *William*, of which Sayle was part owner—and a six-ton shallop specially built, and the pioneering expedition set out for the Bahamas some time in the spring of 1648.[7]

Then the true adventures began. At the first landing place discord broke out, fomented by a young Captain Butler, straight out from England, who, according to John Winthrop, interpreted liberty of conscience to mean complete license and refused to worship or accept any authority. Sayle and the majority of the settlers thereupon shifted to another site but were wrecked in crossing the reef, just like Somers in the *Sea Venture* some forty years earlier. The exact location is not certain, but hallowed tradition and all available evidence suggest it was the north-facing mainland of northern Eleuthera, where the reefs are indeed formidable, a small cove is still called Governor's Bay, and the locals confidently point out Preacher's Cave as the pioneer settlers' first refuge and place of worship.[8]

Only one person was drowned in the wreck, but the main ship was a complete loss, along with all provisions, supplies, and the few stock animals carried. Marooned without the axes, hoes, and saws needed to clear the bush, plant, and provide timber for houses, the seed corn and animals needed for further food, or even enough ready food to sustain themselves, the pioneers, in Winthrop's words "were forced (for diverse months) to lie in the open air, and to feed upon such fruits and wild creatures as the island afforded."[9]

William Sayle meanwhile had gone for relief. Taking the shallop and eight men through stormy seas, he reached Virginia within a week. There he obtained supplies and the loan of a twenty-five-ton pinnace from Independent sympathizers but was not able to persuade them to throw in their lot with their Eleutherian brethren. Reinforcements, however, were on their way from Bermuda. When the news of the execution of Charles II had reached the island in the spring of 1649, the horrified majority declared for Prince Charles and set about expelling the most ardent remaining republicans and Puritans to the Bahamas. A ship with sixty emigrés, including the Independent ministers Stephen Painter and Nathanial White and the lay preacher Robert Ridley, arrived to join the original settlers, though so poorly supplied that they too were soon "subsisting in the woods." Word of their plight reached New England, where Governor Winthrop (though he had dissuaded the mainland Puritans from venturing in person) encouraged the Boston churches to provide moral and material aid. Nearly £800 was raised and laid out on provisions, which were dispatched in March 1650, under the care of two godly agents, in a ship commanded by the Bermudian Captain Chaddock. This lifesaving donation was acknowledged by Sayle, White, and Ridley in a famous letter of gratitude, backed up by a gift of ten tons of braziletto wood. This realized £124 and provided a substantial part of the initial endowment of Harvard College, the first English university in the New World.[10]

Conditions for Puritans and republicans in Bermuda improved once the English Commonwealth asserted its authority there, and most of the Eleutherian emigrés trickled back to Bermuda between 1652 and 1656. Some others went on to Massachusetts, and a few settled in Jamaica after its conquest in 1655. William Sayle himself returned to Bermuda in 1656, or 1657, being appointed governor there for the third time between 1658 and 1662 and seeing the colony through the difficult transition of the Stuart Restoration. William Sayle and his seafaring sons, however, kept up their interest in the Bahamas for many more years, William organizing a quadrilateral trade between Bermuda, the Bahamas, "Cariba" (Barbados), and England in 1658 in the "frigett" *William* (the original or its namesake), commanded by Thomas Sayle, while Nathanial Sayle later claimed that his father had commissioned him as governor of Eleutheria in 1661.[11]

A scattering of colonists, moreover, remained in the Bahamas after the Puritan Adventurers left, and even began to expand their settlements. Such hardy pioneers, including the Adderley, Albury, Bethell, Davis, Sands, and Saunders families whose descendants are still found in the islands, formed a kind of rude elite.[12] Rural (or insular) patriarchs headed loose extended households, whose dependent members included servants and slaves—a dispersed underclass that was intermittently reinforced as a result of the Bermudians' habit of using the Bahamas as a dumping ground for those they regarded as socially undesirable. These deportees included a few poor whites found guilty of social misdemeanors, such as Neptuna Downham, who was transported in 1660 for having an illegitimate child, or Elizabeth Carter, a Quaker banished in 1664 for publicly reproving the Anglican minister in Devonshire Church. But even more important for the shaping of Bahamian society were the nonwhites shipped. The toughest of these were slaves found guilty of insubordination or plotting rebellion, such as the seven blacks transported to Eleuthera in the *Blessing* after the abortive slave plot of 1656. The most numerous, and most useful as colonists, though, were the free blacks and coloreds sent to the Bahamas when the Bermudian regime unrealistically attempted to "extirpate" from Bermuda all nonwhites who were not enslaved.[13]

Northern Eleuthera, where the Sayles kept their house and continued to carry on business and worship "at the cave" through the 1660s, remained an important settlement until razed in a Spanish attack in 1684. But colonists increasingly settled on the neighboring smaller islands, both for security from foreign attacks and for better access to the sea— using the mainland mostly for woodcutting, growing provisions, and running hogs. It was on the Eleutheran mainland too that blacks who could not easily be assimilated into the founding households were settled. The main Eleutheran offshore settlements were founded on Harbour Island and St. George's Cay (Spanish Wells) before 1670, and by the end of the century there were almost certainly settlers on Current Island and Cupid's Cay (Governor's Harbour), as well, perhaps, as the nuclei of the black or colored settlements of the Bluff and the Bogue on the mainland of northern Eleuthera.[14]

Some time around 1666 also, the nucleus of the future Bahamian capital was established some fifty miles due west of northern Eleuthera, on a sizeable island with an excellent sheltered harbor, at the halfway point of the great dog-leg channel that bisects the northern Bahamas between the Florida Strait and the open Atlantic. This was first named Sayle's Island, traditionally because William had twice used its roadstead to escape from storms. But it was soon renamed New Providence—not so much because of Sayle's deliverance or the settlers' residual piety, but in significant reference to the earlier Puritan-privateering colony of Old Providence off the coast of Nicaragua.[15]

By 1670 there may have been a thousand settlers in the Bahamas, two-thirds of them white, in a hundred households, scattered over two hundred square miles of land and two thousand square miles of sea. According to John Darrell, who claimed to have carried two shiploads of colonists from his native Bermuda to Sayle's Island around 1666, there were "near 500 inhabitants" there by 1670, besides "about 20 families of Barmudians" conservatively estimated to be living on Eleuthera, Harbour Island, and Spanish Wells. Darrell (who was promoting the Bahamas, but particularly New Providence, to the Proprietors of Carolina) spoke glowingly of the islands' potential, claiming that New Providence produced "good cotton and tobacco, Sugar Caines and Indico Weed," that Abaco and Andros possessed plentiful cedars and pines, and that Exuma offered salt and spermaceti whales. At the same time, he placed the actual settlement neatly in perspective when he listed the chief needs of New Providence as "small arms and ammunition, a godly minister and a good smith."[16]

Freedom of a sort the Eleutherians certainly had. Far from following the careful plan of the 1647 articles, they were without formal government and lacked even the limited cohesion of the original Puritan settlers. Nearly all had Bermudian antecedents and connections, and cases involving Bahamian settlers were quite often dealt with in Bermudian courts in the early years. But these were tenuous and informal links that were bound to be broken within a generation or two, just as the authority of William Sayle and his sons, lacking royal sanction, faded away in the absence of the Sayles on somewhat more hopeful alternative ventures. Eleutheria by 1670, in fact, was no more than a desperately poor, ill-formed, and informal colony, tending to show that a state of liberty without either order or plenty meant little more than profitless anarchy, and the freedom chiefly to starve.

BY 1670, therefore, some of the salient features of Bahamian life and character had already become delineated: poverty and opportunism, a far greater dependence on the sea than on the land; a preference, indeed, for the unshackled expediency of the maritime life, for all its dangers, over the humdrum certainties of a more settled existence. Quite apart from the intrinsic unsuitability of the Bahamas for forming a colony like Barbados or Jamaica, there was bound to be resistance to whoever attempted to establish colonial authority, a more rigid class structure, and plantations—and thus a growing tension between relatively progressive New Providence and the older Out Island settlements.

Naturally, the scattered and informal colonists of the first, or Bermudian, phase of Bahamian settlement left very few records. Yet their lifestyle can be convincingly reconstructed, not just from the fragments of direct evidence that survive, but also from the similar, and far better documented, experiences of the first Bermudians.

The area first settled had the outward appearance of a flatter Bermuda, with a similar if slightly warmer climate. It was only when the colonists came to clear the trees and bush for cultivation that the impressive primeval vegetation was seen to be set on "hollow rocks" and nurtured by an extremely meager soil. The sea—abounding with fish, mollusks, and turtles—could provide plentiful protein, but only when there were boats and equipment enough to harvest it, whereas the few iguana, agouti, and migratory birds which the land afforded could not compare with the swarms of easily caught cahows and hogs (the latter left by the Spaniards) which sustained the first Bermudians.

With imported provisions for only a few months at best, it was vital

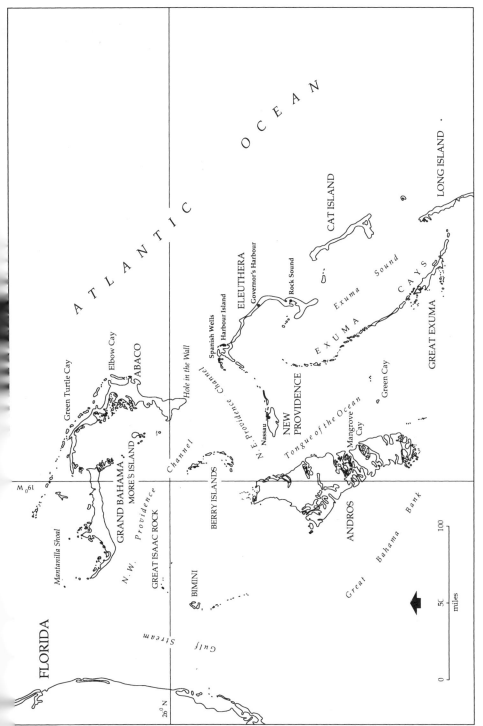

Map 5. Northern Bahamas and early settlements, 1647–1782

for the first colonists to plant food crops immediately. First the land was cleared with fire and axe, and seed corn, peas, and pumpkins planted in the interspersed mode learned from the Indians of Virginia. Seed sprouted quickly—one writer claiming that "the Pease came up in six Weeks Time, and *Indian* corn in 12" [17]—but most plants withered, those which survived the scorching sun and lack of water being eaten by land crabs and the rats that came in the ships. Only by bitter trial and error did the early farmers learn to adapt and more or less unconsciously adopt the techniques of their Lucayan forerunners. The best of the soil and moisture were found in pockets and potholes, and most plants were found to grow best in shade. Soil was consolidated and conserved, fertilized with ash and bat earth from caves, and sometimes piled into mounds between standing trees, while the deeper holes, with perhaps two feet of fertile soil, were most valued of all. But all farming areas had to be rotated after three or four years, so that the process of clearing primary or secondary bush was almost continuous. As visitors noted, even the most successful Bahamian provision grounds were more like a horizontal version of the untidy, ingenious patches of farming found on Antillean hillsides than the neat agricultural husbandry of England, Virginia, or even Bermuda.

Onions and some other European vegetables were eventually found to grow well in the sandy, moist loam next to the sea, but nearly all the main food crops were initially strange to Europeans. Manioc (the growing and processing of which the Bermudians had learned from the first blacks brought from Spanish colonies) was found to be resistant to drought and burrowing creatures, and to produce a form of bread more agreeable to European stomachs than that made from Indian corn. Food plants already introduced into the New World from Africa and Asia by the Spanish and Portuguese, such as bananas, plantains, and yams, were also grown from the earliest years, soon to be followed by guinea corn, groundnuts, pigeon and blackeye peas, and different varieties of root starch plants. The native edible fruits were valued, but neither they nor imported fruit trees were cultivated until later years; even the easily grown indigenous pineapple was regarded as a dispensable luxury. Within a few years some tobacco and sugarcane were grown for local consumption, and some indigo planted, but an export trade in these commodities, or even in the excellent native cotton, was, for the time being at least, quite out of the question. For over a hundred years, Bahamian agriculture was strictly for subsistence, regarded as a necessary evil; backbreaking and scorching work with frequent disappointments.

Shelter was a priority for early settlers, but for a long time houses were no more than flimsy "cabbins." The need for speedy construction, the shortage of tools, and other preoccupations meant that most were of the simplest "puncheon" construction. Posts of Caribbean pine or Lucayan cedar simply split down the middle with axes were planted in rectangles, then bound together with a single "plate rail" under eaves of slimmer split tree stems. Walls were made with wattles of woven mangrove stakes, daubed with a crude "cob" of limestone clay. The roof was covered with overlapped sheaves of stripped palmetto leaves, overhung to let most of the rainwater run off free. Most of the houses had a single doorway, and a window or two close under the eaves, with a door and shutters of simple battens to provide at least a modicum of privacy and security. None of the earliest houses had chimneys, cooking being done, then and later, in a separate shelter or cabin on the leeward side of the house, for safety's sake.[18]

Furniture and utensils were of the simplest; a chest or two, hammocks, perhaps a table and benches, iron cooking pots and trivets, pewter or pottery vessels and plates, pewter or iron knives and spoons. Gourds and simple wooden implements were fashioned from local materials, but crafting in metals developed slowly and the English settlers never matched the Lucayans in developing a native pottery. Anything that had to be imported was treasured and carefully guarded within the house. This included the obvious pioneer necessities; hoes, axes, machetes, and saws; fishhooks, spears, and nets; a musket, gunpowder, flints, and shot. But almost equally valuable were all items of leather, including shoes; all clothes and bed linen; and less obviously irreplaceable objects like needles, thread, and candles. Most settlers had little else; even beds, chairs, dressers, tablecloths, curtains, and muslin netting fine enough to keep out mosquitoes could be heirlooms, along with the family Bible, which in most households was the only book.

A good sense of this pioneer poverty, and the scale of values, is gained from one of the earliest extant Bahamian wills, that of John Darvill of "Islathera," though it dates from 1725, three-quarters of a century after the initial settlement.[19] Clearly a bachelor, Darvill left his meager worldly goods to a dozen different members of his family and neighbors. What should have been his major bequest, his "House and Plantation," was left to his "Friend" William Ingham, probably his uncle by marriage, along with "3 pewter Spoons and a Porringer, for Ever." His single slave, "a Negro Boy named Manuel," was bequeathed to a cousin and namesake, along with "one Silver Spoon markt I.D. for Ever." John Darvill's closest relative, his "well belov'd Sister Sarah Darvill," received only "one Gold

Ring, 4 Pewter Spoons & one Pewter Bason 1 Iron Pott for Ever." This was rather less than the "one Gold Ring and one pr of Silver Shoe Buckles and one Black Hatt and a small parcell of Money for Ever" bequeathed to the daughter of John Bethell (one of the chief Eleuthera settlers), Ann, who may have been Darvill's truelove, or intended wife.

The remaining bequests were even more revealingly picayune. Aunt Ingham was left a gold ring and an "Earthen Pott," and her sons Joseph and Benjamin "about ½ Ton of Brazella Wood" (then worth perhaps one pound ten shillings) and "a Pound of Glaze Powder one Hatchett and one Hoe," respectively. Two other cousins received "one Suit of Cotton Jackett & Breaches and a Sett of Silver Buttons for them," and "a Silver tooth picker." One neighbor, Nathanial Beak, was bequeathed ten pieces of eight (worth one pound fifteen shillings), and another, Matthew Low, "2 bottles of small Shott 1 Gun one Carteuse [i.e., cartouche] Box 2 Horns of Gun Powder and ½ Gourd of Dtto." The will closed with bequests to Mary and James Bun and Paul Nuball of a frying pan and two small parcels of "Hooks for fishing."

A people living close to the shore did not require elaborate roads, and without the constant need to defend themselves against natives such as the mainlanders had, the early settlers did not have an immediate motive, or perhaps the will, to build fortifications. Even when Bahamian settlements proved vulnerable to foreign attack, the settlers found the simplest and safest course simply to take flight into the trackless woods. Their houses thus tended to remain insubstantial: hardly worthy of plunder and easily rebuilt.

The houses of the Darvills and Inghams, even the Bethells, remained starkly simple, if rather more ample than the original "cabbins." As time went on, primitive limekilns and forges were set up and carpentry became more sophisticated, but ships did not come in with a ballast of bricks as in the richer colonies, and the native limestone was rarely cut into building blocks for lack of suitable saws or willing labor. An adequate local mortar, used to cement the abundant freestone rocks, provided a durable building material, but this was used only for fireplaces, ovens, chimneys, cisterns, or the basements of houses. The houses themselves remained timber-built, in the most elaborate cases with frames of stout mastic or horseflesh, pine or cedar planking and shingles, louvered windows and galleries to catch the breeze, and even a second floor. Though the best cabinet woods were exported, the first locally made furniture— a few simple tables, chairs, dressers, and beds—was crafted from Bahamian mahogany, alias madeira.

As houses built in the Out Islands up to the twentieth century testified, Bahamian housebuilding shared much of the technology of shipbuilding. But ships in fact monopolized the best of the wood and the work of the most skilled craftsmen. For this (like its parent Bermuda) was a community dependent more on the sea than the land, where ownership of a small boat was at least as important as permanent shelter and reliable provision grounds, and a share in a larger ship was essential to prosperity, if not survival. In the earliest years, as the early wills testified, even a three-ton shallop might be regarded as equivalent in value to the "houses and plantations" of its three or four owners put together.

A maritime settlement which does not have its own boatbuilding industry is bound to be dependent upon another which has. Nearly all the earliest boats to serve the Bahamas were Bermuda built and owned. But the lack of local capital and the consequent need to be independent, coupled with the availability of suitable woods, meant that ships were soon being built in the Bahamas. Perhaps the first Bahamian-built vessels were simple rowing boats of a type now lost. But the Bermudian-style shallop was the standard early vessel because it was sturdy, relatively simple to build, of shallow draft, and small enough to be rowed and beached, yet large enough to carry cargoes over sizeable stretches of open sea. Only later were more wide-ranging vessels such as sloops constructed, along with the rest of an evolving range of distinctive Bahamian types: dinghies, smacks, schooners, and a few even larger vessels.

The skill and labor of boatbuilding began with the selection of timber and its conveyance to the shore. Vessels far more complex than dugout canoes required much wider range of timber than the Lucayans had used, and the possession of iron tools made such a choice possible. But the early settlers had almost as much difficulty in getting the cut timber out of the woods as their predecessors, since they had few if any draught animals. Keels, stems, and sternposts were made of hardy (and heavy) madeira, horseflesh, or dogwood, and the frame ribs and knees from these woods or the equally tough but lighter corkwood. After trees were felled, timber was cut into sizes suitable for carrying on shoulders or being dragged by small gangs with ropes, but with no rivers and few downward slopes it was a cruelly tough portage.

The ships' keels had to be long and straight, but for the curved pieces great care had to be taken to choose logs in which the natural crook was the right shape and size to allow the grain to follow the boat's own lines. Caribbean pines made fine masts and spars for small vessels, and the largest pines and cedars could be sawed into excellent planks—

tough and resilient, and, with their natural resins, relatively resistant to weather and marine borers. For the parts of the ships most subject to friction, such as pulley-blocks, rowlocks, and rudder posts, local lignum vitae proved ideal, not only being the hardest wood known but having a natural oil that made it virtually self-lubricating.

Cutting and hauling the timber, roughly shaping it with hatchets, or making planks with two-handed saws in rough sawpits, was laborious and time-consuming. But the most time and greatest skills went into the actual construction: shaping and fitting the endposts and frame on to the keel, finishing the planks with their subtle tapers, chamfers, and curves, and bending them to the frame, adding cross-timbers, mast, spars, and rudder—all without plans or sophisticated tools. Nails, rudder hinges, and other iron fitments could be made by local blacksmiths, and seams were caulked with local cotton or kapok from *ceiba* (silk cotton) trees—though not without imported tar. Likewise, though rigging and lines were eventually made with hemp from local sisal plants, Bahamian boatbuilders were, and always remained, completely dependent upon imports for the canvas from which they made their sails.[20] Boats enabled the Bahamian settlers to venture beyond mere subsistence. But their islands' limited resources meant not only that Bahamians played only a marginal role in the expansion of the world economy represented by European colonialism in general, but also that they tended to prefer the chanciest, if potentially most rewarding, pursuits—which lent their maritime activities a somewhat raffish air and reputation.

Of the five potential commodities listed in the 1647 articles, "metalles" were clearly a misapprehension, unless the authors were referring to the possibility of recovering bullion and other metals from Spanish and other wrecks. "Wrecking," indeed, became the perennial favorite activity of Bahamian mariners, in pursuit of which they were prepared to sail close to either side of the narrow line between legitimate and illegal. "As for Wrecks," wrote John Oldmixon in 1708, starting a tradition of mild disapprobation, "the People of *Providence, Harbour-Island* and Eleuthera, dealt in them as it is said the good Men of *Sussex* do: All that came ashore was Prize, and if a Sailor had, by better Luck than the rest, got ashore as well as his Wreck, he was not sure of getting off again as well. This perhaps is Scandal, but it is most notorious, that the Inhabitants looked upon every Thing they could get out of a Cast-away Ship as their own, and were not at any Trouble to enquire after the Owners."[21]

The most sought-after wrecks were, of course, the great treasure galleons which had come to grief in Bahamian waters, such as the fabulous wreck salvaged off Tortuga by Captain William Phipps in 1687, or even whole fleets destroyed by hurricanes, like that led by the *Nuestra Señora de Atocha*, which was still being recovered off the Florida coast in the 1980s.[22] But each year, unwary or unfortunate navigators on their way to and from the Caribbean added to the toll of Bahamian shoals and reefs, and even the wrecks of small freighting vessels carrying out provisions or carrying back produce could yield more returns than years of labor ashore. One early such bounty was that provided by the Spanish wreck on "Jeames man's Iland" (Man Island, just north of Harbour Island) in the summer of 1657, from which a Bermudian, Richard Richardson, and three companions, borrowing William Sayle's shallop, fished cargo and bullion worth at least twenty-six hundred pounds.[23] Most wrecks, of course, yielded far less, but still enough to attract the impoverished Bahamian mariners. News of a fresh wreck, or the discovery of an old one, drew wreckers like turkey vultures converging on a carcass. But it was, almost by definition, hazardous work, and in many cases quite impossible without relatively sophisticated equipment, such as the diving bell invented by Richard Norwood of Bermuda and used by William Phipps in 1687.[24]

Another fortuitous but valuable resource was ambergris. This resinous gray secretion from the intestines of sperm whales, cast up on ocean beaches, was an almost magical fixative for perfumes and at first commanded up to four pounds an ounce in Europe. Lumps weighing many pounds were occasionally found in the early years. But the supply was extremely chancy, not replenished at anything like the rate of collection, and almost exhausted by 1700. The value of ambergris, moreover, was depreciated by the growing supply of spermaceti oil, which possesses much the same qualities, once the fishing for sperm whales was more commercially organized, mainly from New England.[25]

Less immediately rewarding but more reliable returns could be made from turtling, woodcutting, culling the shores and seas for oil-bearing seals and whales, and salt raking—though each activity proved more difficult and the resources less valuable and inexhaustible than the first promoters claimed.

The Bahama Islands were famous for turtles long before the English settled there, and the value of these creatures both for their meat and "tortoiseshell" was one of the factors attracting Bermudian sailors to the Bahamas in the first place. Turtles, indeed, are said to have been critical for the development of the trade and colonization of the West Indies in general, providing an invaluable source of fresh meat for long voyages and for settlements deprived of outside supplies. Turtles were netted or harpooned while swimming at sea, but most easily caught when they crawled ashore to mate and nest between April and July. Immobilized simply by being turned on their backs, they could be kept alive for months on shipboard, or almost indefinitely in ponds called "kraals." Of the four breeds of turtle indigenous to the Bahamas, the largest and rarest, the leatherback (*Dermochelys coriacea*), which can attain a weight of two thousand pounds, and the much more common and scarcely smaller loggerhead (*Caretta caretta*), were the least sought after because their flesh was rank and their shells had little commercial value. The two most important were the green turtle (*Chelonia mydas*) which, being a herbivore, had much the tastiest flesh, and the hawksbill (*Eretmochelys imbricata*), which provided the most prized shell for making into combs, costume jewelry and other luxury items. Turtling was thus an essential feature of Bahamian life from the beginning of English settlement, from the first for food for settlers and transient mariners, but in due course also as part of a limited export trade.[26]

There was some market from the beginning for Bahamian hardwoods —mahogany (*Swietenia mahogani*), horseflesh (*Lysoma sabicu*), and mastic (*Mastichodendron foetidissimum*)—though this soon faded once the Jamaican logcutters opened up the Honduras shore in the 1690s. Rather more lasting was the trade in braziletto (*Caesalpina vesicaria*), a splendid cabinet wood which also produced a red or purple dye, and lignum vitae (*Guaiacum sanctum* or *Guaiacum officinale*), the sap of which was found to have some efficacy against the spirochetes of syphilis. These, however, were slow-growing trees which never grew densely and, being overcut, were seriously depleted even when Mark Catesby wrote his celebrated survey of Carolina and the Bahamas in 1725. Besides lignum vitae, other Bahamian flora were valued for their real or imagined medicinal properties. These included "gum elemi" (*Bursera simaruba*), a tree resin used in Catesby's day for staunching wounds; Winter's bark (*Canella winterana*), a form of cinnamon used in the east for perfume and incense; and, above all, cascarella bark (*Croton cascarella*), used for making incense, laxatives, and tonics, of which up to seventy tons a year was exported by the 1740s and which is still used today as the basis for Campari liqueur.[27]

The Bahamian archipelago in the seventeenth century abounded with monk· seals and various species of whales, the oil from which had a ready and growing market throughout the world before the exploitation of mineral oils. Each monk seal could produce up to twenty gallons of oil, which was particularly in demand as a fuel and lubricant for the sugar mills of Jamaica and Barbados. But the creatures were so unfearful and easily slaughtered (with the six-hundred-pound females preferred by the improvident sealers), that by the early eighteenth century they were depleted below the level of an economic return—though surviving in reduced numbers for another century or more. Whales survived longer because fishing and processing them was far more difficult, requiring large ships and crews, and more capital than Bahamians could muster, to hunt, harpoon, and flense the creatures, boil the blubber, and store and ship the oil. Whaling in the Bahamas therefore tended to be monopolized by Bermudians, who established a whale-fishing consortium independent of the Bermuda Company in the 1660s, the first "husband" (or managing director) of which was Hugh Wentworth, a friend and colleague of William Sayle and himself the first governor of the Bahamas under the Proprietary patent (1670–71).[28]

The same Bermudian dominance applied from the beginning to the salt industry for which the southern Bahamas were especially suited. William Sayle had visualized salt from the Turks and Caicos Islands as being added to the dyewoods, ambergris, and produce from wrecks sent from the Bahamas on to Barbados in the quadrilateral trade proposed for the *William* in 1658.[29] The Bahamian settlers harvested natural sea salt from the earliest days and may have built their first salinas—in southern Eleuthera, Cat Island, and Exuma—well before 1700. But they found the best salt ponds in the southern islands and the onward shipment of salt monopolized by Bermudian ships and crews. Bermudians, indeed, made a permanent settlement in the Turks and Caicos Islands as early as 1676, establishing a subcolonial claim that was not surrendered for another century.[30]

The Bermudians' interest in the remainder of the archipelago, however, was minimal, and the early Bahamian settlers lived a marginal existence, almost marooned. Those who survived were hardy and enterprising but mainly ragged and poor. They lacked some of the most elementary trappings of a civilized life, such as magistrates and regular clergy, teachers, and doctors. In the earliest years there was also a drastic shortage of women.

John Darrell memorably characterized the life of the very first settlers when he complained to the governor of Jamaica in 1672 that the men much preferred to "run a-coasting in shallops which is a lazy course of life and leaveth none but old men, women and children to plant."[31] In a male-dominated society the essential social paradigm might be said to have been the captain and crew even more than the patriarchal family household. For the male majority it was almost an expeditionary life, with regular short trips to provision and fishing grounds, longer forays to cut timber or rake salt, or protracted voyages in search of flotsam, jetsam, or the rarer woods. Co-owners of boats went out with their sons and servants (some of them blacks), often for weeks at a time, camping on distant cays. An inevitable result was the blurring of class, even racial, lines through familiarity and interdependence. The authority of a captain was vital, but the major decisions and the allocation of work and shares were debated and agreed upon, at least by the white freemen. All men took their watch at sea, pulled at the oars and sheets, and colabored in the woods and salt pans—even if the brunt was borne by the servants and slaves, whose ultimate shares were least.

Against this social equalization, though, were set the tensions and heartbreak that stemmed from the lack of enough women to provide wives and the hope of progeny for all of the men—quite apart from the pain of frequent separation for those with wives and children, and the fate of women left behind in the base settlements to care for the provision grounds, the children, the elderly, and the sick. No doubt the power to pre-empt the available women was as potent a socializing factor as material wealth in itself, though the two were inevitably interrelated. Even the most energetic and relatively prosperous male might be doomed to dynastic extinction if he failed to find a wife, but fortunate captains and boat owners could cement their position, or poorer men advance themselves, by making fruitful alliances with well-connected females. At the lower end of the social scale, the ability of white men to attract, or coerce, black women away from male slaves led to a greater incidence of miscegenation and a more relaxed attitude to colored offspring than was later the case—though at the same time the resentment of deprived black males against philandering whites upset any chance of true class solidarity between white servants and black slaves. Similarly, as far as the status of women was concerned, it is difficult to decide whether their scarcity value, or the invaluable independent role they played in the base settlements while the men were absent, ever quite offset the bundle of prejudices against them inherited from England, particularly the tendency to treat them as mere brood chattel.

In any case, conditions were gradually changing in nearly all respects between the 1650s and 1700, with the faint beginnings of a significant and lasting distinction between New Providence and the original Out Island settlements. The general population grew more healthy, not just as the result of its isolation but also through progressive immunization to the tropical disease environment—with the Eleuthera settlements being ahead of New Providence in this respect because they had fewer new immigrants and less outside contact. Overall, in the second and subsequent generations of settlers the demographic balance became more even, as many females being born as men and the number of bachelors declining. At the same time, settlements became more permanent and continuously occupied, while the number of blacks increased through importation, and (some natural resources declining) the early mariners were challenged by a more predatory and lawless breed.

As the Bermuda connection faded, it became vital to establish more formal local structures of laws and courts. At first, houses were so insubstantial and impermanent, and land so poor and plentiful, that legal tenure, surveys, and registration were hardly necessary. But that innocent age was passing as the possession and transmission of houses and land through sale, bequest, and dowry became socioeconomically more important. The original settlements on Eleuthera and its offshore cays always remained outside the legal mainstream, relatively content with a society regulated by its heads of households and by custom rather than by formal laws and courts. For New Providence, with its greater opportunities and aspirations, greater concentration and turnover of population, and greater social ferment, the lack of formal institutions was far more serious.

The colony as a whole, at the very least, needed ministers, magistrates and some kind of police authority, to regularize marriages, process wills, register property deeds, settle disputes, and keep the peace. But the more ambitious settlers demanded more. Though hardly yet even a proto-oligarchy in a mini-metropolis, the chief settlers of New Providence already felt more threatened by political anarchy and social and racial discord than their Eleutheran cousins. They were therefore more attracted to the formal sociopolitical structures already established in other English colonies, particularly that system found in the true plantation colonies whereby the chief colonists legislated quite candidly on their behalf and then, by filling the ranks of the local magistracy, also administered the laws. Such, in their varying degrees, were the changes for which the early Bahamian settlers looked when the tenuous Bermudian link was succeeded by a proprietary form of government—though, for one reason or another, almost entirely in vain.

7

Life Under Proprietary Government,
1670–1700

BENEATH THE PICARESQUE SURFACE of scandal and skulduggery described by John Oldmixon in his *History of the Isle of Providence*, the phase of Proprietary government in the Bahamas illustrated how the highest-sounding principles evaporated before the profit motive.[1] The Proprietors promised rational and orderly government but appointed governors and agents instructed to squeeze the islands' population and resources, and when the returns proved negligible they neglected the islands almost entirely. The governors and agents themselves, if not naturally incompetent, greedy, and unprincipled, were driven to oppression and corruption by frustration and neglect. The disasters which followed, however, can be blamed as much on the ordinary Bahamian settlers as on their would-be rulers. Rejecting Proprietary regulations along with the rigors of a settled life, they followed their bent for instant riches, challenging Spanish authority at the most profitable wrecks or even attacking Spanish ships and towns on the strength of questionable privateering commissions. This inevitably led to reprisals from Havana, which almost extinguished the Proprietary colony and left the Bahamas open to a takeover from outright pirates.

Eight Lord Proprietors had been granted the huge province of Carolina in 1663 by Charles II, and as early as 1668 there was talk of their adding the Bahamas to their grant. But what precipitated the action was the wreck of the *Port Royal* at Abaco on its way to Carolina in January 1670, and a petition to London by John Darrell and Hugh Wentworth just one month later.[2] Sorting out the somewhat obscure sequence of events, it seems that the *Port Royal*, full of settlers and supplies for the mainland colony, was run aground on Munjack Cay through ignorance of the Abaco Cays on the part of Captain John Russell and his Barbadian pilot. Few died in the wreck, but more perished on the Abaco shore when the ships' carpenter was culpably slow to construct another vessel from the timber of the wreck. The survivors made their way first to Eleuthera and then to New Providence, where some elected to stay—the remainder going on to Bermuda in a convenient ship. According to one account, Russell connived with the local colonists to recruit some of those destined for Carolina and to retain most of the *Port Royal*'s supplies for local use. John Darrell wrote from New Providence on behalf of his partner Hugh Wentworth (left behind in Barbados) but was also supported in his plea for moral and material help for the Bahamian settlers by the aged William Sayle, who in the last year of his life had been made the first governor of Carolina.[3]

In response, Lord Ashley (made Lord Shaftesbury in 1672), the chief of the Carolina Proprietors, wrote to tell Darrell and Wentworth that six of the Proprietors had already taken up a patent for the Bahamas, were in the process of forming a Company of Adventurers to develop the islands, and intended to appoint Hugh Wentworth as governor.[4] A set of estimates drawn up at this time, based upon Darrell's overly optimistic view of the prospects for cotton, tobacco, and indigo plantations, called for subsistence for three months for an initial settlement of one thousand whites (in three hundred families) and six hundred slaves, and predicted that hundreds more whites and eight thousand more slaves would be needed over the following two years before a profit might be turned. In all, the cost of recruitment, transportation, subsistence, defense, and public works was estimated at a colossal £633,000.[5]

The grant to the Bahamian Proprietors, dated November 1, 1670, echoed that for Carolina in its curious, and largely impractical, amalgam of feudal and liberal ideas, and is thought to be an early product of the fertile mind of John Locke, then Lord Ashley's private secretary. Like all such Stuart documents, the proprietary patent was couched in terms of the grant of a fief by a monarch to his feudal tenants-in-chief, who exercise nearly all the royal prerogatives, subject to the recognition of the monarch's ultimate suzerainty and the payment of homage and a nominal rent—in this case, one pound of pure silver whenever the monarch visited the colony. The Proprietors' powers included the right to establish a constitution and even a subordinate nobility, to pass laws as long as they were consonant with English law, to administer justice, to collect rents and tithes (though not customs), to coin money, raise troops, exercise martial law, and even make war and peace. At the same time, though, the Proprietors were encouraged to allow some form of political representation for all freemen, to permit freedom of religion, and to promote the settlement of foreigners as long as they were prepared to become British subjects.[6]

In obvious reference to Bermuda as well as Carolina, the proprietary patent specified that the Bahamas was "not to be subject to or depending on any other Government or Colony but immediately upon the Crown of England." Another apparently slight but significant feature was that, unlike the grant of Carolina and the Bahamas to Sir Robert Heath in 1629, the new document specified that the land would be held "in free socage" after the pattern of the king's manor of East Greenwich in Kent, rather than as a county palatine on the model of County Durham. What this meant in practice was that while the form of the grant of the territory to the Lord Proprietors, and of land by them to the colonists, implied that there was no such thing as absolute freehold, those holding land of the Proprietors could freely bequeath and even sell it, as had been the custom in the county of Kent even in medieval times.[7]

The proprietary patent was backed up by a more detailed commission and set of instructions sent to Governor Wentworth in April 1671, both of them in John Locke's handwriting. These were concerned mainly with setting up a government, organizing the distribution of land, and controlling the economy to the Proprietors' (and Adventurers') advantage. There was to be a bicameral parliament on the English model, with a governor's council like a miniature House of Lords, and an elective house of assembly equivalent to the House of Commons. The governor was to summon all freeholders in New Providence, Eleuthera, and any other settled islands to elect twenty representatives "who with the Governor, the deputies as their Lordships' representatives, and five other Councillors as the nobility, are to be their Parliament to make necessary laws, which, ratified under the hands and seals of any three of the deputies, shall be in force for two years, unless their Lordships' pleasure to the contrary be declared in the meantime."[8] This parliament was to meet every other year in November unless it were needed more often, and its laws, once ratified by the Proprietors, were to last three years. There was also to be a grand council—a combination of executive and judiciary—consisting of five of the Lord Proprietors' deputies and five freeholders chosen by the parliament (with a quorum of six) which would settle all local controversies and judge all civil and criminal cases.

Even more important to the individual settler, the governor and his council were empowered to "lett, sett, convey and assure" lands in the colony. Each free person settling before March 26, 1672, was entitled to fifty acres, plus a further fifty acres for each dependent. Thereafter, these grants would be reduced to thirty acres, the same amount as would be granted to time-expired indentured servants. All land grants were to be duly registered and recorded in a registrar's office, and were liable to an annual quit rent of a penny per acre, deferred until 1690.

Two-fifths of all land was to be reserved for the Lord Proprietors and "nobility." Less suitably to the Bahamas than to the Carolina mainland, all land was to be laid out in twelve-hundred-acre squares, with lines running east–west and north–south, called "colonies," one of which was to be granted to the governor in perpetuity. More realistically (perhaps following Bermudian practice), each individual lot was "to be set out in one entire piece, and . . . the front of this land abutting upon the sea or any swamp be but one fifth part of the length running upwards into the country."

As to the resources of the islands, one-third of all ambergris was to go to the Proprietors, and a third of this (that is, one-ninth of each find) was to be given to the governor. No braziletto was to be cut without license except on the settlers' own property.

Events proved these documents to be of limited relevance, and with the Proprietors' failure either to make promised investments or to give their governors the necessary support, settlers and governors went their own ways, as best they could. For a start, Hugh Wentworth had died in Barbados before he could take up his appointment as governor. In his place the settlers chose Wentworth's brother John, a well-known free-booter who had seized Tortola from the Dutch on his own initiative dur-ing the Second Dutch War (1665). The choice angered John Darrell, Hugh Wentworth's partner, who sent a splenetic letter to the Lord Proprietors early in 1671, complaining that John Wentworth debauched himself with drink and encouraged the people in their improvident life. This could only be corrected, argued Darrell, if the number of shallops were strictly controlled, royalties on ambergris and wrecks more efficiently collected, and land allocated freely only to those who could be guaranteed to plant.[9]

In response, the Lord Proprietors, while confirming John Wentworth as governor, firmly instructed him not to allow either the cutting of bra-ziletto and cedar, or "coasting in search of ambergris, whales, whale fishing and wrecks, all which are royalties belonging to the Lord Propri-etors," without a license from the governor and three of the deputies. Besides, a bill was to be drafted for the preservation of turtles. In more general terms, Wentworth was told to ensure against excessive democ-racy. His official instructions ordered that all bills were to be initiated in council and nothing was to be debated or voted on in the assembly "but what is proposed to them by the Council." And in a private letter, Shaftesbury pointedly asked Wentworth: "whether you hold your place of Governor as chosen by the people or us; for if you hold it from the people we shall quickly try how safe the Island will be under another . . . your letter expresses that the Speaker told you in the name of the country that they had chosen you for their Governor. . . . a style for a Republique and not persons that live in a government by virtue of His Majesty's Patent granted to the Proprietors." [10]

In a more conciliatory vein, Shaftesbury told John Wentworth that his selection by the people before the arrival of an official commission from the Proprietors should afford him the double advantage of popular support and royal approval. Shaftesbury hinted that, once the planned orders of nobility were instituted in Carolina and the Bahamas, Wentworth would be the chief among those ennobled, and informed him that he was already a tenth shareholder in the Company of Adventurers, with a portion as large as Shaftesbury's own. In an even more remarkable passage, Shaftesbury (the king's chief minister) suggested that Wentworth might profitably use the Bahamas as a base to engage in an undercover trade with the Spanish colonies—a form of commerce that was as contrary to prevailing English colonial theory as it was to official Spanish policy. Unfortunately, neither admonitions nor verbal inducements were backed up with material support. Far from providing even a fraction of the money said to be needed for extensive plantations, the Proprietors so ignored the Bahamas that at one stage John Wentworth complained that he had received nothing from them in two years and was forced to beg Governor Lynch of Jamaica for the most elementary provisions. [11] Without the means to assert his authority or fulfil the Proprietors' policy, the governor was more or less forced to endorse the settlers' chosen way of life, becoming in effect no more than a *primus inter pares*.

Moreover, in encouraging closer contacts with the Spanish, the chief of the Proprietors was merely precipitating an inevitable conflict, somewhat in the position of a person recommending the search for a gas leak with a lighted match. The Bahamian mariners were quite prepared to smuggle goods to and from Cuba, Santo Domingo, or Puerto Rico but were far more interested in Spanish wrecks or even easier pickings. For their part, Spanish *guarda costas* not only arrested clandestine traders and protected Spanish interests at the sites of wrecks but were not above seizing ordinary trading vessels using the Old Bahama Channel or southern Bahamas, on the grounds that these were Spanish territorial waters. Ostensibly in retaliation, English ships attacked and plundered any Spanish vessels which they outpowered and even planned to make descents upon Spanish coastal settlements, looking to the Bahamian governor for authorization.

John Wentworth, "the people's choice," was as ready to revive the spirit of Drake as he had been to attack the Dutch in 1665. But he was sacked by the Proprietors in 1676 in favor of Charles Chillingworth, whose attempts to enforce his masters' instructions "to persuade the people to plant provisions and clear the ground for cattle and planting tobacco, indigo and especially cotton" brought the settlers' wrath upon his head. As John Oldmixon recounted some thirty years later, the inhabitants of New Providence were "living a lewd, licentious Sort of Life . . . impatient under Government. Mr. *Chillingworth* could not bring them to Reason: They assembled tumultuously, seized him, shipped him off for *Jamaica*, and lived every Man as he thought best for his Pleasure and Interest." [12]

Charles Chillingworth's successor, Robert Clark, was far more complaisant and was soon in trouble with Proprietors and Spaniards alike. The problem stemmed from certain Spanish wrecks on the Florida Cays and the western edge of the Little Bahama Bank, which attracted not only Bahamian shallops but a disreputable range of larger English vessels. These naturally used New Providence as a base and for "refreshment." But Clark went further, using the pretext of the seizure of several English vessels by ships out of Havana to issue letters of marque and reprisal, including one to a Captain John Coxon, who was notorious in Jamaica as an out-and-out pirate. Spanish complaints to London about Coxon's depredations off the Florida coast led to a debate in the king's council about the legality of privateering commissions in times of peace. The Proprietors narrowly avoided the rescinding of their charter by arguing that the charter gave them the right to make war and peace, though it was pointed out to them that this was normally meant to apply only to Amerindians and other native peoples. Robert Clark was dismissed and ordered back to England for trial and Robert Lilburne appointed in his place, with instructions to send a list of all existing privateering commissions to the governor of Jamaica, and an injunction not to issue any new letters of marque against the Spaniards. [13]

Trouble, though, had hardly begun. Another desperado called Thomas Paine, ironically sailing under a commission from Governor Lynch of Jamaica to suppress pirates, had conspired with a French buccaneer to sack Spanish settlements around St. Augustine. Using New Providence as a base, he had sailed back there with his booty, to be welcomed by the inhabitants, including, it was claimed, Governor Lilburne himself.

In retaliation, the governor of Havana sent a punitive expedition of two hundred men in two *barcolongos* under Don Juan de Larco, which quite easily captured and sacked New Providence on January 19, 1684.

The several extant accounts of the Spanish attack also give the best contemporary impression of the settlement and its inhabitants. The population was said to consist of four hundred men capable of bearing arms (though scarcely half in fact possessed guns) and, tellingly, only half as many women. This suggests no more than one hundred white families, with perhaps two hundred children and an equal number of slaves— about a thousand persons in all. Nearly all the inhabitants of New Providence lived in the ramshackle township called Charles Town, just inside the harbor bar. A huddle of houses without real streets stretched from the waterfront to the parallel eighty-foot ridge some four hundred yards inland. There was no fort or any public buildings save, perhaps, a small church perched on the ridge where the house called Greycliff was built much later. The most notable buildings were two or three inns—one of them significantly called the Wheel of Fortune—where the menfolk met and traded, and the visiting seamen "refreshed" themselves. Most houses had their own sizeable yards or gardens, and there were a few further patches of cultivation just behind the ridge and on each side of town. But beyond this, to the far edges of New Providence Island—six miles to the east and south and fourteen miles to the west—was a virtual wilderness of straggly woods, brackish ponds, and limestone ridges.

The Spanish expedition first seized a woodcutting sloop off Andros and forced its captain, William Bell, to act as pilot. Approaching Charles Town from the unexpected eastern side, de Larco landed 150 men a half mile from town at daybreak, while the others went on to attack the six vessels at anchor in the harbor. Robert Clark, whom Governor Lilburne had not yet sent back to England, led a foray against the invaders but was wounded and captured. Lilburne, hearing the sound of musketry from his headquarters in the Wheel of Fortune inn, led the flight of the inhabitants into the woods. Even less gloriously, the New England frigate *Good Intent*, which with its ten guns might easily have repelled the invaders, fled across the bar with another ship, without firing a shot.

The Spaniards pillaged the town and the four remaining vessels, killing three seamen in the process. Loading plunder said to be worth twenty thousand pounds into the largest captured ship and burning the rest, they sailed away before dark, carrying Robert Clark and several other captives suspected of piracy. From New Providence the Spaniards hastened to northern Eleuthera, where they laid waste the chief mainland settlement. But they returned to Charles Town a short while later to complete their work, this time burning most of the houses and carrying off some women and children as well as all the slaves they could capture.[14]

Governor Lilburne and the ships' captains complained to London about an unprovoked attack during time of peace, and the governor sent a delegate, Jonathan Elatson, to Havana to seek restitution. The council in London, though (perhaps bearing in mind Lilburne's own complaint that he could not keep pirates away from New Providence without a stationed warship), merely advised that the captains should sue for damages in the High Court of Admiralty, while the governor of Havana was haughtily unrepentant, claiming that the inhabitants of the Bahamas, from the governor downward, were proven pirates, and that the raid on Nassau was simple retaliation. The unfortunate Robert Clark, whom the Spaniards held responsible for the sack of St. Augustine in 1682 and who may have been tortured to extract a confession, died in captivity—John Oldmixon, indeed, claiming that he had been roasted on a spit.[15]

After the Spanish attacks two hundred homeless settlers from New Providence took refuge in Jamaica, while fifty from northern Eleuthera went to Massachusetts and were temporarily resettled in the very different environment of Casco Bay, Maine.[16] The Bahamian colony, however, was not mortally stricken and recovered to enjoy its most prosperous period under proprietary rule during the reign of William and Mary (1689–1702).

At first it was a bootstrap operation. A small contingent from Jamaica resettled New Providence in 1686, led by a preacher called Thomas Bridges who (like John Wentworth) was elected by the settlers and confirmed, *faute de mieux*, by the Proprietors.[17] A few other colonists came in from Bermuda, and there was some talk of the Bahamas' being formally taken over by either Jamaica or Bermuda. These ideas evaporated, though, when the Bahamas quite suddenly, for the first time, became the focus of interest in the metropolis, with the recovery of fabulous treasure from the wreck of the Spanish galleon *Concepción* off the coast of Hispaniola by Captain William Phipps in 1687.

Phipps, who had already exploited three modest wrecks northwest of Grand Bahama in 1684, arrived off the Silver Shoal wreck in January 1687 and by July was back in England with bullion weighing twenty-six tons. His chief backer, Lord Albemarle, one of the Bahamian Proprietors and recently appointed governor of Jamaica, received a return of ninety thousand pounds on his investment of eight hundred. Phipps himself was instantly wealthy and famous, being rewarded with a knighthood and the governorship of Massachusetts.[18]

Little if any of the Hispaniola treasure stayed within the Bahamas, but the prospect of further windfalls encouraged Lord Albemarle to seek a takeover of the islands from the other Proprietors on a ninety-year lease. This project failed because James II (who as duke of York had been a great colonial promoter) preferred that the Crown itself take over the Bahamas from the Proprietors—an anticipation of royal control that was scotched by James II's flight and dethronement in 1689.[19]

The Lord Proprietors were reprieved, and the Bahamas slid back into obscurity. But the war with France which inevitably followed the accession of William of Orange-Nassau (and his English wife, Mary) made the islands an excellent base for privateers. Some new settlers and many transients flocked to New Providence, which at least temporarily took on the air of a true colonial center. The governors appointed by the Proprietors were an indifferent crew, but one exception by most accounts (especially his own) was Nicholas Trott (1694–96), an enterprising if unscrupulous Bermudian who used the Bahamas as a stepping stone to greater fame and fortune through involvement in the affairs of Carolina.[20]

Under Governor Trott a whole new land settlement was attempted and the land tenure system regularized, at least in theory. The Proprietors retained three thousand acres on each major island, as well as the royalties on braziletto, ambergris, and salt, and the governor was to receive one hundred acres of the best land and the church fifty acres as a glebe, in perpetuity. Each new settler arriving before March 1695 was entitled to twenty-five acres, with an additional twenty-five for each dependent, subject only to the payment of an annual quit rent of a shilling per hundred acres.[21] The earliest land transactions of which we have record date from this period, of which the most notable and controversial was the original conveyance of the whole of Hog Island, the offshore cay which forms the harbor of New Providence, to Nicholas Trott himself, for the lordly sum of fifty pounds and an annual quit rent of six shillings. The actual sale was only made after Trott had left the Bahamas, since the New Providence settlers already regarded the offshore cay as common land and resisted its alienation while Trott was governor. A subsequent act declaring Hog Island common land was disallowed by the Proprietors in 1699, on the grounds of their previous sale to Trott. Interestingly, William Phipps had even earlier applied, in vain, for this valuable piece of real estate, in return for which he had offered to spend one thousand pounds on New Providence's much-needed defenses.[22]

In fact, it was Governor Trott who gave Charles Town its first fort, and a new name. The township was formally laid out for the first time and judiciously rechristened Nassau, in honor of the Dutch William rather than his Stuart predecessor. "By this Time," wrote John Oldmixon,

> the Town of *Providence* was grown so considerable that it was honoured with the Name of *Nassau* and before Mr. *Trott*'s Government expired, there were 160 Houses: So that it was as big as the Cities of *St. James* and *St. Mary's*, in *Maryland* and *Virginia*. The Harbour of Nassau is formed by *Hog Island*, which belongs to Mr. *Trott*. It runs along parallel to it five Miles in Length, lying East and West. At the entrance to the Harbour is a Bar, over which no Ship of 500 Ton can pass; but within the Bar, the Navy Royal of *England* might safely ride.
> In the Town of *Nassau* there was a Church in Mr. *Trott*'s Time, and he began a Fort in the Middle of it, which with his House made a Square. This Fort was mounted with 28 guns and some Demi-Culvers.[23]

According to Oldmixon, the threat of Trott's fort saved Nassau from French attacks on several occasions. Under its protection, the roadstead was crowded with privateering vessels and their prizes, and a few legitimate merchantmen. These were either engaged in trade with Charleston, South Carolina—seven days' sailing there and ten days back—or with Dutch Curaçao and Danish St. Thomas, carrying prize and wreck goods and dyewoods for transshipment, in return for food and other provisions. Oldmixon, like most commentators, was censorious about the dependence upon outside supplies, wondering "why this Place should not produce Provisions for 1000 Souls." He even believed that the Bahamas might develop profitable plantations. During Trott's regime there were between three and four hundred slaves on New Providence, and Ellis Lightwood, one of the chief settlers and slaveowners, "attempted to set up a Sugar-Work, which he brought to some Perfection, the Soil being fertile but shallow. He built a Sugar-Mill, and others were preparing to follow his Example."[24]

Despite the uncouth character of its governors and chief inhabitants, the Bahamas began to claim the form and pretensions of a full-fledged colony, and consequently came into conflict with the Crown as well as the Proprietors. "The Governors talked as big as if they had been Vice-Roys of Peru," claimed Oldmixon, adding that they bragged about having

the power of life and limb over their subordinates, while vehemently rejecting the superior authority of Carolina in local disputes. This was a
response to the Proprietors' custom, in the frequent cases of differences
between the people of New Providence and their governor, of sending
orders to the governor of Carolina to make an inquiry and report back to
them.[25] An assembly also met regularly in Nassau during the later 1690s,
though no direct records have survived. The twenty freeholders elected
by the remainder passed many laws—mainly to their own advantage—
concerning the allocation and sale of lands, the turtling, woodcutting,
and salt-raking industries, and the collection of taxes, though quite a
few were disallowed for infringing the rights of the Proprietors or the
Crown, or the laws of England.

   With even less justification, the colony claimed to possess a fully competent judicial system. "Here were Courts of Justice of all Denomina-
tions, as in Westminster-Hall," wrote Oldmixon, "and the Inhabitants
were so litigious, that not a Borough in Cornwall could compare with
them; which is all the more amazing because they had not much to quar-
rel for or to spare for Law."[26] More important than the regular civil and
criminal courts for a colony that depended on privateering, though, was
the possession of an admiralty court, authorized to adjudicate prizes
seized in wartime and distribute the proceeds among captains, crews,
and shipowners. Such a court the English government was more than
ready to set up in the Bahamas, as an essential part of the sweeping
colonial reforms instituted in 1696, just before the end of King William's
War against the French. Accordingly, in February 1697 Nassau was included as the location of one of the chain of vice-admiralty courts established throughout the American and West Indian colonies, complete with
judge, registrar, and marshal directly appointed by the Crown. In the
same month, Nicholas Webb, Governor Trott's successor, became the
first Bahamian governor confirmed by the Crown, taking his oath and
"kissing hands" with King William III in respect of his vice-admiralty
functions and his duty to impose the Acts of Navigation.

   The imperial reforms of 1696–97, including the institution of a vice-
admiralty court, were, however, a two-edged sword for the Bahamian
settlers. The creation of a separate board of trade and plantations and
the appointment of a surveyor general for North America meant a much
closer scrutiny of colonial behavior, while a comprehensive navigation
act channeled and constrained trade more severely than ever before. As
far as the imperial government was concerned, the primary purpose of
the vice-admiralty courts was the enforcement of the laws of trade, and

this threatened to hamper clandestine traders based on Nassau at the very time that prize court business was suddenly curtailed by the signing of the Treaty of Ryswick (1697). Even more threatening to mariners who were driven to activities outside the law was the third distinct function of the vice-admiralty courts: to serve as supranational tribunals for the trial of pirates by the Law of Nations.[27]

The starting of a war involving Spain as well as France in 1701 promised a profitable revival of privateering. But the failure of the Proprietors or Crown to provide adequate defenses left Nassau helpless before joint French and Spanish attacks, which in 1703 and 1706 so devastated the colony that all semblance of law and order disappeared. Governor Edward Birch, landing in Nassau in 1704, was so distraught to find the inhabitants without "a shift to cover their nakedness" that he did not bother to unroll his commission before taking ship back to England. And John Graves (who had come to the Bahamas with Thomas Bridges in 1686 and served for a time as colonial secretary) reported in 1706 that the few New Providence survivors "lived scatteringly in little hutts, ready upon any assault to secure themselves in the woods." Graves wrote that he had left on the island a mere twenty-seven families, with no more than four to five hundred persons altogether dispersed within a two-hundred-mile radius of the capital, along with the twelve or fourteen small sloops that had escaped the enemy, on Exuma and Cat Island as well as New Providence, Eleuthera, and Harbour Island. "In a little time they will be worse than the Wild Indians," warned Graves, "and at the very best they are ready to succour and trade with Pirates."[28]

The remainder of the war was a period of great distress for law-abiding settlers, driven back into self-sufficiency by the cessation of legitimate trade, with their few vessels outnumbered and threatened by strangers of every nationality, including their own. But if anything the situation worsened after the Treaty of Utrecht in 1713, when the freebooters could no longer make any pretense of being licensed privateers, and for a short while Nassau and the Bahamas became the undisputed center of worldwide piracy.

— 8 —

The Aura of Blackbeard:
Piracy and Its Legacies

THE PIRACY ERA in the Bahamas is usually characterized as a picturesque aberration, a sort of negative state out of which—the pirates being
expelled and commerce restored by a right royal government—emerged
a more positive and progressive, if still impoverished, colony. Rather,
it bears examination as a more formative period in the evolution of the
Bahamian national character: one in which a tendency toward opportunistic self-reliance reached its most extreme, even a brutal, form but was
at the same time lastingly imprinted.

Piracy stands for the opposite pole in the Bahamian lifestyle and character from that implanted by farming, fishing, and other respectable pursuits. But there has rarely been a clearcut or permanent division, even
at the individual level within a single lifetime. Rather, there has always
been an almost schizophrenic tendency to crossovers, particularly when
there has been a recurrence of the conditions of extreme poverty, lack of
profitable alternatives, and the absence of strong forces of law and order
found during the classic era of Bahamian piracy.[1]

The structure of law and order had completely broken down by 1704,
but it is unlikely that it had ever yet been seen as more than a superficial,
sometimes comical, pretence. Hardly a Proprietary governor escaped
censure as a harborer or encourager of pirates, even if he was not
engaged in piratical activity or behavior himself. As we have seen, John
Wentworth was characterized by John Darrell as the unscrupulous captain of a disreputable crew, and the governors of Havana had no doubt
that Robert Clark and Robert Lilburne were inferior piratical replicas of
Francis Drake or Henry Morgan. John Oldmixon in his *History of Providence* provided a gallery of out-and-out rogues, not least of whom was
Colonel Cadwallader Jones, governor between 1690 and 1693. By Oldmixon's account, Jones was a petty tyrant and major crook who almost

provoked civil war. Besides monopolizing the most lucrative offices and promoting "his Favourites, who were usually the *vilest of the People,*" he persecuted some inhabitants and banished others, imposed arbitrary fines, intercepted letters without cause, called the assembly only when it suited him, and on one occasion had his son turn his ship's guns on the assembly building to ensure the passage of unpopular laws. Jones also neglected the defenses, seized and embezzled the treasury and Lord Proprietors' royalties, refused to proclaim William and Mary (being, presumably, a Jacobite), and "declared, *He would have a free Trade,* and nothing to do with the *King's damned Officers.*"

Above all, Cadwallader Jones "highly caressed" the pirates, inviting them into Nassau, giving them commissions against his council's advice, and pardoning and discharging those brought to trial. Law-abiding citizens had Jones arrested and charged with high treason, but "*some desperate Rogues, Pirates and others, gathered together an ignorant, seditious rabble, who, on the 27th of February 1692, with Force of Arms rescued the Governor, proclaimed him again, and restored him to the Exercise of his despotick Power.*" Thomas Bulkley, Jones's chief opponent, was brought to trial under a jury which, by the victim's account, included six pirates, three transient strangers, two "drunken sotts," and a person "arraigned for buggery."[2]

Even Nicholas Trott, who was Oldmixon's chief informant for the period down to 1708 and a relative hero of the narrative, was said by the governor of Massachusetts to be "if common fame lies not extremely . . . the greatest pirate broker that was ever in America." This reputation was largely based upon an episode in 1696 involving the pirate Henry Avery, which featured in a London play and eventually cost Trott his post, though it may not have been all that uncommon an occurrence. In April 1696 a ship called the *Fancy,* carrying over a hundred well-armed men and nearly fifty cannon, appeared off northern Eleuthera. Its captain, calling himself Henry Bridgeman, sent to Trott for leave to come into Nassau for water and provisions. Though it was pretty well known that "Bridgeman" was Avery, notorious for his depredations in the Indian Ocean and clearly wishing for a safe harbor to pay off his crew and disperse his loot, the governor gave permission, on the excuse that the seventy armed men and few guns he could muster were powerless to prevent a forced entry. In fact, the inhabitants of Nassau seem to have welcomed the carousing pirates and the sudden influx of money, and Governor Trott, as befitted his rank, was chief of the local beneficiaries.[3]

The Successful Pirate, the London play about Henry Avery, reflected a tendency to admire at a safe distance picturesque ruffians who commit robberies of foreigners, or even the folk popularity of outlaws who challenge the established order, such as the bandits about whom Eric Hobsbawm has written.[4] Such sentiments were not absent in the Bahamas, but the behavior of Trott and the Nassauvians was probably motivated more by need and greed than by glamor or popular ideology. Rather than moral ambivalence, a pragmatic middle ground was sought between profiting from the pirates and being taken over by them, though such a position proved increasingly difficult during the regimes of Trott's immediate successors.

Governor Webb initiated an act against piracy in 1699 and sent an expedition of five ships, under the command of a mulatto captain, Read Elding, against a pirate called Kelly. But instead of capturing Kelly, Elding returned to Nassau with the Boston-based *Bahama Merchant*, which he claimed had been deserted and was therefore a prize, to be shared among himself, his crew, and the governor. In the subsequent vice-admiralty case, however, the captain of the *Bahama Merchant* (who had miraculously reappeared) asserted that his vessel had been seized in a piratical manner, and his crew marooned on a nearby cay. Completely disillusioned with the Bahamas, Webb gave up his duties and fled to Newcastle, Delaware. But the pirates had the last word, seizing all Webb's worldly goods, worth eight thousand pounds, in his ship the *Sweepstakes*, which they renamed the *Happy Escape* as they sailed off, "firing and drinking the Governor's confusion several times."[5]

Rather surprisingly, Webb appointed as his deputy the mulatto Read Elding, who seems personally to have encapsulated a race/class crossover, as well as the pragmatic ambivalence of the period. Elding owed his position to his energies and capabilities, and combined a freebooting reputation with intermittent zeal against the pirates. Elding ruled in Nassau for almost two years (the first and only nonwhite in such authority for 250 years) and during his regime brought several pirates to trial. Most notably, these included Hendrik van Hoven, alias Hynde, "the grand pirate of the West Indies," who, along with three others, was found guilty of sailing "under a bloody flag, their bloody colours . . . as common pirates and robbers on the high sea," and was hanged at Fort Nassau in October 1699.[6]

Early in 1701, though, the popular Read Elding was superseded by Elias Haskett, who seems to have been a worse tyrant and rascal than Cadwallader Jones. Haskett affected to be horrified by the "disaffection and insecurity of the colony," and by the inhabitants, who were "of an uneasy and factious temper . . . not scrupling to do all manner of villany to mankind, and will justifie and defend others which have done the like." But Haskett's own unscrupulous behavior, in collusion with a new vice-admiralty judge, Thomas Walker, stirred up a violent reaction, led by Read Elding, John Warren, the Speaker of the assembly, John Graves, now collector of customs, and Ellis Lightwood, the most influential would-be planter—all of whom had personal reasons for confrontation. Lightwood, for example, had almost had a sword fight with Haskett in public, while Haskett had once shouted at Graves, "You pitiful custom-house officer, You Rogue, if ever you go aboard any Vessel before my Boat has been, I'll roast you alive, you Dog!"[7]

In October 1701 Haskett accused Elding of piracy and had him thrown into jail but immediately negotiated a bribe to have him released. Instead, Warren led an armed mob which freed Elding, broke into the governor's house, and imprisoned Haskett and Walker in turn. A public tribunal was set up, which declared Haskett deposed and elected Lightwood president of the council and acting governor in his place. Haskett was shipped off to New York in chains in the small ketch *Katherine*, being forced to leave all his money and goods behind on the charge that they had been ill-gotten. In New York and London, Haskett indicted the leading Bahamians with piracy and high treason. But the cases were protracted and never resolved, first on the counter-evidence brought by local witnesses, and finally because Haskett was found to be an undischarged bankrupt and fled from England to the Continent.[8]

In any case, the result would have been purely academic. Quite apart from the difficulty of resolving questions of right and wrong in such a disordered society, even while the Haskett case lingered Nassau was "three times Plunder'd and lay'd in Ashes" by the Spaniards and French, depopulated, and left at the mercy of the pirates. Ellis Lightwood, with some eighty others, was taken prisoner to St. Domingue, though Read Elding (who was still living in the Bahamas in the 1730s) seems to have escaped to the Out Islands in his own ship. Likewise, Thomas Walker had taken flight to Abaco, where one of the northern cays still bears his name, while John Graves went to England to lay his case for a royal takeover of the Bahamas before a largely indifferent audience. "One small Pyrat with fifty Men that are acquainted with the Inhabitants (which too many of them are)," wrote Graves of Nassau in 1708, "shall and will Run that Place."[9] His argument, though, was understated. For the islands were already the headquarters of pirates who hugely outgunned and actually outnumbered the legitimate inhabitants—and who for at least a decade imposed their moral and social economy upon them.

IT IS GENERALLY AGREED that piracy proliferated first once formal colonies were established by the non-Iberian powers and the European nations began to make treaties to end the more or less legitimate free-for-all of the buccaneering era. Piracy increased steadily while the value of new colonies and burgeoning trade was not yet reflected in the numbers of patrolling vessels in times of peace, and it reached its climax after the end of the War of the Spanish Succession (1702–13), when hundreds of privateering ships were suddenly without employment, and the personnel of the Royal Navy alone was cut from 50,000 to 13,500 within two years.[10]

Anglo-American pirates congregated in deserted or ungoverned places which were sheltered yet strategically close to profitable sea lanes. They stayed there until pickings declined, better sites opened up, or they were rooted out by decisive government action. Such conditions explain why the Bahamas succeeded Old Providence, Port Royal (Jamaica), and Tortuga as the ideal pirate base and rendezvous between 1697 and 1718—with subordinate sites as far-flung as Cuba, North Carolina, Sierra Leone, and Madagascar.

Marcus Rediker has estimated that a total of some five thousand men served "under the Banner of King Death" during piracy's heyday; of these about a half, or thirty "companies" of seventy-five to eighty-five men, were active at any one time, worldwide. Of these, up to a thousand, making up a dozen or so fluctuating crews, were normally based in the Bahamas. Certainly, there are records of more than twenty pirate captains who used the Bahamas as their chief rendezvous between 1714 and 1722, if with a fairly high turnover, considerable collaboration, and frequent crew interchanges.[11]

This literally floating community constituted a unique social group. Despite the romanticized activities of the "lady pirates" Ann Bonney and Mary Read, it was almost exclusively male, with a comparatively high average age—nearer thirty than twenty, with some 60 percent being over twenty-five years of age. The age and sex imbalance in the pirate community meant that it was not demographically self-perpetuating. Few active pirates were married, and pirate captains commonly rejected men with wives or families when they recruited. But the arguments of Richard Burg that the pirate community was a kind of "gay republic" do not bear close scrutiny. Moral standards on shipboard were comparatively relaxed, but it is unlikely that sodomy was more common than in either the navy or merchant marine. Severe punishments were meted out to crew members who smuggled bedmates aboard, be they women or boys. Pirate ships were by nature heavily manned, and the lack of living space on shipboard meant that sex, like excessive drinking, gambling, and fighting, was of necessity mainly a shore-based activity. Pirate behavior on shore was, of course, notoriously libertine and seems to have been the result of a conscious policy of captains for "letting off steam." But the fact that pirates ashore had a far wider reputation for "wenching" and "whoring" than for homosexual pursuits suggests that their sex drive was at least as orthodox as that, say, of a professional football team released from training discipline.[12]

What gave the pirate community its distinctive character and coherence—and made it seem especially dangerous to the established order—was not sexual deviance or the rejection of accepted moral standards in general, but its unique social and organizational ethos. Pirates were almost invariably volunteers, recruited from the ranks of ordinary seamen on naval or merchant ships, a brutalized and oppressed class which was itself the scourings of a landborne underclass. They were therefore motivated as much by a rejection of class oppression and by instincts of revenge as by a quest to escape from socioeconomic degradation through instant, if ill-gotten wealth. The leadership of a pirate captain was vital in battle, and, as the reputations of Benjamin Hornigold, Edward Teach, Charles Vane, "Calico Jack" Rackham, and Stede Bonnet show, captains could enjoy almost charismatic (if devilish) power. But pirate captains were elected and ruled by consensus. They could be deposed, even executed, by their crews without taint of mutiny, and they enjoyed very few extra privileges—seldom even a separate cabin, dining table, or bed. Pirate crews met in common council to draw up their initial articles fixing duties and shares, to decide strategy and tactics, to settle disputes, or to determine the fate of captives or of crewmen breaking the pirate code of conduct.

As Rediker remarks, the allocation of shares on pirate ships was not only far more equal than that in either naval or privateering ships but was "one of the most egalitarian plans for the disposition of resources to be found anywhere in the early eighteenth century."[13] No captain received more than twice the share of an ordinary crewman, with gunners, carpenters, boatswains, mates, doctors, and quartermasters receiving between one and two shares apiece. Such socioeconomic leveling—compared with the Royal Navy system whereby an admiral was allocated half of all prizes taken under his command, each captain received 25 percent, and subordinate officers shared half the remainder, while the mass of the crew shared the final 12.5 percent—was probably as offensive to the established order as the act of piracy in itself. For imperialist officials and judges, pirates were not merely parasites upon the mercantile system but also threatened the fundamental rights of property—the preoccupation with which had become the main characteristic of that expansionist age of bourgeois accumulation. Governor Nicholas Trott's nephew and namesake, vice-admiralty judge of South Carolina, vigorously summed up this view while trying the Barbadian-born, Bahamas-based Stede Bonnet and thirty-three of his crew at Charleston in 1718: "The sea was given by God for the use of Men, and is subject to Dominion and Property as well as the Land . . . the Law of Nations never granted . . . a Power to change the Right of Property." Pirates were therefore enemies to humankind, "*Brutes* and *Beasts of Prey* . . . with whom neither Faith nor Oath" need be kept. To the accused themselves, Trott chillingly remarked that "no further Good or Benefit can be expected from you but by the Example of your Deaths."[14]

This crude evocation of a savage (and mythical) State of Nature reflected a conflict noted for reciprocal acts of retribution and revenge. Pirates, knowing that once captured they had little chance of escaping the gallows and gibbet, usually pledged to die fighting rather than surrender. Sailing under the dread ensign of the skull and crossbones, they treated all rival symbols of authority with a ritualized contempt, tearing up official proclamations and drinking damnation and confusion to governor, king, or even God Almighty. Pirates (like naval captains, army officers, or jailers) were capable of acts of sadistic cruelty, but they reserved their worst efforts for captains of merchant vessels and other masters who were known to have treated their crewmen or servants cruelly or unjustly—particularly if the former victims were now members of the pirate crew.[15]

Conversely, captains and masters about whom the reports were good were often treated with leniency and respect. Nor, despite their fearsome reputation, did pirates often fight among themselves. They formed, in fact, a nonconforming, democratic confraternity, none more so than those in that "nest of pirates" the Bahamas, who, as James Craggs noted in 1718, "esteem themselves a community, and to have a common interest."[16] The class divisions of the "straight" world were consciously rejected, and racial divisions were also often ignored as being irrelevant to the pirate life. Captured cargoes of slaves were generally treated—

or maltreated—simply as commercial plunder. But suitable blacks and browns were often recruited along with the white crewmen of captured vessels of different nationalities—all being treated without discrimination. The pirate life, indeed, must have been peculiarly attractive for those who were oppressed, not just for being poor but also because of their color.

Bahamian pirate crews were thus to an extent multicomplexioned and polyglot. The majority of crews and virtually all captains, however, were English-speaking whites. The islands harbored an essentially *English* nest of pirates, and this points up the fact that, despite the pirates' outlandish lifestyle and livelihood, there was a closer than symbolic relationship between them and the other inhabitants. The pirates needed not only places to lurk and shelter, share out their plunder, and lick their wounds, to water, provision, and repair their ships. They needed something more substantial: a permissive shore-based community that would act as a kind of semipermeable membrane between them and the larger society and economy. Such townships as Nassau provided inns and quasi-brothels, stores of provisions, arms, and ships' supplies. But they were also places where cargoes and ships could be disposed of, or through which successful or satiated pirates could filter into a more respectable life.

As early as the Henry Avery incident, the Bahamian tradition of sailing close to the wind was well established. Behind a comparatively respectable façade, shore-based individuals were able to profit from piracy without direct involvement in its brutality and bloodshed. Merchants in Nassau could make substantial profits from selling or bartering provisions at inflated rates, accepting payment in stolen cargoes, plate, or money. This was only one remove from those government and vice-admiralty court officials who made extortionate profits from piracy, privateering, or other prize cases. Several of the Proprietary governors, as we have seen, were even able to "work both sides of the street," taking bribes and a share of the loot as well as more legitimate fees—though this was a delicate and dangerous game.

For some established families the connection with piracy was even more direct. Some pirates "went on the beach" in the Bahamas, changing their names or taking advantage of amnesties, marrying into local families, and attempting to set up as planters. Probably more went the other way, an unknown number of indigent farmer-fishermen joining the pirates, at least for a time. Evidence is scarce, for obvious reasons, but more than a hint of this complex intercourse is conveyed in the correspondence of Thomas Walker, a former vice-admiralty judge, and Alexander Spotswood, pirate-chasing governor of Virginia, quoted by Sandra Riley.[17] In 1715 Walker felt secure enough in Nassau to challenge the set of pirates concentrated in "Ileatheria" under the leadership of the formidable Benjamin Hornigold. Among them was Daniel Stilwell, formerly of Jamaica, who had married the daughter of John Darvill, Sr. Stilwell borrowed the shallop part-owned by his father-in-law, recruited John Darvill, Jr. (aged seventeen), James Bourne, John Cary, John Kemp, and Matthew Lowe (all married men) and two Dutchmen, and set off for the coast of Cuba on a piracy mission. There they seized a Spanish *lancha* said to be carrying 11,050 pieces of eight, taking their booty back to Eleuthera. Alerted to this by the governor of Jamaica, Walker seized Stilwell, his crew, and the vessel, and carried them into Nassau in the hope of a trial. Benjamin Hornigold, however, descended on Nassau, released Stilwell and his men from jail and threatened to burn Walker's house about his ears, claiming that all pirates in the Bahamas were under his protection.

What subsequently happened to Daniel Stilwell was not recorded, though his Eleutheran crewmen seem to have slipped into more respectable activities.[18] In any case, the episode was soon overshadowed by more dramatic events. As Governor Spotswood's informant went on to explain, Hornigold was joined by Henry Jennings and Thomas Barrow, and the pirates had completely taken over Nassau by the middle of 1716. Thomas Barrow was reported as saying "he is Governor of Providence and will make it a second Madagascar, and expects 500 to 600 men from Jamaica sloops to join in." More significantly, though Barrow claimed he intended to sail only against Spaniards and Frenchmen, he allowed his men to plunder ships in Nassau harbor from New England and Bermuda, which had come in for whatever trade was going, however shady. By 1717 the pirates, now joined by Teach, Vane, Bonnet, and Rackham (and also, perhaps, by Mary Read and Ann Bonney), outnumbered the settled inhabitants, who were said to go in fear of their property, their lives, and (in the cases of the women) their honor. Thomas Walker himself fled back to Abaco, by way of Carolina, in August 1716 once the pirates had mounted their own guns on the walls of Fort Nassau and completely controlled both harbor and town.[19]

Such a situation could not last. A pirate entrepot was bad enough; an independent pirate republic was quite intolerable. A chorus of complaints from the mainland colonies and West Indies demanded a government takeover of the Bahamas with sufficient force to root out the pirates and prevent their return. But in some respects the pirates had brought their own downfall, proving that they were no more lastingly viable in economic than in demographic terms. Though always regarded as dangerous outlaws and parasites by the imperial authorities, they had at least served to distribute some of the early wealth of empire around the periphery. Now they were too numerous for the available pickings and were becoming too desperate in their depredations, in effect choking the host on which they lived.

The tales of buried pirate treasure (which abound in the Bahamas as in all former pirate haunts) are instructive legends. They illustrate either the perennial but escalating problem of transforming pirate booty into more acceptable forms of wealth, or, more probably (since so few of the alleged hoards have ever been recovered), the fact that the stories of fabulous returns were almost invariably exaggerated. From the few records we have this was certainly true for those Bahamian settlers who turned their hands to piracy for a time. As may have been guessed already, the John Darvill, Jr., James Bourne, and Matthew Lowe who went a-pirating in 1715 and allegedly shared with five others in the taking of more than eleven thousand pieces of eight were, respectively, the person who had so pathetically little to bequeath in his will ten years later, and those to whom he left simply his gun and fishhooks.[20] The three gold rings, silver toothpick and buttons, and the handful of pieces of eight which John Darvill left in his will might have been the last remnants of his pirate share, but they scarcely seem a rational recompense for the risk of death in battle or on the gallows.

In the end, piracy was self-defeating, not just because of intrinsic faults, and certainly not because of its moral dubiousness, but because it did not pay. It was the very antithesis of an ordered colonial system in its parasitical relationship to the larger economy, its rejection of hierarchical society, and its propensity to violence. The elements ranged against it, in due course, proved overwhelming: not only those officials, merchants, and planters who would gain most from the imposition of law and order, but all colonists who needed security of life, land, and property, and the means to develop a family life and lineage.

At one level, then, the piracy era in the Bahamas was simply an anarchic interlude which pointed up the insufficiency of the Proprietary system and served as a catalyst in speeding the transition from initial settlements to more effective imperial rule. Formal piracy was more or less permanently expunged by 1725. But elements of the piratical ethos remained imbedded in the Bahamian consciousness, to recur whenever conditions were conducive. The survival of Blackbeard's name in a Nassau tavern, a well, and a lookout tower may attest simply to the appeal of a vicarious and romanticized piracy to the modern tourist industry. But what is one to make of the naming of a line of Out Island mailboats after Major Stede Bonnet, the Barbadian desperado executed for piracy in South Carolina in 1718? More curious still, there is the mysterious Abaconian folk figure of Old Bunce—half Guy Fawkes, half mummery monster—paraded through the streets of Green Turtle Cay each New Year's Day to provoke amusement and exact tribute, who is seemingly named after Phineas Bunce, one of the pirates executed by the first royal governor, Woodes Rogers, also in 1718.[21]

Poverty, lack of resources, and the heartbreaking drudgery of alternative occupations meant that Bahamians would recurrently be tempted by the chance of instant or easy riches, irrespective of legal prohibitions or abstract morality. Less obvious and general, but equally important, were the noneconomic legacies; the lure of adventure, the freedom and camaraderie of a life on the open sea, and, above all, the sociopolitical attractions of a life beyond the cramping dictates of orthodox family, social class, and racial distinctions. Piracy and its milder correlatives— privateering, wrecking, smuggling, running blockades—offered most to those who stood to lose most from more respectable pursuits: the poorest of the whites and the mass of the blacks. These occupations therefore provided a perennial, or at least recurrent, factor in the shaping of Bahamian life and character. More than this, such activities represented part of that massive unseen ocean current which, for example, Christopher Hill saw as carrying the radical buccaneering refugees from Charles I and Charles II, Jesse Lemisch the radical maritime underclass of the eastern American seaboard, and Eric Hobsbawm radical bandits and revolutionary peasants almost everywhere.[22]

~ 9 ~

Expulsis Piratis:
Life Under the Old Colonial System

TRANSFORMING THE BAHAMAS into a reputable and efficient component of the British imperial system was to prove a protracted business, with many setbacks. The appointment of governors and other officials who were representatives of imperial authority was bound to provoke friction with the lax and opportunistic Bahamian settlers. Also, in a more subtle way, the concurrent emergence of something like a Bahamian consciousness, and the institution of a small but powerful class of administrators inclined to impose metropolitan ideas, attitudes, and style, introduced a new and lasting social division within the Bahamian ruling classes. On the political plane it was a relationship marked by intermittent conflict, arbitrariness countered by obstructionism, and occasional alliances of convenience, while on the personal and social levels it was characterized on the one side by exasperation, intolerance, even contempt, and on the other by complaints of arrogance, insensitivity, or downright ignorance.

The arrival of the first royal governor on July 26, 1718, however, was a hopeful, and suitably dramatic, beginning. Captain Woodes Rogers, famous as the privateering circumnavigator who had captured the Manila Galleon and rescued Alexander Selkirk (the original for Robinson Crusoe) from Juan Fernández Island, suddenly appeared off Nassau harbor bar with the largest British flotilla yet seen there: a frigate and three smaller naval vessels, escorting a large armed merchantman crammed with soldiers, settlers, and supplies. News of an amnesty for penitent pirates had been sent ahead, but Charles Vane, the chief corsair then in residence, receiving no response from Rogers to a request to keep his booty, fired his prizes and sailed away through the eastern harbor entrance, defiantly flying the skull and crossbones. The settled inhabitants and several dozen instantly reformed pirates (including Jennings, Hornigold, and Cockram), however, cheered Rogers as he read the amnesty proclamation and his royal commission on the flat ground in front of the ruined fort.[1]

Woodes Rogers's immediate tasks were to establish effective government in Nassau, to suppress piracy throughout the Bahamas, and to restore and expand the economy. But his larger mandate was to realize the British claim to effective settlement over the entire archipelago against the French and Spaniards. The Spanish in particular regarded the central and southern Bahamas as their own and were prepared to risk war with Britain to police the islands against pirates and drive away non-Spanish settlers. On the very day that Rogers landed in Nassau, a Spanish force from Havana was in the process of eradicating a small group of pioneers in southwest Cat Island, according to one account murdering all the men and carrying off the women, children, and slaves.[2]

With an initial burst of enthusiasm, Rogers declared martial law, set up a council consisting of six newcomers and six of the most substantial settlers who had not been pirates, and appointed a whole range of officials, from chief justice, provost marshal, colonial secretary, chief naval officer, and vice-admiralty judge, down to justices of the peace, constables, and "overseers of the ways and roads." New settlers, including the dozen or so families of Palatine Germans who had come with Rogers, were given town plots 120 feet square, twenty-five acres of land for gardens, and unlimited rights to cut timber for their houses. The militia was reformed into three companies and ordered to keep a permanent watch, and all able-bodied men were set upon public works, first to mount guns on the fort, to build palisados and houses for the two hundred men of the newly arrived Independent Company, and then to clear the roads and the bush surrounding the houses—so that Nassau once more "began to have the appearance of a civilised place."[3]

The naval captains were reluctant to stay at New Providence longer than they had to and refused point blank to patrol the uncharted shoals of the outer islands. So Rogers riskily commissioned several former pirates and sent them out to proclaim the amnesty and attack the unregenerate. The most notable achievements of this campaign were to drive Charles Vane from his new base at Green Turtle Cay, Abaco, to Honduras (where he was later captured), and to compel the surrender of Vane's quartermaster, the notorious "Calico Jack" Rackham, early in 1719. A more symbolic event, though, was the bringing to justice of John Augur and nine of his crew by Captains Hornigold and Cockram in December 1718. After accepting the amnesty in July, Augur had been sent out by Governor

Rogers on a search for stock animals but had reverted to piracy, marooning his supercargo and others who would not sail under the black flag
on isolated Green Cay, southern Andros. After plundering two trading
vessels, Augur was engaged in a fight at Exuma with a Spanish privateer
and was defeated and put ashore with twelve of his men. Three died
of their wounds, but the remainder were rounded up by Hornigold and
Cockram, brought to Nassau in chains, tried in a special vice-admiralty
court and, after one teenager was reprieved by Rogers, publicly hanged
with exemplary ritual.[4]

Governor Rogers's early energies, though, soon evaporated in the face
of familiar difficulties. Like all unacclimatized newcomers, those who
came with Rogers soon fell prey to tropical diseases, so that within three
months over a third were dead.[5] Others deserted, while the established
settlers soon reverted to their accustomed sloth and misdemeanors. To
Rogers they seemed almost indifferent to the Spanish threat and positively longed for the return of the pirates. "Though they expect the
enemy that has surprised them these fifteen years thirty-four times,"
he wrote in May 1719 (perhaps with some exaggeration), ". . . these
wretches can't be kept to watch at night, and when they do come very
seldom sober, and rarely awake all night, though our officers or soldiers
very often surprise their guard and carry off their arms, and I punish,
fine or confine them almost every day. . . . neither would they willingly
[have] kept themselves or me from the pirates, if the expectation of a war
with Spain had not been perpetually kept up. It was as bad as treason is
in England to declare our design of fortifying was to keep out the pirates
if they were willing to come in and say they would be honest and live
under government."

As for hard work, went on Rogers, echoing at least one of his Proprietary predecessors, the Nassauvians mortally hated it. Subsistence was
easy. All they had to do was to clear a patch to grow a few potatoes and
yams to augment the illimitable supplies of fish. "They thus live, poorly
and indolently with a seeming content, and pray for wrecks and pirates,"
complained Rogers. Few Bahamians had any notion of a "regular orderly
life under any sort of government," and all would clearly prefer to spend
what money they had in a tavern rather than give up as much as a tenth
in taxes, even when it was designed to "save their families and all that's
dear to them."[6]

Woodes Rogers's worst crisis occurred in February 1720, when the
largest Spanish expedition yet descended upon New Providence, under
the command of Don Francisco Cornejo—a veritable armada of two

ships-of-the-line, four smaller warships, and eight armed sloops, carrying thirteen hundred men in all. Rogers summoned all the able-bodied men and arms from Eleuthera and Harbour Island to join the motley force of survivors of the Independent Company, militia, and ex-pirates concentrated in Fort Nassau and Rogers's armed merchantman *Delicia*. This, along with the fortuitous presence of HMS *Flamborough*, was enough to deter the Spaniards from a frontal assault, while a surprise attack from the flank was forestalled by the prompt and heroic action of two black sentries guarding the makeshift fort at Nassau's eastern end.[7] New Providence, however, remained beleaguered for weeks, and the Spaniards roamed the entire Bahamas at will far longer.

The Spanish threat eased with the official ending of hostilities later in 1720, so that Governor Rogers's pleas for military reinforcements and a permanently stationed warship to buttress his authority and prevent a return of the pirates fell on deaf ears at the war office and admiralty. Likewise, the secretary of state and board of trade barely deigned to respond to Rogers's appeals for material aid. This was perhaps understandable, for the colony was still regarded as a semi-private, as well as unprofitable, venture. The Lord Proprietors had surrendered their civil and military responsibilities to the Crown but had retained the rights to allocate land and to collect quit rents and royalties, leasing them to a private development company (of which Woodes Rogers was one of the four major shareholders) for twenty-one years at £150 a year. Because it controlled the land and was obviously looking for a return on its investment (claimed to be £90,000), the company was popular with the inhabitants only while it provided cheap provisions, and Rogers was consequently caught between uncooperative colonists and disappointed copartners. Early in 1721 he was forced to give up, pleading ill health, frustration, and personal losses of £11,000.[8]

After an interval of eight years, spent partly in debtors' prison, Woodes Rogers returned as governor from 1729 until his death, of fever, in 1732. During this second term three things made his reputation as the Founding Father of the Bahamian colony: he convened the representative legislature that has had a continuous existence from that day to this, supervised the first slate of permanent laws, and had the legislature adopt, with some justification, the long-lasting (if somewhat ironic) motto *Expulsis piratis restituta commercia*. The small but steady progress that had been made by the 1730s, however, owed less to Rogers's oft-vaunted achievements and character than to the general economic and imperial expansion that occurred during the two decades of "Walpole's Peace" and to the unostentatious work of Governor George Phenney between 1721 and 1729.[9]

Pirates and Spanish privateers continued to cause concern until at least 1725, and Phenney was almost as much a businessman as his predecessor. But matters of defense and private investment were less pressing than formerly, and the new governor was able to concentrate more on the minutiae of administration—most notably regular responses to the new questionnaires being circulated to all colonial governors. Besides an invaluable account of the trade and industry of the islands, these returns provide the first really accurate demographic picture of the Bahamian people.

It was under George Phenney that the first substantial cargo of slaves was imported directly into the Bahamas, namely, the 295 Negroes brought from Guinea in the *Bahama Galley* (in which Phenney himself held shares) in 1721. With these slaves a handful of plantations were established in New Providence, including the governor's own, built "where the Palatines dwell about five leagues West of the Town of Nassau," which Phenney also designed as a fortified retreat—probably at the location still called Old Fort Bay, not far from Lyford Cay. Under George Phenney shipbuilding also increased, the number of Bahamian vessels over three tons' burden rising from a dozen in 1721 to sixteen in 1725, twenty-two in 1728 and thirty-one in 1731, with up to six built each year. These were nearly all coasting sloops, by far the largest being the ill-fated *Phenney* of eighty tons, built of Bahamian mahogany and cedar in 1727 but lost the following year when it ventured out of the islands into the Atlantic.[10]

During the decade after Phenney's arrival the settled population of the Bahamas rose from under a thousand to almost fourteen hundred, including a 60 percent increase in the number of "Blacks" (mainly slaves). Even a superficial reading of the returns shows a population that, while little larger than that of a sizeable village, was not stable or growing by natural increase. However, comparing and collating Phenney's figures with the much more detailed data sent home by his two successors in 1731 and 1735 allows for a far more subtle analysis of the Bahamian population, not only differentiating New Providence from the Out Island settlements, but distinguishing free whites from black slaves, and both from the allegedly free mulattos and blacks.

In what was almost certainly the first accurate computation of the Bahamian population in February 1722, Governor Phenney listed 427 whites and 233 blacks on New Providence, with a further 150 whites and

Table 2
Population, 1731

| Island | Whites | | | "Negroes" | Total |
| | Adults | | | | |
	Males	Females	Children		
New Providence	190	135	308	409	1,042
Harbour Island]	66	55	181	44	[169
Eleuthera					177
Total	256	190	489	453	1,388

Source: October 14, 1731, C.O. 23/2; *CSP* 38 (1731), 298.

34 blacks on Eleuthera, 124 and 5 on Harbour Island, and 12 and 3 said to be still living on Cat Island.[11] Of this total of 989 persons (probably no more than had been settled during the 1670s and early 1680s) some 67 percent, of whom 35 percent were slaves or other blacks, lived on New Providence. Since only 13 percent of the Out Island population was listed as black, the overall proportion was 28 percent—lower than it was ever to be again.

The census sent home by Woodes Rogers in 1731 for the first time gave totals of free men, women, and children, and of adult and child slaves, and thus provided a clearer picture of the demographic health of the Bahamian population. Even more important, the 1731 census listed all householders by name, giving numbers of men, women, children, and slaves in each household, and this allows for the first analysis of Bahamian household composition.[12]

Of the 1,388 persons totaled in 1731, no less than 1,042, or 75.1 percent, lived in New Providence—a proportion scarcely ever again exceeded. The population of the main island had increased by two-thirds since 1721, whereas Harbour Island, with 169 persons, had grown by only a quarter, and Eleuthera, with 177, had not grown at all (no other islands were permanently inhabited). Overall, 453 persons, or 32.6 percent, were listed as "Negroes"—here clearly used as a synonym for slaves—though since 409 of those listed lived in New Providence and only 44 in the Out Islands, the proportions were about 40 percent and only 12 percent respectively.

In the aggregate adult free population, men outnumbered women by 256 to 190 (that is, 135 per 100), with the disproportion markedly higher

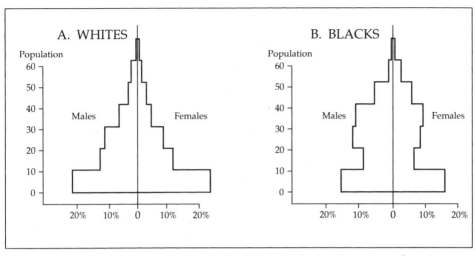

Figure 1. Bahamas, projected population pyramids, 1731 (ten-year cohorts)

in New Providence (141 per 100) than in the Out Islands (120 per 100). This clearly reflected the presence of the small garrison in Nassau and of the reformed remnant of the pirate community, though the proportion of women was almost certainly higher even there than it had ever previously been. Even without miscegenation, at least eight out of ten free men could expect to find mates and establish a family, and this is borne out by the remarkably high number of "children" (probably all those under sixteen years of age) listed. Overall, free children outnumbered free adults by 489 to 446, which suggests a healthily expanding population with a low average age. The disparity between New Providence (with its higher male ratio and greater susceptibility to disease because of more crowded living conditions and closer contact with the outside world) and the Out Islands suggests that the predominantly white population of the Out Islands was already as demographically healthy as any found in the Americas. On New Providence there were 308 free children to 135 adult free females, but on Eleuthera and Harbour Island combined, no less than 181 free children for 55 adult females and 66 adult free males. Over the entire free population (presuming the sexes of the children were more or less evenly divided) the ratio of males to females was about 115 per 100, which boded well for future expansion.

Moving from the tabulated totals to a careful analysis of the nominal list of householders and their households, it is clear that the nuclear family household was already the accepted norm among the free population. No less than 678, or 72.5 percent, of the total free population lived in 130 nuclear family households, containing an average of 3.22 children apiece. Besides this, there were 98 persons living in 33 single-parent households and 25 childless couples. A total of 89 free males and 14 free females were listed as living alone.

The incidence of nuclear families and the size of families were predictably higher in the Out Islands than in New Providence. Whereas on the main island 70 percent of the free population lived in the 92 nuclear families listed, with 2.78 children apiece on the average, in the Out Islands overall some 79 percent lived in 38 nuclear families, with an average of 4.26 children. In Harbour Island, the most tightly knit and insulated island of the three, 121 of the 160 free persons lived in 16 nuclear family households, with a remarkable average of 5.56 children apiece.

The preference for nuclear family households, even if reconstituted, is indicated by the remarriageability of widows, particularly in the Out Islands. Between a third and a half of all marriages recorded during the 1720s involved widows rather than spinsters.[13] Though seventeen of the thirty-three single-parent households recorded in 1731 were shown to be headed by widows, and widows also made up half of the fourteen women listed as living alone, only one of the nine single-parent households in the Out Islands was headed by a widow, and neither of the two Out Island women listed as living alone was a widow.

The information about the slave component of the Bahamian population in 1731 is sketchier than for the free, since sexes were not indicated and the only differentiation was between adults and children. However, since at least a third of the slaves had been imported in the early 1720s, and perhaps a half were African-born, extrapolation from similar Afro-American populations already analyzed by demographers suggests that their average age was higher than that of the whites and free coloreds, with a disproportion of adult males to adult females about the same as for the whites of New Providence.[14] For these reasons alone (quite apart from the effects of dislocation and acclimatization) the blacks would be expected to have been less fertile than the whites. Black adults, indeed, outnumbered children by 275 to 178, which suggests that nubile black females may have averaged less than two surviving children apiece. This indicates a population unable to sustain itself through natural increase, though clearly healthier than the slave populations of the true plantation colonies, which in the early eighteenth century needed about a 5 percent recruitment from Africa each year just to keep up numbers. Demographic conditions for the Bahamian slaves were bound to improve as the proportion of Creoles (that is, island-born) gradually increased, and the number of blacks was also bound to increase through miscegenation. But it was not for a further hundred years that the black population in general became more fertile on average than the white.[15]

As to the concentration of the Bahamian slaves, the 1731 census shows that 188, or some 41 percent of the total, lived in eight units of more than 10, the largest being the 30 adults and 19 children owned by the governor's son, William Whetstone Rogers, in partnership with John Colebrooke (Speaker of the Bahamian assembly), and the 22 adults and 14 children "left on Captain Pheney's Plantation." These sizeable groups of slaves, though mostly listed alongside their owners' families, were clearly gangs employed on the few struggling plantations, growing cotton, sugar, indigo, or large-scale provisions. At the opposite end of the scale were the 43 slaves (33 adults and 10 children) listed singly, and the 24 listed in pairs. These were mainly the domestic servants or helpmates of the poorer whites. In between were the 208, or 45 percent, of the slaves found in 37 units of between 3 and 9—an average of 5.62 blacks in each. These groups seem to have been mainly the slaves owned by the more affluent nonplanter whites, employed in woodcutting, salt raking, and small-scale farming, as well as domestic work.

The census for 1734, sent home by Governor Fitzwilliam in January 1735, differed in some respects from that of 1731 and was superior in indicating adult offspring still living with parents as well as children, and in differentiating male and female adult slaves. Most valuably of all, it also distinguished for the first time the households and families of free mulattos and blacks from those of white freemen, differentiating (as for whites and slaves) adult males and females, and children—thus allowing an initial glimpse into the social life and organization of a group bound to be of gradually increasing size and importance throughout Bahamian history.[16]

One apparent problem with the 1734 census was that it followed, and reflected, a series of serious epidemics. Governor Fitzwilliam himself claimed that "'tis computed we have lately lost by Sickness one third of the White Inhabitants fit to carry Arms." This assessment, though, was exaggerated, and the decline applied even more selectively than the governor suggested. The total population had only declined from 1,388 to 1,378 since 1731, and while the number of free persons in New Providence had fallen from 633 to 538—with a decline, for example, in the number of males listed as living alone from 74 to 43 and perhaps a doubling of the number of widows—the total number of slaves had actually risen from 453 to 491, and the combined population of the Out Islands from 346 to 397. This differential susceptibility to the diseases which arrived (as so often) with a new governor and his recruits is quite consonant with what Kenneth Kiple has discovered about the greater resistance of blacks to certain tropical diseases, and with what is known of the beneficial effects of isolation in the cases of Eleuthera and Harbour Island.[17] An apparent decline in the Bahamian population was also due to Governor Fitzwilliam's own new methods of computation. The total number of free children listed declined from 489 to 397, but this was to a degree offset by the separate listing of offspring over sixteen years of age still living with their parents.

Much more appositely, the drastic decline in the number of men said to be "fit to bear arms" was in part due to the separate listing of white and free colored adult males. Both the separate listing of the nonwhite freemen and their pointed exclusion from the list of those regarded as suitable militiamen (and also, presumably, voters, jurymen, or minor officials) seems to indicate a sociopolitical tightening against them, as against the similarly increasing mass of black slaves, the reasons for which will become apparent at the beginning of chapter 10.

As a result of the relative decline of the New Providence whites, the proportion of slaves in the general population had risen from 32.6 to 35.6 percent since 1731—with 5.6 percent of the population now recorded as coloreds neither slave nor fully free—and the proportion of the Bahamian population living in the metropolis had fallen from 75.1 to 71.2 percent. One healthy indicator for the white population, though, was that the ratio of white men to white women had fallen from 115 to 100 to about 108 to 100.

As to the organization of family and household units, the 1734 census simply corroborates what has already become apparent for the free population in general, further suggesting that the patterns preferred by the free colored population did not differ essentially from those of the whites. Altogether, 77 free mulattos and blacks were identified, representing less than 10 percent of the total free population (or, conversely, a group about a sixth as large as that of the slaves). All nonwhite freemen listed lived in New Providence, which strongly suggests not that there were no free persons of mixed ancestry whatsoever in either Harbour Island or Eleuthera, but that such distinctions were harder to arrive at, and perhaps less important, in the Out Islands than in the colonial metropolis.

The overwhelming majority of the nonwhite freemen listed, 66 out of

77, lived in 16 nuclear-family households, averaging 2.50 children apiece (compared with 2.44 children in the average white nuclear family in New Providence). In 10 of the family households, all members were non-whites, a tightly knit group listed, and perhaps living, close together, and sharing only five surnames—Curtis, Fox, Knowles, McKinney, and Morton. But in the remaining 6 families, one of the two parents was a white—a situation bound to cause social complication. In two cases—those of Nicholas Rowland and the equally Welsh-sounding Nathanial Meredith—the white parent was the father; perhaps soldiers married to free mulatto wives. But even more remarkably, in 4 cases white women (unnamed in the records) were married to, and had children by, free mulatto or black husbands, namely Matthew Morton, Moses and Aaron Sims (almost certainly brothers), and Joseph Watkins. Few free coloreds were likely to have been sufficiently affluent to own slaves, but the fact that 4 of them did—16 slaves in all—illustrates that there was no absolute prohibition against it.

Though only three years had passed since the previous census, the 1734 data show that the slave population had seemingly undergone considerable changes, partly due to social acclimatization and partly, perhaps, as a result of the sociopolitical tightening up already mentioned. There were now 10 units of 10 slaves or more, totalling 181 slaves, compared with 8 and 188 in 1731—figures that were to be raised to 14 and 288 by the end of the decade as more slaves were brought in and further attempts made to establish plantations.[18] But the most obvious change was a remarkable decline in the number of slaves listed singly: from 43 to 19, with a further reduction to 5 by 1740. This was partly accounted for by the increase in the number of two-slave units—rising from 12 to 25 between 1731 and 1734—but it probably also reflected a growing inclination to regard it as sociopolitically undesirable to allow single slaves to be so dispersed throughout the free households.

Whether or not it was a general policy on the part of the whites, the 1734 census certainly illustrates a trend toward having more and more slaves in family units, and this is reflected in the growing rates of natural increase—with 217 slave children being recorded in 1734 against 170 in 1731. Of the 25 units of 2 slaves each in 1734, 8 consisted of a male and female adult slave, and a further 6 of an adult female and a child. Even more tellingly, of the 56 units of more than 3 slaves, only 4 contained no children at all, with the majority of all the units of from 4 to 9 slaves each plausibly consisting of one or two family units. In many cases, the listings suggest almost a social and racial bifurcation, with similar-sized free white and black slave families living (or at least listed) side by side. Even in the larger slave units, the distribution of men, women, and children (with totals of 63, 41, and 77, respectively) was entirely consonant with the existence of at least informal family arrangements.

GOVERNORS PHENNEY AND ROGERS, both traders in slaves, were quite capable of rationalizing a colonial system dependent on slavery. At the same time, they both attributed the fecklessness of the Bahamian white inhabitants to the absence of a normal civilized life, particularly the lack of a secure social order based on land. Without such a basis, they believed, the settlers would neither develop as a people nor attract others to join them. Even after the pirates were driven off, peace with Spain established, and legitimate trade increased, settlers in the Bahamas lacked security of tenure. They could not feel that they really belonged to the place because they could not regard even a part of the land as truly belonging to them. One problem was that the Lord Proprietors had allowed land grants to speculators and absentees (such as Nicholas Trott and Woodes Rogers's copartners) while neglecting the settlers' own rights and tenures. George Phenney in 1723 found three-quarters of the town lots in Nassau apparently untenanted, and very few settlers with actual titles. The general confusion was compounded because Woodes Rogers's first land agent, Samuel Gohier (himself an unscrupulous speculator) had gone back to England with the record books.[19]

What was ultimately needed, argued Rogers and Phenney alike, was an elected assembly, to represent the settlers' interests and to pass laws which, among other things, would permit, define, and protect freehold tenures.[20] Just as the possession of land—plantation, smallholding, or town lot—was an essential factor in establishing a firm social order, so a representative parliament, in all colonies as in the homeland, would be a reflection, and thus reinforcement, of the established social order.

Despite repeated pleas for an assembly, however, the Bahamas was directly ruled by the governor's council until 1729. Perhaps, after all, it was an important preliminary stage. On the surface, Governor Phenney's council seems to have been excessively concerned with the inhabitants' moral well-being, spending much time in the provision of a new church building and a proper minister. This activity, though, was more closely related to the establishment of "civilized order" than it would seem today, since the Anglican church was closely involved with royal authority and as much concerned with local government and such administrative details as the recording of births, deaths, and marriages as with purely spiritual matters. The established church, in colonies as much as in England, was as essential as a parliament in fixing the social order.

Before 1721 the colony had no regular minister, and though marriages at least could be legally performed by any magistrate, or even ship's captain, there were no official records of these, or of baptisms and burials. Along with the first rough census of the Bahamas, and the first recorded wills and inventories (also the first map and drawings of Nassau), Governor Phenney's regime provided the first records of baptisms, marriages, and burials—an invaluable source for local genealogists.[21] The ceremonies were performed and recorded between 1721 and 1726 by one Thomas Curphey, originally styled simply chaplain to the garrison, who was sent back to England for formal ordination by the bishop of London and official endorsement by the Society for the Propagation of the Gospel in 1724.[22]

In 1723 a prefabricated wooden frame for a church was brought over from England at a cost of 450 pieces of eight, and a commission of five councilors and three private citizens was set up to oversee its erection just east of Fort Nassau, on the site of the modern cathedral.[23] A sketch of this modest structure, called Christchurch, is to be found in the Colonial Office papers: a shingled, five-windowed nave said to be capable of holding "upwards of 300 persons," a three-windowed chancel, and a porch, the whole surmounted by a quaint cupola and spire, topped with a gilded vane.[24] A little later, Governor Phenney wrote to the duke of Newcastle, chamberlain of the royal household, begging that since "the Inhabitants have cheerfully at their own Expense errected a decent Fabrick for the Public worship of GOD and there is a Chaplain on the King's Establishment for the orderly performance thereof," the Crown might provide "a service of Plate, furniture of the Communion Table, Pulpit, Desk with such other Ornaments of the Church and the Picture of His Majesty's Person for the Council Chamber as Your Grace's Wisdom shall seem meet."[25] At least some of these luxuries had to await the return of Woodes Rogers, who brought with him in 1729 "two little flagons, one chalice, one paten and a receiver to take the offerings for the Use of His Majesty's Chapel." By that time, though, there was already a decent house set aside for the minister, along with a stipend of forty pounds a year.[26]

Though it was not formally so decreed until 1736, the whole of the Bahamas was regarded as a single parish, and on July 28, 1723, the council had ordered the assembling of all parishioners to "settle the Dues and Perquisites for the Minister and Clergy" and to elect twelve vestrymen, who would then "chuse" two churchwardens. These petty representatives and officials, besides church matters, would be responsible for such parochial concerns as the care of orphans and the poor. The concurrence of civil and ecclesiastical matters was emphasized by the fact that the councilors almost in the same breath decreed that "every Man an Inhabitant of this Island, as well as every Negroe Man" should supply the "posts, rails and Pallisadoes" needed to repair the fort, on pain of a fine of a piece of eight for each deficient item.[27]

The interrelationship between a paternalistic council and an established church in creating a sound social order is even more clearly seen in the first attempts made under Governor Phenney to deal with the social problems posed by the presence of a growing number of slaves and other blacks. The importation of 295 slaves directly from Africa in 1721 alone probably accounted for the first Bahamian "slave laws," a set of regulations decreed by the council on May 2, 1723—clearly an attempt to tidy and tighten up a social-racial situation regarded as having become too easygoing.[28]

Henceforward, no "Negroes" were to be allowed to stray from their homes without their masters' or mistresses' "ticket," and no "Negroes or Indians" were to assemble in groups of more than six, unless they were of the same family or had the permission of a justice of the peace, and the provost marshal or constable had been informed. Blacks or Amerindians meeting whites on the street and not "giving the way" were, on complaint to their masters or mistresses, to be whipped, while instances of overtly threatening behavior or any "great crime" were to be reported to a justice of the peace and punished at his discretion. The only clause protective of the blacks was a qualified one: whichever owner abused his or her slaves in a "barbarous like Manner by burning, cutting or maiming Them" was "upon proof" to be fined forty shillings, for the benefit of the church.

If any black or Amerindian was found carrying and offering goods for sale without written permission from master or mistress, such goods could be seized by "a Constable or any Housekeeper" and ordered by a justice of the peace to be disposed of for the "use of the Poor or Parish," while any free person buying "anything of a Negro or Indian being stolen" forfeited double the value of the goods to their owner and was fined forty shillings for the church's benefit. All owners were to have their slaves' houses searched every fortnight for stolen goods and any "Clubs, wooden Swords, and mischievous Weapons." Goods presumed stolen were to be seized and advertised, while offensive weapons were to be instantly burned. Any persons found selling to a black or Amerindian any "Arms, Powder, Ball, or any offensive Weapons" was liable to a penalty of forty shillings, again to be paid to the church.

Apart from the interesting way in which confiscations and all specified fines were to go to the established church and local government, the 1723 regulations tell us more about the peculiar status and lifestyle of Bahamian blacks at that time. The flexible terminology—"Negroes," "Negroes and Indians," and "slaves"—indicates that while the terms were not quite interchangeable, the regulations applied more or less to all blacks, whether or not they were fully enslaved. "Slaves" were specifically made subject to regular house searches and special punishment for "great crimes," but most regulations, by referring to masters or mistresses, implied that "Negroes" and "Negroes and Indians" also meant slaves. However, the clauses forbidding assembly and enforcing good behavior on the streets implied a more general prohibition by specifying "Negroes and Indians" without any reference to their masters or mistresses.

What seems most likely is that anyone who was unequivocally black (or Amerindian—for Amerindian slaves and their descendants were still quite numerous in the American colonies) was presumed to be a slave unless proof to the contrary was available. Even if not technically enslaved, such persons were treated as inferiors not fully free and were, indeed, normally bound to a master or mistress by ties at least as rigorous as those for white servants. The only possible escape from inferior status for those of mixed race was implied by the absence in the regulations of the term *mulatto*—then used for all blacks with at least a one-half white admixture. This suggests that those of mixed complexion who were not actually slaves might aspire to be practically as free as the whites, and even, after a couple more generations of white admixture, themselves accepted as whites. This, presumably, was the status of such families as the Eldings of New Providence or the Forces of Harbour Island—beneficiaries of a loophole that was to remain open throughout Bahamian history (and actually legislated in 1756),[29] though continually constricted by white racial prejudice.

Already by 1723, it seems, only whites, or those virtually accepted as whites, were supposed to own slaves, to engage in trade, to carry arms, or to assemble without permission. No one, though, had the absolute power of life or limb over slaves. Though closely bound to their masters and mistresses, slaves and other unfree persons seem, moreover, not yet to live under absolute constraints, living, by implication in the 1723 regulations and even more clearly in the censuses of the 1730s, in separate houses and enjoying family life in compact units.

In fact, Governor Phenney's slave regulations seem to have been as much an attempt to "civilize" the Africans within the larger households of their owners, as to constrain them as slaves. The socializing role of the church in this is very clearly brought out in the second set of slave regulations, decreed by the council on February 7, 1726.[30] Masters and mistresses were enjoined to set an example and discourage "Oaths and unseemly discourses" among their slaves. Owners of "Indian and Negro Slaves" who lived in town or within two miles of it were to send them to the Reverend Curphey at 4 P.M. on Saturdays and on Sunday afternoons, for "such Instructions as they are capable of in the Principles of the Christian Religion." When the Minister found "a capacity" in adult blacks they were to be brought for baptism, as were all black children born in the colony. Masters and mistresses of baptized "Negroes and Slaves" were to ensure that they attended church each Sunday and also to do what they could to instruct them at home.

However, Governor Phenney's efforts to make the Africans good Christian slaves were scarcely successful, running up against the theological and practical dilemmas faced in other colonies. One substantial planter, Joseph Watkins, did have his thirty-four slaves baptized en masse in 1723, and Phenney himself, more selectively, had eight of his own slaves baptized: Hannibal, Scipio Africanus, Margo, and Quashebah in 1724, and Elizabeth, two Marys, and John in 1725. But apparently only a handful of other slaves were baptized in New Providence and Harbour Island before the Reverend Curphey left the Bahamas in 1726, and none for a long time thereafter.[31] This almost certainly indicated resistance on the part of most whites to the idea of christianizing slaves, on the grounds of principles rooted in practicality. Africans, it was widely argued, were properly enslaved because they were pagans. Conversely, there was real doubt whether Christians—any more than Britons—could properly be enslaved. In many colonies in the early days, indeed, just as *Negro* and *slave* were virtually synonymous, so *Christian* was used as their antithesis, as well as a synonym for *white*. Even the Reverend Curphey seems to have been numbered among the doubters, including in his parting shots against the governor when he left the Bahamas the accusation that by his policies Phenney had "disturbed the slaves."[32]

What is most certain is that while Phenney and later governors regarded the established church as vital to the social order and managed, with intermittent help from the SPG, to raise the general moral tone above that of piracy days, the Bahamas remained a relatively ungodly place until the end of the eighteenth century. For example, when Curphey's successor, the Reverend Thomas Guy, went on his first visitation to Eleuthera and Harbour Island in 1731, he performed several marriages and baptized 128 persons, but when he celebrated Holy Communion he found only 10 persons ready to receive the sacrament.[33] The evidence of early Bahamian wills—the writing of which surely brought persons as close to the essential concerns of religion as most were likely to come—certainly seems to show that if religious sentiments were present, and gradually becoming more general, they were thinly and unevenly spread. Many wills were strictly businesslike, made no reference to the Deity or the hereafter, and began by simply arranging for the payment of just debts and the provision of a decent funeral. One typical brief document drawn up by the mariner William Thompson in 1756 simply explained that it was occasioned by his "being bound on a foreign Voyage & considering many Dangers of the Seas and the Frailty of humane Nature." Other testators made at least token obeisance to their Maker, consigned their souls to his mercy, or even, like John Graves in 1721, left bequests to charity and the church. Compared, presumably, with most of the original Puritan settlers of the 1640s, true piety was rare, though not entirely unknown. For example, Mary Thompson in 1755, after the usual formula that she was of "sound & perfect Mind, Memory & Understanding," recommended her soul to "Almighty God my Creator, hoping through the merit and Mediation of our blessed Saviour Jesus Christ to have forgiveness of my sins."[34]

Where most of the Bahamian whites were so remiss in their own Christian observance, they were even less than otherwise likely to encourage their slaves to become Christians, since thereby the slaves might be able to challenge their masters' moral, if not also political, ascendancy. The ambivalence of some Bahamians toward slavery and the common doubts about the essential compatibility of Christianity and slavery, however, are underlined by those few slaveholders who made provisions for the Christian education of their slaves or even freed them in their wills. Most Bahamian testators regarded their slaves as no more or less than valuable property, listing them first among their bequests, or between shares in a ship and a house and land, quite often jumbled up with other moveable assets. The Nassau merchant Jacob Cox in 1764, for instance, typically listed slaves and other property together literally without punctuation:

"One thousand pieces of eight in cash a Negro Woman called Diana and her two Children called Jemmy and Sable a Negro Man named Jack Fisher half a dozen Mahogany Chairs."[35]

Yet in the same year, the mariner Thomas Bill freed in his will both his slave Hannah and her son Will (though admittedly Hannah was almost certainly his lover, and Will *his* son too), desiring "that they may Injoy all the Rites and Priviledges of Free Negroes of this Island." His house, land, and another male slave, moreover, were to be sold for the upkeep of mother and son, with the intention "that the Boy Will may be taught to Read and write English, and Arethamatick and Brought up in the fear of God." Even Jacob Cox had manumitted and arranged for the support of his "Negro and Mulatto Slaves old Diana, Grace and her Daughter Susannah," though in his case he also made provision that Susannah (presumably his own daughter or grand-daughter, perhaps even both) "as soon as conveniently may be taken from her Mother and put under the care of my brother Isaac Cox at Philadelphia." No such parental concern, however, can explain the remarkable comment by Governor John Tinker (whose twenty years' residence in Nassau made him almost a Bahamian) when manumitting his faithful servant Abanabah in his 1754 will, that freedom was "the noblest Gift [that] can be conferred on human Kind."[36]

GOVERNOR PHENNEY did what he could to encourage new settlers and expand Bahamian trade. But the new immigrants during his regime, besides slaves, were a few Bermudians who came in to take up lands claimed earlier by their families, to build ships, and to weave palmetto "platt." The scale of trade also remained minuscule. In a typical year (1723), only one ship was reported as coming directly from the United Kingdom, carrying Irish beef and wine picked up en route at Madeira. Most trade was with the other American colonies in short-haul vessels. Local vessels generally ventured no farther than South Carolina, where they bartered Bahamian fruits and turtle meat for provisions, or Jamaica, carrying salt and braziletto wood in return for sugar and rum. Most trading vessels seen in Nassau harbor were from "New England, New York, Rhode Island or Bermuda," looking for Bahamian "Braziletto, Madera Plank, Lignum Vita, Turtle Shell etc.," in return for homegrown provisions or manufactures transshipped from the mother country. A list of these "British Manufactures" which Governor Phenney itemized for the mercantilist-minded board of trade in 1723 (and repeated verbatim in subsequent years) provides both a clear picture of the degree to which the Bahamas was dependent upon the metropole for necessities and marginal luxuries, and of the relative insignificance of the trade—the entire annual value of British imports being computed at £2,320.

Ques: What Quantity and sorts of British Manufactures do the Inhabitants annually take from hence?

Answer: Du roys, Sagathys, Camletts, Shaloons, Bays, Broad Cloths
fine and Coarse, with Thread, Buttons, Silk, Buckram Wadding

and Mohair, valued about	£200
Stockings of all Sorts	200
Shoes, fine & coarse both sexes	200
Ironware and Tradesmens Tools	150
Tin, Pewter and Brassware	60
Earthenware and Glassware	60
East Indian Goods for Apparrel	120
Silks and Ribbands	50
Hatts and Perriwiggs	100
Linen and Ticken	250
Fustian and Callicoes	60
Haberdashery Ware	40
Stationery Ware	50
Gun Powder, Shot and Small Arms	150
Fish Hooks, Nets and Twine	50
Cordage, Anchors, Grapnels, Sail Cloth etc.	300
Provisions from Britain and Ireland besides which come from North America	250
Spicerys and Groceries	30
	£2,320[37]

The petty scale of the Bahamian economy in the 1720s was further borne out by the domestic tragicomedy which—along, perhaps, with complaints about his comparatively easygoing attitude toward the slaves —led to Governor Phenney's recall in 1728. Despite Phenney's personal honesty, Christian good faith, and concern for the proprieties, the governor's authority and reputation were compromised by the mercenary behavior of his wife. No doubt to compensate for her husband's lack of an official salary or share in the Bahamas Company, Mrs. Phenney exploited her position in an attempt to monopolize the export trade in "salt, planking, bark, palmetto and platt," to pre-empt all incoming goods, and to engage in retail trade, even, by the most unfavorable account, going so far as to sell "Rum by the pint and Biscuits by the Half Ryal" out of the back door of Government House.[38]

On his return early in 1729, Woodes Rogers was able to affect a grander style, largely on the strength of a more imposing commission and an official stipend of four hundred pounds a year. But he was able to achieve little that had not been anticipated or proposed by his immediate predecessor. The company had a brief revival, and in place of Mrs. Phenney's petty shopkeeping there was a grandiose scheme to make New Providence a free port in association with the Ostend Company, under the protection of the German emperor. Nothing came of this except squabbles and intrigue, just as Woodes Rogers's continuing hopes to establish a colony of Palatine Germans were dashed by the death or remigration of the few poor German families that came with him in 1718 and 1729.[39]

The most important achievement of Rogers's second term was, of course, the setting up of the old representative system of colonial government in place of rule by governor-in-council, though this change had been long proposed, planned in detail by Governor Phenney, and actually authorized in July 1728. The legislative assembly—destined to survive as long as those of Bermuda and Barbados, on which it was largely based—first met on Michaelmas Day 1729 and sat for only two weeks, but passed twelve important acts. Unfortunately, only those few acts that were still in force when the first edition of the *Laws of the Bahamas* was printed in 1803 are still known in detail. But since the assembly consisted of twenty-four of the most substantial inhabitants not already on the governor's council—eight from Nassau, and four each from the eastern and western districts of New Providence, Harbour Island, and Eleuthera—elected by the 250 or so free white males over twenty-one, this initial raft of legislation represented not just the political will of a new regime but virtually the foundation charter of an emergent ruling class.[40]

Perhaps the most crucial piece of legislation for governor and assembly alike was that voting to the government the financial wherewithal for running the colony, and "Act for leveling divers Sums of money for defraying the publick Charges of these Islands." Like revenue bills in all colonies (for that matter, in Britain also) this did much to establish the fulcrum of practical power and influence. Whereas the colony was responsible for its own support, the costs of administration were to be levied only with the approval of the elected representatives. At the same stroke the governor became to a large degree dependent on the assembly, while those who sat in the assembly became, or represented, a more influential class. Revenue matters, inevitably, were to be a perennial source of conflict between governor and assembly, and this first act was no exception. The levies—which included a poll tax on all adults, including slaves; an annual land tax, distinguishing front and back town lots and farmland; and duties on imports of liquor and slaves and on exports of salt, timber, and fruits—were called "extravagant" even by the solicitor general in England, though the income raised in a normal year at first was little more than one thousand pounds.[41]

Dependence upon voted revenue ensured that the governor had less chance of acting as an arbitrary tyrant—though, paradoxically, the existence of a privileged forum meant that the elected legislators had greater opportunities of describing him as such. Even the governor's chances of acting as a benevolent despot were reduced, and the power of the class of legislators augmented, by the assembly's new partnership in the development of the islands and the regulation of the economy—the concern of three-quarters of the initial laws of 1729. Most of these originated in the mind of a conscientious governor—being initiated either by him or his council—but the fact that they became laws through parliamentary enactment rather than executive fiat made them at least nominally expressions of the will of the legislating class. From the speed they were processed it is unlikely that the 1729 acts were greatly reshaped in the drafting and debating stages, but the potential of the process for creating and reinforcing a ruling class was to prove almost open-ended, especially when dealing with matters involving the special interests of the legislators.

Several of the 1729 acts simply fulfilled policies and proposals for improvements expressed by Rogers and Phenney in their correspondence, or in earlier decrees. Such were the acts "for the Encouragement of Strangers and Foreigners Settling in these Islands," "for the better laying out of the Town of Nassau and regulating the building of the same," "for laying out, regulating, preserving and clearing Publick common highways throughout the Island of New Providence," "to Encourage the Planting of Cotton on these Islands," and "to Encourage the stocking of Keys and Islands with Cattle and to punish Such as destroy the same." But just as many acts were designed to aid, encourage, and safeguard the interests of persons and industries already established in the islands—though not all would necessarily please all settlers at once. Three conservationist acts were plainly designed to aid shipbuilding, timber extraction, and formal plantations by preventing "the Exportation of Timber Plank and other materials fit for the building of Vessels to any American Colony," "the destroying by Fire of all Timber Trees growing on these Islands," and "damages done by Cattle running loose"—though at the same time they might have antagonized some would-be timber exporters and the more casual farmers, whose methods included indiscriminate slash-and-burn agriculture and the running of cattle where they willed.

Two acts, however, were of unequivocal importance to the emergent landowning, slaveowning class. The first was entitled simply "An Act for Settling Claims and the Payment of Quit Rents" but was plainly concerned with the pressing need to establish clear title to land, along with its registration. Under this act and subsequent amendments in the 1730s, machinery was set up for the first time to authenticate land claims, to make rough surveys and "plats," and to record land sales and transfers—not yet through a separate land office but handled by the colonial secretary.[42] The second vital act of 1729 was the first true slave law for the Bahamas, "An Act for the better regulating and governing Negroes and other Slaves." Of all the 1729 acts this is the one for which the precise details are most sorely missed. By inference, though, it seems certain that its purpose and tone came somewhere between the pragmatic simplicity of Governor Phenney's 1723 regulations and the far more systematic and harsher slave law of 1767. Remarks made on the act by the English solicitor general suggest a far greater concern than before—almost an obsession—about the problem of theft by slaves, including clauses allowing the shooting out of hand of slaves caught thieving and the reimbursement of owners of stolen property by the owners of slaves executed for theft (taken out of the reimbursement which the slaveowners themselves received from the treasury for the loss of their slaves).

Most likely, the general model for the 1729 Bahamian Slave Act was the Bermudian code, which itself owed much to the Barbadian law of 1665. By these, for the first time, the slavery of Africans was justified on grounds of racial and cultural inferiority, and real doubt cast on the value, or practicality, of making slaves Christians. Slaves were defined as hereditary chattel property, fit to be bought, sold, and bequeathed, and thus not capable of owning property for themselves and not encouraged to establish formal or permanent families. But at the same time, in a paradox never logically resolved, slaves were regarded as a unique type of chattel property, one that needed to be policed and punished, and against which it was necessary to make restrictions against freedom of movement, assembly, religious observances, and other cultural activities, and against the carrying of arms, raising plantation produce, trading, or hiring themselves out for wages.[43]

~ *10* ~

The Bahamas in Mid-Century,
1733–1767

THE TROUBLED REGIME of Governor Richard Fitzwilliam (1733–38) showed that the changes introduced and proposed by Woodes Rogers were overoptimistic, even premature. The ever-fragile peace with France and Spain was not the economic panacea hoped for, and instead of new settlers and investment the new governor brought with him fresh outbreaks of yellow fever. The effects of poverty, sickness, and the insensitive application of new socioeconomic laws were exacerbated by a governor who was irascible, arbitrary, and tactless. Intermittently facing slave rebellion and military mutiny, Richard Fitzwilliam was also constantly at loggerheads with the local whites and free coloreds. "I am really at a loss how to behave towards them," he wrote after a year, "for in my lifetime I never knew so lawless, profligate and turbulent a People."[1] Relations with the assembly were stormy, particularly over taxation. Little positive new legislation was enacted, and the governor dispensed with the assembly entirely during the last year of his regime— its next meeting being not until 1741. Only with the succession of more capable and tactful (also longer-lasting and more patient) governors did the balance between executive and legislature essential to the old colonial system begin to work. Even more critical was the surge of economic prosperity which, somewhat paradoxically, followed the outbreak of war with Spain in 1739—the beginning of a phase of maritime conflict with France and Spain that lasted almost continuously until 1763, and for more than half the period between 1763 and 1815.

Richard Fitzwilliam did not arrive in Nassau until about two years after Woodes Rogers's death, and the colony had backslidden seriously during the interregnum. In one crucial respect the governor had to start almost completely from scratch. "Soon after the Death of Capt Rogers all the Acts of Assembly of these Islands were secreted or convey'd away;

except one that was left in the Night-time at Mr Fitzwilliam's Door, in a sheet of Clean Paper without any Direction."[2]

Unfortunately, it is not known for certain who it was who had sabotaged Woodes Rogers's legislation or, for that matter, which of the 1729 laws was alone thought worthy of retention. It is tempting to guess that the saboteurs were small farmers or woodcutters—free coloreds as well as whites—who resented the preference shown in the 1729 acts for the more important white mini-capitalists—planters, merchants, and shipbuilders. More likely, they were the normal run of Bahamian settlers, resisting any form of official regulation, particularly when it involved taxation on persons and land, and duties on key imports and exports. At the very least, the new governor would be forced to start from the beginning again, going before the assembly for new, or renewed, legislation. This Governor Fitzwilliam seems to have done, if hardly cap-in-hand, soon after his arrival, so that his first assembly in 1734 passed new versions of most of Woodes Rogers's laws, adding one for the building of a governor's house on land purchased from James Scott, the Speaker. Only two laws were retained from 1729, including that dealing with land claims and quit rents, which seems to be a likely candidate for the manuscript law pointedly left in the night at Governor Fitzwilliam's door.

The records in general were in a deplorable state. "Tis impossible to get an exact Account of the Persons born, christen'd or buried yearly in this Government," complained Fitzwilliam, "because no Register has hitherto been kept thereof, nor could the Inhabitants be prevailed upon to acquaint anybody appointed by the Governor when any such happened."[3] Efforts to repair the records were made through the SPG-appointed Reverend William Smith, and Governor Fitzwilliam set about making a census with his customary mixture of force and tactlessness. The New Providence free coloreds were especially incensed by the governor and council's decision to list them separately. The census was ordered on July 17, 1734, calling for "a Report by all Family Heads on the number of family members, servants, free, unfree, black and white, with all their ages"—rather more details than were, in fact, recorded. On September 23, though, it was found necessary to order the arrest and punishment of those who refused to provide all information, in particular the public whipping of mulattos and free blacks with thirty-nine lashes. "It may be of dangerous Consequence to the Welfare and Safety of these Islands," thundered Fitzwilliam, "to suffer People of their Collor, either to disobey or neglect immediately complying with any Order from the Governor or this Board." At least twelve persons were arrested, kept in jail for twenty-four hours without food, and threatened with whipping, though not actually whipped.[4]

The real danger, though, lay with the slaves, and, indeed, it was a threatened slave revolt only two weeks earlier which had provoked Governor Fitzwilliam's outburst against the free coloreds. An African slave called Quarino had long been a runaway, known to be roaming the bush, but he was not apprehended until he came into town, allegedly to confer with fellow conspirators. Recognized by one soldier, who raised a hue and cry, Quarino killed another with his knife but was overpowered by the guard. On the governor's orders he was closely questioned—probably under torture—and the following day the sergeant of the guard was able to report a confession. From this it seemed that there was a plot for the slaves to take over the island, killing all the white men, beginning with the governor. In a panic, Fitzwilliam ordered the seizure of all the principals named by Quarino and their interrogation in the fort. The accused slaves were uniformly sullen but would confess nothing save a "general knowledge of the plot." What then happened to the accused was not recorded, but it is probable that while Quarino was executed, the remainder were merely deported.

Quarino's plot fortuitously coincided with the opening of Fitzwilliam's first assembly, and the governor was able to use the scare to ensure the immediate passage of a more drastic slave act, tightening supervision and restrictions on movement, and imposing savage punishments for disobedience, insolence, or acts of violence. Possible opposition in England to such measures the governor forestalled by explaining that the new law enacted "no more than what is agreeable to the Laws of our Neighbouring Colonies in the Method of trying and punishing these Savages." At this time, or shortly afterward, a differential tax was levied upon slaves imported from other colonies, not because Africans were regarded as naturally less rebellious, but because of the well-known custom (practiced especially by Bermuda and Jamaica) of dumping their most troublesome slaves on unsuspecting neighbors.[5]

Trouble even more serious than Quarino's abortive plot—and arousing much more concern and interest in England because it involved white men and was written up by John Oldmixon—faced Governor Fitzwilliam two years later, when almost half the Bahamas garrison rose up in violent mutiny. Reading of the conditions under which the soldiers lived, one can only be surprised that it had not happened before. Even Fitzwilliam had complained that the neglected state of the troops was asking for trouble. On February 25, 1735, he went so far as to claim that "the poor Soldiers had much better be condemned as Galley Slaves; for where nothing but Hunger, Sickness and Despair continually stare them in the Face, Slavery, with the common Necessities of Life is preferable to their Condition."[6]

Though every governor stressed the strategic importance of Nassau, the lack of an immediate threat, more pressing needs, and the fact that the garrison was merely an independent company, not a regular unit, meant that the Bahamas came low down on London's list of priorities. The troops were initially of very low quality—including former deserters and other troublemakers—and were not kept up to even their peacetime complement of 150 by recruits. There were few competent NCOs and almost no effective officers—those appointed refusing to take up their commissions, resigning as soon as they saw Nassau, or taking ship to Carolina "to recuperate" at the first excuse. Worse, the soldiers were inadequately housed, chronically short of pay and provisions, and with none of the extra allowances granted to regular units serving overseas. As a result they were forced to shift largely for themselves, and they proved difficult to control and troublesome not only to the regime but to all the more reputable inhabitants. Some of the soldiers were married and lived much like the poorest of the other whites. Others formed liaisons with colored or black women, free or slave, or consorted with the least reputable elements in Nassau's society—drinking and whoring in traditional soldierly fashion on the rare occasions when they had the means. At this worst of times, soldiers roamed the streets in rags, looking for work, handouts, or even easier pickings, or plundered the gardens outside town for provisions, to sell in the market or feed themselves.

Despite his expressions of sympathy, Governor Fitzwilliam himself was scarcely blameless. Complaints spoke of a harshness well beyond the call of discipline, and of soldiers forced to work for the governor without pay or adequate food. One private soldier was said to have committed suicide by drowning rather than continue laboring on the governor's limekiln, and another, found barefoot and in tatters in the bush, was reported fearful of returning to the fort because he had failed to find a lost sheep after which Fitzwilliam had sent him. Punishments inflicted on the governor's orders (as commander-in-chief) included savage floggings and long spells of solitary confinement. By Fitzwilliam's own account, he and Councilor Stuart (captain of militia) had already narrowly averted several attempts at mutiny, though they had not been able to prevent sundry desertions, including those of Peter Owen and four or five others known to be harbored by the Spanish at Havana.[7]

This time the trouble started at 8 P.M. on March 15, 1736, when a private soldier named George Collins attacked the corporal taking the evening roll call. When the corporal ordered him seized, Collins called out, "Who's for Old England?" and nearly all the men on parade came to his aid. The sentinel escaped from the fort and ran the quarter mile to Mount Fitzwilliam to warn the governor. Accompanied by the sentinel and three men set to guard Government House at night, Fitzwilliam marched on Fort Nassau, to be greeted by a volley of musketry that peppered his clothing and cut down two of the men at his side. The governor thereon beat a judicious retreat, on the pretext of raising the militia and guarding a gunpowder store some way east of the fort. The mutineers, some forty in number, broke open the magazine and stores, and trained the fort's guns inward on the harbor to prevent the escape of the four sloops moored there. Then they sallied forth into the town to seize the ships and broke into the jail to release a French captain known to be a competent pilot for the Greater Antilles. After "nailing up" the seaward-pointing guns, the mutineers loaded the largest of the sloops and set sail for Havana at three o'clock in the morning.

Then the mutineers' luck failed them. A fast-sailing sloop owned by one Captain Charles had by chance been anchored off Potter's Cay out of sight of the fort. This Governor Fitzwilliam requisitioned and placed under the command of the veteran pirate chaser Thomas Walker, who filled it with well-armed men and set off in pursuit. Unpracticed sailors, the fugitives had made very poor time and were overhauled and surprised at daybreak. Since their guns were unprimed and their powder wetted by the sea, they were captured without firing a shot and carried back to Nassau by Walker in triumph.

The next day, Governor Fitzwilliam convened a special admiralty court for a piracy trial, ostensibly because the Mutiny Act did not apply in the colonies but also to ensure that the French pilot was condemned along with the mutineers. All those tried were duly found guilty of the capital crimes of piracy and murder, and a third of them were actually hanged— the pilot, George Collins, and eleven others selected for alleged involvement in previous mutinies or desertions. The public hangings, the largest mass execution in Bahamian history, were almost immediate. The flogging of the remaining mutineers before their transportation—they were given up to five hundred lashes at one hundred a time—was a more protracted spectacle, and even more numbing and harrowing.

Even while praising himself for his bravery, promptitude, and efficiency in suppressing the mutiny, and for tempering exemplary rigor with mercy after the trial, Governor Fitzwilliam felt bound to add of the unfortunate troops: "'Tis impossible to keep them . . . faithful to their Trust whilst they remain in the miserable Situation they have hitherto been, without Provisions sufficient to support Life, Barracks to cover them from the Inclemency of the Weather, Fire, Candle, and other Necessarys therein, usually allow'd to other Troops in His Majesty's Service, or proper Medecines to administer them in time of Sickness."[8] Nassau, which was as strategically important against the French and Spanish as Nova Scotia or Gibraltar, deserved at least equal support, argued Fitzwilliam. Indeed, since the supply of locally grown provisions in the Bahamas was far inferior to that in Nova Scotia, Nassau deserved to be placed on the far more generous footing of the Gibraltar garrison.

Since even the most favored units of the British army were in a sorry state during peacetime, Governor Fitzwilliam was praying for a miracle —or at least the onset of a profitable war. The Bahamas colony, indeed, seemed to be a hopeless case, racked by disproportionate turmoils and with a governor more adept at stirring than calming angry waters. As happened so often with the earlier governors, Fitzwilliam's despair and disgust with the colony under his command coincided with the growing conviction in London that the governor himself was not the least of the colony's troubles. Almost inevitably, Fitzwilliam threw in the sponge well before his expected five-year term was up. Returning to England early in 1738, to defend his administration and plead (with perhaps surprising success) the payment of back salary and expenses three years in arrears.[9]

One useful service that ex-Governor Fitzwilliam was able to perform was to forward complaints about renewed Spanish depredations upon British ships in Bahamian waters. For it was on the general issues of Spain's large territorial claims and reluctance to allow Britain a free and expansive trade with Latin America (focused in the popular mind on the case of Captain Jenkins's ear), that Britain decided at last to go to war in 1739. A new governor, John Tinker, did not arrive in Nassau until 1741, but he came with at least some of the means to ensure that Nassau and the Bahamas played an important part in the curtailing of Spanish (and French) claims, and the expansion of British power and commerce in the Caribbean sphere. Tinker brought with him warlike supplies, some recruits for the Independent Company, and the services of an experienced military engineer, the Prussian-born Peter Henry Bruce.

Luckily for us, Bruce wrote an entertaining book of memoirs, and this provides an invaluable, if rather slanted, view of the colony and its people during the first, wartime, phase of the long regime of Governor Tinker.[10] For a person who had never been out of Europe before, the Bahamas must have seemed a far frontier land, as remote from Britain as, say, Antarctica was at the time of Captain Scott. The voyage out, via Madeira and South Carolina, took five months; the travelers were delayed not just by wartime conditions but by three fierce storms and a hurricane. Dozens of men were lost by desertion or disease, the masts and rigging were destroyed off the American coast, and the pilot almost drove them ashore on the Abaco Cays. Crossing the bar of Nassau harbor on April 21, 1741, was a great relief, though accompanied by a violent thunderstorm which sounded like a premonition.

Bruce found Nassau a straggling and makeshift place caught up in a fever of wartime activity. There were still many empty lots and bush on the outskirts but over four hundred houses—mostly of wood and shingle, though some were made of wattle and daub with roofs of palmetto thatch. The population had risen steadily after 1734, then surged to over two thousand after the war began—with almost equal numbers of slave and free.[11] Housing was at a premium, but Bruce was lucky enough to take over a furnished house on which the year's rent of twenty pounds had already been paid by a Royal Navy captain who had gone off to Jamaica in a pique. This house, though close to the center of town, included a garden with a sizeable grove of orange trees.

The engineer's task was to turn Nassau into a Bahamian Gibraltar on a budget of less than four thousand pounds and an almost total lack of local resources. The native rock was ideal for fortifications, cutting like cheese but hardening like flint once exposed to the air. But there was not one stonemason in the islands, or a single wheeled vehicle suitable for carrying the stone from the quarry to the shore. Bruce therefore recruited and retrained two bricklayers from Philadelphia and employed gangs of slaves to quarry the rock and carry the shaped blocks to the building sites on their heads.

The immediate threat from a surprise attack was averted by the completion in July 1742 of Fort Montagu—a squat construction some sixty feet square mounting seventeen guns, guarding the eastern entrance to Nassau harbor where it narrowed to the range of a musket shot. At the same time, the defenses at the eastern end of Nassau were reinforced by the building of a small battery with eight eighteen-pounder guns. Bruce's major achievement, though, was, within another two years, to convert Fort Nassau—guarding Nassau from the west—into a combined bastion and refuge for the garrison and governor. By December 1744 the fortress (located on the present site of the Sheraton British Colonial hotel) mounted no less than fifty-four cannon and twenty-six mortars, supplied from a bomb-proof magazine capable of holding three hundred barrels of powder. Within the fort or the stout mastic palisades on its landward side were stone-built barracks for six hundred troops, a cookhouse, a bakery, two wells, accommodation for gunner, armorer, surgeon, and chaplain, and "above the gate an arched apartment for the governor, with a view of the whole town and harbour." [12]

Peter Henry Bruce was among the first to praise the Bahamas as a health resort, which may have been because conditions were actually improving, or because he was more fortunate with bouts of disease than many first-time visitors. Bruce did complain of the veritable plague of insects—"bugs, cock-roaches, musquitos, flies, sand-flies, ants, and trigers . . . which torment . . . both day and night"—without, of course, recognizing that some at least could carry disease. Most bothersome were the mosquitos and sandflies, which could be reduced by clearing bushes and swamps but were more generally kept at bay by the burning of smoky fires, and the "trigers" (that is, chigoes), which, though "no larger than a mite . . . are very troublesome to strangers; they get through the soles of people's feet and lodge between the skin and flesh where they lay their eggs and breed, if not timely prevented, which is done by picking them out with the point of a needle, at which the negroes are very dexterous." [13]

Even more troublesome than the insects, though, Bruce found some of the inhabitants, with whom he carried on intermittent feuds despite his preoccupation with the forts. His two chief opponents were Councilor William Stuart and James Irving, collector of customs—both cronies of the governor. The gentlemen of Nassau formed a club which met convivially each week at a tavern. But at only the third meeting, Bruce and Stuart, in their cups, had a heated argument, which degenerated into a street brawl, the house arrest of both men, and repeated, though never consummated, offers of a formal duel. With Irving, the argument, concerning Bruce's shares in a cargo of quicksilver seized from the Spanish, had altogether more sinister overtones—Bruce receiving plausible information that the customs officer planned his assassination.

Such tempestuous behavior, particularly the conflict with Irving, was symptomatic of Nassau during the Spanish war. For the town was crowded with roistering privateers, and almost everyone was directly or indirectly interested in the sharing of Spanish prizes. Many of the local shipowners had themselves taken out privateering commissions (called letters of marque and reprisal), armed their vessels as best they could, crammed them with eager local sailors, and sent them to cruise the Windward Passage, Old Bahama Channel, or Florida Straits. Here they would fall upon the smaller and weaker of the Spanish vessels, darting back into the shelter of the nearest Bahamian shoal or line of cays if the opposition proved too strong. The more valuable prizes fell to naval vessels or the larger and better-armed privateers based on the American mainland colonies. A good number of these, however, would choose to bring their captures into Nassau as the nearest port with a vice-admiralty court and reasonably effective means of disposing of booty.

A welcome was assured, as the inhabitants did what they could to gouge the fortunate mariners short of killing the golden goose. Ships and cargoes clearly belonging to the enemy were quickly condemned, though enemy cargoes carried in neutral vessels, and any ship carrying false papers (as most did), took much longer to adjudicate. The vice-admiralty court officials did what they could to complicate and prolong cases to boost their already exorbitant fees, a practice that was much in favor with the tavernkeepers, victualers, and others whose occupation was to entertain the waiting captains and crews. Credit was readily available, and many drank, whored, or gambled their shares away before money actually came to hand, while local grandees like P. H. Bruce speculatively bought up shares from those who could not, or preferred not to, wait for the outcome of pending cases. Much prize business (particularly that of the Royal Navy) was placed in the hands of agents, not many of them local men, and cash share-outs were rare local bonanzas. Despite this, government officials, from the governor downward, showed great ingenuity in tapping prize money, including various forms and degrees of bribery. The largest and most consistent beneficiaries of all, though, were probably the local merchants and shipowners, who bought up condemned cargoes, ships, and tackle in a buyers' market.[14]

Perhaps the most outstanding case, that of the two rich Spanish merchantmen brought in by Captains Sibbald and Dowell of Philadelphia in September 1743, was described in detail by Peter Henry Bruce. There was no doubt that the prizes belonged to the enemy, but in the civilized manner of those days (whereby money ruled, even in wartime) Governor Tinker was empowered by the captors to enter into negotiations with Havana under flags of truce for the redemption of ships and cargoes with silver dollars. This task took four months, during which the privateersmen "were encouraged on shore with rioting and drinking, thereby to run them into debt." Since none of the ordinary seamen were willing to return to their ships, the captains and officers were forced to perform all the necessary work on board. The captains applied to the governor for an order to force the men back to their duties, in vain, and when they entered the town were confronted by resistance and insults from seamen and townsfolk alike.[15]

In February 1744 Spanish delegates arrived in Nassau to redeem the largest vessel, which belonged to the Crown, bringing some forty chests of silver coins, along with a dozen English prisoners in exchange for a like number of Spaniards already sent to Havana. Governor Tinker accepted the money—ninety thousand pieces of eight for the royal cargo alone—despite a valuation two-thirds higher, for which reduction, according to Bruce, he later received a present of three chests of coin (sixteen thousand pieces of eight) and sundry gold ornaments. The Spanish ship was thereupon released, to sail to Havana under prize crew, escorted by the privateers—though Captains Sibbald and Dowell found it impossible to inveigle more than a skeleton crew away from the Nassau taverns.

On returning to New Providence, the privateer captains would not enter the harbor but anchored at Salt Cay and sent word that they wanted their ransom money (which the governor held), and the second vessel and its cargo, to carry back to Philadelphia. This Governor Tinker refused, saying that the vessel had to be adjudicated in Nassau and all the prize money divided there, to guarantee the large debts that the privateers had already run up in the town. He was deaf to the captains' pleas that their articles decreed no share-outs save at their home port, for the benefit of the crews' families as well as the ships' owners and outfitters. Tinker's decision was supported even by some of the beached privateers, "a party of drunken fellows, instigated by some interested persons." These took a local pilot and his boat, went on board the two privateersmen, seized and confined their officers, and brought the vessels into the harbor. There they gave the officers the option: to share out the prizes immediately and suffer no harm, or to refuse and be cut to pieces.[16]

Far from supporting the captains against the mutiny of their men, Governor Tucker cited a petition from the privateers' chief creditor, Mr. Ellis, and "the whole body of the inhabitants," and decreed a share-out under the supervision of Collector James Irving, who would receive 5 percent as an agent's fee. The captains did receive a third share of the proceeds of the royal cargo for themselves and their owners, and each privateersman received 450 pieces of eight. But the disposal of the second ship and the private cargo was so delayed that Captains Sibbald and Dowell sailed off in disgust, leaving most of their crewmen behind. These poor sailors, "when their money was all gone, cursed and damned the government; but they soon found to their cost, now all their money was spent, that instead of being courted as formerly, they were thrown into jail, and very exorbitant fees extracted from them." [17]

It was over the disposal of the second cargo that Bruce fell out with Irving, claiming that he had been cheated of three-quarters of his purchased shares, and that Irving was building a splendid new house and behaving like a nabob with his ill-gotten gains. Tinker and his circle were clearly the chief beneficiaries on this occasion, but much of the money must have spread throughout Nassau—even a few soldiers in the garrison finding the means at this time to purchase their discharge, for a hundred dollars apiece.[18] For his part, Peter Henry Bruce felt more than ready to leave, more out of frustration and chagrin than having suddenly found the means. He quit Nassau as soon as his work on the fortifications was completed, leaving for England by way of South Carolina in January 1745.

Had Bruce stayed (and avoided death at the hands of duelist or assassin) he might have made a modest fortune. For though the pluckings from a single case were never so rich again, the Sibbald-Dowell episode was just one of many similar. Between October 1740 and March 1748, no less than 117 enemy prizes were condemned in the Nassau viceadmiralty court with a combined value, by Governor Tinker's own official computation, of almost three-quarters of a million pounds.[19] This unprecedented influx of money, as even the sober language and statistics of the governor's dispatches admitted, produced almost a transformation in the colony. "The Island of Providence," wrote Tinker in April 1748, "has indeed since the Commencement of the War increased most Surprizingly in Strength and Wealth, and the Town of Nassau Grown Populous and many Edifices that may be called Sumptuous in the Indies." The reason was the commodiousness of New Providence as a privateering base and location for the adjudication of prizes; it attracted adventurers from throughout North America, especially during the winter months. Many privateers were also fitted out and manned by the local inhabitants. As a negative consequence the land defenses and agriculture of the colony both suffered, as potential militiamen were "very frequently out upon their cruises," and no one wished to till the soil, "especially in these Times when a Common Seaman, nay a Negroe Slave, shall step on board a Privateer and in a Six week Cruise return often with a Booty of a hundred pound Sterling to his share." [20]

Already by 1745 the number of local vessels over three tons had risen to forty, half of them displacing between twelve and one hundred tons, and the annual value of imports from England had tripled since 1729. By 1748, though, there were said to be fifty-two locally built or owned ships (against fourteen in 1731), and the Bahamas was said to be consuming thirty thousand pounds' worth of British produce each year, a twelve-fold increase since the time of Governor Phenney.[21] The colonial treasury was in a healthy state, and besides willingly voting more generous salaries to the administration, the assembly passed acts to have Christchurch rebuilt in stone and to establish a "free school" with a salaried schoolmaster. During the 1740s acts were also passed to subdivide local government by creating a second parish, for Eleuthera and Harbour Island; to make landowners in New Providence responsible for maintaining the roads adjacent to their property and clearing vacant town lots; and to order the pulling down of all thatched houses, kitchens, and huts in Nassau (and within one hundred yards of the town boundaries), and their replacement by buildings of plank and shingle.[22]

The great improvement in material conditions is shown by comparing wills surviving from the 1740s with those from two decades earlier, such as that of John Darvill discussed in chapter 6. One typical example was the will of Jonathan Barnett, shipwright of New Providence, who died in 1749, leaving his son, William, and wife, Ann, his sole beneficiaries. To William he bequeathed his work tools, desk, three small arms, a pistol and cutlass, his "wearing apparel," and sundry gold and silver buckles and buttons. The remainder of his "Money Lands Goods Chattles Effects and Credits whatsoever and wheresoever" he left to William and Ann in equal shares, with a reversion to his brother Thomas Barnett, his sister Susanna Frasier, and his friend and executor, John Pinder, Jr.

In all, Jonathan Barnett's worldly goods were valued at 1,787 pieces of eight (approximately £570), of which a third (580 pieces of eight) was in cash. His most valuable possessions were his five slaves, assessed at between 45 and 180 pieces of eight each, and a half share in a sloop called the Two Sisters, worth 250 pieces of eight. But Barnett also left many items indispensable to his trade, including two large saws, eight thousand nails, and a "cab" (leather sack) containing a hundredweight of white lead, altogether worth almost as much as his share in the sloop. Though he left a cow and six goats, Barnett had no land worth bequeathing and seems to have lived in a rented house. This may even have been partly furnished, for though tables (made of madeira or maple), rush-bottomed chairs, cupboards, and chests were listed in the inventory, beds were not. What contrasted most with the goods left by John Darvill in 1725, however, were the rest of the house furnishings. Jonathan and Ann Barnett's home contained a large looking glass, a wide range of bed and table linen, and, besides the usual vessels of pewter and earthenware, china tea- and coffeepots, cups, saucers, plates and bowls, glassware, knives and forks, and a small range of silver tableware—a "pepper box," six large spoons, six teaspoons, and a pair of tongs, together weighing eighteen ounces and worth 27 pieces of eight. In addition to the almost inevitable family Bible, there was an Anglican prayer book and a copy of Stockhouse's *History of the Bible* in two volumes, valued at 10 pieces of eight.[23]

Jonathan Barnett was a Nassauvian of middling rank. Yet even a New Providence bachelor equivalent in status to John Darvill of Eleuthera such as John Stead (or Steed), who died in 1743, left rather more material goods, as well as more slaves, than Darvill had eighteen years earlier. Stead's modest possessions, valued in all at under 500 pieces of eight, were left to three women, almost certainly his sisters, listed under their married names. More than half his estate consisted of four slaves, together valued at 270 pieces of eight: two women called Ruth and Kate, and two children, probably Kate's, named Dick and Moll—the latter listed as a mulatto. Though his house, kitchen, and lot were together valued at only 100 pieces of eight (less than the annual rent of P. H. Bruce's Nassau quarters), his house was comfortably furnished, with bed and table linen and chinaware. Stead also left a silver-hilted sword, silver watch, and gold rings, besides a decent set of clothes.

Perhaps the most intriguing aspect of John Stead's will, though, is the evidence that he lived in the lowest stratum of New Providence freemen, with relatives who were colored as well as white. Quite apart from the presence in his household of a mulatto child, daughter of one of his female slaves (presumably not Stead's own child since he did not free her in his will), two of John Stead's three female beneficiaries were married to men called Sims, closely related to each other, one of whom, Moses, was listed in the 1734 census as a black or mulatto freeman married to a white woman, with three mulatto children.[24]

This complex social milieu—in fact the very same familial network—is illuminated even better by the will of Benjamin Sims, written within a year of John Stead's. For Sims, a mariner who was probably a privateer or even a former pirate, seems to have been a colored freeman "passing" for white, among whose beneficiaries were undoubted whites as well as his "cousins" Moses and Aaron Sims and several other persons listed as free

blacks or mulattos in 1734. Benjamin Sims, like John Stead, was technically a bachelor (or widower), who probably lived most of his life at sea,
for he left neither house nor land. Besides nine slaves, his most valuable
asset was his half-share in the sloop *Two Brothers*, which he bequeathed
to Aaron Sims, along with sixty pieces of eight. His possessions included
such odd items as a large canvas mainsail and three hundredweight of
brown sugar, but most of his personal effects were crammed into a large
sea chest. These consisted mainly of wearing apparel—including no less
than thirty-one pairs of breeches—and a range of weapons: three small
arms, three pistols, a blunderbuss, and two silver-hilted swords. Most
exciting to Benjamin Sims's legatees, however, was the veritable trove of
gold and silver coins that he left, stored away in a jar, a tin canister, a
calabash, and a sock—English guineas, Spanish pieces of eight, pistoles,
and doubloons, worth altogether almost fifteen hundred pieces of eight.

The most unusual feature of the will was that Benjamin Sims manumitted all his slaves at his death. "Item: I will that after my Decease all my
Negroes vizt. Moll Satyra Hannah Pompy Moll junr Casinda Peter and
Sarah [to whom the infant John was added in a codicil] be all made free
and . . . be no longer Slaves to any Person whatsoever, and I do hereby
enjoin my Executors to see the same performed according to Law and
the Custom in like Cases." Sims's two executors were John Howell (once
acting governor and said by one enemy to have been "surgeon to the
pirates") and Benjamin Watkins, both listed as planters and substantial
slaveowners. As time went on it was almost inconceivable that persons
of such a class would agree to manumit a whole household of slaves,
and even in the 1740s it seems unlikely that they would have acceded to
such a provision unless the slaves were the will maker's mistresses and
children.[25]

Certainly, the fact that Benjamin Sims's slaves included at least three
grown women and only one grown man makes it plausible that they
were his own "outside family." What therefore seems most likely is that
Sims was a member of that small but growing class of Bahamians who
found it impossible to fit exactly into social and racial categories, having
spouses, lovers, children, and other relatives who were white, colored,
and black, and slaves as well as free—and who were thus a growing
problem for the emergent Bahamian ruling class.

The situation would have deteriorated through the natural increase
of Bahamian blacks and the normal degree of miscegenation between
the races. But it was exacerbated by the importation of slaves captured
during the wars—not just cargoes of blacks on their way from Africa

to the Americas but parcels of Spanish and French Creole slaves, who were frequently of mixed racial origins (and often, of course, pretended to be free). In sum, not only did the black population of the Bahamas rise from about 250 in 1720 to about 1,250 in 1750, with a further rise to about 2,250 in 1780 (representing a proportional increase from 35 to 56 percent), but the proportion of persons who were neither unequivocally black nor white, and neither slave nor fully free, was bound to have risen from as few as 5 percent in the 1720s, to perhaps 20 percent in the 1770s. These developments led both to new and more comprehensive slave laws, and to the first and all-important attempt legally to sharpen the indistinct lines between black and white, slave and free.

A preference for native African slaves (who, presumably, could be mistreated with a clearer conscience and molded more easily) over slaves from other colonies, especially Creoles (who, though more "seasoned," would be less easily controlled and might even be deportees) had long been shown by differential import duties. In 1741 this was extended to place an almost prohibitive duty on slaves from Spanish or French colonies, who were regarded as extremely difficult to reacculturate. And in 1763, after a severe slave plot was uncovered in Bermuda, an absolute ban was imposed on "the importing into these Islands any Negroes, Mulattoes and Indians from Bermuda or any other of His Majesty's Colonies in America, who have been convicted of or Transported for any high Crimes or Misdemeanours." [26] Concurrently, the internal regulations controlling Bahamian slaves were progressively tightened. The 1748 Slave Act was distinctly tougher than those of 1734 and 1729, to the point that the English attorney general, while nonetheless approving the act, felt bound to comment: "The Powers therein given are very Extensive over the Negroes in Respect of Punishing them But are such as are usuall in other Colonys and Plantations." The same could have been said of the comprehensive Bahamian slave law passed in 1767, though, as we shall see, its provisions were in fact marginally less severe than those found in colonies more subject to slave unrest, including Jamaica or even Bermuda.[27]

Slaves, at least in legal theory, could be placed under absolute control. But restricting the nonwhite freemen was far more difficult, particularly since, as we have seen, many had become persons of substance in the community. The attempted solution was the act of 1756 "to ascertain who shall not be deemed Mulattoes," which, though containing some conciliatory phrases, was in fact designed to limit upward mobility and reinforce white dominance, both by reasserting that only whites could be fully free and by implying that only a strict biological description (rather than economic status or customary acceptance) could define a white. The preamble to the act claimed that it was passed because "many good subjects were deprived of doing themselves justice by being deemed Mulattoes," going on to enact that "all Persons who are above Three Degrees removed in a lineal descent from the Negro Ancestor exclusive shall be deemed white, and shall have all the Privileges and Immunities of His Majesty's White Subjects of these Islands, Provided they are Free, and brought up in the Christian Religion." [28]

This vital and subtly racist act, which remained in force until 1824, did both more and less than it seems at first glance. Like the similar Jamaican legislation, it did not decree, as is sometimes claimed, that no one with the specific proportion of white antecedents could be a slave, or that a slave who could prove the right admixture was automatically freed. It only applied to those "mulattoes" already free. Moreover, it placed the onus of proof on the claimant, an extremely difficult task in a colony with such deficient birth records, not to mention some extremely complex genetic mixes. Conversely, the provisions of the act could be used to deny white status to those already passing as white, if any negro ancestry within the forbidden degrees could be proved. All in all, the act placed great stress on the social importance of aspiring to the white phenotype, ascribing disproportionate value to regular (and well-recorded) white liaisons, while conversely devaluing and degrading all sexual relationships involving blacks. More subtly and damagingly, it was a white male chauvinist enactment. A white male could "upgrade" a black female's offspring and thus had great opportunities for philandering outside his marriage, which, for dynastic reasons, was almost invariably with another white. On the contrary, the offspring of a white female by a black could only be "regressive" in the eyes of the dominant whites, besides bringing such social obloquy on the woman involved that such relationships were almost unknown.

The degree to which Bahamian slaves and other blacks were controlled in the mid-eighteenth century, as well as the ways in which the lines between black and white, slave and free, were legally drawn, can best be discovered by a brief analysis of the 1767 "Act for governing of Negroes, Mulattoes and Indians," and the amending act passed in the following year.[29] "Because of the baseness of their condition," slaves were said not to deserve the protection or normal provisions of the English law, and because of the problems of prolonged imprisonment (including the danger of escapes as well as expense) were to be summarily tried and punished. Slaves were subject to "correctional" punishment solely at the whim of their masters without hope of appeal, and they could be publicly whipped with up to one hundred lashes by order of a magistrate simply on an application by their masters. But for offenses regarded as more serious they were to be tried by a bench consisting of two justices of the peace and three freeholders—any three of whom, including one justice, constituted a majority. This scanty tribunal, which did not necessarily include a single qualified lawyer, had absolute authority to judge a very wide range of offenses regarded as capital crimes: not only murder, poisoning, rape, arson, cattle maiming or rustling, breaking and entering, burglary, and theft of articles worth six shillings or more, but also mere attempts to commit such offenses, or being accessory to them.[30] For offering violence to a white, a slave was to be whipped for the first offense, have "his or her Nose Slit, ears cut off or Face branded with a hot Iron" for a second, and executed for a third offense.

The 1767 act specifically stated that its provisions against "heinous and grievous crimes" were occasioned by the frequency with which they were committed. Likewise, the severe prohibitions against slaves' carrying offensive weapons, assembling riotously, gaming, or tippling in taverns strongly suggest that slaves were accustomed to stretch the law in these respects. In forbidding slaves to trade or plant on their own account, the law referred quite directly to their habitual tendency to do so. The former was prohibited because, in the act's words, "many evil minded and covetous People of these Islands make a practice of Trading with Negro and other Slaves." The prohibition against slaves' planting on any land save that belonging to their owners similarly arose because it had "hitherto been customary for Slaves to make Plantations for themselves." Thus, like all West Indian slave legislation, the 1767 act tells us as much about customary practice and the prevailing conditions as it does about the law itself.

Not remarkably in a colony so difficult to police, with such practical mobility possible for the slaves and so many refuges available, the 1767 act was obsessively concerned with the problem of slaves' running away. Slaves were permanently under curfew, not being allowed out between 9 P.M. and daylight without a ticket from their owners or employers. Slaves who absented themselves for more than fourteen days were deemed outlaws, and owners were required to advertise their runaways "in the usual publick places." Any slave out after curfew, seen carrying arms, or thought to be a runaway, could (and should) be stopped, questioned, and, if necessary, apprehended, by any freeman.

Known outlaws had a price of twenty pounds placed on their heads, dead or alive. In general, the killing of a slave by any freeman was not a crime unless it was done willfully, in which case the killer was supposed to be tried "according to the Laws of England"—though such an occurrence was almost inconceivable.

Curiously, and in contrast to most other colonies, Bahamian slaves were allowed to carry firearms when it suited their owners—for example, for fowling, hog hunting, or protection against Spaniards or pirates—as long as they carried permits to produce on a demand from any freeman. Bahamian slaves were also specifically permitted to serve under arms against foreign enemies in times of war. If slaves were killed during war service, compensation was to be paid out of the colonial treasury, though to the owner, not the next of kin, of course—slave families having no legal existence. Even less justly, owners were to be compensated up to sixty pounds for slaves killed as outlaws or executed after due legal process—provided that a special investigatory tribunal of two justices of the peace and three freemen did not find that the slave had been provoked into crime by being "inhumanely used" by his or her owner or employer. This latter negative and indirect penalty, along with the provision against willful killing and the suggestion that the most severe correctional whippings should be under the supervision of a justice of the peace and the provost marshal, were the only clauses in the 1767 act even vaguely protective of the slaves. There were no clauses establishing standards of food, clothing, or work conditions, nor were there any provisions for family life or even Christianization, and the question of slave manumission was apparently ignored.

Though objectionable by absolute standards, the slave provisions of the 1767 Bahamian act were relatively less severe than those in similar acts in the true plantation colonies. The Bahamian free coloreds and blacks, however, were treated with relative harshness—a reflection of the socioeconomic and political threat they were thought to pose. Remarkably, the provisions threatening, successively, whipping, mutilation, and execution for offering violence against a white applied equally to all "Negroes, Mulattoes and Indians," and the only concession in the regulations against abusing a white person was that a free colored person might be fined fifteen pounds in lieu of a public whipping. Free coloreds and blacks also faced an absolute ban on gaming, were forbidden to sell liquor, and suffered from restrictions on trading and planting. Their oaths and evidence were not valid in court except in cases of debt, though evidence of slaves might be used against them. Most dramatic of all was the scarcely credible provision that any free black, mulatto, or Amerindian who harbored a runaway slave was liable to forfeit his or her freedom and suffer deportation. In an inversion worthy of Lewis Carroll, this was the severest punishment exacted for such a "crime." Whites who harbored runaways were normally to be fined (albeit heavily), while slaves (of whom it was presumably thought completely natural) were merely to be whipped.[31]

The only theoretical mitigation of the provisions against free coloreds and blacks was the presumption that "Negroes, Mulattoes and Indians" who had been born free could expect to be tried for serious crimes by a regular court, using normal judicial processes, rather than by the arbitrary tribunal of two justices of the peace and three freeholders decreed for slaves in the act. Such an implied advantage (which in cases tried by jury might well be a two-edged sword) did not apply, however, to all free coloreds and blacks. For the act singled out for special severity those "Negroes, Mulattoes or Indians" who had been freed during their own lifetime. Such *freed* (as opposed to free-born) persons were specifically subject to trial by the slave tribunals. Freedmen were liable for most of the penalties imposed on slaves and, unlike other free coloreds and blacks, suffered an absolute ban on planting cotton, coffee, or indigo.

Besides this, moves were afoot to ensure that the number of freedmen, never high, increased even more slowly. A notable deficiency of the 1767 Act was an absence of regulations governing slave manumissions, which seem to have occurred, as far as they did, through customary practice rather than formal law. The deficiency was remedied by an amending act in 1768 which, predictably, made manumission more difficult and hedged the freed persons with tougher restrictions. Henceforward, except for special acts of assembly, slaves could be manumitted only by their owners, and the custom implied in the 1767 act that freedmen continued to be tied to their former owners by a form of apprenticeship was now made law. This was enforced, and the practical self-manumission of slaves by paying off their owners made almost impossible, by the requirement that the former owner post a ninety-pound bond for each manumitted slave, to ensure good behavior and avoid any possible future burden on the colonial treasury.

In the above ways, the legislating class in the Bahamas attempted both to discourage manumission and to defuse any potential threat from too rapid a change by separating out those who were at least a generation closer to the status of the fully free. The price of this distinction, though, was a further complication of the social matrix, adding yet another subclass. Indeed, Bahamian society, with the existence of subclasses within the white section as well as racial and class crossovers within families at all levels, was already more like a complex social spectrum than the tripartite system claimed by many commentators for Latin America and the Caribbean in general, let alone the simply bifurcated society developing in the American mainland colonies.[32]

A final significant aspect of the 1767 act—not previously noted by writers on slavery, in the Bahamas or elsewhere—was the copious use of informers. In nearly all cases, presentments against wrongdoers— whites and free coloreds as well as slaves—were expected to be made not by constables or other officials but by civic-minded free persons, who were thereupon rewarded either with half the fines levied, or an assessed equivalent sum. In the case of information leading to the conviction of a white person found harboring a runaway this could be as much as thirty pounds—equivalent to the annual wage of a professional man and thus a sore temptation to any poor white or free colored person. This obnoxious feature of the act clearly stemmed not just from the lack of a formal police machinery but from a calculated plan to have the society regulate itself. In practice, however, far from ensuring a more orderly social system, it was bound to produce a society even further divided against itself.

~ 11 ~

The End of the Old Regime,
1763–1783

WARTIME PROSPERITY and interwar slumps during the mid-eighteenth century set the pattern of "boom and bust" which was to characterize all subsequent Bahamian history and have a lasting effect upon the character and psychology of the Bahamian people.

The Treaty of Aix-la-Chapelle in 1748 brought an immediate halt to the surge of good fortune during the wars with Spain and France over Jenkins's ear and the question of the Austrian succession. But the trough was followed by an even greater crest during the Seven Years' War (1756–63) and the regime of Governor William Shirley. As a reflection of Britain's triumphs in what might be called the first world war—which in the Caribbean sphere saw the capture of Cuba and Guadeloupe and the acquisition of Florida and the "Neutral Islands" of Dominica, St. Vincent, Grenada, and Tobago—effective British control was extended for the first time over the entire Bahamian archipelago.

This progress was not sustained over the subsequent decade, as relations between Britain and her American mainland colonies deteriorated, and the French rather than the British became the beneficiaries of the decline of Spain in the region. Nor, for the first time, did the return of wartime conditions revive the colony's fortunes. The Bahamas, its own loyalties divided, was briefly captured by the American rebels in 1776. It did recover, to become once more, for a time, an important privateering base. But when Britain, confronted by all the European maritime powers as well as the Americans, lost control of land and sea in 1781, the Bahamas suffered the crowning indignity of a takeover by Spain—a power that had seemed eclipsed in 1763.

The pattern of alternating expansion and decline, indeed, was reversed in this phase. The complete ebb of Bahamian fortunes at the end of the maritime war was the prelude, not to prolonged misfortune, but to the greatest of all forward surges, as the defeat of the British cause on the American mainland and the loss of Florida led to the influx of American Loyalists into the Bahamas after the Treaty of Versailles.

The need to tighten belts and buckle down to work with the sudden slump of 1748 called forth from John Tinker one of the most memorable of all speeches from a Bahamian governor: "The war now at an end we must have recourse to Industry and Frugality. Nature has been sufficiently liberal in furnishing these Islands with the Means of amply rewarding the laborious but I am afraid the War has introduced and left us two formidable Enemies, I mean Luxury and Sloth. The Country is almost drained of its Currency, the extravagant Wages given to all Tradesmen and the Excessive dearness of every Necessary of Life would make a Stranger at first sight imagine we had golden Mines no further than the blue Hills."[1] Tinker's exhortations, though, fell on deaf ears, and some time later he felt bound to report that he found the "genius" of the people "repugnant." They would not farm, culled the woods with no thought of conservation, and left the islands for greener pastures with no sense of loyalty. Trade was at a standstill, defense was neglected, and even the assembly had become almost moribund. "I have used every inviting method in my reach to bring people hither during the recess from the late war" concluded Tinker, but the lack of "money, protection and assurance" meant that his efforts were doomed to failure.[2]

A more convincing argument for imperialists, and all those who wished for a return to wartime conditions, was the evidence that the Bahamas was slipping back under Spanish and French domination. Tinker reported that Cat Island was greatly superior for plantations to either New Providence or Eleuthera, and that a planter from Carolina called Laroche had actually settled on Exuma with his slaves.[3] But no permanent expansion was possible without greater security from foreign attacks. In 1753, for example, a father and son called Sturrup complained that while sailing from Nassau on a wrecking voyage, their sloop *Tatem* had been boarded and seized by Spaniards in the central Bahamas. They also gave a graphic account of a Bermudian sloop that escaped its Spanish pursuer only by expertly dodging between the Exuma Cays. In general, they claimed, ships' crews cutting wood, "fishing boats and most other vessels of a commercial type" were frequently "harassed by enemy ships being Pirates, Spanish or French."[4]

In fact it was the French threat which now seemed greatest, with a focus of conflict in the islands commanding the Windward Passage into the Caribbean. Governor Tinker complained of French landings on

Inagua in 1749 and in 1754 argued that French designs on the Turks and Caicos Islands could only be scotched by placing those islands officially under the command of the government in Nassau. Tinker claimed to have made such a plea as early as 1740, only to be opposed by the Bermudians, who, while salt raking and wrecking there, could do nothing to defend the islands.[5] Tinker, however, did not explain how the Bahamas government could any better protect islands so far to windward and so close to St. Domingue—which could in fact be reached almost as quickly from Bermuda or Jamaica as from Nassau.

When the Seven Years' War broke out in 1756, the business of privateering instantly revived, though with less than universal approbation. In one of his last dispatches, on leaving Nassau after nearly twenty years, Governor Tinker reported "at present the spirit of privateering has taken possession of these people, and extinguished every other industrious and commercial application." What lay behind Tinker's disapproval was not just distrust of instant and temporary riches but the potential of privateering for dividing the Bahamian mercantile community. For the first five years of war Spain was ostensibly neutral, and many mainland American shippers—with their Bahamian and Bermudian associates—became involved in the profitable contraband trade being carried on through the port of Monte Christi, just on the Spanish side of the border of French St. Domingue.

The suppression of this clandestine trade, which at its peak was said to engage ninety British ships carrying five hundred cargoes a year, was one of the chief tasks assigned William Shirley, formerly governor of New England and commander-in-chief in North America, when appointed Tinker's successor in 1758. From the beginning of the war, Spanish ships as well as French were brought into Nassau for adjudication, and those found to be carrying French cargoes were automatically condemned. But Spanish vessels carrying American cargoes, or American vessels seized in suspicious circumstances (for example, carrying dubious documents or claiming to sail under flags of truce) did not all suffer the same fate. The privateering interests, including twenty-three Nassau merchants, blamed Samuel Gambier, the vice-admiralty judge, who, they claimed, "was lately sent here from Philadelphia, fee'd, hired and employ'd by the Philadelphians concerned in holding Correspondence and Communication with, aiding, supplying, supporting, relieving, comforting and assisting the . . . French . . . having openly and avowedly both in Court & Out of Court declared the . . . Flag of Truce a fair, honest and legal Trade."[6]

In support of his decision to sack Samuel Gambier (whose brother John had been acting governor before Shirley arrived) the new governor agreed that the judge "had a direct Tendency to Support and Encourage the Owners of English trading Vessels concern'd in carrying on a General Illicit Commerce with the French Island of St. Dominique." Even more rebelliously, Gambier had asserted that neither king nor governor had the right to prevent trade by British subjects, and that since neither Parliament nor colonial assembly had passed a law specifically banning the Monte Christi trade, it should be regarded as "legal and beneficial."[7]

These premonitions of future conflict, however, soon faded in the light of larger events. As Britain's mastery of the seas became absolute, the Monte Christi loophole was closed, and Nassau's vice-admiralty court business multiplied. The governor of Havana called William Shirley a "Bastard" for his support of "piracy" against Spanish ships, and Madrid threatened London in rather more diplomatic language. The unwisdom of this now that France was defeated on land and sea was underlined when Britain herself declared war against Spain in 1761. In the following years, in an apparent resurgence of Cromwell's old "Western Design," a huge expedition under the earl of Albemarle sailed through the Bahamas to capture Havana and bring out plunder worth over a million pounds.

Mainland Americans and many Bahamians alike saw the capture of Havana as a great opportunity for widening their legitimate trade. They were therefore dismayed when first Cuba was returned to Spain by the Treaty of Paris in 1763, and then Britain further restricted the freedom of colonial trade on strictly mercantilist principles. The ensuing conflict between doctrinaire imperialists and colonial free traders which was one of the underlying causes of the American War of Independence also had its repercussions in the Bahamas. In the war itself the Bahamas (like the other island colonies) remained nominally loyal but divided, and the natural tendency toward conflict between imperial executive and native whites became entrenched as an almost permanent feature of Bahamian life.

The emergent conflict of interests was encapsulated by the vexed question of the Turks and Caicos Islands. Despite the ending of the Seven Years' War, the French Admiral d'Estaing had raised his flag on Grand Turk in June 1764 and was persuaded to depart only after strong diplomatic pressure was applied between London and Paris. William Shirley, as a staunch imperialist and francophobe (who as governor of Massachusetts had been responsible for the capture of Louisburg in Nova Scotia in 1745), argued that the time had come for the extension of effective British authority over all islands in the Bahamian archipelago. Though the Spanish retained control of Cuba, they no longer posed a military threat, since Britain now controlled both sides of the Florida Strait. France in St. Domingue, though, was permanently dangerous to the Bahamas and the Jamaica trade as long as the Turks and Caicos Islands were only tenuously held. These islands, argued Shirley, should therefore be annexed to the Bahamian rather than Bermudian government, and defended by the permanent installation of a naval force. For this, an ideal base could be Great Exuma, which not only possessed the best and safest harbor in the entire Bahamas, but was centrally located and an island highly suitable for cotton plantations.[8]

London agreed that the Turks and Caicos Islands should come under the authority of Nassau but in 1766 appointed as local agent a man with ambitions to create a virtually independent colony.[9] Andrew Symmer laid out on Grand Turk a township judiciously named after Lord Shelburne, president of the board of trade, and attempted to control the salt and wrecking industries and to attract settlers to plant cotton in the Caicos Islands. These efforts failed, as few legitimate settlers arrived and the Bermudian and Jamaican salt rakers resented the taxes and regulations. The chief difficulty, though, was that the islands were a natural entrepôt for the increasingly illicit trade with Spanish Cuba and Santo Domingo and French St. Domingue—in which Bahamian as well as mainland American traders were deeply involved, and toward which Andrew Symmer found himself forced to turn a blind eye.

Whitehall complained of smuggling, but the Royal Navy did nothing to suppress it. And during the postwar depression even those legislators in Nassau who were not directly involved in the clandestine trade saw the expense of ruling such a distant outpost as the Turks and Caicos Islands as a foolish extravagance. Far more agreeable was the notion of making both Nassau and Grand Turk official free ports—a rational scheme even for mercantilists since the balance of trade was almost certain to be in Britain's favor. The chief beneficiaries, however, were likely to be colonial not metropolitan merchants, and such legislation was not likely to emerge from an imperial parliament capable of passing the Sugar, Molasses, and Stamp acts against the interests and wishes of the colonials. Governor William Shirley did endorse the application to make Nassau a free port when he forwarded the assembly's unctuous message of thanks to the Crown for the repeal of the Stamp Act in 1767, but with predictably negative results.[10]

The able but authoritarian William Shirley, now aged and sick as well as disappointed, gave up the struggle to reconcile colonial realities with imperial theory in 1768 and retired to his native Massachusetts to die. The unresolved conflicts inevitably intensified during the five-year regime of Thomas Shirley, who lacked his brother's charisma and skill and was faced by ever-worsening economic, political, and social conditions. Thomas Shirley's first reports were downright alarmist. Many settlers had left the Bahamas since the last war, and the level of poverty was such that the colony might have to be abandoned. The garrison was reduced to twenty-three men, the surviving remnant of the Independent Company, which was dangerous because of the threat not so much of foreign attack as of internal disorder. Reinforcements of troops should be sent (as they were to Boston at much the same time), argued Shirley, because a great proportion of the inhabitants were "Blacks, Mulattoes and Persons who live by Wrecking and Plunder and a People of very bold daring Spirit." [11]

Thomas Shirley's pleas of depopulation and fears for its effects were exaggerated, though his concern over the potential for discord over economic and political policies was probably not overstated. The new governor's own report in 1768 estimated that there were 3,130 persons living in the Bahamas, exclusive of the Turks and Caicos Islands, but a more accurate compilation in 1773 arrived at a total of 4,143 (with 150 more living in the Turks), an increase of 80 percent since the time of P. H. Bruce.[12] This rough census, showing the Bahamian population at its peak before the Loyalist influx of the 1780s, did, however, indicate several significant trends. Some time during the Seven Years' War the black population had overtaken that of the whites and now constituted 52.9 percent of the total—reason enough for the passage of the Slave Act of 1767. This growth was especially notable on New Providence, where the white population had remained almost static at 1,024, but the number of blacks (probably including free blacks as well as slaves) had almost doubled to 1,800 since the 1740s and was now 63.7 percent of the total New Providence population.

There were also now at least twice as many blacks in the Out Islands (including forty in Cat Island and twenty-four in Exuma), though the healthy growth of the Out Island white population kept the proportion of blacks to just under 30 percent. Overall, the proportion of the Bahamian population living outside New Providence had risen from 25 to 34 percent since 1734. To a certain extent this reflected the first tentative development of Out Island plantations. But it chiefly stemmed from the relatively healthier birthrates of the Out Island populations—as Thomas Shirley acknowledged and explained in a surprisingly perceptive note. With many soldiers, sailors, and other transients, including merchants and planters likely to transplant their families to more hopeful locations, a settled family life was not the absolute norm on New Providence, wrote Shirley, whereas "the Inhabitants of the other Islands, called the Out Islands, being in general Natives of them, and attached to their own manner of living, never think of emmigrating and are therefore continually multiplying."[13]

Some of the persons who had deserted Nassau were merchants and traders who had gone to enjoy the laxer climate of the Turks Islands, and Thomas Shirley made resolute efforts to bring them, and the other Turks Islanders, under Nassau's control. Instructions from Shirley to Symmer in 1769 asserted that the Turks and Caicos Islands must obey Bahamian laws, particularly those regulating the raking of salt and the taxing of foreign shipping.[14] But a petition from the islanders to the king pointed out that the Turks Islands had been settled for at least a generation before the advent of Andrew Symmer and had been effectively governed by local custom. They should not be subject to Bahamian laws as the interests of the Turks Islands and the Bahamas proper were incompatible, and Turks Islanders could not expect to receive justice or understanding from distant Nassau. For his part, Thomas Shirley attempted to place the dispute in context by suggesting to Lord Hillsborough, the secretary of state, that Andrew Symmer was himself involved in illicit trade and behind the petition. He also recounted that on a visit to Grand Turk in March 1770 he was told by Symmer that he could expect to meet with the inhabitants only of a morning because they were so addicted to drink as to be incapable by noon.[15]

Lord Hillsborough duly rejected the Turks Islands petition, ordering Thomas Shirley to legislate for and tax the Turks Islanders even if they did not enjoy direct representation. "As the whole body of People belonging to the British Empire are represented by the Commons of Great Britain," he asserted provocatively, "so are the inhabitants of the Bahamas in general represented in the Assembly of that Government." This doctrine was highmindedly spurned by the assembly in Nassau, taking the mainland American position that colonists should not be governed, let alone taxed, without representation, and refusing to pass laws intended to apply to the Turks and Caicos Islands proposed by the governor. Thomas Shirley responded by angrily dissolving the House of

Assembly in October 1770, going so far as to suggest to Hillsborough that the whole system of representation be revoked and the Bahamas return to rule by governor-in-council.[16]

Such a drastic solution was not found necessary, and a new session of the assembly did pass the required laws in 1771, if with limited effect. The dispute sputtered on even after Andrew Symmer left the islands in 1772, until it was overwhelmed by the larger issues and events of the American War of Independence in 1775. Indeed, what opposition Thomas Shirley faced increasingly focused on what was happening to the north, not the south, as the situation on the mainland rapidly deteriorated. The governor felt obliged to dissolve the assembly for a second time when it refused to pass a militia and night watch bill—the majority feeling that it infringed their liberties or fearing that it was aimed against their American fellow colonists rather than the French or Spanish. Similarly, the pro-American element, led by the Gambier brothers and others with close mercantile and family connections to the mainland, resented the reinforcement of the garrison by a whole company of regular troops in 1773 and resisted the employment of up to five hundred of their slaves in forced labor on the forts.[17]

But in at least one respect the growing colonialist opposition agreed with their imperialistic governor. Though their interests were concurrent rather than exactly coincidental, both deplored the powers still held by the Bahamian Lord Proprietors, and repeated petitions from the colonists asking for the abrogation of the charter were cordially endorsed in Thomas Shirley's last dispatches. A joint petition from the council and assembly, forwarded by Samuel Gambier, council president, in February 1773 complained that the Proprietors had virtually abandoned the Bahamas, yet still retained the theoretical monopoly of land allocation and the right to collect quit rents. The legislators complained that the supply of native woods was almost exhausted but that plantations were not a viable alternative because of the difficulty in obtaining certain tenure and title to the land. A telling comparison was made between the Bahamas and Georgia, which under the proprietory trusteeship was said to have been "reduced to the like Degree of Poverty and Distress," but to have prospered greatly since the revocation of the grant.[18]

In November 1773, just before he left to be governor of Dominica, Thomas Shirley also argued that until the dead hand of the Proprietors was prised away the Bahamas would "remain in a state of Inactivity and supineness with regard to their progress in Commerce, Cultivation, and Inhabitancy."[19] For Shirley too the crux of the problem was the anarchic state of land tenure, which not only denied security to the settler and retarded development but also deprived the Crown of profit and control. The situation was bad enough on New Providence, the most developed island, but was worse on the Out Islands, the essential bases for future expansion.

In the first-ever general analysis of Bahamian tenures, Thomas Shirley noted that while only a fraction of the lands were held with any sort of title, there were at least four forms of claim: original Proprietary grants, grants by Proprietary delegates such as the copartners of 1718–39, grants by former royal governors, and "warrants of survey"—that is, claims based upon uninterrupted possession and acknowledged development. There were some records of the grants by governors and by warrants of survey, but the Proprietors and copartners had carried back to England any records they might have made, and since had done nothing. A search of the secretary's office in Nassau revealed grants totaling some five thousand acres, but these were limited almost entirely to town lots in Nassau and tracts on New Providence, Rose, and Hog islands. "The Inhabitants of the other Islands," wrote Shirley, "except two or three Families who hold by Warrants of Survey, have no other Title to their lands but that of Possession; and there being much waste Ground about them seldom improve one Tract longer than two or three Years, when they explore some new Spot and cultivate the same, until it begins to grow impoverished, so that it is impossible to remark with the least degree of exactness what number of Acres is cultivated." [20]

A compounding complication was the question of quit rents. The local act of 3 Geo II (that is, the third year of the reign of George II, 1729) had established that an annual quit rent of one shilling and nine pence per hundred acres of cultivated land, and a similar sum for each developed town lot, was payable to the Lord Proprietors. But there was a disingenuous haziness about what constituted either cultivation or development, and besides, no one seemed to be certain whether the rents applied only to direct Proprietary grants—some of which, moreover, specifically required only a peppercorn rent. In any case, no quit rents seem to have been paid for many years, and the 1729 act was commonly regarded as obsolete.

To Thomas Shirley's mind, the only solution was to cut the Gordian knot. Only after the Proprietors' rights had been expunged and the fundamental ownership of the land resumed by the Crown could the system of title and tenure be clarified. The Crown could then take responsibility for all land titles, surveys, and registration, as well as assuming control over all unadopted lands—perhaps in the process setting up a formal land-registry office. Only in this way could owners be made secure and more willing to settle and stay in the Bahamas, plantations replace casual cultivation, and new islands be developed. As far as the Crown was concerned, it would also have the advantages of facilitating control by tying owners (and their slaves) more closely to their lands and of enabling the more efficient collection of a regular revenue from quit rents and taxes on sales and other transfers. These last features, of course, were not quite what the Bahamian petitioners of 1773 were looking for; and in any case the reform called for by Thomas Shirley was delayed for fourteen years, when the arrival of a very different breed of settler, in very large numbers, made such a change imperative.

The decade after 1775—the final phase of early settlement—was the most eventful in the entire history of the Bahamas. Yet the material for the social history of this period is relatively scanty. Government was disrupted and records were dispersed by the American invasions and Spanish occupation, but what official records there were had to sail gingerly around the fact that many Bahamians behaved very equivocally throughout the War of American Independence. As ever, the grounds were opportunistic self-interest rather than ideology. There were as few ardent republicans as there were dedicated loyalists among the early settlers, and the war did not produce any great changes in this respect. It was, indeed, the easygoing pragmatism of the original settlers as much as the accidents of war and diplomacy and the influx of more committed Loyalists that shaped the emergent national character: a sense of ideological detachment, of belonging there and nowhere else, and the calculated balancing of the advantages of continuing British protection, over the ties of trade and family with the mainland.

At least the salient events of the period are well known, and sufficient hints linger between the lines adequately to sketch out the social implications. The Bahamians were tested very early in the American War of Independence, when Nassau became the first target of the infant American navy, and immediately showed their reluctance actually to come to blows with the rebels. Even Governor Montfort Browne, a Tory with aristocratic connections who had already served as lieutenant governor of West Florida (1767–69), proved pacific, if not an out-and-out poltroon.

Nassau had ample warning of the impending attack but did nothing to arm itself, and when the American fleet of seven small warships under the command of Admiral Esekial Hopkins appeared off the bar early in the morning of Sunday, March 3, 1776, the governor was in a complete dither. Called to the door of Government House in his nightshirt, he ordered the firing of warning guns from Fort Nassau to summon the militia. The shots deterred the Americans from a frontal assault, but few of the militia rushed to Nassau's defense, and in the firing two of the guns fell from their mountings. Knowing that the chief purpose of the attack was to capture warlike stores, Browne was inclined immediately to dispatch all the powder in the magazine to St. Augustine in a fast sloop but delayed giving the order when Samuel Gambier suggested the powder might be necessary for defending the fort.

The Americans, guided by two Bahamian captains dragooned off Abaco, sailed through the narrows into Montagu Bay, and three hundred marines were landed in whaleboats in Fox Hill Creek, a mile east of Fort Montagu and three miles from Nassau. Browne sent a detachment to defend Fort Montagu and a larger force of troops and volunteers to confront the attackers. But the Americans were seen to be formidable, and Fort Montagu in worse condition than Fort Nassau. So both columns of defenders fell back on the town after spiking the guns in Fort Montagu, without firing a shot in anger. Far from retreating into Nassau's main fort and bastion, most men then retired to their own houses "to provide for the security of what is dear to every man," while the minister of Christchurch actually "went on with the duty of the church in the usual manner." Told by his council that the defense of Fort Nassau was futile and advised to take flight himself, Governor Browne now ordered the shipment of the powder and the spiking of the guns but retired to Government House to await the American takeover, complaining of an attack of colic.

The following morning the Americans quietly entered Nassau, taking the governor and expatriate officials prisoner but distributing leaflets promising civilians security of life and property. Montfort Browne later claimed that he had been roughly seized and dragged like a "felon to the gallows in the presence of a dear wife and an aged aunt, both near relatives of the Earl of Dartmouth, who were treated with such abuse and such language as could not be heard in Billingsgate."[71] Many of the prominent inhabitants, including members of council, however, were said to have welcomed and "elegantly entertained" Admiral Hopkins and his officers, while the ordinary people had eagerly catered for the carousing marines and sailors in their traditional way.

The rebel fleet spent a fortnight loading the Nassau ordnance and some remaining barrels of gunpowder before sailing back to the Chesapeake, carrying Governor Browne and a dozen other hostages. Unwittingly, many of the Americans also carried gifts from the Bahamian mosquitos, and 140 died or fell sick of fever before they reached home. This setback their officers blamed on overindulgence or the baleful effects of local "obeah" magic.[22]

Montfort Browne was not imprisoned long, being exchanged for "the rebel chief who calls himself Lord Stirling." But he seems to have been in no hurry to return to the Bahamas, serving at the siege of Rhode Island and spending some time in Florida before resuming his Nassau post in July 1778. Pretty soon, charges and countercharges were flying: that the governor had surrendered Nassau in 1776 through incompetence and cowardice, and that the council had virtually kept open house for the Americans during the interregnum. Certainly, the rebel cruisers seem to have roamed the islands freely until the entry of the French into the war led to an increase in Royal Navy activity. On one occasion late in 1776 an American privateer sailed into Nassau harbor to cut out prizes, threatening to rake the town with its guns. And in 1778 Lieutenant Rathburn of the USS *Providence* actually reoccupied Fort Nassau, failing to ambush HMS *Gayton* only when loyal inhabitants sent frantic signals to prevent the naval vessel's crossing the bar. Harbour Island was even more vulnerable, the local minister complaining that rebel privateers sailed in and out of the roadstead at will, exchanging provisions for Bahamian salt and terrorizing the inhabitants with their rough behavior.[23]

Clearly, sentiments in the Bahamas were divided, at least until the Americans signed treaties with the French and Spaniards, the few dedicated republicans left to fight on the rebel side, and the first Loyalist emigrés began to appear in Nassau. By that time also, the Bahamas had a rather more forthright governor, Montfort Browne having been replaced by John Maxwell in 1780 after Browne had taken the desperate and unprecedented step of dismissing his council. Under Governor Maxwell, Nassau enjoyed a brief revival as a privateering base, at least twenty-seven enemy prizes being condemned in the vice-admiralty court during 1780 and 1781. This brought renewed prosperity for some but was dangerous for the colony as a whole. After the British defeat at Yorktown and French victories at sea, the protection of the Royal Navy faded from little to nil, and late in 1781 the Americans and Spanish combined to eradicate the threat that the Bahamas posed to their trade.

Ironically, Maxwell had cobbled together the most substantial defense force that Nassau had yet seen. The 247 regular troops (mainly "invalids" from the fighting on the mainland) and 338 militiamen were augmented by 800 armed sailors in a dozen privateering vessels, deploying 150 cannon in all. Yet defense was deemed futile against the overwhelming armada which appeared off Nassau on May 6, 1782, under the command of Don Antonio Claraco y Sanz, and Maxwell accepted honorable surrender terms without a fight. The Bahamas were declared to be under Spanish suzerainty, though the inhabitants were guaranteed protection for themselves and their property, and the exercise of their chosen religion. The governor and other officials were sent to Havana as hostages, though soon released on parole. The troops, and civilians who wanted to leave immediately, were shipped off under flag of truce, and all who did not wish to remain under the Spanish flag were given a year to wind up their affairs.

Most inhabitants in fact decided to stay and soon were giving the Spanish governor such a rough time that he called them "these wretched portions of mankind" and came to refer to Nassau as "one of the miserable spots of the universe." Claraco's tenure was in fact doomed, for no sooner was he installed in Nassau than Admiral Rodney won the decisive Battle of the Saints against the French, and the last tides of the war flowed resolutely in Britain's favor. As peace negotiations were begun late in 1782 it became clear that while Britain might give back East and West Florida to the Spaniards, she would regain the Bahamas. The preliminaries to the Treaty of Versailles along these lines were signed on January 20, 1783, to come into effect in Europe one month and in America two months later. This was well known, at least in outline, by English and Spanish alike, in Florida and the Bahamas, by the end of March. Yet it did not forestall the pre-emptive strike against Nassau by the first and most aggressive of the Loyalists, Colonel Andrew Deveaux, in April 1783. Deveaux's coup has been traditionally regarded as a heroic reconquest and a kind of "foundation charter" for the Bahamian Loyalists as a whole.[24]

Andrew Deveaux was the twenty-five-year-old son and namesake of a substantial planter and stock farmer of Beaufort, South Carolina—owner of fifty-one slaves, 1,000 black cattle, 200 pigs and 250 sheep on 9,225 acres of Prince William's Parish and Port Royal Island. Joining the British forces under Major-General Prévost in 1779, Andrew Deveaux, Jr., was supposedly commissioned by Lord Cornwallis to raise a regiment called the Royal Foresters after the siege of Charleston. Little came of this save to give Deveaux the title of colonel and the command of a small band of Loyalist irregulars, who gained a reputation as wily guerrillas and captured two American generals in woodland ambushes. In December 1782, though, the British evacuated South Carolina, and Deveaux went with his men to St. Augustine, the capital of East Florida. Disappointed by the prospects there, they dreamed up the almost piratical project of seizing the Bahamas for the British and themselves.

Deveaux and seventy followers set out from St. Augustine on April 1, 1783, in six vessels, of which the *Perseverence* (twenty-six guns) and *Whitby Warrior* (sixteen guns) were the largest. Reclaiming uninhabited Abaco, Deveaux landed at Harbour Island, where he recruited almost the entire male population and most of the local ships. Altogether, 170 "Brilanders" joined in the enterprise, led by the white militia officers Robert Rumer, Samuel Higgs, Joseph Curry, and Gideon Lowe, and including free coloreds and black slaves. What incentives Andrew Deveaux was able to offer for such a madcap venture as the seizure of Nassau from a Spanish force perhaps three times as large as his own is not certain, but they are suggested by the outcome. Deveaux's white officers received substantial grants of new land from the Crown well in advance of Lieutenant Governor Powell's proclamation of general grants to Loyalists in September 1785. All Harbour Island freemen, colored and black as well as white, also assumed a much firmer title to the six thousand acres of farming land on the mainland of northern Eleuthera which they had been working informally for many years,[25] as well as receiving town lots in their various degrees in the new township laid out by Governor Dunmore in the 1790s. The slaves in Deveaux's Nassau expedition—who were, presumably, the ninety or so listed as being without firearms, armed only with cutlasses, clubs, and pikes—may have been involuntary Loyalists, simply ordered along by their owners to man the boats and perform pioneering and back-up duties. Equally likely, they may well have gone willingly, even voluntarily, on the general, if vague, expectations of such rewards as were often given to slaves who behaved loyally in campaigns against their owners' sovereign's enemies.

The story of Deveaux's success in wresting Nassau from Claraco and his forces between April 10 and 17, 1783, has been often told, with exaggerated color—not least by the Bahamian Liberator himself.[26] Clearly, Claraco was tricked and outmaneuvered by the guerilla methods of Deveaux and his second-in-command, Archibald Taylor, and there was at least one prolonged cannonade, if very little bloodshed. But the decision to surrender was probably based mainly on Claraco's sense of the futility and inhumanity of resistance when the handover of the Bahamas had already been ordained at Versailles. Accordingly, Claraco received terms as generous and gentlemanly as those given to Maxwell just under a year earlier. To the great relief of the Nassauvians, the six hundred occupying troops and their camp followers sailed back to Havana within a few days, paving the way for the return of Governor Maxwell later in 1783. Antonio Claraco was held hostage in Nassau for a few weeks until the exchange of prisoners had been effected. But his return to Havana was far from a relief. He was immediately charged on the evidence of those who had preceded him with the unwarranted surrender of Nassau and the Bahamas to a greatly inferior force. He was imprisoned in Cuba and Spain for no less than eight years before his case was finally heard in 1791.[27]

Fortune smiled far more kindly on the victors, most notably their leader and his family. Though Andrew Deveaux, Jr., left the Bahamas for England as early as September 1783—revisiting the islands often but spending the last years of his life back in the United States, at Red Hook, New York—he and his family were the foremost of the developers of the new plantation islands. Though he had sold off some of his Bahamian lands before he died in July 1812, Andrew Deveaux, Jr., still left in his will 1,380 acres at Red Pond and Boatswain Hill, Cat Island, and the whole of the islands of Little San Salvador (340 acres) and Highborn Cay (430 acres), as well as a sizeable tract of 420 acres on eastern New Providence. Deveaux's younger brothers Nathanial, William, and John all seem to have been settled on Bahamian lands, though all were dead by 1810. The chief of the clan, in every respect, though, was Andrew Deveaux, Sr., who, having forfeited all his lands in South Carolina, transferred most of his slaves and stock to southern Cat Island. There he built a mansion, the impressive ruins of which can still be seen in the settlement of Port Howe (named after the British commander-in-chief in North America). And there he remained, outliving all four of his sons and outlasting nearly all the other Loyalist planters, to die on December 23, 1814, at the age of seventy-nine.[28]

After the departure of the Spaniards, Nassau quickly returned to its prewar normality, and we have an excellent description of the town and New Providence just before the descent of the majority of the Loyalist emigrés, in the memoirs of Johann David Schoepf.[29] He was an Ansbacher German who spent four months in the Bahamas on his way home from serving as a surgeon to the British forces during the Revolutionary War. Of Nassau he wrote that there was "but one tolerably regular street, or line of houses, which runs next to the water." This main road (Bay Street) was unpaved, though paving was scarcely necessary since all the streets were cut down to the island's native rock. Even in town, the chief houses stood apart, "surrounded by trees, hedges and gardens." The houses were all of wood, lightly and simply built; because of the climate, attention had been given only "to roof, shade, space and air." In most cases there was simply a single planking covering the wooden house frame. "The best are boarded double," wrote Schoepf, "but even then the covering is light. . . . Any of our light summer-houses would serve as a comfortable dwelling at Providence in all seasons." Chimneys were even rarer than glass windows.

Even the governor still lived in a rented house—built by Fitzwilliam at his own expense and leased by his heirs—though this was the most imposing residence in Nassau, commanding the highest point of the coastal ridge and recently fortified by Don Antonio Claraco. Apart from the forts guarding each end of the harbor, "a church, a gaol, and an Assembly-House make up the public buildings of the town," reported Schoepf. The commercial hub of town, though, was the open-sided building grandly styled the Bourse (later the Vendue House), where sales were made of all goods brought in, as well as slaves, and all public notices and regulations were posted. Here were to be found throughout the day "buyers and sellers, ships' captains, and other persons, of affairs or of none," who came to transact business, to hear or retail the latest news, or simply to gossip.

According to Schoepf, the inhabitants of Nassau consisted of "a few royal officials, divers merchants, shipbuilders and carpenters, skippers, pilots, fishermen, and what laborers are needed, with several families who live on the returns from their lands and the work of their slaves." The real planters, though of lesser consequence, lived on their estates in the nearby countryside. Eastward of town along the waterside were scattered houses occupied by sailors and fishermen, and several miles out (near the northern, seaside end of the present Fox Hill Village) was "a little village, to which the name of New Guinea has been given, most of its inhabitants being free negroes and mulattoes."

In the main the inhabitants were a healthy and easygoing crew, flourishing in wartime from privateering but in peacetime subsisting on "wrecking," woodcutting, turtling, and fishing, with a minimum of farming and few plantations. The general poverty did not seem to inhibit a hearty contentment, at least among the slaveowning whites. Every freeman, claimed Schoepf, had the right to fell wood as it pleased him and wherever he found it, and many families made a considerable livelihood by keeping their slaves constantly at work on woodcutting expeditions. Fishing was a common employment of the poorer whites as well as many blacks, and this, which Schoepf seems to have regarded as a pleasant diversion rather than real work, made for easy sustenance.

The industrious German fresh from the American mainland was impressed by the way that most of the whites of New Providence were able to live happily and well despite their relative indolence—though their idleness, he admitted, was largely bought by "the sweat of their slaves." Schoepf reckoned that even the "so-called planters" worked no more than two, at most three months in the year. "They fell some wood, catch fish, sell what they raise—drink up their gains and dance away the time, for not even the hottest weather can keep them from this diversion. They are amiable, courteous, and according to their circumstances hospitable—but of severe work they know nothing and do not want to know anything." If it was axiomatic that the harder and more tedious the life of a country was, the less did its population increase, Schoepf concluded, the lifestyle of the majority of Bahamians should guarantee the opposite result.

Though they did most of the hardest work, "even the blacks here take part in the general contentment," claimed Schoepf on his all-too-brief acquaintance. They were everywhere of a better appearance and seemingly happier than those he had encountered on the southern mainland, "strong, well-fed, and of a decent demeanour." There was a considerable number of free blacks, some of whom owned houses and plantations or were commanders of small vessels. But even slaves were able to earn money for themselves in their free time, being left "undisturbed in the enjoyment of what they gain by other work" on the payment of "a small weekly sum" to their owners. Bahamian slaves, asserted Schoepf, had "never experienced the inhuman and cruel treatment which draws so many sighs from their brethren in the neighbouring sugar-islands or the rice plantations of the main-land."

Schoepf did not notice schools in Nassau and probably regarded it as a cheerfully illiterate place compared with the more substantial mainland towns. Yet compared with Nassau at an earlier time and the Out Island settlements then, progress had been made. In 1770 the minister reported that Christchurch School, which met from eight to twelve and two to five each day, had fifty-four pupils (all baptized), including six black children. Besides, there were said to be two other schools of more modest size.[30] On the eve of the American war, a dissenter from "Cambridge College, New England" with the engaging name of P. Belcher Noyes kept a school with twenty-three pupils, including six "Latin scholars."[31] And when the churchgoers of Nassau and Harbour Island signed a testimonial in 1779 on behalf of a minister whose allegedly bigamous past had caught up with him (Richard Moss), all but two of the seventy-five who signed in New Providence could write their names on the document, whereas thirty-six of sixty-one parishioners of Harbour Island could only provide a mark.[32]

Unfortunately, Johann Schoepf did not venture away from New Providence, except for a picnic trip to Rose Island. But we do have some account of social conditions in Harbour Island and Eleuthera from the missionary correspondence of the SPG, particularly that with the enterprising if unconventional Mr. Moss, the first resident minister, who served from 1767 until his dismissal in 1780.[33] The Out Island settlements had been constituted a second parish by Governor William Shirley in 1764, but they had no regular minister until Moss arrived in Harbour Island. At first he preached under a tamarind tree but soon built a church, St. John's, which was opened on March 16, 1769. Moss found the settlement a tight and orderly community of some sixty families, living mainly a maritime life, building their own ships, and growing subsistence crops and raking salt on the nearby mainland of Eleuthera. Of the 438 inhabitants in 1769, he reported that only 6 were guilty of swearing and only 2 habitually broke the Sabbath, though his communicants never totaled more than 42. There was a small school, but Moss's first schoolmaster, John Petty, he found "very profane in conversation and of a loose character." Petty's successor, William Lawes, was preferable, and his classes were attended by some 30 to 50 of the settlement's children. Richard Moss also trained a local catechist, Robert Curry, whom he frequently praised to the SPG as an able and godly man. His only complaint about his Harbour Island parishioners was their persistent preference (so consistent with the nature of the early settlements) for holding baptisms and marriages not in the church but in their own houses, "on any day, at any time of day."[34]

The far more scattered population of Eleuthera was a very different case. Already the six or seven hundred inhabitants (one third of whom were listed as "coloured" in 1776) lived in nearly a dozen separate settlements, strung out along a hundred miles of the leeward coast of the attenuated island. Isolated from each other almost as much as from Nassau, they were almost beyond Moss's pastoral care. In order to visit them he found it necessary to go first to Nassau and wait weeks for a boat, and he rarely made the effort more than once a year. Compared with the Harbour Islanders, the minister found the Eleutherans ignorant, uncivilized, and guilty of "sinful habits and heathenish practises," as well as levels of profanity and drunkenness exceptional even by Nassau standards. "The People stupify their senses with drinking spiritous Liquors to excess, & even the Magistrates are profane to the highest degree and the Settlements being so scattered I find it very difficult to collect the

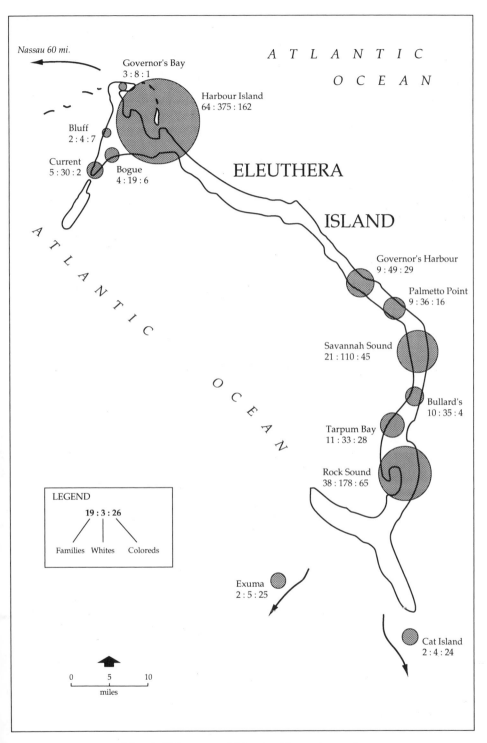

Nassau 60 mi.

A T L A N T I C

O C E A N

Governor's Bay
3 : 8 : 1

Harbour Island
64 : 375 : 162

Bluff
2 : 4 : 7

Current
5 : 30 : 2

Bogue
4 : 19 : 6

ELEUTHERA

ISLAND

A T L A N T I C

O C E A N

Governor's Harbour
9 : 49 : 29

Palmetto Point
9 : 36 : 16

Savannah Sound
21 : 110 : 45

Bullard's
10 : 35 : 4

Tarpum Bay
11 : 33 : 28

Rock Sound
38 : 178 : 65

LEGEND

19 : 3 : 26

Families   Whites   Coloreds

Exuma
2 : 5 : 25

Cat Island
2 : 4 : 24

0   5   10

miles

Map 6. Bahamas out island settlements, 1776

People together," Moss wrote in despair in 1771. There were no schools that Moss knew of, and church services were rarely held. Even Thomas Craig, the layman who occasionally read services at Savanna Sound, was reproached by Moss for living in sin and being frequently drunk— though he later repented and was reported by Moss to have died "in hope of salvation." [35]

Even discounting Richard Moss's obvious professional bias, his account of the Eleuthera settlements does suggest a poor, rough, and loosely organized pioneer community on the outer margins of Bahamian society, ethnically mixed and living as best it could off land and sea. It had, however, pre-empted most of the land and permanently stamped its special character on Eleuthera, which was more or less leapfrogged by the Loyalist planters and their slaves who flocked to the Bahamas after 1783.

III

Loyalist Slavery,
1783–1834

~ 12 ~

Threatened Transformation:
The Loyalist Impact

THE RESETTLEMENT of American Loyalists and their slaves in the Bahamas after the Treaty of Versailles was undoubtedly one of the most crucial phases in Bahamian social history. Of the grand total of about one hundred thousand refugees from the new United States, only some sixteen hundred whites and fifty-seven hundred slaves and free blacks migrated permanently to the Bahamas. Yet this modest influx trebled the colony's population, raised the proportion of slaves and other blacks from one-half to three-quarters of the whole, and increased the number of permanently settled islands from three (or five) to a dozen.[1]

As most local histories and the bicentennial celebrations of the 1980s have testified, the Loyalist era was a phase rich in symbol and myth. Yet in fact it represented a process different from what the legend would have us believe, and more complex. The coming of the Loyalists to the Bahamas was formerly characterized as the transformation of the islands by a new and more progressive type of white colonist. It could as easily be portrayed as the transformation of such Loyalists in the Bahamas— even *by* the Bahamas. Moreover, the "Loyalist" immigrants were far from being a single type, or even just a range of whites. Indeed, it was probably the slave and free black majority of newcomers who most indelibly shaped the social history of the Bahamas.

In an oft-quoted passage, Governor John Maxwell in May 1784 distinguished two basic types of Loyalist arriving in the Bahamas: "(a) Farmers who have set themselves down on the out Islands with large families and from 10 to 100 slaves each. These merit particular attention. (b) Officers, merchants and people who hope to return to the continent after peace there—nothing can satisfy this lot. They demand everything immediately—land, stores and employment, in fact they almost wish to take over the government. . . . These are the most tormenting, Dissatisfied people on earth."[2]

Table 3

Population, 1773–1807

Island	1773		1788				1807[a]			
	Whites	"Reputed Blacks"	Old White Household Heads	Old Slaves	New White Household Heads	New Slaves	Male Slaves	Female Slaves	Free Coloreds and Blacks	Whites
New Providence	1,024	1,800	131	1,024	165	1,264	1,810	1,470	1,035	1,720
Harbour Island and Spanish Wells	410	90	94	142	—	—	215	210	35	650
Eleuthera	509	237	119	310	26	679	570	515	125	575
Exumas	6	24	11	75	28	442	595	490	45	50
Cat Island	3	40	12	16	49	198	375	320	55	30
Abaco	—	—	—	—	29	476	8	7	2	250
Long Island	—	—	42	306	—	—	380	355	65	140
San Salvador and Rum Cay	—	—	—	—	22	132	190	190	6	20
Andros	—	—	4	56	5	357	100	80	5	10
Crooked and Acklin's islands	—	—	—	—	6	214	470	400	30	20
Caicos	—	—	1	5	—	—	540	530	7	20
Turks Island	40	110	18	40	—	—	855	440	75	40
Total	1,992	2,201	430	1,974	330	3,762	6,128	5,007	1,485	3,525

Sources: 1773, C.O. 23/22, 59–72; 1788, William Wylly, A Short Account of the Bahama Islands (London: N.p., 1789), 7; 1807, C.O. 23/48, 144, and 23/59, 37.
[a] Data for 1807 are estimated.

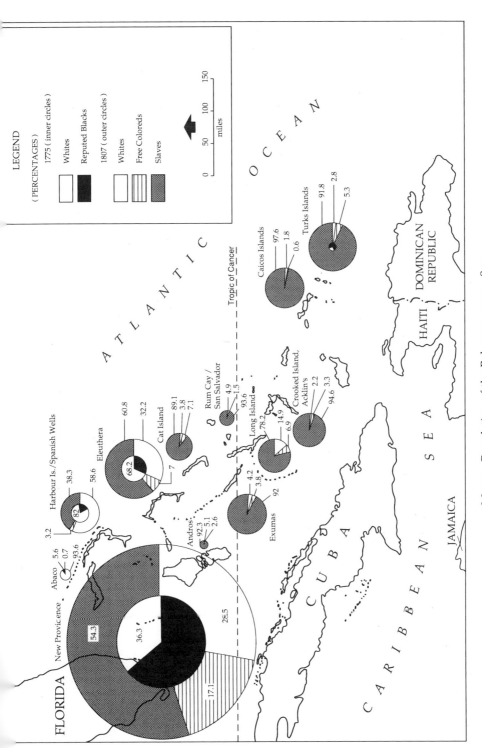

ATLANTIC

OCEAN

Tropic of Cancer

CARIBBEAN   SEA

FLORIDA

CUBA

JAMAICA

HAITI

DOMINICAN
REPUBLIC

New Providence

54.3

36.3

17.1

28.5

Abaco
5.6   0.7
93.6

Harbour Is./Spanish Wells
3.2
38.3
82
58.6

Eleuthera
60.8
32.2
68.2
7

Cat Island
89.1
3.8
7.1

Andros
92.3
5.1
2.6

Rum Cay /
San Salvador
4.9
1.5
93.6

Long Island
78.2
14.9
6.9

Exumas
4.2
3.8
92

Crooked Island,
Acklin's
2.2
3.3
94.6

Caicos Islands
97.6
1.8
0.6

Turks Islands
91.8
2.8
5.3

Map 7. Population of the Bahamas, 1775–1807

Quite apart from the fact that it was the "farmers" as much as the townsfolk who fled the islands when they could, Maxwell's list ignored the very different type of Loyalist who had landed in Abaco and found more affinities with the old inhabitants of Harbour Island and Eleuthera than with Nassauvians or the planters of the southern islands. It also failed to acknowledge the critical importance of the "Loyalist" blacks, a quarter of whom were settled on New Providence and the rest used to clear and plant seven new islands—where they outnumbered their white masters by twenty to one.

As we have seen, Andrew Deveaux, Jr., and his father were part of a spearhead of Loyalist adventurers who pre-empted some of the best lands in Cat Island, Long Island, and Exuma, as well as setting up a base on New Providence. But the bulk of the Loyalist planters who had fled the Carolinas and Georgia for East Florida were slower to migrate, some because they could not really believe that Britain had given East Florida back to Spain and awaited the publication of the definitive treaty (signed in September 1783), some because they hoped to receive acceptable terms to remain from Spain, but most because they hoped for a more favorable destination. The first large organized migration to the Bahamas in fact came not from the southern plantation colonies but from New York, in the summer of 1783.

The British had held New York throughout the War of Independence but by the terms of the peace were to give it up in November 1783. Many of the inhabitants were compromised by their Tory affiliations, and the city was also crowded with Loyalist refugees. These included petty officials, professionals, and small planters from most of the former colonies; military volunteers such as the veterans of the unsuccessful siege of Pensacola; and many former slaves who joined the British forces on the promise of freedom. The British authorities did what they could to relocate those who wished to leave. The majority who could not sail with the troops and officials to England were destined for Nova Scotia. But others, reluctant to leave the New World yet dismayed by the prospect of the Canadian cold, were attracted by exaggerated reports of the undeveloped potential of Abaco circulated by canny promoters.

In June 1783 a committee said to represent four hundred Loyalists who had already prospected a site at Little Harbour, Abaco, sent a petition to Sir Guy Carleton, the British commander-in-chief in North America, asking for a ship, provisions, tools, arms, and troops. The petition, and advertisements that appeared at the same time in the *New York Royal Gazette* claimed that Abaco not only was strategically located, with excellent harbors and a perfect climate, but also possessed soils of wonderful fertility, "Capable of Producing all the West India Produce." Besides this, the island abounded with turtles, whales, and many valuable timber trees, "Fir, Madeira Wood, Mahogany, Fustick, Lignum Vitae, Brazeleto, Logwood, and . . . Red Cedar large enough to Build Ships of Three Hundred and fifty Tons."[3]

A pioneer group, provisioned by the commissary general and placed by Carleton under the command of Captain Thomas Stephens, late of the Pennsylvania militia, sailed from New York in the transports *Nautilus* and *William* on August 21 and 22, 1783, arriving at Abaco about ten days later. It consisted of perhaps 250 settlers, of whom 95 were blacks ostensibly free, though "apprenticed" to white masters. For some reason they landed not at Little Harbour, south of the bend of Abaco, but some forty miles farther north at Black Point (at the northern edge of what is now called Treasure Cay), founding a settlement which was called Carleton after the commander-in-chief. They were followed there by at least two larger ships with more settlers, the *Charlotte* in September and the *Hope* in October.[4]

In all, about 1,000 settlers sailed from New York to Abaco between August and October 1783, augmented by about 650 persons who reached Abaco from St. Augustine, Florida, rather later and settled on the south Abaco mainland between Spencer's Bight and Eight Mile Bay.[5] The composition of the two groups was clearly distinct. Whereas the southern settlements seemingly consisted mainly of would-be planters and their slaves, the northern enterprise consisted of modest white families— former soldiers, townsfolk, and farmers—with very few slaves and a high proportion of blacks of equivocal status. In the best contemporary compilation, the total of 941 settlers sponsored from New York was said to include 217 men, 118 women, 203 children (108 of them under ten years of age, and 403 "servants." If, as seems likely, all blacks were listed as servants and all the rest were whites, this indicates a proportion of blacks even smaller than in the existing Bahamian population, and only a third as large as in the Loyalist migration to the Bahamas as a whole.

The peculiar status of the majority of the blacks who went to northern Abaco is also shown by an analysis of the detailed list of those who sailed on the *Nautilus* and *William* in August 1783, drawn up by the commissary general by the orders of Sir Guy Carleton.[6] The two ships carried ninety-five "Negroes," of whom twenty-one were under fifteen years of age. As in the demographic profile of a typical slave grouping, there was a high proportion of persons in the middle age range, with 56 percent aged between twenty and forty, and among the adults males outnumbered females by three to two (forty-five to twenty-nine). Yet these were not slaves, and it was a group more or less randomly gathered. The comments about each of the blacks indicated that they derived from eleven of the former mainland colonies, with other individuals from Bermuda, Barbados, Jamaica, and Haiti. Even more notably, they were all described in ways that indicated that none were any longer strictly enslaved. A fair number were said to have been born free, to have purchased their freedom, or to have been granted it by official decree. The majority were listed as "formerly the property" of specific owners—many of them from the plantation colonies, especially South Carolina and Virginia.[7]

Certainly, the transported blacks were far from the undifferentiated chattel found, for example, in Jamaican slave lists of the period. The indications are that few of them were African-born, and most were substantially creolized. There was a sprinkling of mulattos, and more than three-quarters of the adults had Christian names and surnames, rather than the single names characteristic of unacculturated slaves. Fourteen of the adult blacks were listed as couples with the same surnames, though a majority of the young children belonged to single women. However, there were several healthy nuclear families, most notably that headed by the most distinguished of all the passengers carried on the *Nautilus* and *William*, white or black. This was Joseph Paul, who had heard George Whitefield preach and was to be the apostle of popular Christianity to Bahamian blacks. He was listed as a "Stout low Man" aged thirty, alongside Susannah Paul, a "Stout Wench" of the same age, married and with children aged thirteen, five, and two.

Sir Guy Carleton had ordered lists of all black emigrants to show the grounds under which they claimed their freedom, specifically to ensure that no black already free, or who had come within the British lines on the promise or expectation of being made free, might subsequently be re-enslaved.[8] The lists of those blacks who were carried to Nova Scotia left no doubt that they were no longer owned—whatever was to be their subsequent fate. Those transported to colonies where slavery was more firmly entrenched were a more delicate matter. Consequently, in the Abaco lists (like those of blacks taken to the true plantation colonies of the West Indies) against all blacks were the names of white persons "in whose possession they are now." This was clearly intended to be a form of apprenticeship, or of that continued responsibility required of the former masters of manumitted slaves in all plantation colonies, though it was potentially dangerous to the freedom of the Loyalist blacks.

In all, thirty-one white masters were listed for the ninety-five *Nautilus* and *William* blacks. Of these masters, twenty "possessed" only one or two blacks, but a handful held control of small gangs. George Antill, Thomas Cartwright, Alexander Dean, and Patrick Kennedy among them held possession of thirty-six blacks from the two ships and may well have augmented the numbers for whom they were held responsible from the later arrivals. In quite a few cases, the white person listed as possessing a particular black was also listed as the former owner, even purchaser of that individual. In such cases, particularly where the controlling white had aspirations to be a planter or had made an actual financial investment in a black, there was every incentive to reduce the subject black to absolute bondage if possible.

At the very least, the different understandings and expectations of the dominant whites and such "black Loyalists" as were carried to Abaco were bound to produce social friction. On the part of the whites who needed laborers and domestics, the possession of legal authority, if not also "the custom of the country," disposed them to regard and treat all black dependents as actual slaves. Inevitably, this would come in conflict with the aspirations toward independence and individuality which had led the blacks toward the Loyalist camp, if not actually to fight for their freedom. Even where the limited political freedom obtained by the black Loyalists was not reversed, the attitude of the dominant whites was an affront to that hope of gradual upward mobility and of "civilization" through Christianity that, as we shall see, so powerfully motivated Joseph Paul and his followers.

The first discord in Abaco, however, stemmed not from race relations but disappointment with the island's resources and disgruntlement at the system of martial law imposed on the first settlement. The expedition's leaders had no immediate plans, or indeed the authority, to distribute lands; and the settlers, suffering from the attacks of fever inevitable for unacclimatized newcomers, lacked both adequate means and the will to labor at communal tasks. The situation was not made easier by the heavyhandedness of Captain Thomas Stephens and the other militia officers.

To say the least, the Carleton settlers were desperately ill provided and ill prepared. Within a few days of their arrival, they found themselves "in want of many necessities that cannot be obtained at any Price" and complained that it would be "impossible for them to clear the Land, Plant it, and Reap the Fruits of their Labour Sooner than Twelve or Fourteen months." They therefore begged Sir Guy Carleton to order the shipment of an additional six months' provisions, as well as some medicines, a few rolls of osnaburg cloth (a coarse type of linen), a thousand pairs of military shoes, a cross-cut saw, a dozen whipsaws and six casks of nails for cutting lumber and building houses, some horned cattle and horses, and "two Setts of Tools for Black Smiths, and some coals." They also asked for a competent surveyor to help lay out the town and survey building and farming lots.[9]

Some supplies were sent, and Carleton also ordered General Archibald McArthur, whom he had appointed to supervise the Loyalist transfer from East Florida to the Bahamas, to check up on conditions on Abaco. Early in 1784 McArthur sent to Abaco an engineer lieutenant, John Wilson, who reported that not only had the settlers chosen the very worst part of the island but they appeared "to have attended more to politics than to Agriculture."[10] A dispute had arisen over the labor required to build the township provision store. This had deteriorated almost to civil war, with the whites on both sides arming their black dependents. A section of the townsfolk had thrown off the authority of Thomas Stephens and the other militia officers and appointed a rival board of police. Then, when they feared retribution from General McArthur and his detachment of the Thirty-seventh Regiment, they deserted Carleton Town to form a rival settlement eighteen miles southeast at Marsh's Harbour. This, in an attempt at conciliation, they christened Maxwell Town, after the recently returned governor of the Bahamas.

Lieutenant Wilson made a careful survey of the Abaco coastline and settlements, and praised the island's harbors and marine resources. But he concluded that while the soil at Marsh's Harbour was slightly better than at Carleton, and that in the areas farther south where the East Florida Loyalists had recently landed it was the best on Abaco, there were not really any "extensive tracts of land fit for cultivation anywhere in this Island. Generally the soil was composed of nothing more than vegetable bodies rotted on the surface of the rocks."[11] This reality had already discouraged most of the Abaco Loyalists, and those who had the means began yet another migration, to New Providence, other Bahamian islands (particularly Long Island or the Caicos), or even the West Indies proper. This accounted for most of the would-be planters with gangs of slaves, inveterate townsfolk with some savings, and even a few of the Loyalist blacks, such as Joseph Paul, who seems to have contrived to migrate with his family to Nassau as early as 1784.[12]

For the whites who remained, the formal granting of lands to Loyalists after September 1785 was a decided relief, and many tracts of the Abaco mainland and cays were taken up. As elsewhere in the Bahamas, cotton was the most hopeful crop. But the most urgent problem was the short-age of suitable laborers. Since there were very few slaves remaining, this meant that the new landowners attempted to coerce the Loyalist blacks. This was an explosive situation, for the blacks, hitherto neglected by the authorities, not only had enjoyed practical freedom but were even accustomed to carrying arms.

As early as 1784, Governor Maxwell reported that the Loyalist whites were attempting to re-enslave all free Loyalist blacks,[13] and in June 1786 a sympathetic white called John Barry wrote: "It is with great Pain of Mind that I, every day see the Negroes, who came here from America, with the British Generals' Free Passes, treated with unheard of cruelty by Men who call themselves Loyalists. These unhappy People, after being drawn from their Masters by Promises of Freedom and the King's Protection, are every day stolen away."[14]

When Governor Dunmore—whose 1775 proclamation while he was governor of Virginia had first promised the mainland slaves freedom if they fought for the British—arrived in the Bahamas in the following year, one of his first actions was to set up a tribunal to examine blacks' claims to freedom.[15] This procedure, though, was seen by whites and blacks alike as a means of re-enslavement and on Abaco at least was fiercely resisted by the blacks. On November 28, 1787, Dunmore wrote to Lord Sydney: "I am just now informed from the Island of Abbaco that a number of outlying Negroes went about with Muskets and fix'd Bayonets, robbing and plundering, so that the white inhabitants had to collect themselves in a body and having come up with the Negroes had killed, wounded and taken most of them Prisoners, three of the latter they immediately executed."[16]

Dunmore went in person to Abaco early in 1788, set up his tribunal to examine the claims to freedom of thirty rebellious blacks, and declared all but one of them slaves. Returning to Nassau, he claimed that his action had made Abaco permanently peaceful. In reality, not only were plantations never successfully established in the island, but the conflict of the mid-1780s had established a permanent racial divide.

Though William Wylly claimed that over eighteen hundred acres of Abaco had been cleared and cultivated by 1788, he also reported that the last of the true planters were "moving off."[17] The remainder of the whites were rapidly turning to a lifestyle similar to that of Harbour Island and northern Eleuthera, and moving from the Abaco mainland to the offshore cays. Here they established a chain of all-white settlements, leaving the remaining blacks scattered along the mainland shore and engaged, for the most part, in subsistence farming. Though the majority of these Abaco blacks—whose numbers remained similar to those of the whites[18]—were technically regarded as slaves, the links between ostensible master and slave were tenuous, amounting at most to a sharecropping claim by the whites, some trade in ground provisions and fruit, and occasional help from the blacks in cutting wood and hunting wild hogs.

At Cherokee Sound (cut off from the mainland by a creek), Hope Town on Elbow Cay, Man-o-War Cay, and Great Guana Cay, small communities of poor whites built their own ships and eked out a living through fishing and wrecking, visiting the Abaco mainland only as frequently as necessary for provisions and lumber, and having closer social and trading connections with the similar white settlements of northern Eleuthera than with the Abaco blacks. The only exceptions to this pattern were the settlements at Marsh's Harbour, in the center of the Abaco mainland, and on Green Turtle Cay, almost opposite the deserted site of Carleton Town. These two settlements were racially mixed, or rather bifurcated, with a rigid racial separation within the settlement—a variation on the general pattern of Abaconian apartheid that probably stemmed from the fact that the original black and white settlers came from New York rather than directly from southern plantation colonies.

Throughout Abaco, however, the local environment and the traditional way of life of the Bahamian Out Islands can convincingly be said to have transformed the lifestyle of the Loyalist newcomers, rather than vice versa. To a somewhat lesser degree this may also be argued of the "Loyalist" period on New Providence and the other Bahamian islands: a phase of conflict between old inhabitants and Loyalist newcomers, a losing fight against intractable local conditions, painful adaptation, and, in the end, only qualified change.

By far the largest number of Loyalists—and the largest groups of slaves—came into the Bahamas from East Florida by way of New Providence. They totaled some three hundred families of whites, of whom more than a hundred owned ten or more slaves—perhaps five thousand slaves in all.[19] Of these migrants, more than half of the whites stayed on New Providence, while two-thirds of the slaves ended up on Out Islands hitherto undeveloped. But the resettlement was a protracted and troublesome process. As early as December 1783, Lord North had sent orders to Governor Patrick Tonyn of East Florida to encourage and aid migration to the Bahamas, stating that the British government intended to buy out the rights of the Lord Proprietors and make generous land grants. At first, however, it was mainly those without a stake in Florida who volunteered, and it was not until several months after the Spanish flag was raised in St. Augustine in July 1785 that the last Loyalist planters accepted the inevitable and set sail for the Bahamas.

Their reluctance was realistically based. Some planters had already migrated twice—typically from South Carolina and Georgia before East Florida—losing each time, and reports from the Bahamas did not encourage hopes of improvement. The first shiploads of refugees arriving in Nassau had found it a strange and backward town, unable and unwilling to cope. Not only was there a desperate shortage of housing, provisions, and essential supplies, but the townsfolk were unfriendly and the governor and council unwilling to make grants of land without formal authorization. One Loyalist planter wrote disparagingly to a friend about those in the Bahamas in 1784 that "much of the Dregs of an unfortunate and Licentious Army are now interspersed or incorporated among the Natives of this Country, the Offspring and Successors of the famous Blackbeard the Pirate." He went on, though, with more optimism. "This ought now to be considered a new Country. For the Old Inhabitants ever followed Wrecking, Privateering, Fishing, Turtling and some little Trade to the American Continent, and at this moment know as little as you do, of the Soil and interior part of these Islands."[20]

The same writer also described Governor John Maxwell as "ignorant, illiterate and Avaricious, full of low Duplicity of Conduct and really uncapable of well governing a private Family, much less so large a Body of People as the Bahama Islands now contains."[21] Maxwell certainly lacked capacities, but he was also unlucky. He had pressed the British government on the land question and the need for supplies before leaving England but awaited further instructions in vain.[22] Some supplies reached Nassau from Barbados and Ireland, but the ship with the largest consignment from England was wrecked coming over Nassau harbor bar. To relieve the dearth of provisions, Maxwell opened Nassau to mainland traders, only to have a Loyalist mob tear down the American colors. Other Loyalists, attempting to establish themselves in the Out Islands, though, engaged in a clandestine trade with the Americans in complete disregard of the government in Nassau.[23]

But if the white Loyalists were troublesome, it was the great influx of blacks which gave most immediate concern to the old regime. When Governor Maxwell reconvened the assembly in April 1784, he piously commended the plight of the Loyalists to the members, but also stressed the need for tighter social controls. A new militia act was passed which required much stricter observance in times of peace and gave the militia special duties and powers in suppressing civil riots. The 1767 Act for the Governing of Negroes, Mulattoes, Mustees and Indians was also re-enacted, with even tougher restrictions against slaves and freedmen alike.[24]

The most significant piece of new legislation, however, was that with the innocuous title "An Act to exempt Sundry Negroes that have purchased, or otherwise obtained their Freedom from the payment of the penalty imposed on them by an Act passed in the Eighth Year of his present Majesty's Reign."[25] This act suspended the payment of the freedom bond of ninety pounds required by the 1768 Manumission Act, in return for requiring all black and colored males aged between fifteen and sixty who had been freed since 1768 to serve, for the first time, in the militia. Far from being integrated with the white majority of the militia, though, these freedmen were to be formed into a special Free Company, under their own officers, with the specific duty of pursuing slave runaways. Each eligible freedman, moreover, was to wear a special metal badge, on one side of which would be inscribed the word FREE and the date, and on the other the freedman's name and militia number. In this way the legislators not only recruited those blacks already free into the forces of law and order by a valued concession but subtly distinguished them both from the old Bahamian blacks who had been born free and from the "Loyalist" blacks, whether enslaved or claiming freedom.

Andrew Deveaux and other pioneer Loyalists already sat in the 1784 assembly, but the majority of the white newcomers felt themselves almost totally unrepresented. Somewhat ironically for alleged Loyalists, they stood on the principles of representation which had motivated the mainland republicans, behaving in a manner that allowed their opponents to claim that they plotted treason and secession. The leader of the radicals was James Hepburn, former attorney general of East Florida, who formed a Board of Loyalists to promote their cause through public meetings and handbills, and most of all in the columns of Nassau's first newspaper. This was the *Bahama Gazette*, a weekly founded in August 1784 by John Wells, an ambitious bookseller and printer from Charleston, South Carolina.

Governor Maxwell vacillated between petulance and concession but was unable either to quell or to conciliate the opposition. Hepburn and other Loyalist lawyers complained of being excluded from practice in the Bahamian courts, but when Maxwell tried to appoint several as magistrates they refused to stand. Some of the Loyalists made such a set at

Chief Justice Atwood that Maxwell closed down the general court. But at the same time the governor signed a decree that there would be a major revision of constituencies for the next assembly. The seats for New Providence, Harbour Island, and Eleuthera were reduced from twenty-four to fourteen, while there were to be eleven new Out Island seats, distributed among Cat Island, Exuma, Long Island, Abaco, and Andros.

At the general election held between December 1784 and February 1785, at least nine of the Hepburn faction were elected for the new seats, including James Hepburn himself as a member for Cat Island. However, the dissidents remained outnumbered by old inhabitants and moderate Loyalists and immediately challenged the election's validity, at the same time redoubling their demands for Maxwell's recall. In exasperation the governor threw in his hand and sailed for England, leaving James Powell, himself a Loyalist, as acting governor, to face the new assembly.

Lieutenant Governor Powell died of fever within a year, but his brief regime saw the resolution of the two most urgent problems. The members of the Hepburn faction boycotted the assembly and campaigned against it in the press, but in September 1785 they were expelled for nonattendance or contempt by the vote of the remaining members. In the resulting by-elections more temperate Loyalists were chosen and party strife faded, with the assembly resuming its more usual role as a more or less united interest group. The 1785 assembly, in fact, was the longest-lived in Bahamian history, lasting until 1794.

Concord was aided by the long-overdue announcement of government grants of unoccupied lands to all would-be planters, made by Lieutenant Governor Powell at the same time as the Hepburn expulsions. This was made possible by the piecemeal purchase by the Crown of lands from the Lord Proprietors after 1784, completed by the final conveyance of all rights by the heirs of the original Proprietors on March 14, 1787—for a total payment of twenty-six thousand pounds.[26] Each head of household (old inhabitant as well as Loyalist) was entitled to a basic block of forty acres, with an additional twenty acres for each dependent, white or slave, subject only to an annual quit rent of two shillings per hundred acres. In the case of displaced Loyalists, grants were to be exempted from all initial charges and even quit rents for the first ten years.[27] Once the Lord Proprietors were finally bought out it was also possible to establish a regular registry office, responsible for surveys, registration, and the keeping of records, and in 1789 an act was passed to come to terms with the difficult problems of resolving claims to land.[28]

As a result of these changes, there was an explosion of land grants and claims between 1785 and 1790, with only a slight diminution in the subsequent five years, which together accounted for almost all the developable land in the settled islands and laid the basis for all later land transactions. Because of deficient records, subsequent sales, and, above all, the resumption by the Crown of unimproved land, it is difficult now to know quite how much land was taken up in the first wave. But one partial modern compilation listed 43,000 acres in 114 patents taken out before the end of 1789, for an average of 382 acres.[29] This total of new holdings, which included almost all the unadopted lands in New Providence, Long Island, and Exuma, and some of the best lands in Cat Island, Crooked Island, Acklin's, San Salvador, Rum Cay, and Andros, but comparatively few plots in Eleuthera or Abaco, is beguilingly close to the total number of new settlers arriving with ten or more slaves counted by William Wylly in 1788—allowing at least a rough estimation of the size and population of a typical new plantation.[30]

Certainly, the later 1780s were a period of great expansion and optimism. Wylly calculated that already the area of cultivated land had risen from 3,434 to 16,322 acres between 1783 and 1788, and that total was probably doubled to a peak around 1793. As early as 1785, the new plantations produced 124 tons of cotton from 2,476 acres, rising steadily to 219 tons in 1787 and 442 tons in 1790, from perhaps 12,000 acres. Thereafter, growth was slower and intermittent, with a peak of production around 1810, when, according to Bryan Edwards, the Bahamas exported 602 tons—around 6,000 bales—to the already-voracious Lancashire mills. With the export of logwood reflecting the clearing of land for plantations, and production of salt and stock animals becoming important adjuncts to cotton production, the value of Bahamian exports soared above prewar levels, reaching £58,707 as early as 1787, compared with a trifling £5,216 in 1774. Largely as a result of the imperial Free Port Act of 1787, which for a few years made Nassau a profitable entrepôt for trade with the French and Spanish colonies, but also because of the expanded needs and more refined tastes of the Loyalist newcomers, the surge in the value of imports was even more impressive, totalling £136,359 in 1787, a forty-fold increase since before the American War.[31]

While the dynamic energies of the Loyalist newcomers were concentrated on setting up plantations, Nassau must have seemed very much a frontier town, bursting at its seams and rapidly changing but very far from the solid and elegant colonial capital which McKinnen was to praise in 1802.[32] The population of New Providence more than doubled in less than five years, and with the establishment of plantations throughout

BAHAMA-ISLANDS, }
NEW-PROVIDENCE. } ss.

By His Honour JAMES EDWARD POWELL,
*Esq; Lieutenant-Governour and Commander in
Chief in and over the said Islands, Chancellor,
Vice Admiral, and Ordinary of the same, &c. &c.*

A PROCLAMATION.

WHEREAS it is His Majesty's
Royal Will and Pleasure, signified by his Instructions bearing
date at his Court at St James's,
the tenth day of September 1784,
that the Lands within his said
Bahama-Islands, shall be surveyed
and granted on the following conditions; that is to
say, That forty acres of land be granted to every
person, being master or mistress of a family, for
himself or herself; and twenty acres for every
white and black man, woman or child, of which
such family shall confist at the actual time of granting such warrants; That all grantees be subject to
the payment of two shillings sterling quit rent for
every hundred acres, to commence at the expiration of two years from the date of their respective
grants, to be paid at the end of every year thereafter, in default of which the grants to be void:
But his Majesty has been graciously pleased, as an
encouragement to his Loyal Subjects who have
been residents in any of the Colonies or Provinces
now the United States of America, and who on
account of their loyalty to his Majesty, shall or
may willingly, or by compulsion, remove into his
said Islands, to order, that the quit rent to be
reserved in ....
to his said Subjects, shall not commence and be
payable until after the expiration of ten years from
the date of their respective grants; which said
grants it is his Majesty's Royal Will and Pleasure
shall be delivered to the several grantees free of all
expence whatever: I DO THEREFORE, by and
with the advice and consent of his Majesty's
Honourable Council, issue this my Proclamation,
hereby making known to all persons concerned,
that upon application to me in Council, they will
receive Warrants of Survey for running out their
lands, agreeable to his Majesty's said Instructions,
and their family rights.

GIVEN *under my Hand and the Great Seal of
the said Islands, at Nassau, this fifth day of
September, in the Year of Our Lord One thousand seven hundred and eighty five, and in the
twenty-fifth Year of His Majesty's Reign.*
JAMES EDWARD POWELL.

By his Honour's Command,
STEPHEN HAVEN, pro Secretary.
GOD SAVE THE KING.

Lt. Gov. Powell's proclamation of land grants to Loyalists,
including headrights, September 5, 1785

the island, the area under cultivation increased by twelve times, to some thirty-five hundred acres. To serve these new plantations, Governor Maxwell was persuaded by the Loyalists in 1784 to appoint commissioners to supervise the building of roads and to introduce the principle, applied in all plantation colonies, that landowners were responsible for the upkeep of the public roads passing their lands—a system that was extended to the Out Islands by an Act of 1789.[33] Gradually, on New Providence and all the chief Out Islands at least one "carriage" road was completed—that on Long Island being said to be one hundred miles in length—though even on New Providence heavy goods continued to be transported mainly in coasting vessels, white planters normally traveled by horse, and market produce and small items were usually carried by donkey or mule, or on the heads of slaves.

In Nassau too, new roads were built and old ones improved, as wheeled vehicles became a more common sight and the town became an increasingly important market center and entrepôt. As evidence of Nassau's surge of mercantile activity, including a greatly increased trade in slaves, the first new public building erected was the Vendue House (still in existence), a handsome small structure with open colonnades for the auction of produce and slaves, raised in 1787 on the site of the Bourse mentioned by Schoepf. Two years later, an act was passed to set up and regulate a public market, situated on the waterfront adjacent to the Vendue House.[34] There were several new warehouses, taverns, and shops, including Nassau's first bookshop, in the building where John Wells printed the *Bahama Gazette*. This newspaper in the later 1780s also reported the establishment of several schools and societies, a lending library, and Nassau's first attempts at forms of "polite entertainment."

In general, though, there was a desperate shortage not only of living accommodation but of public buildings. This was emphasized by Lord Dunmore, who, accustomed to the elegant spaciousness of Williamsburg, Virginia, complained in 1789 that Nassau's Assembly House (at the juncture of Bay Street and Prison Lane) consisted of two meager rooms, in one of which the courts of justice and assembly were held, with the other serving as the town jail. A committee appointed in the same year to report on Bahamian conditions also noted that the one church and small workhouse were quite inadequate for Nassau's needs, and that the Out Islands possessed not a single public building (the church at Harbour Island apparently having been destroyed in a storm).[35]

The first detailed map of Nassau, dated 1788, depicts a place about the size of a small English country town, stretching about a mile along the waterfront and a quarter mile south to the parallel ridge.[36] Within this rough quadrilateral nearly all the streets still found between the present Victoria Avenue in the east and Augusta Street in the west were already in existence, though the buildings were by no means continuous even in the center of town. This twenty-acre downtown core, which contained perhaps a third of Nassau's buildings, was bounded on the north by Bay Street, which then fronted on the harbor, and to east, south, and west (in unconscious homage to the Butcher of Culloden) by Frederick, Duke, and Cumberland Streets. Bay Street, then as now, was Nassau's chief thoroughfare, extending in this section between Fort Nassau and its Parade, past the Vendue House, to the multipurpose assembly building. The symbolic axis of Nassau, however, was the north–south line of George Street, extending from the commercial focus of the Vendue House on the waterfront, past Christchurch, the sole house of worship, to the governor's house on Mount Fitzwilliam.

The more substantial New Providence whites who did not reside out of town on plantations lived for the most part in the more secluded streets outside Nassau's commercial center, where the house lots seem to have averaged about a quarter acre. The very best houses were on the upper slopes or crest of the ridge, along East and West Hill streets. The poorer whites and most prosperous free coloreds lived above or among the downtown shops, or in small houses in the crowded streets just east of East Street or west of West Street, outside Nassau's official boundaries. However, despite the novel dispersion of plantations throughout New Providence, the majority of Nassau's population were not whites or prosperous free coloreds, but slaves and the poorer free blacks, including those who believed themselves freed during the American War. As an index of the new pressures on space in downtown Nassau, and of the more rigorous concern for racial separation which came in with the Loyalists, most of these no longer lived in the yards of their owners or employers, but in two distinct areas just "over the hill," on either side of the southward-stretching grounds of the governor's house. Most of the old slaves and some of the freedmen seem to have clustered around the southern slopes of Society (later Fort Fincastle) Hill. But the area which caused the white establishment the most concern was the stretch of former bush "behind the hospital" on West Hill Street later to be called Delancey Town. For here were not only many of the new slaves, but most of the Loyalist blacks who claimed their freedom. It was here too that the Wesleyan Joseph Paul and certain "Black Baptists" preached, and, as William Wylly complained in 1789, so many runaway slaves were harbored that the rest of Nassau was "actually overawed" by them.[37]

～ 13 ～

Cotton and Conflict: The 1790s

THE DISTRIBUTION of lands, the redistribution of seats in the assembly, and the preoccupation of old and new whites alike with developing an oligarchic system quelled discord among the ruling class and should have allowed for rapid and peaceful progress. Advances were made, in the modernization of the administration and the improvement of facilities in Nassau. But progress was slowed and made turbulent by the failure to establish a prosperous plantation economy, by the difficult personality and behavior of Governor Lord Dunmore, and by the social and racial discord that reflected the first whispers of liberal reform in the metropolis, the revolutions in France and St. Domingue, and the outbreak of war with revolutionary and Napoleonic France.

As the Arawaks had discovered long before, the climate of the central Bahamas was ideal for growing sea island cotton, and early reports suggested that it might prove a bonanza for Loyalist planters. For example, one of the first settlers in Cat Island, Oswell Eve, wrote in May 1784 that a planter who six years before was in "debt and ruin" had gone to Long Island with six slaves and had already grown enough cotton "to establish a fortune of £5–6,000." More soberly, William Wylly in 1789 claimed that while cotton production was suitable for neither the northern nor southern Bahamas, the area between Cat Island and Acklin's promised to be such an important "cotton belt" that Exuma ought to be made an official port of entry, if not the colonial capital.[1]

As early as 1788, though, cotton production fell drastically short of predictions. At first this was attributed solely to the appearance of the chenille bug, a cotton-eating "worm that looks like a caterpillar . . . variegated with beautiful colours and many legs."[2] But the real and lasting reason for failure was the inadequacy of Bahamian soils. These were so thin, scattered, and easily exhausted that while first growths were often encouraging, productivity rapidly declined. Besides, the clearing of the natural cover for making cotton fields, coupled with the occasional heavy rains, speeded erosion and the leaching of what soils there were. Bahamian cotton production did not suddenly fade and was sustained by high wartime prices between 1793 and 1815. Productivity was also aided by the invention of a wind-powered version of the mechanical cotton gin by a Bahamian Loyalist, Oswell Eve's son Joseph, who was also the second editor of the *Bahama Gazette*.[3] As we have seen, a peak of over six hundred tons of cotton, worth some seventy-five thousand pounds, was produced in the Bahamas as late as 1810. But this level was achieved only through a steady increase in the area cultivated, and despite a disastrously declining average acreage yield. Though the demand from the British textile industry increased hugely after 1815, the decline of Bahamian cotton was also speeded by the introduction of free trade and the consequent inability to compete with those areas of very large and economical production, such as the U.S. cotton belt.

To a certain extent, the decline of Bahamian cotton was cushioned by the profitable development of salt production. Turks Island had been one of the major producers of salt in the Americas since the seventeenth century, and in the remainder of the archipelago small salinas had been unsystematically harvested since John Darrell reported a salt pond in Little Exuma in 1670. Now, planters found that they could take advantage of the very sea-connected marshes and ponds, the low rainfall, and the continuous baking temperatures that lowered the agricultural value of their land and retarded cultivation, while at the same time providing their slaves with employment during lulls in the cultivation cycle or periods of agricultural failure. Consequently, many of the more substantial planters, such as the Rolles of Exuma, developed small salinas alongside their cotton fields. A few Loyalists even went into salt production on its own, such as Duncan Taylor, the brother of Andrew Deveaux's chief lieutenant, who set up the industry on arid and infertile Ragged Island as early as 1783.[4]

The optimal production of salt, however, required large operations and more capital than most planters could muster. The most successful Bahamian salinas therefore tended to be owned and developed by combinations of planters. As the troubled history of the Turks Islands showed, the government also had an interest in controlling salt production and not allowing individuals too much latitude. Salt was a proven revenue raiser, yet it could very easily slip through the mercantilist net if production and shipments were not carefully monitored. Consequently, known or even potential salinas were not normally included in grants of agricultural land, were rarely granted to individuals, and were covered

by special terms and regulations. In 1781, even before the Loyalists arrived in the Bahamas, Governor Maxwell passed an order-in-council to
establish rules for the leasing and regulation of salinas. Special commissioners were appointed, drawn from the local grandees, who were as
often as not the lessees themselves, to allot tasks and timetables, to keep
records, collect taxes and duties, and settle disputes. This order was converted into an act in 1789 and was reviewed and revised at intervals
thereafter.[5]

In 1802 an assembly inquiry reported that there were twenty-five major
salt ponds in the Bahamas (excluding the Turks and Caicos Islands),
with a potential annual production of three million bushels, or one hundred thousand tons. To carry this harvest, worth an estimated £250,000,
would permanently employ as many as one hundred vessels averaging
two hundred tons' displacement.[6] In order to develop these resources,
a major salt act was passed in 1803. This placed the chief salt ponds in
the rest of the colony on exactly the same footing as those in the Turks
Islands, including the provision that foreign vessels could obtain salt directly, rather than having to trade through Nassau. In fact, Bahamian
production before the twentieth century rarely reached half the level
projected in 1802, and increased production, peacetime conditions, and
free-trade policies drastically brought down prices after 1815. But in its
value, and the amount of labor and shipping required, Bahamian salt
production actually exceeded cotton in importance by 1800 and ran increasingly farther ahead of it until the end of slavery, with important
social as well as economic implications.

On the model of the mainland colonies they had left behind, Loyalist
planters judged their success by the degree to which they were able to
establish (or re-establish) themselves, their families, and their retinues
of slaves in a quasi-feudal style in the Bahamian Out Islands. Their ideal
was an efficient, self-contained agricultural unit, centered on a "great
house," sustained by simple and contented slaves, but regulated and
given tone by the resident planter and his family. The Out Islands as a
whole would be transformed into an ordered and "civilized" province
by a whole constellation of such mansion-based units, by an increasingly
interrelated network of white families, and, above all, by a class of paternalistic family heads who at the same time were planters, slave owners,
justices of the peace, militia captains, commissioners of roads, harbors,
and ponds, and members of the House of Assembly representing their
island constituencies.

Elements of this imagined edifice were realized, but in fragmentary, temporary, or parody form. The ideal faded with the knowledge that neither cotton nor any other plantation crop could provide the means for a baronial lifestyle in the Bahamas equivalent to that in Virginia, Carolina, Brazil, or Cuba, and that wringing a bare livelihood from the stony soil or, even more, the sun-baked salt pans with the labor of slaves was inimical to the creation of a "polite" society. Those disappointed planters who did not abandon the Bahamas altogether (and their numbers would have been greater had it proved easier to find a market for Bahamian assets), tended to desert their lands and slaves and gravitate with their families to the colonial capital. Here they looked for alternative, or supplementary, opportunities in government, law, and business, for a somewhat more elegant and comfortable lifestyle, and even such elementary components of "civilization" as schools, churches, and clubs. This process of reconcentration was reinforced by the number of substantial landowners who held estates in several islands, by those engaged in selling and speculating in land and slaves who found that such business required far more time in Nassau than in the islands, and by those engaged in colonial politics who discovered that to spend too much time on their estates was to invite political oblivion.

Thus, after the first flush of pioneering optimism, the whites in the newly settled Out Islands consisted mainly of those too poor to move, those managing estates for others, absentee owners rotationally visiting their scattered and decaying plantations, or white families spending time in the healthful quiet of Out Island estates to escape Nassau's clamor and occasional sieges of epidemic disease. Far from the decentralization envisaged by William Wylly and others, Nassau not only remained the hub of business and government but became the concentrated focus of the energies and evolving lifestyle of a new and enlarged Bahamian elite. Inevitably, there was a renewal of competition, tension, and conflict. But these no longer stemmed chiefly from differences between old and new inhabitants, or even (as in Jamaica and other West Indian colonies) between merchants and planters. Instead, they followed from the formation of the reconstituted oligarchy, flexing its muscles in the enlarged assembly and eager to assert its authority, its concepts of social order and progressive administration, and its sectional interests, in confrontation with an arrogant, aristocratic, and imperialistic governor and against a troublesome majority of urban slaves and ambitious free coloreds.

John Murray, Lord Dunmore arrived as governor in October 1787 and was almost immediately embroiled with the white slaveowners. He retained from Virginia an exaggerated reputation of being a "friend to the blacks" which was not reduced by his recent residence in the land of William Wilberforce or by some of his initial actions. However, these probably stemmed more from an aristocratic attitude of protective paternalism toward the underclasses and a concomitant contempt for such bourgeois behavior and values as exhibited by the Bahamian whites, than from any real commitment to liberal principles, or even direct orders from the secretary of state. As he reported in his first dispatch to Lord Sydney, Dunmore received complaints that runaway slaves and blacks claiming freedom were creating havoc by "plundering and committing Outrages upon the Inhabitants of this and several other Islands." But on inquiry he had found that much of the trouble was occasioned by whites, "who had detained several of these poor, unhappy People under various pretences in a State of Slavery" and were in the habit of sending out posses to round up blacks whom they suspected of being slaves.[7]

Only two weeks after his arrival, Dunmore had been awakened in the night at Mount Fitzwilliam by screams and cries of "Murder!" from the adjacent black quarter. He had sent out to the scene some of his servants, who had found five or six "gentlemen" armed with swords and pistols in the act of breaking into the house of a free mulatto woman with seven or eight children, beating the woman and one of her daughters and threatening to fire the house. The whites' leader was one Josiah Tatnall, who claimed to have an official warrant to search for runaways and arms, and boasted he cared not for Dunmore, the king, or anyone else. Brought before a magistrate the following day, Tatnall threatened to burn all the black houses in that quarter if necessary.[8]

Determined, as he said, to put an end to this type of lawlessness, Dunmore issued a proclamation of amnesty for all runaways who would give themselves up, and set up his tribunal for investigating challenged claims to freedom. As we have seen, the whites bitterly resented these moves, though in fact a large proportion of the cases went against the black claimants. Even with such an outcome, Dunmore was blamed. Since some masterless men were either declared slaves of the Crown or sold on behalf of the treasury, the governor was accused of re-enslaving blacks for his personal benefit.[9]

With rather more justice, some whites charged that Dunmore was trying to revive the animus against the Loyalists and was fomenting party strife on the principle of "divide and rule." However, he was more successful in the long run in uniting all local whites in a party against his government. In April 1788 Dunmore contended that the assembly should be dissolved and the Bahamas placed under martial law. He quoted evi-

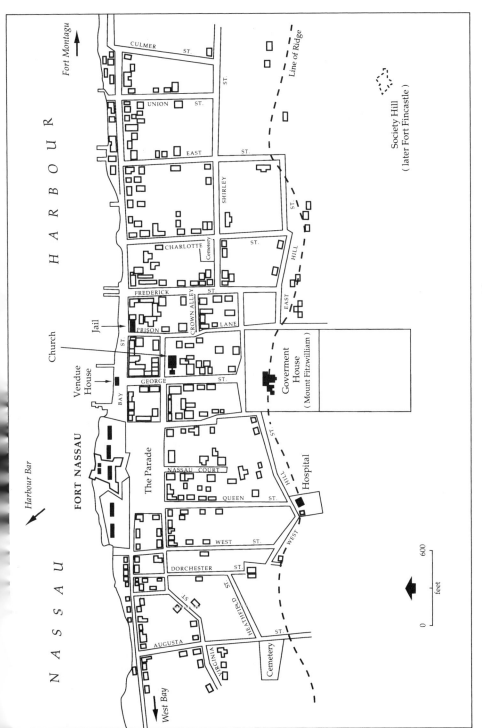

Map 8. Nassau in transition, 1788

dence from his unreliable friend William Augustus Bowles, "Director General of the Creek Nation," that the Loyalists were plotting to make the colony independent with the help of the Americans.[10] When his suggestion about martial law was ignored, the governor concentrated on turning the assembly against itself.

In this phase, as for much of the next thirty-five years, a key figure was William Wylly, a Georgia Loyalist and relatively enlightened slaveowner, who had first fled to New Brunswick but was now attorney general of the Bahamas. Determined to be neutral, as he had been in Canada, Wylly was offended by a demand from the governor, channeled through Chief Justice John Matson, that he should "take a party" in return for a lucrative post in the vice-admiralty court. The affair rapidly escalated. Wylly abused Matson in public, was thrown into jail, and resigned as attorney general; Dunmore closed the courts after the Wylly case got out of hand; and both Matson and Wylly went to London to place their cases before the privy council. Wylly aired his views publicly (if pseudonymously) in his *Short Account of the Bahama Islands* (1789), which claimed that "the interests, the reputation, and the laws of a valuable Colony" were being "sacrificed by the arbitrary mandate of a Madman to serve the infamous purposes of a Knave," and memorably characterized Lord Dunmore as greedy and licentious, with a "capacity below mediocrity, little cultivated by education, ignorant of the constitution of England . . . the lordly Despot of a petty Clan."[11] The intercession of Anthony Stokes, colonial agent for the Bahamas, saved Lord Dunmore's position, but William Wylly returned to the colony to carry on his campaign in the House of Assembly, as a private lawyer and New Providence planter.

Lord Dunmore provided ever more plentiful fuel for his opponents. Besides quite shamelessly exercising patronage—favoring, it was said, his cronies and the husbands of his lovers—he was guilty of nepotism and using his privileged position to speculate in land. He eased one of his sons into a safe assembly seat for Eleuthera, and appointed another first agent for the Turks Islands and then, without official approval from London, lieutenant governor. Despite theoretical limits on the size and number of land grants, Dunmore rewarded himself and his family with substantial parcels of prime land in all the settled islands, profiting by numerous subsequent transactions, especially after automatic grants to Loyalists came to an end in 1790. Though he failed with a cotton plantation on southern Long Island (near the settlement still called Dunmore's), Dunmore laid out a new township on Harbour Island (also named after himself), building a summer retreat on the crest of the ridge and parceling the adjacent lots to the chief of the local inhabitants, at an annual rent of two shillings and sixpence apiece. In New Providence he built an elegant small mansion called the Hermitage in the best seaside location on the Eastern Road and in 1793 obtained the finest remaining Crown lands site in Nassau, thirteen acres from the ridge southward, immediately to the west of Mount Fitzwilliam.[12]

What brought down most trouble on Dunmore's head, though, was his extravagant use of public funds to finance his obsession with building new forts—none of which, as it happened, was ever to fire a shot in anger. Chief of these was Fort Charlotte and its outworks, built between 1787 and 1794, at eight times the originally estimated cost, to replace Fort Nassau. But Dunmore also fortified Harbour Island and, after war broke out in 1793, added batteries at Clifton, Winton, Hog Island, and Potter's Cay, and on Society Hill in Nassau, began yet another fortress, named Fort Fincastle after one of his family's subsidiary titles.[13]

The Bahamian whites complained bitterly of the taxes and slave labor levied to complete Lord Dunmore's fortifications. But in fact the governor's follies underwrote the power of the new oligarchy. The demands for extraordinary expenditures united almost all assemblymen in opposition, and with the imperial government providing only meager assistance, it was Dunmore's financial need which enabled the assembly to assert its control over the allocation and spending of the colony's budget and thus to establish the practical ascendancy of the locally elected legislature over the Crown-appointed executive.

During the struggle over financial control and the relative prerogatives of governor and assembly—at its most bitter between 1791 and 1793— Lord Dunmore several times prorogued the assembly. But he was reluctant to dissolve it altogether because he realized that the few remaining supporters of the governor would be swept away in a general election. The outbreak of war in 1793 distracted the colony, but the hope of a reprieve for the governor was scotched by the replacement of Anthony Stokes as colonial agent by George Chalmers, who was faithfully to represent the interests of the Bahamian assembly from 1792 to 1825. The old regime effectively ended in 1794, when London ordered the governor to approve a septennial act and, the assembly having already sat for nine years, Lord Dunmore was at last forced to proclaim a dissolution and call a general election.[14]

The aging and increasingly irascible Lord Dunmore was finally recalled in 1796. But the new assembly had already set about passing a whole raft of new and overdue legislation, which the governor resignedly endorsed. The financial victories over the executive were entrenched by acts concerning the funding of government expenses and the payment of official salaries, including a special act to provide an annual salary of five hundred pounds for William Wylly, who, by a nice irony, was now appointed chief justice. An act to forbid the appointment of absentee officials was aimed at reserving lucrative posts for local residents and cutting down a notorious form of executive patronage, while a tax on land sales was, almost certainly, another sideswipe at the governor. The assembly's concern to promote a revision of the system of law and order was reflected in acts to regulate and reform the militia, the office of provost marshal, the lower courts, and the jury system, and to build a new jail and workhouse. More objectively progressive were the acts to set up and regulate the town market, to erect new public buildings, to improve Bay Street and the Nassau waterfront, once more to forbid the keeping of hogs and the erection of thatched houses within Nassau's boundaries, and to extend and keep clean the roads throughout New Providence. Acts were also passed concerning quarantine, pilotage, the regulation of printing, and the promotion of schools.[15]

The assembly was more than ever concerned about the proper licensing of teachers and the promotion of established religion, not just because the Bahamas was more deficient than any other British colony in these respects, but because of the growing fear that unlicensed dissident preachers and teachers—even blacks—might fill the gap. For the first time, non-Anglican Christians were given official sanction when the kirk established by Loyalists of Scottish extraction was given government aid. But this was, and remained, an exclusively white congregation. Intended to be of far more general importance was the great extension of the parochial system of the established Anglican church. An act of 1795 proposed a second parish for New Providence and added six new Out Island parishes to St. John's, Harbour Island: St. Patrick, south Eleuthera; St. Salvador, Cat Island; St. Andrew, Exuma; St. Paul, Long Island; St. David, Crooked Island; and St. George, Turks and Caicos Islands.[16] However, the vision of a society fixed in its ranks through the "civilizing" medium of the Anglican church was not fulfilled, since the provision of the act that the existing churches be extended and repaired and new ones erected was for long a dead letter, for years there were no more than three Anglican ministers in the Bahamas, and for even longer the Anglican church did little or nothing to proselytize the blacks.

For those now represented in the Bahamian assembly, moreover, the social-racial situation in the 1790s was sufficiently serious to require a more direct solution. The problem, from their point of view, was not just that of controlling slaves and free blacks who had increased vastly in numbers since 1783, but also two complicating threats: the French Revolution and the related slave revolution in Haiti, and the more insidious influence of British humanitarianism. The solution was legislation which would subtly satisfy the latter, while deflecting and defusing the former.

The first hint of imperial concern about slave conditions had come within a year of Lord Dunmore's arrival, in the form of the long questionnaire sent out as part of the great Parliamentary Inquiry of 1788–89. Dunmore's scrupulous answers to the committee's fifty-four questions would have displeased few Bahamian slaveowners. The general picture that emerged was one of a healthy, scarcely overworked, and largely contented slave population, with masters who fed, clothed, and housed their slaves well and never treated them harshly. Perhaps most impressive of all were his claims that Bahamian slaves suffered from no diseases unknown to the whites, lived just as long on the average (some sixty to seventy years), and had at least as many children. As a result of this, in contrast to Jamaica and other West Indian colonies, it had not been necessary to import slaves from Africa within human memory.[17]

Bahamian slave conditions may indeed have been rather less dismal than in many other colonies, and the slaves not completely demoralized. But by absolute standards, and on closer inspection, there were serious flaws and widening cracks in the smooth surface presented by Lord Dunmore. Adherents of the recently founded Society for the Abolition of the Slave Trade would have been skeptical of the bland generalities in Dunmore's account, eager to read between the lines, and completely dissatisfied by many of the slaveowners' implicit assumptions. Even those moderates, on both sides of the Atlantic, who reflected on Lord Dunmore's replies must have been struck by the dangerous degree to which relations between master and slave in the Bahamas were a matter of custom, not statutory laws. With justice, the English friends of the slaves pointed out the almost complete absence of protective clauses in the Bahamian slave laws. Bad masters might do almost what they willed with their slaves. Bahamian slaveowners, on the other hand, while claiming that such protective clauses had not hitherto been necessary, had to admit that their absence might give the wrong impression, as well as allow for abuses.

"The Proprietor has a legal and absolute right to dispose of his Slave," conceded Lord Dunmore in answer to the very first question. Besides being subject to all the penalties of the English criminal law, though tried in a special court consisting only of two justices of the peace and three other white freeholders, slaves could be freely "corrected at the will of their Master." While whites might theoretically be convicted and fined for assaulting a slave, they could be prosecuted only by another white, since neither slaves nor free blacks could sue or bear witness against a white in such cases. The same catch practically negated the provision that a white master whose cruelty led to the death of his slave could be tried for murder in the general court.[18]

Bahamian slaves were fed at their masters' expense and generally were issued six to eight quarts of Indian corn per week apiece, or rice or guinea corn in proportion; but the amounts depended on the "generosity or good Nature of the Master." Slaves were "in general Clothed by their Masters and Lodged and secured against the inclemency of the Seasons," they were allotted "small portions of land" to grow their own provisions, and "allowed the Sunday only for themselves." But in all these respects, there was said to be "No Law but Practice." When slaves were old or disabled their masters were bound to maintain them so that they would not be a general burden. And when slaves were sick they were "in general taken very good care of," though this was mainly because it was in their masters' interest. There was "no Law or regulation for that purpose." Likewise, there was no legal provision for slaves to be married, baptized, or (any longer) given religious instruction, though by the same token there was no law which said they might not be.[19]

The outbreak of the revolution in France did not immediately alarm the Bahamian whites any more than it did the regime in England. To most it seemed simply that the politically backward French were catching up with the more progressive English—imposing a constitutional relationship upon the French monarch and giving the colonial planters the chance of greater self-determination. Alarm began to spread only when the doctrine of the Rights of Man encouraged the free coloreds in St. Domingue to rise up for their civil rights, when the conflict between the St. Domingue whites and free coloreds allowed the slaves to start a colonywide revolution, and when the triumphant Jacobins in France overthrew the monarchy and declared their alignment with the slaves who had seized their freedom.[20]

Almost certainly, it was news of the mulatto rebellion in St. Domingue led by Vincent Ogé that persuaded the Bahamian assembly to demand late in 1789 "that all free Negroes, Mulattos, Mustees and Indians should register with the Secretary their name, age, address, their family, sex and colour, under forfeit of their freedom." Once registered, Bahamian free coloreds were to be issued with tools and required to work on the public roads for a daily wage of two shillings, being subject to a fine or corporal punishment if they refused. After the completion of their symbolic *corvée,* and only then, they were to be given a certificate that they were both free and exempt from the ninety-pound bond levied on the newly freed since 1768. This menial treatment was in notable contrast to the enrollment of the freedmen in a special company of the militia only five years earlier.[21]

Having thus humbled those whom they regarded as their greatest threat, the Bahamian whites were perhaps unduly complacent about the dangers inherent in the tremendous slave revolt that broke out in St. Domingue early in 1791. Chauvinistically convinced that slave revolution was far less likely in their own regime than under the harsher French conditions, they were also confident that they could prevent the revolution from spreading by cutting off all communications between the Bahamas and St. Domingue. As late as April 1792 Governor Dunmore wrote to Secretary of State Dundas: "I am happy to inform you that there is not the least appearance of any disorderly behaviour among the Slaves in this Government and that we have very little communication with any French West India Islands."[22]

Even when war broke out with revolutionary France in 1793, the Bahamian whites were reassured that the eradication of the threat from the French West Indies was a priority for Prime Minister William Pitt. They felt even safer as the Nassau garrison was raised to its highest level ever, and the largest expeditionary force ever sent out from Britain sailed through the Bahamas on its way to conquer St. Domingue in the first campaign of the war. Many Bahamian planters continued to see it as an international rather than class and racial conflict, and even considered that their own slaves would fight loyally against the French—both black and white—in defense of their British masters and their lands. Such an optimist was the East Florida (and Devonshire) Loyalist Denys Rolle, who late in 1793 was chiefly concerned that the French would descend upon the underdefended Out Islands in the traditional way, to plunder and destroy the settlements and carry off the slaves. Rolle went so far as to argue that his slaves in Exuma should be armed and sent on patrols, since they would defend their master's land as if it were their own. They would also feel, he claimed, that they were protecting their own wives and children, as well as "riches gained by extra Labour."[23]

Such optimism, though, was never general and evaporated altogether once the British expedition to St. Domingue turned into a fiasco, the

Jacobin exslaves under Toussaint l'Ouverture gained control of most of the island, and more and more blacks from St. Domingue filtered into the Bahamas, either as prisoners of war or as slaves accompanying their refugee French masters. Already in July 1793, Governor Dunmore had issued a proclamation prohibiting the admission into the Bahamas of "French Mulattos and Free Negroes,"[24] but by 1795 pressure had mounted to exclude all "French" blacks, for fear of revolutionary infection. In May 1795, for example, the planters of Long Island (who were almost as close to St. Domingue as they were to Nassau) asked for better protection because they feared that their slaves might be incited into insurrection, either by a French invasion or by the slaves of French refugee planters.[25] In the very same week Governor Dunmore reported the unmasking of a plot by certain "French Negroes" in Nassau to burn the town, free the French prisoners of war, and kill all the white inhabitants. What happened to the plotters was not recorded, but the militia was placed on permanent alert, and shortly afterward the imposition of a prohibitive duty virtually ended the further importation of French slaves.[26]

Such alarms were clearly behind some of the new legislation put forward by the reformed assembly between 1795 and 1797: the tightening of the militia system and police regulations, the building of a new jail and workhouse, and the Deficiency Law, which attempted to maintain a safe proportion of whites to blacks, especially in the Out Islands.[27] The chief outcome, both of the immediate threat of revolutionary infection and of the need seen to disarm the metropolitan liberals of the Wilberforce school, was, however, the first Consolidated Slave Act for the Bahamas, which passed into law on May 11, 1797.

The first third of the new law—nearly half the clauses—ostensibly concerned the slaves' protection, though very few provisions added anything to what was claimed to be normal practice, except to specify fines for infractions. Masters were to provide twenty-one pints of flour, seven quarts of rice, or fifty-six pounds of potatoes each week for every slave over ten years of age, with half as much for those under ten. Slaves were also to be allotted sufficient land on which to grow additional ground provisions. The custom of allowing them Sunday free was not made law, though Christmas Day and the two following working days were decreed a holiday. Each slave was to receive two suits of clothing a year.[28]

Strangely in a colony where cruelty toward slaves was said to be virtually nonexistent, no less than six clauses dealt with excessive punishments by masters. No maiming punishments were allowed, and no more than twenty lashes at any one time, unless in the presence of the workhouse superintendent. The use of iron collars and chains was outlawed, except in cases "of strict necessity." The malicious killing of a slave remained a capital crime, and a master could be fined as much as one hundred pounds for willful mutilation. Even more remarkably (though it doubtless remained a dead letter), the vestry in each parish was to set up a "council of protection" to inquire into cases of cruelty. This body could even decree that a slave victim be made free, and the guilty master could be forced to pay maintenance of ten pounds a year for the rest of the slave's life.[29]

It remained the duty of masters to maintain their sick, maimed, or elderly slaves, but the parishes were responsible for masterless slaves. The practice of consigning slaves to the workhouse for trivial offenses was discouraged by the levying of an initial fee of three shillings plus a shilling a day, payable by the master to the workhouse keeper for each slave sent. The encouragement to masters to have their slaves instructed in the Christian religion, and "sensible" slaves baptized, was revived, though without any enforcement. There were no provisions encouraging masters to promote marriage among their slaves and nothing directly to encourage a healthier birthrate. But for the first time, masters were to send in to the colonial secretary on January 1 each year a list of all births and deaths among their slaves, with a penalty of fifty pounds for noncompliance.[30]

Masters could still impose limited corporal punishment in the "rightful correction" of their slaves, and magistrates could order summary punishment for minor offenses. More serious cases, though, were dealt with by a reconstituted slave court, consisting of two justices of the peace and five free jurors, meeting for five days four times a year, beginning on the first Thursdays of January, May, July, and October. The court was officially charged with looking after the slaves' interests, but it is unlikely that in practice the removal of three lay white freeholders from the bench served the slaves any better, for the two justices were, almost inevitably, members of exactly the same class. When slaves were charged with capital crimes they were to have a five-man jury, though since all jurymen were bound to be whites, this was a merely nominal concession.[31]

The final two-thirds of the 1797 law, moreover, made little or no pretense to liberalization. The majority of the clauses overall dealt with the policing and punishment of the slaves, imposing regulations and penalties that were at least as severe as those previously enacted. The legislators were clearly still obsessed with the fear of conspiracy and the threat of violence. Slaves were forbidden, on pain of fifty lashes, to carry guns, lances, or cutlasses, even for hunting, unless accompanied by a white or with a ticket from their master. They were to be severely whipped for concealing "any Fire arms Gunpowder Sluggs or Ball." Slaves were to suffer death, or at the very least transportation, for striking a white, unless they were defending their master at his orders. Death was also the penalty for any slave who mixed a poison which resulted in the death of a white.[32]

The largest number of clauses dealt with the problems of controlling the slaves' movements, particularly their tendency to run away. All slaves absent from their homes had to have tickets from their owners, unless they were collecting firewood, rounding up stock, or carrying produce to market. All slaves absent more than ten days or found more than eight miles from their homes without a ticket were deemed runaways, could be apprehended by any freeman, and were severely punished. Slaves who were absent up to six months were punished by whipping and terms in the workhouse, but those absent for more than six months (and presumably "spoiled" as slaves) were subject to transportation. Generous rewards were paid for capturing and returning runaways, and severe penalties decreed for harboring, aiding, or employing them. Helping slaves to escape by boat was regarded as especially heinous, being itself punished by transportation. Slave masters were compensated for runaways who were not returned, but only if they had properly advertised their disappearance within fourteen days. The workhouse superintendent was entitled to a payment of one shilling and sixpence a day for each slave's food and medicine but was bound regularly to advertise all unclaimed slaves. Slaves not claimed within a year were to be sold for the benefit of the public treasury.[33]

Slaves, being regarded as property themselves—almost nonpersons—could hardly be expected to regard either the property of the master class or its sense of propriety as sacrosanct. At the same time, slaves were constantly exposing as a legal fiction the concept that, as property, they could neither own property nor earn money for themselves. In the 1797 act the Bahamian slaveowners were therefore as concerned with defending their property against their slaves as they were with preventing slaves' stepping out of line. Cattle stealing by slaves was decreed a capital crime, but even the possession by slaves of food for which they could not give an adequate explanation (not just beef, veal, or mutton, but also the flesh of "horse, mule or donkey") was severely punished. By inference, slaves could trade in provisions and hire themselves out, with their masters' permission and ostensibly for their masters' benefit.

But they were forbidden absolutely to trade in dry goods and could not sell liquor without special permission. Besides, slaves were forbidden to drink liquor after 8 P.M., to play at dice, or to engage in gambling. Slave drunkenness was harshly punished.[34]

The final purpose of the 1797 act, as of all such laws, was to divide the black community against itself. Besides being punished for transgressions against the masters' code, slaves were rewarded for fulfilling the masters' concept of their duty. Slaves who returned runaways were rewarded in the same manner as free blacks. And those who served against rebel slaves were not only to be paid five pounds for each rebel killed and ten pounds for each captive, but were to be awarded "a Blue Cloth Coat with a red Cross on the right Shoulder." The same divisive purpose (as well as the logical nonsense or injustice of decreeing differential penalties for different classes and races) was shown in the extraordinary penalties ordained for those freedmen who aligned themselves with the slaves. For example, any "Free Negro Mulatto or Indian" who concealed a runaway or forged a ticket of leave was liable to lose his freedom and be transported, as well as any other punishment the court decreed, "short of life or limb." Freedmen aiding runaways to escape by boat not only were to suffer transportation but were threatened with death if they returned to the Bahamas.[35]

Lieutenant Governor John Forbes, who took over from Lord Dunmore at the end of 1796, was sufficiently confident of improved security to recommend early in 1797 that the larger islands still uninhabited should be settled by refugee French planters and their slaves: sixty families on Inagua, fifty on Andros, and forty on Acklin's. He was candid enough to mention, though, that many planters might still resist the introduction of more French blacks.[36] That this reluctance was not ill founded was shown when, just three months after the passage of the Consolidated Slave Act of 1797, President Robert Hunt (who had succeeded as acting governor when Forbes succumbed to yellow fever) announced the discovery of a second, and more serious, plot among French blacks in Nassau.

On August 21, 1797, a slave called Francis Montell informed two militia officers of a plan by certain "French Negroes from captured ships" to take advantage of an epidemic of fever among the garrison troops of the Thirty-second Regiment and the militia, to kill their guards at Fort Charlotte, seize weapons from the ordnance store, and set fire to the town, before sailing off in a captured ship. Francis Montell, with others, had been approached for help, on a promise that coconspirators would be put "in the same situation the black people were in at the Cape" (that is, at Cap François in Haiti), but he had agreed only in order to act as a spy. At a meeting in the black quarter, only twenty of the expected seventy to eighty conspirators had appeared, so the plan was postponed to the following day, giving Montell the chance to raise the alarm.

On Montell's information Robert Hunt doubled the guard on the fort, ordered two gunboats to cover the ordnance stores, and sent patrols into the black quarters. Eight alleged conspirators (including a woman) were arrested in a house rented to "a Mulatto Fidler called Stephen . . . in the Western part of town"; they had been found sitting round a table with a candle on it, in possession of a musket, a sword, a fuse, and a powder horn. After interrogation and trial, five of the accused were sentenced to death and three to transportation, though none had confessed to the plot. Baptiste Perpall, Baptiste Tucker, and Police Edgecumbe were hanged the following day, and Tom Bethune and Tom Lockhart one week later. Presumably, Francis Montell was rewarded with money and a blue cloth coat, as provided for in the recent act.[37]

Despite the equivocal names of those executed and the absence of a detailed confession, President Hunt reported on September 7 that the plot was entirely limited to the French blacks. The mass of the English-speaking slaves were said to be loyal, or at least quiescent.[38] Though to us the occurrence of the plot so soon after the passing of the 1797 act suggests that it was caused at least in part by the tightening of the cords binding the slaves, for the white regime the failure of the plot clearly demonstrated the effectiveness of the act—especially, perhaps, the clauses enrolling the blacks in their own suppression.

~ 14 ~

The Decline of Cotton
and Formal Slavery, 1800–1834

WHEN DANIEL MCKINNEN TRAVERSED the southern Bahamas in
1802, on his way back to England from the West Indies during the
eighteen-month interlude in the last French war, he found cotton plantations reverting to bush or a less intensive form of agriculture, and
poor white Out Islanders ("Conchs") returning to casual salt raking, log-
cutting, and "racking." On Long Island alone "eight or ten plantations
were entirely quitted and thirteen others partially given up" since 1795.
Nassau, on the other hand, McKinnen found a lively, interesting, and
handsome colonial town, "as well built as any I saw in the West Indies."
Peace had led to a revival of trade with Cuba, the recent renewal of land
grants had enlivened the dealings in real estate, and the arrival of several
African cargoes added to the normal turnover in slaves. Conditioned by
a proplanter viewpoint and knowledge of the social turmoil which two
decades of war had brought to the Caribbean, McKinnen found the Nassau ruling class genteel and self-confident, and the black majority of the
population healthy, quiescent, and seemingly content.[1]

McKinnen's account was used by Bryan Edwards as an appendix to
the third edition of his West Indian history to counter the abolitionists'
negative view of the British slave colonies.[2] But it was an accurate enough
description of Bahamian conditions, which, at least for Nassau and the
ruling class, actually continued to improve for another decade. This was
despite—even because of—the renewal of war against France in 1803.
Napoleon's surrender of Haiti to the blacks and Louisiana to the Americans removed the threat to the southern Bahamas and opened up new
avenues of trade through Nassau. But most important, the naval hegemony won by Britain at Trafalgar (1805) was the prelude to a phase of
unprecedented activity for the Nassau vice-admiralty court. In less than
a dozen years, 503 vessels, worth millions of pounds, were condemned

in Nassau. More than half of these were adjudicated during the two years of the war with the United States (1812–14)—a bonanza that more than offset the brief loss of American trade and the unrealized threat of an American invasion.[3]

The wartime tide of prosperity, which persuaded many failed planters to involve themselves in business as well as privateering, further united the Bahamian oligarchy and cemented its power. This entrenchment was symbolized by the completion of Nassau's architectural transformation, begun by the Loyalists nearly thirty years earlier.

Broadly speaking, the change was from a town built almost entirely of wood, using shipbuilding skills and features, to one in which the architecture married the technologies of wood and cut stone. As befitted a mercantile center, many of the first stone buildings were warehouses fronting the harbor, constructed of squared stone blocks, with internal timber frames. Many of the shops on Bay Street and in the center of town were similarly built but were houses too, with covered arcades on wooden pillars on the ground floor at the front, surmounted by jalousied galleries on the second (or even third) stories. All roofs in town were cedar shingled, often long in pitch, with an attic story and dormer windows.

All-wood houses—often of unpainted timber bleached gray by the sun—predominated in Nassau until early in the twentieth century. But the characteristic "Loyalist" townhouse for substantial inhabitants was a stone shell encased, and made light and airy, by elegant woodwork: a wooden piazza gallery approached by central stone stairs, with an upper gallery above it, partially enclosed with louvered shutters. Depending on the location of the house, these galleries might be only at the front, at front and back, on three sides, or even (if the house was on a large lot on the top of the ridge) running all round the house. The flat stonework of the finest houses was plastered, sometimes in pastel shades of blue, green, or yellow, with the distinctive stonework coigns picked out in white. The inner windows had Nassau's first glass panes, and the main doorways were often framed by elegant pilasters and porticos, fashioned in wood or plaster.

This "Loyalist" style of domestic architecture lasted for at least a century, some of the most impressive and lasting examples—such as Greycliff, Jacaranda, and Cascadilla—being built between 1825 and 1850. But the most notable changes in Nassau's appearance were the new public buildings completed between 1799 and 1811. The first after the Vendue House was the new jail, a surprisingly elegant octagonal building (since the 1870s housing the Nassau public library and museum), said to have been modeled after the Old Powder Magazine at Williamsburg, Virginia. The two-story building, containing only twelve tiny cells, was crowned by an eight-sided lantern and cupola (now surrounded by a covered gallery), which contained the bell used to summon the members to the House of Assembly or raise a public alarm.

The most handsome of all Loyalist buildings was Nassau's second parish church, St. Matthew's, designed by the versatile Joseph Eve and built with a grant from the House of Assembly to serve the large number of white families who now lived on Nassau's eastern outskirts. Consecrated in July 1802, St. Matthew's (as perhaps befitted a church voted for by an alliance of old and new inhabitants) was a curious but aesthetically successful mixture of Neoclassical style and Gothic proportions. The nave and side aisles were contained under a single roof but with separate barrel vaulting, supported on imposing Corinthian columns. The chancel, at the proper eastern end, was enclosed in a small apse, with excellent windows, while the baptistry and west door stood beneath an elegant small octagonal tower, much like the lantern of the jail, though surmounted not by a metalled cupola but (from 1816) by a shingled steeple. As in all Anglican churches, the seating arrangements carefully reflected the society which St. Matthew's served. The most substantial parishioners rented the high-backed pews at front center, the poorer whites occupied the rest of the nave and side aisles, and blacks sat in a special upstairs gallery. Since Christchurch was rebuilt in the 1840s, St. Matthew's is now Nassau's oldest church building, its churchyard and adjacent public park containing the remains of many Loyalists and some even earlier tombstones transferred from Nassau's first burial place near the center of town.[4]

This period also saw the building of a suitably imposing new Government House. The house and gardens on Mount Fitzwilliam which had been rented by successive governors since 1737 were at last purchased between 1798 and 1802, and a completely new house was constructed between 1803 and 1806. This building, not remodeled until almost blown away by the hurricane of 1929, was for long the largest, if not the most handsome, in Nassau. It was a two-story edifice having a frontage of nearly a hundred feet, with an upper gallery supported on ten tall columns. From here the governor could survey the whole of Nassau and much of New Providence, proudly display the Union Jack on its fifty-foot pole, and march his red-coated guard from the garrison to and fro for all the inhabitants to see. To approach the governor, though, meant a climb from George Street up a flight of almost fifty steps—in the middle of which Governor Carmichael Smyth was to erect the famous statue of Christopher Columbus in 1830.

Most important of all architectural changes, however, and in symbolic counterpoint to the creation of the new Government House at the head of the George Street axis, was the erection of a new complex of government buildings some four hundred yards to the east. The site had been selected as early as 1790 and was purchased a few years later from John Brown, an old inhabitant and former president of the council. It consisted of four acres with a frontage of one hundred yards on Bay Street and the waterfront, running back two hundred yards to the foot of the ridge on Shirley Street. It was on the back of this spacious lot that the jail had been built in 1799. Four years later were laid the foundations of a trio of large buildings, forming three sides of a square open to Bay Street and the harbor, on a design said to be based on Governor Tryon's winged palace at New Bern, North Carolina, once called "the most beautiful building in Colonial America."[5] The two side buildings were completed in 1805. That on the east contained the treasury and the offices of colonial secretary and registrar general. Downstairs in the western building were the offices of surveyor general and provost marshal, while the upper floor became the permanent home of the House of Assembly. The splendidly porticoed central building, not finished until 1816, came to house the post office, as well as the general court and the governor's council.

Thus, this compact group of buildings (to which were later added a separate supreme court building and the main police station) became the focus—and for a century was almost the circumference—of the colony's government. It neatly concentrated the functions of making the laws and applying them through the police and courts, raising taxation and spending the revenue, distributing land, and all the ordinary business of running the colony. The concentration of government functions also symbolized the concentration of power in the hands of a unified ruling class, the completion of a process of socioeconomic reshuffling spread over thirty years. It was therefore fitting that in the most imposing of this range of new buildings—the Council Chamber and its anterooms—were also held annual balls at Christmas and New Year's, which rivaled those at Government House and were the glittering highlights of the social season of the new ruling class.

The establishment of the Bahamian oligarchy, however, was not the prelude to an era of social and political concord, any more than of economic success. The final ending of the French wars in 1815 and the gradual triumph of free trade and laissez-faire principles in the metropolis were the antecedents to an era of colossal, if largely informal, imperial expansion. Yet for one of Britain's poorest colonial possessions these changes brought few benefits, many detriments, and much disturbance. While the prevailing imperial theory expected colonies to be economically self-sufficient, the new liberal ideology in regard to slavery permitted greater interference in the affairs of colonies in which previous conditions had created powerful local oligarchies. Thus, the complete collapse of the Bahamian plantation economy (along with a decline in mercantile activity) was accompanied by increasing tension and paranoia among the Bahamian ruling class, and increasing conflict with the colonial governor, as the imperial government moved inexorably through a phase of "ameliorating" slave conditions toward slave emancipation.

The first major expression of imperial interference in the slave system of the plantation colonies was the abolition of the slave trade from Africa, directly imposed on the Crown colonies in 1805 and on the rest of the British Empire in 1807. This did not seriously affect the Bahamas, since the decline of plantations and steady natural increase of the slave population had long made the importation of African recruits unnecessary. The Bahamian legislators, like those of Bermuda and Barbados (also colonies in which slaves were increasing naturally), were even inclined to garner virtue by approving of the abolition of the African trade—though their real motives included the fear that African imports would further depress internal slave prices and disturb the social situation.

Of rather more direct interest to the Bahamian slaveowners were the subsequent measures by the British government to restrict the movement and sale of slaves between colonies, which seemed to threaten both the custom of shifting slaves freely among the islands of the Bahamian archipelago and the important continuing internal market in slaves, and also the increasing tendency, initiated as early as 1811, to dump on the Bahamas Africans seized from foreign or illegal British slave-trading vessels.[6] While the French war continued, though, these matters were of less concern to the Bahamian whites than the problems involved in the British government's decision to garrison Nassau with black troops from the British West India regiments—a practice that began in 1801 and was to continue until 1891.

Since the beginning of the French war, the free colored militia had been reactivated and formed an essential component of Nassau's defenses. Their general decorum, as well as their indispensability, had reassured the nervous whites. But the arrival of 272 black troops from the Fifth and Sixth West India regiments in May 1801, while Britain and France were at peace, led to an explosion of complaints. From 1795 many black units—including, in due course, no less than twelve regular West India regiments—had been formed to fight the white man's war in the Caribbean. These troops, though mainly consisting of slaves levied from the plantations or bought directly from Africa, had proved invaluable, often displaying great hardihood on campaign and gallantry in battle. Despite this, they were regarded as a temporary expedient (and expendable) by the West Indian whites, who vehemently resisted their being permanently garrisoned upon them.[7] Predictably, the Bahamian whites, who had never yet seen black regular troops and were already paranoid about the dangers from "French Negroes," were at least equally incensed.

"It is not easy," wrote Acting Governor Robert Hunt on May 9, 1801, "to conceive a more general panic than the appearance of these Detachments has excited . . . the agitation of the public mind could not have been greater had Toussaint himself have come with all his force." Hunt had been presented with a petition against the black troops, signed by "almost everyone" in Nassau. The colony had recently been flooded with French blacks "as well as slaves from other countries," who were "of the very worst description . . . cunning and artful." The petitioners feared that if the foreign slaves joined with the black troops, "the situation of these Islands would be truly alarming." At the very least, many planters would leave the Bahamas with their slaves for greater security. The War Office responded that it would reduce the number of black troops and try to keep up the proportion of white troops in the garrison. In April 1803, however, Governor Halkett almost hysterically complained of the arrival of a troopship carrying 270 black reinforcements. The black troops already in the garrison, he claimed, were partly responsible for the recent desertion to the United States of several planters with six hundred slaves, and these new arrivals threatened "the very existence of this little Colony." He therefore intended to prevent them from landing.[8]

In October 1803 Governor Halkett reported thankfully the removal of almost all the black troops from Nassau. But within a few weeks, with the renewal of war with France, he was almost comically to change his tune. The removal of the black troops, coupled with an epidemic of fever among the whites, he complained, had left the Bahamas almost defenseless. Halkett and the white inhabitants were therefore relieved when fresh detachments were sent to Nassau from Jamaica.[9]

Despite occasional alarms, the colony remained safe from foreign attack for the rest of the war, but the garrison continued to be a perennial source of friction and concern, even after peace returned. While white troops formed a part of the garrison, brawls occurred between the soldiers themselves, which was not surprising considering the discriminatory way in which the blacks were treated. For example, Major Darling, senior officer of the detachment of the Ninety-ninth Regiment, complained to the governor in July 1806 that his own troops were forced to share the hospital at Fort Charlotte with the blacks, though it was a building "unfit for Europeans to inhabit."[10] The white soldiers were unpopular enough with the local inhabitants, who complained about their arrogant and aggressive behavior and, getting no satisfaction from the military authorities, sometimes proceeded against them in civil court. But it was the black troops who provoked most trouble, particularly once their officers gave them permission to wear side arms in town "and repel any Insult that might be Offered to them by the Inhabitants."[11]

Governor Cameron forwarded many complaints from white inhabitants early in 1807, adding his own unfavorable comments on the behavior of the black soldiers. To his surprise, he received a severe reprimand from Downing Street. This expressed extreme displeasure at the conflict between black troops and white locals and claimed that the accounts given by governor, assembly, and townsfolk alike were prejudicial and one-sided. They should remember that the soldiers of the Second West India Regiment had been sent to Nassau for its protection, and should behave in a more enlightened manner and show more respect to the king's troops, "whatever may be their description or colour."[12]

This rap over the knuckles did not quell the complaints, though it modified them. Henceforward, the whites stressed the ways in which, to their mind, the presence of the black troops was detrimental to the society at large. In September 1808, for example, a report was forwarded from the chief constable, J. H. Smith, complaining of a serious affray between the black troops and some town slaves. On the morning of August 29 the constable saw a black soldier of the Seventh West India Regiment in a fight outside the Vendue House with a slave belonging to a Mr. Begbie. When Smith attempted to separate the two, the soldier drew his bayonet but was disarmed by a crowd of black bystanders. Smith then attempted to take the two fighters into custody, but before he reached the police station a body of black troops appeared, drew their weapons, and released their fellow soldier by force. This was bad enough, but when Constable Smith reported the incident to Major Naismyth, the commander of the detachment at Fort Charlotte, the officer was said to have retorted: "Oh, the Honourable Mr. Begbie's Negro! The

Scoundrel I suppose insulted the Soldier. The Soldiers have my Orders to go to town with side arms, and to run the Bayonet hilt home into every buggering Inhabitant offering to offend or insult them." [13]

Apparently nothing came of this episode, and such incidents became fewer as the black troops became more integrated with the local black community. As the war lingered on without their being relieved or adequately supplied, the black troops also seem to have become demoralized, with their officers less willing to take their side against the local whites. Even their poor health conditions were used as an argument against them. In May 1815, for example, Governor Cameron wrote of "a very alarming mortality" that was raging through the black troops in the garrison, carrying off twenty men in a week, though it was not yet affecting either the white officers or the townspeople. The medical officer admitted that the disease was probably due to the unhealthy location of the black barracks, but because of the fear of contagion Cameron had ordered that all dead soldiers be buried on deserted Silver Cay rather than in the garrison cemetery, which was dangerously close to town. [14]

Similarly, once the war was over, Governor Cameron used the justified complaints of the black troops about their deficient supplies to argue for their removal from Nassau. The discontent, he argued in January 1816, should be considered in the light of their long term of duty, but also their "intimacy with the black population, particularly with the indentured Africans" landed from captured slave ships. Apart from having much practical freedom, many of the black soldiers were themselves native Africans, and all such had an aura of power and prestige among the black community as a whole. This was especially dangerous in the light of the growing unrest in the colony occasioned by the renewed activities of the metropolitan abolitionists and the campaign for slave registration, of which the soldiers were fully aware. Far from being a bulwark for the defense of the colony, the black troops might be a Trojan horse within the gates. [15]

The black soldiers of the West India regiments were rotated but not removed. They remained in Nassau a further seventy-five years, a picturesque feature for tourists in their zouave uniforms. But they were never allowed to stay long enough to become fully integrated with the local blacks, and the local whites never entirely trusted or adequately appreciated them. This was despite behavior that was almost invariably correct and loyal throughout the periods of greatest social stress—allowing them to be regarded, and sometimes used, as the military backup arm for the civilian police. Indeed, the black peacetime garrison of Nassau down to 1891 was the first of several manifestations in the Bahamas of a tactic of control used throughout the history of the British Empire: the employment of a policing force itself drawn from the subject classes but recruited in distant parts.

After the defeat of Napoleon, the British government came increasingly under the influence of the antislavery lobby. Consequently, the universal abolition of the slave trade became a major concern for British diplomacy, and the condition of British slaves the predominant issue in imperial policy. Prompted by a Colonial Office infiltrated by the humanitarians, the secretary of state gave more positive instructions to colonial governors and even began to appoint governors who were personally opposed to slavery. In the Bahamas case this meant that even the proslavery Cameron came into conflict with the assembly toward the end of his long tenure (1804–20), his conciliatory successor, Grant (1820–29), was hard put to keep the peace, and the climax was reached during the regime of the liberal and uncompromising Carmichael Smyth (1829–35), who left the Bahamas on the eve of slave emancipation. For their part, the Bahamian oligarchy—like their West Indian counterparts—organized an increasingly desperate rearguard action, standing on two principles that they regarded as essential: their dearly won rights to self-legislation and their property rights in their slaves.

The conflict was first joined over the general matter of slave registration, but it gained intensity from a series of specific issues involving Attorney General William Wylly. Slave registration was intended both to enable a statistical inquiry into the demographic condition of West Indian slaves and as a prelude for measures to prevent illicit transfers of slaves. Apart from the general question of imperial interference, it was of special concern to Bahamian slaveowners because they feared restrictions on slave mariners and on the transfer of slaves from island to island within the Bahamas, as well as to other territories. Slave registration had been imposed on the Crown colonies of Trinidad, British Guiana, and St. Lucia in 1812, an act to create an imperial slave registry had been passed in 1815, and most self-legislating colonies in the West Indies had been pressured to pass their own slave-registration acts by 1817. But the Bahamian legislators were able to resist the introduction of an effective system of slave registration until 1822, being helped in their procrastination by the conflict and confusion over what became known as the Wylly case.

William Wylly had changed from being the most outspoken opponent of the governor to a zealous upholder of imperial policy through having become one of the most prominent Bahamian converts to Methodism and a paternalistic humanitarian with respect to the slaves. White Methodist missionaries had been active in the Bahamas since 1799 and were known to proselytize the slaves. But they were careful not to assert that the conversion of slaves implied any change in the social order, let alone challenge the institution of slavery itself.[16] For Wylly, however, slavery could now be justified only if it were reformed, and slaves themselves brought within the Christian community. Accordingly, in 1815 he published for the slaves on his New Providence estates a set of regulations which included more generous allotments than those provided by law, inducements and penalties to promote marriage and family life, and provision for baptism, regular church services, and Sunday schooling.[17]

Even such blatant paternalism was anathema for the majority of Bahamian slaveowners, who were therefore disposed to see Wylly as an agent of an abolitionist conspiracy in all his official actions. The initial cause of disruption was the case of a slave called Sue, brought to the Bahamas from Georgia in 1809 and left there. In 1815 Sue's master returned to the Bahamas with a male slave called Sandy, who promptly fathered a child with Sue. The master then attempted to return to Georgia with all three slaves, but Sue and Sandy absconded with their child. When they were recaptured and brought before the slave court, Wylly brought a charge of illegal importation against the slaves' owner and obtained a judgment that while Sandy and the child might be carried away to Georgia, Sue must stay.[18] This decision ran counter to the slaveowners' contention that they had an absolute power to transfer their slaves at will.

In a similar case in the same year, Wylly ordered the collector of customs (who happened to be Alexander Murray, the son of Wylly's old antagonist the earl of Dunmore) to seize four blacks who were said to have run away from East Florida and to be in danger of re-enslavement. These blacks—Boatswain, his wife, Rose, and their two children—were owned by one Perpall, whose brother John, a Nassau resident, intended to claim them. Wylly, as attorney general, gave his opinion that if Perpall was successful it would amount to the illegal importation of slaves under the Abolition Act of 1807. In support of his case he had evidence that the blacks had in fact been shipped involuntarily and brought to shore by the Perpalls' agent. For his part, Perpall pointed out that if the slaves were declared free, it would provide a dangerous precedent and an inducement for foreign slaves to take flight to the Bahamas in order to obtain their freedom. This argument was telling but not sufficient to make Wylly give up the case. Instead, to the anger of Bahamian slaveowners, he decided that it should be heard by the High Court of Admiralty in London, rather than the vice-admiralty court in Nassau.[19]

Even more inflammatory were Attorney General Wylly's actions in bringing charges against owners and overseers for mistreatment of slaves, particularly since he singled out two of the owners with the largest slave holdings. As Wylly himself noted in 1815, it was very easy to violate the protective clauses of the 1797 act without detection, and very few persons had ever been prosecuted for mistreating slaves. An 1812 report listed a mere fourteen charges brought between 1800 and 1811, with only one person, a free colored, actually imprisoned. Five of those charged were found guilty and fined; the rest, all whites, were acquitted.[20] It was therefore a bold move when in 1816 Wylly brought charges against James Moss, who owned one thousand slaves in all, for persistently undersupplying the forty-two slaves on Perseverance Estate, Crooked Island. Evidence was brought forward that Moss rarely provided more than half the provisions required by the 1797 law and was in the habit of withholding a proportion when his slaves did not work on Saturdays. Moss, however, claimed that his slaves were so well supplied that they often sold some of the issued food back to him and so underworked that they often finished their tasks before midday. When other planters also testified that Moss was a benevolent master, giving his slaves more privileges than they did for their own, Moss was acquitted.[21] Wylly was rather more successful when he prosecuted Richard Evans, the overseer of Burton Williams's Eleuthera estate, for gross cruelty toward a slave called Dick. Evans had ordered the slave bound to a ladder in the broiling sun and whipped for three hours by two slaves, including Dick's son. He then had bird peppers rubbed into Dick's wounds, eyes, and fundament. Evans was found guilty, sentenced to eighteen months in jail, and fined forty pounds, despite the testimony of his employer that he was a humane man whose only fault was that he drank to excess.[22]

Clearly, William Wylly and the majority of Bahamian slaveowners were headed for a general confrontation. The collision occurred when the attorney general appeared before an assembly committee convened to discuss the registration bill—or rather, to procure evidence that a registration act was not necessary for the Bahamas. In testimony Wylly quoted statements that he had made in a letter addressed to the abolitionist African Institution, which the committee regarded as irrelevant and dangerous, if not erroneous. These included opinions that the black people in the Bahamas were inadequately protected in criminal cases because they were not able to give evidence, and that no person "with one drop of black blood" could testify against a white person.[23] Though Wylly moderated his stance and denied that he had actually sent off the offending letter, the assembly was incensed when similar statements were circulated in London.

On January 22, 1817, the Speaker issued a warrant for Wylly's arrest with an order to appear before the bar of the house, for "injuriously and scandalously" misrepresenting the actions of the assembly before the African Institution. When the sergeant-at-arms, Chisholm, appeared at the gate of Clifton Estate, he was denied entry by Wylly's slaves, who were carrying their cutlasses and birding guns. The following morning Wylly went voluntarily to town, but on finding that he was subject to a second warrant committing him to the common jail, he returned to Clifton. On January 25 he was summoned by Governor Cameron to explain his actions, but as soon as he reached Government House he was arrested by Chisholm and the provost marshal. Immediately, the chief justice drew up a writ of habeas corpus and Wylly was released on bail, only to be faced by a third warrant for his arrest a few days later. At this the exasperated governor declared the writs *ultra vires*, dissolved the assembly, and suspended the provost marshal. Four days later, Wylly was accosted and horsewhipped on Bay Street by a member of the house.[24]

The Wylly case dragged on for many more months, with the courts and the assembly at loggerheads over the question of privilege. George Chalmers, the colonial agent, resolutely supported the assembly's cause but was overruled by a Colonial Office angry over the assembly's foot-dragging over slave registration. A satisfactory registration act did not become law until after Governor Cameron retired and Acting Governor Munnings (the chief justice who had released Wylly in 1817) had again been forced to dissolve the assembly. The animus against Wylly lasted even longer, dogging him until he left the Bahamas on appointment as chief justice of St. Vincent in 1822.[25]

At least some Bahamian slaveowners, though, had reason to be grateful for the Wylly case. Thanks to the legal distractions and delay, a minimum of twenty-three hundred Bahamian slaves, some 20 percent, were transferred to more profitable territories before an efficient registration system could disclose the traffic and the imperial government move to stop it.[26] The most promising destination was nearby Cuba, with its fertile underdeveloped soils. Quite a few Bahamian planters wished to transfer there but were frustrated by the absolute ban on shipping plantation slaves to foreign colonies. There was, however, a loophole. The laws against slave trading did allow a master to carry two slave domestics with him while traveling, and the Bahamian customs officers interpreted this as allowing any free person to leave the colony with any two slaves. As Governor Grant reported to Secretary of State Bathurst in August 1821, some planters were persuading their friends to take pairs of slaves to Cuba for them or even hiring free coloreds for the purpose. In theory, there was nothing to stop would-be migrants from manumitting a third of their slaves as ostensible apprentices, to legitimize the transportation of the remaining two-thirds. In such ways, if not by outright smuggling, an Exuma planter, William Forbes, had already transferred at least twenty-nine of his slaves and could not be extradited for any offense.[27]

Because of the clandestine nature of the trade, it cannot be known with any certainty how many Bahamian slaves were carried to Cuba and other foreign colonies, but it was probably no more than 200 in all.[28] By far the largest number of transferred slaves were carried to other British colonies. This was then quite legitimate as long as the slaves were accompanying their owner to set up a new plantation. This process, though, was open to finagling, and quite the biggest transfer broker was James Moss, who seems to have built up his vast slave holding very largely with the aim of arranging its profitable transportation elsewhere. In 1818 Moss was given permission to carry up to 1,000 slaves to the developing sugar colony of Demerara, and before his death in 1824 he had actually managed to ship out 823—most to Demerara, but at least 128 to Jamaica. Burton Williams, the second target of William Wylly in 1816, was scarcely less active in the transfer business. In five cargoes between 1821 and 1823 Williams shipped off 336 of his slaves to Trinidad, where he had bought land to set up sugar plantations for himself and his four sons.[29]

Altogether, there were official records of 2,229 Bahamian slaves' being transferred to other British colonies between 1816 and 1823. Fewer than half of these slaves (939) were destined for the labor-hungry sugar colonies of Demerara and Trinidad, which, being Crown colonies, offered at least nominal Colonial Office supervision over working conditions. A surprising number (632) were taken to the underdeveloped but far less promising self-legislating colonies of St. Vincent and Grenada. But the most remarkable, and reprehensible, fact was that the largest single total (649) were transported to Jamaica, where, since the rapid decline of the sugar industry, there was, strictly speaking, no labor shortage at all. Wherever they went, the victims of this minidiaspora were in for traumatic changes and generally far harsher conditions. Moreover, their transfer, though it had only a marginal influence on the colonies

Table 4
Slaves Transferred from the Bahamas to Other British Colonies, 1816–23

Colony	1816	1817	1818	1819	1820	1821	1822	1823	Total
Jamaica									
Males	50	57	37	58	0	28	99	—	328
Females	45	48	34	56	1	16	121	—	321
St. Vincent									
Males	—	280	3	—	—	2	—	—	285
Females	—	244	11	—	—	3	—	—	258
Trinidad									
Males	—	—	59	18	—	76	15	62	230
Females	—	—	77	14	—	106	20	61	278
Demerara									
Males	—	—	—	—	—	49	49	116	214
Females	—	—	—	—	—	53	51	113	217
Grenada									
Males	—	23	18	—	—	—	—	—	41
Females	—	35	13	—	—	—	—	—	48
Bermuda									
Males	—	—	5	—	—	—	—	—	5
Females	—	—	—	—	—	—	—	—	—
Antigua									
Males	—	—	2	—	—	—	—	—	2
Females	—	—	1	—	—	—	—	—	1
Barbados									
Males	—	—	1	—	—	—	—	—	1
Females	—	—	—	—	—	—	—	—	—
Total males	50	360	124	76	0	155	163	178	1,106
Total females	45	327	136	70	1	178	192	174	1,123
Total Slaves	95	687	260	146	1	333	355	352	2,229

Source: C.O. 23/72, 25, and 23/75, 50–52.

Note: Figures are those given in official records; there were almost certainly unofficial transfers as well.

of destination, had a drastic, if localized, impact upon the Bahamas and its population. Overall, the slave population of the Bahamas suffered its first decline ever, probably falling from over 12,000 in 1815, to less than 11,000 a decade later.[30] Several islands, particularly Crooked Island, Acklin's, Watling's, and the Caicos Islands, were so depopulated that all chances of a true plantation economy were lost. A far worse effect was that although the slaves were generally transferred with their immediate kin, many slave communities and extended families, painfully constructed over the previous decades, were suddenly broken apart.

The ascendancy of the Evangelical abolitionist James Stephen at the Colonial Office, the lobbying activities of the newly formed Anti-Slavery Society, and the tenure of the forthright Lord Bathurst as secretary of state meant that much more rigid controls were applied on the British slave colonies after 1823. After the first registration returns and searching inquiries into transfer practices, the intercolonial trade in slaves was almost completely halted between 1824 and 1826. In the latter year, restrictions were also placed upon the movement of slaves between the Bahamian islands.[31] The Tory Bathurst and his Whig successor, Goderich, also sent out an escalating series of directives on slave amelioration, in the form of instructions to the Crown colonies and arm-twisting recommendations to the self-legislating colonies. Coming at the same time that the remaining protective duties on colonial produce were being removed, these were seen by the West India interest as part of a concerted attack, calling for equally well-coordinated resistance.

Though the Bahamas could no longer aspire to be a true plantation colony, the Bahamian legislators showed at least as much vigor and ingenuity as those of Jamaica and Barbados in defending their socioeconomic system. Like the West Indian plantocrats, their tactics were three-pronged. Through their tireless colonial agent and the West India Committee of Merchants and Planters, they supported the campaign of counterpropaganda against the abolitionists and lobbied as best they could at Westminster. In these activities their purpose was, first, to paint their slave system in the most favorable possible light; second, to delay the amelioration and emancipation programs as much as possible; and finally, once slave emancipation was only a matter of time, to argue that there should be a transitional phase of "apprenticeship" between slavery and full freedom, and that slaveowners should be generously compensated. On the home front, the Bahamas assembly spent more and more time in stalling and modifying the imperial directives, coming as close as it dared to the threatened abrogation of its cherished rights to self-legislation. The many laws and amendments passed between 1824 and 1833 were progressively more liberal but always as close as possible to existing customary practice, or relying on the notorious difficulty of implementation under Bahamian conditions. Even more subtly, and far more important in the long run for Bahamian society, the ruling class used the time that remained before slavery ended to do what it could to co-opt the rapidly expanding section of free coloreds and blacks: to create a buffer class, if not actual allies, against the threatening tide of emancipated slaves.

In this complex rearguard action, the Bahamian legislature passed no less than three consolidated slave acts within six years, in 1824, 1826, and 1830, as well as many ancillary and amending laws. At each stage, the concessions grudgingly made to Bahamian slaves were greatly outweighed by those made to the free coloreds and blacks—to the point that those already freed finally achieved full equality before the law just as the slaves were entering what was planned to be a six-year phase of apprenticeship to their former owners.

The free coloreds and blacks had been permanently enrolled in the militia since the Napoleonic War, though the 1814 experiment of having fully integrated companies, with forty free coloreds or blacks per company of one hundred, seems to have been soon discontinued in favor of a separate company of free blacks and a company of brown rangers.[32] Restrictions continued for some time on the issue of firearms and ammunition to these nonwhite units, but the legislature did not hesitate to use them as an auxiliary police force. In 1816, for example, an act authorized the governor to order out patrols of the colored militia in Nassau on Sundays, since it had "of late been a common practice for white persons as well as free people of colour, free blacks and slaves, to meet and assemble together upon the public grounds and other places in and about this town and suburbs, for the purpose of playing at ball, and other sports and pastimes, thereby profaning the Sabbath or Lord's Day."[33]

This combination of maintaining social order while preserving the Sabbath was fully consonant with the type of reformist sentiment expressed in the Bathurst circulars, which were as concerned with the slaves' moral well-being and social behavior as with their material conditions. Since the status of slavery before the law, particularly the way that differential slave codes challenged the presumption that law was absolute, was another burning issue in the metropolis, much emphasis was also laid on the rights of free coloreds and blacks, as well as slaves, before the courts. All three of the last consolidated slave acts contained clauses extending the slaves' legal privileges, but the rights of the nonwhite freemen were expanded even more rapidly. In 1822 their evidence was accepted against whites in all civil cases, and in 1824, in an act passed immediately before the slave act of that year, this was extended to criminal cases as well.[34] Progressively, moreover, colored and black freemen were excluded from the provisions and penalties applying to slaves, so that by 1830 the Consolidated Slave Law was almost as exclusively concerned with slavery and slaves as its name implied.

The form of the 1824 slave act, which itself admitted to being "due to good policy, as well as to humanity and justice," was similar to that of 1797, in that the harsher clauses were preceded and softened by nearly as many ostensibly concerned with the slaves' protection. The provisions against slave violence and running away continued very strict, and for the first time there were specific prohibitions against riotous and unlawful assemblies of slaves. Owners or those in charge of slaves were to be penalized if they allowed more than twelve "strange" slaves "to assemble together, or beat their drums or blow their horns or shells." In other respects, though, penalties were moderated and protective clauses extended, with a canny emphasis on the promotion of Christianity and "Christian" values—as long as they remained firmly under the aegis of the established church.

For the first time since the days of Governor Phenney, owners were enjoined to provide Christian teaching for their slaves and to have them baptized as soon as they were ready. This was a belated recognition of the fact that an increasing number of slaves, particularly in Nassau, were being converted and baptized by unlicensed black preachers, despite the law of 1816 against such "illiterate, ignorant and ill disposed persons."[35] Besides, slave marriages were to be recognized and positively encouraged, and even the marriage of slaves and free persons was made legally possible. Yet more important, slave couples were not to be separated by sale or transfer, or slave children under fourteen years of age taken from their mothers. From now on, slaves were not to be given more than twenty lashes unless their owner or an official was present, and no more than thirty-nine lashes in a day under any circumstances. Furthermore, in changes that were more important in legal principle than in effect, charges of cruelty against a white could now be prosecuted in the general court, and all slaves charged with capital crimes were also to be tried in the general court, rather than in the special slave court, with its two justices of the peace and five free jurors.[36]

The 1826 Slave Act made additional concessions to the abolitionists by banning Sunday markets and further humanizing the official system of corporal punishment. Henceforward the use of the whip was banned at work, females were not to be whipped in the presence of any males except their masters, and solitary confinement was suggested as an alternative to whipping. Some restrictions were added to the right of slaves to marry, in that marriages could occur only with the owners' permission and were not to interfere with the slaves' duties to their masters. Slave marriages, moreover, had to be in virtually the same form as those of free persons, and no marriage between slaves (or between a slave and a free person) was to be valid that would be void between two free persons. However, vital legal concessions were made (or customary practices acknowledged) with respect to slaves' owning property, appearing before the courts, and obtaining their freedom.

The 1826 act recognized that it "had been the custom of the Bahamas for slaves to have been able to hold and keep property free from the owners," and this custom was now to be legalized. Slaves were declared "competent to hold, inherit, purchase and dispose of land, money, cattle of what value soever, and maintain and defend their rights in respect thereof as were persons of free condition." The only specific restrictions on ownership were that slaves could not themselves hold slaves and were not allowed to possess firearms, gunpowder, or ammunition without their owners' permission. Slaves also could not make personal suit in the courts in respect of property, having to be represented by a free person as a "guardian."

Though not allowed to bring personal suits in the general court, slaves were for the first time allowed to give evidence in court in civil and criminal cases, if under very strict conditions. Slave witnesses had to have a certificate from a minister of the Church of England or the Church of Scotland, duly registered with the clerk of the court, that they were Creole-born, had been in the Bahamas at least five years, and were baptized Christians capable of understanding the oath. Slaves could not give evidence in a case involving a capital charge against any white, a criminal case against a slaveowner, a libel case against any free person, or any case concerning the manumission of a slave. Moreover—almost a catch-22 situation—slaves were not permitted to give evidence in court on any matters that had preceded the award and registration of their certificate of competency to attest. On the other hand, freedmen (that is, those who had been granted freedom rather than being born free) were to be treated virtually the same as those fully free, rather than like slaves, in giving evidence in court.

Indeed, the most important sections of the 1826 Slave Act were those which quite suddenly increased the number of freed coloreds and blacks, while at the same time ensuring that freedom was granted only to those types most likely to sustain the social system. The old requirement of a bond of ninety pounds was replaced by a simple enrollment fee of eight shillings, and for the first time the practice of slaves' purchasing their own freedom was legalized. The snags were that manumission could now be obtained only by the owner's will or deed, and that the price paid by a slave for manumission had to be at a rate and on terms agreeable "between the parties." This meant in practice that only those slaves whom the masters deemed to be worthy of freedom and who had sufficient means and incentive to enter the intermediate class of the black petty bourgeoisie were given their freedom.[37]

The final Bahamian slave act in 1830 (made necessary mainly because that of 1826 was scheduled to last only three years) made fewer important advances. It did make a further concession to the sabbatarian abolitionists by decreeing that the prevailing custom of giving slaves freedom from work on Sunday be extended actually to forbid any slave labor on that day. But it did not go far enough in relaxing slave punishments to satisfy the ever more vocal antislavery sentiments in Britain, particularly over the question of the flogging of female slaves, which caused a tremendous furor between Governor Carmichael Smyth and the assembly in the early 1830s. In any case, the Slave Act of 1830 was probably regarded on all sides as a merely temporary and temporizing measure, soon to be swept away by the now inevitable legislation freeing the Bahamian slaves, which was to come into effect on August 1, 1834.[38]

Not that it was a period of relaxed anticipation. As we shall see, during the very last years of Bahamian slavery the restlessness of those about to be legally freed clashed with the determination of the more diehard masters and their poor white supporters not to relinquish the reins of power and privilege. In this phase, however, the more astute members of the ruling class did their best to maneuver the now very large section of free coloreds and blacks at least into a position of social neutrality, by convincing them that they had almost as much to lose from general slave emancipation as had the whites. The first manifestation of this was the act of 10 Geo IV, c.10, dated January 11, 1830, which gave colored and black freemen the vote, provided they had been born free and were not of African birth. However, there was much evidence that, while nonwhite freemen still suffered from civil disabilities, many of them— persons born free as well as those freed during their own lifetimes—

tended to take the side of the slaves against the slaveowning class. For example, hundreds of free coloreds and blacks signed petitions in 1831 and 1832 to counter the calls by white Bahamians for the recall of Governor James Carmichael Smyth for being too "soft" on the slaves, too hard on the masters. Carmichael Smyth himself (never quite the liberal his most ardent friends and enemies considered him to be) told London that he believed that only by giving the most prosperous of the blacks full civil rights could a polarized society and almost certain racial conflict be avoided in the future.[39]

Therefore, of greater significance for Bahamian society than the 1830 Slave Act, or even the act in the same year extending the franchise to some colored and black freemen, was the act of 4 William IV, c.1, which became law on September 27, 1833, "To relieve His Majesty's free Coloured and Black Subjects of the Bahama Islands, from all Civil Disabilities." By this act, all coloreds and blacks born free were immediately to "have and enjoy all the rights, privileges and immunities whatsoever, to which they would have been entitled, if born of, and descended from white ancestors." More remarkably, those persons "who had been born slaves but had been manumitted through behalf of their owners, by deed, will, or otherwise, or by judgement of the General Court, or sentence, order or decree in the Court of Vice-Admiralty," were to enjoy the same rights once they had been free for two years, excepting only the African-born, who were to wait six years.[40] To put this legislation in context, it should be pointed out that the free coloreds and blacks, who in 1810 had constituted less than 10 percent of the Bahamian population, compared with the slaves' 67 percent and the whites' 27 percent, now made up 23 percent of the total, compared with the 26 percent who counted as whites and the 50 percent who were slaves.[41] Thus in 1833, by what was virtually the last law passed by the Bahamian assembly before the Emancipation Act, the Bahamian oligarchy—with the help of an almost Machiavellian governor—made a last desperate effort to separate from the mass of the black slaves a section of the population now almost as numerous as the whites, thereby creating an intermediate class which might help to sustain its hegemony once the remaining ten thousand slaves were freed.

Right, Colonel Andrew Deveaux, Jr. (1750–1815) from Beaufort, South Carolina, by way of Florida, Abaco, and Harbour Island. In the background, Fort Nassau, flying the Union Flag. *Below*, John Murray, fourth earl of Dunmore, shown in a 1756 painting by Sir Joshua Reynolds.

Panorama of Nassau from Fort Fincastle, 1800, from a drawing by John Irving

John Irving's view toward Nassau's ridge and Fort Fincastle in 1800. At that time, the great silk cotton tree and the New Gaol dominated open spaces between Charlotte and East streets, where many new public buildings were erected over the following two decades. The silk cotton, sometimes known as Blackbeard's Tree, more than three hundred years old, survived into the 1970s.

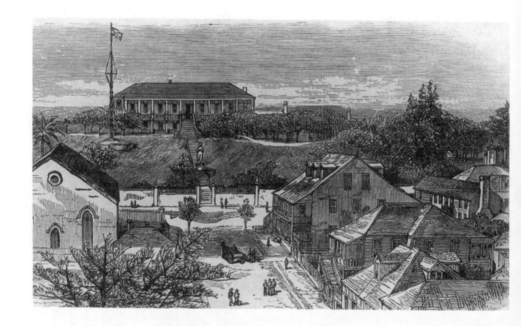

Top, a mid nineteenth century view from Christchurch tower looking south toward Government House, in front of which is the statue of Christopher Columbus erected by Governor Carmichael Smyth in 1832. *Bottom*, Bay Street, Nassau. Though this print dates from the mid nineteenth century, it depicts a building and social scene similar to that which Johann Schoepf described seventy-five years earlier.

Private soldier of Second West India Regiment. During the last French wars many slaves were enrolled, but after 1815 complements were largely made up with Africans liberated from foreign slavetraders.

Lord John Rolle in his baronial splendor

Mid nineteenth century lithograph of Nassau from Fort Charlotte. In the foreground, soldiers mount a casual guard; between fort and town are their barracks and tented encampment.

Nassau from the harbor just after the end of slavery

Sebastiano del Piombo portrait of a man said to be Christopher Columbus (The
Metropolitan Museum of Art, Gift of J. Pierpont Morgan, 1900 (00. 18.2).

Theodore de Bry engraving of
Columbus's landing (1594)

Ponce de Leon

Edward Teach, alias Blackbeard. Note the battery of side arms, ornate naked sword, shorn locks of a victim's hair, and smoking slow matches attached to the hat. The instrument on which Blackbeard's clawlike left hand rests seems to be a captured Admiralty Court ceremonial oar, symbolizing authority overthrown.

Mary Read, Lady Pirate. The dress, accoutrements, and early eighteenth century ships depicted are probably authentic, but the character herself may be fictional. What she symbolized, though, was a double rejection of conventional values: those of established bourgeois society and women's traditional subjugation.

Facing page: top, the hamaca; *bottom,* the cacique's, or communal, batey (Oviedo, 1526).

Left, copper blanca of Henry IV of Castille, glass bead, and belt buckle found on Watling's Island by Charles Hoffman and his archeological students at Long Bay Lucayan site, June-July, 1983; *below,* three duhos discovered in 1988 by Carleton Cartwright near Mortimer's, Long Island.

Left, petroglyph showing Atabeyra, the chief Arawak goddess, in characteristic crouched posture; *below,* typical triangular depiction of Jocahú, the chief god of the Arawaks, in a petroglyph from Layou.

Above, a five-person dugout canoe propelled by "paddles like a baker's peel" (Benzoni, 1563); *right*, a modern reconstruction of a bohio in cross-section.

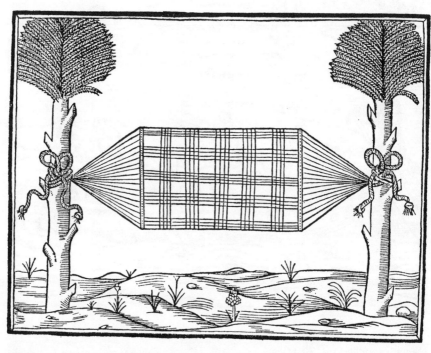

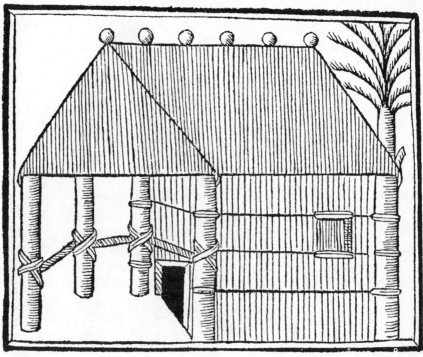

~ *15* ~

The Lifeways of the Loyalist Elite

THE WAY OF LIFE of the ruling class and the social life of the Bahamian capital during the Loyalist slavery era are preserved, as in amber, by the three earliest sets of private documents still surviving: a series of letters by the women of the Kelsall family (1804–47) and two parallel but dissimilar journals kept in 1823–24 by American visitors, a doctor and a young woman of leisure.[1]

The Kelsalls were almost the quintessential Bahamian Loyalist family. The patriarch was John Kelsall, owner of Great Ropers Plantation near Beaufort, South Carolina, whose sons Roger and William compromised themselves during the Revolutionary War and migrated to the Bahamas after the American victory. Roger, the older son (1738–88), was the pioneer. A widower since 1770, he had already resettled in Georgia, where he became a councilor in the Loyalist government and "a Commissioner to take possession of the Negroes and other property of active Whigs." Having sent his children John and Anne to England for their education, he went to the Bahamas around 1783 with a handful of slaves, establishing an estate called Pinxton adjoining the great salina on Little Exuma. During this rough initial stage, the middle-aged bachelor, isolated from his family and fellow planters, fathered a girl called Portia with his black slave housekeeper, Eleanor, commonly called Nelly. The struggle to clear land, raise cotton, and rake salt broke Roger's health, and he went to England in 1786, to die two years later.[2]

Roger Kelsall's legitimate children returned to the Bahamas after their father's death, dividing their time between Pinxton and Nassau. Anne, no great heiress, married a modest doctor called Lewin, but John, with his Cambridge degree and legal training, married Lucretia, the daughter of John Moultrie, former lieutenant governor of East Florida. He failed as a planter but enjoyed a distinguished if brief public career, becoming vice-admiralty judge and Speaker of the assembly before his tragically early death in 1803. His private life, promising so well, was also clouded, since his restless wife became dissatisfied with the Bahamas and left in 1800 to live in London with his mother, accompanied by their four young children and a black wet nurse, Statira. Anne Lewin and her husband also left the Bahamas forever after John Kelsall's death.[3]

Roger Kelsall's brother William, who had married into a family with "Whiggish" connections, was not forced out of South Carolina until well after the war ended. On February 5, 1790, however, he arrived at Georgetown, Exuma, in the schooner *Eliza*, direct from Beaufort, with his wife, Mary Elizabeth, and his four daughters, Mary (sixteen), Charlotte (thirteen), Henrietta (four), and Eliza (two), as well as his slaves and stock animals. This household settled on Little Exuma, where William began to develop an estate adjacent to Pinxton called the Hermitage, which also fronted on the great salina. Besides, he planted cotton and raked salt on Rum Cay. But like his brother, William was soon worn down by the effort and died, aged only fifty-two, in 1792.

Mary Elizabeth Kelsall was left in genteel poverty, to maintain the family estate as long as she could while bringing up her almost dowryless daughters to marriageable age. Their time was divided between Exuma and Nassau, while an agent and overseers carried out the actual management of the land and slaves. Mary, the eldest daughter, married a naval captain in Nassau in 1797,[4] and in the following year Mary Elizabeth went to England with the other girls, looking for better doctors and schools than could be found in Nassau for Henrietta and Eliza, and for Charlotte, perhaps, a husband or respectable domestic employment. Charlotte, in fact, never married and remained in England in a state of dependence and poverty which distressed her mother.[5] Mary Elizabeth herself had returned to the Bahamas in 1802, placing herself under the short-lived protection of her nephew-in-law, John Kelsall. It was at this stage that she began the correspondence with her relatives, carried on after her death mainly by her daughter Henrietta, which forms the as yet unpublished collection "Henrietta, My Daughter," edited by Mary K. Armbrister.[6]

In the letters, complaints about economic prospects and the lack of civilized amenities were mixed with family news and local gossip. The Exuma estates never made a profit and were constantly threatened with sale, if buyers could be found. However, the prospect of selling out was specially daunting to those to whom the possession of land and slaves remained their chief pretensions to membership in an aristocratic class, complete with its notions of honor and attitudes of paternalistic solicitude toward faithful retainers. "Everything here remains just as it was," wrote Mary Elizabeth to her niece Anne Lewin from the Hermitage in April 1804, "tho I think it will not be kept together another year." After all the fine prospects, there would be no more than thirteen tons of clean cotton produced by the Hermitage and the Rum Cay estate together, which would not nearly pay even the interest on the family debts. Despite all the efforts of Mr. Forbes, the agent, time was running out for what Mary Elizabeth termed "this fine Estate."[7]

To the genteel owners it seemed that the collapse of the estate would be almost as dire an outcome for their faithful black servants, whom they regarded as a sort of family, as for themselves. "The negroes are in general in good health," wrote Mary Elizabeth, "and they all dread the idea of being sold." What, for example, would happen to "Poor old Nelly," the aged domestic (and mother of Roger Kelsall's mistress) who was "not long for this world," she wondered. Nelly was extremely feeble and not able to do anything for herself, but because she had "been a faithful servant in her time" she was indulged with a black female attendant and the help of her grandson (or great-grandson) George, who, though old enough to work in the fields, was allowed to stay round the house to run errands and perform odd jobs for Old Nelly.

Even before retailing personal news, Mary Elizabeth went on to provide Anne Lewin with news and gossip about other family slaves. Anne's former servant Eve was sadly afflicted with epilepsy, the convulsions seemingly having impaired her intellect. She had grown so thin that Anne would scarcely recognize her. Worse luck, Eve's husband, Joe, Anne Lewin's former "waiting man," had actually been enticed away by her own mother, Flora, with whom he was now living as husband and wife, leaving Eve to look after her two small children alone. Flora's behavior in general was probably the worst of any of the women on the plantation. Of other slaves, Little Jenny now had four fine children, Old Mary was as well as ever, but Big Nanny had grown even more monstrously fat. Old Strap, another of the South Carolina veterans, had lost the sight of one of his eyes, allegedly from a cold.

As to Mary Elizabeth and her two daughters, they lived in "a very sober, Methodical way," without any intrusion from visitors. The girls were accustomed to rise at five or earlier, to bathe in the sea while the air was still cool and then go riding until seven. Breakfast was at eight, after which they alternated between reading to their mother and playing the piano for six hours. This was followed by an hour and a half of French and an hour and a half of geography, leaving just half an hour to dress before dinner, which was on the table by five. After dinner and before dark the girls went out riding again, often accompanied by their mother, either on horseback or in the gig. Her own time, summed up Mary Elizabeth, was "tolerably well-filled" so that she could truly say that she never found the days too long or tiresome.

With the further decline of cotton, efforts were made to increase salt production, though this was scotched by an American trade embargo, so that up to twenty thousand bushels at one time piled up at the Little Exuma salina. With creditors pressing and her field slaves growing restless because of harder work under shorter rations, Mary Elizabeth went to live almost permanently in New Providence, taking up residence at a small "farm" called Blair, three miles east from town. In 1807 Eliza married a local white named Robert Duncombe, ambitious and efficient but almost as poor as herself, and scarcely a gentleman. A representative of a new class of "improving" overseers, Duncombe took over the management of the Hermitage, Pinxton, and other Exuma estates, while holding the minor post of collector of customs at Williamstown. It was a hard life for masters as well as for slaves, made harsher by the attacks of fever which reduced Duncombe to "a mere anatomy" and led to the death in infancy of two of Eliza's three children.

Even then, for the whites, there were occasional distractions. "Wonderful to tell," wrote Mary Elizabeth of Eliza in July 1808, "she had a ball at their house about a fortnight ago; she had five ladies and a good many more gentlemen, and what makes it more surprising, all these ladies had received their education in England." The mother reported that she was more pleased than she had formerly been with her daughter's choice of spouse; Robert Duncombe seemed a "truly worthy man" and an excellent husband. All Eliza needed was more company to make her more comfortable. She had only one white female neighbor on Little Exuma; the other ladies mentioned were on a visit from Long Island, and the ball had presumably been arranged to mark the special occasion.[8]

Yet for Henrietta and her mother, life at Blair was little better, and during the American war conditions grew almost desperate. They had few invitations and fewer visitors, and were even dependent on gifts of clothes from their English relatives. Prices became so inflated that they could hardly afford meat, let alone books. A hurricane which struck Nassau in September 1813 was almost the last straw. Blair Cottage was almost totally destroyed and its contents scattered, including Henrietta's party dresses and few ornaments, her treasured copy of Milton, and the last mementos of her cousin John Kelsall. Her "poor old mother" fell seriously ill "in consequence of the colds caught from being exposed to the fury of the elements," while Henrietta herself suffered from a "depressing indisposition."[9]

With the ebullience of youth, Henrietta was able to look on the bright side of the enforced move into town while Blair was being rebuilt. "The succession of visitors is the thing of all others I like best," she wrote to her cousin Eleanor (John Kelsall's sister). Three miles had been too far to make casual visits or send a servant, so that invitations and calls were now more frequent. Eleanor now felt better in the evenings, that being the time for parties, and she had been to several recently. Ladies were almost excluded from dinner parties, but she had been to some charming soirées at Government House, where she found Governor Charles Cameron and his family delightful company. The Camerons also had a large collection of books newly sent out from England, and no treat was so great for Eleanor as a book she had not read before. In recent weeks (this in December 1813), she had particularly enjoyed two novels: one, which she found amusing and instructive, called *The Countess and Gertrude*; the other, "much lighter and highly entertaining and funny," called *Pride and Prejudice*.[10]

Poverty and dependence, however, remained galling. "I have long been thinking of my future destiny & trying to find employment," wrote the twenty-eight-year-old Henrietta a few months later, "but there are so few means by which a female may hope to earn even bread!" The local schools were overstaffed, and needlework would not serve because her eyesight was less than perfect. Henrietta had heard by chance that the vice-admiralty court paid well for transcriptions, had applied for the job through the medium of a friend, and had been able to present her mother with sixty-four dollars as a result. But the work was demeaning as well as short-lived. "This position & confinement are oppressive beyond any idea I had formed," concluded Henrietta.[11]

It was a situation that Jane Austen herself would have recognized, and Henrietta found the only solution. On April 18, 1814, she married Captain Joseph Eysing of the Second West India Regiment after a short engagement, to her mother's heartfelt approbation.[12] Captain Eysing, a German-born veteran of the Caribbean campaigns of the Napoleonic War, continued to serve for a few years after the peace, at Harbour Island (a healthful resort which Henrietta referred to as "the Montpellier of the Bahamas")[13] as well as Nassau. In town, thanks to Governor Cameron, they lived in the commander's apartment in old Fort Nassau. "They are delightful quarters," wrote Henrietta when she sent her cousin the news of the birth of their first child, "healthy, roomy, airy, and all that a poor soldier can desire, & all for nothing." Mary Elizabeth stayed often with the Eysings, and Henrietta believed that she would immediately sell Blair if she could, alternating her time between the apartment in Fort Nassau and the Duncombes' home on Little Exuma. The chance of selling Blair advantageously, though, was almost nil. Times were "deplorably bad" since the peace, with Nassau "quite deserted." White people were continually migrating, each ship seemingly "taking away whole cabins full." Though the price of slaves was as "wonderfully depreciated" as that of land, there were few if any purchasers for houses, estates, or slaves. Soon, reckoned Henrietta, the minuscule local white society would be even more limited and impoverished.[14]

Captain Eysing resigned his commission when threatened with a distant foreign posting, but in 1821, like several others around that time, he and his wife forsook the Bahamas to settle in Cuba. Taking the now aged and ailing Mary Elizabeth and the last of the Kelsall slaves, they purchased some four hundred fertile undeveloped acres athwart the Cacuyugin River near Candelaria in Holguin province and started a small sugar plantation. There Mary Elizabeth died in 1823, but Henrietta stayed for the remaining twenty-six years of her life. The sugar estate never really flourished, and Henrietta, widowed in 1832, was, like many Loyalist former planters in the Bahamas, not above turning to commerce, setting up a small store to retail English goods imported through Nassau (they were in fact closer to the Bahamian capital than was Inagua or the Turks and Caicos Islands). But despite her modest income and increasing political turmoil in her adopted country, Henrietta strove to preserve, or re-create, a polite quasi-plantocratic society among her emigré Bahamian and Cuban neighbors, and remained in touch with her distant relatives to the end. Alone of the Kelsalls, her sister Eliza Duncombe remained in the Bahamas, tied to a husband unwilling or unable to move and forced to adapt as best she could to inexorably changing conditions. Robert Duncombe, indeed, was a minor, perhaps tragic, actor in Bahamian slavery's last dramatic phase. Rescued from Exuma by a rather more lucrative post "under government" in Nassau shortly after the peace, he was to become one of the most obstreperous opponents of Governor Carmichael Smyth's attempts at liberal reform, and the police magistrate sacked in 1830 over the flogging of female slaves.[15]

An inevitable counterpoint to the decay of a mainland style of plantocracy—epitomized by the fate of the Bahamian Kelsalls—was the deterioration of relationships between masters and slaves, and the mutual decline of morale. In the Kelsall case, these changes were almost too neatly encapsulated in the gradual change in the relations of the white

Kelsall women with the mulatto girl Portia, daughter of Roger Kelsall by his black slave Nelly.

Since a child took the status of the mother, not the father, Portia was technically a slave to Roger Kelsall's family. However, she was treated almost as free by the Kelsalls, while her mother, Nelly, received even more privileges than Old Nelly the grandmother, because she had been Roger Kelsall's mistress—despite a notable drinking problem. John Kelsall was particularly generous to his half-sister and her mother. But after John's death, Mary Elizabeth Kelsall felt that she neither could nor should continue such privileged treatment. In 1804 Portia, aged about twenty, "hired herself to a decent family in Nassau," the Havens, having decided not to stay with her mother, whom Mary Elizabeth now called "a worthless drunken hussy . . . from whom she could learn no good."[16] Another motive was that the Havens were planning to go to England, where Portia might well pass as completely free, if not obtain her freedom from John Kelsall's family. "I had forgot to say you will see Portia, who goes home with Mr. Haven's family," wrote Mary Elizabeth to Anne Lewin in England in August 1804. "I understand that she has conducted herself well. The only thing I found fault with her was for her always saying 'my brother' whenever she spoke of my dear nephew to me. Since then I have reason to think that he gave her every encouragement. I believe she was disappointed that I did not take her home with me. As I thought it was time for her to endeavor to provide for herself, I knew it would be doing her an injury by taking her out of the way of doing so. It was out of my power to maintain her as she had been accustomed to, for your poor brother was, I am sorry to say, more liberal than he ought to have been."[17]

Portia did not obtain her freedom while in England, and in 1805 the Havens brought her back to Nassau with them. There she found herself in imminent danger of being sold with the rest of John Kelsall's slaves, and perhaps turned out to the fields or salt pans. "Poor Portia is in great distress," wrote Mary Elizabeth to Anne Lewin early in 1806, "for Mr. Forbes has said unless you purchase her freedom, she must be sold with the other Negroes, as she has nothing to show that she is free." Poor Portia had fretted so much that Mary Elizabeth had told her that she would at least endeavor to prevent her being sold at the public auction block if the sale had to go through before the necessary manumission fee and authorization arrived from England. For Portia's sake, Mary Elizabeth hoped that they would hear from Anne Lewin soon, adding that Portia was "a good girl & a favorite with many people."[18]

The record is silent, but it is clear that Anne Lewin must have heeded her half-sister's plea, for by 1807 Portia was no longer a slave but a self-employed seamstress.[19] Her mother too was seemingly freed at the same time. Their entry into the ever-growing ranks of Nassau's free colored population, perhaps predictably, led to a quite sudden worsening of relations between Portia and the white Nassauvian Kelsalls. This estrangement was blamed on Portia herself by the Kelsall letter writers, though a less biased and more generous interpretation might have explained her behavior as that of an insufficiently meek spirit having difficulty in adjusting to her new status and the problems of making an independent living.

"I am sorry to say anything to lessen Portia in your good opinion," wrote Mary Elizabeth to her niece in May 1807,

> but as you particularly requested me to inform you, I can only say that we never see her, for she has behaved very ill to us. We have heard of a number of lies that she has told on Eliza and Henrietta, even at the time that I was serving her and her worthless drinking mother by maintaining old Nelly. When the negroes were sold, Mr. Forbes had her brought down here and sent to her daughter, who would not receive her. The poor old woman has been with me ever since.
>
> I have been told that she has behaved with *impertinence* to ladies that she works for, that she has lost a good deal of work by it, and got hardly enough to pay for the bread they ate. Soon after I came here, I let her have a nice little yellow girl about ten years old, whom they almost starved to death before I could take her away; the child did not get a sufficiency to keep her alive, and must have died if she had not begged from neighbors. My own negroes gave her, whenever they could do it secretly, for Madam had quarrelled with them and said she would murder the child if she came here for victuals.[20]

Mary Elizabeth was convinced that neither Portia nor her mother had any sense of gratitude towards the Kelsalls, even to Anne Lewin, who had obtained their freedom. Mary Elizabeth wrote that she had heard Portia speak disrespectfully of Anne, and that Portia had sulked when reproved for it. She behaved tolerably well only until she was certain of her freedom. "I shall not be at all surprised if she was to take to drinking," concluded Mary Elizabeth maliciously. "She is now, I believe, free from that vice, but her mother being a determined sot, is a bad example for her."

A few months later, in August 1807, Mary Elizabeth also wrote to Lucretia Kelsall (John's widow and daughter of ex-Governor Moultrie), the most aristocratic surviving member of the clan, adding waspish reports on Portia to straightforward news of other old family retainers. She asked Lucretia to tell her aunt, Miss Moultrie, that "poor old Nab" had recently died, apparently from old age, having just wasted away with no obvious illness. Mary Elizabeth had visited Nab at the last, found that she complained of nothing but weakness, and reported her "sensible of her approaching end and quite resigned." Nab had asked Mary Elizabeth if she had heard from England and inquired after the health of her former owners and employers, particularly Miss Moultrie. Of another elderly servant, Old Statira, Mary Elizabeth wrote that she had arrived back from England in remarkably good health and spirits, adding the opinion that "if she will keep herself sober she will always get as much work as she can do."

Sustaining the temperance train of thought, Mary Elizabeth went on to inform Lucretia that Portia and her "drinking mother" were still living together, and to repeat the belief that the daughter would very likely follow the alcoholic example of the mother. She had "taken a great deal of notice of this girl," she added self-righteously, but on the strength of this Portia had given herself many airs and had repeatedly "behaved very insolently to Eliza and Henrietta." She often boasted that she used to sleep over at John and Lucretia Kelsall's house, invariably spent weekends there, and always drank tea in the drawing-room when the Kelsalls had company—all claims which Lucretia must know to be obvious fabrications. "She has the character of being a great liar," asserted Mary Elizabeth, completely reversing her opinion of less than two years earlier by concluding that Portia "is not a favorite with any person I know of."[21]

Mary Elizabeth never made reference to Portia again, but five years later Henrietta responded to queries from her cousin Anne Lewin about her:

> To your enquiries respecting Portia, I will relate what I have heard. She left this country with a taylor, a Mr. Smith (who, I am sorry to say has a wife in Charleston) about 4 years ago, & returned here about a twelvemonth since. Two years of the time she was absent she was in St. Domingo. She has a child which appears 4 or 5 years old born before she left this country. We often meet her, but she never notices us. I suppose shame restrains; we never deserved anything but gratitude from her; she always sat at table with us, & *now* I think we treated her with too much of the consideration due to a relative. Her mother still *drinks* & goes on as usual; she takes the name and title of Mrs. Kelsall, and we were once much annoyed at "Mrs. & Miss Kelsall's compliments" being sent with enquiries after a young officer, in whose health we were interested.[22]

Henrietta remarked at first that Smith the tailor seemed devoted to the mother of his child, regretting only that he would not marry her. But a few weeks later, in July 1814, she had to report that Portia seemed to have another partner. "I have seen her only once or twice since her return to this country," she wrote in the last reference to Portia in the Kelsall letters, "& a while ago passed near her, but she has never recognised me since her faux pas; she was leading her boy, a dark mulatto, by the hand. Mr. Tudor is the name of her lover, & I think he must be constant for they still hang together. Portia has lately set up a huckster's shop; if she does not acquire her mother's vice she may do well, for that is a flourishing business in this country." [23]

The two American visitors, Dr. Townsend and Miss Hart, who arrived on the same boat for the winter season of 1823, naturally provide a different perspective of Nassau and its society from that of the Kelsall women. Their accounts lack the personal involvement and intimate gossip of the Kelsall letters, and they were also describing a subtly changed milieu. But they were privileged outsiders, being guests of two of the leading members of Bahamian society. The doctor's journal is especially valuable, for his sex and profession gave him rather greater mobility, and, unlike the overly romantic Miss Hart, he did not write for publication.

They set sail from wintry New York in the brig *Trent*, bound for New Orleans, on November 30, arriving in a Nassau where it was seemingly still summer, just over a week later. Miss Hart accompanied the Honorable Patrick Brown and his wife, and Dr. Townsend the even grander Honorable James Moss, who traveled with his white manservant and black slave coachman, as well as a "fine span of carriage horses." [24] The Mosses, in fact, were as typical of a new age as the Kelsalls were of the old. With an English slave-trading rather than American slave-plantation background, they had been somewhat ridiculed by Mary Elizabeth Kelsall as mercantile *nouveaux riches*, who boasted of their familiarity with "titled folks." James Moss was the same person prosecuted by William Wylly for maltreatment in 1816, when he had already augmented his fortune by selling off nearly all his slaves to the sugar colonies. With strong ties to Liverpool, where his family owned a bank, and to Havana (which Mary Elizabeth Kelsall in 1808 called "that money-making place . . . quite an Elfin Hill for all merchants who go there"), James Moss was the linchpin of Nassau's new mercantile oligarchy—though the family remained sufficiently involved in planting for Moss's nephew Henry to be found guilty, with his wife, of gross cruelty to one of his female slaves on Crooked Island, in a notorious case in 1827. [25]

Such bleak features of social life were not even hinted at in the visitors' first impressions of Nassau, which approached enchantment. The *Trent* anchored two hundred yards off Nassau's waterfront in brilliant moonlight. The passengers were handed down into a small boat with some of their essential luggage and rowed to one of the small piers built out from the shore—marveling at the greenness and transparency of the water, through which they could see white coral many fathoms down by the light of the moon. Townsend's party reached James Moss's town house after a short walk through a lumber yard and down Bay Street. Situated on one side of the oblong open green called the Parade in front of Fort Nassau, it must have been one of the grandest residences in town, though like most merchants' homes it had offices below and living quarters above. "Its gable ends were as usual in the tropics placed North & south," wrote Dr. Townsend, "& the house long and narrow & three stories with five windows in front, a larger number than usual for buildings of this size, but very necessary in the climate."

The front door was opened before they arrived, and several sprightly young slave menservants were ready with candles to conduct them up the grand and gleaming mahogany staircase. There they entered first the great dining parlor, which occupied half the length and the entire breadth of the building, and then the even more impressive *salon de reception* occupying the rest of the second story. "This is a charming room with high ceilings, window casements of solid mahogany which with the side board & tables of the same material vied in the brilliancy of their surface with the stair-case," reported Dr. Townsend. The floor was covered with oilcloth, and on a central table were two large candles with high cylindrical shades, the utility of which was immediately recognized when Mr. Moss ordered the servants to open the windows to provide a cooling breeze on that summery evening. "Of course no fireplaces or grates were visible," commented the newcomer, "nor did our feelings make us wish to see them."[26]

In the morning, Townsend looked out of his top-floor window at the prospect that was to delight the watercolorist Winslow Homer sixty years later, and still delights: coconut palms, the brilliant blues and greens of the harbor, the lighthouse on its rocky spit, and the brilliant white of the breakers creaming across the bar. After a typical breakfast at nine o'clock, of "Snapper, Margate (a native fish & very good), also hashes, etc. & coffee, tea etc.," the Mosses and their guest went by gig to make the obligatory call at Government House, left their cards, and then drove eastward along the ridge to visit the Browns and Miss Hart. This gave

Dr. Townsend the opportunity to enjoy and describe one of the handsom-est mansions on the suburban fringes of Nassau—a stone-built house with elegant piazzas, galleries, and jalousied windows, set in spacious and well-tended grounds. "The room we were received in was very pret-tily furnished," he wrote enthusiastically, "& the beautiful rich bouquets of roses etc. on the central table of glistening mahogany charmed the eye & scattered a delightful fragrance thro the air." The lawn around the house seemed to Townsend "as green as our northern meadows in Spring," though made exotic by the foliage, fruit, flowers, and scents of coconut palms, tamarind, orange and lemon trees, hibiscus and bou-gainvillea shrubs, and ornamental trees such as the Pride of India.

After Miss Hart and the Browns had entertained them for hours with chatter and tea, Dr. Townsend was brought home by a tourist's route through the narrow lanes "in the back part of town." Here the glar-ing white of the roadway accentuated by the white-plastered walls, the white-, blue-, or yellow-plastered houses of the well-to-do, and the luxuriant gardens, reminded the well-traveled Townsend of Nice on the French Riviera. Nothing in his experience, though, had quite prepared him for the formality and plenitude of the eight- or ten-course dinner that awaited him at five, so soon after his return from the hot afternoon drive.[27] Such elaborate early dinners, often extended into the small hours by talk, drinking, cards, or dancing, were the most common feature of Nassau's high society. As respectable visitors, Dr. Townsend and Miss Hart were invited, together, to Government House within a week of their arrival. This was a splendid but rather formal occasion, with Governor Grant dressed in the "full uniform of a major general, long tailed red coat with superb massy gilded trappings," and about forty guests, including the Murrays, Munningses, Wyllys, and Kerrs, as well as the Mosses and the Browns. The Mosses' own dinners were sometimes more sumptu-ous, if with fewer diners. For example, one "modest repast" on Friday, December 19, consisted of "about 30 covers (vegetables included) ham, turtle, lamb, fish, pidgeon pie etc etc. Next course yam puddings (very good) jellies, tarts, custards etc. Next fruits—in short a more elegant & splendid dinner than the Governor's. Plenty of Madeira, Champagne, Claret etc."[28]

The interlocking permutations of guests at these frequent dinner par-ties suggest a limited social circle that surely palled after a time, not to mention the cumulative effect of such strenuous eating and drink-ing. Even before Christmas, the initially enthusiastic Dr. Townsend was beginning to show traces of ennui. On December 23 he went with the

Mosses to the Browns'. There were about twenty persons at the dinner party, including the governor "in undress uniform & his trappings"; Mr. Irving, colonial secretary; "Mr and Mrs Chief Justice Munnings"; Colonel Murray, son of Lord Dunmore, with his wife; the chaplain of the garrison, Mr. Hepworth; and "a jolly fat Englishman," Captain Graham, R.N., of the visiting "brig-of-war" HMS *Icarus*. Dr. Townsend was fortunately seated between Mr. Hepworth, "a dry humorous sensible companion," and a Mrs. Bunch, "an interesting pretty little woman, daughter to the late Dr Richard Bailey of Newyork." Miss Hart, he also noted, "looked very well." The food, though, was fairly humdrum, with "a good round of American corn beef" being favored over the local turtle and a goose that had been one of Townsend's "fellow passengers" on the *Trent*. The dessert was "very tasty," but the madeira, claret, and malmsey only "tolerably good."

The men rose from the table at nine to join the women in the drawing room, where they found a considerable number of additional young ladies and gentlemen who had been invited for "tea" and dancing. The rest of the evening was reported as "rather dull," with Dr. Townsend teaching Mrs. Munnings to play the two-handed card game écarté, before joining some twenty dancers on the piazza. The style of dancing was probably distinctively Bahamian but was not to Townsend's taste. He described it as "a country dance to dull music on the piano" and expressed surprise that the locals preferred such to cotillions. All in all, he was more than content to take his leave at a quarter hour past midnight.[29]

A favorite daytime diversion for Nassau's elite—then as for another century—was the "maroon" or picnic, an excursion either by horseback and carriage into the countryside or, less frequently, by boat to one of the offshore cays. One day-long outing just before Christmas to the Honorable Alexander Murray's country estate on Prospect Ridge and James Moss's farm, the Grove, nearby were enjoyed by both Miss Hart and Dr. Townsend. The lady of leisure described it in typically gushing style, with the black slaves encountered having minor parts in a romantic *fête champêtre*; the doctor, as ever, was more realistic and able to see just a little beneath the surface. "Yesterday we passed at the country-place of the Honourable Colonel M[urra]y," wrote Miss Hart under her pen name, Adela Del Lorraine. "He is the son of the Earl of D[unmore], and his wife is a beautiful young woman, a native of the island. The Colonel possesses all the pride of hereditary rank, of which he is very tenacious; but he is affable and courtier-like in his manners, is an indulgent master, and a kind father. Mrs. M[urray] has five sisters residing here, all of them intelligent and well-educated young ladies, and from them we have received many proofs of friendship."

The Murray country residence was four miles west of town on top of what was then called Prospect Hill (now Prospect Ridge). Reversing the usual sequence, the Murrays spent the winter months there, preferring their house in town during the summer, when Prospect Hill was accounted unhealthy. The ascent to the house was steep over limestone ledges, but citrus trees grew in profusion on the slopes, and on the level ground between hill and sea (the present site of Nassau's chief golf course) was "an extensive lawn" studded with various cultivated trees and shrubs, and surrounded by a neat stone wall. To the south and east of the house, though, was an untamed "Pine Barren," through which a short walk suddenly opened up the picturesque vista of a large and tranquil lake (Lake Cunningham, by the side of the highway to Nassau International Airport), nestling in trees, with its waters "seldom disturbed, excepting when a little boat passes silently over them."

The house itself, not with disparagement but to satisfy the romantic sensibilities of Adela Del Lorraine, was described as looking "almost like a ruin," and the view from its terrace was pictured in terms of the conventionally sublime: "The country all around is broken and uneven; hills and valleys, the masses of rocks, the negro huts scattered over them, and the broad blue sea, which meets the eye at every turn, boundless as the wildest imagination, terrific almost in its infinity, lies in front, and its never ceasing roar, which is distinctly heard, is imposing, if not always inspiring."

The "cottage" and plantation of James Moss, which the "marooners" stopped at on their way back to town and revisited many times later, was described by Hart in scarcely less overblown and myopic terms. The Mosses treated the Grove—which, subdivided since the 1920s, is still one of the most fertile and luxuriant areas close to Nassau, with many fine houses and gardens—more as a country retreat than a commercial venture, and it was this aspect, of course, which Hart emphasized. The thatched roof of the cottage was first glimpsed "through groves of oleander, mahogany, and cocoa-nut trees" and approached along a shady tree-lined avenue through well-cultivated gardens and orchards. The gardens were "filled with rose and myrtle trees," and although the soil was sandy, it produced "the most beautiful flowers and the best European vegetables" Miss Hart had seen in New Providence. This paradise was seemingly created without toil or hardship, though clearly somewhere on the plantation lived a great number of slaves, whose "comfort

and happiness" the lady visitor was "gratified to witness." In an unconscious repetition of the famous scene when the naive absentee proprietor
Matthew Gregory Lewis first visited his Jamaican estate,[30] as soon as the
Mosses' carriage was seen driving up the avenue the children ran "with
their little baskets to gather the choicest fruits and flowers, as a grateful
offering to their 'young massa' and 'missee'" and appeared "quite wild
with joy" when they received "some cakes and sugar-plums" in return.
"I have never seen an instance of cruelty to the slaves since my residence here," added Hart from her limited viewpoint; "on the contrary,
they are well fed and clothed, and appear always cheerful and happy.
They have but little employment, as there are neither sugar nor coffee
plantations on the island, but they are civil in manners, and very kind
and obliging."[31]

Townsend's parallel description of the Grove did not totally contradict
Hart's Panglossian account but provided more telling detail. The "several
acres" of subtropical plants were carefully itemized: "the cocoa, sapa-
dillo, orange, lemon, lime, tamarind, pappaw, Sago, myrtle (growing 30
feet high), roses (in full bloom & in great abundance), the marigold,
myrtle, rosemary & lavender, peas etc etc." Townsend noted besides "a
collection of geese, muscovy ducks, fowls & pidgeons all in excellent
order" and described a lawn adjacent to the garden where there was "a
stag tied by a rope & a fawn his mate whom they are obliged to shut up
as the husband never comes near but he fights her." But he also observed
that the Mosses' farm was partly cleared for corn, and made the remarkable discovery that the garden manager was a dark mulatto slave woman
called Phillis, who in the previous year had returned James Moss about
four hundred dollars from the sale of fruit in Nassau market.

While the Mosses were visiting the Grove with their guests they held
"a sort of levee," at which they received about a dozen male and female
slaves with their children, on their return home from gathering guinea
corn from the provision grounds. The slaves were making plans for
Christmas, when they were to receive extra rations and a special issue
of rum, and were thus, presumably, on their best behavior. That evening
a religious meeting was planned, about which James Moss made close
inquiry, since the question of "the propagation of Christianity among the
W. Indie negroes" (that is, the acceptable forms of religious observance)
was at that moment "a serious subject of deliberation in the colonial legis-
latures." All of the Moss slaves, like the rest of those Townsend had seen
in New Providence since his arrival, were "comfortably dressed." But the
visiting doctor was not impressed with their looks, on which their slave

condition seemed indelibly printed. "None of the blacks whom I saw today, & very few whom I have seen, are good looking," he wrote. "Generally their physiogomy is marked by a painful expression, the effect probably of their degraded condition, which descending from generation to generation has distorted their features and destroyed the natural symmetry of the human countenance."[32]

Dr. Townsend's account of Christmas itself also gave some hint of social life beyond that of the white elite. On normal evenings, the sergeant's guard of black soldiers stationed in Fort Nassau cleared the streets of blacks, or rather prevented any walking about after 8 P.M. without a pass. But "being Christmas our ears were assailed with the noise of the black & white boys playing on the green before our house," he wrote on the evening of Christmas Day, in what was perhaps the first foreign description of the traditional Junkanoo. "We should not have noticed ten times as much sound in Newyork but in this still town it seemed quite grating. We were also regaled last night at Christmas eve until 3 or 4 in the morning with some bad music on hoarse cracked drums & fifes by groups of negroes parading the streets."

At eleven on Christmas morning, Dr. Townsend had received a note from Mr. Hepburn, one of the Mosses' neighbors, inviting him to witness a black baptism in the sea "some distance up the bay" (probably along West Bay Street, where such traditional baptisms are held to this day). The party, which included Henry Moss and Sophie Hepburn as well as Hepburn and Townsend, took a boat from near the marketplace but found that the ceremony was over before they reached the scene. Instead they saw a tumultuous procession of the several hundred blacks who had attended the baptism returning to town, following "a white banner with a cross as if they were bound on a crusade to the holy land."[33]

This lively scene was in marked contrast to that in the two parish churches which Townsend attended. At the "Eastern church" (St. Matthew's) on Sunday, December 14, he heard the Reverend Hepworth give a poor sermon "in an awkward sleepy tone" to a congregation of only thirty or forty, mostly poor whites. The following week he was rather more impressed with the service at Christchurch, not for anything in the religious ceremony but because of the attendance of the governor, with his "mace guard of black troops," the turnout of the fashionable whites, and the fact that the organist was reputedly paid five hundred dollars a year. "The people dress as much to go to church as if they were in a populous city or as if all the world were looking at them," he reported. "There was quite a parade of all the gigs & curricles in town before the church door, with starved diminutive horses arrayed in burnished harness & accompanied with plenty of black equerries, all of which ostentation appears ludicrous when contrasted with the meanness of the cavalry." One splendid exception, however, was Mr. Moss's pair of carriage horses recently imported on the *Trent,* which matched his coach to make "the only decent entire equipage in town."[34]

A similar parade occurred at the funeral of a prominent white woman, except that it was an occasion for blacks and whites alike. "Two black persons went before with lanterns which are used in case night should come before the service is over, for darkness sets in soon after sundown," wrote Townsend. "The negroes like to go to funerals. It seems as rich a treat for them as they were to the poor crazy Lord Portsmouth. They followed to the number of 20 or 30 couple male & female. Some dozen gigs driven by servants brought up the rear. . . . The burial ground is Potter's field in the Western skirts of the town [still Nassau's Western Cemetery], where all the whites are placed without distinction of rank."[35]

Townsend, who, unlike Hart, was able to roam Nassau on horseback or even on foot, provided a few other glimpses of ordinary social life. These included some impressions of the poor whites and free coloreds engaged in fishing and "racking." On one of his horseback explorations along the Eastern Bay he passed "thro' a small collection of mean houses" about four miles from town, "occupied by fishermen & wreckers whose small craft are moored out a few yards from shore & make quite a little fleet. Most of them have a dash of dark blood in their veins & many are mulattoes."[36] The wreckers' product Townsend had already inspected at the Vendue House, where he and Henry Moss had twice attended a sale of allegedly salvaged goods just before Christmas. The heterogeneous items displayed, which included "flour, wine, black walnuts, hickory nuts, paper etc.," were sold duty free, ostensibly for re-export, or because they were damaged or perishable. However, reported Townsend, those "in the know" knew that this "is all a humbug, and that the goods tho' pretended to be reexported will all find their way back & that the town now on the verge of bankruptcy would go entirely to ruin if it were not for these occasional windfalls." None of the goods appeared damaged, and few were really perishable. Townsend reckoned that the Bahamian wreckers were "no better than licensed smugglers," or perhaps worse, repeating the common gossip that vessels were sometimes purposely wrecked "and that the Captain & those concerned purposely keep out of the way." To this was added a version of the reproach so often repeated by foreigners: "It is affirmed that Nassau was first settled by a colony of pirates under the celebrated Blackbeard. Smuggling and wrecking as they are practised in these islands are next-a-kin to piracy or no better than a refined species of it. The Bahamians are very expert and adroit at it, it is said, perhaps owing to a hereditary predisposition and tact, for if tradition is to be believed all the inhabitants are either lineally or collaterally descended from the founder of Nassau & his associates." [37]

Townsend's account, however, almost as much as that of the sheltered Hart, concentrated on the more respectable members of the Bahamian elite, and their social life through the official season, which lasted from Christmas, through the legislative session, to the start of the hot weather. For the whites, the highlights were the formal balls, the assembly prorogation ceremony, and the celebration of the king's birthday on April 23, which rounded off the season. Describing such occasions, Hart was in her element. "I have been at two charming balls since I wrote you last," she reported in her eighth epistle,

> The first was given by Mr. I[rving], who is the "Secretary" and "Treasurer." It was at the Assembly Room, which is in the "Public Buildings," and was beautifully decorated and splendidly lighted. It was arched at one end, and in the recess were placed orange and lemon trees in full bearing, and lights were tastefully arranged among the branches, producing the most enchanting effect imaginable. . . . I went under the protection of my kind friends, Mr. and Mrs. James [Moss], and when I entered the room, I stood still a moment to enjoy the novelty of the scene. The ladies were seated on side benches, and the profusion of flowers and feathers, and the gay dresses, and the splendour of the light, and the freshness of the perfume from the flowers, and the music, all made me imagine that I had suddenly been transported to some fairy spot.

When the governor and his suite arrived, the band saluted him first with the "King's March" and then "God Save the King," awakening in many hearts, thought Hart, "dear delightful thoughts of country and of home." The ball was opened by Governor and Lady Murray, and then "young and old, gay and sad, all joined in the merry dance." The glitter and swirl, the "fantastic dresses and unique appearance of some who were there," demanded the "pencil of a Hogarth." About a hundred persons sat down to supper late in the evening, the tables, laid out in a separate room, being "prettily ornamented and abundantly filled." Hart and her coterie obtained plentiful supplies of champagne. "You may be sure," she concluded, "when we rose from the table, there was no trace of gloom or sadness left."

The other social high point for Hart was the Birth-Night Ball, given at Government House on April 23. This was "both splendid and charming." The ladies were decked in their most gorgeous finery, and the gentlemen resplendent in uniforms, formal dress, and decorations. At midnight there was a fireworks display on the lawn in front of the governor's mansion, with the colored flashes lighting up the town below and the harbor beyond, where all the boats were decked out with flags, gaily waving in the light breeze. To the impressionable visitor, the panoramic display, with the accompanying sound of fireworks, signal guns, and occasional bugle calls, was "quite enchanting." The supper, though, fueled a somewhat snobbish condescension, as "a scene of indescribable hilarity." For the occasion of the fête "made it necessary to invite many [whites and near-whites] who did not generally mingle with the gentry; and nothing is more amusing than the assumed consequence of those persons, when they are admitted to the society to which they are unaccustomed."[38]

Far more solemn and symbolic were the public ceremony in the council chamber on January 28 at which the governor gave assent to bills and closed the annual session of the assembly, and the formal display on April 23 in honor of the king's birthday. Hart attended the former as the guest of Councilor James Moss, accompanied by the wife of the chief justice, though it was not customary for women to be present and, like the members of the House of Assembly, she had to stand throughout. Typically, she was far more interested in the outward trappings of the occasion than its inner significance, which included the passage of the vital new Slave Act of 1824. They had waited an hour, she told her American correspondent, when a fine flourish of trumpets and a roll of drums announced the arrival of Governor Grant. He was in his carriage, a plain equipage with two liveried servants, but preceded by a file of black soldiers in gaudy yellow uniforms and attended by all the staff officers in their full dress. The soldiers ranged themselves on either side of the door, and the governor passed through them, richly caparisoned but "without the proud and lofty demeanour which often distinguishes a man of power."

Everyone stood still until Governor Grant had taken his seat at the head of the council table and had taken off what Miss Hart called his "imperial hat." Then the Speaker, in his black robes and cap, advanced with a huge roll of papers, each of which bore the royal signet. He bowed "gracefully and reverentially" to the governor and read each bill that had been passed by the assembly and council, to which the governor affixed his signature, turning it into an act. Governor Grant then made

a "short and handsome" speech, addressed to the seven or eight gentlemen of the council rather than the legislature as a whole. He thanked
them for the assistance they had rendered him in performing the duties
of his office, "modestly attributed to their wisdom, more than to his own,
the prosperous and tranquil state of the colony" and kindly invoked for
them "the blessings of peace and union, and the approbation of His most
gracious Majesty, King George the Fourth." The governor then retired,
attended to his carriage by the council and his officers, amidst the loud
applause of the assembly and spectators, and to the repeated strains of
the national anthem.[39]

The Birthday Parade was a more public and even more obviously significant exercise, in that it included a demonstration of the actual power
of the entire regime—intended to impress and overawe the ordinary
people—rather than symbolizing the merely nominal superiority of the
governor and his council over the House of Assembly. Predictably, it
was Townsend rather than Hart who gave the better sense of this. "The
King's birth day was celebrated today by the militia," began his entry for
April 23, 1824,

> whose uniform is that of the regular—consisted of about 200 in all, two
> companies of which were artillery with field pieces. One of the comps. of in-
> fantry was the Brown Rangers, being mulattoes commanded by Capt. Kerr
> (Speaker) & Lieut Butler, a gentleman whom I know very well. The whole
> was commanded by Lieut. Col. Armbrister father of the young man shot
> by General Jackson of the United States army during the Seminole war. The
> troops marched several times round the parade passing by the Governor
> who was mounted on a white charger in full British uniform, being a long
> red coat, high cocked hat with three or four tall ostrich plumes, large full
> white pantaloons coming over his boots & held down by straps. . . . The
> firing of the field pieces as well as of the small arms was executed with a
> precision & regularity which would have done honour to veterans.[40]

One is immediately reminded of the sense of the comments made by
Richard Ligon of a similar occasion in Barbados some 180 years earlier:
that the guns were fired to strike terror into the heart of the slaves, and
that an efficient militia was worth any number of laws for social control.[41]

With the end of the season and the advent of the hot weather, the enthusiasm of both American visitors for Nassau and its society noticeably
faded. Townsend was more fortunate in being able to exercise his profession, but Hart became quite clearly bored. "I now scarcely know how
to fill up a letter to you," she wrote some time in May, "for there is no
variety in our amusements, having become accustomed to the common

round of visiting, riding, sailing, and marooning, and our occupations are from day to day much the same." It was not a truly literate society. New books were seldom received, except by a few private individuals, and the monthly packet from Jamaica bringing letters and papers was only intermittently augmented by merchant ships carrying periodicals for the public reading room. Books could not be purchased, for there were no book stores, and only one printing office, from which "a small gazette" was issued twice a week.

The reading room was in the public buildings, alongside the legislative and administrative offices. Its location made it a "disagreeable resort for ladies," though it might have become a greater "source of pleasure and improvement" were more of them to patronize it. "But really, every thing in such a climate tends to depress intellectual exertions," complained Miss Hart, "and a drive in the evening along the bay is more refreshing than a morning passed in the public reading-room." In fact, many of the wealthier residents had valuable private libraries, and the ladies were not totally lacking in "intellectual cultivation and taste," since many of them had been educated "'at home', that is, in England," and had useful accomplishments. But there was nothing in Nassau to remind anyone of the fine arts; "neither pictures, nor statues, nor artists." This the prim Miss Hart considered a major misfortune, for such were "among the highest sources of improvement to the taste," affording "a delightful and classical gratification to the mind, as well as to the imagination." [42]

One diversion which Hart did not mention but in which Townsend, with some trepidation, did become involved, was amateur dramatics. As the doctor reported, a stage was set up in a room at the courthouse and many "of the finest people in town" acted "to beguile the time, as there are no sports & amusements of any description in this place." [43] The leading lights were the Speaker, "Lewis Kerr" (more than something of an actor in real life, for he was really Herman Blennerhassett, one of the associates of the notorious Aaron Burr),[44] who was stage manager, scene painter, and makeup artist, and Assistant Judge Lees (later suspended by Governor Carmichael Smyth at the same time as Robert Duncombe), who was scene shifter and prompter.

Townsend accepted the walk-on part of Heartly in "Who Wants a Guinea," but only once he was convinced of the respectability of the other players. The performance, after less than two weeks' rehearsal, on Wednesday, January 14, was as amateur as could be, though 160 persons, including the governor and all "the first people in town—females in great abundance," had each paid a dollar to see it. Most of the players performed tolerably well, but Mr. Malcolm the schoolmaster, who played Torrent, "on whom the interest of the play turned & who had most to say & oftenest to appear," had conceived the part so poorly and committed so little of it to memory that "the prompter's voice was almost constantly substituted for his own." Townsend reckoned that the whole cast would have been hissed off the stage for having allowed Malcolm to ruin the performance had the audience not all been the actors' friends and in a tolerant mood. William Wylly, the solicitor general, goodhumoredly told the company that it had done admirably, except for the schoolmaster, who deserved a good whipping. Townsend himself was not feeling well on the night—probably an attack of nerves—but managed to stumble through his small part without "rendering it ridiculous," which he considered "a great escape."[45]

There seem to have been no more organized sports in Nassau than in an English country town a century earlier, for much the same reason, that they were regarded as socially disruptive; and the absence of regular visits from professional entertainers was due partly to Nassau's isolation but mainly to the regime's fear that they might similarly disturb the people. An earlier visit from a Cuban circus and pantomime troupe, reported in the *Bahama Gazette*, may well have been a cautionary experience. On April 22, 1813, the following advertisement appeared in the paper:

THEATRE
By permission of his Excellency the Governor
Dona Delores Miranda
Has the honor to inform the public, that
This Evening,
At the Theatre, on the lot of Mr. James
Hollywood, in the road leading
to Fort Fincastle.
Don Jose Miranda's Company
will perform for her
Benefit
A VARIETY OF
Feats of Agility
On the Tight and Slack Rope
during which the performers will do their utmost
to gratify the public.
A CHILD
will balance itself on its' head
on the rope.

Don Francisco Lopez
will dance on the tight rope with a
pair of eggs attached to his feet.
DON JOSE LOPEZ
will especially exert himself on the rope
to please the spectators.
DONA MIRANDA
will balance herself sitting in a chair
and walk on a plank on the rope.
DON JOSE MIRANDA
Will Conclude
With an elegant English Hornpipe
on the rope.
The evening's entertainment to close with
the much admired pantomime of
BLACK BEARD.
The Scenery will represent the Sea, the Island of N. Providence
with the adjacent cays. An English frigate with her commander
on board will combat the Pirates, firing broadsides, &c.
Doors to be opened at 4 o'clock and the performance to begin
precisely at half past 7.
TICKETS to be had at the Theatre—price, six shillings for
white persons, three shillings for coloured people.[46]

Three weeks later, however, one "Bonefish" wrote a letter to the *Gazette* complaining of the effects of the above extravaganza upon the pockets, minds, and behavior of "the prodigal and unthinking part of the community." Don and Dona Miranda's company was termed

a parcel of Rope Dancers, who have been performing in this town for some time past, in a kind of rude booth, patched up with rough boards and partially covered with old sails and bagging. The price of entrance to this ragged theatre has been lowered, so that the poorest and most dissolute persons of every description can by some means raise as much as will procure them admission. The example thus held out to our servants is perceivable every hour; for in passing the parade or any open place, you observe dozens of clumsy fellows attempting to tumble and throw sommersets & the little boys in every yard about town, instead of cleaning their knives and candlesticks, are seen standing on their heads and tumbling over.

A gentleman who has a number of vessels and many Sailor Negroes, on coming home, a few days ago, found that his people, instead of attending to the work laid out for them (which was laying rope to make rigging for his vessels) were all idle, and laughing heartily at one of them who had set up a tight rope and was attempting to cut capers on it for the amusement of his fellow idlers. If a family take a walk abroad in the fine evenings of the season, they find on returning the servants are not to be found and are gone to the maroma in the road leading to Fort Fincastle, These are, perhaps but a few of the ill effects produced by this nuisance, and although it is not liable to be indicted in our Courts of Law, ought nevertheless, in my humble opinion, to be suppressed by some means or other.[47]

Such rough entertainment was obviously out of bounds to such a delicate flower as Miss Hart, though Townsend may well have become familiar with at least the more respectable members of the Mirandas' audiences through his medical practice. As a foreigner, with unknown qualifications, he was not readily admitted into the small circle of established local practitioners—whose own qualifications he in turn regarded with some skepticism.[48] Townsend, though, did gradually earn respect by his willingness to give advice and assistance without pay and by being prepared to minister to colored servants, or even slaves. He also seems to have been something of an expert on vaccination against smallpox— still a bit of a novelty in 1824—having brought some vials of vaccine with him from America, and keeping a record in his diary of "Successful Vaccinations (Gratuitous) Colored People's Children."[49]

On April 1 Dr. Townsend even reported that he had deserted a dinner, "being obliged to meet Dr Tynes in consultation at that hour on the case of difficult parturation in a servant woman of Hon. Patrick Brown."[50] Perhaps as a reward for his unpaid help, Tynes appointed Townsend as his *locum tenens* when he went on a visit to Crooked Island on June 19. This left Townsend responsible not only for Tynes's private practice but for attendance at the poor house, jail, and health department. For two months the American doctor was kept so busy that he left the comfort of the Mosses' house for a separate office and lodging. When Tynes returned on August 20, however, he took back all his work. Either through lack of profitable employment or because he now shared Hart's disenchantment with Nassau, Townsend's diary entries grew sparse and perfunctory, fading out on September 24, 1824, just as he was preparing to return to New York.[51]

In this falling off there is hint of a deeper melancholy. Even in the spare medical prescriptions with which Dr. Townsend's journal ends there is a sense of unbridged, unbridgeable distances and impotence just as poignant as Henrietta Kelsall's profitless invocation of the world of *Pride and Prejudice*, or Miss Hart's echoes of the Romantic novelist and Jamaican slaveowner Matthew Gregory "Monk" Lewis; not just of the distance between a relatively progressive American doctor from New York and the life of a sleepy British colony on the edge of the tropics, but of the gulf between the cultural and material lifestyles of whites and blacks, which early nineteenth-century medicine was powerless to cross. For the child of the free mulatto Ann Paul, suffering from a persistent unexplained swelling, the best that Dr. Townsend could do on leaving Nassau was to prescribe a lancing and some ineffectual medicine; and for Charlotte, the "native African" slave of Mr. Armbrister, said to be suffering from "Scrophula," he could do no more than leave "advice in writing." [52]

～ 16 ～

The Slave Majority:
Demographic Patterns

WHEN TURNING from the world of Nassau and its elite to look in detail at the Bahamian Out Islands and the slaves, one is faced by the problems confronting all would-be historians of the great majority—those who did not, could not, write their own historical account. Inevitably, the persons who wrote about Bahamian slaves, or even of the poor-white "Conchs," were mainly white outsiders. There is only one relatively objective description of the day-to-day life of an Out Island slave plantation equal to the Kelsall letters or the Townsend journal—a Watling's Island planter's diary that dates from the very last days of formal slavery. For the remainder, direct accounts of Bahamian slavery were written by whites whose view was subjective and impressionistic, if not overtly biased, either to defend or, less commonly, attack the institution.

The best of these accounts were undoubtedly those of William Wylly, himself a slaveowner as well as attorney general, who in 1815 gave a brief conspectus of Bahamian slavery and Bahamian slave law to the House of Assembly, and also published a somewhat idealistic account of the regime on his own New Providence estates.[1] Unusually, Wylly set out to attack the worst abuses of the system, while at the same time denying that he was attempting to dismantle it. His version was also distinguished by both a respect for the independent qualities of many Bahamian slaves and, as a true Loyalist, a thoroughgoing contempt for many of the poorer class of Bahamian whites.

Wylly acutely recognized that in 1815 there were four distinct classes of slaves: black seamen, domestics, slaves belonging to petty farmers, and plantation slaves. Of these, he pointed out, the seamen enjoyed the most practical freedom. They were allowed a percentage of the profits of their fishing and turtling and were treated almost exactly the same as ordinary white seamen. For this reason, despite better than average opportunities, they rarely attempted to escape. Domestics too, he claimed, had as easy and comfortable a life as any free domestics in other countries. The petty farm slaves were mainly engaged in supplying the Nassau market with vegetables, fruit, and poultry. These slaves lived in small groups, on a footing almost of equality with their masters—not infrequently, indeed, being smarter than they. The lot of the majority who were plantation slaves was naturally harsher but still very dependent on their special circumstances, and in no cases as severe as in the true West Indian colonies. Wylly asserted that the work on a Bahamian cotton plantation was "mere play" compared to that on a sugar estate in the West Indies. Bahamian plantation slaves worked on a task system, were given three hours a day for meals, and rarely worked after dark. Their punishments were less severe than in the British army, the use of the brutal cowskin whip had been discontinued (in favor of the cat-o-nine-tails), and they generally enjoyed three days off at Christmas. The most fortunate of plantation slaves were those whose owners were resident. Plantation slaves were "well attached" to resident masters, who looked on their slaves almost as children and protected them against the overseers, who as a class were generally "low and ignorant." [2]

Wylly's 1815 account, however, was obviously slanted and somewhat Panglossian. It was far from comprehensive, being based on very limited experience of Out Island conditions. He not only was wrong in some of his sweeping generalizations but also wrote at a time when the Bahamian economy and slavery system were undergoing rapid changes. To gain a fuller and truer picture, it is necessary not only to read between the lines of subjective descriptions, governors' dispatches, plantocratic laws, and newspaper articles, but also to adopt the techniques of the so-called cliometric revolution: to analyze the telling minutiae of runaway advertisements and police returns, and, above all, to look with a new eye, fresh questions, and modern methodology at demographic statistics drawn up for different purposes by old-fashioned counting methods. In this last respect, the social historian of the Bahamas is fortunate in being able to call upon and redeploy the detailed if incomplete population censuses of 1805, 1810, and 1819, and the even better slave registration returns for the last dozen years of slavery (1822–34)—a set of data so accurate and comprehensive that one can not only learn more of Bahamian slaves than the owners (or even the registrar) knew, but, paradoxically, far more in crucial demographic respects than can ever be known of the other sections of the Bahamian population, free coloreds and blacks as well as whites of every social level.

The slave census of 1805 and the census of the entire population in 1810,[3] which were the first to be broken down in rough age groups, not only provide a clearer picture than before of the distribution of all sections of the population throughout the colony, including whites, but allow for some comparative analysis of the balance of ages and sexes. By 1810 little more than a third of the Bahamian population of over 17,000 lived on New Providence.[4] The New Providence total of 6,084 was made up of 1,820 whites (including 100 foreigners), 1,074 nonwhite free persons (of whom 565 were listed as black and 509 "coloured"), and 3,186 slaves (146 of them colored). Whites thus now made up no more than 30 percent of the New Providence population, being outnumbered 5 to 3 by the island's slaves and outnumbering by little more than 3 to 2 the steadily increasing section of free blacks and coloreds. Nonetheless, no less than 43 percent of the 4,250 Bahamian whites lived on New Providence, and 67 percent of the nonwhite freedmen, compared with only 28 percent of all Bahamian slaves.

The only other Bahamian islands with a balance of population comparable to New Providence's were the Turks Islands—almost a self-contained satellite colony with a separate free port until 1823, though not politically detached (with the Caicos Islands) from the Bahamas until 1848. In the Turks Islands there were 1,935 persons in 1810, of whom 540, or 28 percent, were whites; 1,308, or 68 percent, slaves; and 87, or 4.5 percent, free persons of color.

The remaining Out Islands had become quite clearly separable into the few mainly old-established islands with a high proportion of whites and comparatively few free coloreds and blacks, and those newly settled islands where black slaves hugely outnumbered both whites and nonwhite freedmen. Harbour Island, Eleuthera, and Abaco, along with their inhabited offshore cays, together contained some 1,500 whites, 1,800 slaves, and 130 free coloreds and blacks, percentages of 44, 52, and 4 respectively. The other dozen or so Out Islands settled since the Loyalist influx contained about 44 percent of the total of Bahamian slaves, some 5,000, compared with only 385 whites and 240 nonwhite freedmen—percentages of 89, 8, and 2 respectively. In other words, in the islands settled since the American Revolution (with the exception of Abaco) black slaves outnumbered whites by 13 to 1 and nonwhite freedmen by over 20 to 1, whereas in the old-established islands (plus Abaco), the ratio was no more than 1.5 slaves to each white, or 3.8 slaves to each nonwhite freedman—with the slaves outnumbering the free of every complexion by only 6 to 5.

Table 5
Population, 1810, by Islands

Island	Whites			Slaves			Free Nonwhites			Total	Whites per 100 Slaves	Free Coloreds per 100 Whites
	Males	Females	Total	Males	Females	Total	Males	Females	Total			
New Providence	—	—	1,820[a]	—	—	3,190	—	—	1,074	6,084	57	59
Harbour Island	324	337	661	271	268	539	26	26	52	1,252	123	8
Eleuthera	302	274	576	557	541	1,098	79	64	143	1,817	52	25
Abaco (1807)	—	—	250	—	—	150[b]	—	—	10[b]	410	167	4
Exumas	60	36	96	681	580	1,261	21	34	55	1,412	8	57
Cat Island	30	24	54	354	308	662	31	27	58	774	8	107
Long and Ragged Islands	83	58	141	379	355	734	30	37	67	942	19	48
San Salvador	12	9	21	233	253	486	2	3	5	512	4	24
Rum Cay	7	0	7	102	75	177	0	0	0	184	4	0
Andros (1807)	—	—	10	100	80	180	—	—	—	195	6	50
Crooked and Acklin's islands	19	4	23	547	595	1,142	27	26	53	1,218	2	230
Inagua	1	0	1	17	11	28	0	0	0	29	4	0
Caicos Islands	19	13	32	275	247	522	3	3	6	560	6	19
Turks Island	290	250	540	741	567	1,308	32	55	87	1,935	41	16
Total	2,232[b]	2,000[b]	4,232[b]	6,095	5,382	11,477	829[b]	786[b]	1,615	17,324	37	38

Source: C.O. 23/59, 37.
[a] Includes 100 "foreigners."
[b] Estimated.

Both the 1805 and 1810 censuses give the numbers of different sections of the population in each island, males and females, who were aged one to twelve, twelve to twenty, twenty to sixty, and over sixty. Though providing too rough a division of ages to allow for the construction of convincing population "pyramids," these data do show how the sex and age balance—that is, the demographic health—of slaves compared with that of whites and nonwhite free persons, and how that of the people in New Providence compared with those in the Out Islands, in the period midway between the coming of the Loyalists and the ending of formal slavery.

Unfortunately, for neither year was an age or sex breakdown provided for the New Providence whites, so that it is not possible to compare their situation with that of the New Providence slaves and freedmen. However, the data which are provided for the whites of the other Bahamian islands in 1810 (including Turks Island) do show remarkable similarities with those for Out Island slaves—suggesting that in at least some demographic respects the Bahamian slaves were catching up with the whites.

In both the white and slave Out Island populations, though for different reasons, there was a slight "bulge" in the number of males and of persons in the middle age range. Among the slaves this was, of course, accounted for by the continuing presence of Africans (still about 25 percent of the slave population in 1810), who were nearly all imported as young adults, with a proportion of roughly three males to two females.[5] But this imbalance was matched in the Out Island white population by a tendency for there to be a comparatively high proportion of adults, especially males, because of the need for slave overseers, many of whom were bachelors. The similarity in the low proportions of elderly folk may also slightly mislead since, unlike slaves, some elderly whites would have had the chance to migrate from the Out Islands before they died.

A more telling similarity, though, was the high proportion of children in both populations. The 394 male and 330 female Out Island whites under thirteen years of age in 1810 constituted 35.1 percent of the total of Out Island whites. Though a relatively healthy figure, this was almost matched by the Out Island slaves, whose 1,273 males and 1,264 females under thirteen made up 31.9 percent of the total of Out Island slaves. This, moreover, was a significant advance over the figure of 30.6 percent only five years earlier and suggests that the fertility of Out Island slaves was rapidly increasing at this period.

Though no certain figures are available, Out Island slaves may well already have become as fertile as the majority of the white population who lived on New Providence. But how did the New Providence slave population compare both with the New Providence whites and the Out Island slaves in this and other respects? Although complete data on the New Providence slaves exist only for 1805, these do, predictably, show that there was less of an age and sex bulge in the middle age range than for Out Island slaves, because the proportion of African slaves was much lower than in the Out Islands (perhaps already as low as 10 percent). Only 45.8 percent of New Providence slaves in 1805 were aged twenty to sixty, compared with 53.8 percent for the newly settled islands, and New Providence slave males in this age range outnumbered females by only 109 per 100, compared with 133 per 100 for the newly settled islands.

Nonetheless, this ostensibly healthier demographic statistic for New Providence was not matched by a comparatively higher proportion of slave children. The 492 slave males and 546 slave females under thirteen in New Providence in 1805 made up 29.5 percent of the New Providence slave total, which was actually 1.1 percent lower than the Out Island slave average at that time. It is unlikely, however, that the New Providence slaves' fertility was less than that of the island's white population, because of the well-attested fact that the proportion of slaves there was steadily increasing without fresh importations—though the emigration of whites may well have had some bearing on the matter.

The absence of age and sex data for the great majority of Bahamian free coloreds and blacks who lived in New Providence does not allow us to test whether the contemporary impression was correct that they were demographically healthier than either the local slaves or whites. The data for the minority of nonwhite free persons who lived in the Out Islands in 1810 do not suggest significant differences from either whites or slaves, except that there were rather more in the over-sixty bracket, some 5 percent of the total, compared with 3 percent of slaves and whites alike.

Another contemporary impression, however, was certainly borne out by the 1805 and 1810 data: that Harbour Island and Eleuthera were healthier than either Nassau or any other Out Island. Though there was a notable shortage of persons over sixty years of age (a fact that lacks sufficient explanation), in the key indicator of the proportion of the total population represented by children, Harbour Island and Eleuthera were perceptibly ahead of the rest of the Bahamas in respect of whites and slaves alike. In 1810, 38.0 percent of the combined white population of Harbour Island and Eleuthera was under the age of thirteen, compared

Table 6

Slave Population, 1805, by Islands and Broad Age Cohorts

Cohort	Males				Females				Total Males and Females
	Nassau	Harbour Island and Eleuthera	Other Out Islands[a]	Total Males	Nassau	Harbour Island and Eleuthera	Other Out Islands[a]	Total Females	
Over 60	140 (1.5)[b]	16 (0.2)	54 (0.6)	210 (2.2)	66 (0.6)	14 (0.1)	78 (0.8)	158 (1.7)	368 (3.9)
20–60	846 (8.9)	347 (3.7)	1,393 (14.7)	2,588 (27.3)	778 (8.2)	251 (2.6)	1,050 (11.1)	2,079 (21.9)	4,667 (49.2)
12–19	373 (3.9)	114 (1.2)	435 (4.6)	922 (9.7)	312 (3.3)	121 (1.3)	245 (2.6)	678 (7.2)	1,600 (16.9)
Under 12	492 (5.2)	266 (2.8)	649 (6.8)	1,407 (14.8)	546 (5.8)	251 (2.6)	644 (6.8)	1,441 (15.2)	2,848 (30.0)
Total	1,853 (19.5)	743 (7.8)	2,531 (26.7)	5,127 (54.1)	1,702 (17.9)	637 (6.7)	2,017 (21.3)	4,356 (45.9)	9,483 (100.0)

Source: C.O. 23/59, 37.

[a] Includes all islands except Nassau (New Providence), Harbour Island, and Eleuthera.

[b] Figure in parentheses is percentage of total males and females in all age cohorts (9,483), rounded to nearest decimal point.

with 30.8 percent of the whites of the other Out Islands of which there were records. More surprisingly, the figures for the Harbour Island and Eleuthera slaves were marginally higher, 38.2 percent being under thirteen (up from 37.5 percent in 1805), compared with 30.2 percent in the other Out Islands (28.4 percent in 1805), and 29.2 percent in Nassau.[6]

These findings, suggesting significant variations in demographic health (especially fertility and infant mortality) and a quite rapid relative improvement in the average health of Bahamian slaves, are quite consonant with known causes and trends: Nassau's reputation for being relatively subject to contagious diseases (though, of course, far healthier than any West Indian colonial capital), the comparative unhealthiness of intensive plantation agriculture, well-known tendencies toward stable marriages and large families, the decline of plantations, and the inexorable, partly related, decline in the proportion of Africans in the slave population.

The census of 1810 was the last before Bahamian slaves began to be re-exported or manumitted in considerable numbers. The total of slaves probably reached a peak of just over 12,000 around 1815, but the largest number actually counted was the 11,155 listed in the tables sent home by Acting Governor Munnings in 1819—the last compilation before the much more detailed and accurate triennial returns that began in 1822. This final rough census is chiefly useful in showing the advance made by the general slave population since 1810, and for being the first to divide the slave population into African and Creole components.[7]

Though the figures may have been slightly skewed by the export and manumission of a greater number of mature slaves than children, the proportion of slaves under thirteen years of age had risen to 35.7 percent from 31.9 percent in 1810 (and 30.2 percent in 1805). This was despite the fact that Africans, of whom only 1.3 percent were under thirteen, still made up 23.9 percent of the total slave population. Remarkably, nearly half (46 percent) of the 8,589 Creole slaves (who made up 76.1 percent of the total) were under the age of thirteen in 1819. Perhaps just as surprising, though, was that only 1.7 percent of Creole slaves were over sixty, compared with 9.8 percent of Africans—Africans over sixty actually outnumbering Creoles by 252 to 145. Predictably, there were still 152 African males per 100 African females. This contrasted with the superfluity of females among the Creoles of 100 to 93, attributable to the somewhat lower mortality of Bahamas-born female slaves in each age range.

When the Triennial Slave Registration Act was finally passed by the Bahamas House of Assembly in April 1821, it required all masters to

Table 7

Out Island Population, 1810, by Broad Age Cohorts

| Cohort | Slaves | | | Whites[b] | Free Coloureds[b] | Total Population[b] |
	Harbour Island and Eleuthera[a]	Other Out Islands[a]	Total Out Islands[a]			
Over 60						
Males	24 (0.3)	99 (1.2)	123 (1.5)	30 (1.4)	16 (3.1)	
Females	20 (0.3)	103 (1.3)	123 (1.5)	30 (1.4)	11 (2.1)	
Total	44 (0.6)	202 (2.5)	246 (3.1)	60 (2.9)	27 (5.3)	333 (3.2)
20–60						
Males	380 (4.8)	1,776 (22.3)	2,156 (27.1)	489 (23.6)	111 (21.6)	
Females	361 (4.5)	1,499 (18.8)	1,860 (23.4)	520 (25.1)	121 (23.6)	
Total	741 (9.3)	3,275 (41.2)	4,016 (50.5)	1,009 (48.7)	232 (45.2)	5,257 (49.9)

12–19						
Males	119 (1.5)	486 (6.1)	605 (7.6)	135 (6.5)	53 (10.3)	
Females	107 (1.3)	445 (5.6)	552 (6.9)	143 (6.9)	45 (8.8)	
Total	226 (2.8)	931 (11.7)	1,157 (14.5)	278 (13.4)	98 (19.1)	1,533 (14.5)
Under 12						
Males	305 (3.8)	968 (12.2)	1,273 (16.0)	394 (19.0)	73 (14.2)	
Females	321 (4.0)	943 (11.9)	1,264 (15.9)	330 (15.9)	83 (16.2)	
Total	626 (7.9)	1,911 (24.0)	2,537 (31.9)	724 (35.0)	156 (30.4)	3,417 (32.4)
Total (all cohorts)						
Males	828 (10.4)	3,329 (41.8)	4,157 (52.2)	1,048 (50.6)	253 (49.3)	
Females	809 (10.2)	2,990 (37.6)	3,799 (47.8)	1,023 (49.4)	260 (50.7)	
Grand total[c]	1,637 (20.6)	6,319 (79.4)	7,956 (100.0)	2,071 (100.0)	513 (100.0)	10,540 (100.0)

[a] Number in parentheses is percentage of grand total for total out islands (7,956), rounded to the nearest decimal point.

[b] Number in parentheses is percentage of grand total for column, rounded to the nearest decimal point.

[c] Nassau totals: 1,720 whites (plus 100 foreigners), 565 free coloureds, 509 free blacks, 3,044 black slaves, and 246 coloured slaves, for a total of 5,084.

Table 8

Slave Population, 1819, by Broad Age Cohorts and Male/Female, African/Creole Ratios

Cohort	Creoles		African-born		Total				
	Males	Females	Males	Females	Males	Females	Creoles	African-born	All Slaves
Over 60	72 (0.6)[a]	73 (0.6)	155 (1.4)	97 (0.9)	227 (2.0)	170 (1.5)	145 (1.3)	252 (2.3)	397 (3.6)
12–60	2,122 (19.0)	2,370 (21.2)	1,375 (12.3)	906 (8.1)	3,497 (31.3)	3,276 (29.4)	4,492 (40.3)	2,281 (20.4)	6,773 (60.7)
Under 12	1,954 (17.5)	1,998 (17.9)	18 (0.2)	15 (0.1)	1,972 (17.7)	2,013 (18.0)	3,952 (35.4)	33 (0.3)	3,985 (35.7)
Total	4,148 (37.2)	4,441 (39.8)	1,548 (13.9)	1,018 (9.1)	5,696 (51.1)	5,459 (48.9)	8,589 (77.0)	2,566 (23.0)	11,155 (100.0)

Sources: Governors' Dispatches (Duplicate), 1818–25, 755; Bahamas Archives; Gail Saunders, Slavery in the Bahamas, 1648–1838 (Nassau: Privately published, 1985), 52.

[a] Figure in parentheses is percentage of total slaves in all age cohorts (11,155), rounded to nearest decimal point.

make a sworn return of all the slaves they owned on January 1, 1822, and each third January 1 thereafter, on pain of a penalty of one hundred pounds for non-compliance.[8] The location of each slave holding was to be specified, and each slave was to be listed by name, sex, color (black or mulatto), age, and origin (African or Creole). Owners were also to list the increase and decrease in their holdings over the preceding three years, whether by birth, death, purchase, gift, manumission, transportation, or desertion. A separate column entitled "How disposed of, etc." was intended to indicate the names of persons from whom slaves were purchased or inherited, and to whom they were sold, deeded, or bequeathed, but was sometimes used to indicate causes of death. Slaves' mothers were also very occasionally listed, but since very few slaves had (and even fewer were listed as having) a second or family name, it is generally impossible to trace family connections. Yet, as we shall see, a minority of the owners of sizeable numbers of slaves did list their slaves in such a way that family or household groupings were clearly indicated.

Excluding an incomplete trial run for 1821, five Bahamian slave registration returns were made, for 1822, 1825, 1828, 1831, and 1834. A sixth complete slave census, made in July 1834 for the purpose of compensating the owners, provides valuable additional information about the slaves' employment. Two complete sets of all these returns still exist: the original collations made by the Bahamian registrar of slave returns, James Ambrister, long kept in the Nassau Public Library and now in the Bahamian Archives; and the copies sent to the imperial registrar of colonial slaves in London, now lodged in the Public Record Office at Kew.[9]

Altogether, the Bahamian slave registration and compensation returns (like those of all the British slave colonies) are an invaluable source.[10] With painstaking work, they allow for an almost illimitable range of demographic analysis. At the macro level, for each of the five registration years a static demographic portrait of the overall slave population is easily obtainable, employing at least six standard variables: location and size of holdings, sex, age, color, origin, and categories of employment of slaves. From this, other general demographic features such as fertility, mortality, and life expectancy can be processed for each of the variable categories. Even more valuably, the demographic picture can be dynamically enhanced—as if graduating from snapshot to movie— by using the sequence of five triennia. In addition, valuable information can be garnered, in a more or less random or sample manner, about causes of death, manumission, sale and other forms of transfer, transportation, desertion, punishment, family and household patterns, and naming practices. Nor does the value of the material end there. At the micro level it is possible to trace the history of small groups and families of slaves, or of individuals, over the entire period of the last twelve years of formal slavery—in exceptional cases even to trace the fate of slaves transferred from the Bahamas after they reached their colonies of destination.[11]

The accuracy of the data was more or less guaranteed by the fines for irregularities and the threat of losing compensation in 1834. Very few slaves were missed or double-counted, and those who were can normally be traced through corroboration with other triennial returns. Naturally, the ages given for slaves were not always accurate, as the "clumping" for round numbers suggests, but were clearly more accurate for Creoles than for Africans, and for Creoles born in the Bahamas were almost entirely reliable. Moreover, the errors in giving slaves' ages almost certainly evened out, because there was no consistent motive for either under- or overstatement. The worst deficiencies, potentially affecting all estimates of fertility and mortality, were that children who were born and died within the same triennium were not invariably recorded, and that purchasers in registering new slaves sometimes left out those who had died or been born since the previous census. These problems, though, seem to have been less a feature of the Bahamian registration returns than those of the sugar colonies, both because the Bahamian system was more scrupulous and because infant mortality was less severe in the Bahamas than elsewhere.

Ultimately, indeed, it is in comparing the Bahamas with other slave colonies that the registration and compensation returns have perhaps their greatest value. As James Stephen suggested in *Slavery Delineated* as early as 1830, and Barry Higman has recently demonstrated in his magisterial *Slave Populations of the British Caribbean, 1807–1834*, the material from one slave colony is massively illuminating in itself but tells us even more about one colony's slave system and the life of its slaves when placed in a comparative context.[12]

As in all populations for which ages and sexes are known, the most graphic means of display is the population pyramid (really triangle), showing the balance of males and females in each age cohort. The Bahamas slave data are sufficiently full and detailed to allow for five-year cohorts for almost every island in each triennium, making a further distinction between the African and Creole components of the population. The resulting pyramids give a visual impression not only of the age and sex balance of each sample population (African as well as Creole), but also some idea of fertility, mortality, and life expectancy—more precise figures for which can be generated from the raw data on which the pyramid diagrams are based.

To place the pyramid diagrams in comparative context, however, it should be remembered that, as the name implies, for a perfectly stable population (in which the sexes were equally balanced and the birthrate sufficient to balance an equalized deathrate geared to a life expectancy of seventy years), the diagram would be in the shape of a stepped equal-sided triangle, while for the most extreme of Afro-Caribbean slave populations (in which nearly all adults were Africans with a low average fertility rate and at least two-thirds of all adults were males) it would be more like a lopsided Christmas tree than a recognizable triangle.

By 1822 the slaves of the Bahamas already exhibited most of the characteristics of a healthy and stable population which, but for the continuing presence of a minority of Africans and notable shortage of elderly persons, would compare favorably with any modern West Indian population. Only in the middle and upper age ranges was there a slight disproportion of males, because these cohorts included most of the Africans (who made up 22 percent of the total), of whom, originally, only a third were females. All in all, there were 106 males for each 100 females, compared with 152 African-born males for each 100 African-born females. This was an even better balance than might be predicted, because of the slightly lower female than male infant mortality figures, and the tendency of females to live rather longer than males.

The overall birthrate of Bahamian slaves in 1822—helped by a relatively healthy balance of sexes in the fertile age range for females and the fact that many African females were still of childbearing age—so far exceeded the deathrate as to ensure a population healthily expanding by natural increase. The crude annual birthrate (or rate of survival to become recorded) seems to have been about 27 per 1,000, or 56 per 1,000 females, and 193 per 1,000 females aged between fifteen and forty-five—with the fertility of African-born females in this age range being little if any lower than for Creoles.[13] The crude annual deathrate was a comparatively modest 14 per 1,000, leading to a natural increase of 13 per 1,000—compared with the natural decreases as high as 25 per 1,000 in the sugar colonies which so shocked the emancipationists when the first results of the registration of slave returns were computed around this time.[14]

In fact, it was the comparatively low mortality in the Bahamas even more than the relatively healthy birthrate that led to this substantial natural increase. As Higman and Kiple have demonstrated for all West Indian

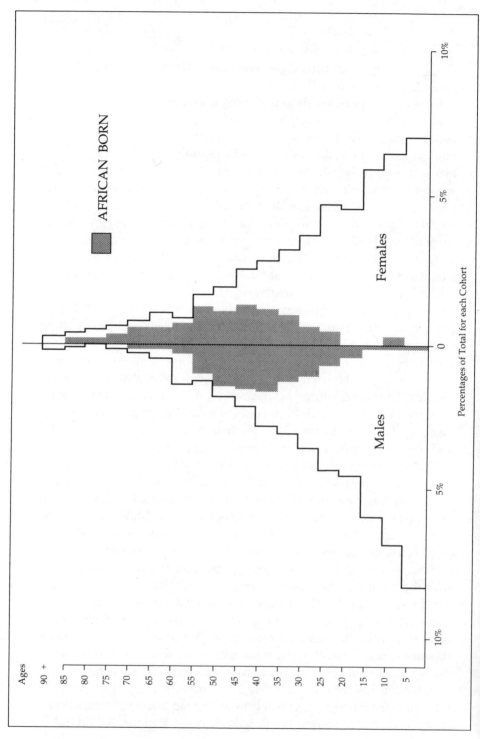

Figure 2. Bahamas slave population, 1822 (five-year cohorts)

Table 9
Age-Specific Deathrates for Slaves,
1831–34 (Registered Deaths per 1,000)

| Age Cohort | Africans | | Creoles | | Total | | |
	Males	Females	Males	Females	Males	Females	All Slaves
Under 10	—	—	16	16	16	16	16
10–19	—	—	3	4	3	4	4
20–29	—	—	7	5	7	5	6
30–39	2	1	8	10	10	11	11
40–49	9	5	8	3	17	9	13
50–59	22	10	5	8	27	18	23
60–69	34	15	12	10	46	25	37
70–79	51	28	12	19	63	47	56
80–89	150	21	30	21	180	42	98
Over 90	270	—	—	—	270	—	180
Total	48	20	10	9	14	11	13

Sources: Register of Returns of Slaves, 1831–34, Public Record Office, London; Barry Higman, *Slave Populations of the British Caribbean, 1807–1834* (Baltimore: Johns Hopkins University Press, 1984), 657.

slave populations, there were two peaks of mortality in early childhood, in the first few months and around the age of two, and a steadier but still high rate of erosion among slaves of working age.[15] The mortality rates for Bahamian slaves in all age brackets, though, were lower than for almost all West Indian slaves, except that the rate of survival beyond working age seems to have been little if any higher for the Bahamas than elsewhere. The rate of survival for Africans in the Bahamas in 1822 was notably higher than in the West Indies—largely because so few had been imported in the last phase of the legitimate trade—and those Africans who had already survived to the age of sixty had a notably greater life expectancy in the Bahamas than had Bahamian Creoles of that age range.

In all, the life expectancy at birth for slaves in the Bahamas in 1822 was probably forty years, and on reaching the age of five, some fifty years. These figures compared with twenty-five and thirty-five years in Jamaica around this time, twenty and thirty years in British Guiana, some twenty and thirty years for English cities, and thirty-five and forty-five years for English country districts.[16]

The balance of the Bahamian slave population between 1822 and 1834 was somewhat affected by three extraneous factors: the last wave of slave transhipment between 1822 and 1825, the crescendo of manumissions, and the "aging and wasting" of the African-born component. Very largely because of the loss in this triennium of up to two-thirds of the 3,000 slaves exported in all after 1815, the total Bahamian slave population actually fell from 10,705 in 1822 to 9,233 in 1825. Over the remaining nine years of the registration period, when large-scale exportation was vetoed, it climbed again to just above 10,000, but at a rate increasingly slowed by manumissions. The average annual rate of manumission, which had been about 20 between 1774 and 1806, and 45 between 1808 and 1825, rose to 78 between 1827 and 1830, and 130 in the last three years of slavery.[17]

During the period 1825–34, the number of African slaves in the Bahamas fell from 1,900 to 938, that is, from 20.7 percent of the total to 9.4 percent. This decline had several significant demographic effects. Since the surviving Africans lived on the average at least as long as Creoles, the former bulge in the population pyramid rose up the age cohorts with the increasing average age of the remaining Africans. By the end of the registration period, nearly all African females had passed out of the fertile age range, but this loss to the potential crude birthrate was more than offset by the aging of the Creole component and the consequent increase in the proportion of females in the cohorts from age fifteen to forty-five— as well as by the general equalization of sex ratios. The crude birthrate of the Bahamian slave population thus rose steadily from 27.3 per 1,000 between 1822 and 1824, to 32.5 between 1825 and 1827, 37.3 between 1828 and 1830, and to an extremely healthy 44.6 per thousand between 1831 and 1834. With the crude deathrate holding steadily around the average of 13.4 per 1,000 between 1822 and 1834, this led to rates of natural increase rising steadily from some 14 per 1,000 in 1822–24, to 19 per 1,000 in 1825–27, 24 per 1,000 in 1828–30, to an almost incredible 32 per 1,000 in 1831–34. Thus, though it was some of the healthiest slaves who were transferred or manumitted between 1822 and 1834, by the time of emancipation the predominantly Creole slave population of the Bahamas enjoyed a natural rate of increase in advance of nearly all modern West Indian populations.

The overall Bahamian slave population at the time of formal emancipation was extremely stable and healthy despite the continuing presence of 9.4 percent of elderly Africans. Excluding these, the Creole slave population pyramid for 1834 scarcely looks like that of a slave population at all. Its broad base was aided by the fact that comparatively few persons

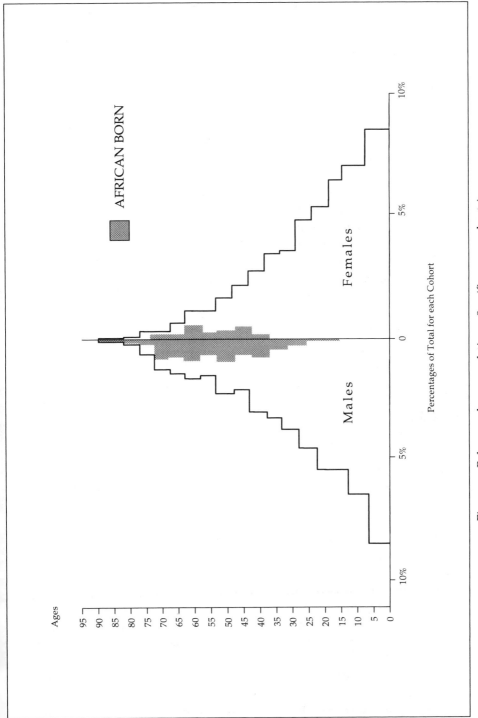

Figure 3. Bahamas slave population, 1834 (five-year cohorts)

lived beyond sixty years of age, but it was nonetheless an extremely rapidly expanding and "young" population. No less than 40.0 percent of the slave population was under thirteen years of age in 1834, compared with 35.7 percent in 1819 and 30.2 percent in 1805—though the figure for Creole slaves alone was not quite so high as it had been in 1819. Natural increase was aided both by comparatively low mortality rates among infants, children, and young adults, and by the highest fertility rates yet achieved. This, in turn, was aided by the general swing to a preponderance of females, who now outnumbered males by 103 to 100 overall, and by 110 to 100 in the crucial age range between fifteen and forty-five. Consequently, the annual birthrate was now approximately 35 per 1,000 for the entire slave population, 70 per 1,000 females, and 233 per 1,000 females aged fifteen to forty-five.

The overall Bahamian figures for 1834, however, disguise significant variations in demographic patterns within the general picture. Besides the substantial differences between Africans and Creoles, males and females already noticed, there were slighter but perceptible differences between black and mulatto slaves. Even more obviously, demographic patterns and performance varied according to the size of holdings and the occupations of the slaves—with these factors relating to, and partly accounting for, the notable differences to be found between Bahamian islands.

Bahamian practice (as demonstrated, for example, in the slave runaway advertisements in the newspapers) did recognize degrees of genetic mix and gradations of visible color among the slaves who were not unequivocally black. The terms *mulatto, quadroon, octaroon,* and *sambo* were used, more or less precisely, for those who were one-half, one-quarter, or one-eighth black, or a mixture of any of those with another black, respectively. Vaguer terms, such as *yellow* or *brown,* were even more commonly used. The Bahamas Registration Act of 1821, however, acknowledged no fine distinctions of color. Though a few owners ignored the ruling and were more precise, owners were instructed to list all nonblack slaves simply as mulattos. This may have led to some confusion and considerable undercounting. Colored slaves also made up a disproportionate number of those manumitted—perhaps half, or five times their due proportion in the slave population. Nonetheless, the proportions of those slaves listed as mulattos in the slave registration returns does suggest that miscegenation, though far from general, was on the increase. It also varied significantly from island to island.

In all, there were 966 slaves listed as mulattos in the 1834 registration returns, or 9.7 percent of the total number of slaves. The proportions varied considerably between islands, though, and not always in obvious ways. The proportion on New Providence, with its seemingly ample opportunities for miscegenation, for example, was no higher than the Bahamian average, with 220 mulatto slaves out of a total of 2,250. This comparatively low figure was almost certainly accounted for by the relatively high rate of manumission on New Providence—probably a third of all slaves manumitted being mulattos.[18] In all, there were probably 1,000 mulattos, slave and free, living on New Providence in 1834—nearly a quarter of the nonwhite inhabitants. This was a much higher proportion than in 1810, when the 124 mulatto slaves were only 4.8 percent of the total New Providence slave population, and the total number of mulattos on New Providence, free as well as slave, was 633 out of 4,264 nonwhites, or 14.8 percent. Another indicator that miscegenation was on the increase was that no less than 70 percent of the New Providence slaves listed as mulattos in 1834 were under the age of twenty, compared with 42 percent of the New Providence slave population as a whole.[19]

The proportion of mulattos in the slave populations of Eleuthera, Long Island, and the Turks Islands, where miscegenation was known to be common, was relatively high, around 13 percent. On Eleuthera, with its comparatively high proportion of free coloreds, mulattos probably made up an even higher proportion of the nonwhite population than on New Providence—quite apart from the likelihood that many of those who passed as whites on Eleuthera might have been accounted mulattos in the capital. On Harbour Island, by contrast, only 8.4 percent of the slaves were listed as mulattos, and with comparatively few free coloreds in the population, the proportion of mulattos to other nonwhites was almost as low as anywhere in the Bahamas, around 10 percent. This was an early indicator of the racial separation which increasingly characterized that and similar settlements.

More or less predictably, the proportion of mulattos was low on such islands as Cat Island, Exuma, Watling's, and Rum Cay, which had not long been settled and had a very high proportion of blacks to whites—averaging less than 5 percent mulattos to other slaves. Somewhat strangely, though, the islands with the highest proportion of mulatto slaves were Crooked Island, Long Cay, and Acklin's, where 14.8 percent of the slaves were listed as mulattos in 1834. This, paradoxically, was mainly the result of comparative isolation. The few resident whites were mainly males who practiced quite open miscegenation, while the chances of their mulatto offspring's being manumitted were relatively small. To these factors were added the incidence of miscegenation between black female slaves and the transient white (or near-white) mariners who stopped at Pitt Town on Long Cay, situated on the route between England and Jamaica and the site of the general post office for the Bahamas since 1800.

For a colony with such a modest-sized slave population, the Bahamas did show a surprising variation in demographic patterns between islands, though these were far less than the overall differences between the Bahamas and other slave colonies. Both internal and external differences were partly attributable to differential proportions of Africans and rates of manumission. But much more crucial determinants were the differing economies and patterns of employment. As far as the Bahamas is concerned, these can be more than adequately illustrated from the data on the sizes of slave holdings and the categories of slave employment drawn from the slave registration and compensation returns for 1834.

Compared with the sugar colonies, Bahamian slave holdings were nearly all of modest size, and even then the largest holdings were split between different locations. This, of course, reflected the decay of plantations and the low fertility of Bahamian soils. Many of the larger holdings—such as the Mosses'—had already been split up or transferred, and by 1834 there were altogether only 24 Bahamian holdings of more than 50 slaves. These accounted for 25.6 percent of the total Bahamian slave population, compared with the 80.0 percent of Jamaican slaves in holdings of similar minimum size. There were only 9 Bahamian holdings of more than 100 slaves in 1834, and only 1 equal in size to any of the top 100 Jamaican sugar estates.[20] Lord Rolle held 330 slaves in Exuma in 1834, but they were divided among his 5 estates.

There were 32 Bahamian holdings in 1834 of between 31 and 50 slaves each, accounting for 11.8 percent of the slave total. But almost half of all Bahamian slaves (4,834, or 48.4 percent) were found in 402 holdings of from 6 to 30 slaves, with nearly 2,000 (19.1 percent) in 238 groups of from 6 to 10 slaves. Only the largest of these modest groupings constituted the labor force of what might be termed a true plantation. The majority were employed in smaller enterprises, belonging to petty farmers, salt rakers, boat captains, shipbuilders, logcutters, or those who lived by hiring out their slaves. The remaining 1,420 Bahamian slaves in groups of 5 or fewer (14.2 percent) were divided into no fewer than 710 holdings, averaging just 2 slaves each. These, it would seem, were mainly domestics.

Clearly, slave ownership was spread very widely throughout the free Bahamian population, and it was a rare white adult who did not own at

Table 10

Mulatto Slaves, 1834, by Age Cohorts

Island	0–19			20–44			Over 44			Total Mulatto Slaves	Mulattos as % of All Slaves
	Male	Female	Total	Male	Female	Total	Male	Female	Total		
New Providence	63	90	153	30	30	60	5	2	7	220	9.78
Eleuthera	59	61	120	16	25	41	2	5	7	168	13.09
Harbour Island	13	18	31	3	3	6	3	3	6	43	8.41
Turks and Caicos	50	62	112	36	24	60	0	8	8	180	13.08
Long Island	33	31	64	4	6	10	2	0	2	76	12.44
Cat Island	8	18	26	3	6	9	0	0	0	35	5.28
San Salvador	14	11	25	2	2	4	0	0	0	29	8.12
Rum Cay	9	6	15	5	1	6	1	2	3	24	3.71
Exumas	16	9	25	1	4	5	1	0	1	31	3.57
Crooked and Acklin's Islands	29	32	61	11	7	18	5	0	5	84	14.79
Inagua	0	1	1	0	0	0	0	0	0	1	2.00
Abaco	16	22	38	6	7	13	0	0	0	51	12.91
Grand Bahama	4	6	10	1	3	4	0	0	0	14	10.14
Spanish Wells	1	0	1	0	0	0	0	0	0	1	2.63
Ragged Island	3	2	5	0	1	1	0	0	0	6	4.17
Andros and Berry Islands	0	1	1	0	1	1	1	0	1	3	2.91
Total	318	370	688	118	120	238	20	20	40	996	9.66

Sources: Register of Returns of Slaves, 1834, Bahamas Archives; Gail Saunders, "The Slave Population of the Bahamas, 1783–1834" (M.Phil. thesis, University of the West Indies, 1978), 225.

least one slave. There were 432 separate slave holdings on New Providence alone, of which 306 were of groups of 5 or fewer—some 43 percent of the Bahamian total—most of whom would have been located in or around the town of Nassau. The slave population of New Providence, though, was surprisingly diversified. Three-quarters of the New Providence slaves were found in holdings of more than 5, and nearly half in units of more than 10. Some of the smaller units might have been families or laboring gangs working in town, but most of the larger groups lived and worked on country estates such as the 3 owned by William Wylly, of which there were said to be more than 50 on New Providence even after slavery ended.[21]

On all islands some slaves were found in holdings of fewer than 5, but predictably it was on the older-established islands that there was the highest proportion of smaller holdings and on the most recently settled that the most large groups were found. While Eleuthera had attracted a few large holdings of slaves, on Harbour Island, though there were 104 separate slave holdings, there were none larger than 20, and an average of only 4.9 slaves per holding. On Cat Island, in contrast, there were only 27 slave holdings, but 14 of these were of more than 10 slaves, with an overall average of 24.2 slaves per holding. On New Providence, Eleuthera, Harbour Island, and Abaco added together, there were 4,470 slaves in 769 holdings, an average of 5.8 slaves, whereas in the remaining islands, the 5,519 slaves were divided among only 389 holdings, an average of 14.2 slaves apiece.

The work categories into which Bahamian slaves were divided for registration and compensation purposes provide considerable refinement to William Wylly's rough general analysis of 1815, as well as adding to the interpretation of the marked differences between islands.

The slave registration returns recognized seven slave work categories, besides the "nil" that designated slaves under six years of age or too old or sick to work, and the very small categories of "sundry" and "unknown." The seven true work categories were domestics, field laborers, mariners, salt laborers, drivers and overseers, nurses and midwives, and tradesmen and craftsmen. In order to place a more exact valuation on Bahamian slaves, the 1834 compensation computation refined the categories further by distinguishing superior from inferior domestics, laborers, mariners, and tradesmen/craftsmen, and by placing all slaves into three general categories: predial attached (for those agricultural and salt workers directly attached to an estate), predial unattached, and nonpre-

Table 11

Number of Slave Holdings, 1834, by Size and Island

Island (Sq. Mi.)	Holdings by Number of Slaves in Holding										Total Slaves (est.)
	1–5	6–10	11–20	21–30	31–40	41–50	51–100	101–150	151–200	Over 200	
New Providence (80)	306	81	30	10	4	1	0	0	0	0	2,145
Eleuthera (200)	89	37	24	3	4	1	2	1	0	0	1,369
Harbour Island (5)	66	28	10	0	0	0	0	0	0	0	506
Turks and Caicos (166)	91	21	13	8	6	0	3	0	1	0	1,355
Long Island (173)	34	18	10	3	2	2	0	0	0	0	597
Cat Island (150)	10	3	6	2	0	0	2	2	0	0	654
San Salvador (63)	1	1	0	1	1	1	2	1	0	0	390
Rum Cay (30)	10	2	2	1	3	0	3	1	0	0	721
Exumas (72)	13	10	4	7	1	0	1	1	0	1[a]	906
Crooked and Acklin's Islands (92)	11	7	5	4	2	0	2	0	1	0	473
Inagua (645)	4	2	0	1	0	0	0	0	0	0	49
Abaco (649)	42	16	5	3	0	1	0	0	0	0	411
Grand Bahama (530)	12	4	2	3	0	0	0	0	0	0	151
Spanish Wells (2)	3	1	0	1	0	0	0	0	0	0	39
Ragged Island (9)	11	4	3	0	1	0	0	0	0	0	134
Andros and Berry Islands (2,300)	10	3	3	0	0	0	0	0	0	0	89
Total holdings	710	238	117	47	26	6	15	6	2	1	
Average slaves per holding (approx.)	2	8	15	25	35	45	75	125	175	330	
Total slaves (est.)	1,420	1,904	1,755	1,175	910	270	1,125	750	350	330	9,989

Sources: Register of Returns of Slaves, 1834, Bahamas Archives; Saunders, "Slave Population of the Bahamas," 197–99.

[a] Lord Rolle's Exuma estate employed 330 slaves in 5 settlements.

dial (many of whom, like the predial unattached, might be hired out rather than directly employed by their owners).

The valuations placed on Bahamian slaves in 1834 provide an index of the relative importance accorded to different types of slave by the master class, if only a very rough guide to their actual socioeconomic rank and no more than a hint of their relative importance in the eyes of their fellows. The valuations varied from five pounds for aged or diseased "noneffectives," to eighty pounds for "head people" on plantations (all presumed to be males). Head tradesmen were thought to be worth sixty-five pounds, head mariners or wharfsmen sixty pounds, and head domestics forty-five pounds, whereas their respective "inferiors" were valued at fifty, thirty-nine, and twenty-five pounds. Ordinary laborers (either agriculturalists or salt workers) were valued at twenty-five pounds, irrespective of sex, inferior laborers at nineteen pounds, and all children under six years of age on August 1, 1834, at ten pounds apiece.[22] Luckily, many of the individual returns added more specific details of employment to the general categories required, showing the wide range of occupations followed by Bahamian slaves—who were, of course, the indispensable sinews for all types of economic enterprise. Correlation of the occupational categories with the colors, ages, and sexes of slaves also adds an important social dimension to the analysis.

Though a handful of the wealthiest whites (such as James Moss and his wife) employed indentured white servants as butlers or ladies' maids, almost all Bahamian domestics were slaves. The great majority of these, moreover, were black. Somewhat surprisingly, the proportion of mulattos among the slaves listed as domestics was scarcely higher than in the population at large.[23] Though the general classification may have hidden a preference for the lighter-colored slaves in the most confidential positions, this does seem to run counter to the West Indian case, where to be a nonblack slave multiplied the chance of becoming a domestic—and thus suggests that the Bahamian whites came closer to lumping all nonwhites together in the American manner than to thinking of coloreds as forming an intermediate class as in the West Indies.[24]

Male domestics, who made up less than a quarter of the total, included butlers, waiters, coachmen, and grooms, while female domestics were waitresses, maids, laundresses, or cooks. Naturally, most of those slaves called nurses or midwives were females, though there were fourteen males listed in the category. These may have filled the role of the "black doctors" found assisting the white medical practitioners on many Jamaican estates. Eight out of nine in the category of nurses and mid-

Table 12

Slave Occupation Categories and Valuations, 1834

Categories	Males	Females	Totals	Estimated Valuation (£)
Predial attached				
1. Head people	68	0	68	5,400
2. Tradesmen	0	0	0	0
3. Inferior tradesmen	0	0	0	0
4. Field laborers	1,292	1,376	2,668	93,380
5. Inferior field laborers	734	546	1,280	24,320
Predial unattached				
1. Head people	3	0	3	240
2. Tradesmen	0	0	0	0
3. Inferior tradesmen	0	0	0	0
4. Field laborers	88	96	184	6,440
5. Inferior field laborers	43	30	73	1,387
Nonpredial				
1. Head tradesmen	162	0	162	10,530
2. Inferior tradesmen	48	0	48	2,400
3. People employed on wharves, shipping, etc.	459	0	459	27,540
4. Inferior, employed on wharves, shipping, etc.	244	77	321	12,543
5. Head domestic servants	165	1,099	1,264	56,880
6. Inferior domestics	471	715	1,186	29,650
Children under 6 years	960	1,032	1,992	19,920
Aged, diseased, or otherwise ineffective	151	142	293	1,465
Total	4,888	5,113	10,001	292,135

Sources: Slave Compensation Returns, 1834, Bahamas Archives; Saunders, "Slave Population of the Bahamas," 250.

wives were blacks rather than mulattos. Nurses, besides the few who had specific medical duties, included wet nurses and child minders, some of whom were very young themselves. A few of those listed as nurses also tended sheep or were engaged in light agricultural tasks, such as weeding.

Both the poorer Bahamian whites and the slaves were employed in maritime activities and the crafts, though few whites were in subordinate positions, and it was only in the upper reaches of the slaves' achievement, and in the colonial capital, that there was real competition in these fields. "Tradesmen," however, included a large number of slave carpenters and boatbuilders, and also blacksmiths, masons, sawyers, coopers, mechanics, basketmakers, and seamstresses, as well as such unique occupations as wine and liquor corker, and sugar maker. The eleven slaves listed in the "sundry" category included watchmen, warehousemen, and two working in the ordnance yard, as well as three castor-oil boilers. Those slaves who worked on wharves were lumped together with true mariners, and most slave mariners were generally engaged "in vessels wrecking, wood-cutting, droughing [that is, coastal or interisland transportation], fishing and turtling."[25] But distinctions were sometimes made among ordinary sailors, fishermen, droughers, and (the elite of all slave mariners) pilots. Several mariners were also listed as shipbuilders, and one Cat Island slave combined seagoing with specialized pigeon shooting.

Needless to say, slaves exclusively monopolized the role of laborer in the Bahamas, with blacks being in the overwhelming majority, and male laborers only marginally outnumbering females (by 1,778 to 1,722 in 1834). Virtually all the head laborers were blacks and, despite the balance of sexes in the fields, only one was a female. Distinctions were rarely made among the agricultural laborers between those who tended the fields and those who looked after the stock, presumably because virtually all were engaged in diversified tasks and very few were specialists. The slave registration returns did make a valuable distinction, though, in separating salt laborers from other rural laborers—for full-time work at the salt pans was clearly both harder and less healthy than the normal Bahamian type of agricultural labor. This surely explains the marked differences in demographic patterns and performance between the predominantly agricultural islands and those, like the Turks and Caicos Islands, almost wholly dedicated to salt production.

The breakdown of the Bahamian slaves' occupations in 1834 shows a considerable modification of William Wylly's four categories of 1815. Overall, three-quarters of the slaves were listed as "effective"—a higher proportion than in most slave colonies—though only a third were agricultural laborers, compared with something more like two-thirds in Jamaica and the other sugar colonies. Even with the salt laborers added, the manual labor force was no more than 45 percent of the slave total— though still a more dominant proportion of the slave population than Wylly acknowledged. Wylly was right to mention the importance of the Bahamian slave mariners, though in fact they made up less than 6 percent of the slave total, being outnumbered by domestics more than four to one. Wylly was also probably right in claiming that Bahamian slaves had more practical independence than those elsewhere, but he could hardly have claimed the existence of an exceptionally large slave elite. Even when the owners made their evaluations for compensation, only 265 Bahamian slaves were listed as specialist craftsmen, and the total of those deemed to be worth the top price of eighty pounds on the market, the drivers and overseers, numbered just 80, or 0.8 percent of the total slave population.

William Wylly's analysis was largely based on his knowledge of New Providence, an island which differed substantially from the Bahamian average and even more from some of the more distant islands. New Providence naturally had the highest proportion of nonpredial slaves and of the slaves most valued by the master class, as well as an extremely high proportion of domestics and the largest proportion of slave mariners. The older-established and more traditional Out Islands of Eleuthera, Harbour Island, and Abaco, taken together, had a lesser but still high proportion of domestic and maritime slaves, and a far higher, though still not predominant, proportion of agricultural slaves. The comparatively recently settled island of Exuma contained all working categories of slaves, including a few engaged solely in salt raking, and a fair number of mariners and domestics. The predominant category, though, was field laborer, the large number of laboring gangs and the shortage of white overseers being suggested by the comparatively high number of black drivers and overseers. The slave population differing most from New Providence, and from all other Bahamian islands, though, was that of the Turks and Caicos Islands. Though there were a few mariners and craftsmen, and a considerable number of field laborers (nearly all in the Caicos Islands), almost half the slave population was listed as given up to the production of salt.

This dangerous predominance was clearly reflected in the demographic statistics of the Turks and Caicos slaves, especially when compared with those living in the other types of Bahamian island. The 1834 population pyramid for the slaves of New Providence was a steeper-sided version of that for the Bahamas as a whole, while that for Eleuthera was almost grotesquely broad-based and attenuated, and for Exuma shaped somewhere in between. These differences reflected annual gross birth- and deathrates over the registration period that varied from 30.2 and 17.6 per 1,000 for New Providence, to 41.1 and 8.1 for Eleuthera and 40.4 and 7.8 for Exuma. The Turks and Caicos pyramid for 1834, though, was less triangular than those for any other Bahamian islands,

Table 13
Slave Occupations by Ages, 1834

Occupation	Age									All Ages	% of Total Slaves
	0–10	11–15	16–24	25–29	30–39	40–49	50–59	Over 60	Unknown		
None	2,420	15	2	2	2	2	14	76	0	2,534	25.33
Domestic worker	450	402	440	141	231	162	109	66	2	2,003	20.03
Field worker	368	536	758	292	543	410	319	273	1	3,500	34.99
Mariner	9	58	219	85	94	79	30	11	0	585	5.85
Salt worker	15	85	309	97	190	131	59	28	2	916	9.16
Driver/overseer	1	0	4	10	20	23	13	9	0	80	0.80
Nurse/midwife	54	13	0	0	1	6	10	10	0	94	0.94
Trade/craftsman	2	15	57	33	53	48	27	30	0	265	2.65
Sundry	1	0	1	1	1	3	3	1	0	11	0.11
Unknown	3	0	2	1	5	2	1	0	1	14	0.14
Total	3,323	1,124	1,792	662	1,141	866	584	504	6	10,002	100.00

Sources: Register of Slave Returns, 1834, Bahamas Archives; Saunders, "Slave Population of the Bahamas," 259.

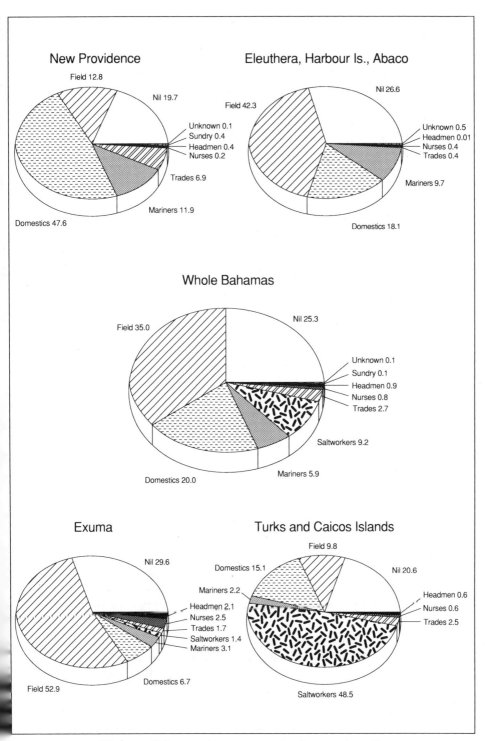

Figure 4. Bahamas slaves, occupational categories, 1834

more closely resembling a jagged Christmas tree in a tub. This indicated an imbalance of sexes and ages, an annual gross birthrate of only 24.0 per 1,000, and a gross deathrate of 21.6. The annual net increase of 2.4 per 1,000 was 19.2 per 1,000 below the Bahamian average and 37.5 per 1,000 below the rate for Abaco, the island with the most rapidly rising rate of natural increase during this period.

The demographic performance even of the Turks and Caicos slaves in 1834, however, was superior to that of the slaves in any West Indian sugar island, in only one of which, Barbados, was there a natural increase by the time slavery ended. Barbados, the earliest British sugar colony, had the most creolized population, having ceased to import Africans even before the slave trade officially ended in 1808. Yet even creolization did not necessarily lead to a natural population increase in a sugar monoculture. Jamaica, which developed as a sugar island several generations after Barbados, had only 60,000 Africans (or 20 percent) among its 311,000 slaves in 1834. Yet Jamaican slaves as a whole could achieve an annual birthrate of only 23.3 per 1,000 and suffered a gross deathrate of 28.3, for a net annual decrease of 5.0 per 1,000. In the still-developing sugar island of Trinidad, where more than 40 percent of the population was African-born, the statistics were even more dire. Despite living in a Crown colony under the watchful eye of the supposedly humanitarian Colonial Office, Trinidadian slaves were dying at the rate of 28.0 per 1,000 per year, against a birth rate of only 18.7 per 1,000, for an annual net decrease of 9.3 per 1,000.[26]

Much more similar to the Bahamian case were the demographic statistics of the slaves of the nonsugar and nonplantation colonies of the region. Though, as Barry Higman has shown, when a colony's stage of development and the proportion of town to country slaves are taken into account, the slaves of diversified colonies tended to perform better than those of sugar monocultures, nonplantation slaves performed better than those engaged in any form of plantation agriculture, and those on islands with economies and climates most similar to the Bahamian performed best of all.[27] Of those islands so far analyzed in detail, the highly creolized populations of the nonplantation Leeward Islands of Anguilla and Barbuda were closest to the Bahamian model. But almost certainly, the slaves who were demographically most similar to those of the Bahamas were the Bermudian slaves, who lived in a colony with a comparable history, society, and economy, and with an even more temperate climate. The demographic performance of the Bermudian slaves (who scarcely outnumbered the Bermudian whites, were found in small average units,

Table 14
Bahamas Slave Population, 1822–34

Island	1822			1825			1828			1831			1834		
	Male	Female	Total	Male	Female	Total	Male	Female	Total	Male	Female	Total	Male	Female	Total
New Providence	1,453	1,482	2,935	1,122	1,270	2,392	1,192	1,270	2,462	1,224	1,266	2,490	1,068	1,182	2,250
Eleuthera	627	614	1,241	614	609	1,223	579	579	1,158	617	635	1,252	611	672	1,283
Harbour Island	234	224	458	207	207	414	202	224	426	220	247	467	230	281	511
Turks and Caicos	1,074	872	1,946	719	682	1,401	750	661	1,411	716	727	1,443	698	678	1,376
Long Island	304	314	618	274	289	563	272	272	544	323	294	617	309	302	611
Cat Island	334	379	713	344	292	636	221	261	482	262	293	555	301	362	663
San Salvador	197	158	355	142	146	288	156	186	342	165	164	329	185	172	357
Rum Cay	102	127	229	251	218	469	266	264	530	286	282	568	317	330	647
Exumas	353	348	701	402	334	736	349	357	706	398	382	780	439	429	868
Crooked and Acklin's Islands	494	423	917	326	211	537	284	204	488	231	223	454	304	264	568
Inagua	25	26	51	26	26	52	25	14	39	29	20	49	30	20	50
Abaco	124	93	217	153	131	284	170	145	315	197	169	366	194	201	395
Andros and Berry Islands	108	65	173	81	49	130	92	57	149	70	50	120	54	49	103
Grand Bahama	21	12	33	15	14	29	51	32	83	63	68	131	74	64	138
Spanish Wells	18	20	38	16	12	28	27	18	45	21	13	34	24	14	38
Ragged Island	43	37	80	23	28	51	41	33	74	54	59	113	63	81	144
Total	5,511	5,194	10,705	4,715	4,518	9,233	4,677	4,577	9,254	4,876	4,892	9,768	4,901	5,101	10,002

Sources: Register of Returns of Slaves, 1822–34, Bahamas Archives; Saunders, "Slave Population of the Bahamas," 97.

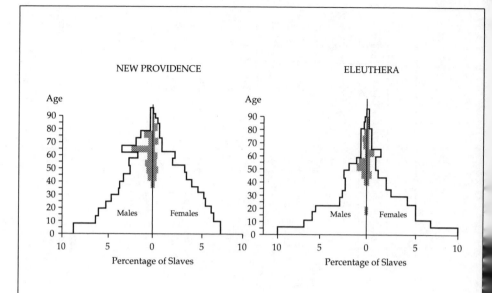

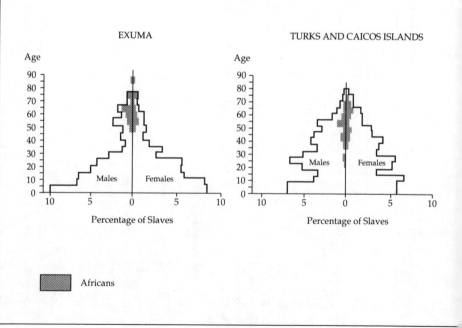

Figure 5. Slave populations of select Bahamian islands, 1834 (five-year cohorts)

and were even less engaged in harsh forms of labor than were Bahamian slaves), indeed, was probably more like that on Eleuthera or Harbour Island than that of the Bahamian slaves as a whole.[28]

That the Bahamian regime was naturally healthy in demographic terms, and that there was something intrinsic to the climate and socio-economic regime of sugar-plantation colonies that affected demographic performance even more than disproportions of sexes, ages, and place of birth, can convincingly be shown by tracing the fortunes of slaves transferred from the Bahamas to West Indian sugar colonies whose sequential records occur in the registration returns of both places. This has so far been done, at least in part, for the slaves of Burton Williams who were transferred mainly from Watling's Island to Trinidad between 1821 and 1823.[29]

In 1821 Burton Williams and his sons owned at least 450 slaves in the Bahamas, most located on Watling's Island, but others on Cat Island and Eleuthera. Between July 1821 and June 1823, some 330 of these slaves were transferred to Trinidad in five shiploads and placed on three estates near San Fernando called Williamsville, Picton, and Cupar Grange. Fortunately, all the Williams slaves were included in the Bahamian trial census of 1821, so that their demographic characteristics can be analyzed and compared with those of the transferred slaves, as revealed by the Trinidad returns of 1825 and subsequent triennia.[30] Besides this, the demographic performance of the transferred slaves can be compared with that of the Williams slaves who remained in the Bahamas, as shown in the Bahamian returns of 1825 to 1834.

Rather than just selecting those slaves who would be most economically valuable in Trinidad, Burton Williams was constrained by British and Bahamian law not to break up families and at least nominally obtained the slaves' agreement to the transfer.[31] Thus, as the Trinidad and Bahamas returns for 1825 demonstrate, both the slaves transferred and those left behind remained healthily balanced groups. Though with a slightly larger proportion of Africans (14 percent) and older slaves than before, the Williams slaves left in the Bahamas were quite comparable with the Bahamas Out Island average population, and continued to perform well demographically until 1834. The transferred slaves, conversely, included few Africans and an even greater majority under forty-five years of age. However, they were far closer to a Bahamian-type population than to the Trinidadian averages, with only 6 percent Africans (compared with 48 percent) and females outnumbering males by 100 to 86, rather than being actually outnumbered by 122 to 100.[32]

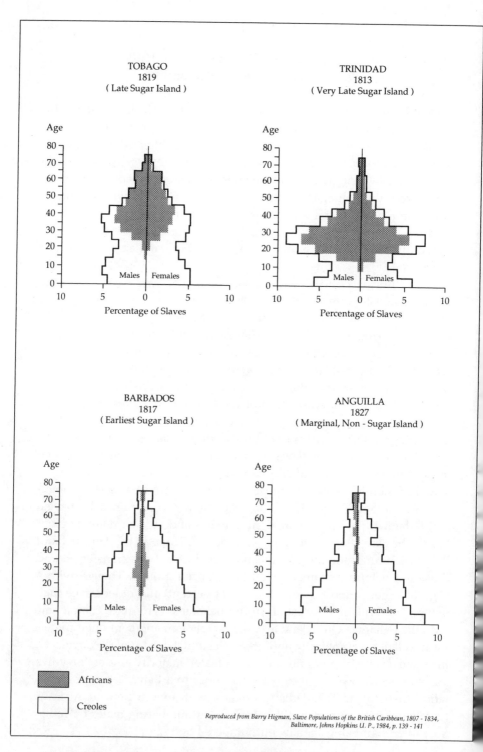

TOBAGO
1819
(Late Sugar Island)

TRINIDAD
1813
(Very Late Sugar Island)

BARBADOS
1817
(Earliest Sugar Island)

ANGUILLA
1827
(Marginal, Non - Sugar Island)

Africans

Creoles

Reproduced from Barry Higman, Slave Populations of the British Caribbean, 1807 - 1834,
Baltimore, Johns Hopkins U. P., 1984, p. 139 - 141

Figure 6. Late slave populations of select British West Indian islands, 1813–32
(for comparison with Bahamas)

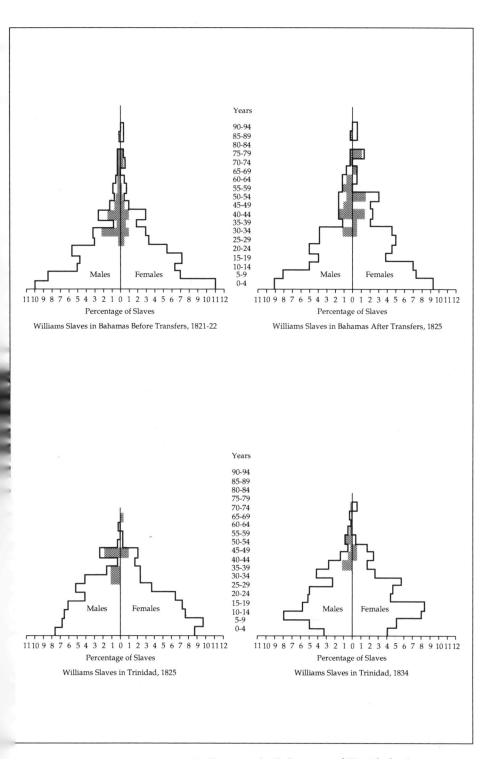

Figure 7. Slaves of Burton Williams in the Bahamas and Trinidad, 1821–34

Other comparisons are made possible by the requirement that the Trinidadian registration returns give the heights of all slaves, to the nearest quarter inch, and that slaves' mothers and siblings be indicated where possible. The transferred Bahamian adult slaves averaged 68.0 inches in height for males and 62.6 for females, compared with the Trinidadian averages of 64.2 and 61.4 (65.4 and 61.8 for Creoles). The height data for young slaves viewed over triennial intervals also indicated a faster maturation by Bahamian-born slaves, with a suggested age of the onset of menarche for females of 16.2 years, compared with 16.6 years for other young females living in Trinidad. The data also suggest that something like 80 percent of all female Williams slaves became mothers, with an average of more than three surviving children each, born at average intervals of 2.2 years—statistics far in advance of those for Trinidad and other sugar islands.[33]

On January 18, 1825, Burton Williams provided valuable, if severely biased, information about his slaves and management practices in evidence before the Trinidad Council.[34] He was tortuously intent to show that while his regime in the Bahamas had been benign and Bahamian conditions were generally healthy, the transfer had been in the slaves' own interests, and that Trinidad was even preferable to the Bahamas. Certainly, the Trinidadian soil was infinitely more fertile than that in the Bahamas—the best that Williams had ever seen. This, he claimed, not only made plantation labor easier but facilitated the growing of food on the slaves' own allotments. Besides, more profit for the planter meant the chance of better provision for the slaves. In the Bahamas, asserted Williams, he had made so little money from plantation agriculture that he had difficulty feeding and clothing his slaves adequately, "though he possessed 13,000 acres."

Burton Williams admitted that the transferred slaves were sickly for the first few months in Trinidad (with "fevers and Agues and bowel Complaints") and later complained that it was two or three years before transferred slaves could be expected to do a proper day's work because of "the effect the change of Climate, and of food have upon their Constitutions." But he claimed that he had lost only 7 out of 329 transferred slaves in the first two years, and that by 1825 there had been 34 births, from which 30 infants had survived.

Williams was also bound to admit that, after being contented for the first two years, the slaves had become disenchanted with Trinidad and that many of them would have preferred to return to the Bahamas. But by a superb plantocratic rationalization he attributed this to the undermining by enemies at home and abroad of the paternalistic power he had formerly enjoyed. Ignorant meddlers in England had been responsible for such measures as the recent orders-in-council, which had been intentionally misinterpreted by certain "designing negroes" to imply that all slaves were entitled to three days to themselves each week. This inevitably led to discontent and misbehavior, and thus to a level of punishment greater than had ever been necessary in the Bahamas. "They do not live as harmoniously together as before," testified Williams; "the more Sensible amongst the slaves observe the change, and would gladly return to the Bahamas, where the Power of the Master is less limited."

With rather more plausibility, Burton Williams asserted that the health of his slaves was related to their tendency toward monogamous marriages and the maintenance of stable nuclear families. But as usual he gave himself most of the credit and indulged in paternalistic moralizing. The natural decrease of Trinidadian slaves, he believed, was due both to the disparity of the sexes and to the fact that insufficient care was "given to their living together as Man and Wife, by giving a feast to the Gang when they come together and a sharp punishment when they part. . . . I have found," added Williams, "that the Men and Women can only be coerced to remain together by the fear of Corporal Punishment; already I begin to see a Material Change in their manners and the Women are using profane Words and Swearing which I never allowed before and had not heard for years." Asked if he did not believe that English experience had shown that better treatment of the laboring classes led them to respect themselves more, Williams made an emphatic denial. "Our female Slaves have no sense of Shame or the least Idea of Morality and Chastity," he asserted; "the fear of Punishment from the Master is the only thing which keeps them in tolerable Decency and Decorum; and as to their Sense of Modesty they may be seen every day free as well as Slave, bathing and exposing their persons at mid-day with only a Handkerchief round their Waist, at the Wharfs in Port of Spain and at the Rivers in its Vicinity, in the most open places at the Crossings of the Public Roads." [35]

Burton Williams deluded his listeners and himself about the healthiness of his slaves in Trinidad as much as he exaggerated his own contribution to his slaves' health, happiness, and good behavior in the Bahamas. An official return in 1826 showed that in fact 33 of Williams's transferred slaves had died by the middle of 1826. Over the same period, there had been 57 births, from which 49 infants had survived. This represented an average annual net increase of only 1.6 per 1,000. This was a better result than for Trinidad as a whole (which suffered a net annual decrease of over 5 per 1,000 at that time) but worse figures than for the sugar island of Barbados and only a fraction of the former rate for the Williams slaves, or for the Bahamas overall.[36] Moreover, the subsequent statistics for the Williams slaves in Trinidad make even more melancholy reading. Over the last nine years of slavery the population increased hardly at all. The fertility figures were so low, and infant mortality so much worse than before, that the final population pyramid for the Williams slaves in Trinidad bore no resemblance to what it had formerly been. It was, in fact, almost typical of any developing sugar plantation colony in its middle years.

A final and poignant irony was reflected in the name which the Williams exslaves chose for their settlement once they left Williamsville for the life of squatters in the nearby hills with the coming of emancipation. It was the name of the estate in Watling's Island from which many of them had come: Hard Bargain. A truer choice might have been Even Harder Bargain.

~ 17 ~

The Lifeways of the Slaves

IN STATISTICAL TERMS, as we have seen, the slaves of the Bahamas were a relatively healthy population. However, one needs to know much more yet of the conditions under which the slaves lived and worked, both to see how the statistical results came about and to estimate whether a healthy demographic performance necessarily meant a satisfactory, let alone satisfying, life. The causal factors were, of course, interrelated. But it is vital for the present enterprise to discover to what extent slave conditions were determined (as masters and the opponents of slavery alike presumed) by the legal and customary system imposed upon the slaves; to what degree they were the result of fortuitous external factors (as objective cliometricians might be inclined to argue); and how far they were in fact (as we would like to believe) shaped by the slaves themselves.

Those humanitarians who, like James Stephen, perused both the slave registration returns and the colonial slave laws after 1815, had no doubt that the unhealthiness and unhappiness of the slaves were the result of the extensive powers given to slaveowners, the cruel punishments allowed by the laws, and the lack of protective clauses. Most slaveowners agreed that the welfare of the slaves was almost entirely in their masters' hands, but while asserting their need for plenary powers, they denied the need for specific protective legislation. Custom, practical experience, and the masters' own interest in keeping their slaves alive and fit were sufficient, if not the only practical, safeguards for the slaves.

Bahamian slaveowners as different (and as opposed) as Burton Williams and William Wylly concurred in believing in a policy of strict paternalism toward their slaves, differing perhaps only in the greater willingness of Wylly to concede that the decline in the value of Bahamian plantations reduced the owners' self-interest in the welfare of their slaves and thus made at least minimal protective legislation necessary. Neither of them had much faith in the slaves' will to self-improvement or the slaves' chances of succeeding on their own. Burton Williams smugly recounted to the Trinidad Council in 1825 the case of the twenty-six slaves who had been manumitted by the will of Christopher Neely in 1807 with as much land as they needed but had so neglected cultivation that eighteen years later only four or five were still alive.[1] Even Wylly's relatively enlightened 1815 regulations for the slaves on his three New Providence estates combined force with generosity, and a few years later Wylly was quite capable of condemning and punishing the "skulkers" among his slaves, as well as bending the provision clauses of the slave laws to his own advantage.

In some ways, Wylly's regulations[2] anticipated the amelioration legislation recommended in the Bathurst and Goderich circulars and incorporated into the Bahamian slave laws of 1824–30. But all of his concessions were purposeful, and most were made strictly conditional. A Protestant clergyman (of whatever denomination) was to be paid twenty pounds to visit the estates four times a year, and slaves were to be baptized once properly prepared. There were no estate tasks on Sundays (or on Good Friday and at Christmas) but slaves were not allowed to work on their own grounds either, being given half tasks on Saturday instead. A chapel was built at Clifton, which the slaves had to attend each Sunday morning at eleven, when the driver was to read them prayers. Defaulters' names were listed, and those without a sufficient excuse were given a full task the following Saturday. Prayer books and spelling books were made available and the "people" encouraged to read and write, though mainly for godly purposes. The driver, or any other suitable literate person, was to be paid three guineas for each pupil (up to ten a year) who could be taught to read a chapter of the Bible and recite the Lord's Prayer and Creed.

Each man on taking his first wife was entitled to "a well built stone house, consisting of two apartments." He also received "a sow pig, and a pair of dunghill fowls, as a gift of the proprietor." Adultery, though, was severely punished. The man was to forfeit his hogs, poultry, and other movable effects, which were to be sold for the benefit of the injured husband. Both offenders, moreover, were to be whipped, their heads were to be shaved, and they were to be forced to wear sackcloth (that is, smocks and caps made of cotton bagging) for six months, during which they were forbidden to leave the estate. Similar punishments were also decreed for running away, with the money raised from the sale of forfeited goods being used to purchase books for the school.

Besides being expected to be literate Christians, the drivers were given special privileges and powers. The head driver at Clifton and the chief herdsman at Tusculum were each allowed a brood mare "for the purpose of enabling them the more frequently and expeditiously to ride over the pasture grounds and other Lands." They could not sell the mares but were entitled to any foals they might produce. More remarkably, as long as no free overseer was employed on the Wylly estates, these two chief slaves were to be given an annual allowance of twelve guineas each, payable quarterly, in addition to their regular provisions and clothing. Drivers could impose corporal punishment on the other slaves but were forbidden to inflict more than a dozen lashes without the owner's permission, and all punishments, however minor, had to be entered into a special journal. Major punishments were to be administered "with due solemnity, in the presence of all the slaves of the plantation, and with the common Military Cat." West India cartwhips and American cowskin whips were expressly forbidden, and no punishment was to exceed the legal limit of thirty-nine lashes.

As much land was set aside for the use of the slaves as was needed for their provisions. Half an acre was allotted as a garden for each house, "as the property of the occupant for the time being," with further pasturage for hogs and fowls. Keeping the number of small stock under control was obviously a problem. Each family head was allowed one breeding sow, as long as it was kept in a pen, but for those who had one, a quart of corn was stopped from the slaves' weekly allowance, to be fed to the free-running hogs. Further to prevent overgrazing, all these hogs were to be sold as soon as they were "fit for the spit," with the exception of one that might be kept in a pen for the slaves' consumption. The owner had the right of pre-emption of all hogs, poultry, and eggs but agreed to pay Nassau market prices, as fixed by the driver and two persons chosen by the seller.

The people were free to work their own grounds whenever their official tasks were finished, and on Saturday afternoons they were generally expected to do so. On Saturdays, though, they could also get permission to attend market in town (over a dozen miles from Clifton), as long as their grounds were in good order, they had provisions to sell, and the weather was not inclement. At Christmas there were three days free from work, and the slaves were "at liberty to go where they please." The owner also ordered the killing of an ox, "or a competent number of hogs," for a Christmas feast, with a special issue of "Rum, Sugar, Pipes and Tobacco."

Each week, the slaves were issued with the more or less official ration of eight quarts of corn per adult, with half that amount for children under twelve.[3] During the course of each year they were given three new suits, two made of osnaburg or some other coarse linen and one of wool. Every third year they received a new blanket. No hats were mentioned in the regulations (the slaves probably made their own of straw), and as far as the owner was concerned, the slaves went shoeless.

These were fairly basic provisions. For any refinements, the ordinary slave had to depend on what he could purchase from the meager earning the regime allowed. In an obvious attempt to keep his slaves at a healthy number, however, the owner did make some special provisions for expectant mothers, young children, and the sick. Pregnant women were given an extra blanket and a straw palliasse for their lying-in. The midwife's fee was three dollars, but she received nothing if the infant died within the first month. On working days, mothers of children under six years of age were to take them early in the morning to the nursery, collecting them in the afternoon once the day's task was finished. Mothers still suckling their young were not to be employed far from the homestead. Slaves falling sick enough to be excused from work were to be listed. Those on the sick list were not allowed to stay in their houses but were to go to the hospital. There they would be "properly supplied with tea, gruel, broth, and other necessaries," though while they were sick they would not receive their normal issues of food.

In the prevailing circumstances, the ideal of Wylly's regulations worked to the satisfaction of neither master nor slave, and by 1818 Wylly's tinkering with his own system was also providing fuel for his many enemies in Nassau.

A healthy natural increase (which raised the number of his slaves from forty to sixty-seven in a decade) meant that Wylly had more slaves than he needed for the labor of his three New Providence farms, or could easily feed. In 1818 he told Acting Governor Munnings that he no longer attempted to grow any plantation crops. On his two smaller estates, Tusculum and Waterloo, he ran cattle and sheep, and only on Clifton was there much tillage. This, however, was given up almost entirely to the production of Indian and guinea corn for the sustenance of his slaves and stock.[4]

Besides the three drivers, the only men continuously employed (and none were really overworked) were eight cowherds and dairymen, five shepherds, three plowmen, two carpenters, and two masons. Except for the busiest seasons and hardest tasks, most of the field work was done by the women, but it was far from continuous even for them. At times, Wylly was almost reduced to inventing tasks, such as the building of walls, at which all his slaves were adept. The owner scarcely employed the numerous children at all, though he was legally entitled to their labor from the age of six.

The slaves themselves (of whom three-quarters lived at Clifton) had twenty-two family allotments, totaling sixty acres, well planted in ground provisions. All the slaves grew Indian and guinea corn, yams, potatoes, pumpkins, squash, peas, beans, and okras, and most also produced benny, eddoes, groundnuts, melons, plantains, and bananas. Nearly all had poultry, and more than half owned hogs, for which areas of rough pasturage were allocated.[5] Though much of the area on each farm was "white land" or swamp, and the slaves' provision grounds were not in the best locations, it was possible for a family to sustain itself through the labor of the women and children alone, and the more industrious families produced considerable surpluses for the market in Nassau.

This was an activity which Wylly and most of his slaves wished to expand. It offended Wylly's sense of economy that he was forced to employ and feed unprofitable slaves who were quite capable of working to feed themselves. It was also, he claimed, a demoralizing form of dependency and an invitation to sloth. As long as they had their guaranteed issues of corn, there was insufficient incentive for lazy slaves to work their own grounds. For their part, though, the more ambitious slaves only wanted more time to work for themselves, and some means of getting their surplus produce more easily to market.

Accordingly, in August 1818 William Wylly made a decision that he would give those slaves whose work was not permanently needed the option of having three taskless days each week (from Friday to Sunday), in return for giving up their weekly issues of corn. He also allowed the use of his boat to transport to market produce too heavy to send by road. Only a slave called Caesar and certain other unnamed "skulkers," who had neglected their grounds and malingered at their tasks, were excluded from the offer: they would get their corn but work six days each week, without choice. In times of scarcity, though, all slaves could opt to obtain corn from Wylly's storage barn, but at a price of four shillings a peck, repayable in labor at a rate of a shilling for each day's task.[6]

Besides being technically illegal (much the same offense with which Wylly himself had charged James Moss in 1816), this type of flexibility was probably doomed to failure. The master's attempt to maximize his own returns (or at least cut losses) by giving the slaves incentives was scarcely compatible with either the open-ended drive of the industrious slave to become more independent, or the skulker's will to retreat into the abject lethargy of complete dependence. Indeed, most whites probably felt more comfortable with the latter type of slave, "proving his natural inferiority," than with an "uppity nigger," eager to enter and compete in the master economy. Wylly's own attitude may have been hypocritical (as his enemies alleged), or simply self-deluding. Certainly, the subsequent fate of his slaves suggests mutual disenchantment, if not the complete emptiness of Wylly's brand of self-serving paternalism.

Caesar and his fellow skulkers were probably whipped into submission; the record is silent. It was one of Wylly's trustiest slaves who most conspicuously ran away, probably going off with the master's boat and not returning. On January 24, 1821, the following advertisement appeared in the *Bahama Gazette*:

> Clifton, 17 January, 1821
>
> Absconded from this place, on the night of Saturday last, a man named Boatswain and his wife Chloe—and they carried off with them their four children, viz. Harriet, about 12 years of age, Phillis, 9 years, Matilda, 5 years, and St. George, 3 years.
>
> The Man is a tall slender African, about 48 years of Age, a mason by trade; of an upright carriage, and has lost two or three of his upper front teeth. The Woman is short corpulent, a cook and washerwoman, about 42 years old— of a tawney complexion, and has a remarkably good countenance. Both are well known about Town—and they are supposed to be harboured by some of the Baptist Negroes about Sambo Scriven's Meeting House.
>
> One dollar for each of them will be paid upon their being delivered to the keeper of the Work House in Nassau.
>
> Wm. Wylly[7]

Whether or not the meager reward had proved an inducement to a slave catcher, Boatswain and his family were rounded up and remained in bondage until slavery ended. Indeed, for virtually all his slaves, Wylly's alleged liberalism did not extend to actual manumission, either when he left the Bahamas in 1823 or in his will when he died in 1828.[8] Some of his slaves were shipped off to St. Vincent when he was appointed chief justice there, and four members of one family, the Peages from Tusculum, were drowned on the way in the wreck of the schooner *Resolution* off Acklin's Island in October 1821. The remainder of Wylly's slaves were sold, some of them, with tragic irony, to the same Henry Moss who, with his wife, was convicted of gross cruelty in 1826.[9] Among these unfortunates was the entire family of Boatswain, the ambitious African Baptist and mason. Sold to Moss on February 3, 1823, they were shipped by their new master to Long Cay, Crooked Island, where they toiled at the fields and salt pans till the end of slavery, almost a world away from Clifton, Nassau, and Samuel Scriven's chapel.[10]

In material terms, William Wylly's slaves probably existed toward the upper end of a spectrum of Bahamian slave conditions. They lived relatively close to Nassau and had a master who was concerned to behave correctly toward them—or to be seen to do so. But these were mixed blessings. Wylly's almost constant oversight saved his slaves from serious maltreatment and complete exploitation but also reduced their chances of bending the system to their own advantage. They had less work required than most laboring slaves, and more time to themselves. But their provision land was of indifferent quality, and the market too far to provide easy rewards. They also had few opportunities to hire themselves out, or to develop craftsman skills. In these respects, Nassau beckoned and tantalized; the healthier regime of the far western edge of New Providence was insufficient compensation.

Except for the slave quarters adjacent to town houses or country mansions, or formally integrated into the few more elaborate plantation complexes (built by slave craftsmen but under their masters' orders), slaves were responsible for building, as well as furnishing, their own houses. The quality of accommodation therefore depended on the slaves' own skills, ingenuity, and industry, as well as the materials available. The farther away from Nassau, the less sophisticated and more rudimentary slave houses and furniture tended to be, though this did not necessarily mean they were less healthy, because of the more generous allotment of space. Accommodation designed and built entirely by the slaves themselves was also more likely to reflect their own chosen style of family life.

From the evidence of the few "slave houses" still found in the courtyards of the oldest Nassau town houses, many urban domestics lived in very cramped quarters in close proximity to their owners. For example, the house called the Deanery, said to have been originally built in 1710 but mainly dating from the 1820s, shows the remains of a slave "dormitory" just twelve feet square (with slits for windows almost like a castle or prison) at one end of the stone-built kitchen, just behind and at a lower elevation than the main house. In this case, white masters and black slave servants—perhaps a dozen in all, with the latter at least as numerous as the former—shared a living and working space no larger than thirty by ninety feet, suggesting a very complex, tight, and tension-fraught arrangement of spaces and dividing lines.

Large houses on the outskirts of town, such as Dunmore House or the Hermitage, gave slaves greater spatial separation from their masters, though nothing like that distancing and informality enjoyed by the town slaves who lived "out," Over-the-Hill in Nassau. There, because the slaves wished to live as close as possible to town and their workplaces yet could not own any land, the houses tended to be simply constructed, almost temporary, crowded together, and unsanitary. Yet the slaves were also gregarious partly from choice. The Over-the-Hill pattern was reminiscent of the "yards" of West Indian towns, in which informal and extended family arrangements, and a vibrant social life, could flourish.

In these respects the settlements huddled under Fort Fincastle and behind the hospital were more like the quasi-villages of the largest and most decayed Out Island plantations—such as those of Lord Rolle on Exuma—than the tighter and closely knit communities on smaller and more tightly supervised estates—such as William Wylly's Clifton, Tusculum, and Waterloo. On the latter type of estate, where the master supervised the layout and building style as well as attempting to regulate his slaves' marital arrangements, the standard stone-built two-room cottage was likely to enforce, or at least reinforce, a tendency among the slaves to establish the tight-knit twin-headed nuclear family as the social norm. In much the same way, Western bourgeois industrialists have been accused of promoting the type of simple nuclear family that was most effective both for the capitalist mode of production and for social control—in contrast to the larger family units and extended family groupings of traditional preindustrial societies.

In the most carefully planned country or Out Island estates, the house of the owner or overseer pre-empted the highest ground, with its views and breezes, and was surrounded by the most important plantation buildings: produce store, granary, stables, smithy, slave lockup, and hospital (the chapel at Clifton seems to have been unique). On a more or less distant knoll, or, more likely, in some infertile nearby dell, were the slave houses, rarely in rows, but clustered, each with its garden and most with a pen for the family sow and an outhouse privy. Some of the stone-built slave houses that have survived have internal fireplaces and chimneys, but cooking was almost invariably done outside, either in a separate kitchen of wattle and thatch, or, with infinite ingenuity, simply on three rocks in the open air.

Those slave quarters located on the flat lowland close to swamps were notoriously unhealthy. This was not (as was commonly said) because of "miasmas" arising from the marsh but from the mosquitoes breeding in stagnant water and not blown away by a breeze and from the way that cooking and drinking water from the shallow wells was mixed with the effluent from wastewater, garbage, and earth privies. Obtaining sufficient fresh water was always a problem, particularly in the southern islands. But paradoxically, the need to trudge miles to a suitable well, which has always been such a wearisome feature of daily life in the Bahamas Out Islands, was probably healthy, since distance from settlement reduced the chances of pollution.

Similarly, it was sometimes on the poorest and most neglected estates, where the slaves had no competition for the limestone ridges, that some of the healthiest slave communities lived, even though their houses were built of wattle, daub, and thatch rather than stone and shingle, or even almost entirely of thatch like Amerindian huts. The least fortunate of all Bahamian slaves, though, were those unable to establish a permanent home, whether on ridge or plain, because they were constantly being split into gangs and shifted by masters in search of elusive profits, from season to season and year to year. Such, it seems, were the seasonal salt-raking gangs of the southern islands, whose sun-scorched toil while living in palmetto bothies or barracks by the side of the salt pans was almost reminiscent of the fate of the Lucayan pearl divers described by Bartolomé de las Casas. One of the few Bahamian slaves ever able to give testimony to the outside world, Mary Prince, who raked salt in the Turks Islands for ten years, described how she was put to sleep "in a long shed, divided into narrow slips, like the stalls used for cattle." [11]

Since they left no wills or inventories, it is difficult to establish with certainty the range of material possessions owned by Bahamian slaves. But the indications from the archeology of slave house sites, and such sources as the newspaper advertisements for runaways (which often mentioned how slaves were dressed and what personal or purloined goods they chose to take with them when they fled), are that in terms of worldly goods they ranged between poverty and destitution. For long denied the right to own goods at all, and never having much surplus cash, slaves were also discouraged from building up personal possessions by the lack of space and security, and the likelihood of being shifted from place to place. Even more demoralizing, the system so encouraged a dependence on the masters for issues and hand-me-downs, and such a "slavish" imitation of the masters' living style, that the slaves failed to develop skills—for example, in pottery, woodcarving, weaving, and leatherwork—that would have helped them supply themselves. In terms of domestic craftsmanship and in adapting to native materials, the Bahamian slaves were greatly inferior both to the ancient Lucayans and to

their African forebears. What adaptations and survivals there were—
African-style thatching, calabash utensils, stone corn mortars, palmetto
plait, sisal rope—occurred mainly of necessity, and in ratio to the distance from the colonial capital. Paradoxically, the Nassau slaves, marginally richer in material terms, were the most dependent and imitative
of all—at the poorest, almost the "refuse," end of a material culture based
on imports from the industrializing European motherland.

The chief item of furniture in most slave houses was the foursquare
marital bed, which took up most of the sleeping half of the typical two-
room layout; the bedstead of planks in a hardwood frame, with a grass-
stuffed sacking mattress and the well-worn issue blankets. The youngest
children slept with their parents, the rest on palliasses laid on the earthen
floor, spreading throughout the house and overflowing into the houses
of grandparents or spinster aunts as the family increased. In general,
these crowded houses would be more sparsely furnished than those of
the seventeenth-century Adventurers: besides the bed, probably only a
rough table, benches, a wooden safe or casks to store food, and a cut-
down barrel for washing in; a few iron pots and knives; basins, plates,
and mugs of rough imported earthenware; a single lamp and a couple of
candle holders; cutlasses, hoes, and fishing gear; working clothes hanging from the rafters; and, hidden under the thatch, perhaps, a fowling
gun with its flints and powder. An iron-bound chest for special clothes,
and a large Spanish jar for storing grain or keeping water cool, would be
family treasures.

Little of the slaves' waking life was spent indoors. Eating as well as
cooking was often outdoors. Houses were mainly for sleeping and shelter from the rain. Since lamps, lamp oil, and candles were scarce, the
nights were long. Expected to rise before daylight, families generally retired well before nine, closing their shutters tight against the "night airs,"
insects, and prowlers. Very few slaves possessed netting, and on still,
damp nights fires of green leaves were left smoldering all night to keep
the mosquitoes and sandflies at bay—so that many slaves suffered from
persistently red and weeping eyes.

Except for those domestics who were dressed by their owners in smart,
if distinguishing, uniforms, Bahamian slaves during the working week
were shabby and threadbare, and sometimes almost naked at their tasks
in the field. Young children too were often issued no clothes and wore
borrowed rags or went completely naked up to the age of puberty. The
minimum legal issue of "two suits of proper and sufficient clothing"—
generally woolen jackets and linen trousers for the men, a woolen wrap-

Havana, with a Cargo of Dry Goods, Wines, Spices, &c.

A Cartel Schooner returned yesterday from Havana, with nineteen exchanged Prisoners; amongst whom are Capt. Frith, late of the Hezekiah Privateer of Bermuda, and Capt Clunes, late of the Hindostan Privateer Ship of Jamaica.

To be Sold at Public Auction,

At the Tavern in Georgetown,

On Saturday, the 27th of *May*, 1797,

A GANG of valuable NEGROES, between 30 and 40 in Number.

Any Person desirous to treat for them at Private Sale, may apply to Messrs. *Forbes, Munro,* and Co. in Nassau.

Exuma, 27*th April,* 1797.

For Sale by Private Contract,

A PLANTATION on *Great Exuma,* containing Six hundred Acres, with the Buildings and Improvements thereon.— About 140 Acres are well laid out in small Cotton Fields, 40 Acres formerly planted in Corn, and 26 in Pasture.—The Land fronts on the Sea, has a convenient Landing Place,

Slave sale advertisement (Bahamas Archives)

per and linen petticoat for the women—scarcely survived a year's hard work in the fields and were insufficient to keep slaves warm in the coldest months between October and March. Some masters, like William Wylly, issued a third annual suit or a few lengths of the cheaper cloth (cotton duck, woolen pennistones, linen osnaburg), which the more dexterous and industrious female slaves could make into extra suits or children's clothing, or use for patching.

However, to put on a more dignified or elegant appearance, slaves had to fend for themselves. A large part of the small sums of money earned through extra work or selling produce went in purchasing a pair of shoes and at least one set of decent clothing for dances, funerals, or church-going: for the men, good woolen trousers, shirt, waistcoat, topcoat, and top hat; for the women, a dress and petticoats of good East Indian cotton, colorful handkerchiefs for headties, perhaps even a pair of stockings. Similarly, the more fortunate and industrious slaves would boast a pitiful handful of extra possessions and marginal luxuries: scissors and dressmaking materials, some specialist tools, a glass or two, and some chinaware (some of it cracked or chipped and passed on from the master), a mirror, combs and trinkets, and a store of clay pipes (which were smoked by women and men alike when they could). But slave houses rarely contained pictures or books, unless it was the treasured Bible and prayer book in the home of the few literate Christian slaves.

If Bahamian slaves were relatively well fed on the average, this too was due to their own augmentation of the official issues. The most fortunate were sleek and strong, though those worked hardest, with little spare time or provision land, were seriously undernourished. On its own, the official minimum issue of twenty-one pints of flour, seven quarts of rice, or fifty-six pounds of potatoes for each adult (with half as much for those under ten) provided an average of between twenty-one hundred and thirty-two hundred calories a day but was seriously deficient in protein, fat, vitamins, and essential minerals.[12] On this diet alone, laboring slaves would not have starved but would have lacked energy and been constantly hungry. Over the longer run, they would have suffered and died from deficiency diseases and the effects of reduced resistance. Luckily, nearly all Bahamian slaves were able to augment their diet, with root starches, peas and beans, green vegetables, fruits, fish, mollusks, and some animal meat—though for one reason or another, few slaves enjoyed a perfectly balanced, or even consistently adequate, diet.

From Mary Prince's account, the least fortunate Bahamian slaves were those working permanently at the salt pans in the southern islands.

During her ten-year ordeal on virtually barren Grand Cay, Mary Prince subsisted almost entirely on a diet of corn. On the very first day, she recounted,

> I was given a half barrel and a shovel, and had to stand up to my knees in the water, from four o'clock in the morning till nine, when we were given some Indian corn boiled in water, which we were obliged to swallow as fast as we could for fear the rain should come and melt the salt. We were then called again to our tasks, and worked through the heat of the day; the sun flaming upon our heads like fire, and raising salt blisters in those parts which were not completely covered. Our feet and legs, from standing in the salt water for so many hours, soon became full of dreadful boils, which eat down in some cases to the very bone, afflicting the sufferers with great torment. We came home at twelve; ate our corn soup, called *blawly*, as fast as we could, and went back to our employment till dark at night. We then shovelled up the salt in large heaps, and went down to the sea, where we washed the pickle from our limbs, and cleansed the barrows and shovels from the salt. When we returned to the house, our master gave us each our allowance of raw Indian corn, which we pounded in a mortar and boiled in water for our suppers.[13]

Most Bahamian slaves, though, had access to provision grounds, kept some small stock, and were able to fish. For these persons, a diet that included each week on the average eight pints of corn or peas, twenty pounds of yams or similar starchy roots, three pounds of fish or pork, and such green vegetables as okra or benny, would have provided a daily intake of three thousand calories, with an adequate balance of protein, minerals, and vitamins. If somewhat overweighted with carbohydrates and deficient in calcium (like most tropical diets), this was a diet well above modern Caribbean or African averages.[14]

The ideal pattern, however, was not attainable everywhere, or permanently possible anywhere. Town slaves had limited chances to grow food, keep animals, or fish for themselves, and had to depend on extra allowances, scraps from the master's table, or purchases in the market. For their part, rural slaves often saved their best produce for sale, or had it pre-empted by the master—especially pork, poultry, or fruits. In any case, as we have seen, even the best masters were in the habit of cutting down their issues of food to compensate for time spent by the slaves in producing their own. Masters were always quick to complain when shortages through war or bad harvests raised the price of corn but notoriously slow in responding to the loss of slave-grown produce through prolonged drought, flood, or hurricane. On such occasions, the diet of any Bahamian slave might quite suddenly deteriorate to the level normal for the salt-raking slaves of the Turks and Caicos Islands.

Besides, as Kenneth Kiple has argued, even the availability of healthy foodstuffs did not necessarily mean their optimum use by the slaves. The custom of cooking all food damaged or destroyed some essential nutrients, and the use of iron pots, while it increased the intake of iron, further decreased the amount of vitamin C in green vegetables. Vitamin A, as well as being present in much smaller amounts in the guinea corn issued by some masters instead of the Indian variety, depended on a relatively high intake of fats for efficient conversion in the body. Furthermore, while the prevalence of a high-carbohydrate, low-protein diet greatly increased the slaves' need for vitamin B_1 (thiamine), the lack of sufficient B_1 decreased the effective absorption of vitamins B_2 and B_3 (riboflavin and niacin).[15]

Thus, while the far better average health and demographic statistics for Bahamian slaves compared with slaves from the sugar colonies reflected the better average diet they enjoyed, the levels both of diet and of morbidity, mortality, and fertility were far from uniform, or as sound as they might have been. Nowhere are the effects of diet deficiencies coupled with excessive work under extreme conditions seen more clearly than in the Turks Islands salinas. But other more general features, particularly a poor level of resistance to cold and damp, and a far higher rate of infant mortality than suggested by the official returns, may also be at least partly diet-related.

The effectiveness of a slave's diet, of course, related mainly to the type and amount of work required, with most Bahamian slaves benefiting from the converse of that inexorable equation that said that the more work demanded by the master the more food was needed by the slave yet the less time was available to grow it. The steady decline of the plantation economy thus meant, in general, the steady improvement in the slaves' diet, and consequently in the statistics of health and demographic performance.

The Loyalists' slaves had been hard worked in clearing the land of trees and rocks, and cotton fields had priority over provision grounds. Then, as long as cotton production still seemed an economic possibility, a large proportion of Bahamian slaves were subjected to a plantation regime at least as rigorous as that left behind on the American mainland. Not that cotton cultivation and harvesting could ever compare with the almost year-round gang labor of sugar production—especially the backbreaking toil of cane holing in stiff clays, or cutting and carrying the cane to the pitiless tempo of the mill. Cotton bushes are planted as seeds and grow easily in lightly hoed land. Plucking and cleaning the cotton bolls are tedious tasks, but not desperately strenuous, and the pace of the crop is not driven by either a short flowering season or a tendency of the product to decay as soon as picked.

Yet cotton production under Bahamian conditions was always hard work, most efficiently performed by gangs of slaves, and it actually grew harder before it was virtually given up. The poverty of the soil and the prevalence of parasites meant that the density and productivity of the bushes was always low and grew progressively lower, forcing the slaves to cover an increasing area. The preference for the long-staple Anguilla cotton, which grew all the year, with two crop peaks in February and early summer, also meant more continuous seasons and a more difficult cleaning process than with the Persian type generally grown on the mainland. Even the introduction of Joseph Eve's cotton gin after 1793, which multiplied the amount of cotton wool which one slave could process in a given time (up to 360 pounds in a day), increased the total work by making it possible to grow a larger crop.

At its peak, Bahamian cotton involved perhaps three thousand working slaves, producing six hundred tons a year from twelve thousand acres. The most monocultural plantations would have two-thirds of their slaves in the cotton fields or at the ginning shed, from sunup to sundown, nine months in the year. An efficient estate could produce five hundred pounds of cotton per acre, and an efficient slave fifteen hundred pounds a year, worth perhaps £150. But the averages were less than a quarter of this at the best of times and rapidly declined after 1800, when the world price also fell. However hard slaves were driven, plantations faced collapse unless they diversified—into salt production, raising stock animals, or growing provisions for the Nassau market. By 1810 there were no pure cotton plantations left. Cotton was a marginal product, employing a smaller number of slaves for fewer days in the year, plucking cotton from "ratoon" rather than replanted bushes, and working by tasks rather than in supervised gangs. Except in cases where estates switched to producing almost nothing but salt, all these changes were improvements for the slaves.

The extent of the diversification of Bahamian agriculture between 1810 and the end of formal slavery, and the comparatively small degree of variation from island to island, is most clearly seen by looking at the statistics of Bahamian production in 1832 calculated by Robert Montgomery Martin (table 15).[16]

Table 15
Agricultural Produce, 1832

Island	Horses	Horned Cattle	Sheep and Goats	Swine	Indian and Guinea Corn (bu.)	Potatoes and Yams (lbs.)	Peas and Beans (bu.)	Pineapples (doz.)	Pumpkins and Lemons	Okras (lbs.)	Cassava and Arrowroot (lbs.)	Onions, Garlic, Shallots (lbs.)	Cotton (tons)
New Providence	200	300	1,000	250	800	1,700	3,500	500	2,000	15,000	10,000	400	—
Turks Islands	175	240	100	50	1,000	—	—	—	—	—	500	—	—
Caicos Islands	120	300	700	100	500	300	50	—	1,000	1,000	700	150	—
Eleuthera	50	200	500	450	10,000	70,000	2,000	40,000	20,000	8,000	30,000	1,000	4
Crooked Island	45	350	400	200	2,000	3,500	1,100	—	1,500	1,000	2,000	100	5
Rum Cay	150	250	1,000	250	1,700	2,200	220	200	8,000	700	1,000	100	5
San Salvador	140	150	1,000	300	1,500	1,700	100	220	3,000	600	500	70	—
Long Island	250	1,000	700	400	1,500	8,500	200	200	7,000	3,000	700	150	11
Exumas	40	200	500	200	2,500	4,500	250	80	2,500	1,700	300	50	12
Inagua and Mayaguana	10	25	50	100	1,500	2,700	70	45	1,200	700	500	30	3
Grand Bahama and Berry Islands	10	50	100	200	4,500	1,700	80	25	2,700	4,500	1,100	1,000	—
Andros	—	—	10	150	1,700	2,500	200	—	8,000	1,700	1,200	100	—
Ragged Island	20	100	200	100	50	400	—	—	600	700	300	—	—
Cat Island	120	550	1,500	300	2,000	1,700	450	50	3,500	6,000	1,700	200	2
Abaco	—	—	50	500	2,200	20,000	900	20	11,000	8,500	1,000	700	—
Harbour Island	60	50	50	200	—	—	—	—	—	—	—	—	—
Total	1,390	3,765	7,890	3,750	33,500	121,400	9,120	41,340	72,000	53,100	51,500	4,350	42

Source: Robert Montgomery Martin, Statistics of the Colonies of the British Empire (London: W. H. Allen, 1839), 110.

Although nearly all planters tried to develop salt production as a substitute for cotton, and important salinas were constructed as far north as Rose Island, Salt Cay, and the Berry Islands, the chief Bahamian salt pans were to the south and east of Great Exuma—on Little Exuma, Long Island, Rum Cay, Ragged Island, Long Cay, and Great Inagua, as well as in the Turks and Caicos Islands. With an annual capacity in excess of five million bushels, the Bahamas was one of the largest producers of salt in the hemisphere. But only in the Turks Islands was the industry virtually a monoculture. Elsewhere, islands producing salt were also self-sufficient in agricultural produce, with few if any slaves worked as continuously or as hard at the salt pans as Mary Prince and the other slaves on Grand Cay, Turks Islands. Rum Cay, for example, with salinas totaling 650 acres capable of producing a half million bushels a year, became the second most important Bahamian salt island, and so many slaves were transferred there that it became one of the most densely populated Out Islands. But, as table 15 shows, Rum Cay became one of the most diversified Bahamian Out Islands and, as a consequence, was much more healthy than the Turks and Caicos Islands in demographic terms.[17] Even Ragged Island, which had limited agricultural land, was not entirely dependent on salt—its inhabitants being also mariners famous for the more or less illicit trade with nearby Cuba.

Another result of the decline of cotton was the increase in stock production. Though requiring long hours and continuous employment throughout the year, stock husbandry was a healthier and more popular occupation for slaves than any form of manual labor. But it was a far from open-ended development. The sweltering summers and scarcity of fresh water and good grass made for meager animals, which needed large grazing areas and, in times of drought, ate into the never-plentiful supplies of estate-produced food. To this were added the limited markets and the difficulty of transporting the animals there. Besides, the preference for the hardy goat and the almost goatlike Caribbean sheep, with their voracious and indiscriminate appetites, meant that what grazing there was rapidly deteriorated even further.

The most efficient diversified estates, such as in Eleuthera, produced ground provisions, fruit, and stock for export to Nassau. But those farther afield, on the poorer soils, and without access to large salinas, were little more than subsistence farms by the end of slavery. Masters worked their slaves as hard as they could, but most found that with a steadily expanding population on soils of declining fertility, more and more time was needed to produce the food which the slaves required.

The practice favored by William Wylly of giving slaves extra free days in lieu of food never became general because it was technically illegal. But most masters found themselves constrained not only to give their slaves progressively more time each day to produce food on their own, but to allot more and more land and official working tasks to producing the food crops they were legally bound to provide for their slaves.

Thus, not only was the improving demographic health of the Bahamian slaves related to the declining plantation economy, but to the average planter's declining expectation of profit from his estate was coupled the slaves' rising expectation of being left on their own. Perhaps the most extreme case was that of Lord Rolle's estates in Exuma. Here, on four of the least infertile tracts of the island, totaling five thousand acres, some 150 slaves in 1791 had grown thirty tons of cotton, worth perhaps £3,000.[18] By 1825, though cotton production had almost ceased, the population had all but doubled and was increasing by 3 percent a year. In making a plea to transfer his slaves to Demerara, Jamaica, or Trinidad, Lord Rolle claimed that expenditure on the obligatory issues of clothing and food to his slaves had exceeded income from the estate by £3,378 over the previous seven years.[19] Five years later, when troops were sent to quell unrest among the Rolle slaves after rumors had reached them that they were about to be moved, a police officer reported that though turned out to the fields each day at 6:30 A.M., nearly all slaves had finished their tasks and were back in their huts by 1 P.M., ready to work their own grounds, to look after their stock, go fishing, or simply relax.[20]

Since masters would have driven their slaves harder with less food if they could, they cannot justly be given credit for those conditions of work and diet that made Bahamian slaves relatively healthy. Similarly, the masters cannot be given credit (or, for that matter, blamed) for the effects of epidemiological and etological factors of which they were ignorant or which were beyond their control. Furthermore, since they provided almost no medical treatment for their slaves, the masters can only be awarded a left-handed accolade: that in the prevailing state of medical ignorance, a lack of formal medicine of the European (and North American) type was positively benign.

As Kenneth Kiple has persuasively argued, the decline in the proportion of African-born slaves and the end of direct links with Africa resulted in the disappearance of diseases which depended on purely African vectors (such as the tsetse-borne sleeping sickness), and the progressive reduction of other epidemic and contagious diseases brought directly from Africa, such as yaws and leprosy. At the same time, the genetic inheritance that made black persons relatively resistant to such diseases as malaria (because of the sickle-cell trait) and yellow fever, and capable of working efficiently on relatively low levels of protein and fat, were positive factors.[21]

Against this, however, were the medical drawbacks of entering a new work regime and environment under the pressure of attacks from European as well as American (and later, even Asiatic) diseases. Under the worst conditions found in the Bahamas, slaves would have suffered almost as much as those in the West Indies from deficiency diseases, such as night blindness, pellagra, beriberi, and even scurvy (due, respectively, to shortages of vitamins A, B-2, B-3, and C), from rickets and other bone afflictions caused by calcium deficiency, and even, in some circumstances, from anemia due to a shortage of iron. Such deficiencies would have been especially damaging in childbirth and the nursing of infants, with the demographic effects that can be traced in the Bahamian regions most affected, such as the Turks Islands. It was the same harsh regime, as Mary Prince testified, that produced such distressing, if not directly life-threatening, symptoms as diarrhea, dermatitis, and leg ulcers that ate down to the bone.[22]

Bahamian slaves had much closer and more continuous contact with Europeans than with Amerindians, and their prolonged and incomplete immunization to European diseases was complicated by the African's special susceptibility to cold. Contacts with Europeans which long antedated the settlement of the Bahamas had led to Africans' being little more subject to smallpox, measles, mumps, and diphtheria than Europeans were themselves, with these diseases also mitigated by the comparative dispersion of the Bahamian slave population. Yet the common cold, influenza, pneumonia, and any other disease affecting the lungs continued to find all blacks vulnerable, especially during the coldest months, when clothing or food were insufficient, or where slaves were forced to live in exceptionally cramped and unhygienic conditions.

Generally speaking, Bahamian slaves were much less subject to intestinal and parasitical disorders than slaves elsewhere, and some African and West Indian afflictions, such as hookworm and guinea-worm infestation, were almost unknown. But all diseases that owed their origins and spread to high population densities, unclean living quarters, and polluted water supplies were, naturally, far more common in Nassau than in any Out Island, and least common in the most distant and most sparsely settled islands. Though cholera, the great nineteenth-century urban killer from Asia, did not reach the West Indies until 1833 or the Bahamas until the 1840s,[23] this category included the water-borne typhoid, amoebic, and bacillary dysentery; the insect-borne typhus, scabies, and chigger infections; and intestinal parasites such as tapeworms and roundworms—all of which continued and even increased after slavery ended.

Worst of all afflictions, though, causing perhaps as great a mortality as all other diseases put together, and totally baffling medical science, was lockjaw, alias tetanus. Blacks seem to have been especially susceptible to this disease, which was spread from long-lived organisms carried in the soil into open wounds and almost invariably killed those infected after a week's progressive paralysis. Newborn infants were the most vulnerable of all, commonly being delivered under extremely unhygienic conditions and infected through the umbilicus. It was also a disease which affected Out Island slaves at least as much as those in Nassau, because the infection was usually carried through the droppings of stock animals, particularly horses.[24]

Burton Williams told the Trinidad Council in 1825 that in the Bahamas he had come to expect the death of one-third of all slave infants from lockjaw within their first nine days. Though this statement was no doubt exaggerated (in order to argue the greater healthiness of Trinidad), it would support the contention of Barry Higman that both birthrates and infant mortality figures in the Bahamas were greatly understated by the registration returns. Higman's elegantly argued corrections suggest a Bahamian slave infant mortality rate as high as 34 percent, and an overall annual slave mortality rate of 35.8 per 1,000, rather than the figure of 13.4 per 1,000 indicated by the registration returns and quoted in the last chapter.[25] Given the actual natural increase of 32.0 per 1,000 per year, this indicates not only a relatively low child and adult mortality rate but a gross fertility rate even higher than previously thought—an almost incredible 69.4 per 1,000 per year. Thus, since the adjusted overall mortality rates for Bahamian slaves were considerably higher than the fertility rates for most West Indian slave populations, Higman concluded that it was not the general healthiness or low mortality of Bahamian slaves which accounted for their natural increase so much as their quite exceptional fertility.[26]

As Dr. Townsend noticed in the 1820s, there were no more than a handful of medical practitioners in the Bahamas, and these spent most of their time ministering to the white population. Slaves in the Out Islands could, at most, expect a visit from a doctor once or twice a year. "When we were ill, let our complaint be what it might," testified Mary Prince, "the only medicine given to us was a great bowl of hot salt water, with salt mixed in it, which made us very sick." [27]

Yet such an emetic probably did less harm than some of the medicine which doctors commonly applied. At best, they were competent surgeons and gynecologists for simple cases, but complex operations, most internal disorders, and the diagnosis and treatment of tropical ailments were quite beyond them. Still shackled to humoral theory, they let blood, blistered, and purged their patients with careless abandon, and administered medicines, such as mercury and opium derivatives, that were dangerously toxic, if not addictive. Dr. Townsend himself noted the serious side effects of mercurials—which had some value in treating venereal disease and yaws but were used indiscriminately, particularly for purging—and even gave the symptoms a name: *hydrargyra*. Townsend also mentioned the gossip about a Scots doctor in Nassau called Blair, who had just lost one of his patients, a "respectable merchant" called Dunshee, who had "ailed nothing till he died."[28]

Dr. Townsend was in advance of most local doctors in his concern for all classes of patients, his careful observation, his skepticism of some traditional remedies, and his willingness to consider local specifics. He often prescribed aloes and tamarind water, and on one occasion jotted down a medicinal recipe from one Judah Forbes consisting of rat root, milkweed, sarsaparilla, and another local plant, dismissing it only because the labor needed in its preparation was "worth at least five dollars."[29] Most impressively, Townsend was also a skilled practitioner of vaccination against smallpox—one of the few positive achievements in preventative medicine up to that time. But he was no more able than the other doctors to solve difficult surgical problems, to save patients from serious infections or tropical fevers, or to prescribe palliatives, let alone cures, for such "African" afflictions as the dropsy suffered by Ann Paul's child (perhaps beriberi), or the slave Charlotte's "scrophula" (probably either yaws or leprosy).[30]

Slaves, for good or ill, had largely to rely on traditional African medical lore, compounded with local "bush medicine." By trial and error they built up an impressive pharmacopeia of teas, tinctures, and ointments. At best, these had real efficacy against mild fevers, minor intestinal troubles, or the lesser skin complaints; at worst, they were useless but harmless. Bahamian slaves, like their masters, also pragmatically recognized the advantages of living on the dry and airy ridges in preference to the mosquito-ridden swamps, of personal cleanliness, and of frequent sea bathing. Only as time went on, though, did any slaves have the choice of quite where and how they lived. And they had no more science than the white doctors to identify the true causal connections between lethal tropical diseases and the prevalence of mosquitoes, polluted water supplies, and cramped living conditions. In parallel with the pseudoscience of humoral theory and practice (mercifully applied in very small doses), they suffered from the worst effects of the lingering legacies of African sorcery and antisorcery medicine. In nothing was this more apparent, sadly, than in the way that the ancient African custom of smearing the umbilical stump of newborn babies with earth and ash, and wrapping it in "leaves or any old piece of cloth" inevitably contributed to the prevalence of neonatal tetanus.[31]

Nonetheless, the general trend in the medical health of Bahamian slaves was ever upward, until it equaled, and in some respects surpassed, that of the whites. Some diseases characteristic of slavery, such as yaws, leprosy, and neonatal tetanus, continued, survived the ending of slavery and lasted into modern times. But these were more the product of poverty and overcrowding than the African heritage or slave conditions as such. Other "slave" afflictions, such as worm infestations and tuberculosis, were found among all sections of the population in the century after slavery ended and were probably more common among poor whites than among the more affluent blacks. And leprosy, though rare, was probably as common in the poor white settlements of the northern Bahamas at the end of the nineteenth century as among the black former slaves. Likewise, cholera was a scourge that in the 1840s and 1850s attacked whites and blacks without discrimination, concentrating its fury on Nassau and the more densely settled nearer islands.

Just as the improving medical and demographic health of Bahamian slaves were interrelated, so both were the products of creolization. As we have already seen, improving health conditions and a very low level of mortality through the ages of female nubility helped to produce fertility rates so high that they were able to sustain serious losses among newborn infants. These factors were probably as influential as the purely demographic results of creolization: the decline almost to zero in the proportion of Africans in the slave population, the equalization of the sex ratios (in fact, a slight preponderance of females), and the healthy balance of ages.

Almost certainly most important of all, though, were the prevalence of stable monogamous marriages, the predominance of nuclear households, and the entrenchment and spread of patterns of extended family among the slaves. These conditions were, of course, aided by the virtual guarantee of a long life for marital partners and by the survival of a very high proportion of all children who lived beyond their first ten days. They were also facilitated by the encouragement of many of the masters, by the regulations that decreed that families should not be split up, and by the conditions that made it increasingly uncommon to shift slaves from place to place. Yet the evidence that a stable family lifestyle was at least as common among African as among Creole slaves, that it flourished where the masters' control and concern were minimal, and that it continued to be the prevailing custom after slavery ended, surely shows that it was predominantly the creation of the slaves themselves—at the same time the result of a will to live more like free peasants than slaves and the very means of making such a "protopeasantry" possible.

Bahamian owners, unlike those in Trinidad, St. Lucia, and British Honduras, were not required to indicate their slaves' family relationships in the registration returns.[32] It would, in any case, have been an almost impossible task, given the small numbers of slaves in the majority of Bahamian slave holdings. All the same, in twenty-six of the holdings listed in 1822, including a quarter of all Bahamian slaves, the owners did choose to list their slaves in what were clearly their family groupings, rather than in alphabetical order, by age or sex, or by any other system of categorization.[33]

Though skewed toward the larger holdings, and including the slaves of the two owners who claimed to have promoted slave families—William Wylly and Burton Williams—this was clearly a more or less random cross-section of the Bahamian slave population. Distributed over eleven islands, the 3,011 slaves were in holdings averaging 116, but with a range between the 20 slaves owned by Phillip Bullard in Exuma and James Moss's huge holding of 840 on Crooked Island, Acklin's, and Long Cay. The combined age, sex, and African-to-Creole profile of the twenty-six slave holdings was very similar to that of the total population of Bahamian slaves.

From the 1822 evidence, the great majority of Bahamian slaves lived in some type of family unit. On the sample of twenty-six holdings, no less than 71.9 percent apparently lived in nuclear families (that is, a man and woman living together, with or without children or parents), while 13.0 percent were listed in single-parent families (overwhelmingly, a woman and her children), and only 15.1 percent were listed outside a family grouping. These figures contrasted starkly with those computed by Barry Higman for Trinidad, where in 1813 just over half the slaves seem to have lived outside a family grouping, and less than a quarter in a nuclear family. They also contrasted with one of the most paternalistically managed Jamaican estates, Montpelier in St. James, where in 1825, 77.6 percent of the slaves lived in some type of family household,

Table 16

Slave Household Patterns, 1822: Rolle Slaves and 26 Other Holdings

Family Type	Rolle Slaves, Exuma				26 Bahamian Holdings			
	Total Slaves	Number of Units	Mean Size of Units	% of Total in Type	Total Slaves	Number of Units	Mean Size of Units	% of Total in Type
Nuclear family								
Man, woman, children	110	26	4.23	46.6	1,629	308	5.29	54.1
Man, woman	14	7	2.00	5.9	178	89	2.00	5.9
Three-generation groups	29	5	5.80	12.3	358	46	7.78	11.9
Total	153	38	4.03	64.8	2,165	443	4.89	71.9
Denuded family								
Woman, children	40	12	3.33	16.9	377	95	3.97	12.5
Man, children	11	2	5.50	4.7	16	3	5.33	0.5
Total	51	14	3.64	21.6	393	98	4.01	13.0
No family								
Men alone or together	11	—	—	4.7	264	—	—	8.8
Women alone or together	9	—	—	3.8	173	—	—	5.8
Children separately	12	—	—	5.1	16	—	—	0.5
Total	32	—	—	13.6	453	—	—	15.1
Total for all types	236	—	—	100.0	3,011	—	—	100.0

Sources: Slave Registration Returns, 1822, Bahamas Archives; Michael Craton, "Changing Patterns of Slave Families in the British West Indies," Journal of Interdisciplinary History 10 (Summer 1979): 9.

Note: The 26 Bahamian holdings are those for which families are indicated in returns.

Table 17

Slave Family Structure: Williams Slaves Transferred to
Trinidad, 1825, Compared with Trinidadian Total, 1813

Family Type	Williams Slaves, 1825				Trinidadian Slaves Total, 1813			
	Total	Units	Mean Size	% in Type	Total	Units	Mean Size	% in Type
Man, woman, children	142	24	5.9	57.4	4,675	1,162	4.0	18.3
Man, woman	6	3	2.0	2.4	1,036	518	2.0	4.0
Woman, children	15	3	5.0	6.0	5,690	2,066	2.8	22.2
Man, children	0	0	—	—	357	138	2.6	1.4
Polygynists	0	0	—	—	31	7	4.4	0.1
Three-generation and extendedᵃ	47	8	5.9	18.9	445	97	4.6	1.7
Siblings	14	4	3.5	5.7 ⎱	547	197	2.8	2.1
Siblings, children	9	2	4.5	3.6 ⎰				
Man, woman, cousins	5	2	2.5	2.0	0	0	—	—
No familyᵇ	10	—	—	4.0	12,892	—	—	50.2
Total	248	—	—	100.0	25,673	—	—	100.0

Sources: Register of Returns of Slaves, T. 71/501–13, Public Record Office, London; Barry Higman, "African and Creole Slave Family Patterns in Trinidad" (Paper presented at the Tenth Conference of Caribbean Historians, 1978).

ᵃ In the Williams population, category includes man, woman, children, and their children (8 slaves); man, woman, children, man's sister, and her children (7); man, woman, children, man's sister, and her children (7); man, woman, children, woman's brother, and his spouse (6); man, woman, child, man's brother, and his spouse (5); man, woman, man's sister, and her child (4); woman, children, children's spouses (5). The Trinidadian total includes woman, her children, and her grandchildren (227); and "extended" (218).

ᵇ In the Williams population, category includes men and women living alone and unrelated separated children.

but those in single-parent households (40.3 percent) outnumbered those in nuclear families (37.3 percent). The nearest parallel to the Bahamian family pattern of 1822, in fact, was that calculated by Edith Clarke for the Jamaican peasant village of "Mocca" in 1955.[34]

The strength of the slave family in the Bahamas was related to the very positive fertility characteristics of female Bahamian slaves. On the twenty-six holdings in which families were shown, 66 percent of all females between fifteen and forty-nine were indicated as mothers, with an average of almost exactly three children each. But overall, probably 80 percent of all adult Bahamian female slaves in the 1820s became mothers, of whom perhaps three-quarters were partners in a nuclear-family household at least part of their adult lives. Over a third of the 3,011 slaves in the twenty-six holdings were children in the 308 nuclear

Table 18

West Indian Family Structure, 1813–1955: A Comparison of Trinidad, Jamaica, and the Bahamas During Slavery, Barbuda Immediately After Slavery, and Modern Rural Jamaica

	Trinidad, 1813				*Montpelier, Jamaica, 1825*			
Family Type	*Total Slaves*	*Number of Units*	*Mean Size of Units*	*% of Total in Type*[a]	*Total Slaves*	*Number of Units*	*Mean Size of Units*	*% of T… in Ty…*
Nuclear family								
Man, woman, children	4,675	1,162	4.0	18.3	204	50	4.1	25.
Man, woman	1,036	518	2.0	4.0	76	38	2.0	9.
Three-generation groups	445	97	4.6	1.7	24	6	4.0	2
Total	6,156	1,777	3.5	24.0	304	94	3.2	37
Denuded family								
Woman, children	5,690	2,066	2.8	22.2	328	70	4.77	40
Man, children	357	138	2.6	1.4	0	0		0
Others[c]	578	204	2.8	2.2				
Total	6,625	2,408	2.8	25.8	328	70	4.7	40
No family								
Men alone or together Women alone or together Children separately	12,892	—	—	50.2	182	—	—	22
Total	12,892	—	—	50.2	182	—	—	22
Total for all types	25,673	—	—	100.0	814	—	—	10

Sources: Trinidad: Register of Returns of Slaves, T71/501, Public Record Office, London; Higman, "African Creole Slave Family Patterns." Montpelier: Barry Higman, "Household Structure and Fertility on Jamaican S Plantations: A Nineteenth Century Example," *Population Studies* 27 (1973): 527–50. Bahamas: Slave Registr Returns, 1822, Bahamas Archives. Barbuda: Dolin Clarke and David Lowenthal from Codington Records, Glo ter County Records Office, England (Private correspondence). Jamaica: Edith Clarke, *My Mother Who Fathere* (London: Andre Deutsch, 1957), 191–94; Craton, "Changing Patterns," 28–29.

	Bahamas, 26 Holdings, 1822			Barbuda, 1851				Rural Jamaica, 1951	
al ves	Number of Units	Mean Size of Units	% of Total in Type[a]	Total Slaves	Number of Units	Mean Size of Units	% of Total in Type[a]	"Sugartown": % of Total Population in Type[b]	"Mocca": % of Total Population in Type[b]
29	308	5.3	54.1	425	76	5.6	67.7	[46	41
78	89	2.0	5.9	28	14	2.0	4.5		
58	46	7.8	11.9	90	18	5.0	14.3	18	30
65	443	4.9	71.9	543	108	5.0	86.3	65	71
77	95	4.0	12.5	50	12	4.2	8.0	16	17
46	3	5.3	0.5	6	1	6.0	0.7	3	3
93	98	4.0	13.0	56	13	4.3	8.6	19	20
54	—	—	8.8	7	7	1.0	1.1	[17	9
73	—	—	5.8	10	10	1.0	1.6		
6	—	—	0.5	13	6	2.2	2.1		
53	—	—	15.1	30	23	1.3	3.1	17	9
1	—	—	100.0	629	—	—	100.0	100	100

unded to nearest tenth of a percent.

unded to nearest whole percent.

ludes children living with adults other than parents.

Table 19
Child Spacing and Ages of Mothers at
Births: Averages for 26 Holdings, 1822

Birth Order of Child	Number of Mothers	% of Total Mothers in Group	Average Age at Births	Average Spacing (years)
1st	479	100.0	22.37	
2d	356	74.3	26.53	3.36
3d	244	50.9	30.00	2.93
4th	170	35.5	32.60	2.93
5th	105	21.9	33.38	2.42
6th	59	12.3	35.22	2.81
7th	31	6.5	40.10	2.95
8th	8	1.7	43.46	2.67
9th	2	0.4	38.75	1.87
10th	1	0.2	38.00	1.00
Average			34.84	3.02

Sources: Register of Returns of Slaves, 1822, Bahamas Archives;
Craton, "Changing Patterns," 10.

families, with an average of 3.29 children in each family. This compared with the average of 2.97 children living with each of the 95 mothers listed as living without a partner.[35]

Though the average indicated age of slave mothers at the birth of their first surviving child was just over twenty-two years, the true average age when the first child was born was probably well under twenty.[36] The peak of fertility was between the ages of eighteen and twenty-seven, and a considerable number of slave women continued to have children until after they were forty. The spacing between surviving children averaged exactly three years, which was remarkably short given the high incidence of neonatal tetanus and the survival of the African custom of prolonged lactation.

The census of a single year (1822) gives a merely static view of the pattern of Bahamian slave families; much more detailed information over a long period would be needed to provide a dynamic life-cycle view. It is clear, however, that once they were established, Bahamian nuclear slave families were remarkably stable and long-lived. In the Wylly, Burton Williams, and Rolle slave holdings over the entire registration period, for example, there are very few examples of slave nuclear families breaking up for any reason save parental death or the departure of children to form a family of their own.

From the presence of teenaged mothers with one child in their parents' household, but the almost complete absence of young mothers with more than one child in the parental home, there is a strong hint that premarital intercourse was common and that girls married and left to form their own households only after the birth of the first child. This would have been entirely consonant with a society in which personal and inheritable property was too scarce for the development or retention of systems of dowry or bride price.

On an average, husbands in nuclear slave families were almost four years older than their wives.[37] This suggests the custom prevalent in many poor peasant societies of marriage occurring only once the male has "made his way in the world," that is, after he has cleared a ground of his own, acquired stock, and built a family house.

Very few of the ninety-five mothers listed as living with their children alone were necessarily women who had failed to find a husband or had been deserted. A fair number were widows. Others had permanent liaisons with partners from another slave holding (a situation extremely common, of course, in Nassau or wherever else slave holdings were small). A very few apparently single mothers were the extra wives of slave males practicing polygyny—an African custom which, though rare in the Bahamas, was seemingly, and strangely, more common among Creole than among African-born males.

In general, the pattern of slave family in the Bahamas seems closely akin to that promoted by certain masters, such as Burton Williams or William Wylly, upon grounds of efficiency, "civilization," or "Christian principles." Yet the evidence is that it was the slaves' own choice and the special circumstances of the Bahamas which actually determined this pattern, rather than the will of the masters—many of whom were ignorant of, or indifferent to, precisely what was going on.

Burton Williams and William Wylly may have believed in the socioeconomic value of encouraging slave family formation, but the incidence of stable nuclear families was equally high on such estates as Lord Rolle's, which had negative economic value to the master and were very loosely supervised by the 1820s. Lord Rolle's voluminous correspondence about his slave holdings in Exuma was greatly concerned with socioeconomic tinkering but said nothing about attempting to regulate the slaves' family organization. On the contrary, Rolle often complained that his slaves ordered their own affairs without any reference to the will of their nominal owner.[38]

Such powerlessness on the part of the masters is congruent with what is known of the sugar colonies of the British West Indies. However hard the masters there tried to impose "pronatalist" practices upon their slaves, including formal marriage and stable monogamy, they were frustrated both by the prevailing conditions and the will of the slaves, who, as John Quier testified as early as 1788, were "universally known to claim a Right of Disposing themselves in this Respect, according to their own Will and Pleasure without any Controul from their Masters."[39]

A final argument against the shaping of Bahamian slave family by the master class is the curious fact that "European-type" nuclear families were proportionately more common among African than among Creole slaves. Although by 1822 only 21 percent of Bahamian slaves were African-born, on the twenty-six slave holdings studied, 1,198 of the 3,011 slaves were in families headed by at least one African parent, compared with 1,360 in Creole-headed families. Among the African-headed component, simple nuclear families included 61.0 percent of the slaves, compared with 48.4 percent for the purely Creole component (and the overall average of 54.1 percent). It is true that Bahamian slaveowners favored elderly Africans as drivers and other "confidential" slaves, but in so doing they were merely capitalizing on the fund of "reputation" (that is, authenticity and authority) which such persons retained. The masters were thus almost bound to adopt the Africans' preferred forms of family organization, whether or not these coincided with what they themselves willed.

Prevailing nonhuman conditions were also critical and at least as important as the slaves' and masters' choices. Such conditions were rarely as favorable to family formation anywhere in the slave colonies as they were in the Bahamas Out Islands during the last decades of slavery. In the sugar plantations the high mortality rates, the gang system (which normally separated husbands from wives and parents from children), and the liability to shifting and sale militated against the formation of stable nuclear families. In Nassau too, the comparatively high mortality rates and the predominantly small slave units meant that the incidence of nuclear families was lower, and that of female-headed families higher, than in the Out Islands—though the way that each owner had to send in a separate return may have somewhat disguised the true picture.

In contrast, the situation in the Out Islands, particularly in the larger

TABLE 20

Comparison Between African-Headed and Creole Families, 26 Slave Holdings, 1822

Family Type	African-headed Families[a]				Creole Families			
	Total Slaves	Number of Units	Mean Size of Units	% of Total in Type[b]	Total Slaves	Number of Units	Mean Size of Units	% of Total in Type[b]
Nuclear family								
Man, woman, children	830	154	5.39	61.0	799	154	5.19	48.4
Man, woman	138	69	2.00	10.2	40	20	2.00	2.4
Three-generation groups	128	19	6.73	9.4	238	29	8.21	14.4
Total	1,096	242	4.53	80.6	1,077	203	5.31	65.2
Denuded family								
Woman, children	91	21	4.33	6.7	278	72	3.86	16.8
Man, children	11	2	5.50	0.8	5	1	5.00	0.3
Total	102	23	4.43	7.5	283	73	3.88	17.1
No family								
Men alone or together	114	—	—	8.4	150	—	—	9.1
Women alone or together	48	—	—	3.5	125	—	—	7.6
Children separately	—	—	—	—	16	2	8.00	1.0
Total	162	—	—	11.9	291	—	—	17.7
Total for all types	1,360	—	—	100.0	1,651	—	—	100.0

Sources: Register of Returns of Slaves, 1822, Bahamas Archives; Craton, "Changing Patterns," 18.
[a] African-headed families were taken to be those in which both parents, either parent, or the single parent was of African birth. Thus mixed couples are included in the African-headed nuclear family categories.
[b] Rounded to nearest decimal point.

slave holdings, was almost ideal for the development not only of small nuclear families, but also extended family "yards" and "villages" along protopeasant lines. Moreover, contrary to the usual interpretation, which sees slave family as being essentially a development of the mature slave system, it is probably more accurate to see it as a carryover from African practice, merely reshaped by conditions in the New World.

Slaves certainly carried from Africa very strong traditions of family organization and kinship affiliations, if not also of an easily transferable peasant lifestyle. Although existing families and kinship networks were broken up by the Middle Passage, and tribal identities mixed almost beyond recovery, family and kinship were reconstituted as soon and as well as possible in the new environment. The initial stages were those of the "fictive kin" of the "shipmate bond" (that is, the identity forged among those arriving on the same ship), which in the sugar colonies at least was soon reinforced by the sense of kinship engendered within the cohesive plantation units. At the same time, actual families were engendered by the Africans' predilection for the simple pairing and nuclear family as the essential building blocks of a more extended system. As generations passed, actual kinship networks replaced the more fictive kind, though still largely constrained by the enforced endogamy of the self-contained plantation units.

In the Bahamas case, the preference for the simple nuclear family was reinforced by the standard type of accommodation provided and by the availability of provision grounds that were most efficiently worked, like peasant holdings, in small family units. As elsewhere, each group of families within a single holding developed a sense of identity, often recognized by the adoption of the owner's surname by the people (or, after slavery ended, retaining it for the settlement too). At the same time, the healthy growth of the population, the loosing of the master's bonds, and the insufficiency of the nearby soils led to expansion and other forms of nucleation: the extended-family yard, the village-type group of related families, and satellite villages. Thus, for example, Lord Rolle's slaves multiplied and spread, in their families, to five small village settlements in Exuma, including Rolleville and Rolle Town. Whether strictly related or not, all of them, and their descendants, proudly took the surname Rolle. This was not out of gratitude to their master, or, of course, in remembrance of slavery as such. Rather, it was a recognition of that bond that gave them a new kinship identity, and a peasant lifestyle, based on a Bahamian "family island."

Masters who did not positively encourage stable slave families did not often discourage them, and the formation of families was also facilitated by the amelioration legislation emanating from London between 1824 and 1830. Bahamian slaves gladly adopted such trends, just as they had taken advantage of the masters' increased willingness to allow them provision grounds and the keeping of stock for their own subsistence. Similarly, the more frequent identification of formal marriages and stable families with "civilized Christian values" was also to the slaves' advantage—endowing their preferred lifestyle with a useful mantle of respectability.

Nothing, indeed, so encapsulates the slaves' adaptation of institutions to their own purposes and ways of thought as their enthusiastic ascription to Christianity in the half century after 1783. In the process, they benefited from the filtering down from England of the principles of Christian humanitarianism and took advantage of those growing numbers of the ruling class (such as William Wylly or Governors Grant and Carmichael Smyth) who believed that promoting Christianity among the slaves would not only dignify and justify the institution of slavery by making the slaves "respectable" but actually "reinforce the status quo, rather than disrupt it."[40]

Joseph Paul, the first black preacher in the Bahamas of whom details are known, was a follower of John Wesley. But the most numerous black evangelists, preaching a much more popular faith, were Baptists. Wesleyan Methodism was essentially a nonestablishment variation of Anglicanism, dispensing with bishops and stressing a more personal and direct approach to the deity, and a less structured—though still highly respectable—form of service. Baptists, on the other hand, adopted a far more charismatic style of worship, centered on the preacher but with fervent participation by the congregation and great stress on the ceremony of baptism by total immersion. Such forms of worship and faith were far more congenial to Afro-American slaves than the staid formulae and precepts of the Church of England, since they harkened back to African forms of religious belief and practice, and offered cathartic relief from the irksome bonds of servitude. In these respects the ceremony of baptism in the open sea—which strangers like Dr. Townsend or Miss Hart saw merely as a picturesque and somewhat outlandish spectacle—was crucial. Attuned to the common African belief in the sacredness of the natural elements and the deeply cleansing effects of living waters, and establishing a symbolic link with the distant African heartland across the ocean (as well as with the Christian Holy Land), it thus provided a sacrament of escape and regeneration.

Undoubtedly, Baptist preachers came in numbers with the Loyalist slaves and continued their informal ministry from the time of arrival. As early as August 1785, a Loyalist owner placed the following advertisement in the *Bahama Gazette:*

FOUR DOLLARS REWARD

Run away about nine months ago in St. Augustine, a Negro Man named SAMBO; he is an old fellow about 55 years of age, has a remarkably long under lip and chin, is knock-kneed, and has a large flat foot, is well known by the Negroes as a Baptist Preacher, calls himself a freeman, and is often seen in Nassau. Also a Negro Man called PRINCE; he is a little bow legged and turns on his great toes, has his Country marks down his face; went away about four days ago. Whoever takes up the Said Negroes or either of them and delivers them to Mr. Peter Dean, merchant of Nassau, or at the Blue Hills, shall receive Two Dollars reward for each.

Isaac Baillou

Refugee Hill, August 6, 1785.[41]

These two runaways were almost certainly the two chief founders of the black Baptist congregation in the Bahamas, later known as Samuel Scriven (c. 1730–1822) and Prince Williams (c. 1760–1840). Both had achieved their freedom by 1790 and after many years of preaching in the open air or private houses Over-the-Hill, were prominent members of the Anabaptist Society, which in 1801 purchased lots 20 and 21 in the township formed out of the 150 acres "behind the hospital" acquired by Chief Justice Stephen Delancey in 1789.[42] Here was constructed the first Baptist chapel, called Bethel (built of wood until 1847), of which Samuel Scriven was pastor till his death. Prince Williams was Scriven's successor, but after three years there was a schism in the Bethel congregation (seemingly occasioned by the separation of Prince Williams from his wife and the question of whether the pastor ought to be allowed to maintain a "housekeeper" in her place) which led to the secession of Williams and his supporters and the foundation of St. John's Baptist Chapel, just three hundred yards down Meeting Street, on Delancey Town's lot 76.[43]

Already by this time, the Baptist faith was widely disseminated. A more shadowy evangelist called Frank Spence had established a "New Chapel" among the blacks living behind Fort Fincastle,[44] and other preachers had so effectively planted the word in the Out Islands that the ministers of the established church were concerned to condemn and ridicule their efforts. As early as 1799, for example, the Reverend D. W. Rose reported to the SPG that the slaves on Long Island "had been misled by strange doctrines. They called themselves Baptists, the followers

of St. John. . . . Their preachers, black men, were artful and designing, making a merchandize of Religion. One of them was so impious as
to proclaim that he had had a familiar conversation with the Almighty,
and to point out the place where he had seen Him. At certain times
of the year the black preachers used to drive numbers of negroes into
the sea and dip them by way of baptism, for which they extorted a dollar, or stolen goods." According to Rose, some of these Baptist sectaries
were so attached to their practices that when their masters attempted to
"check their proceedings," they "absconded and concealed themselves
in the woods." [45]

Official Methodist missionaries were at work in the Bahamas from the
1790s but took a decade to establish themselves. The first who were sent
were not worthy of the call, and the first to persevere, William Turton,
sent by the Manchester Methodist Conference in 1800 in answer to a
plea from Dr. Thomas Coke, was a Barbadian colored man who had the
temerity to convert and marry a local white woman. However, John Rut-
ledge and William Dowson, Turton's white missionary reinforcements,
were a great success among the poor whites of Harbour Island and Abaco
as well as among the blacks, and the Methodist missionaries began to be
encouraged by some of the slaveowners (such as William Wylly), who
considered that despite the dangers inherent in preaching to the slaves,
the white ministers could be fairly easily controlled and might well drive
the black preachers out of business. [46]

Indeed, one such victim was Joseph Paul, though not in the expected
way, since he was apparently persuaded to defect to the Anglican church.
From the time of his arrival in Nassau, Paul had held services in the
poor sections of the western district, though on the more respectable
northern side of the ridge. There he and his congregation had erected
the first Methodist church in the Bahamas around 1793, at the junction
of Augusta and Heathfield streets, and Paul had established the Associates School, the first Bahamian day school for blacks. By the time of
his death in 1802 (when he was succeeded, in order, by his sons Joseph
and William), Joseph Paul had fallen out with the other Wesleyans, and
the Pauls' chapel, fittingly called St. Paul's, had become an unofficial
black annex to Anglican Christchurch—attracting those blacks and free
coloreds who wanted the respectability of belonging to the established
church without the dishonor of having to worship on the fringes of a
white congregation. [47]

Though Wesleyan missionaries were regarded as preferable to black
Baptist preachers, a majority of Bahamian whites were in favor of rig-

orous controls for all forms of nonconformist activity among Bahamian blacks. In 1816 the assembly passed the self-explaining "Act for the preventing the profanation of Religious Rites and false worshipping of God, under the pretence of preaching and teaching, by illiterate, ignorant, and ill disposed persons; and also for the better regulation of Methodist missionaries and other dissenting preachers, within these islands." [48] Henceforward, no person would be allowed "to preach or teach or offer up public prayers, or sing psalms in any meeting or assembly of negroes or persons of colour" without an annual license from the governor, "specifying the particular district and place, chapel or chapels, meeting house or meeting houses expressly appropriated for divine worship." Such preachers, moreover, were required to make an oath and enter into a bond of four hundred pounds with two other freeholders that "no doctrine or opinion shall be inculcated, preached or circulated by him unfriendly to the system of government established in this Colony, or inconsistent with the duty which slaves owe their masters." At the same time, a clause in the Police Act made it illegal for any church service to be held between the hours of 6 P.M. and 6 A.M., which in effect denied any form of organized worship to the slaves, save during the hours of daylight on Sundays.

The following few years were critical for the independent black Christians. Only the crudest members of the ruling class continued to practice overt oppression. Mary Prince, for example, testified how in the Turks Islands during the 1820s, "the poor slaves had built up a place with boughs and leaves, where they might meet for prayers, but the white people pulled it down twice, and would not even allow them even a shed for prayers." Yet by 1830 black Baptist missionaries from Nassau had built a permanent wooden chapel there, which attracted large numbers of slaves. [49] The more subtle members of the ruling class, following the lead of the governors, sailed a far trickier course, persuading the Anglican church to drive home its advantage by actively proselytizing the slaves, while doing what they could to reshape the nonconformist churches by the skillful exercise of the licensing process and the selective encouragement of the missionary societies. In 1824, for instance, Governor Lewis Grant reported to Lord Goderich that besides the white Methodist missionaries, there were three licensed "Anabaptist and Baptist" preachers in New Providence. "They are Black Men," he added, "and their Hearers comport themselves in a very creditable manner when attending worship. It nevertheless, if it can be temperately effected, would be desirable that the last description of persons were brought on a different footing and embodied into either the Established Church or the Wesleyan Mission. But though this may be kept in view, it is too soon, perhaps, at present to take any immediate steps regarding it. I mean any steps savouring of compulsion because I think it possible to bring it about otherwise by degrees."[50]

In 1827 the rector of Christchurch, William Strachan, was appointed to the executive council, with the express purpose of extending the influence of the established church. In the same year St. Paul's was made an official chapel of ease of the Church of England, and its black preacher was granted an annual allowance. By 1829 it was reported that since the expiration of the 1816 act against evening services, the 6:30 P.M. Sunday service was attracting so many black and colored persons that an extension to the building was planned. A few years later, in response to an accusation that the Church of England was indifferent to the conversion and moral condition of Bahamian blacks, Strachan reported that since his incumbency began, there had been 3,895 blacks and coloreds baptized and 600 black and colored couples married in the two Nassau parish churches, compared with 1,221 white baptisms and the marriage of 320 white couples.[51]

With the urging of the Colonial Office, the monopoly of the Anglican church was eroded when in 1826 dissenting ministers were for the first time allowed to perform and record marriages, as well as baptisms and burials. These privileges, however, were specifically limited to white ministers of the Presbyterian kirk and the official missionary societies. This militated severely against the black Baptists, who had their own baptism and burial rites, many of whose adherents were living in consensual rather than formal marital unions, and who had no white ministers before 1833.

The judicious behavior of the Methodist missionaries steadily increased their favor among the white community, but any proposals to extend the number of licenses for black Baptist preachers was met with resistance and ridicule. In 1830, for example, a circular from Secretary of State Lord Goderich told the governor· "Your duty will be, to encourage, as much as possible, those religious teachers, in whose good sense and sobriety of mind, you can place the greatest confidence; and not to refuse your license to any man of honest intentions and decorous conduct, whom the Slaves themselves may be disposed to receive as a Teacher."[52]

However, Governor Carmichael Smyth's subsequent proposal to use "his special license to introduce a few Baptists, or any other species of

Sectarian preachers, among the Out Island negroes," was turned down flat by the assembly. This was reinforced by an editorial in the *Bahama Argus* which poured scorn on what would happen if more black Baptist preachers were given official sanction and showed a predictable lack of sensitivity for the nature of black worship and ritual. "A quick and apt sense of the ludicrous, and of its concomitant combinations, are the leading features of the mind in a state of ignorance," it pontificated, "more particularly so of that of the Bahamas negro; and although temporary fear of censure may induce a degree of demure decorum among them, yet there would be a proportionate want of real reverence for what they will deem a 'John Canoe' exhibition. That there will be an abundance of followers we admit; but their worshipping would be more in conformity with the noisy rites of Bacchus, than with the sober doctrines of the Christian faith." [53]

The chief threat to the independence of the black Baptists in the last years of slavery, indeed, came not directly from the regime but from their need to have white missionary supervisors in order to gain official sanction and respectability. The first official white Baptist missionaries, Joseph Burton and Kilner Pearson, did not arrive in the Bahamas until 1833, having found conditions in Jamaica "too warm" (that is too intolerant) for their liking. Within a few months they had demanded a reformation in the management and practice of the Baptist churches, including the regulation that only those who were properly married could be full members. [54]

Less than a month before the ending of formal slavery, Sharper Morris, the black pastor of Bethel Chapel, moved a resolution that henceforward a white missionary would take his place. This surrender was accomplished with the agreement of a majority of the congregation, the committee of the Baptist Missionary Society were appointed trustees of the Anabaptist Society of New Providence, and the foundations of an imposing new chapel, Zion, were built on the northern slopes of the ridge. The aged Prince Williams and his congregation, however, would have nothing to do with this shift and went into the era of formal freedom from slavery free also from white supervision, their church in due course being proudly rechristened St. John's Particular Church of Native Baptists. [55]

~ 18 ~

Socioeconomic Symbiosis:
Charles Farquharson and His Slaves,
San Salvador, 1831–1832

IN THE STRAGGLY BUSH on the eastern side of San Salvador (alias
Watling's Island), four miles from the beach where Columbus landed
and a mile from the Lucayan village site on Pigeon Creek, are the scanty
remains of the only Bahamian slave plantation for which a day-to-day
record survives. This was the estate of Charles Farquharson, a resident
owner whose journal for 1831 and 1832 was rescued from oblivion in
1903 and locally published in 1957.[1] Though fairly unusual for the period
in still being directly managed by its owner, Farquharson's plantation
was otherwise typical. Despite some tantalizing omissions, Charles Farquharson's unique manuscript, in conjunction with archeology and the
public records, thus provides an invaluable insight into the daily life of
Bahamian Out Island slave society on the eve of emancipation.[2]

Charles Farquharson (1760–1835) was a Loyalist of Scots extraction
and limited formal education who obtained one of the original grants of
land on San Salvador, two hundred acres between the Great Lake and
Pigeon Creek, in 1803. Making the island his home for more than thirty
years, Farquharson extended his estate to some fifteen hundred acres
as almost all of his white neighbors gave up the struggle to wrest a fortune from the meager soil. Poverty, lack of attractive alternatives, and
sheer Scots determination may have contributed to Farquharson's perseverence. Another likely factor, though, was his unconventional domestic
situation. Either deserted by his wife or left a widower, Charles Farquharson had spent most of his years on San Salvador in common-law union
with a colored woman, Kitty Davies or Dixon. Politely referred to on the
island as Mrs. Farquharson, but by Farquharson himself (in his will) as
his "faithful companion," Kitty was the mother of John Dixon, a planter

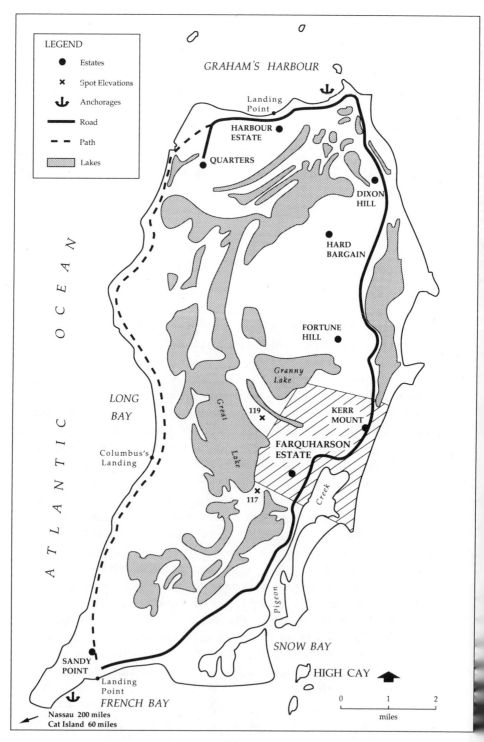

LEGEND

● Estates
✕ Spot Elevations
⚓ Anchorages
── Road
--- Path
▒ Lakes

GRAHAM'S HARBOUR

Landing
Point

HARBOUR
ESTATE

QUARTERS

DIXON
HILL

HARD
BARGAIN

A T L A N T I C   O C E A N

FORTUNE
HILL

Granny
Lake

LONG
BAY

119
✕

KERR
MOUNT

FARQUHARSON
ESTATE

Great
Lake

Columbus's
Landing

117
✕

Creek

Pigeon

SNOW BAY

HIGH CAY

SANDY
POINT

Landing
Point

FRENCH BAY

0   1   2

miles

Nassau 200 miles
Cat Island 60 miles

Map 9. Farquharson estate, San Salvador, 1831–32

neighbor, as well as of James Farquharson, Charles's chief assistant, and perhaps four other Farquharson children, including William Farquharson, drowned in the wreck of the schooner *Eleanor* on the Ragged Islands in 1824.[3]

For years San Salvador's senior justice of the peace, Charles Farquharson was probably the last permanently resident white slaveowner on the island. Two of Burton Williams's sons still owned land and slaves on San Salvador but spent most of their time in Nassau and on Cat Island. After the owner of Fortune Hill, the widow Sarah Lowther, alias Lauder, left with her slaves in March 1831, Charles Farquharson's only planter neighbors were the colored Dixons of Dixon Hill and the black owner (perhaps overseer) of Sandy Point, Prince Storr. Except for his twice-yearly visits to Nassau, the aging Farquharson was thus almost completely isolated from "polite society," driven by tightening economic circumstances, shared experiences, and sheer propinquity ever closer to his slaves. Charles Farquharson gained the reputation of being a stern but just, even generous, owner.[4] But, especially as the racial lines blurred, the necessary minimum distance between master and slave was maintained only at the cost of increasing tension and occasional conflict.

The Farquharson slaves were almost a microcosm of the Bahamian population at large during formal slavery's last decades. In 1822 Charles Farquharson owned thirty-five slaves, of whom thirteen were Africans and twenty-two Creoles. Eight of the Africans were males and only five females, whereas among the Creoles females outnumbered males by fourteen to eight. The average age of all the slaves was 21.1 years, but the Africans averaged 38.3 years against the Creoles' 10.9 years—seventeen being under 20 years of age, and twelve under 10. The dominance of the Africans up to that time was very apparent in the formation of families and households. Only four of the Africans, three males and a female, lived without spouses. The remaining nine made up five couples (one African male having a Creole wife), two without children and the remainder heading three of the five nuclear families on the plantation. In all, nuclear families accounted for twenty-seven of the thirty-five slaves, and all of the children (unusually, there were no women listed alone with their children). The exceptionally tight-knit nature of the Farquharson slave population in 1822 is evident from the fact that certainly one and possibly both of the two Creole nuclear families were headed by slaves who were both the offspring of African couples on the same estate.[5]

Over the period between 1822 and 1834, the Farquharson slave population increased at the general Bahamian rate, with predictable results in

Table 21

Charles Farquharson's Slaves, San Salvador,
with Ages As Listed in the Slave Returns, 1822–34

Name of Slave	Year of Return				Comments, Including Employment (1834)
	1825	1828	1831	1834	
Dennis*	38	41	44	47	
Cloa*	39	42	45	48	
Charles*	53	56	59	62	
Rachel*	39	42	45	48	
March	19	22	25	28	Herd Man
Sally	18	21	24	27	
John	1	4	7	10	Stock Boy
Isaac	9	12	15	18	
Jacob	3	6	—	12	Stock Boy
George*					Died 1822
Maria*	—	52	55	58	
Harry*	38	41	44	47	
Mary	40	43	46	49	
William	21	24	27	30	Herd Man
Catherinell	14	17	20	30 (?)	
Mary Ann	12	15	18		Sold to Vass 1832
Liddy	10	13	16	19	Domestic
Soffey	8	11	14	17	
Betty	5				
Cloa	1	4	7	10	Nursing
Charlotte†					Manumitted 1824
Patty		8	11	14	
Suky					Died 1823
Bacchus	27	30	33	36	
Flora	27	30	33	36	
Diana	10	13	16	19	
Nanny	7	10	13	16	
James	3	6	9	12	
Margaret	9 mo.	4	7	10	Domestic
Alexander	25	28	31		Sold to Vass 1832
Eliza	24	27	30	33	
Lucy	6	9	12	15	About Yard
Alexander	4	7	10	13	Herd Boy
Samuel	2	5	8	11	Stock Boy
Cato*	33	36	39	42	
Cumba*	32				Died 1825
Betsy	6	9	10 (?)	15	Hired Out

Table 21—Continued
Charles Farquharson's Slaves, San Salvador,
with Ages As Listed in the Slave Returns, 1822–34

| | Year of Return | | | | Comments, Including |
Name of Slave	1825	1828	1831	1834	Employment (1834)
Jack*	33	36	39	42	
Peter*	31	34	37	40	
Charles*	38	41	44		Died 1832
Tina*	51	54	57	60	
Juliann			5	8	b. 1825 Nursing
Sue			5	8	b. 1825 Nil
Agnes			4	7	b. 1826 Nursing
Cicely			4	7	b. 1826 Domestic
Charles					b. 1827 died 1830
Harry			3	6	b. 1827 Nil
Richard			3	6	b. 1827 Nil
Matilda			33	36	Bought 1825 House Cook
Terace			15	18	Bought 1825
George			7	10	Bought 1825 House Servant
Rachel					Bought 1825 died 1826
Amelia				6	b. 1828 Nursing
Silvester					b. 1829 died 1832
Johnston				4	b. 1829 Nil
Rose				4	b. 1829 Nil
Louisa					b. 1830 died 1833
Douglas					b. 1830 died 1832
Ritty					b. 1831 Nil
Philip					b. 1831 Nil
Janey					b. 1832 Nil
Beck					b. 1833 Nil
William					b. 1833 Nil
Phoebe					b. 1833 Nil
Edmond					b. 1833 Nil

Note: Brackets indicate family; asterisks, African; dagger, mulatto. Parents of those born after 1825 (beginning with Juliann in list) were not indicated in records.

Table 22
Summary of Farquharson Slaves
for Compensation, 1834

Employment Classification	Males	Females	Total	Valuation (£)
Effective field	9	12	21	735
Inferior field	6	4	10	199
Head domestic	—	4	4	180
Inferior domestic	3	4	7	175
Under six years	4	5	9	90
Aged, etc.	—	1	1	5
Total	22	30	52	1,384

Sources: Register of Returns of Slaves, 1822–34; Slave Compensation Returns, 1834, Bahamas Archives.

creolization and increased endogamy. One slave, an infant mulatto girl, was manumitted in 1824, four were purchased in 1825, and two sold in 1832, for a net gain of one. Only nine slaves died over the twelve-year period (four of them infants under three years old), and no less than twenty-five were born and survived, so that the population had risen from thirty-five to fifty-two almost entirely by natural increase.[6] This was more than a seventh of the total slave population of San Salvador, which, despite such depredations as the removal of the Burton Williams slaves, had remained fairly steady through natural increase. Only three of Farquharson's Africans died between 1822 and 1834, but their proportion in the group fell from a third to a fifth, as their average age rose to 50.1 years—compared with 14.4 years for the Creole slaves.

The Farquharson population remained a close-knit group—almost a single extended family—though household groupings showed an apparent decline in the predominance of the simple nuclear family, and some diffusion. According to the slave-registration returns, by 1834 there seem to have been only four nuclear family households instead of five (accounting for nineteen slaves instead of twenty-seven), with four households headed by a single parent (in one case, grandparent). In the 1834 return no less than sixteen children were listed apart from their immediate families—seemingly living in single-sex groups. One single-parent household was the result of the purchase of a mother and her three children in 1825. Another resulted from an unusual instance of polygyny: the sale of the chief driver, Alick, with a second young wife and infant child in 1832, leaving his long-standing wife Eliza and their three children behind.[7] The other cases may be an indication of the increasing shortage of acceptable (that is, nonincestuous) mates on the Farquharson plantation. The journal itself records one instance of marriage outside the original group, when on September 17, 1832, Farquharson "sent out Diana to John Dickson to work and be the wife for his Cuffey as it appears that she is already with child for Cuffey."[8] The apparent separation of children from their parents, on the other hand, may reflect no more than space constraints—the existing slave houses being too solidly and closely built to be expanded to contain the greatly enlarged Farquharson families.

The latter conclusion, and the general pattern of slave families suggested by the register of slave returns, neatly fit the archeological evidence. The slave quarters at the Farquharson estate were located some 300 yards behind the ridge on which the main buildings stood—close enough to be supervised when necessary but sufficiently far to be out of normal earshot, and close together. Today there remain the ruins of fifteen stone-built dwellings, spaced out in a 130-yard row, with walls suggesting a half-dozen "yard"-type subdivisions. Eight of the houses were small-family-sized homes, some twenty-two feet by fourteen feet square, gable-ended but single-storied, with two or four windows and two doors each—three with a single large room, four with two rooms, and one with three. The other seven buildings were single-room dwellings some eighteen feet by twelve feet square, with two windows and a single door. All houses were constructed of uncut stone roughly mortared together and plastered inside. Unusually, most homes had a chimney and fireplace, though this was probably for heat in the winter and greenleaf fires against mosquitoes, rather than for day-to-day cooking. Roof and chimney beams, window and door frames were of local hardwood logs and planks, and the roofs were palmetto-thatched, probably on a frame of mangrove stakes.

The slave houses faced eastward, toward the master's house and the prevailing breeze, with the walled yards behind. A few smaller structures in the yards suggest animal pens, and the quarters were backed by the slaves' own gardens and rough pasture for their hogs and goats. The slaves' latrines were probably in this area. Fresh water was taken from a nearby well in a natural sinkhole (located by John Winter in 1981), and rainwater collected in tanks cut in the rock.

The main buildings on the Farquharson estate, forming a compact group around the modest "great house" of the owner, looked out over the most fertile fields toward the glittering expanse of Pigeon Creek and the sea beyond. Today, the rectangular two-story shell of the great house is just thirty feet by fifteen feet in area, and twenty feet high, but it would have been rather more impressive with its long-vanished wooden carapace of piazza, gallery, and shingled roof. From the evidence of Charles Farquharson's will, though, its furnishings were far from luxurious. All that was thought worth valuing in 1835 were a mahogany table, sofa and sideboard, a dozen chairs, some silverware, glass and books, together assessed at thirty-nine pounds.[9] Behind the great house was a solidly built two-room kitchen building, with a large open hearth and adjacent oven, lined with imported bricks. The master's stone-built latrine, placed over a deep sinkhole, was located a discreet seventy yards to the south of the great house.

On the other side of the great house, but much closer, was a large two-story barn, probably what Farquharson called the corn house; cemented flat barbecues for drying corn and peas; and a stable with three stalls for the master's horses. Nearby were sited the barn called the pigeon pea house and cowsheds, probably made of wood, now disappeared without trace. Balancing the corn house to the south of the great house was the stone building sometimes called the bakery (because it contained a fireplace and chimney) which more likely was the so-called cotton house. This was fronted by the cemented ginning circle, once covered by a thatched roof raised on poles. On the lower slopes of the ridge were another barn and a cartshed, from which a farm road descended the short distance to the island-encircling public road. Here this ran alongside Pigeon Creek, where Farquharson kept canoes and a shallow-draught coasting vessel.

The Farquharson family thus lived at the working hub of their estate, in daily, day-long contact with their slaves but painfully isolated from their fellows. Fortune Hill, a grander estate but empty after March 1832, was three miles to the north, and Dixon Hill and Sandy Point were six miles in a straight line to north and south. Visitors came rarely. Except for Christmas Day 1832, when ten sat down to dinner, the only guests recorded in two years were Captain Richard Owen of the survey ship HMS *Blossom* and three of his officers, who were invited to dine on May 29 and 30, 1832, after the captain had sent boats into Pigeon Creek to cut firewood and the purser had come to Farquharson's to purchase some hogs.[10] Ships which came from Nassau to San Salvador about every second month but anchored no closer than French Bay or Graham's Harbour were eagerly awaited for the mail and newspapers they brought.

How often over the years Charles Farquharson and his family must have paced their hill or sat on their verandah, scanning the distant blue sea for some sign of contact with the outside world! This is conveyed by the most poignant of the relics preserved in the Farquharson estate ruins. As elsewhere in the Out Islands, graffiti of sailing ships are scratched in the plaster of the great house and nearby buildings. These realistic portrayals of sloops, schooners, barques, or warships are sketched as if from life but are more likely drawn from memory, symbols and signs of a desperate loneliness and of the tenuous links between such distant outposts and the larger world of European commerce, culture, and civilization. In this respect they were the correlatives of those fading survivals of African culture—the songs, stories, fragments of religion, and medicine—that continued to be heard and practiced in the slave quarters, literally behind the master's back.

Charles Farquharson clearly recognized that only by vigilance, hard work, and careful management of land and slaves could such a marginal estate as his be kept in being. More intuitively, he recognized the delicate balance between his own dependence on his slaves and their dependence upon him, above all, for food and clothing. This probably accounted for Farquharson's pragmatic unwillingness to drive his slaves through sickness and inclement weather, his reluctance to resort to corporal punishment on the estate, and, more privately, his invariable practice of referring to his workers not as slaves but—as on a ship or an English farm—as "the people," or "the hands."

Nonetheless, Farquharson's journal does reveal how important it was for the owner to keep his slaves continuously at work throughout the day, the week, the year, in a system as close to gang labor as the estate's conditions allowed. Unfortunately, the journal is vague about precise tasks or hours, but work was assigned every day of the week except Sunday, throughout the year, with exceptions only at Christmas, "cropover," and such special occasions as the funerals of prominent slaves—even if on distant estates.[11] Moreover, on a small estate where the only "specialists" were a handful of domestics and three or four stockmen, and the most skilled craftsman tasks were usually performed by Farquharson's son James, efforts were made to assign as many of the hands as possible to the same jobs in the same area, under the direct supervision of the drivers, Alick and Bacchus, if not of Charles or James Farquharson themselves.[12]

The Farquharson estate incorporated Kerr Mount, two miles to the north, and some of the back pastures and southern fields were even more distant. But most of the main fields were close enough for the slaves to return to their quarters for "breakfast" midway through their official working day. In all probability, the slaves worked for their owner from sunup until midafternoon, with a single break of an hour for food, leaving two or three hours to work their own provision grounds, tend their stock, or gather firewood before darkness fell. On rainy days— which rarely occurred more than once a month—slaves were excused labor in the open field but were given work under cover instead, such as ginning cotton or shucking corn. Slaves who declared themselves in- jured or sick—usually of fevers or colds—were not forced out to work, but their names were carefully noted and their progress checked, with a view to reducing malingering. Children worked in the fields from the age of six, and infants were normally carried out by their mothers. One preg- nant woman, Flora, the driver's wife, came in from the field only when she began labor, though she was then off work for almost a month.[13]

Farquharson estate was a typical diversified operation, and remarkably self-sufficient. It was well known for its stock but grew a large quantity of corn (mainly for subsistence) and as much cotton as it could. Peas, beans, ground provisions, and other vegetables were grown for food, and some castor oil processed for export. The estate produced its own lumber, thatch, rope, and salt, and seined fish from Pigeon Creek to augment the meat that could be spared for the slaves. As a careful hus- bandman, Farquharson had his slaves cut down what stands of lignum vitae they could find, though it waited two years till it could be shipped out for sale. Opportunistically, he also sent several of his men to scour the wreck of the brig *Enterprise*, driven ashore at Graham's Harbour in March 1832 on its way from Savannah to Jamaica, though all they recov- ered was some tackle and rope—the cargo having been stripped by the Williams slaves.[14]

The cattle, sheep, and pigs required year-round attention, with extra work during periods of drought. The cycles of planting, harvesting, and processing the main crops were also spaced out over much of the year. The interim periods, however, were always easily filled, by the perennial chores of weeding, "blanking" (planting between the rows of growing crops), and picking "volintere" crops (that is, the remnants growing out of season), or by such periodic tasks as clearing new fields, building walls, repairing buildings, or "cleaning" roads. Most of these activities could engage most of the slaves together; but from time to time a few slaves might be employed in cutting and carrying wood, gathering for- age, fishing, raking salt, or carrying produce and luggage to and from the dock.

With the decline of cotton, stock animals were the remaining hope for a regular, if small, economic return for the Farquharson estate. In the two years 1831–32, only 12 bales of cotton were shipped to Nassau (worth perhaps £200), but at least 24 cattle, 70 sheep, and considerable numbers of pigs and poultry, worth at least twice as much. When Charles Farquharson died he owned 45 head of horned cattle, 7 horses and 250 sheep, as well as a few goats and pigs, valued in all at £674 (compared with the less than £1,000 which Farquharson had received in compensation for his slaves).[15] Except for the horses and a couple of milk cows kept under cover, the stock were left to roam more or less freely over the estate's thousand acres of rough pasture and adjacent untenanted areas, foraging where they could and drinking from the few freshwater ponds and cisterns cut in the rock. It was poor sustenance at the best of times, and in summer, or when rains failed, even the hardy Caribbean sheep suffered severely.

Animals destined for market were brought into the small area of improved pasture called the guinea-grass patch for a month or so to fatten, and when the ponds dried out and the island turned brown, all the stock had to be watered, and fed from precious stocks of hay and corn. The Farquharson "cowboys" and shepherds, almost as free-roaming as their charges, spent much of their time in the bush, searching for or rescuing errant animals. Three times in two years, steers were so badly injured in falls or scrapes that they had to be slaughtered—such a bonus for the slaves in the way of extra meat that one is almost as suspicious of the circumstances as Farquharson was himself.[16]

Cotton would doubtless have declined in any case, but its virtual demise was assured by the insatiable demands of corn production. With an annual requirement of seven hundred bushels of corn (or its equivalent) for the slaves' official rations, and perhaps as much again for the stock, corn and its production cycles had come to dominate the agricultural resources of Farquharson's estate and the lives of its people. It was a domination, indeed, firmly established in most Out Islands by the 1830s, and destined long to survive slavery, lasting in many places till the present day.[17]

Of the two main types of corn, guinea corn, originally from Africa, was much the more important. Though rather less productive than Indian corn, less easily harvested (being taller), and less favored as food, it was preferred by planters because it was more drought resistant than the hardiest local varieties of native American corn. It also grew slightly more quickly and was less susceptible to attacks from weevils, rats, and other predators.

For both types of corn there were two planting and reaping seasons, with Indian corn following guinea corn in every phase. The main guinea-corn planting was between April and June, with a second planting in August or September. Nearly all Indian corn was planted between May and July, though a second crop might be added between September and December. The main guinea-corn crop was ready for harvest at the turn of the year, as early as mid-December (hence its somewhat confusing designation as "late" rather than "early" corn), but was most commonly cut in mid- or late January, being immediately followed by the first crop of Indian corn. The two harvests of so-called "early" corn followed each other between May and August.

On Farquharson's estate corn was planted in four or five large fields or "pieces." Since the soil was more or less worn out within five years, a new corn piece was prepared each year, and at least one left fallow or planted in guinea grass. In 1831 the creation of a new corn piece out of virgin bush took the labor of most of the slaves for several weeks in the lull after the main corn, cotton, and pea harvests. Between April 22 and May 13 the trees were felled, the stumps and bush being burned in mid-June. The piece was not planted until the following year, when the secondary bush and weeds called for another week of slash-and-burn.[18]

On the best "white soils" corn was planted at one-foot intervals in rows three feet apart, though in the poorer areas those planting took advantage of the crannies and pockets in the rocks. Holes were prepared with dung or bat earth, carried to the fields in carts and baskets. Two or three seeds were dropped into each well-watered hole to ensure germination. The transplanting of excess shoots, constant weeding, and watering and redunging when necessary ensured that the growing plants had ample space and nourishment. Once the corn shoots were well established, beans and peas were planted in the spaces between the rows (as well as in separate areas) the runners freely using the growing canestalks. This secondary crop, which used different nutrients from the soil, matured just after the corn, and its leaves and stalks provided a far better mulch or animal fodder than the dry corn trash.

Both types of corn were left to ripen and dry as much as possible on the stalk before harvesting, children and dogs being employed to keep rats and birds at bay. But the timing of the harvest was critical within a few days, depending on ideal weather, and the main corn harvest was the most intensive period of work in the year. First, the cobs were cut, "trashed" (that is, divested of leaves), and stacked in the fields to dry further for a week or so. Then they were humped back to the corn barns in sacks, carried on horseback or the heads of the slaves. There the corn was shucked as soon as possible by all the slaves not needed in the fields, either by beating the sacks with flat wooden paddles, or, more laboriously, rubbing the cobs together and picking out the stray kernels by hand. If properly dry, with all the weevil-infested kernels discarded, corn could then be stored up to three years in barrels or sacks, though it was normally needed long before then. The dry cobs were kept for fuel, and the chaff saved for the pigs and poultry.

The main guinea-corn harvest of 1831 was especially busy since there was hardly any early corn planted that year, and rain and cool weather delayed the start until Wednesday, January 19. Then in fine dry weather with the omens good, all hands were turned out, starting in the well or corn-house field. Two days later, Prince Storr of Sandy Point sent over eleven slaves to help, "to return the work for the time our people was there cuting Corn on the last days of the old year and the first days of the New year which was 8 working days of Eleven hands."[19] Working twelve hours a day, the slaves finished the well field on Saturday night and, after their usual rest day, began cutting the big field at daylight on Monday. This they completed late on Wednesday evening, despite losing the whole of Monday afternoon to rain, before making a final two-day assault on the sage field, the last of the guinea-corn pieces. On the evening of Friday, January 28, Charles Farquharson proudly recorded:

> Employed cuting Corn in the sage field and finished cuting it all to a few bags weather fine and dry wind easterly a Moderate breeze
>
> Got 273 Bags of Corn out of the Well field
>   "   210 Do "   "   "   "   " Big field
>   "   200 "   "   "   "   "   " Sage field
> which makes 683 Bags, which at half a Bushel each Bag makes 341½ of clean Corn.[20]

The following day, a Saturday, Farquharson gratefully "gave the people a half sheep and 2 flasks of rum to make them a super." One week later, he employed two men to clear the paths from the corn pieces, and on Monday, February 7, having borrowed horses from Sandy Point and Dixon Hill to augment the four of his own, set all the "able hands" to bring the corn to the lower barn. This mammoth task took four full days, after which the barn was filled to the rafters.[21] The estate was safe from hunger for half a year at least, though, as it transpired, it was the last time that Charles Farquharson was able to exact such a period of prolonged extra labor from his slaves without provoking resistance.

The production of cotton on Farquharson's estate was a far from intensive activity. Nearly all the cotton was on a single large piece, called
the Blanket Field by the slaves, though in July 1831 Charles Farquharson did begin the planting of a new cotton piece, prepared the previous
year, which had not come into production before the journal ended. In
1831 there were two short periods of concentrated picking by the entire
workforce, in the week in February between the cutting and carting of
the main guinea-corn crop and at the end of June, after the main harvest of peas and Indian corn. These two main cotton harvests, though,
were preceded and followed by many weeks of intermittent picking by
a few hands at a time, including the culling of what was called "one
one cotton" (that is, bushes located and bearing "one here, one there").
As they picked the last cotton wool, the hands would take out some of
the oldest bushes and plant fresh seeds, but after the picking was finished the only maintenance of the Blanket Field was some trimming and
occasional weeding.

Placed in sacks, the harvested cotton wool was carried to the cotton
house for ginning and baling. After the two small peaks of the crop, this
was a fairly leisurely process, employing only those hands not needed
elsewhere, and larger numbers only on rainy days. The first harvest
was processed between March and May, the second between July and
September, the finished bales being ready for the two main annual shipments to Nassau, in June and November, before and after the traditional
hurricane season.[22]

Three ships serviced San Salvador fairly regularly during 1831 and
1832, the sloops *Liberty* and *Shearwater* and the schooner *Traveller*. Passengers preferred the smaller and faster sloops, which could sail down
to Nassau in a couple of days and back in five. But the vessel used for
family moves and all four shipments of produce during the two years
was the larger and less mobile *Traveller*, of one hundred tons' displacement, owned by Burton Williams's son Henry and commanded by Captain Moxey. Primarily used as a link between Nassau and the Williams
estates on Cat Island and San Salvador, the *Traveller* was always ready to
take on extra cargo and could even be chartered outright for seventy-five
dollars the round trip.

The *Traveller*'s visits to San Salvador were an important punctuation
in the life of Farquharson's estate. The schooner would generally arrive
first at Graham's Harbour, and a Williams slave would ride the ten miles
south to Farquharson's estate with the news and whatever letters and
packages the captain had brought. If Charles Farquharson had freight

for Nassau, the *Traveller* would then sail to French Bay in the south of the island and send its boat up to Pigeon Creek to help Farquharson with his loading.

On Friday, May 20, 1831, for example, Charles Farquharson heard that the *Traveller* was at Graham's Harbour when the slave Toby Williams arrived with some letters and newspapers from Nassau. Having sent word back to Captain Moxey, Farquharson set his chief driver Alick to sewing up the last bale of cotton and sent the cowboys to round up the heifers most ready for sale. On the Monday, as the *Traveller* was seen passing Farquharson's estate toward French Bay on a northerly breeze, nearly all the men were employed in transporting the cotton, cattle, and other stock—first down to Pigeon Creek and from there to French Bay in Farquharson's shallow-draft boat. On Thursday, May 24, Farquharson was able to record: "Shiped on Board the Traveller 7 Bails Cotton 4 head of Cattle and 16 sheep for Market and a Cup [coop] with 5 Pigs in it as presents 2 for Mrs Dean 2 for Miss Sarah Lowther and one for Mr Vass. Wind Southerly."[23]

Because the wind from the south made the French Bay anchorage uncomfortable, Captain Moxey was eager for a quick turnaround. But the breeze shifted to the west before loading was finished, and the *Traveller* was detained a further thirty-six hours—setting sail for Cat Island and Nassau with some difficulty on the morning of Thursday, May 26.

Later in the year, after the *Traveller* had been laid up for the three months of the hurricane season in Hawk's Nest Creek, Cat Island, Charles Farquharson chartered the schooner for his exclusive use. This was because, besides his produce and some baggage left behind by Miss Lowther, he intended to send his family down to Nassau for the winter season. This time, Captain Moxey came straight to Snow Bay, near the mouth of Pigeon Creek, on Sunday, November 20. From here he sent word to Farquharson by boat and then careened the almost empty *Traveller* so that her bottom could be scoured throughout Monday, "she being very foul." Loading the schooner took the whole of Tuesday and Wednesday. Some stock, fodder, and Miss Lowther's baggage were put aboard at Snow Bay, but the *Traveller* then had to go to French Bay to take on some firewood, the cattle, and the passengers. Mrs. Farquharson, her grown children Christian and James, and her daughter-in-law Mary Dixon, along with Mrs. Dixon's maid Cora and the two Farquharson slaves George and Henry as "waiting boys," went down to French Bay on Wednesday afternoon but had to stay the night with the Storrs at Sandy Point.

The *Traveller* set sail at 8 A.M. on Thursday, November 24, on a fine easterly breeze. Besides Miss Lowther's goods, the fodder, firewood, and the "3 Trunks, Beding and Seastores" for the four passengers and their slave servants, the schooner was crammed with "6 head of Cattle 23 Sheep 9 Turkeys 2 Cups of Foules 18 Bushels of Guinea Corn [and] a pair of Cart Wheels for repairs." With continuing luck with the wind and the briefest possible stop at Port Howe, Cat Island, the passengers could hope to be in Nassau (two hundred miles from San Salvador) within three days, where they expected to be joined by Charles Farquharson himself some time before Christmas.[24]

Farquharson's brief visits to Nassau generally involved legal or commercial business but were welcome social breaks too, taken, if possible, when other Out Island planters were most likely to be congregating in the colonial capital. The Farquharson slaves could not look forward even to such limited mobility. For most of them, the only reason they might be sent to Nassau was to be tried before the slave court and suffer a spell in the workhouse, if not to be sold and sundered from their larger family and familiar island. The absence of their normally vigilant master in Nassau, though, must have been an occasional relief, especially since it usually coincided with comparative lulls in the estate's work routine.

The weeks leading up to Christmas and the beginning of the corn harvest (during which, in 1831, the Farquharsons were in Nassau) was, in fact, the nearest to an intermission in the estate's agricultural year. This was the time when Charles Farquharson expected the slaves to undertake maintenance tasks, in their own quarters as well as on the estate's buildings, walls, fences, and roads. During much of October 1831, for example, slaves were employed in cutting thatch and wattles "over the Creek," belatedly to make good the damage caused by a hurricane in the previous year to the cotton house, the ginning circle, the "mistress's shed," and some of their own houses. On other days in October and November, slaves were employed in mortaring and plastering certain slave houses that had fallen into disrepair. In such respects the owner does not seem to have drawn a very fine distinction about what was his responsibility and what was to be left entirely to the slaves—though from the evidence of his journal he paid no specific attention at all to the slaves' provision grounds.[25]

Before going off to Nassau in December 1831, Charles Farquharson supervised the rebuilding of walls and clearing of estate roads, especially the back road to Kerr Mount and "the road or path back to the fields and round to the lake side as far as the well field."[26] As a local justice of the peace, Farquharson was also concerned that his slaves fulfil his obligation to maintain the public road past his property. For two days in December 1831, and for a whole week in December 1832, all the able hands were deployed in clearing and repairing the road as far as the "Fortune Hill gait" and in patching the bridge that crossed the head of Pigeon Creek.[27]

December was also the month for domestic economy, particularly the making of clothes for the new year. With the exception of Christmas gifts of handkerchiefs for the women and waistcoats for the men, the slaves were expected to make up all their own clothes from issues of coarse linen cloth. The only general cloth issue recorded in the Farquharson journal (which has a few crucial gaps) was made on November 28, 1831, when Charles Farquharson reported the handing out of 198½ yards of cloth. Six yards were given out to each of twenty-five adult men and women, and amounts varying from one to five yards to each of the children and younger slaves, according to age and sex. If these meager quantities were the sole annual issue, as seems likely, they suggest that the Farquharson slaves were very poorly clothed—bearing out the common observation that Out Island slaves toiled almost naked in the field, and never looked better than shabby.[28]

The Farquharson slaves' clothing deficiencies, and their material poverty in general, must have been made worse by the almost complete lack of opportunities on San Salvador for slaves to make money and purchase clothes and other items for themselves. Indeed, though the Farquharson journal is an incomplete record, the overall impression is of a very stark contrast with life in Nassau and the longer-settled islands. Living almost outside the cash economy, the Farquharson slaves were not only more dependent on their owner but suffered in a magnified way from his own relative poverty. Less certainly, the Farquharson slaves seem also to have been beyond the widening mantle of Christianity, retaining remnants of older spiritual beliefs and practices through the lack of missionaries and their master's seeming indifference to religious matters, as well as being bound by less subtle forms of master-slave relationship than those conceived by such as William Wylly.

Predictably, Farquharson's journal provides even less insight into the private and inner lives of the slaves than of the owner himself. Even if he knew what the slaves did on their own, Charles Farquharson did not often think it worthy of note. What ailed his people when they were not working, and what they did after finishing their tasks on working days, was sometimes recorded. This gives us at least a partial view of the slaves' pattern of sickness and of the working of their provision grounds. But the record is almost invariably silent after Saturday's half-day task was completed, and there is not a single entry for a Sunday during the whole two years.[29]

The journal's lacunae may thus hide the existence of a regular market system (marketing elsewhere being the traditional activity of slaves on Saturday afternoons) and of more or less regular attendance at church meetings on Sundays, though this seems unlikely. It is far more plausible that the Farquharson community was still small enough to be bound together by its common dependence on the owner and by sharing, and linked to the other San Salvador slaves only by occasional bartering forms of exchange—though the manifest attractions of the wider market economy must have begun to impinge by the 1830s. Similarly, African-based forms of religion probably still predominated, including a reverence for the spirit world and such natural elements as the earth, fire, and sea, a deep-set belief in sorcery magic (especially what was commonly called *obeah*), and great stress on the passage rites of birth and death in relation to the "tribal" group—though the syncretic potential of the teachings and practice of such Christian sects as the black Baptists had almost certainly begun to be felt. Even where planters did not insist on specific Christian observances (and Charles Farquharson for one does not seem to have been a practicing believer), the development of the slaves' own form of Christianity was also, surely, reinforced by the coincidence of the official weekly "day of rest" with the Christian sabbath, and of their one annual holiday with the Christians' celebration of the birth of Christ.

Besides each Sunday and the Christmas holiday (not to mention days of excessive rain), Charles Farquharson felt himself bound to allow his slaves a whole day off, and permission to leave the estate if necessary, in order to attend slave funerals. This occurred at least twice during 1831–32. On Thursday, August 18, 1831, Farquharson reported that almost all "the people" had gone down to Sandy Point to attend the funeral of a respected elderly African slave called Old Corker, who had died the previous afternoon. And on Saturday, December 1, 1832, he recorded that almost no work was done because "most of the gang" had gone up to Polly Hill to attend the funeral of another senior slave called Ben Storr, who had died suddenly the day before.[30] These occasions, especially the latter because it was followed by a rest day, were rare extra occasions for all the San Salvador slaves to get together, doubtless to enjoy a wake as well as the more solemn Afro-Bahamian obsequies.

The only regular opportunity for time off work, feasting and celebration, and license to roam came once a year, at Christmas. The record of Christmas 1831 is missing from the Farquharson journal, but that for the following year, when Christmas Day fell on a Tuesday and there were only two full days of work between Saturday, December 22 and Monday, December 31, is fairly full:

> Monday 24. Doing nothing today but killing our Christmas meat for the people and sharing it out to them, we killed a hog weighing 120 lbs and a young heifer weighing 260 lbs the hog and the half of the beef 130 lbs served out to the people which came to 4 lbs of pork and 4 lbs of Beef to each share allowing the children half a share each, and a Bottle rum to each of the grown hands and a large cup full of sugar to each and a half to each child, and a handkerchief to all the grown people and to the big boys and girls and a good westcot to each of the men.
>
> Tuesday 25. Being Christmas day had nothing to do but enjoy ourselves having served out everything to the people befor, had Mr and Mrs Dickson to dinner and Mr Edward Stevenson and Miss Nex. who are here on a visit. Besides our own family being ten in Number at Table. Weather very fine and dry.
>
> Wednesday 26. Some of our people gon abroad to see some of their friends and some at home amusing themselves in their own way threw the day, but all of them home in the evening and had a grand dance and keep it up until near daylight.
>
> Thursday 27. Everything very still today the people mostly sleeping being much fatigued in dancing last night had a pritty good shour yesterday P.M.

The following day, Friday, and on Saturday morning, Farquharson had the slaves out on minor tasks: planting potato slips and guinea grass in Hercules field, cutting thatch over the creek, carrying dung from the cowpen to the great-house garden, and weeding the guinea-grass patch. But after the normal Sunday rest day on December 30, the slaves enjoyed a New Year's Eve bonus when it rained hard all day Monday, almost no work being done on the last day of 1832—which was also the last day recorded in Farquharson's journal.[31]

In the perennially delicate balance of social and industrial relations, the prolonged holiday period and the continued presence of the owner over the turn of the year augured for peace in the early months of 1833. This was in contrast to 1832, when a short period of turmoil occurred in the middle of the corn harvest, with resistance actually led (in an echo of similar disturbances in the sugar islands) by the senior and "confidential" slaves.

Though the crucial pages are missing from the Farquharson journal,[32] the trouble was probably hatched while Charles Farquharson was absent in Nassau and his son James was left in charge. The owner himself had sufficient difficulty controlling his slaves—having on one occasion decided against punishing a female slave, Katherine, for manifest "empidence" because of the "threatening manner with deffiance" of Alick, Bacchus, and another male slave.[33] But James lacked his father's discretion and, as a colored man who was technically illegitimate, much of his natural authority. His compensatory harshness alienated all the slaves and aroused the special animosity of those upon whom Charles Farquharson most relied. Only a few days before the outbreak there had been an incident when James had spoken harshly to Alick's wife Lisey in the kitchen after her refusal to come into the main house after dark to put more oil in the lamps.[34]

Apparently, there had been great difficulties at the start of the crop because of intermittent rain, and many slaves had reported sick.[35] The explosion, however, occurred on Monday the week after the corn cobs had been cut and stacked, at the end of the first day of carting the corn back to the barns. It had been a hard day's work, with seven "horse-kind" and all the slaves making at least seven round trips from the fields. In the evening, when the boys were leading the horses to be watered, James Farquharson had an argument over a trivial matter with Alick's brother Isaac, backing it up with two or three lashes with a palmetto switch. At this, Alick, who had been sick "or pretended to be sick and had been laid up in the kitchen for a week before and was blooded for a pain, or pretended pain in his breast this morning," emerged from the kitchen and angrily asked James why he was attacking Isaac so. James demanded of Alick what right he thought he had to call him to account and moved as if to strike Alick too.

Alick's response was to draw out a heavy bludgeon concealed under his arm and make as if to defend himself. James asked him if he intended to use his weapon, and Alick replied, "By God! if you strike me I will knock you down." Though armed with only a light walking stick, James gave Alick a single cut with it. Alick then went for James with the bludgeon and gave him three heavy blows before he was dragged off by another slave, Matilda. He later admitted that but for the restraint he had every intention of killing the owner's son.

By this time, the entire gang had come into the great house yard "like so many furies threatening revenge against James." Chaos reigned all night, during which Charles Farquharson and his son went to summon John Dixon, Prince Storr, and some of their most reliable slaves "to try to reason with our people in the morning." As soon as day broke, "every Black soul on the plantation that could walk with the exception of 2 old women and the driver [Alick] turned out, the men with there clubs and even some of the women had sticks in there hands particularly Alick's wife Lisey. Katerine, her sister and Diana they were all very noisy and repeted a great deal of the threats and abuse that they used the night befor and would not harken to any advice or counsel that was given them." [36]

The slaves were persuaded to go to carry corn later in the day, but Alick remained sulking in his house, and the two senior remaining slaves went armed with their clubs every time they passed through the yard. This threatening behavior continued until the afternoon of the following day, with five other slaves besides Alick pleading sickness.

Alick went back to work on the Saturday morning, but if the immediate mutiny was quashed, the matter was far from over. The three chief mutineers, Alick, Bacchus, and Peter, were sent up to Nassau and the slave court on the first available boat. But this was a month later, and the departure of the mutineers in the custody of James Farquharson on the sloop *Traveller* on March 21 was the signal for further trouble. In an urgent letter written to his son that very night, Charles Farquharson reported that as soon as the news that the *Traveller* had sailed reached the estate, "we had a Great riote in the Yard with a Great deal of abuse and threatning to Kill every body and Burn the House and all in it." The two chief dissidents were Alick's brother March and March's wife, Matilda, but even the most elderly slave, Old Charles (respected, of course, by the slaves but termed by Charles Farquharson "as hard-headed and mulish as ever"), denied that the prisoners "did anything deserving of punishment." In his immediate pessimism, Charles Farquharson doubted that he could get any useful estate work done without help, or permanently control his slaves without a detachment of troops on the island.[37]

Having left the slaves in the Nassau workhouse, James hurried back to San Salvador within two weeks. There he and his father decided that March and Matilda too must be taken to Nassau. But since the slaves protested their innocence and James Farquharson as a person officially listed as colored might have some difficulty prosecuting them, James requested his father and his half-brother John Dixon to return with him to Nassau to give supporting evidence to the court. Father, son, and son-in-law left San Salvador with the two slaves (and Matilda's infant child) on the *Traveller* on April 19.

A speedy resolution by the court was denied both by the somewhat equivocal status of James Farquharson and by the intervention of the governor, Sir James Carmichael Smyth. As he explained in his dispatch to London, Smyth recommended lenient treatment on five counts, including those of expediency. Not only was James a free man of color and a bastard who had been living on "familiar" terms with his father's slaves, but he had exercised corporal punishment for "trifling reasons," without his father's knowledge or authority. Even more cogently, argued Governor Smyth, on an island like San Salvador, so far removed from authority and having only a few resident whites, the slaves would not, indeed need not, submit to the kind of treatment meted out by James Farquharson. Finally, it should be taken into account that the slaves, after their initial resistance, had voluntarily given themselves up to the authority of the slave court, expecting justice if not leniency.[38]

The Farquharsons returned to San Salvador at last on May 10, almost three months after the original incidents. They brought with them Bacchus, Peter, and March, obviously chastened from their punishment of lashes and a sojourn at hard labor in the Nassau workhouse. Matilda (and her child) were left in the workhouse for a further six weeks in lieu of a lashing. Alick never returned to San Salvador and was apparently separated from Lisey and their children. He was ordered to be sold after his punishment was completed, but instead of his main family being sent to share his fate, another young woman named Mary Ann was sent to Nassau "to be sold with Alexr as one of his wives by permission from the governor," along with the infant, named Eliza, she had borne for Alick while he was away, on March 31.[39]

The rapid return to normal routine by the Farquharson slaves, the inexorable punishment of the mutineers, and, above all, the banishment of the slaves' chief leader, could be portrayed as an unequivocal victory for the owner and his son. Yet, as Farquharson's own journal unintentionally shows, the situation was far less clear-cut. The slaves' return to bring in the corn harvest on the second day, while their leaders remained angry and armed, was an acknowledgment that the corn was as much for their subsistence as for the master's profit. The fact that it was Matilda, herself later punished as a mutineer, who intervened to save James Farquharson's life on February 20, indicates a recognition that while protest and negotiation were necessary features of master-slave relations, violent resistance and bloodshed were clearly counterproductive. An overt rebellion was bound to bring down the colonial forces on the slaves, but even the more gradual defeat and departure of the master would cut off the organized supplies and issues of food and clothing so vital in present circumstances.

On their side, no masters could succeed under Bahamian conditions in slavery's last days, or even make a livelihood, by the exercise of naked power. Alick was banished, but no master could manage his slaves without drivers as mediators, privileged on the one side, respected on both. Under provocation, Alick had gone too far in the interpretation of his role. Previously treated with great reliance (the only slave, for example, allowed to go out fishing on his own), he had eroded his master's trust by suspected malingering even before he physically assaulted his owner's son. But James Farquharson too had overstepped the delicate line between effective mastery and oppression. Young and insecure, like a tyro schoolmaster he made the mistake of resorting to the kind of physical correction which Charles Farquharson, through expediency rather than genuine enlightenment, had virtually given up.

While there had to be masters, Charles Farquharson was perhaps the best possible type from the point of view of the slaves; a long-resident planter lacking the will or ability to leave. Older than any of his slaves and having lived in San Salvador for half a lifetime, he was tied to his land and slaves by economic necessity as much as by a sense of proprietorship, and by familiarity if not affection. He was at least as dependent on the slaves as they on him, and his relationship with them was more an implicit informal contract than one of absolute domination. The slaves would labor steadily, if not with enthusiasm, as long as the master observed well-established limits on hours and tasks, did not expect work during sickness or bad weather, scrupulously observed the official requirements as to issues of food and clothing, and rewarded extra performance as far as his means allowed.

It was a temporizing situation, but also a temporary one, probably recognized as such by master and slave alike. For formal slavery had less than two years to run when Farquharson's journal ended, and the owner himself died in 1835 at the age of seventy-five, before the transitional experiment of apprenticeship had been completed. The graves of both Charles Farquharson and his wife, Kitty, are still pointed out among the crumbling ruins of the Farquharson estate, preserved (or at least not destroyed) by his former slaves and their descendants, however equivocal their feelings were.[40]

~ 19 ~

Slaves' Resistance
and the End of Loyalist Slavery

THE FARQUHARSON JOURNAL clearly disproves two hitherto-common assumptions: that Bahamian slaves were entirely quiescent (having no need to rebel) and that effective slave resistance was limited to outright rebellion. A more general examination of Bahamian slave behavior also points up two related paradoxes: that it was not necessarily the most oppressed slaves who most vigorously resisted and that slave resistance actually increased—rising almost to a climax—in the very last phase of formal slavery.

The Bahamian case bears out what the more intelligent West Indian planters acknowledged: that slave resistance was inevitable and endemic wherever slavery existed and as long as it lasted.[1] Only the form of resistance varied from place to place and time to time. Open rebellion and widespread plots, moreover, were exceptions rather than the rule in all slave colonies. Until formal slavery's last phase, when a consciousness of antislavery allies in England made a bloodless type of mass industrial action seem (misguidedly) realistic, such actions were utterly desperate. They occurred only when slaves (such as newly landed Africans) were ignorant of the almost inevitable outcome, where conditions were so intolerable that it seemed preferable to die in rebellion than to live in chains, or where (because of unusual concentrations of slaves or the temporary weakness of the forces of law and order) there seemed a reasonable chance of success.

Defining slave resistance merely as plots and acts of rebellion, though, is unduly limiting, giving a misleading impression of the effectiveness of slavery as a socioeconomic system. To discover fully how slaves modified and shaped slavery, contributed to its evolution, even helped to speed its demise, it is necessary also to study and understand forms of resistance short of actual (or proposed) revolt. The chief of these was what the French called marronage: running away, either en masse to live over an extended period in the wild (*grand marronage*), or, more commonly, singly or in small numbers, not very far, and for a short period (*petit marronage*). But resistance also involved less obvious manifestations, shading from covert violence, through forms of internal rejection and anomie, to modes of apparent (though simulated) accommodation and acceptance that were, perhaps, as subversive as any other forms. In the last analysis, the effectiveness of slave resistance was determined by the degree to which the enslaved were able to overcome the constraints of the master system and "make a life of their own"—an aspiration which, of course, put them at one with all oppressed peoples, before, during, and after the phase of formal enslavement.

As we have already seen, there were slave plots and disturbances in the Bahamas at predictable times before 1800; once when the influx of new Africans first upset the balance of slave and free, again when "black Loyalists" resisted their re-enslavement, and on two occasions at the instigation of "French revolutionary" slaves.[2] But these outbreaks were limited in scope, uniformly unsuccessful, and easily squashed, telling us more of the exaggerated fears of the master class and the repressive power of the regime than of the ideas and aims of the would-be rebels. Even the disturbances of the last decade of formal slavery, which, as we shall see, were more numerous, more rational, and with hope of at least some form of success, were localized, limited in their aims and tactics, and almost pacific. By far the most common, telling, and perhaps effective means of slave resistance in the Bahamas was running away, a complex and changing phenomenon for which rich evidence can be collated and analyzed from the almost five hundred slave-runaway advertisements that survive from the newspapers of the period 1784–1834.[3]

Since no person would remain in bondage who had a realistic chance of escape, the list of Bahamian runaways covered an entire spectrum of characters, from violent desperadoes to the most privileged and respected slaves. Certain salient types of runaway and patterns of flight emerge, however, depending on the slaves' own personalities and circumstances, the motives and special opportunities for flight, and the prevailing conditions in the colony and colonial slave system at large.

The most colorful gallery of runaways, though a decided minority, were those natural rebels, rogues, and misfits whose deviant behavior would have kept the courts busy and filled the jails in any free population, and today would keep psychiatrists in profitable employment. Such were the "young Negro Man called Cuffy, well known about Town for his wickedness"; the "Mulatto Villain Jack, well known, as he has been, and still remains, a perfect Pest in the Neighbourhood"; Robin, formerly employed at the ordnance department, "a short thick Black fellow, chews a great deal of tobacco, is much addicted to strong liquor, and very insolent when drunk"; and an eighteen-year-old boy called Hamlet, notorious around town, who had "lately been discovered to frequent the Negro Dances, to furnish himself for such Entertainments, he has committed several robberies."[4]

Many of the small-criminal underclass were advertised after they had actually broken out of the jail or workhouse. Such were Jim Pinder, who was awaiting "Public Punishment" and transportation from the Bahamas in October 1814 but "Broke Jail on Sunday Night the 30th. Inst. at the Time the Bell was Ringing" by "breaking the lock from the iron grating of his cell door"; two slaves named Harry Malcolm and Jacob Patton who escaped in 1824 "by cutting their irons and breaking through the iron grating windows"; and the even more ingenious Charlotte Pinder, who in 1833 was "supposed to have secreted herself in the Well, aided by certain implements belonging to the Establishment."[5]

At least an equal number of runaways were those slaves whose unfortunate appearance or afflictions made them as much rejects of the society as true escapees. Such surely included Mungo, "about 5 feet 9 inches high, very stout made, a little knock-kneed, and has remarkable large Feet; appears to be very much swelled, and has large holes in his ears"; a "New Negro Wench" named Sarah, "five feet four inches high, from 30 to 40 years of age," who had "a small sleepy Eye . . . a Mark also on her left Waist, and one Bone being slipt above the other"; and a "mulatto Man Slave" named Hughey, "about five feet 4 inches high, hobbles in his gate and has a hump back." Many other runaways were distinguished by injuries, such as lost fingers and toes or scars on their bodies, sustained at work or in "lawful correction" for alleged misdemeanors. Among the most disgracefully disfigured of the Bahamian runaways was a black woman named Maria who escaped from Benjamin Tynes in September 1808. She was said to have been branded by her former owner in Jamaica (clearly a British patriot), with "NEL on the right breast and SON on the left."[6] But perhaps the most desperate of all Bahamian escapees was one of the earliest recorded (before the use of chains, collars, and manacles by masters was outlawed):

TEN DOLLAR REWARD. RUN AWAY from the Subscriber, on Tuesday night last, a Negro Man named JACKSON, about 5 feet 8 inches high, square made, and has the look of a compleat villain; had on when he went off, a large Chain and iron Collar fastened with a double bolted padlock round his ankle. Whoever delivers the said fellow to the Subscriber, or secures him in Nassau jail shall receive Ten Dollars, and the like sum to those who will discover the person or persons who assisted in knocking off his irons; he was seen going with his irons on towards that harbour for villains, the Negro Town behind the Hospital.

   Masters of Vessels are cautioned against carrying him off the Island.
Nassau, Nov, 2, 1786   JOHN MORRIS[7]

   A number of runaways equal to those who were natural deviants and misfits, though forming a less constant category, were those who had special reasons for not assimilating into the Bahamian slave system, and whose motives and actions in running away had much in common with the plotters and rebels of 1734, 1787–88 or the 1790s: newly imported African, French, and other "foreign" slaves brought into the Bahamas during the last French wars, and the Loyalist and other blacks who claimed that they were free but wrongfully re-enslaved.

   The history of the British West Indies demonstrates the tendency of African slaves (notably the Akan-speaking "Coromantees" from the area of modern Ghana) to run away and rebel, and of the plantocratic regimes to counter the threat by placing an embargo on Coromantees, breaking up groups of the same African ethnicity, and spreading new African slaves among the Creoles. In the Bahamas there were few if any Coromantees, those slaves imported were especially heterogeneous,[8] and native African slaves made up less than 10 percent of the population by the end of slavery. But a remarkable number of Africans did still attempt to escape by running away, especially soon after their arrival and sale. In 1800, for example, when many new slaves were being brought in by privateers, there were at least ten different new African runaways reported, a typical example being the "New Negro Man" apprehended by the watchmen at the Look Out Farm in the Blue Hills of New Providence, who was described as "a likely stout Negro, with a pleasing Countenance, and appears to be from 20 to 25 years of age. . . . cannot tell his Owner's name."[9]

   Naturally, most African runaways spoke little or no English, and some were ignorant not only of their owners' names but of the English names which their new owners had tagged them with. So small were their chances of escaping detection that the owners usually speculated that they had simply roamed and got lost. Such were the unnamed "New Negro Man purchased at the Sale on the ship Colonial Cargo" in June 1794, of whom it was said both that he had "absented himself" and "it is suspected that he lost himself in the woods"; and the slave Dublin, "about 5 feet 7 inches high, lively countenance," with "a Scuff on his Skin, supposed to be the effect of scurvy, and Lump on his left side, occasioned by a wound," reported "Missing, supposed to have lost himself" one week after "the Sale of Prime Negroes" in September 1797.[10]

Other owners guessed that unscrupulous fellow planters simply rustled roaming new Africans, in the belief that they could not be identified and claimed. In 1792, for example, John Morris of Long Island offered a fifty-dollar reward

> to whoever will inform who harbours two of the Subscriber's Negroes named Jack Kie and Sandy on conviction of the offender if white; they are both of the Angola Country, the former a tall young Fellow with a pleasant Countenance, has a kind of Scar on one of his Breasts, besides other of his country marks on the same side, a few small marks on his temples near his Eyes; and his teeth are filed. Sandy is a strong built young Fellow, not so tall as the former, with many of his country marks about him, and has also a facetious Countenance.
>
> It may be supposed by those who harbour them that they being New Negroes, may be easily forgot; to the contrary, they lived in the house for some months and are known by many in the Neighbourhood, so that the employers of these Negroes, if any, can expect nothing but infamy, and as severe a Prosecution as the Law will admit of.[11]

In fact, most of the new African runaways, if ignorant of Bahamian conditions and overestimating their chances of success, were as determined not to assimilate as their owners were to attribute other causes for their running away. Such obdurate slaves included the unnamed runaway boy who "either cannot or will not speak English"; the slave, renamed Isaac by his master, who would only be known by his "country name," Mompier; and the female runaway called Sarah, "a stout likely Wench, with a good Countenance and pleasant appearance, about twenty or twenty-five years of age," of whom it was said "she speaks very little if any English and it is doubtful she can tell her owner's name," though she had already lived in Nassau as long as three years.[12]

Many of the foreign slaves brought to the Bahamas—the majority from French colonies during the period 1793–1807, while the Anglo-French wars raged in the Caribbean—may have been inculcated with French revolutionary ideology, as well as feeling a disinclination to be taken over by another brand of European. But at least some were runaways simply because their experience of other islands and imperial systems gave them a greater awareness of alternatives and practical knowledge of the ways, means, and chances of escape. The expressed intention of the black French would-be rebels of August 1797, it should be remembered, was less the conversion of the Bahamian slaves to Jacobinism and the takeover of the Bahamas than the seizure of a boat to escape to St. Domingue. Similar aims clearly motivated such foreign slaves as the unnamed "Negro Man, black Complexion, about Twenty Years of Age," said to speak "a little Negro French," who in 1799, after receiving "a Punishment sometime before" absconded from Golden Grove estate on Crooked Island in a "four Oared Cedar built Boat."[13] An altogether superior runaway, though, was the "short Mastee Man named Thomas, about 30 years old, small featured," reported as having run away from Captain Dean in September 1793, carrying "a Quantity of good Clothes." Thomas was said to be a Jamaican Creole who was fluent in French, Spanish, and Dutch as well as English—a true Caribbean Man, as rare then as now.[14]

Bridging the small class of polyglot, well-traveled runaways and those runaways who more or less truthfully claimed to be free was an equally remarkable slave called Castalio, for whose return his master advertised in Charleston, South Carolina, in January 1785. Castalio was African born, of "a clear black complexion" with "country marks on each side of his face," but was a "waiting man and shaves and dresses hair" who spoke "good English, also the Dutch and French language distinctly." He first belonged to a Dutch planter in St. Thomas but had spent some time in Holland before being carried by another owner from St. Thomas to New York in 1783. There he ran away with a slave from Dominica called Dick, was caught but escaped again, and was finally "supposed to have been carried to Abaco, or some other of the Bahama Islands, by some white person."[15]

No further trace of a slave called Castalio appears in the Bahamian newspapers or public records, but he may simply have been the first of many ingenious runaways claiming freedom in the Bahamas without sufficient legal evidence—prepared if necessary to change their names, their appearance, or even their personalities in order to sustain their claim. A few runaways arrived from other island colonies, even Bermuda (which some have asserted to have had the most benign slave regime), in the mistaken belief that freedom was easy to obtain in the Bahamas. Such a person was the "Black Woman who calls herself Clarissa Hall" who secreted herself aboard a ship leaving Bermuda and landed in Nassau in May 1812, claiming that she was free but having no documents to prove it. Brought to the workhouse, she was advertised in the *Bahama*

Gazette as being recoverable by her owner "on proving the property and paying the charges according to law."[16] An even more hopeful escapee was the male slave "of a yellowish complexion," colorfully dressed in "a red flannel shirt and blue Trowsers" when he ran away in December 1807. He called himself Tom Freeman, though it was well known that he was "a New Negro Man" from Africa. He was also so little regarded as a worker that his owner offered only three dollars for his recovery.[17]

By far the most numerous of the runaways claiming they were free, though, were blacks from the American mainland, who were, above all, loyalists to themselves. Some of them at least were simply plausible rogues. These included the "remarkably likely and well made" black man named London, who ran away in June 1786 in a "blue jacket with metal buttons and a pair of long trowsers" and was said to be "very artful and sensible, and speaks good English with the accent of the back country people of South Carolina"; and the "Mulatto Man named Mike Devraux, alias Armstong," who deserted John Armstrong in September 1800 and was said to be "well known as an idle vagabond, and it is supposed will endeavour to get to the Continent, where he alledges he was born free."[18]

Most of the black Loyalist runaways were males born in the American colonies, but at least one such artful escapee was an African female, for whom Alexander Inglis of Charleston, South Carolina, offered a ten-pound reward in November 1789. She was, as the advertisement said, "a Negro woman named Dumba, but very probably will call herself Bella, of the Angola Country, aged about 35 years, five feet two or three inches high, slim made; has her country marks on her temples; is sensible and very artful, and may attempt to pass for a free woman—having many acquaintances in Georgia and New Providence, it is supposed that she will endeavour to get to one or either of those places."[19]

Many of the re-enslaved black Loyalists who ran away had worked well enough as long as they had been allowed to do so as more or less free persons. A typical case was that of the woman called Nancy who ran away from Dr. Allan in January 1789 after working about town for two years under the name Free Nancy, because she had been "lately adjudged a slave by the Court attempting to assertain the Freedom of Negroes." This may well have been the same "lusty Negro Woman named Nancy," now owned by John Morris and "the hair on her haid a little sprinkled with grey," who ran away seven years later and was thought to be harbored among "the free crew that came from the Carolinas . . . being a tolerable washer and ironer [she] may employ herself in that way during the time she can absent herself."[20] Three others claiming freedom ran away as a group once they were transferred by their new master from Nassau to Exuma in May 1791. The owner, Zachariah Allen, advertised in the *Bahama Gazette*: "Ran away from the Subscriber's Place on Great-Exuma, Andrew, a stout well made Fellow, has rather a dull look, and is known in Nassau, having for a considerable time worked at Fort Charlotte as a Free Man. John, a Fellow extremely artful and well known in Providence, by the appelation of Free John, and Sue his Wife, a very dark Mulatto; they took with them a small carib capot [a type of small canoe], a steel corn mill, nearly a bolt of Oznaburgs, and several other Things." For the return of the trio, Allen offered a reward of only fifteen dollars, though this was raised to twenty dollars if "the boat and articles mentioned" were also saved.[21]

The king of the artful dodgers described in the Bahamian runaway advertisements, however, was surely Sandy, "also known as Elic or Alexander," for whose return the Loyalist general Charles Cunningham was prepared to offer $150 in 1816: "He is about 5 feet 8 inches high, stout made, yellow complexion, his lips very thick and prominent, his forehead high, small whiskers and bushy hair, is about 30 years of age, speaks good English and lisps a little and is very plausible. He perhaps may change his name and endeavour to pass as a free man; had on when he went away white pantaloons, a bottle green coat, and a glazed leather hat; but as he has taken other clothes with him, he may change his dress."[22]

Besides the natural rebels, the unassimilable, and those who refused to accept re-enslavement in the Bahamas was the large category of runaways resisting the conditions that separated them from their loved ones, kin, or familiar acquaintances. Most of these did not run far or stay away long enough to be recorded as runaways, and in fact many masters who did not own large numbers of slaves were tolerant of visiting customs, perforce. But the importance of affective bonds as a motive for running away was also understated in the slave-runaway advertisements because the owners were often unaware of, or not interested in, the reasons for flight. Many of the runaways simply listed as "harboured," and a high proportion of the hundreds who ran away in couples or groups, were also making their protest against the tendency of slavery to treat them as machines or animals, not sensitive social beings.

Many of this general class of fugitives were not, in a strict sense, running *away*, but rather running *to* a lover, spouse, parent, family, kinship group, or group of acquaintances equivalent to kin. This occurred most notably in Nassau, where such runaways could be hidden, at least for a time, in the increasingly crowded suburbs to east and west and Over-the-Hill—which, if not actually "no go" areas, seem to have been virtually *terra incognita* for whites. Five cases within little more than a year provide a sample cross-section. In February 1799 Christopher Neely advertised for the return of a black boy named Sam, a carter by trade, who had been absent some weeks but frequently seen "near the Eastward Fort, where his Mother lives. His Mother belongs to Mr. Bethel." Five dollars was offered for the return of Sam, but double that amount for information that would lead to the conviction of the person harboring him. Similar rewards were offered by Mary Willcocks in June 1799 for the return of a black woman named Mary, "well known in the Neighbourhood" who ran away with her five-year-old son and was "supposed to be harboured by her husband," while a few months earlier, Thomas Johnston had offered ten dollars for the return of a black man named Mott, "well known about Town . . . good looking, had a deep scar on his Chin," who was said to have "a wife in the Western Suburbs." In May 1799 Robert Smith offered six dollars on behalf of Wade Stubbs of the Caicos Islands for the apprehension of a young black man named Harry, who was "supposed to be harboured by some of his old Comrads in the Eastern Suburbs," while in August 1800 John Anderson offered ten dollars for the return of a "Negro Wench" named Dianna, "about thirty-five years of age, 5 feet 5 inches high, and of a yellow Complexion. She speaks very good English, being a native of this Country, and having some relations, and many acquaintances, it is suspected that she is harboured." [23]

From the time of the earliest advertisements, the favorite refuge for Bahamian *petits marrons* was that growing settlement called "the Negro Town behind the Hospital," where the runaway Jackson in 1786 was, presumably, able to find fellow American blacks willing to cut off his chains and hide him. It was to Negro Town in 1800 that the black man Cesar, formerly the property of Lord Dunmore (and for that reason, perhaps, regarding himself as virtually free), was thought to have fled from his new master, Edward Shearman, to be harbored by the free blacks living there. But the most notable Negro Town refugees were those like William Wylly's slave Boatswain and his family, who in 1821 sought sanctuary (and perhaps a more symbolic loosing of chains) with the black Baptist preachers who by then dominated the area. Boatswain, indeed, had at least one notable predecessor, the "short, elderly man, well known about Town" called James, who with his wife, Venus, and their daughters Hannah and Eve (aged sixteen and eight) absconded from Nathanial M'Queen in March 1818. Three months later they were still at large, though it was confidently reported that "James is connected with Black Preachers and is supposed to be harboured by them."[24]

Of the 463 Bahamian slave-runaway advertisements collated by Godwin Friday in 1984, 383, or 82.7 percent, concerned single slaves, of whom 295 were males and 88 females. But this still left 80 cases where slaves absconded in pairs or groups, accounting for 246 slaves (including children), 39.1 percent of the total of runaways, of whom 193 were males, 53 females. In at least 30 of the 80 cases of pair and group runaways, the bonding agent was wholly or partly a familial one—husband and wife, nuclear family, parent and children, siblings—with the proportion, predictably, higher among the minority of runaway females than among the males. There were at least 19 cases of husband and wife running away together, 11 of them being couples unaccompanied by children and the remaining eight in nuclear family groups. No less than 12 single mothers (and apparently few if any single fathers) ran away with one or more of their children—the most resourceful of them being perhaps Charlotte, who ran away with her three daughters, Hetty, Queen, and Rooty, in January 1793, shortly after they were sold to a new master on the death of their owner, James Rose.[25]

Some of the couples and families went on their own; others were part of a larger group. The largest of all advertised runaway groups, the fourteen slaves belonging to Wade Stubbs of Grand Caicos who took flight in September 1800, for example, was led by an "American Negro" named Harry, who was accompanied by his wife, Abigail, and three children, Jack, Hector, and Hannah, aged five, three, and two respectively. The group also included a Fulani African, Jupiter, his American wife, Pender, and son, Stephen, aged three, as well as six single males. The largest of the nuclear families running away on their own was that made up by the slaves Jem and Jenny and their six children, who managed to escape from their owner, John M. Kelly, on Eleuthera in April 1817, though the most celebrated were undoubtedly the slaves Sandy and Sue, who had absconded with their infant child when threatened with removal to the United States; their status had became a famous test case in the hands of Attorney General William Wylly just two years earlier.[26]

Most of the single mothers, some of the single runaways without children, and a few of the nuclear family groups were simply running to join a mate or a larger family grouping. But the majority of Bahamian slaves who took flight, including many of the whole or partial families, were running away in a stricter sense. Most of them, too, were not natural rebels, not especially unassimilable, or even necessarily persons with a specific reason for running away, but sheer opportunists, seizing a chance of escape as it presented itself, using what means came to hand, going where they could, and sustaining themselves by their wits.

Very few of the Bahamian runaways could expect to live like the *grands marrons* of the larger Antillean islands or the American mainland, though, surprisingly, a few did manage to sustain themselves in small groups in the bush for months or even years at a time, even on densely populated New Providence. The earliest case recorded involved the "stout made Negro Fellow named Jackson, about thirty years of age, a little pitted by the small pox, and . . . well known about town" who went missing in October 1785. Three months later, his owner, John Morris, offered twelve pieces of eight for his return, stating that he had "associated himself with several runaway Negroes who are encamped in the bushes somewhere behind the hospital."[27]

Like "bush Negroes" even in such ideal maroon habitats as Jamaica, St. Domingue, Dominica, or Guiana, runaways aiming for permanent escape had to possess a refuge far enough away from the whites, or sufficiently impregnable, to frustrate recapture; but they also had to be sufficiently close to the established settlements, and their more settled black brethren, to steal or carry on trade for necessities, or to obtain female companions, who were sometimes wooed, sometimes taken in more predatory manner.[28] Jackson and his fellows clearly lived such a symbiotic life, at least for a time. But with the expansion of Negro Town, and the spread of plantations round the shores of New Providence, as through many of the other islands, would-be maroons were pushed ever deeper into the tangled and marshy interior of New Providence and the undeveloped parts of the larger Out Islands.

The thirty armed black Loyalists rounded out of the bush of mainland Abaco and re-enslaved at the behest of Lord Dunmore in 1788 were the first recorded Out Island would-be maroons.[29] But the runaway advertisements and other newspaper items suggest other examples on Long Island, Exuma, Andros, and Inagua. In June 1789 Messrs. Forbes and Stevens were forced to advertise that two of their "New Negro" slaves, called George and Toby, had been absent from their Long Island plantation since the previous July. "From their Huts being frequently discovered on the north side of the Island since their elopement," they reported, "at the back of the settlements where Negro fields are, there is every reason to believe some encouragement must be shewn them." Nine years later, in advertising for the return of Villain Jack, John Morris of Mount Morris, Long Island, stated that "it is supposed by his fellow Servants, that he is harboured by the Negroes of three or four neighbouring Plantations, having no White Person residing on them, as the law directs." [30] Similarly, slaves from the island of Little Exuma seem to have been able easily to wade or swim over to Great Exuma and hide out in the undeveloped bush or decayed plantations. This seems to be what happened to a six-foot slave called Tom, who had been missing for months when advertised for by Thomas Forbes in July 1790, and to six slaves belonging to General Sir John Stuart of the Hermitage estate, who were "supposed to be lurking about the west end of Great Exuma" when advertised for by John Forbes, Thomas's son, in June 1813.[31] The other two islands were so vast and undeveloped that, while they provided only a meager sustenance, maroons could live on them undetected and undisturbed. The west coast of Andros, indeed, harbored a whole settlement of fugitives from the Seminole Wars (the ancestors of the modern Bahamian family of Bowleg), whose existence for years was little more than a rumor in Nassau. The African-born Hamlet and his French-speaking companion, Jem, who ran away from their owner on the Turks Islands and subsisted for a time "on the East End of Heneagua," were less fortunate, being rounded up by John R. Smith in June 1817 and sent to Nassau for trial, though a third Inaguan maroon named Bright, alias Tony, escaped the net and remained at large.[32]

On New Providence so many slaves were "lurking" on the fringes of Nassau and the outlying plantations in the later 1790s that the Look Out Farm in the center of the island became a semiofficial maroon-hunting outpost. In February 1796, for example, "a French Negro Man named John Lewis" (Jean-Louis?) was thought by his Nassau owner, J. B. Perrault, to be "lurking around the Plantations to the Westward." There he may have joined up with a black man named Drogheda, reported in May 1796 to have been hiding in the same area for the past three months. Two years later, in June 1798, another black man named Aubo was "suspected to be lurking about some of the Plantations to the Westward, having formerly had a Wife at General Cunningham's Place."[33] At the very same time, "a stout Negro Man" was reported by Joseph Smith to have escaped from his custody at Look Out Farm and was "supposed to have joined other deserted Slaves in the Neighbourhood of Town." Just a year later, in two separate advertisements in August 1799, Joseph Smith reported that besides the two "New Negro" men (mentioned earlier) who were ignorant of their owners' names, two other runaways were being detained at Look Out Farm: "an old Negro Man with his front Teeth out" who spoke "a few words of broken English" and said he belonged to a

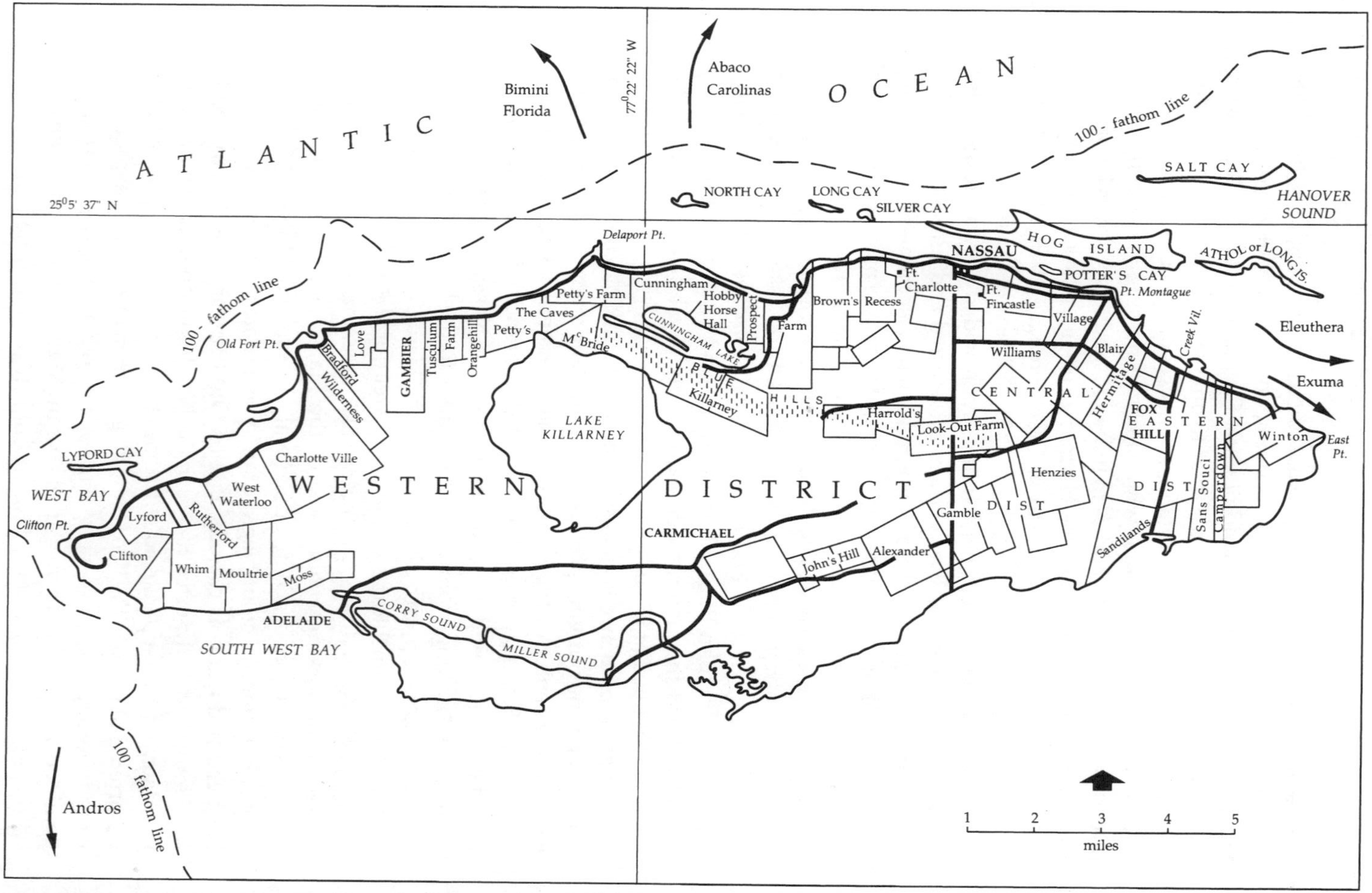

Map 10. New Providence, mid nineteenth century

Mr. Dean of Long Island, and "a Country born Negro Man named Will," who said he belonged to Captain Sergeant and had been placed in the punishment stocks for three or four days.[34]

Look Out Farm was clearly not an unequivocal success, for it was much the same area that saw the most authentic Bahamian incidence of *marronage*, occurring, remarkably, as late as 1823. On May 17 that year, a detachment of the Second West India Regiment, while searching the interior of the island for naval deserters, suddenly came on a party of well-armed maroons. As the *Royal Gazette* reported: "They discovered five black men coming towards town, with baskets of provisions on their heads, one of whom being recognised by a soldier as a runaway, he was called to by name, but threw down his load and ran off. . . . he however soon turned about and fired at the soldiers, the ball passing through the trousers of one of them, and after a little further pursuit another of the runaways fired his gun at the party." Since the soldiers carried no firearms, they gave up the pursuit after being fired upon by the remaining three maroons. Even more interestingly, the newspaper continued:

> It is said that there are upwards of twenty of these desperados in the interior of the island, who partly subsist on killing Cattle, and are headed by a notorious fellow named Jem Matthews, who has been in the woods for several years. This outlaw has his wife with him and has such influence over any runaways who may join his party, that they dare not desert him under the fear of death if again met with him, and there is little doubt but he is often in town at night and would have opportunities of putting his threats into execution.[35]

Perhaps, as Godwin Friday suggests, Jem Matthews was the Bahamian equivalent of the Jamaican maroon bandit Three-Fingered Jack—a mythical hero to the ordinary folk but (for much the same reasons) almost a figure of terror to the regime. Jem's fate, though, was significantly different from that of his Jamaican soul brother (who was killed like a dog by fellow blacks). A party of heavily armed soldiers was sent in search of the maroon camp, found it, and, after a fight, captured four maroons, including a woman. Jem Matthews escaped, but, probably because his wife was in custody, surrendered soon afterward, claiming that his name was not Jem Matthews and that he was a free man named McDonald. By law he should have been transported out of the Bahamas, if not executed, but in fact he was merely given a lashing and a comparatively short spell in jail. Even more surprisingly, when he ran away again in August 1824, his owner, Paul Drouet, advertised only the derisory reward of three dollars for his return.[36] Most likely, as was sometimes done in the case of

troublesome slaves elsewhere, the owner was merely fulfilling the minimal requirements of the law and would have been quite content if Jem
Matthews had remained quietly at large. Perhaps only the comparative
civilization of the Bahamas by 1824 prevented M. Drouet's following the
earlier practice in other colonies of advertising a larger reward for a dead
runaway than for one returned alive.

As befitted an archipelagic colony (and in line with what happened in
the Lesser Antilles, most notably the Virgin Islands)[37] a high proportion
of Bahamian fugitive slaves did not run away by land but attempted to
escape by sea. Naturally, nearly all slaves who had lived any time in the
Bahamas were familiar with the sea, many were adept seafarers and had
easy access to boats—even the personal use of them—and some were
employed in and about ships with little or no supervision. It might even
be surprising that marine *marronage* was not more common than it was.
The ocean horizon was a constant temptation to persons constrained by
slavery, but flight by sea was fraught with risk. Many Bahamian slave
mariners were already almost free in practice and would not readily
chance what they had, and perhaps most slaves would not gamble the
loss of a now-familiar island and a family—even the security of having
a master who was bound by law to provide food and clothing—for the
dangers of an ocean voyage and the uncertainty of landing on their feet
in a foreign land. When looking at those who did in fact attempt to
escape by sea, one should therefore expect to discover signs of intolerable hardship, desperate flight, or, most common of all, sudden, special,
or specially hopeful opportunity.

Over the fifty years of Bahamian slave-runaway advertisements, there
was almost every permutation of types of marine runaway, boats used
for flight, and destinations sought. But the Bahamian would-be marine
maroons fell into two broad categories. A particular threat to Bahamian
owners were those fugitives, generally acting in company, who seized
a boat and sought out another island, colony, or independent country
where they might live unmolested or pass as free. But at least an equal
number were individual mariners who went off on a non-Bahamian
vessel on the promise or hope of a life as a free sailor, or the chance of
going ashore in a freer land.

The boats taken by maritime fugitives varied from two-man canoes,
through two- or four-oared rowing boats, single-masted skiffs, dinghies
or whalers, small-draft droguers such as William Wylly's provision boat,
up to a small schooner, a fishing smack of eight tons' displacement, and
Lord Rolle's salt boat, capable of carrying more than forty persons. Many

A uonc jau, mau receive the above Reward.

Matters of Veffels and others are cautioned againft carrying the faid Negro off this Ifland.   †

January 15, 1790.   **JAMES LOWTHER.**

Twenty or Fifty DOLLARS Reward.

WHEREAS a NEW NEGRO MAN

named C A T O,

has abfented himfelf from this Place, ever fince April laft. I hereby offer a Reward of *Twenty Dollars* to any one who will deliver him to Mr. VINCENT ROCHE, my Overfeer upon this Plantation. And as there is fome Reafon to fuppofe he is harboured, from his having been feen near the Croffing, I will pay *Fifty Dollars* to whoever can give me fuch Information as may enable me to profecute the Offender.

The faid Negro is rather underfized, has many of his Country Marks on his Face and Breaft, and is remarkable in having fmall Feet.

         ALEXANDER MAIR.

Banchory-Lodge, (Long- Ifland,
    February 20, 1790.   †

Runaway slave advertisement (Bahamas Archives)

were leaky and ill-found, having had their oars, rigging, or sails removed for security reasons. Few therefore were suitable for long voyages or for beating against the prevailing winds and currents, factors that as much as anything determined directions of flight and destinations. Both because security was tighter and the temptation to escape rather slighter on New Providence, the majority of boats were taken from Out Islands, following the easiest routes to the nearest safe island or out of the Bahamas altogether.

Some of the earliest advertisements dealt with American-born slaves so completely disgruntled with their new location and employment on Out Island plantations that they would risk escape by sea. Skilled and enterprising, they probably aimed in due course to return to the mainland, but at first they went where they could. The very first case of a maritime flight advertised provides such an example. In May 1785 a black man named Peter, "by trade a house carpenter," led an escape from his owner's plantation at Alligator Bay, Long Island, along with his wife, Pindar; their four sons, July, Gilbo, Robin, and Peter; another American-born couple named Toby and Venus; and "a young Negro fellow this country born" named Robin. "They went off in a new luggage boat, about 3½ tons and are supposed to be amongst the Keys," it was reported. "The mainsail of the boat is remarkable, being made of crocus [that is, coarse sacking] and Peter has a quantity of tools with him."[38]

Three cases within a six-month period in 1789 provide variations upon the same theme, involving Africans and Bahamas-born slaves as well as Americans. On June 17 three African slaves called James, Jack, and Qua stole a small boat from James Wallace's plantation and bravely set out from the west end of Cat Island. "It is hoped," wrote the advertiser, "that they will get to Eleuthera or some other island." On October 12 two Creole blacks, "late the property of Lieut. Col. Brown"—Will, a carpenter with "a very remarkable defect in one of his eyes, and most of his fore Teeth decayed or gone," and his wife Mary, alias Lytha, who had recently been passing as a freewoman—fled with two Africans named Caesar and Agrippa from John O'Halloran's plantation on Derby Island. "They went off in a small schooner, owned by Mr. Carey," wrote O'Halloran, "and carried with them a small skiff with a white bottom, the gunwale and inside painted Red. As they had no provisions with them, nor water, it is imagined that they must be lurking somewhere about the Keys, between Providence and Exuma." A week before Christmas, a Carolina-born slave called John Sampson led two Creoles, Tom and London (who was also "late the property of Col. Thomas Brown"), and a "Guinea born" African, Dunco, in an escape from Henry Glenton's plantation on northern Long Island. "They went off in an old boat about 12 feet keel, all black, full bow'd, square stern, and marked W. They had no oars, but an old sail cut like a boat's foresail."[39]

After 1800, as the Haitian blacks began to establish their independence, the island of St. Domingue was a possible safe haven for Bahamian slave fugitives, though it is unlikely that many except French-speaking slaves or those from the nearer Bahamian islands took their chance there. Haiti would certainly have been the logical destination in maritime terms for the fourteen slaves who fled from Grand Caicos in September 1800 crammed into a small one-masted vessel. But their American-born leader, Harry (incidentally described as "a good boat-man, [who] has worked some time at the sail making business"), may have had the more reckless intention of trying for the American mainland by way of the Old Bahama Channel. Among those who were more likely to have made Haiti their destination, though it was a journey to wind-ward taking more than a week in normal conditions, were the unknown number of New Providence slaves who in April 1808 took "an American built Whale Boat, belonging to Mr. Henderson, branch pilot . . . built of white cedar, painted yellow, with a black streak on top" from "General Cunningham's Wharf" on Cable Beach. Their leader was said to be Henderson's own slave Will, who not only was a practiced sailor but spoke French fluently.[40]

The most popular foreign destination for Bahamian slave fugitives, however, seems to have been Cuba. Not only was it the easiest foreign landfall from most Bahamian islands, but it was an island so large, fertile, and undeveloped that blacks could live unmolested as free peasants in many parts. Non-Spanish-speaking slaves could also apparently easily pass as free men, and even the conditions for slaves in Cuba (before about 1815 at least) were no worse than in the Bahamas, and probably better than in the United States. It was only after British slavery ended that the Cuban sugar monoculture really developed and conditions for Cuban blacks, slave as well as free, deteriorated—with formal slavery actually continuing until 1886.[41]

The motivation of the fugitives who occasioned the first mention of Cuba as a runaway's destination hardly needs speculation. In February 1794 three male slaves, two of whom, Janviet and Congo, were "French Negroes," absconded in a fourteen-foot boat from the plantation of their recently deceased owner, Isaac Baillou, on Big Wood Cay in central Andros—little more than a hundred miles from the nearest point in

Cuba. Five years later, an even more interesting fugitive group also set out for Cuba from Andros, crammed into a stolen canoe. This consisted of an African, Sambo, his Creole wife, Betty, and their three children, under the leadership, or direction, of a French black called Dennis. A rather less adventurous method was used by the slave called Mott, formerly owned by Thomas Johnson of Eleuthera, who left James Moss's schooner *Harriot* while it was actually lying in the harbor of Havana in May 1812. The reward of fifty dollars offered by James Moss suggests that Mott was regarded as a valuable, if troublesome, piece of property.[42]

At least as late as 1816, Bahamian fugitives were still aiming for Cuba. On April 20 that year, an American brig sailing near the Berry Islands was approached by three young black men in a leaky ten-foot cedar rowboat. These men, who were actually three New Providence slaves named Neptune, Vulcan, and Ben, asked for passage to Cuba, claiming that they were free. When they were unable to produce their free papers, saying that they had left them at home, the captain ordered them off his boat. The three men were last seen rowing resolutely for the Joulter Cays, on the northern end of Andros, in the direction of Cuba. Similar methods had apparently been tried at the other end of the Bahamas by the two slaves Israel and Bacchus, who fled from John Mowbrey's plantation on Crooked Island in August 1795, taking a "small two-oared poplar canoe, with a white bottom, black sides, and red gunwales." Their owner supposed that "they would endeavour to get on board of some Vessel going through the Crooked Island Passage," to land in Haiti, Cuba, or some other island in the Caribbean.[43]

The willingness of non-Bahamian captains to take on black crewmen and craftsmen without too many questions asked, as well as the ease with which Bahamian sailors could jump ship (if not steal the ship itself) were perennial problems for Bahamian slaveowners—particularly since the skilled sailors, shipwrights, and dockside workers involved were among the most valuable slaves. The Bahamian slave-runaway advertisements abound with examples of such fugitives, which seems on the surface to contradict William Wylly's contention in 1815 that since Bahamian slave mariners were allowed a percentage of the profits from their work and were treated "exactly as white seamen would be," they "rarely attempted to escape."[44]

Some of this class of fugitives were unruly and drunken types who might have stepped out of the pages of *Treasure Island* and would have given trouble to Blackbeard himself. Such were Jack, "about 30 years of age, five feet, eight or nine inches high, squints with one Eye, and has a remarkable roguish look," who had been "brought up to the Sea, and was dressed in a Sailor's Habit" when he ran away; or Belfast, "about 5 feet eight inches high, 20 or 21 years old, has a large cut across his nose, is a good Sailor and much addicted to drinking of rum"; or the Bermuda-born Sam, who ran away from the sloop *Governor Hamilton*, "a carpenter by trade, aged about 40 years, of a yellowish complexion, and is a very great Drunkard." [45]

The majority of marine fugitives, though, were more respectable types (one was called Trusty). They included experienced interisland sailors such as Pollydore of Governor's Harbour, Eleuthera, "a little of a yellowish complexion, about five feet ten inches high," who was "well known in most of the islands" and suddenly had a reason or chance "to get off in some vessel going to America"; a number of slaves presumed to have been pressed aboard Royal Navy vessels in wartime; and exprivateersmen like Stepney, also "of yellowish complexion" and tall, "lately employed on board the Bellona, hired armed schooner," who went off with his share once cruising was done, in January 1810. But a remarkably large number were also marine craftsmen: sailmakers, caulkers, sawyers, and, above all, ships' carpenters—a trade which, like those of shoemaker and cobbler in the history of English radicalism, seems to have provided a disproportionate number of restless men. [46]

William Wylly's suggestion that Bahamian slave mariners rarely ran away was only true in relation to their opportunities. They were, indeed, only a fraction of the 629 runaways recorded in the fifty years after 1784, who themselves were no more than 3 percent of all Bahamian slaves. But the Bahamian marine maroons, apart from illustrating the axiom that no slaves were ever immune from the temptation to escape from slavery if they could, were only a part of the final, most interesting, and steadily increasing general class of Bahamian slave runaways: those who ran away not only as a protest against slavery itself but as a form of industrial action—over working conditions, the amount and type of work expected, and sudden changes in accepted custom that amounted to the frustration of rising expectations. These, in turn, were only the leading, activist edge of a more general and rising wave of more subtle slave resistance, that which by continuous pressure on customary relationships and terms of employment, and by the constant threat of more overt action, made the slave at least equal to his master in the shaping of slave society.

"It has long been the custom in this Colony to permit the more intelligent of the Slaves, and more particularly Artificers, to find employment for themselves," wrote Governor Carmichael Smyth in 1832, "& to pay to their owners either the whole or such a proportion of what they may gain as may be agreed between the Parties. Almost any slave is anxious to enjoy this Species of Liberty."[47] Inevitably, though, the custom was the cause of increasing friction, particularly on New Providence, where the proportion of artisan slaves, and of slaves surplus to their owners' domestic requirements, was greatest. Independently employed or "jobbing" slaves were always likely to stay longer away than they should, to keep more of their wages than their owners decreed, and to take advantage of offers to "harbor" them in conditions of virtual freedom.

Self-employed runaways included such female "higglers" as the "two Mulatto Wenches named Judy and Meg" who had "been in the habit of daily selling vegetables through the town" and ran away from William King in July 1810. In a similar category there were surely some female slaves accustomed, with or without the connivance of their owners, to sell more intimate wares, and who were unwilling to surrender all, if any, of their ill-gotten pay. Certainly, a few of the advertised runaways were young girls of bankable charms, persuaded to escape into a life of easy virtue rather than hard labor. Such seem to have been the "Negro girl named Maria, between eighteen and nineteen years of age, an African by birth, rather small and good looking," who had "frequently been seen about the Barracks at Fort Charlotte" in 1810; and the "Negro Wench named Kate, about 16 years old" who in 1815 was "supposed to have been inveigled on board some vessel."[48] There was also the intriguing case implied by the following cryptic advertisement in 1804:

CAUTION

Absented herself from the Subscriber a few days ago, a Mulatto Girl named Matilda Baldwin. Pretty correct information has been given where she is harboured, and this is meant by way of a HINT to the Gentleman who is said to be the cause—that the young lady is a Slave, and that upon sufficient proof he will be liable to be exposed by the General Court.

Thos. Bill[49]

The great majority of self-employed runaways, though, were male artisans. These included masons, plasterers, wall builders, a butcher, a baker, and a "segar-maker." But again, ship, house, and "jobbing" carpenters outnumbered the rest of the craftsman runaways added together. Typical of more than a dozen such advertisements was the following, dated June 1799:

Run away on Monday last, immediately after receiving his wages for some days hire, from Mr. Richie, which he carried off, a Negro Man named Dick, belonging to the Subscriber, a Ship Carpenter by Trade, and well known about Town. He frequently saunters about the Western Suburbs, there is reason to suspect that he is occasionally employed there. Ten Dollars reward will be paid on his being secured in Gaol. The same Sum will also be paid for Information that will lead to conviction of any Person harbouring or employing him.

Timothy Cox, Senior Ship Carpenter[50]

As can be seen from the above, owners were often far more minatory toward those who harbored their slaves than toward the runaways themselves—a sure indication of the value of such slaves to their owners, and of the ways in which the slaves were able to take advantage of competition for their services. For example, Thomas Johnson, seeking the return of his mulatto carpenter slave Paris, advertised in May 1800: "All persons are hereby forwarned from harbouring or employing him without a written order from the Subscriber. Masters of vessels are cautioned from carrying him off the Island as they will be dealt with according to the Law." And by the end of slavery, in June 1832, Sarah Poitier was reduced to the following plaintive cry: "The Subscriber again finds it necessary to forbid any person employing or paying wages to any of her Negroes, without a written order from herself, or in her absence from Henry Greenslade Esq."[51]

Though slaveowners could be censorious towards their slaves if they thought they had gone off without due cause, a remarkable number were not only willing to forgive valuable runaways but to advertise the fact in the newspapers. The very first advertiser, the old inhabitant John Russell, calling for the return of eight of his slaves in October 1784, went even further and uniquely offered them not only "a free pardon" but the choice of a new master if they returned. William Wylly, with his tortured sense of reciprocal duties, was typically capable of taking apparently contradictory positions. When his black woman named Sue ran away in June 1800, his advertisement in the *Bahama Gazette* thundered: "As this Woman has gone off without any Cause of Complaint, and has been guilty of great Insolence, she will be prosecuted against as an Outlaw should she not return to her Duty." But when the more valuable black man named John, who was known to have "a Field and Hut near Buen Retiro," had run away in February 1792, Wylly had promised, "If he returns on his own accord in the course of ten days from this date, he will be forgiven." Similarly, in October 1795 Alexander Wildgoos advertised for the valuable man named Tom he had recently purchased from a Mr. Lorimer of Cat Island: "He has been seen in Town several times since he went off, at night. He is Carolina born and is a very plausible Fellow.

Should he voluntarily return before the End of the ensuing Week, and offer any tolerable excuse for absenting himself, he will be forgiven."[52]

By the last few years of slavery, not only were disgruntled slaves more likely to protest, but slaveowners had a further excuse for their slaves' disobedience—the activities of the emancipationists in England and of their alleged agent in Government House. Probably the most tortuous and hypocritical of all Bahamian runaway advertisements was that published by the assemblyman John Wildgoos, Alexander's son, in June 1831, at the very same time that he was being arraigned by Governor Carmichael Smyth for ordering a female slave to be whipped with seventy-nine lashes in the Nassau workhouse:[53]

NOTICE

Whereas, Forres a slave, by trade a plasterer and mason, the property of the subscriber, who has always until the last twenty-five days conducted himself to the satisfaction of his master, but in consequence of having been slightly corrected for a fault viz. sleeping during working hours, has absented himself from my services.

And whereas I have reason to believe that Forres has been induced to commit this fault which is of so unpardonable a nature, under the influence of an improper feeling which has of late spread itself within these Islands much to the prejudice of that description of property, and with a view of its depreciation of value, and not from a natural inclination to be disorderly or disobedient.

Now therefore, being actuated solely by feelings of humanity, and being on all occasions most willing to extend pardon when solicited for.

I do publicly declare that should Forres return to his duty within ten days hereof and humbly ask to be forgiven, he shall be pardoned, but should he continue absent after the expiration of the above period, he shall be punished to the fullest extent the law will allow.

And the reward of Five pounds will be paid to any person who will apprehend and lodge him in the common Jail of this Town.

John Wildgoos[54]

Apart from extending and protecting favorable work conditions and their right to earn wages, and (as we also saw with the Farquharson slaves) resisting what they now considered unacceptable forms of punishment and correction, a final category of Bahamian slave protesters ran away, paradoxically, because they wished to be left where they were. Such were the black man Primus, who in May 1791 "made his escape while going from the Subscriber's house to the Caicos Packet, on board of which he was to have been sent to the Grand Caicos"; or the mulatto woman Nancy and the mulatto boy Jack, who in 1794 and 1798 respectively escaped from boats on the point of sailing for Long Island; or another mulatto boy named Joseph, "by trade a Carpenter, and very lately brought from Antigua in Mr. Fisher's brig" who in May 1807 was "supposed to have concealed himself in Town, from an aversion to go to the Country, to his master in Exuma." [55]

But the most notable of such Bahamian resisters were those Exumian slaves who at the very end of slavery refused to be transferred in the other direction and were prepared to rise up in concerted action to make their point. Just as those slaves who had experienced the comparative freedom of life as townsfolk, craftsmen, or wage earners were increasingly reluctant to be returned to the Out Islands as plantation laborers, so those ostensible plantation laborers who had become rooted in what were virtually peasant communities were increasingly reluctant to have their lifestyle disrupted. The boldest and most effective of all these protesters were, not coincidentally, the largest of all such communal groups; the 350 slaves of the absentee Lord Rolle, established at Steventon, Rolleville, Mount Thompson, and Rolle Town, Exuma. [56]

These slaves were descended from the fewer than 150 blacks brought to the Bahamas from East Florida by Lord Rolle's father, Denys Rolle, in 1784. With the decline of cotton, the slaves were worked less hard, left more to themselves, and expected to be more self-sufficient. Distributed among the four Rolle estates in Exuma, with only the largest group under the direct supervision of the sole white overseer, they were organized by their own choice mainly in nuclear families, with the chief family heads enjoying much popular authority in the four villagelike settlements. Although 60 percent were listed as field laborers (as high a percentage as in the sugar colonies), only a few hours a day at most were spent on estate tasks, including the growing of subsistence foods. Much of the remaining time the slaves spent in their own provision grounds, running their own small stock, fishing, and even hunting. As a result of this healthy lifestyle, the original slaves had multiplied to 254 by 1822, and were to increase even faster to 357 by the end of slavery—an annual average rate of natural increase of 34.5 per 1,000. [57]

From his splendid estate in Devonshire, the absentee owner grew ever more vexed about the expanding gap between the cost of sustaining his slaves and the income which they generated. By 1825 Lord Rolle was complaining of a net loss averaging five hundred pounds a year since 1818 and was making a series of proposals to transfer his slaves to more profitable colonies: Cuba, Jamaica, Demerara, and Trinidad. Most imagi-

native of all was Rolle's offer that if allowed to shift his slaves to Trinidad
(as Burton Williams had done before the clampdown in 1824) he would
allow them to earn wages and pay off the cost of their manumission in
installments. This proposal, though it had the qualified approval of Governor Lewis Grant (himself transferred to Trinidad in 1828), was, like the
others, turned down by a skeptical Colonial Office.[58] But the Trinidad
plan was even more adamantly rejected by the slaves themselves when
news of it was tactlessly leaked by a temporary agent of Lord Rolle's
called Munnings on his first visit to Exuma in 1828.

For by now not only were the Rolle slaves firmly established in their
Exumian home, but they had had time to create, or embroider, a claim
to a special status bequeathed to them by Lord Rolle's father. "There is a
prevailing opinion in the Bahamas," wrote Governor Lewis Grant to the
colonial secretary in December 1828,

> that the predecessor of Lord Rolle who brought them from America to the
> Bahamas, had provided in his Will that they should never be sold or sepa-
> rated or otherwise severely dealt with. They themselves have this impres-
> sion and, for many years, it has been much confirmed in many quarters,
> by the extraordinary indulgent treatment they have received in having their
> labour chiefly applied to their private benefit while the expense of their
> maintenance etc. was supplied by Lord Rolle. After such a state of things
> it is not to be wondered at that they should startle at a proposal abruptly
> made to them by strangers.[59]

The Rolle slaves' reaction to Munnings's announcement about Trinidad caused Thomas Thompson, the overseer, to send an urgent SOS to
Nassau. "I never in my life saw anything to equal it," he wrote to Rolle's
factor on November 21. "They have kept it up ever since & have been
doing what they please since the morning Mr. Munnings left." On Sunday afternoon, forty-five slaves had assembled of their own accord "on
the parade ground (as they call it)," performing military drill and firing
off their muskets about fifty times. On Monday and Tuesday very few
turned out for work, and those only for an hour. On Tuesday evening,
after noisy debates in the slave quarters, an angry crowd surged round
the overseer's house, and for a while Thompson believed they had come
to murder him and his family. He tried to remonstrate with the ringleaders, but while the slaves offered no physical violence, they would
not listen and dispersed only when they were ready. "They say they
want the land to maintain themselves," he reported, "and they won't be
flogged by any white man, neither will they remove from this place."[60]

Governor Grant's last action before leaving for Trinidad in HMS *Barham* was to order a detachment of the Second West India Regiment to Exuma under the command of Captain Thomas McPherson. Landing at Steventon from the armed schooner HMS *Monkey* late on December 8, McPherson ordered the slaves to assemble the following morning. After a long delay only a third of the slaves appeared, and none of the nine ringleaders.[61] Asking those assembled what their grievances were, McPherson was told by the slaves' spokesman, an elderly carpenter called Isaac, that they had no argument with the overseer over the levels of work and punishment, but that they did not wish to be removed to Trinidad and had received no new clothes for eighteen months. They regretted the uproar of the recent past and promised that it would not be repeated as long as they were not shipped off to Trinidad and were properly supplied. Isaac, though, did admit that he was scared of the ringleaders and thought that it might be best if they were removed to another place in the Bahamas.[62]

Captain McPherson concluded that while the immediate crisis had passed, the situation remained inflammable. Nine of the most troublesome slaves had fled to the bush, but as many as 90 of the 318 Rolle slaves had access to firearms, and the overseer in practice was almost impotent. "As to obeying his orders," wrote McPherson in his report on December 10, "they comply so far as to go out to the Grounds, which they immediately quit, and go to their own plantations, notwithstanding his remonstrances." Thomas Thompson agreed with McPherson that the best solution would be a permanent small garrison of troops at Exuma— there being a building highly suitable as a barrack for thirty to forty men and an officer only two hundred yards from the slave quarters at Steventon.[63]

This recommendation was not implemented at that time, and on Governor Grant's suggestion that bad management was chiefly at fault, Lord Rolle's regular agent, A. J. Lees (who was also a member of council) went down to Exuma in person early in 1829. He reported to Lord Rolle that although the slaves refused to be transferred to Trinidad, "they stated they had no objection to removing to any other of the Bahama Islands." Accordingly, Lees planned to ship off twenty slaves, mainly the 1828 ringleaders and their families, to the much less attractive and almost unpopulated island of Grand Bahama. When the time came for the move, though, the chosen slaves refused to embark on Lord Rolle's sloop, despite having been promised money for their crops and being allowed either to sell their hogs and fowls or carry them with them. At Lee's request, troops were again dispatched to Exuma, and the twenty slaves transferred by force. In describing the events to the colonial secretary, Lord Rolle had no hesitation in blaming the antislavery climate of the time. "These disturbances amongst the Negroes," he complained, "are occasioned by the new unfortunate System [promoted by the] Liberals and Saints as they are termed. . . . I wish I had been as fortunate as one of that Sect Mr W—— to have disposed of my Property in the West Indies before this."[64]

Much worse trouble, however, lay in store for Rolle and Lees at the hands of the Exuma slaves and the new "antislavery" governor, James Carmichael Smyth. Early in 1830 the ingenious agent planned to transfer seventy-seven more of Rolle's slaves to Cat Island. There they were to be rented as a jobbing gang to a planter called Thompson, though to comply with the law Lees claimed that they were being resettled on another of Lord Rolle's estates. In making the transfer Lees made sure that no husbands and wives were being separated, or any children under fourteen separated from their parents. But the slaves were informed of the move only three days in advance and given just one weekend to pick their crops of peas and beans, thrash their corn, and dispose of their poultry and pigs. Besides this, they would have to abandon whole fields of Indian corn just planted for the following season.[65]

Under the leadership of a thirty-two-year-old slave called Pompey, most of the selected slaves fled to the bush, remaining there until their provisions ran out five weeks later. Then forty-four of them—nine families and three single slaves—seized Lord Rolle's salt boat and sailed it to Nassau, hoping to put their case to Governor Carmichael Smyth. Approaching the capital, the salt boat was chased in by a Harbour Island sloop, and the slaves were seized and thrown into the workhouse without access to the governor. Almost immediately, the adult slaves were tried before the general court as runaways. Most of them, including five of the women, were found guilty and ordered to be flogged.

Initially kept in ignorance of these events, Carmichael Smyth was incensed when he heard of them, particularly the flogging of the female slaves—two of whom had babies at the breast. Police Magistrate Robert Duncombe and the two justices of the peace sitting on the case, John Anderson and William Vass, were sacked from the bench, and when A. J. Lees sprang to their aid and was insolent to the governor, he was suspended from the council. On making inquiries, Carmichael Smyth discovered not only that Lord Rolle owned no land in Cat Island, but that Lees had perjured himself to obtain the governor's signature on the transfer permit. In consequence, Carmichael Smyth ordered that Pompey and his crew be carried back to Exuma.[66]

The arrival of the rebels at Steventon after a two-month absence "caused a considerable degree of rejoicing and exaltation amongst their comrades." All the slaves refused to work, and Thomas Thompson sent a desperate message that made it seem that armed rebellion was imminent. Somewhat regretting his leniency, the governor forthwith dispatched Captain McPherson once again, with fifty regular soldiers, in the armed schooner HMS *Skipjack*, accompanied by Patrick Grace, the chief constable of the Bahamas, in the sloop *Lady Rolle*.[67] Arriving off Steventon in the middle of the night of Monday, June 20, the two vessels docked at 6 A.M. on Tuesday, to find the slaves quiet but making no preparations to go to work. The armed soldiers rounded them up in the overseer's yard, where they were harangued by Grace, who later reported, "They all appeared to be very much dissatisfied as they understood they were to be free." Meanwhile, a detachment of soldiers made a thorough search of the slave houses and discovered twenty-five "very indifferent muskets" and small quantities of powder and shot.

Later that day Captain McPherson and half the soldiers set out overland to search the second slave village at Rolleville, five miles to the north. The Steventon slaves were not released until two hours after McPherson's party left, but Pompey, "knowing a Short cut to Rolle Ville along the Beach, got there before the Party and by giving the Alarm frustrated the intent of the Expedition." Most of the slaves hid in the bush, and only three more muskets were found in the huts. Pompey, however, was taken and brought back to Steventon early the next day.[68]

That morning, Patrick Grace ordered Thomas Thompson to set the slaves back to work, but "the greater part refused under a plea that they had been for the last three years at work for themselves and wished still to remain so." Only when Pompey was given a public punishment of thirty-nine lashes were the slaves persuaded to go to their allotted tasks. This was at 9:30 A.M., and at 2:30 P.M. the slaves returned with their drivers, announcing that they had completed the day's tasks. The two following days they were turned out for work at 6:30 A.M. but were back again in their houses by 1 P.M., going about their own business throughout the afternoon. During this period Grace interviewed many of the slaves individually and reported that their lack of cooperation was "in consequence of information received from George Clarke and William Neely, Free Black Men, that they were to be Free, and the land was to be divided among them." Having, he believed, convinced the slaves of the falsity of these stories (which seem to have been a combination of wish fulfilment and distorted rumors of Rolle's Trinidad proposals), Grace returned to Nassau on Saturday, June 26, with McPherson and all but twenty of the soldiers, reporting, with some exaggeration, that he had left Lord Rolle's slaves "quiet and industrious." [69]

In retrospect at least, Pompey's miniature rebellion was the first substantial victory for Bahamian slave resisters. It firmly established the principle that Bahamian slaves could not be moved with impunity against their will. The flogging of the Rolle women in April 1830 also created such a stir in antislavery circles that it accelerated protective legislation, if not the emancipation bill itself. But in more general terms, the resistance of the Rolle slaves—which continued after 1830 and was emulated elsewhere—reinforced underlying trends in the relationship between masters and slaves that laid the basis for similar relationships between landowning employers and their workers, and between the white regime in general and black peasants and urban workers, after formal slavery ended.

Just as the owners of town-dwelling slaves could expect little from their slaves unless they allowed them considerable practical freedom and a share of the product of their labor and skills, so the experience of Lord Rolle with his Exumian slaves illustrated that by 1830 Out Island slaveowners could expect little cooperation from their slaves unless they treated them humanely, gave them generous allotments of land, and issued them their full quotas of food and clothing as provided by the law. Harsh treatment and attempts to transfer slaves from their established settlements would provoke outright rebellion, and any attempts to cut down on the official issues of food and clothing would be acceptable only in conjunction with compensatory reductions, or the complete abrogation, of formal work tasks. In extreme cases, such as that of the Rolle estates, the slaves had been able to establish the lifestyle of proto-peasants well before 1838, or even 1834. Elsewhere, the structures and habits of dependency were more firmly entrenched, with slaves handing on to their apprentice and exslave successors the tradition of reliance on allotments of land and handouts of food, seed, tools, and clothing, in return for labor or a share of produce. Yet, at worst, this remained a system of qualified and negotiable interdependence, rather than that type of absolute socioeconomic (and psychological) dominance by which slavery is properly defined.

The period between Pompey's revolt and the end of formal slavery was the most restless phase of readjustment in Bahamian history between the coming of the Loyalists in the 1780s and the emergence of the blacks' Progressive Liberal party in the 1950s and 1960s. It saw some episodes of violence, most notably the uprising of the slaves of the Hunter estate on Cat Island in December 1831, provoked by bad treatment and a rumor (so similar to those circulating in the sugar colonies around that time) that the slaves had been freed but their freedom withheld by the local white regime. A refusal to work and rioting climaxed in the firing of a gun at the Honorable Joseph Hunter, the owner. After troops were sent to restore order, seven men and two women slaves were tried by the general court. All the men were condemned to death by hanging, but only Black Dick, the driver, was actually executed.[70] Similar incidents, involving complaints of failure to issue food and clothing, claims of freedom, refusals to work, and military intervention, occurred on William Thompson's estate on Eleuthera, on Crooked Island, and on the Ragged Islands in 1833 and 1834.[71]

Although on New Providence there was less violence, there was a constant threat of violence, and much white paranoia, as the growing number of the manumitted adjusted gingerly to their equivocal freedom and the remaining slaves tested the declining strength of their restraining bonds. In January 1832 was held the first general election after free coloreds and blacks became eligible to vote, and there was near rioting in Nassau on both voting days. Trouble began with the scrutiny of voting qualifications and the blatant disqualification of far more of those favoring the "liberal" candidates than of those who supported "pro-slavery" candidates such as John Anderson and Robert Duncombe.[72] Rival bands of poor whites and blacks, armed with cudgels, noisily paraded the streets to intimidate or encourage the voters (whose voting choices, of course, were public), and only the presence of armed patrols of the Second West India Regiment prevented actual clashes.

On Monday, January 9, when the elections for the western district were held, the disturbances climaxed at the Vendue House, when a gang of drunken whites celebrating their victory by setting off fireworks were surrounded by "a most vociferous and motley collection principally of women and boys and girls, black, white, brown and yellow who drowned the cheerings within with other cheerings of their own, on the outside, of an opposite character."[73] The following day, the eastern district elections were even more rowdy. After the declaration of winners, the successful voters, "after partaking pretty freely of the good things prepared for them by the members elect," came into town, as was customary, for the purpose of visiting at their own houses the gentlemen returned to represent them. . . . Early in the evening, an immense number of negroes, men, women, and children, collected below the Government House, and opposite the house of John Anderson Esq., where the voters then were, armed with sticks and stones, who behaved in a most riotous manner, and committed several breaches of the peace. All this took place within a hundred yards of the residence of the Police Magistrate, who was at home, and perfectly aware of what was doing, but would not attempt to disperse the mob, until required to do so by two gentlemen.

After dark the streets were again crowded with black and coloured persons, who conducted themselves in the most riotous manner. . . . several white persons were attacked, and two persons, Conrad Duncombe Esq. and Mr. John Sherry, severely maltreated. . . . Parties of the 2nd. W.I. Regiment patrolled the streets, during the whole night.[74]

This effervescence subsided, but three months later there was a short-lived scare of a slave uprising, "having plunder and conflagration for its leading objects." The magistrates were awakened in the middle of the night, and parties of soldiers and militia patrolled the streets till dawn. The regime was just congratulating itself on "providentially" averting "so awful a visitation of calamity" when the "plot" was discovered to be either a hoax or almost comic misapprehension. As the *Royal Gazette* somewhat shamefacedly explained, the chief informant, who was somewhat hard of hearing, had overheard an old black woman relating a dream and thought that she was detailing a violent conspiracy.[75]

All this was a prelude to the oligarchy's last attempt to divide non-white freemen from slaves by the act that granted the freemen full civil rights just a year before the slave emancipation bill came into effect (and thus five years before all exslaves achieved similar rights). In the same few months before the passage of the emancipation bill there was an epidemic of running away, which Governor Carmichael Smyth was at pains to diffuse. Favorite refuges were the extension of Negro Town south of Government House called Grant's Town since 1825 and the settlement of liberated Africans called Carmichael in the center of New Providence, six miles from town. So many slaves ran away and were harbored in Carmichael that the governor issued a proclamation on April 24, 1833, recalling the slaves to their "duty" and promising amnesty for all those out fewer than six months who returned within twelve days. As a result, fifty-five had returned voluntarily to their masters before May 18, and Chief Constable Grace rounded up twenty-two more, "mostly of the ages of 12 to 16 years." The problem, though, remained unsolved, and after Carmichael Smyth left for British Guiana on June 1, Acting Governor Balfour had to issue another stern lecture on July 29, pointing out how far off full freedom for slaves still was. An amnesty proclamation on August 15 named more than fifty specific runaways.[76]

On Exuma there had been almost a carbon copy of Pompey's revolt in February 1833. A large boat crowded with thirty-five slaves was stopped off Fort Montagu on the eastern approaches to Nassau. These were running away from Mrs. Ferguson's plantation on Great Exuma because they objected to a plan to shift them to the desolate salt-producing island of Norman's Pond Cay in the Exuma Cays and wished to present their case to the "Gubna." To their dismay, they discovered that Carmichael Smyth had already given his assent to the move and refused to change his decision, though when they were returned to Exuma by force, they were relieved to find that Mrs. Ferguson's agent had changed his mind about the wisdom of the move.[77]

The Ferguson slaves were clearly emulating their Rolle neighbors, who continued to be the spearhead of all the activist Bahamian blacks during the transition from formal slavery through apprenticeship to nominal freedom. In October 1833, for example, Balfour reported Lord Rolle's slaves once more "refactory," after Taylor, the attorney for the estate, had informed him that they refused to work and offered violence. On inquiry Balfour decided that Taylor was as much to blame as the slaves. "The details which he gave me," he wrote to the Colonial Office, "proved that although the Slaves on the property are not ill-treated in the Article of Labour, yet that sufficient care had not been taken to supply them with the quantities of food allowed by law." Taylor was firmly told "that if the literate Manager neglected the law, what response could you expect from the illiterate slave?" Balfour, though reluctant, was still prepared to send soldiers if necessary to quell the slaves. "Their passive resistance will no doubt cease on the sight of the King's Troops," he concluded, "but I dislike extremely to use the arm of power unless when urged by necessity."[78]

Such a soft approach was of little avail. As the emancipation bill passed in London and awaited implementation by the Bahamian legislature, the Rolle slaves became even less tractable. In January 1834 Lord Rolle wrote to the colonial secretary that he had heard from Taylor that his slaves in Exuma had "severely beaten and bruised" Thomas Thompson's successor as overseer, one Hall, and had calmed down only on the arrival of a special magistrate who threatened to send troops. "I attribute the disorderly Change in the Conduct of my Negroes," wrote Rolle, conveniently forgetting all the previous incidents of insubordination, "to the Encouragement they experience from what passed in the last Sessions of Parliament . . . that they were all free and were to be found everything by me."[79]

During the transition from full slavery to apprenticeship, Lord Rolle's slaves proved more troublesome than almost all others in the British West Indies. As Balfour wrote to London on September 13, 1834, he had been compelled to send troops to Exuma three times that year because of the insubordination of Lord Rolle's "gang" and now decided to station a detachment permanently on the island. Rolle's slaves, who became officially apprentices on August 1, 1834, had not committed any overt acts of rebellion but were said to be "content with refusing to work, so long as the Troops are absent. But the mere presence of the latter has always been sufficient to restore discipline."[80]

Lord Rolle himself echoed and added to this assessment. On August 11, 1834, he wrote from Devonshire to the colonial secretary—in a scraggly scrawl that suggests an old man at the end of his tether—that he had heard from Taylor that his "slaves" still would not work, "except the Soldiers are on the Spot—the Moment the Troops leave the Island they are again in a State of Insubordination as before—in Consequence of this Representation I am inclined to send out Instructions to discharge the Negroes from their Apprenticeship but first to request through you the Cooperation of Government—My Instructions would be in my Power of Attorney that it should contain full Powers to convey the lands for the use of the Negroes during their Apprenticeship."[81]

Such a unilateral act of emancipation, or abrogation of responsibility, was, of course, unacceptable. Lord Rolle's offer was officially rejected. However, even more than most other Bahamian Out Islanders, Rolle's exslaves served a purely nominal apprenticeship, and when they became "full free" on August 1, 1838, they assumed full possession of their ex-owner's lands under a self-determined commonage system. As already mentioned, all of Rolle's exslaves also assumed the surname Rolle, and to this day any of the five thousand Bahamian Rolles can theoretically claim a house lot or provision grounds on Exuma. Over the years since 1838 a quite spurious legend has grown up about the alleged philanthropy of John, Lord Rolle, who is commonly said to have been one of only two Bahamian masters who deeded their lands to their exslaves at emancipation.[82] In fact, no such deed has ever been traced. It may well have been a convenient fiction (like the legend of Denys Rolle's will) invented by the first generation of black peasant farmers called Rolle—

Pompey's brethren. Rather than giving credit to a querulous and self-serving absentee, it should surely be argued that by their uncooperative behavior and actual resistance the slaves Lord Rolle ostensibly owned virtually won independence and land for themselves—setting a proud example for all Bahamian blacks.

It remains to be seen, however, whether the subsequent history of the Bahamian people demonstrates either that the Rolle example was suitable for all exslaves, or even an unequivocal and lasting victory for the Rolles themselves.

Epilogue:
Muted Celebrations, 1834–1838

THE TRANSITION out of formal slavery was justifiably anticipated with extreme nervousness, by the white Bahamian master class and the black majority alike. The crescendo of slave unrest in the Out Islands during the early 1830s, epitomized and spearheaded by the Rolles of Exuma, carried over from an opposition to actual slavery to a rejection of the system of apprenticeship. The ethnopolitical ferment of the general election which followed the political emancipation of the free coloreds in 1830 gave some inkling of what might be expected once the franchise was extended to the far larger number of former slaves. Besides this, there was the unresolved question, worrying to former slaves as well as former masters, as to the response of the liberated African apprentices once they too achieved full freedom by the expiry of their involuntary indentures in August 1838. All elements knew that the transition augured substantial economic as well as social and political changes, and feared the worst. On one side, at least some of the ruling class feared that economic disaster might be accompanied by mass uprisings; on the other, the more pessimistic of the black majority feared extreme economic hardship accentuated by ethnic discord and fierce repression.

The most immediate indicators of attitudes and responses of all elements in Bahamian society to the ending of formal slavery would seem to have been the first annual ceremonies celebrating emancipation, held over the two days of July 31–August 1, 1834 to 1838. Perhaps surprisingly, by all accounts that have survived, these were far more muted than expected—indeed, less tumultuous than the annual Emancipation Day celebrations were to become later in the century. The actual day that formal slavery ended in 1834 apparently passed quietly, both on the Out Islands and in Nassau. A Methodist missionary wrote home from Abaco that on "that memorable day in the annals of British history I walked from one end of the place to the other and . . . not a disorderly person was to be seen nor a voice to be heard. It appeared as if a general silence was commanded to hear the falling chain struck into annihilation." Another missionary wrote of Harbour Island: "The 1 of August—*Memorable Day*—passed away, without the least excitement whatever, or disposition toward it." On making his official report in September 1834, Acting Governor Balfour informed London that the state of the entire colony was tranquil, with the single exception of the "trifling insubordination of Lord Rolle's gang of apprentices," which was quashed immediately a detachment of troops was sent to Exuma.[1]

On August 1, 1835, Governor Colebrooke was able to report that the first anniversary of emancipation had likewise passed with "utmost tranquillity" throughout the colony and felt able to claim that apprentices were well behaved and well disposed toward their masters. Three years later, on the coming of full freedom, his successor, Governor Cockburn, wrote to the colonial secretary, Lord Glenelg, that "the 1st of August has passed off to my entire satisfaction—everything has been quiet—those set free have rejoiced in their new state but without the slightest disposition to tumult or insubordination and as far as I have yet been informed there appears every disposition on the part of those who were of late owners and apprentices will continue together."[2]

Once again, these accounts were substantiated by Methodist missionaries. The Reverend Thomas Lofthouse wrote from Harbour Island to the Methodist Missionary Society that "the 1st Aug. passed off . . . among the coloured people in a manner highly creditable to themselves and satisfactory to all who had the pleasure to witness their orderly upright and religious proceedings as well as the joy and gladness they manifested on that memorable and never to be forgotten day." And the Reverend William West reported from Nassau in the same week that Emancipation Day was hailed with joy by all the liberated, but that "it was not a joy expressed by noises and tumult but displayed in a mild, becoming, and I may add, Christian manner. . . . All the places of worship were opened and unusual numbers of black and coloured population attended and listened with devout and serious attention to the interesting subjects that were being brought before them. . . . Singing was unusually lively."[3]

To what can be attributed the general quiescence and respectable behavior reported on what later writers often call "The Day of Jubilee"? To a certain extent the reports reflected their provenance. Neither colonial governors nor Methodist missionaries were likely to exaggerate the disorderliness of the people committed to their charge. Accounts from the

PROCLAMATION AND ADDRESS,

TO THE POPULATION OF THE BAHAMAS.

• By *His Excellency* BLAYNEY TOWN-
    LEY BALFOUR, *Esquire, Lieutenant*
    Governor and Commander in Chief
    in and over the Bahama Islands,
    Chancellor, Vice Admiral, and Or
    dinary of the same.

FELLOW SUBJECTS AND FRIENDS.

IN a few weeks Slavery will be at an
end, and I therefore address you, that
you may all know the chief points in the
new system, and that you may not offend the Laws through ignorance.

MASTERS, remember that you
must feed and clothe your Apprentices, and otherwise provide them, according to Law.—Remember that you have
no right to strike or imprison an apprentice; but if he deserve punishment, you
must take him to a Special Justice.

SLAVES, you will, on the 1st of
August, lose this name, and become
free; but as I told you last year, you
will not be altogether free, but for a
few years you will have to work for
your Masters as Apprentices: that is, to

Balfour Proclamation, 1834 (Bahamas Archives)

silent majority were far more likely to have stressed the sense of chains unloosed, if not to express a riotous sense of new-won license. Acting Governor Balfour's account, besides expressing relief, also provides more than a hint that the quiescence of the celebrations was achieved by the manifest presence of the forces of law and order—military and naval detachments as well as magistrates and police.

However, the quiet and orderly behavior seems to have been real enough, and achieved without undue recourse to force. One salient explanation is that the celebrations were not just a spontaneous expression of the people's feelings but were increasingly well orchestrated occasions controlled by the more subtle agents of social order themselves. In a sense, the missionaries, and through them the officers of the colonial government (if not members of the local ruling regime), had *captured* the emancipation celebrations from the people actually freed—just as metropolitan philanthropists (and social conservatives) took over the emancipation movement and its subsequent historical interpretations from more dangerously radical and revolutionary forces and theorists, from the time of Wilberforce, Macaulay, and Buxton down to Reginald Coupland, G. R. Mellor, or even Seymour Drescher.[4] How else can we explain that the only sanctioned celebrations in Nassau and the Out Islands consisted of well-clothed and well-organized parades along well-defined and well-controlled routes, and services in respectable churches, where the people would be subjected to salutary and self-serving homilies, and encouraged to sing uplifting hymns? It was only later that the Emancipation Day celebrations took on a more popular, populist, and secular form, when they came to express a more generic attitude toward slavery and its legacies.

Yet there remained another important reason why the earliest Emancipation Day celebrations were decidedly muted: real doubts about what the occasion meant and whether the future held any real improvement. For those slaves who were already virtually free, who had become dependent on their statutory allowances of food and clothing, or who had been able to use the conditions peculiar to the last phase of formal slavery to negotiate better terms, the status of full independence in a highly competitive wage market, without the assurance of free access to land or houses, emancipation was an especially hypothetical benefit. In competing for land and work, moreover, the exslaves were in contention with a body of liberated Africans a quarter as numerous as themselves— a people whom they affected to despise as unacculturated Africans but who themselves claimed a greater ethnic authenticity and who pointed out that they had never had to undergo the degradation and demoralization of full chattel slavery.

This ethnic subplot in the social history of the Bahamas was already of long standing when formal slavery came to an end, for the first liberated Africans had been landed as early as 1811. This volume has not treated the relationship between former slaves and liberated Africans in detail, not just because the anomalies of having an increasing number of African-born nonslave Bahamians would unnecessarily confuse the consideration of "Loyalist" slavery on which this volume has concentrated, but because Africans saved from slavery continued to be settled in the Bahamas until the 1860s, and the fascinating story of their gradual integration into a newer and richer society of black Bahamians essentially belongs to the later nineteenth and early twentieth centuries. To provide just one cogent example, it was to be the secular lodges and "friendly societies," many of them organized on different African ethnic lines, that not only changed the nature of the Emancipation Day celebrations but provided an increasingly creolized and homogenized black Bahamian people with the opportunities of self-help, protopolitical organization, and sheer human dignity denied to them by the ruling Bahamian classes until the 1950s.

Notes

Preface

1. For typical earlier histories see, for example, James H. Stark, *History and Guide to the Bahama Islands* (Boston: Stark, 1891), 11–105; A. Talbot Bethell, *The Early Settlers of the Bahamas* (Nassau: Privately published, 1914); Sir Harcourt Malcolm, *History of the Bahamas House of Assembly* (Nassau: House of Assembly, 1921); Mary Moseley, *The Bahamas Handbook* (Nassau: Nassau Guardian, 1926), 16–36; H. M. Bell, *Bahamas, Isles of June* (New York: McBride, 1934). The first scholarly historical work, by the American James M. Wright in 1905, though entitled "History of the Bahama Islands," turned out to be little more than an account of the political struggle over slave emancipation. For years, scholars were warned off by the unsubstantiated rumor that a definitive history was being written by Mary Moseley. In the 1950s, during the last days of the Bay Street regime, a committee of the House of Assembly commissioned the English historian Hilary St. George Saunders to write an official history. After employing two researchers two years in the London archives, Saunders went to Nassau to write the book but died six weeks later. The famous English novelist engaged to complete the work made such a botched effort, and ran his employers such a merry dance, that the manuscript was never published. For a fuller discussion of Bahamian historiography, see Michael Craton, "The Historiography of the Bahamas, Cayman Islands, and Belize," in vol. 6 of the forthcoming UNESCO general history of the Caribbean, edited by Barry Higman and Jean Casimir.

Chapter 1

1. There is some controversy over the terms used for the aboriginal peoples. The inhabitants of the Bahamas at the time of Columbus, who called themselves Lucayans ("island peoples"), were ethnically, culturally, and linguistically related to the majority of the people then inhabiting the Greater Antilles, whom British scholars have traditionally called Arawaks, in distinction to the more warlike Caribs of the Lesser Antilles. There were, and still are, ethnic groups on the South American mainland calling themselves Arawaks and Caribs, with distinct languages and cultures, but island Caribs and Arawaks alike spoke Arawakan

languages, though practicing different cultures. Although the Antillean natives at the time of Columbus seem to have had no consistent generic names for themselves, most modern ethnographers and archeologists divide the majority into Island Caribs and Taino (the latter taken from the people's own word for "a virtuous man"). The Taino are divided into the Classic Taino, inhabiting Puerto Rico, most of Hispaniola, and far eastern Cuba, and the Sub-Taino, including the Bahamian Lucayans, along with the people inhabiting central Cuba, Jamaica, the islands between Puerto Rico and Guadeloupe, and perhaps parts of the southern Lesser Antilles (where they are also called Igneri). The only other peoples in the Antilles at the time of Columbus of whom there is certain knowledge were those of the preceramic culture and distinct language now termed Guanajatabey (formerly called Ciboney, from a Tainan word said to mean "cave dwellers") found in far western Cuba, who were almost certainly the Meso-Indian predecessors of the Neo-Indian Tainos. There is, though, still some doubt about the correct classification of the people called Ciguayo whom the Spaniards found in northeastern Hispaniola.

After due consideration, we continue to use the terms *Arawak* and *Taino* interchangeably, as we do *Ciboney* and *Guanajatabey*. We also refer to Neo-Indian, Meso-Indian, and Paleo-Indian cultures rather than to use the more trendy terms *ceramic, preceramic,* and *lithic*. No one, surely, can gainsay our use of the term *Lucayan*. For as clear an exposition of the terminological debate as is possible, see Irving Rouse, *Migrations in Prehistory: Inferring Population Movement from Cultural Remains* (New Haven, Conn.: Yale University Press, 1986), 106–56, and "Whom Did Columbus Discover in the West Indies?" *American Archeology* 6, no. 2 (1987): 83–87.

2. Besides Christopher Columbus himself, whose account is limited to the first voyage, and Ferdinand Columbus, biographer and apologist of his father, the chief early Spanish commentators were Dr. Diego Chanca, Guglielmo Coma, and Michele Cuneo, who wrote letters concerning the second Columbian voyage; the Benedictine friar Roman Pane, commissioned by Columbus to describe the natives' beliefs and rituals; Andrés Bernáldez and Peter Martyr, who never visited the Indies but carefully retailed first-hand accounts; Bartolomé de Las Casas, whose father and uncle accompanied Columbus in 1493 and himself lived in the Indies from 1502 to 1550, and Fernández de Oviedo y Valdez, who lived on the Spanish Main and in Hispaniola between 1514 and 1542. See Cecil Jane, L. A. Vigneras, and R. A. Skelton, eds., *The Journal of Christopher Columbus* (London: Anthony Blond, 1960); Robert H. Fuson, ed., *The Log of Christopher Columbus* (Camden, Me.: International Marine, 1987); Benjamin Keen, ed., *The Life of the Admiral Christopher Columbus by His Son Ferdinand* (New Brunswick, N.J.: Rutgers University Press, 1959); Martín Fernández de Navarrete, ed., *Collección de los viages y discubrimientos que hicieron por mar los españoles desde fines del siglo XV,* 5 vols. (Madrid: Imprente Nacional, 1825–37); *Raccolta di documenti e studi publicati dalla R. Commissione Columbiana per il quarto centenario della scoperta dell'America,* 14 vols. (Rome: Commissione Colombiana, 1892–96); Andrés Bernáldez, *Histo-*

ria de los reyes católicos D. Fernando y Dona Isabel, 2 vols. (Seville: Geofrin, 1870); Alberto Salas, *Tres cronistas de Indias* (Mexico City: Fondo de Cultura Economica, 1959); Francis A. MacNutt, ed., *De Orbe Novo: The Eight Decades of Peter Martyr D'Anghera*, 2 vols. (1912; reprint, New York: Burt Franklin, 1970); Bartolomé de Las Casas, *Historia de las Indias*, 3 vols. (Madrid: Fondo de Cultura Economica, 1875–79); Gonzalo F. Oviedo y Valdez, *Historia general y natural de las Indias*, 5 vols. (Madrid: Graficas Orbe, 1959). For our account of Lucayan-Tainan culture, we have relied also on the following salient modern works: Sven Loven, *Origins of the Tainan Culture, West Indies* (Goteborg: Elanders, 1935); Irving Rouse, "The West Indies," in *Handbook of South American Indians*, vol. 4, *The Circum-Caribbean Tribes*, ed. John H. Steward (New York: Cooper Square, 1963), 495–565; Jesse W. Fewkes, *The Aborigines of Porto Rico and Neighboring Islands* (1907; reprint, New York: Johnson, 1970); Fred Olsen, *On the Trail of the Arawaks* (Norman: University of Oklahoma Press, 1974).

3. MacNutt, *De Orbe Novo*, 1: 170.

4. For a brief survey of Bahamian geology, including an evaluation of competing theories, see Neil E. Sealey, *Bahamian Landscapes: An Introduction to the Geography of the Bahamas* (London: Collins Caribbean, 1985), 9–44.

5. See, for example, George J. Benjamin, "Diving into the Blue Holes of the Bahamas," *National Geographic* 138, no. 3 (September 1970): 346–63.

6. A thorough study of the land resources of the Bahamas, including rocks, landforms, soils, fresh water, climate, and vegetation, running to eight volumes, was produced by the British Ministry of Overseas Development between 1969 and 1976, but only a 178-page summary has been made available to the public: B. G. Little et al., *Land Resources of the Bahamas* (London: Ministry of Overseas Development, 1977).

7. For a fine popular account of the evolution of the ecology and natural history, see David G. Campbell, *The Ephemeral Islands: A Natural History of the Bahamas* (London: Macmillan, 1978).

8. Ibid., 19–36.

9. José M. Cruxent and Irving Rouse, "Early Man in the West Indies," *Scientific American* 221, no. 5 (1969): 42–52.

10. The most ardent advocate of a Meso-Indian or even earlier presence in the Bahamas is the imaginative paleolinguist-archeologist Julian Granberry, who mentions Herbert Krieger's claim of Ciboney sites in Andros and the Berry Islands (1936) and his own possible discovery of preceramic sites in New Providence and Grand Bahama. Underwater burial sites, reported from Grand Bahama and Andros as well as the Caicos Islands, are currently undergoing scholarly investigation. Julian Granberry, "Antillean Languages and the Aboriginal Settlement of the Bahamas: A Working Hypothesis" (Paper presented at the conference "Bahamas 1492: Its People and Environment," Freeport, Grand Bahama, November 1987); Herbert W. Krieger, "The Bahama Islands and Their Prehistoric Populations," *Smithsonian Institution, Explorations and Field Notes, 1936*, 93–98.

11. Tony Aarons of the Bahamas Archives is currently working on a bibliog-

raphy of Bahamian archeology, though it is a project that needs almost monthly updating. To the time of writing, the following have been among the most notable contributions toward a comprehensive overview: William K. Brooks, "On the Lucayan Indians," *Memoirs of the National Academy of Sciences*, no. 4, pt. 2 (1888), 215–22; Theodoor De Booy, "Lucayan Artifacts from the Bahamas," *American Anthropologist* 15 (1913): 1–7; Krieger, "Bahama Islands"; John M. Goggin, "An Anthropological Reconnaissance of Andros Island, Bahamas," *American Antiquity* 5 (1939): 21–26; Julian Granberry, "The Cultural Position of the Bahamas in Caribbean Archeology," *American Antiquity* 22 (1956): 21–26, and "A Brief History of Bahamian Archeology," *Florida Anthropologist* 33 (1980): 83–93; Charles A. Hoffman, Jr., "Bahamas Prehistory: Cultural Adaptation to an Island Environment" (Ph.D. diss., University of Arizona, 1967), and "The Palmetto Grove Site on San Salvador, Bahamas," *Publications of the State Museum*, no. 16 (Gainesville: University of Florida, 1970), 1–26; James C. MacLaury, "Archeological Investigations on Cat Island, Bahamas" (M.A. thesis, Florida Atlantic University, 1970); William H. Sears and Shaun D. Sullivan, "Bahamas Prehistory," *American Antiquity* 43 (1978): 3–25; Irving Rouse, "The Concept of Series in Bahamian Archeology," *Florida Anthropologist* 33, no. 3 (1980): 94–98; Shaun D. Sullivan, "Prehistoric Patterns of Exploitation and Colonization in the Turks and Caicos Islands" (Ph.D. diss., University of Illinois, 1981); Richard Rose, "The Pigeon Creek Site, San Salvador, Bahamas," *Florida Anthropologist* 35, no. 4 (1982): 129–45; John Winter, "Preliminary Results for a Cuban Migration" (Paper presented at Third Bahamas Conference on Archeology, San Salvador, 1982); William F. Keegan and Steven W. Mitchell, "Archeological Research in the Bahamas Archipelago, 1984," Report to the Bahamas Government, 1985; William F. Keegan, "Dynamic Horticulturalists: Population Expansion in the Prehistoric Bahamas" (Ph.D. diss., University of California, Los Angeles, 1985).

12. For the sites known in June 1990, see map 3, compiled by Tony Aarons of the Bahamas Archives Department. The most spectacular archeological growth area is the northern Bahamas, where dozens of sites are being located in islands previously thought uninhabited or merely visited by the Lucayans.

13. Keegan, "Dynamic Horticulturalists"; Sears and Sullivan, "Bahamas Prehistory."

14. Michael Halkitis, Steven Smith, and Karen Rigg, *The Climate of the Bahamas* (Nassau: Bahamas Geographical Association, 1980); Little, *Land Resources*; Sears and Sullivan, "Bahamas Prehistory"; Keegan, "Dynamic Horticulturalists," 74–121.

15. Sears and Sullivan, "Bahamas Prehistory"; Winter, "Cuban Migration"; Keegan, "Dynamic Horticulturalists," 189–299.

16. Carl O. Sauer, *The Early Spanish Main* (Berkeley and Los Angeles: University of California Press, 1966), 51–69.

17. Most commentators have jumped to the conclusion that the aggressors of the Guanahaní Lucayans were the Caribs, and hence that the threat must have

come from the southeast. The actual words of Las Casas's transcription of Columbus's entry for the first day after landing at Guanahaní are: "They showed me that other people from nearby islands came there and tried to capture them and that they defended themselves. And I believed and still believe that people come here from the mainland to take them as captives." This would seem to indicate enemies much closer than the nearest Caribs, such as the Taino of Hispaniola or Cuba, and not to exclude even fellow Lucayans. Indeed, later for the same day's entry, Columbus was quoted as writing, "Some of the other islands are more distant, some less. They are all very level, without mountains [which would have excluded Cuba and Hispaniola], and very fertile. They are all inhabited, and the people make war against each other." Recent suggestions, by Aarons and others, that the attackers may have been Indians from the mainland of Florida, that is, from the northwest, are as yet unsubstantiated, though they are backed up by the third quotation from Columbus's entry for October 14, 1492, often ignored or misquoted: "According to many of them . . . there would be land to the south, southwest and northwest. They said that the people from the northwest had come to fight them many times, then [had gone on] to the southwest to search for gold and precious stones." S. Lyman Tyler, *Two Worlds: The Indian Encounter with the European, 1492–1509* (Salt Lake City: University of Utah Press, 1988), 38–42.

18. Hoffman, "Palmetto Grove Site."

19. Sears and Sullivan, "Bahamas Prehistory." As already noted, the Lucayan occupation of the northern islands may have been hitherto understated. Sears and Sullivan also probably overstate the climatic susceptibility of manioc, which, in variant types, is today grown successfully in the southern United States. A final view of the extent and nature of Lucayan colonization in the Bahamas must await archeological study of northern sites so far merely located, as well as the scientific analysis of the evidence for corn and manioc cultivation.

Chapter 2

1. Richard Rose, "Pigeon Creek," "Lucayan Lifeways at the Time of Columbus," in *Columbus and His World: Proceedings of First San Salvador Conference, October 30–November 3, 1986,* ed. Donald T. Gerace (San Salvador: College Center of the Finger Lakes, 1987), and "Trade and Economy in the Lucayan Bahamas" (Paper presented at conference "Bahamas 1492: Its People and Environment," Freeport, Grand Bahama, November 1987). Also, De Booy, "Lucayan Artifacts"; M. K. Pratt, "Prehistoric Archeology of San Salvador: Preliminary Reports, 1973, 1974," in *Island Environmental Studies* (Corning, New York: College Center of the Finger Lakes, 1974); Ruth G. Durlacher-Wolper, "Columbus' Landfall and the Indian Settlements of San Salvador," *Florida Anthropologist* 35, no. 4 (December 1982): 203–7.

2. Besides the main contemporary and modern sources listed in chap. 1, n. 2 above, the following have also proved valuable: Julian H. Steward, ed.,

Handbook of South American Indians, vol. 3, *The Tropical Forest Tribes* (Washington, D.C.: Smithsonian Institution, 1948), 799–881; Bradley Smith, *Columbus in the New World* (New York: Doubleday, 1962); Sauer, *Early Spanish Main*; Alfred W. Crosby, *The Columbian Exchange: Biological and Cultural Consequences of 1492* (Westport, Conn.: Greenwood, 1972), and *Ecological Imperialism: The Biological Expansion of Europe 900–1900* (Cambridge: Cambridge University Press, 1986); Donald W. Meinig, *The Shaping of America: A Geographical Perspective on Five Hundred Years of History*, vol. 1 (New Haven, Conn.: Yale University Press, 1986); David Watts, *The West Indies: Patterns of Development, Culture, and Environmental Change Since 1492* (Cambridge: Cambridge University Press, 1987).

3. MacNutt, *De Orbe Novo*, 1:66, 367.

4. Keegan, "Dynamic Horticulturalists," 41–73, and "Structural Determinants of Lucayan Taino Settlement Patterns" (Paper presented at the Fifty-second Annual Meeting of Society for American Archeology, Toronto, 1987).

5. Keegan, "Dynamic Horticulturalists," 32–40; Sauer, *Early Spanish Main*, 65–69; Sherburne F. Cook and Woodrow Borah, "The Aboriginal Population of Hispaniola," in *Essays in Population History*, vol. 1, *Mexico and the Caribbean*, ed. Sherburne F. Cook and Woodrow Borah (Berkeley and Los Angeles: University of California Press, 1971).

6. The same argument applies to the Caicos Islands, the only other location of multiple duho finds. George Anthony Aarons, "Report on Long Island Expedition, Cartwright Duho Cave Excavation (LN-37), 22–28 September, 1988" (Unpublished report, Bahamas Department of Archives, 1988), and "The Lucayan Duhos: 1828–1988," *Journal of the Bahamas Historical Society* 11, no. 1 (October 1989): 3–11.

7. Sauer, *Early Spanish Main*, 51–69; Watts, *The West Indies*, 53–63.

8. Columbus was certain that the Lucayans of Fernandina (Long Island) planted and harvested corn throughout the year, though he was, of course, not familiar with the type of corn he saw for the first time on October 17, 1492, calling it *panizo* (panic grass). Tyler, *Two Worlds*, 45. Coma and Peter Martyr made it clear that the Tainos of Hispaniola grew maize and processed it into flour, and it seems unlikely that maize cultivation would have been entirely absent in the Bahamas. Sauer, *Early Spanish Main*, 55.

9. Campbell, *Ephemeral Islands*; Sullivan, "Prehistoric Patterns"; Keegan, "Dynamic Horticulturalists," 120–31.

10. There is tantalizing evidence that the Lucayans may have imported and domesticated the agouti (*Geocapromys ingrahami*, alias hutia, or "Bahamas coney") for eating—based on the discovery of large numbers of skeletons of identical size in the food-refuse middens, the Spaniards' reports of a domesticated "small, barkless dog," and the apparent speed with which the agouti followed the Lucayans into extinction. The only remaining colony is on uninhabited East Plana Cay, between Acklin's Island and Mayaguana. Garrett C. Clough, "A Most Peaceable Rodent," *Natural History* 82, no. 6 (1973): 66–79.

11. Rose, "Trade and Economy"; Sears and Sullivan, "Bahamas Prehistory."

12. Campbell, *Ephemeral Islands*, 40. Watts, *The West Indies*, 65; aloe, from the agave plant (*Agave bahama trelease*), though it differed from the Mediterranean species later introduced (*Aloe vera*), was, with cotton, one of the few useful indigenous flora that Columbus recognized on his first voyage, noting it first on Crooked Island (Isabela) on October 21, 1492. Mary Jane Berman, Perry L. Gnivecki, and Deborah Pearsall, "Paleoethnobotanical Investigations at an Early Contact Site, San Salvador, the Bahamas: A Preliminary Study" (Paper presented at the Fifty-third Annual Meeting of the Society for American Archeology, Phoenix, Arizona, 1988).

13. Watts, *The West Indies*, 61–65; Keegan, "Dynamic Horticulturalists," 131–33.

14. William F. Keegan, "Lucayan Fishing Practices: An Experimental Approach," *Florida Anthropologist* 35, no. 4 (1982): 146–61, and "Dynamic Horticulturalists," 111–21, 133–64, 170–73.

15. Columbus, however, did mention at least one Lucayan canoe capable of carrying forty to forty-five persons, as well as the common type, suitable for one or two persons. Jane, Vigneras, and Skelton, *Journal of Columbus*, 25–26.

Chapter 3

1. The material for this chapter is derived mainly from the writings of the early Spaniards, particularly Columbus, Pane, Peter Martyr, Oviedo, and Las Casas, with the help of the chief modern commentators, notably Fewkes, Loven, Rouse, and Olsen, all cited in chap. 1, n. 2. Sauer's *Early Spanish Main* and Samuel Eliot Morison's *Admiral of the Ocean Sea: A Life of Christopher Columbus* (Boston: Little Brown, 1942) have also been invaluable here, as throughout part 1.

2. Tyler, *Two Worlds*, 46–51, quoting the entries in Columbus's journal for October 17, 19, and 21, 1492.

3. See chap. 1, n. 16.

4. Oviedo was the first man to connect the virulent outbreak of syphilis in Europe in 1493 to the return of Columbus's first expedition; *Historia*, bk. 2, chap. 8. Modern historians, though, have hotly debated whether syphilis was indeed "the Arawaks' revenge," whether it was actually brought to the New World by the Europeans, or whether it was a case of the catalytic mingling of two strains of the disease. For a full statement of the first position, see Saul Jarcho, "Some Observations on Disease in Prehistoric North America," *Bulletin of the History of Medicine* 38 (1964): 11–15; for the second, Charles C. Dennie, *The Gift of Columbus* (Kansas City, Mo.: Brown-White, 1936); and for the "unitarian" position, E. H. Hudson, "Treponematosis and Man's Social Evolution," *American Anthropologist* 67 (1965): 885–991. For a balanced discussion of this and other questions concerning indigenous and exchanged diseases, see Percy M. Ashburn, *The Ranks of Death: A Medical History of the Conquest of America* (New York: Coward-McCann, 1947); C. W. Dixon, *Smallpox* (London: Churchill, 1962);

Crosby, *The Columbian Exchange*, 35–63; Kenneth F. Kiple, *The Caribbean Slave: A Biological History* (Cambridge: Cambridge University Press, 1984), 7–12, 190–94.

5. Kiple, *Caribbean Slave*, 104–34.

6. Irving Rouse, "The Arawak," in *Handbook of South American Indians*, ed. Steward, 4:531–32.

7. Ibid., 535–38.

8. Ibid., 533–34.

9. Olsen, *Trail of the Arawaks*, 91–120, 170–71, 223; no equivalent has yet been found in the Bahamas for the remarkable anthropomorphic duho from Hispaniola in the British Museum, in the form of a prostrate man, face down, with upraised legs and a rampant penis, as if offering sexual congress. Quite what this signified has not been speculated so far in the literature.

10. Campbell, *Ephemeral Islands*, 34–36.

11. Olsen, *Trail of the Arawaks*, 89–120, 215–24.

12. Ibid., 102–34.

13. Ibid., 103–14.

14. There has hitherto been almost no consideration of Lucayan iconography along the lines pioneered for the Taino by Fred Olsen's *Trail of the Arawaks* and Irving Rouse's "Ceramic and Religious Development in the Greater Antilles," *Journal of New World Archeology* 5 (1982): 45–55. This situation is only partly due to the relative paucity of suitable artifacts in the Bahamas. Most artifactual forms and decorative patterns in ceramics, wood, stone, and shell have been treated descriptively and, at most, comparatively, with the mere intention of discovering stylistic derivations and thus inferring historical developments. This is true of the few attempts at generalization as well as almost all reports concerning specific archeological sites. See, for example, Julian Granberry, "A Preliminary Ceramic Typology and Chronology for the Bahamas" (Manuscript, Peabody Museum, Yale University, 1952); Ripley P. Bullen, "Similarities in Pottery Decoration from Florida, Cuba, and the Bahamas," *Proceedings of Americanists' Congress, San José, Costa Rica, July 1958* (San José: N.p., 1959), 2:107–10; Charles A. Hoffman, "Petroglyphs on Crooked Island, Bahamas," *Proceedings of the Fourth International Congress for the Study of the Pre-Columbian Cultures of the Lesser Antilles* (Castries: St. Lucia Archeological and Historical Society, 1972), 9–12. For a start, much more work needs to be done from a basis of comparing Lucayan artifacts by types, along the lines of Tony Aarons's painstaking 1989 survey of all known Lucayan duhos.

Chapter 4

1. We fully subscribe to the belief that Guanahaní–San Salvador, the island of Columbus's landfall in the New World, was that formerly called Watling's and now (since 1926) San Salvador. In this, and in tracing the Discoverer's onward voyage through the Bahamas in October 1492, we follow the itinerary described

in Samuel Eliot Morison's *Admiral of the Ocean Sea,* emphatically not because on a former occasion, when asked for permission to use material from his book, the great Harvard historian insisted on the condition that his interpretation be followed absolutely, but rather from a long and careful weighing of the evidence. No other candidate for the landfall fits more completely the description given in Columbus's log, as retailed by Las Casas. The chief seeming discrepancy is the quoted statement of Columbus that many other islands could be espied from San Salvador, when in fact none can be seen from near sea level on Watling's–San Salvador. The best explanation for this is that the statement is an erroneous interpolation, either by Las Casas or by Columbus himself, in writing up or revising the account of the landfall some time after the event. For us, the clinching evidence is the unique discovery, in July 1983 at the site of the Lucayan village adjacent to the almost certain location of Columbus's first landing, of Spanish artifacts including a copper *blanca* coin of Henry IV of Castille (1454–74), two bronze buckles, several iron nails and majolica fragments, and ten tiny glass beads of the very type Columbus described as being used to trade with the Indians. See Charles A. Hoffman, "Archeological Investigations at the Long Bay Site, San Salvador, Bahamas," in *Columbus and His World,* ed. Gerace, 237–45; and Robert H. Brill and Charles A. Hoffman, "Some Glass Beads Excavated on San Salvador Island in the Bahamas," *Annales du 10e Congrès de l'Association Internationale pour l'Histoire du Verre, Madrid-Segovie, 23–28 septembre 1985* (Madrid: N.p., 1986), 373–400.

The embers of the Columbus Landfall Controversy were increasingly fanned as the quincentennial of October 1992 approached, with the *National Geographic* magazine placing its huge resources behind the choice by its senior associate editor, Joseph Judge, of Samana Cay, first suggested by one Gustavus Fox in 1882. Although Watling's–San Salvador has had the most, as well as the most persuasive, advocates, dating back to Juan Bautista Muñoz in 1792, and including R. H. Major, A. B. Becher, and J. B. Murdock in the century before Morison, at least eight islands have been put forward over the last two centuries. First of these was Cat Island, favored among others by Washington Irving and actually called San Salvador from the early 1700s until 1926. In 1990 the Cat Island claim was revived by local residents and their parliamentary representative, in the hope of attracting the international attention being monopolized by neighboring Watling's–San Salvador. Much the same motivation explained the revival of the long standing claims for two islands outside the political jurisdiction of the Bahamas: Grand Turk, suggested by Navarrete in 1825, George Gibbs in 1846, Pieter Verhoog in 1947, and Robert Power and Robert Fuson in the 1980s; and East Caicos, first proposed by Edwin and Marion Link in 1958. Other claimants have included Mayaguana (proposed by Francisco Varnhagen in 1864), Conception Island (R. D. Gould, 1927), and, most outlandish of all, Egg Island, off the northern anvil of Eleuthera (Arne Molander, 1986).

The literature on the Landfall Controversy is as extensive as that arguing the claims for Columbus's birthplace (or, for that matter, his claim to priority in the "discovery" of America). But see, for example, Samuel Eliot Morison and Mauricio Obregón, *The Caribbean As Columbus Saw It* (Boston: Little Brown, 1964); Louis De Vorsey and John Parker, eds., *In the Wake of Columbus* (Detroit: Wayne State University Press, 1985); Joseph Judge, "Where Columbus Found the New World," *National Geographic* 170, no. 5 (November 1986): 563–99; Robert H. Fuson, "The Turks and Caicos Islands as Possible Landfall Sites," in *Columbus and His World*, ed. Gerace, 173–84; and Arne B. Molander, "Egg Island Is the Landfall of Columbus: A Literal Interpretation of His Journal," in *Columbus and His World*, ed. Gerace, 141–72.

2. Jane, Vigneras, and Skelton, *Journal of Columbus*, 23–24.

3. Ibid., 28.

4. Ibid., 26–28. The purpose of the ships' sails, which must have seemed to them like great birds' wings, would, of course, have been unclear to the Lucayans. Had Columbus been less ingenuous, he might have translated the Lucayans' words more along the lines of "Heavens! Look what the wind's blown in! Bring these creatures food and gifts and perhaps they'll go away."

5. All probably soon perished, though one, christened Diego Columbus, accompanied the Discoverer on his second voyage, and was an invaluable interpreter wherever the Arawak language and its dialects were spoken.

6. Jane, Vigneras, and Skelton, *Journal of Columbus*, 28–29.

7. Ibid., 32–43; Morison, *Admiral of the Ocean Sea*, 222–53; Morison and Obregón, *Caribbean*, 14–43.

8. For the Spanish colonization of Hispaniola and its effect, see Sauer, *Early Spanish Main*, 37–108, 147–60, 196–217; Troy S. Floyd, *The Columbus Dynasty in the Caribbean, 1492–1526* (Albuquerque: University of New Mexico Press, 1973).

9. Sauer, *Early Spanish Main*, 101.

10. Kiple, *Caribbean Slave*, 9–12.

11. Sauer, *Early Spanish Main*, 65–66.

12. C. Edwards Lester, *Life and Voyages of Americus Vespucius* (New Haven, Conn.: Mansfield, 1855), 169–70.

13. King Ferdinand to Diego Columbus, August 14, 1509, *Collección de documentos inéditos relativos al discubrimiento, conquisto y organización de América*, 42 vols. (Madrid, 1864–84), 31, 438.

14. Floyd, *Columbus Dynasty*, 133–35.

15. MacNutt, *De Orbe Novo*, 2:270.

16. Bartolomé de Las Casas, *The Tears of the Indians*, trans. John Phillips (London, 1656), 84–85.

17. Sauer, *Early Spanish Main*, 160.

18. MacNutt, *De Orbe Novo*, 2:249–50.

19. Ibid., 1:274; E. W. Lawson, *The Discovery of Florida and Its Discoverer, Juan Ponce de Leon* (St. Augustine: Privately published, 1946).

20. Sauer, *Early Spanish Main*, 190–92.

21. Las Casas, *Tears of the Indians*, 86–87.

22. Ibid., 87; MacNutt, *De Orbe Novo*, 2:252.

23. Floyd, *Columbus Dynasty*, 97.

24. These Arawaks, who call their language Lokono, are found in dispersed settlements within a hundred miles of the coast, between the rivers Orinoco and Marowyne, in the modern countries of Venezuela, Guyana, and Surinam. Steward, *Handbook of South American Indians*, 3:799–881.

Chapter 5

1. Meinig, *The Shaping of America*, 1:244–54. For the general processes of European expansion into the New World, and the effects of the African diaspora, see J. H. Parry, *The Age of Reconnaissance, Discovery, Exploration, and Settlement, 1450–1650* (New York: World, 1963); Philip D. Curtin, *The Atlantic Slave Trade: A Census* (Madison: University of Wisconsin Press, 1969); Charles Verlinden, *The Beginnings of Modern Colonization* (Ithaca, N.Y.: Cornell University Press, 1970); Crosby, *The Columbian Exchange*; Ralph Davis, *The Rise of the Atlantic Economies* (Ithaca, N.Y.: Cornell University Press, 1973); Kenneth G. Davies, *The North Atlantic World in the Seventeenth Century* (Minneapolis: University of Minnesota Press, 1974); Immanuel Wallerstein, *The Modern World-System*, vol. 1, *Capitalist Agriculture and the Origins of the European World-Economy in the Sixteenth Century*, vol. 2, *Mercantilism and the Consolidation of the European World Economy, 1600–1750* (New York: Academic Press, 1974, 1980); Jack P. Greene, *Pursuits of Happiness: The Social Development of Early Modern British Colonies and the Formation of American Culture* (Chapel Hill: University of North Carolina Press, 1988).

2. For Spanish imperialism in the region see J. H. Parry, *The Spanish Seaborne Empire* (London: Hutchinson, 1966); J. H. Elliott, *The Old World and the New, 1492–1650* (Cambridge: Cambridge University Press, 1970); Kenneth R. Andrews, *The Spanish Caribbean: Trade and Plunder, 1530–1630* (New Haven, Conn.: Yale University Press, 1978); James Lockhart and Stuart B. Schwartz, *A History of Colonial Spanish America and Brazil* (Cambridge: Cambridge University Press, 1983). Though legendary, belief in Spanish occupation of the Bahamas has a long history and dies hard. Both Governor Woodes Rogers in 1721 and Peter Henry Bruce in the 1740s reported Spanish ruins on Cat Island. Vernon-Wager Papers, reel 2, 155–56, Peter Force Collection, Library of Congress, Washington, D.C.; Peter Henry Bruce, *Bahamian Interlude* (1782; reprint, London: Culmer, 1949). Local legend at The Bight, Long Island, reinforced by the 1972 ordnance survey map, claims that the ruined Anglican church there was originally Spanish. It is said that the date 1611 is scratched in the plaster of the tower, and that the original Spanish settlement was wiped out by a tidal wave. There was in fact a disastrous tidal wave in 1832, which washed away the village and destroyed the southern wall of the church; but settlement and church alike were almost certainly founded by anglophone Loyalists in the 1780s. The story of "Spanish" settlers

may well originate in the presence of illegal Cuban migrants in Long Island during the nineteenth century. Delmore Cartwright (catechist and local informant), personal communication, 1983; *Royal Gazette*, January 13, 1832; *Nassau Quarterly Mission Paper*, no. 1, June 1, 1886, 17–22.

3. Laudonnière had actually been preceded in Florida by Jean Ribault, another Huguenot, who attempted in vain to set afoot a joint Anglo-French expedition in 1563. For this, and for French imperialism in the region in general, see J. Saintoyant, *La Colonisation française sous l'Ancien Régime (du XVe siècle à 1789)*, 2 vols. (Paris: La Renaissance du Livre, 1929); Herbert I. Priestley, *France Overseas Through the Old Regime: A Study in European Expansion* (New York: Appleton-Century, 1939), 44–54; William J. Eccles, *France in America* (Vancouver: Fitzhenry and Whiteside, 1972); Jacques-Nicolas Bellin, *Description geographique des Isles Antilles possedées par les Anglois* (Paris: Didot, 1758), 142.

4. Saintoyant, *Colonisation française*, 2:116–20; Priestley, *France Overseas*, 253. In 1755 the French governor of Saint Domingue felt free to send Admiral de Vaudreuil to extirpate an alleged pirate base in the Bahamas, and as late as 1768, a French geographer wrote of the islands that they were "almost all deserted" and that "the English pretend that they belong to them." Antoine Bruzen de la Martiniere, *Grand dictionnaire geographique, historique, et critique*, 6 vols. (Paris: Libraires Associés, 1768), 3:920. For the French claim to the Bahamas in 1754 and the occupations of 1764 and 1783, see Governor Tinker to Lords Commissioner of Trade and Plantations, April 20, 1754, C.O. 23/6, 38–40, and Halifax to L.C.T.P., July 1, 1764, C.O. 23/7, 138, Public Record Office, London; Craton, *History of the Bahamas*, 134, 144.

5. For the early phases of English expansion, especially as regards Ireland, see K. R. Andrews, N. P. Canny, and P. E. H. Hair, eds., *The Westward Enterprise: English Activities in Ireland, the Atlantic, and America 1480–1650* (Liverpool: Liverpool University Press, 1978); Angus Calder, *Revolutionary Empire: The Rise of the English-speaking Empires from the Fifteenth Century to the 1780s* (New York: Dutton, 1981); K. R. Andrews, *Trade, Plunder, and Settlement: Maritime Enterprise and the Genesis of the British Empire, 1480–1630* (Cambridge: Cambridge University Press, 1984).

6. David Beers Quinn, *Raleigh and the British Empire* (London: Hodder and Stoughton, 1947), *The Roanoke Voyages, 1584–1590*, 2 vols. (Cambridge: Hakluyt Society, 1955), and *Set Fair for Roanoke: Voyages and Colonies, 1584–1606* (Chapel Hill: University of North Carolina Press, 1985).

7. Andrews, *Trade, Plunder, and Settlement*, 209–11; Mary F. Keeler, ed., *Sir Francis Drake's West Indian Voyage, 1585–86* (London: Hakluyt Society, 1981).

8. Quinn, *Raleigh*, 61.

9. W. Noel Sainsbury et al., eds., *The Calendar of State Papers, Colonial Series, America and West Indies, 1574–1737* [hereinafter abbreviated *CSP*], 43 vols. (London, 1860–1963), vol. 9 (1675–76), addenda (1574–1674), no. 151, pp. 70–72; Craton, *History of the Bahamas*, 50–52; James A. Williamson, *The Caribee Islands Under the Proprietary Patents* (Oxford: Oxford University Press, 1926).

10. Frank Kermode, ed., *The Tempest* by William Shakespeare, The Arden Shakespeare (London: Methuen, 1954), xi–xciii. For the early history of Bermuda in general, see John H. Lefroy, *Memorials of the Discovery and Early Settlement of the Bermudas or Somers Islands, 1515–1685*, 3d ed., 2 vols. (1879; reprint, Toronto: University of Toronto Press, 1981); Vernon A. Ives, ed., *The Rich Papers: Letters from Bermuda, 1615–1646* (Hamilton: Bermuda National Trust, and Toronto: University of Toronto Press, 1984); Henry C. Wilkinson, *The Adventurers of Bermuda: A History of the Island from Its Discovery Until the Dissolution of the Somers Island Company in 1684*, 2d ed. (Oxford: Oxford University Press, 1958); Charles M. Andrews, *The Colonial Period of American History*, 4 vols. (New Haven, Conn.: Yale University Press, 1934–38), 2:214–48; Wesley Frank Craven, "An Introduction to the History of Bermuda," *William and Mary Quarterly* 17 (1937): 176–215, 317–62, 437–65, and 18 (1938):13–63; Cyril O. Packwood, *Chained on the Rock: Slavery in Bermuda* (Hamilton, Bermuda: Baxter's, 1975).

11. Wilkinson, *Adventurers of Bermuda*, 77–79. The 1615 Bermuda Charter is given in Lefroy, *Memorials of the Bermudas*, 1:83–96.

12. Lefroy, *Memorials of the Bermudas*, 1:98–100.

13. Ibid., 68–69, 108–10, 193; Lefroy, *Memorials of the Bermudas*, 1:140–43, 228–30.

14. Packwood, *Chained on the Rock*, 1–9. Lefroy cites a case of a black man who was enslaved for assault as early as 1617, and Ives points out the ambivalence of the status of the black tobacco experts at much the same time, calling them slaves. An act was passed "to restrayne the insolencies of the Negroes" by the second Bermudian Assembly in 1623—called by Packwood "the first law anywhere in English specifically dealing with Blacks"—but the first real slave ordinances were promulgated in 1656, following the slave plot in that year; Lefroy, *Memorials of the Bermudas*, 1:127, 2:95–97; Ives, *Rich Papers*, 59, 81, 233–34; Packwood, *Chained on the Rock*, 6–7, 117–30.

15. Wilkinson, *Adventurers of Bermuda*, 140–42, 163–67, 194–203, 259–62, 318–31, 346–49.

16. Ibid., 218–48; Arthur P. Newton, *The Colonising Activities of the English Puritans* (New Haven, Conn.: Yale University Press, 1914).

Chapter 6

1. Wilkinson, *Adventurers of Bermuda*, 246–80. Personally, Sayle seems to have been an arch-pragmatist, being accused of being a dangerous Independent in the 1640s, a Royalist in the later 1650s, and a republican in the early 1660s, though more or less exonerated each time. Lefroy, *Memorials of the Bermudas*, 2:4, 108–10, 117–18, 195.

2. William Rener to John Winthrop, March 1646, in *Winthrop Papers*, ed. Samuel E. Morison, 5 vols. (Boston: Massachusetts Historical Society, 1929–85), vol. 5; W. Hubert Miller, "The Colonization of the Bahamas, 1647–1670," *William and Mary Quarterly*, 3d ser., 2, no. 3 (January 1945): 33–46, 34.

3. Miller, "Colonization of the Bahamas," 34–35. A copy of the 1647 articles is given in Robert A. Curry, *Bahamian Lore* (Paris: Privately printed, 1930), 115–22. The fullest contemporary account of the initial Eleutherian adventure was given by Governor John Winthrop of Massachusetts; James K. Hosmer, ed., *Winthrop's Journal 'History of New England' 1630–1649*, 2 vols. (New York: Barnes and Noble, 1946), 2:351–53.

4. *Journal of the House of Commons*, August 21, 31, 1649; Lefroy, *Memorials of the Bermudas*, 2:10–11.

5. The descendants of John Bolles, one of the original signatories, in 1899 possessed a letter of attorney dated 1654, which claimed that a parliamentary act of 1650 had given all twenty-six original adventurers a joint proprietary right in the Bahamas. This was never substantiated. The proprietorship issue came to a head in 1665, when Nathanial Sayle failed in his claim that his father had enjoyed proprietary rights in the Bahamas by virtue of a commission under the Great Seal, and that he had been appointed his father's deputy and heir. Lefroy, *Memorials of the Bermudas*, 235–36; Miller, "Colonization of the Bahamas," 37–38; John T. Hassam, "The Bahama Islands: Notes on an Early Attempt at Colonization," *Proceedings of the Massachusetts Historical Society*, March 1899.

6. Wilkinson, *Adventurers of Bermuda*, 266–72.

7. Hosmer, *Winthrop's Journal*, 351–53.

8. Ibid., 352; Paul Albury, *The Story of the Bahamas* (London: Macmillan Caribbean, 1975), 42–43.

9. Hosmer, *Winthrop's Journal*, 352.

10. Ibid., 352–53; Lefroy, *Memorials of the Bermudas*, 2:9; *CSP*, vol. 5 (1661–68), 1110; Samuel E. Morison, "The Strange History of the Eleuthera Donation," *Harvard Alumni Bulletin*, June 1930; Miller, "Colonization of the Bahamas," 39–40.

11. Miller, "Colonization of the Bahamas," 40–41; Lefroy, *Memorials of the Bermudas*, 2:20, 84–89, 98, 108–10, 137, 235–36; *CSP*, vol. 1 (1574–1660), 453, 468; *CSP*, vol. 5 (1661–68), 1110; Wilkinson, *Adventurers of Bermuda*, 279. The form of the proposed voyage in 1658 is instructive. Thomas Sayle was ordered by William Sayle and the five merchant co-owners of the *William* to sail from his anchorage in the Thames to Bermuda, to augment his crew there with woodcutters and sealers, to scour the Bahamas for braziletto, seal oil, ambergris, and the produce of wrecks, and to sail on to Barbados, where the oil (needed in the sugar mills) would be sold to make up the return cargo for London with tobacco and sugar. Thomas Sayle was expected to make this voyage a second, third, or even fourth time, and was authorized to make side trips to Florida or Surinam if opportunities of profit presented themselves there. Lefroy, *Memorials of the Bermudas*, 108–10.

12. The very first member of these founding families of whom we have record is Peter Sands, who in 1665 testified that he had heard William Sayle read his commission "in the cave" in Eleuthera around 1648; Lefroy, *Memorials of the Bermudas*, 2:235–36. The claim to descent from the very earliest settlers depends

largely on family tradition. Though members of the Davis, Saunders, and Albury families from Eleuthera were among those who took refuge in Massachusetts after the Spanish attack in 1684, and scattered records exist for the subsequent forty years, the earliest authentic census for Eleuthera dates no earlier than 1730 (not 1671, as claimed by Bethell). Bethell, *Early Settlers*; Miller, "Early Colonization of the Bahamas," 43–44; Craton, *History of the Bahamas*, 66–67; Sandra Riley, *Homeward Bound: A History of the Bahama Islands to 1850, with a Definitive Study of Abaco in the American Loyalist Plantation Period* (Miami: Island Research, 1983), 241 n. 27.

13. For Neptuna Downham and the complex fortunes of Elizabeth Carter, see Lefroy, *Memorials of the Bermudas*, 2:133, 227, 374, 377, 379, 434, 453. For the fate of the 1656 slave rebels, see Wilkinson, *Adventurers of Bermuda*, 280; and Packwood, *Chained on the Rock*, 142–43.

14. For the Spanish attack of 1684, see Craton, *History of the Bahamas*, 70–71. The spread of settlements within Eleuthera remains an obscure subject, especially in relation to Spanish Wells. Local tradition claims this to have been one of the earliest settlements, if not the first. Yet the first definite surveys of Eleutheran settlements in the mid-eighteenth century do not even mention Spanish Wells or St. George's Cay. Most likely, it was then regarded as an outlier of the foremost, and earliest, permanent settlement, on Harbour Island. The later distinction and rivalry between Harbour Island and Spanish Wells really dates from Loyalist times.

15. The exact date of first settlement in New Providence remains uncertain. Lefroy retailed the story of William Sayle's discovery of a safe harbor there from the *Universal History*, 36:287, but this was attributed to the year 1667. Lefroy elsewhere quotes a brief description of the island dated 1668 which describes it as already well settled by Bermudians and named New Providence. A petition for aid made to Jamaica in 1672, signed by 25 inhabitants, said that they had settled New Providence from Eleuthera in 1666, numbered 250 by 1668, and 500 by 1672; Lefroy, *Memorials of the Bermudas*, 255, 265; *CSP*, vol. 7 (1669–74), 916. The documentation of the early settlement of the Bahamas was not simplified by the fact that the first editor of the *Calendar of State Papers*, Geoge Sainsbury, originally confused Old and New Providence islands—thus attributing the settlement of the Bahamas to the Providence Island Company, between 1630 and 1641.

16. *CSP*, vol. 7 (1669–74), 153.

17. Mark Catesby, *The Natural History of Carolina, Florida, and the Bahama Islands*, 2 vols. (London: Privately published, 1731–43), 2:51.

18. Ives, *Letters from Bermuda*, 74, 202, 245; Norman M. Isham, *Early American Houses* (New York: Da Capo Press, 1967).

19. Wills, "A" Copies, 1700–55, Bahamas Archives.

20. William R. Johnson, *Bahamian Sailing Craft* (Nassau: Explorations, 1974); Steve Dodge, *Abaco: The History of an Out Island and Its Cays* (Miami: Tropic Isle, 1983), 34–61.

21. John Oldmixon, *History of the Isle of Providence*, ed. Jack Culmer (London: Culmer, 1949), 10. Culmer's edition comprises the Bahamas section of Oldmixon's *The British Empire in America*, 2 vols. (London: Brotherton and Clarke, 1741).

22. Cyrus H. Kairaker, *The Hispaniola Treasure* (Philadelphia: University of Pennsylvania Press, 1934); Peter Earle, *The Wreck of the Almiranta* (London: Macmillan, 1979); *National Geographic* 126, no. 1 (January 1965): 1–37; 149, no. 6 (June 1976): 787–809; 161, no. 2 (February 1982): 229–43.

23. Lefroy, *Memorials of the Bermudas*, 2:112; Miller, "Colonization of the Bahamas," 41–42; Riley, *Homeward Bound*, 32–33, 237 n. 39.

24. Wilkinson, *Adventurers of Bermuda*, 372.

25. Ambergris in the early years was as good as money. In 1656 a vessel was commissioned to sail between Bermuda and the Bahamas on the payment of £20 in ready money and "15 lbs in Ambergreece of the best sorte at 25s p ounce." As late as 1670, John Darrell sent back four pounds of ambergris from the Bahamas to Bermuda, where it realized £4 an ounce, or £256. Lefroy, *Memorials of the Bermudas*, 2:86, 108; Wilkinson, *Adventurers of Bermuda*, 50–52, 57–62, 280, 337.

26. Campbell, *The Ephemeral Islands*, 34–36.

27. Ibid., 37–43; Catesby, *Natural History*.

28. Campbell, *Ephemeral Islands*, 28–34; Wilkinson, *Adventurers of Bermuda*, 328–31, 337–39.

29. Lefroy, *Memorials of the Bermudas*, 2:108, 169–70.

30. Ibid., 465–66; Wilkinson, *Adventurers of Bermuda*, 317, 339.

31. Egerton MSS, 2395, British Museum.

Chapter 7

1. Culmer's edition, entitled *History of the Isle of Providence*, is a reprint of the Bahamas section of Oldmixon's *The British Empire in America*. For the Carolina Proprietors in general, see Andrews, *Colonial Period*, 2:199–240; M. Eugene Sirmans, *Colonial South Carolina: A Political History, 1663–1763* (Chapel Hill: University of North Carolina Press, 1966); Robert M. Weir, *Colonial South Carolina: A History* (Millwood, N.Y.: KTO, 1983).

2. *CSP*, vol. 7 (1669–74), 153, February 17, 1670.

3. Ibid., 434, March 4, 1671; 1388, November 20, 1674; 86, July 27, 1670.

4. Ibid., 308, October 29, 1670.

5. Ibid., 312, November 1, 1670.

6. Ibid., 311, November 1, 1670.

7. *CSP*, vol. 9 (1675–76), 384, July 11, 1670.

8. *CSP*, vol. 7 (1669–74), 509, 510, April 24, 1671.

9. Ibid., 510, April 24, 1671.

10. *CSP*, vol. 9 (1675–76), 561, May 17, 1675.

11. *CSP*, vol. 7 (1669–74), 916, August 23, 1672.

12. Commission and Instructions to Charles Chillingworth, *CSP*, vol. 9 (1675–76), 970–71, July 1, 1676; Oldmixon, *History of Providence*, 12–13.

13. *CSP*, vol. 11 (1681–85), 769, November 6, 1682; 948, February 17, 1683; 963, February 22, 1683 (also nos. 552, 627, 668, 673, 712, 895, 912, 948, 1303).

14. Ibid., 1590(i), March 15, 1684; 1924, November 7, 1684; 1927, November 7, 1684.

15. Ibid., 1942, November 17, 1684; Oldmixon, *History of Providence*, 13.

16. Petition of Nicholas Davis, Nathanial Saunders, John Albury, and Daniel Saunders to Governor Edmund Andros of Massachusetts, September 15, 1686, and Petition of Jeremiah Dunmer and others to Andros, January 6, 1687, Usurpation vol. 126, no. 387, Massachusetts Historical Society, 3d ser., 7:158–68, Massachusetts Archives, quoted in Stark, *History and Guide*, 143–44.

17. *CSP*, vol. 12 (1685–88), 1128, February 11, 1687; 1449(i), August 23, 1687; 1831–32 (Commission and Instructions to Thomas Bridges), July 12, 1688; 1835, July 16, 1888.

18. Kairaker, *Hispaniola Treasure*; Earle, *Almiranta*; Dumas Malone, ed., *Dictionary of American Biography*, 20 vols. (New York, Scribner's, 1943), 14:551–52.

19. *CSP*, vol. 12 (1685–88), 1772, June 1, 1688.

20. Nicholas Trott, Sr. (1658–c. 1730) was a Bermudian merchant and sea captain, related to one of William Sayle's chief trading partners and, like Sayle, engaged in the West Indian trade with England. He was chiefly known for an acrimonious commercial dispute with Governor Isaac Richier. In 1698, after he left the Bahamas, he married the daughter of Thomas Amy, the Proprietors' chief agent in Nassau, who himself became one of the Carolina Proprietors and passed on his rights to his enterprising son-in-law. Trott is, however, not to be confused with his distinguished nephew, Nicholas Trott, Jr. (1663–1740), attorney general of Bermuda in 1696, who became, successively, attorney general, Speaker, and chief justice of South Carolina. Henry C. Wilkinson, *Bermuda in the Old Empire: A History of the Island, 1684–1784* (Oxford: Oxford University Press, 1950), 37–40, 79–83. Paul Albury, *The Paradise Island Story* (London: Macmillan Caribbean, 1984), 15–22; *Dictionary of American Biography*, 14:551–52.

21. George Chalmers, *The Bahama Islands: Account of Them from Their Settlement to 1728* (London: Hansard, 1803); Craton, *History of the Bahamas*, 79–82.

22. Albury, *The Paradise Island Story*, 21–22.

23. John Oldmixon, *History of Providence*, 18.

24. Ibid., 20

25. Ibid., 21.

26. Ibid.

27. Michael Craton, "Indispensable Agents of Empire: The Caribbean Vice Admiralty Courts, 1713–1815" (Ph.D. diss., McMaster University, 1968); Andrews, *Colonial Period*, 4:222–318.

28. C.O. 23/12, 76; John Graves, *A Memorial or Short Account of the Bahama Islands* (London, 1708); Craton, *History of the Bahamas*, 94.

Chapter 8

1. The literature on piracy is huge, but not much of it is of scholarly quality or value. However, the following are useful to very good: Charles Johnson [Daniel Defoe], *A General History of the Pyrates* (London: N.p., 1724); Shirley C. Hughson, *The Carolina Pirates and Colonial Commerce, 1670–1740* (Baltimore: Johns Hopkins University Press, 1984); Don Carlos Seitz, *Under the Black Flag* (New York: Dial Press, 1925); H. C. Christie, *Blackbeard: A Romance of the Bahamas* (London: Press Printers, 1930); Philip Gosse, *The History of Piracy* (New York: Longman's Green, 1932); George Woodbury, *The Great Days of Piracy in the West Indies* (London: Elek, 1951); Patrick Pringle, *Jolly Roger* (New York: Morrow, 1953); P. K. Kemp and Christopher Lloyd, *Brethren of the Coast: Buccaneers of the South Seas* (New York: St. Martin's Press, 1960); Neville Williams, *Captains Outrageous: Seven Centuries of Piracy* (London: Macmillan, 1961); Stanley Richards, *Black Bart* (Llandybie, Wales: Davies, 1966); Hugh Rankin, *The Golden Age of Piracy* (New York: Holt, Rinehart and Winston, 1969); James G. Lydon, *Pirates, Privateers, and Profits* (Upper Saddle River, N.J.: Gregg Press, 1970); B. Richard Burg, "Legitimacy and Authority: A Case Study of Pirate Commanders in the Seventeenth and Eighteenth Centuries," *American Neptune* 37 (1977): 40–49; Marcus Rediker, *Between the Devil and the Deep Blue Sea: Merchant Seamen, Pirates, and the Anti-American Maritime World, 1700–1750* (Cambridge: Cambridge University Press, 1987).

2. C.O. 23/12, 26.

3. Craton, *History of the Bahamas*, 80–82.

4. Eric Hobsbawm, *Bandits* (London: Weidenfeld and Nicolson, 1969).

5. C.O. 23/12, 57; *CSP*, vol. 18 (1700), 211, 250, March 11, 25, 1700; 61, January 29, 1700.

6. Craton, *History of the Bahamas*, 84.

7. Ibid., 84–87, Cole to Council of Trade, *CSP*, vol. 20 (1702), 120, February 17, 1702, pp. 81–86.

8. Craton, *History of the Bahamas*, 87; Oldmixon, *History of Providence*, 21.

9. Graves, *Memorial of the Bahama Islands*, 48.

10. Rediker, *Deep Blue Sea*, 281–82.

11. Ibid., 256–68.

12. B. Richard Burg, *Sodomy and the Perception of Evil: English Sea Rovers in the Seventeenth Century* (New York: New York University Press, 1983); Michele Landsberg, "Let's Face It: A Jock's a Jerk with Money," *Toronto Star*, Friday, July 13, 1990, B1.

13. Rediker, *Deep Blue Sea*, 264–65.

14. Ibid., 273–75; *The Tryals of Major Stede Bonnet and Other Pirates* (London: N.p., 1719), 2–4, 34.

15. Rediker, *Deep Blue Sea*, 276–81.

16. Ibid., 275–76; *CSP*, vol. 31 (1719), 31, January 29, 1719.

17. Riley, *Homeward Bound*, 55–57.

18. *CSP*, vol. 27 (1712–14), 651, April 22, 1714; vol. 28 (1714–15), 276, March 14, 1715.

19. Governor Spotswood to Council of Trade, *CSP*, vol. 29 (1716–17), 240, July 3, 1716.

20. Above, chap. 6, pp. 83–84.

21. *Tryals of Bonnet*; Rediker, *Deep Blue Sea*, 273–74; Riley, *Homeward Bound*, 74–75, 240 n. 20.

22. Christopher Hill, *The World Turned Upside Down: Radical Ideas in the English Revolution* (London: Temple Smith, 1972); Jesse Lemisch, "Jack Tar in the Streets: Merchant Seamen in the Politics of Revolutionary America," *William and Mary Quarterly*, 3d ser., 25 (July 1968): 371–407, and "The American Revolution Seen from the Bottom Up," in *Towards a New Past: Dissenting Essays in American History*, ed. Barton Bernstein (New York: Pantheon, 1968), 3–45; Eric Hobsbawm, *Bandits*, and *Primitive Rebels: Studies in Archaic Forms of Social Movement in the Nineteenth Century* (New York: Praeger, 1963).

Chapter 9

1. Rogers to Council of Trade, *CSP*, vol. 30 (1717–18), 737, October 31, 1718; Bryan Little, *Crusoe's Captain: Being the Life of Woodes Rogers, Seaman, Trader, Colonial Governor* (London: Odhams, 1960), 182–223; Craton, *History of the Bahamas*, 93–101.

2. *CSP*, vol. 30 (1717–18), 737, pp. 372–81, C.O. 23/1, 10.

3. *CSP*, vol. 30 (1717–18), 737, p. 373.

4. Rogers to Craggs, *CSP*, vol. 30 (1717–18), 807, p. 376, December 24, 1718; Roger to Craggs, *CSP*, vol. 31 (1719–20), 33, January 30, 1719; C.O. 23/28, 76–82; Johnson [Defoe], *History of the Pyrates*, 144–47, 620–41; Riley, *Homeward Bound*, 72–76.

5. *CSP*, vol. 30 (1717–18), 807.

6. Rogers to Council of Trade, *CSP*, vol. 31 (1719–20), 209, May 29, 1719.

7. *CSP*, vol. 32 (1720–21), 47, April 20, 1720.

8. Ibid., 390, February 25, 1721, C.O. 23/1, 35; Little, *Crusoe's Captain*, 193–96; Craton, *History of the Bahamas*, 100–101.

9. For the generally underrated regime of Governor Phenney, see C.O. 23/1–2, 12–13. From Phenney's time on, until newspapers begin in the 1780s, the series of Governors' Correspondence becomes the main and indispensable source for Bahamian history, particularly since the *Calendar of State Papers* has not been carried beyond 1737.

10. C.O. 23/1–2; *CSP*, vols. 32–36 (1720–29).

11. C.O. 23/1, 54 iii.

12. C.O. 23/2, Woodes Rogers to Lords Commissioner of Trade and Plantations, October 14, 1731; *CSP*, vol. 38 (1731), p. 298.

13. "List of Christenings, Marriages and Burials, 1721–1726," November 13, 1726, C.O. 23/13, 267–70.

14. C.O. 23/14, 60–70, April 20, 1727. For slave demography in general, see Robert W. Fogel and Stanley L. Engerman, *Time on the Cross: The Economics of American Negro Slavery*, 2 vols. (Boston: Little, Brown, 1974); Barry W. Higman, *Slave Population and Economy in Jamaica, 1807–1834* (Cambridge: Cambridge University Press, 1976), and *Slave Populations of the British Caribbean, 1807–1834* (Baltimore: Johns Hopkins University Press, 1984); Michael Craton, *Searching for the Invisible Man: Slaves and Plantation Life in Jamaica* (Cambridge, Mass.: Harvard University Press, 1978).

15. Higman, *Slave Populations of the British Caribbean*, 31, 40–41, 120–23, 136, 300–302, 307, 355–56, 365–68, 376, etc.; D. Gail Saunders, "The Slave Population of the Bahamas, 1783–1834" (M. Phil. thesis, University of the West Indies, 1978).

16. Census of December 25, 1734, in Fitzwilliam to L.C.T.P., March 11, 1735, C.O. 23/3, 129–32.

17. Kenneth F. Kiple, *The Caribbean Slave: A Biological History* (Cambridge: Cambridge University Press, 1984).

18. Census of 1740–41.

19. *CSP*, vol. 33 (1722–23), 284, September 14, 1722.

20. For example, *CSP*, vol. 31 (1719–20), 523, Governor and Council to C.T.P., January 15, 1720, C.O. 23/1, 22; *CSP*, vol. 32 (1720–21), 758, Phenney to C.T.P., December 26, 1721, C.O. 23/1, 42; *CSP*, vol. 33 (1722–23), 45, 284, 612, 801; vol. 34 (1724–25), 2.

21. "List of Christenings, Marriages and Burials, 1721–1726," C.O. 23/13, 267–70; Riley, *Homeward Bound*, 79–80, 240 n. 1.

22. *CSP*, vol. 33 (1722–23), 368, December 3, 1722, C.O. 23/12, 81.

23. C.O. 23/12, 81.

24. C.O. 32/13, 93–104.

25. *CSP*, vol. 34 (1724–25), 449; C.O. 23/12, 86.

26. *Calendar of Treasury Books and Papers*, vol. 1 (1729–30), 57, 65, 260, 276, 282; C. F. Pascoe, *Two Hundred Years of the S.P.G.: An Historical Account of the Society for the Propagation of the Gospel in Foreign Parts* (London: S.P.G., 1901), 216–17; Little, *Crusoe's Captain*, 209.

27. Minutes of the Governor in Council, July 28, 1723, Bahamas Archives.

28. Negroes Imported into the Bahamas, 1718–26, *CSP*, vol. 35 (1726–27), 515, April 20, 1727; Council Minutes, May 2, 1723, 284–85.

29. Act of 27 Geo III, c. 43. See below, chap. 10, pp. 151–52.

30. "Further Regulations Concerning the Negroes and Slaves," Council Minutes, vol. 1 (1723–29), 74, February 7, 1726.

31. C.O. 23/13, 267–70.

32. *CSP*, vol. 36 (1728–29), 358, 460; C.O. 23/2, 152, and 23/12, 97–101, October 1, 1728.

33. The Reverend Guy had been recruited by Woodes Rogers when he went to

Charleston, South Carolina, to recover from a bout of fever in 1731; *CSP*, vol. 38 (1731), 83; Pascoe, *Two Hundred Years*, 216–17.

34. Wills of William Thompson and Mary Thompson, Wills, 1758–66, 4–8, 15–18, Bahamas Archives; John Graves (1718 and 1721), Wills, Copies, 1700–1750, Wills "A" copy, 1700–1755.

35. Wills, 1758–66, n.p.

36. Wills "A" Copy, 1700–1755, 55–58.

37. *CSP*, vol. 33 (1722–23), 801, December 24, 1723; C.O. 23/1, 54.

38. *CSP*, vol. 36 (1728–29), 358, 371, 373; C.O. 23/2, 148–70; *CSP*, vol. 37 (1730), 480; C.O. 23/14, 137–42; Little, *Crusoe's Captain*, 205–6; Craton, *History of the Bahamas*, 104–5; Riley, *Homeward Bound*, 83.

39. Little, *Crusoe's Captain*, 209–23; Craton, *History of the Bahamas*, 105–11.

40. Woodes Rogers to Board of Trade and Plantations, *CSP*, vol. 36 (1728–29), November 12, 1729; C.O. 23/2, 210–12.

41. List of Laws passed, C.O. 23/2, 210–12.

42. Act for Quit Rents and Surveys, 2 Geo II (1729), Manuscript Laws, 1729–92, n.p., Bahamas Archives.

43. 2 Geo II (1729), ibid.

Chapter 10

1. February 10, 1730, C.O. 23/3, 113–15.

2. C.O. 23/3, 112.

3. March 11, 1735, C.O. 23/3, 128–33.

4. C.O. 23/3, 242, 244; "The Case of the Inhabitants of the Bahamas Islands," C.O. 23/3, 277–81.

5. C.O. 23/3, 123; Michael Craton, James Walvin, and David Wright, *Slavery, Abolition, and Emancipation: Black Slaves and the British Empire, A Thematic Documentary* (London: Longman, 1976), 175–80; Michael Craton, *Testing the Chains: Resistance to Slavery in the British West Indies* (Ithaca, N.Y.: Cornell University Press, 1982), 137–38.

6. February 25, 1735, C.O. 23/3, 173–74; Oldmixon, *History of Providence*, 28–30.

7. C.O. 23/3, 170–72.

8. C.O. 23/3, 174.

9. Craton, *History of the Bahamas*, 123.

10. Bruce, *Bahamian Interlude*.

11. Ibid., 49.

12. Ibid., 50.

13. Ibid., 47.

14. Craton, "Indispensable Agents of Empire," 151–88.

15. Bruce, *Bahamian Interlude*, 32.

16. Ibid., 33.

17. Ibid., 35.

18. Ibid.

19. C.O. 23/5, 125.

20. C.O. 23/5, 95–98.

21. C.O. 23/5, 39, 95–98.

22. Manuscript Laws, 1729–92, 17–26, Bahamas Archives.

23. Will and Inventory, Wills (Copies) 1700–1750, 120–28, Bahamas Archives.

24. Wills "A," 1700–1755, 75–76.

25. Ibid., 80–82.

26. 3 Geo III (1763), Manuscript Laws, 1729–82, 48–50.

27. 19 Geo II (1748), November 2, 1748, C.O. 23/5, 141.

28. 27 Geo II, c. 43 (1756), Manuscript Laws, 1729–92, 43.

29. 7 Geo III, January 4, 1767, Manuscript Laws, 1729–92, 57–60.

30. They were not necessarily executed if found guilty; the tribunal could order "such other punishment as in their judgment they shall think meet." Executions were to be immediate and public, and carried out by a specially commissioned "Negro Man Slave," but the form of death was not specified. Hanging is presumed. There were not the horrific provisions for death by slow fire, mutilation, or the gibbet, or even the noncommittal "by hanging or any other method" found in the slave codes of some other islands. Sir Fortunatus Dwarris, *The Substance of Three Reports into the Administration of Civil and Criminal Law in the West Indies* (London: Butterworth, 1827).

31. Theoretically, whites too could be whipped, being liable to sixty stripes if they could not pay the fine of sixty pounds. It is extremely unlikely, though, that this punishment was ever actually exacted, particularly since it would have been administered by the public hangman, a black slave.

32. Magnus Mörner, ed., *Race and Class in Latin America* (New York: Columbia University Press, 1970); David Lowenthal, *West Indian Societies* (Oxford: Oxford University Press, 1972); Harry Hoetink, *Slavery and Race Relations in the Americas* (New York: Harper and Row, 1973).

Chapter 11

1. Votes of the House of Assembly, 1748. The Blue Hills are the low ridges in the center of New Providence due south of Nassau. They, and the road leading to them, were not, as is sometimes said, named after Isaac Baillou, a much later settler.

2. October 27, 1755, C.O. 23/6, 71–72.

3. May 15, 1753, C.O. 23/5, 282–83.

4. April 14, 1752, C.O. 23/5, 65–66.

5. April 20, 1754, C.O. 23/6, 38–40.

6. Petition of twenty-three New Providence merchants to Governor William Shirley, October 1760, C.O. 23/7, 51–53.

7. Craton, *History of the Bahamas*, 132–33.

8. October 3, 1764, C.O. 23/7, 166–67.

9. November 5, 1766, C.O. 23/7, 226.

10. Craton, *History of the Bahamas*, 135; Symmer to Board of Trade and Plantations, August 3, 1767, C.O. 23/7, 275; Governor Thomas Shirley to B.T.P., December 9, 1768, C.O. 23/8, 3–5.

11. December 9, 1768, C.O. 23/8, 3–5.

12. C.O. 23/22, 59–72.

13. Ibid.

14. C.O. 23/8, 21-22.

15. C.O. 23/8, 153; October 21, 1770, C.O. 23/8, 132.

16. Craton, *History of the Bahamas*, 137; October 2 and 11, 1770, C.O. 23/8, 102, 108.

17. Craton, *History of the Bahamas*, 138–39.

18. October 10, 1771, C.O. 23/21, 2–11; February 11, 1773, C.O. 23/9, 53; C.O. 23/22, 18.

19. Governor Thomas Shirley to Lord Dartmouth, November 28, 1773, C.O. 23/22, 57–58.

20. November 1773, C.O. 23/22, 59–72.

21. Lydia Austin Parrish, "Records of Some Southern Loyalists: Being a Collection of Manuscripts About Some Eighty Families, Most of Whom Immigrated to the Bahamas During and After the American Revolution" (Typescript, Widener Library, Harvard University), 179.

22. For the American invasion of 1776, see Gardner W. Allen, *A Naval History of the American Revolution*, 2 vols. (New York: Russell and Russell, 1962), 1:100–120; Craton, *History of the Bahamas*, 140–42; Riley, *Homeward Bound*, 99–103.

23. Craton, *History of the Bahamas*, 142; Riley, *Homeward Bound*, 103; Albury, *Story of the Bahamas*, 99; Fulham Papers, Society for the Preservation of the Gospel [hereinafter abbreviated SPG], 1767–1822, Lambeth Palace Library, London.

24. Michael Craton, "Hopetown and Hard Bargain: The Loyalist Transformation in the Bahamas," in *Settlements in the Americas: Cross-Cultural Perspectives*, ed. Ralph Bennet (Newark: University of Delaware Press, 1991); and *History of the Bahamas*, 143–44; "The Spaniard Who Won and Lost the Bahamas," *Bahamas Handbook*, 1971–72, 16–25.

25. Mary Moseley, in her *Bahamas Handbook*, 72, retails the story that the land was granted as a reward for the Deveaux exploit. Yet a formal grant was not obtained until after a petition was made by certain Harbour Islanders in 1840, when the petitioners claimed that they had in fact been working the land for more than a hundred years as customary commonage. Michael Craton, "White Law and Black Custom: The Evolution of Bahamian Land Tenures," in *Land and Development in the Caribbean*, ed. Jean Besson and Janet Momsen (London: Macmillan, 1987), 12–13.

26. "The Colonel from Carolina: Andrew Deveaux, Rascal and Redeemer,"

Bahamas Handbook, 1977–78, 14–31; Craton, *History of the Bahamas*, 146–47; Riley, *Homeward Bound*, 131–34; Albury, *Story of the Bahamas*, 104–8; Wilbur H. Siebert, *Loyalists in East Florida, 1774–1785: The Most Important Documents Pertaining Thereto*, 2 vols. (1929; reprint, Boston: Gregg, 1972), 2:146; Catherine S. Crary, *The Price of Loyalty: Tory Writings from the Revolutionary Era* (New York: McGraw Hill, 1973), 354–56; C.O. 23/26, 42–43.

27. *Bahamas Handbook, 1971–72*, 24.

28. *Bahamas Handbook, 1977–78*, 25.

29. Johann David Schoepf, *Travels in the Confederation, 1783–1784* (Philadelphia: Campbell, 1911).

30. Hunt to SPG, 1770, SPG Papers, reel 1, Bahamas Archives.

31. Ibid., 1771.

32. Ibid., 1780.

33. He may have stayed on as an unlicensed preacher until his death at the age of sixty-seven, in 1784. A former Wesleyan, Moss may therefore have been responsible for the establishment of Methodism at Harbour Island and its later dominance over Anglicanism there.

34. April 11, 1769, SPG Papers, reel 1.

35. Moss to SPG, May 30, 1771, SPG Papers, reel 1.

Chapter 12

1. For the Loyalists in general, see Lorenzo Sabine, *The American Loyalists; or, Biographical Sketches of Adherents to the British Crown in the War of the Revolution*, 2 vols. (Boston: Little and Brown, 1847); Wallace Brown, *The Good Americans: The Loyalists in the American Revolution* (New York: Morrow, 1969); Mary Beth Norton, *The British-Americans: The Loyalist Exiles in England, 1774–1789* (Boston: Little, Brown, 1972); Robert McCluer Calhoon, *The Loyalists in Revolutionary America, 1760–1781* (New York: Harcourt Brace Jovanovich, 1973); Ellen Gibson Wilson, *The Loyal Blacks* (New York: Putnam, 1976); James St. G. Walker, *The Black Loyalists: The Search for a Promised Land in Nova Scotia and Sierra Leone, 1783–1870* (Halifax, Nova Scotia: Dalhousie University Press, 1976). Unfortunately, there is not yet a general study of the Loyalist migration to the West Indies at large. For the Bahamas, see Crary, *The Price of Loyalty*; Thelma P. Peters, "The American Loyalists and the Plantation Period in the Bahama Islands" (Ph.D. diss., University of Florida, 1960); Parrish, "Records of Loyalists"; Riley, *Homeward Bound*; Gail Saunders, *Bahamian Loyalists and Their Slaves* (London: Macmillan Caribbean, 1983); Siebert, *Loyalists in East Florida*, vol. 1; *The Loyalist Bi-Centennial*, Handbook of Archives Exhibition, Department of Archives, Nassau, February 1983.

The population changes brought about by the Loyalist migration are difficult to assess with complete accuracy because of inefficient censuses and constant re-migration. But see the accompanying table, based upon C.O. 23/22, 59–72 (1773); William Wylly, *A Short Account of the Bahama Islands: Their Climate, Productions,*

&c, to Which Are Added Some Strictures upon Their Relative and Political Situation, the Defects of Their Present Government &c. (London: N.p., 1789), 7; C.O. 23/48, 144; C.O. 23/59, 37 (1807). See also C.O. 23/30, 334 (1790).

The islands permanently settled before 1783 were New Providence, Harbour Island, and Eleuthera (including almost certainly Spanish Wells and Current Island), though there had been some intermittent settlement in Cat Island and Exuma. Besides permanently settling in the last two of these, Loyalists before 1800 also opened up Abaco (and its cays), Andros, Long Island, San Salvador, Rum Cay, Crooked Island (including Long Cay) and Acklin's in the Bahamas proper, and added settlements on Salt Cay and in the Caicos Islands to that long established on Grand Turk. Grand Bahama, Bimini, the Berry Islands, Ragged Island, Mayaguana, and Inagua were almost certainly not settled until the nineteenth century, and very thinly then.

2. Maxwell to Sydney, May 12, 1784, C.O. 23/26, 103–4.

3. Memorandum to Carleton, June 25, 1783, Carleton Papers, no. 8227; New York Public Library, *New York Royal Gazette*, June 28, July 5, 1783; "The Loyalist Bi-Centennial," 8–9.

4. Ibid., September 13, October 25, 1783; Riley, *Homeward Bound*, 141, 145.

5. An analysis of the ninety-seven white family heads settling in Abaco whose origins are known shows that thirty-seven were originally from New York, twelve each from South Carolina and Georgia, nine from East Florida, six from West Florida, four from Maryland and Massachusetts, three each from Virginia, Pennsylvania and Scotland, two from England, and one each from New Jersey and Ireland. Of fifty-six who sailed from New York to Abaco, thirty-seven were originally from New York, fifteen had resided in another colony, and four in two others. Of thirty-six sailing from East Florida to Abaco, only nine were originally from that colony; seventeen had come from one other colony, and ten from two others, typically from South Carolina by way of Georgia. Riley, *Homeward Bound*, appendix E, 270–74.

6. Carleton Papers, no. 10,427, vol. 83, no. 2; Riley, *Homeward Bound*, appendix D, 266–69.

7. Of this category, eighteen Negroes were said to have originated from South Carolina, fourteen from Virginia, four each from Georgia, Maryland, and New Jersey, three from New York, two from Pennsylvania, and one each from East Florida, Massachusetts, Rhode Island, and Jamaica. Of those said to have been born free or to have obtained their freedom, eight were from New York and one each from Connecticut, Bermuda, Barbados, Jamaica, and Haiti. Riley, *Homeward Bound*, appendix D, 266–69.

8. Riley, *Homeward Bound*, 139–40, 248 n. 17.

9. Carleton Papers, no. 9266; Craton, *History of the Bahamas*, 149; Riley, *Homeward Bound*, 143–44.

10. Report, 1784, 8, Wilson Papers, Boston Public Library; C.O. 23/26, 26–28; "Loyalist Bi-Centennial," 11.

11. Report, 1784, 8–9, Wilson Papers.

12. An analysis of seventy Loyalist whites who originally settled in Abaco and whose subsequent histories are known shows that only five stayed and died in Abaco. For twenty the next destination was Nassau, with nineteen going to the Caicos Islands, eleven to Long Island, three each to Cat Island and England, two each to Exuma and Rum Cay, and one each to Harbour Island, Eleuthera, Crooked Island, West Florida, and South Carolina. Most of these migrated at least once again. Ten settled or eventually died in Nassau, six in Long Island, five in Georgia, two in St. Vincent, and one each in Cat Island, San Salvador, Crooked Island, Ragged Island, Inagua, and England. Riley, *Homeward Bound*, appendix E, 270–74.

13. N.d. [1784], C.O. 23/25, 197.

14. June 30, 1786, C.O. 23/26, 225.

15. Order-in-Council, December 8, 1787, C.O. 23/28, 3.

16. Dunmore to Shelburne, December 28, 1787, C.O. 23/27, 75.

17. Wylly, *Short Account*, 7.

18. In 1788, William Wylly stated that there were 49 white family heads and 198 "New Slaves" in Abaco (a total of perhaps 450 persons). In 1822 there were said to be 217 slaves in Abaco, and in 1834, 361 slaves and 61 free coloreds against 499 whites. The interim figures given in 1807 of only 15 slaves and 2 free coloreds against 250 whites was almost certainly a gross misstatement. Wylly, *Short Account*, 7; Register of Returns of Slaves, 1822–34, Bahamas Archives; *Blue Book, 1834*; C.O. 23/48, 144; C.O. 23/59, 37.

19. Wylly, *Short Account*, 7 (3,762); C.O. 23/29, 172–77 (5700).

20. C.O. 23/26, 26–28, 204–5.

21. C.O. 23/26, 161–64.

22. Maxwell to North, November 21, 1783, C.O. 23/25, 64.

23. Maxwell to Shelburne, June 4, 1784, C.O. 23/25, 108; C.O. 23/26, 209.

24. C.O. 23/25, 99; Manuscript Laws, 1729–92, 109–13, 121–23.

25. Manuscript Laws, 1729–92, 115–17.

26. Craton, *History of the Bahamas*, 156–57.

27. Proclamation of Lieutenant Governor Powell, *Bahama Gazette*, September 10, 1785; "The Loyalist Bi-Centennial," 12.

28. Manuscript Laws, 1729–92, 1:27–28, 181–83.

29. Bethell, *Early Settlers*, 46–50; Craton, *History of the Bahamas*, 151.

30. Wylly, *Short Account*, 7.

31. *Bahama Gazette*, March 14, April 11, 1789, June 15, 1790; Edwards, *History of the West Indies*, vol. 5, appendix 38; Saunders, *Slavery in the Bahamas*, 23–27; Craton, *History of the Bahamas*, 156.

32. Daniel McKinnen, *A Tour Through the British West Indies in the Years 1802 and 1803, Giving a Particular Account of the Bahama Islands* (London: J. White, 1804), 213.

33. Wylly, *Short Account*, 7; Maxwell to Shelburne, June 29, 1784, C.O. 23/25, 243–76; Manuscript Laws, 1729–92, 131–36.

34. Manuscript Laws, 1729–92, 165–71.

35. Dunmore to Grenville, August 31, 1789, C.O. 23/29, 168; Manuscript Laws, 1729–92, 172–77.

36. Nassau, Department of Lands and Surveys, Plan of Nassau and Its Environs, 1788; "The Loyalist Bi-Centennial," 52.

37. Wylly, *Short Account*, C.O. 23/28, 191–213.

Chapter 13

1. May 29, 1784, C.O. 23/26, 204–5; Wylly, *Short Account*, 4.

2. Saunders, *Slavery in the Bahamas*, 44 n. 44.

3. Riley, *Homeward Bound*, 254 nn. 23, 44.

4. *CSP*, vol. 7 (1669–74), 153; Original grant to Duncan Taylor, Nassau, Department of Lands and Surveys, Book KP 91, 1805; *Loyalist Bi-Centennial*, 41.

5. June 29, 1781, C.O. 23/25, 34; December 31, 1803, 43 Geo III, *The Salt Industry of the Bahamas* (Nassau: Department of Archives, 1980), 10. For a typical joint grant (Rose Island, to fifteen New Providence merchants and planters, including James Moss, William Wylly, and John Anderson, 1806), see *Salt Industry*, 20.

6. *Journal of the House of Assembly*, December 21, 1802, *Salt Industry*, 8.

7. Dunmore to Shelburne, November 28, 1787, C.O. 23/27, 75. Also C.O. 23/26, 225.

8. Dunmore to Shelburne, October 20, 1787, C.O. 23/27, 92–93.

9. Proclamation, C.O. 23/27, 78; Order-in-Council, November 8, 1787, C.O. 23/28, 3. For typical Negro appeals, C.O. 23/27, 46–47, C.O. 23/29, 282; Wylly, *Short Account*, 21.

10. Dunmore to Shelburne, April 8, 1788, C.O. 23/27, 122, 159.

11. Wylly, *Short Account*, C.O. 23/29, 191–213.

12. Craton, *History of the Bahamas*, 158–59; Riley, *Homeward Bound*, 169–88. The local belief that Lord Dunmore built both the Priory on West Street and Buena Vista in Delancey Town appears unfounded; Grant to Lord Dunmore, April 8, 1793, C.O. 23/33.

13. Harcourt Malcom, *Historical Memoranda Relating to the Forts in Nassau* (Nassau: Privately published, 1913).

14. Craton, *History of the Bahamas*, 160.

15. Manuscript Acts, 1794–97, 78–341, Bahamas Archives.

16. Ibid., 101.

17. Answers to Questions 11, 13, 15, Additional Question 1, July 30, 1788, C.O. 23/28, 31–34, later published in *British Sessional Papers, Accounts and Papers, 1789, Part III*.

18. Answers to Questions 1–4, C.O. 23/28, 31–34.

19. Answers to Questions 5–7, 8, 12, 13, 17, C.O. 23/28, 31–34.

20. For the Haitian revolution, see C. L. R. James, *The Black Jacobins: Toussaint L'Ouverture and the San Domingo Revolution*, rev. ed. (London: Alison and Busby,

1980); Eugene D. Genovese, *From Rebellion to Revolution: Afro-American Slave Revolts in the Making of the Modern World* (Baton Rouge: Louisiana State University Press, 1979); Jean Fouchard, *The Haitian Maroons: Liberty or Death* (New York: Blyden Press, 1981); David Geggus, *Slavery, War, and Revolution: The British Occupation of Saint Domingue, 1793–8* (Oxford: Oxford University Press, 1981); Robin Blackburn, *The Overthrow of Colonial Slavery, 1776–1848* (London: Verso, 1988).

21. Minutes of Assembly, 1789, C:O. 23/30, 16–18.

22. Dunmore to Dundas, April 11, 1792, C.O. 23/31, 109.

23. 1793, C.O. 23/32, 261–63.

24. Dunmore to Dundas, July 1793, C.O. 23/32, 124.

25. Petition to Dundas, May 9, 1795, C.O. 23/34, 48. Also, Settlers of Crooked Island, 1799, C.O. 23/39, 40.

26. Dundas to Portland, May 10, 1795, C.O. 23/34, 45.

27. The proportion was one white male aged sixteen to sixty per thirty slaves; Manuscript Laws, 1794–97, 310.

28. Consolidated Slave Law, 1797, clauses 1, 4, 13, Manuscript Laws, 1794–97, 265–80.

29. Ibid., clauses 6–10.

30. Ibid., clauses 11, 12, 2, 3, 5, 14.

31. Ibid., clauses 31, 30, 33.

32. Ibid., clauses 16, 23–25.

33. Ibid., clauses 15, 17, 18, 20, 22, 28.

34. Ibid., clauses 26, 27, 29.

35. Ibid., clauses 17, 19, 21, 28, 32.

36. Forbes to Portland, 1797, C.O. 23/35, 97–99.

37. Hunt to Portland, November 7, 1797, enclosing deposition of Montell before the council, C.O. 23/36, 104–10.

38. Hunt to Portland, September 7, 1797, C.O. 23/36, 117–18.

Chapter 14

1. McKinnen, *Tour*, 112–272. See also C.O. 23/44, 6–9 (1802).

2. Edwards, *History of the West Indies*, 5th ed., 5 vols. (London: Whittaker, 1818–19), vol. 5, appendix A.

3. Craton, *History of the Bahamas*, 167.

4. Gail Saunders and Donald Cartwright, *Historic Nassau* (London: Macmillan Caribbean, 1979), 26.

5. Ibid., 19.

6. See Epilogue, below.

7. Roger Buckley, *Slaves in Redcoats: The British West India Regiments, 1795–1815* (New Haven, Conn.: Yale University Press, 1979).

8. Hunt to Portland, May 9, 1801, C.O. 23/39, 133–34; Petition of Nassauvians, May 18, 1801, C.O. 23/40, 118; Downing Street to Nassau, August 10, 1801, C.O. 23/40, 30; Halkett to Hobart, April 20, 24, 1803, C.O. 23/43, 145, 147.

9. Halkett to Hobart, November 7, 1803, C.O. 23/44, 100.

10. Dundas to Cameron, July 23, 1806, C.O. 23/50, 14.

11. C.O. 23/50, 124–25.

12. C.O. 23/50, 139; Downing Street to Cameron, May 9, 1807, C.O. 23/51, 60.

13. Testimony of Chief Constable Smith, C.O. 23/54, 292–93.

14. Cameron to Bathurst, May 8, 1815, C.O. 23/62, 29–30.

15. Cameron to Bathurst, January 24, 1816, C.O. 23/63, 69–71.

16. Colbert Williams, *The Methodist Contribution to Education in the Bahamas* (Gloucester: Privately published, 1982).

17. 1815 Regulations, C.O. 23/67, 154–60.

18. February 4, 1817, C.O. 23/64, 118; James M. Wright, "History of the Bahama Islands, with a Special Study of the Abolition of Slavery in the Colony," in *The Bahama Islands*, ed. G.B. Shattuck (Baltimore: Geographical Society of Baltimore, 1905), 433; Craton, *History of the Bahamas*, 184.

19. C.O. 23/63, 187–88.

20. C.O. 23/63, 38–41; C.O. 23/59, 40.

21. C.O. 23/67, 103–14.

22. C.O. 23/67, 115–16.

23. Wylly to African Institution, December 26, 1815, C.O. 23/64, 230–32.

24. C.O. 23/64, 59–91, 112–19, 229–32; Riley, *Homeward Bound*, 203–5.

25. Parrish, "Southern Loyalists," 477–81.

26. David Eltis, "The Traffic in Slaves Between the British West Indian Colonies, 1807–1833," *Economic History Review*, 2d ser., 25, no. 1 (February 1972): 55–64; Higman, *Slave Populations of the British Caribbean*, 79–85.

27. Grant to Bathurst, August 1, 1821, C.O. 23/70, 51–53; C.O. 23/71, 5–6; C.O. 23/72, 5.

28. Eltis, "Traffic in Slaves," 58.

29. C.O. 23/78, 232–36; C.O. 23/75, 50–52; Michael Craton, "Changing Patterns of Slave Families in the British West Indies," *Journal of Interdisciplinary History* 10 (Summer 1979): 1–35.

30. C.O. 23/72, 25; C.O. 23/75, 50–52.

31. Eltis, "Traffic in Slaves," 53.

32. Acts 55 Geo III c.9 (1814); 57 Geo III c.9 (1816); 7 Geo II c.5 (1826).

33. 57 Geo III c.9 (1816), 204.

34. 2 Geo IV c.37 (1822), 70–73.

35. 57 Geo III c.9 (1816), 223–26.

36. 4 Geo IV c.6 (1824), 223–55.

37. 7 Geo IV c.1 (1826), 335–65.

38. 10 Geo IV c.13 (1830), 239–60; 4 Will IV c.21 (1834), 122–67.

39. Memorial to King from Free People of Colour in Nassau, 1831 (with 337 signatures), April 1832, C.O. 23/86, 147–60; from Andros (50 signatures), May 7, 1832, C.O. 23/86, 250–52; from Current Island, 1832, C.O. 23/68, 270–71; Carmichael Smyth to Goderich, September 3, 1832, C.O. 23/86, 430, and November 2, 1832, C.O. 23/87, 41–43. In fact, a very small number of colored if not black

freemen had enjoyed the vote before 1830, but could only do so if authorized by a special act of the Assembly. One such person was Murray George Farquharson of Crooked Island, extended the privilege in 1829 (*Journal of the House of Assembly*, December 11, 1892). Nonwhites, though, could not sit in the Assembly until after the passage of the civil liberties act of 4 William IV, c.1 in 1833, the first three, including Stephen Dillet, being elected in January 1834.

40. 4 Will IV c.1 (1833), 3–5.

41. Munnings to Peel, December 12, 1810, July 16, 1812, C.O. 23/59, 37; *Bahamas Blue Book, 1828–1834*, C.O. 27/26–32; Saunders, *Slavery in the Bahamas*, 53.

Chapter 15

1. Mary K. Armbrister, ed., "Henrietta, My Daughter" (Typescript, Bahamas Archives); [Dr. P. S. Townsend], *Nassau, Bahamas, 1823–24*, (Nassau: Bahamas Historical Society, 1980); Adela Del Lorraine [Hart], *Letters from the Bahama Islands* (Philadelphia, 1827).

2. Armbrister, "Henrietta, My Daughter," v., vii; Sabine, *The American Loyalists*; *Bahama Gazette*, April 5, 1790.

3. Armbrister, "Henrietta, My Daughter," xiv–xv. John Kelsall's obituary was in the *Bahama Gazette*, April 15, 1803. He was buried in St. Matthew's churchyard, where his headstone can still be seen.

4. Captain George Fowke, R.N., *Bahama Gazette*, July 10, 1797; Armbrister, "Henrietta, My Daughter," xiv.

5. Mary Elizabeth Kelsall to Lucretia Kelsall, Blair Cottage, June 10, 1802, in "Henrietta, My Daughter," ed. Armbrister, 119.

6. Deposited in the Bahamas Archives, 1980.

7. Mary Elizabeth Kelsall to Anne Lewin, April 1804, in "Henrietta, My Daughter," ed. Armbrister, 80–81.

8. Mary Elizabeth Kelsall to Anne Lewin, July 21, 1808, in "Henrietta, My Daughter," ed. Armbrister, 83–84.

9. Henrietta Kelsall to Eleanor Kelsall, September 26, 1813, in "Henrietta, My Daughter," ed. Armbrister, 130.

10. Henrietta Kelsall to Anne Lewin, December 4, 1813, in "Henrietta, My Daughter," ed. Armbrister, 132–33. The arrival of Jane Austen's *Pride and Prejudice* was remarkably prompt. Though written in an earlier draft entitled "First Impressions" as early as 1797, it was not published until early in 1813.

11. Henrietta Kelsall to Anne Lewin, February 4, 1814, in "Henrietta, My Daughter," ed. Armbrister, 135.

12. Henrietta Kelsall to Anne Lewin, July 8, 1814, in "Henrietta, My Daughter," ed. Armbrister, 137, 143; *Bahama Gazette*, April 20, 1814.

13. Ibid., 165. Whether this referred to the hill resort of Montpellier in southern France, or the resort town in Vermont named after it (or even to James Madison's mountain estate of the same name, near Richmond, Virginia) is not exactly clear.

14. Henrietta Kelsall to Anne Lewin, 1815, in "Henrietta, My Daughter," ed. Armbrister, 165.

15. Ibid., 223–300; below, chap. 19, p. 384.

16. Mary Elizabeth Kelsall to Anne Lewin, the Hermitage, Little Exuma, April 25, 1804, in "Henrietta, My Daughter," ed. Armbrister, 36.

17. Mary Elizabeth Kelsall to Anne Lewin, the Hermitage, Little Exuma, August, 1804, in "Henrietta, My Daughter," ed. Armbrister, 48.

18. Mary Elizabeth Kelsall to Anne Lewin, 1806, in "Henrietta, My Daughter," ed. Armbrister, 60–61.

19. Ibid., 63, 67.

20. Mary Elizabeth Kelsall to Anne Lewin, Nassau ("By Captain Sands, with a box of preserves"), May 11, 1807, in "Henrietta, My Daughter," ed. Armbrister, 72–73.

21. Mary Elizabeth Kelsall to Lucretia Kelsall, Nassau, August 31, 1807, in "Henrietta, My Daughter," ed. Armbrister, 74–75.

22. Henrietta Kelsall to Anne Lewin, May 1814, in "Henrietta, My Daughter," ed. Armbrister, 144.

23. Henrietta Kelsall to Anne Lewin, July 1814, in "Henrietta, My Daughter," ed. Armbrister, 149.

24. Entry for December 10, 1823, *Nassau, Bahamas, 1823–24*, 12.

25. Armbrister, "Henrietta, My Daughter," 94; Munnings to Bathurst, May 5, 1827, C.O. 23/776, 224.

26. December 8, 1823, *Nassau, Bahamas, 1823–24*, 9–10.

27. December 9, 1823, *Nassau, Bahamas, 1823–24*, 11.

28. December 19, 1823, *Nassau, Bahamas, 1823–24*, 16.

29. December 23, 1823, *Nassau, Bahamas, 1823–24*, 18.

30. Matthew Gregory Lewis, *Journal of a West India Planter, Kept During a Residence in the Island of Jamaica* (London: Murray, 1834), 60–63.

31. Del Lorraine, *Letters*, no. 9, 41–43.

32. December 24, 1823, *Nassau, Bahamas, 1823–24*, 19–20.

33. December 25, 1823, *Nassau, Bahamas, 1823–24*, 20–21.

34. Entries for December 14, 21, 1823, *Nassau, Bahamas, 1823–24*, 13, 17.

35. March 22, 1824, *Nassau, Bahamas, 1823–24*, 36.

36. January 16, 1824, *Nassau, Bahamas, 1823–24*, 25.

37. Entries for December 20, 21, 1823, *Nassau, Bahamas, 1823–24*, 16, 17.

38. Del Lorraine, *Letters*, 35–37. See also January 1 and April 23, 1824, *Nassau, Bahamas, 1823–24*, 24, 38.

39. Del Lorraine, *Letters*, 56–57. See also January 28, 1824, *Nassau, Bahamas, 1823–24*, 28–29.

40. Friday, April 23, 1824, *Nassau, Bahamas, 1823–24*, 38.

41. Richard Ligon, *True and Exact History of the Island of Barbados* (London: N.p., 1657), 46.

42. Del Lorraine, *Letters*, no. 9, 40–41.

43. January 3, 1824, *Nassau, Bahamas, 1823–24*, 23.

44. Del Lorraine, *Letters*, no. 11, 57–58; Riley, *Homeward Bound*, 256 n. 6; Stark, *History and Guide*, 183–85.

45. Wednesday, January 14, 1824, *Nassau, Bahamas, 1823–24*, 24.

46. *Bahama Gazette*, April 22, 1813.

47. Ibid., May 16, 1813. The popular emulation of such novelties, often with very rapid success, is a recurrent theme in Bahamian social history. For one example, see the introduction of the triple jump in athletics in the mid-twentieth century and the rapid achievement of world-class performances by Bahamians, described in part 3 of vol. 2.

48. May 16, 1824, *Nassau, Bahamas, 1823–24*, 17–18.

49. June 30, 1824, *Nassau, Bahamas, 1823–24*, 44.

50. April 1, 1824, *Nassau, Bahamas, 1823–24*, 36–37.

51. April 1 and September 10, 1824, *Nassau, Bahamas, 1823–24*, 36–46.

52. September 10, 1824, *Nassau, Bahamas, 1823–24*, 46.

Chapter 16

1. C.O. 23/63, 37–41; William Wylly, *Regulations for the Government of the Slaves at Clifton and Tusculum in New Providence* (Nassau: Royal Gazette, 1815), and in C.O. 23/67, 154–60.

2. C.O. 23/63, 37–39.

3. C.O. 23/47, 51, 23/48, 144–46 (1805); C.O. 23/59, 37 (1810).

4. The 1810 census listed only 16,617 but did not include either Abaco or Andros. C.O. 23/59, 37.

5. B.S.P., *Accounts and Papers*, 1789, XXVI, iv, 15; Michael Craton, *Searching for the Invisible Man*, 72–73.

6. The figures for Abaco were not given either in 1805 or 1810 but were almost certainly similar to those for Harbour Island and Eleuthera.

7. Governors' Dispatches, duplicates, 1818–25, 755, Bahamas Archives, Nassau; Saunders, *Slavery in the Bahamas*, 52. The total for 1810 given in table 5 is slightly higher, but the figures for Abaco and Andros were estimates.

8. Act of 2 Geo IV c.16 (1821), amended by 3 Geo IV, c.13 (1823), 9 Geo IV c.4 (1828), and 4 William IV, c.17 (1834).

9. Register of Returns of Slaves, 1822–34, 9 vols., Bahamas Archives, Nassau; Register of Returns of Slaves, T/456–60, Public Record Office, London.

10. They were also pioneer materials in the history of demography and demographic theory. See Barry W. Higman, "Slavery and the Development of Demographic Theory in the Age of the Industrial Revolution," in *Slavery and British Society, 1776–1846*, ed. James Walvin (London: Macmillan, 1982), 164–94.

11. See below, pp. 291–96.

12. James Stephen, *The Slavery of the British West India Colonies Delineated*, 2 vols.

(London: 1, Butterworth, 1824; 2, Hatchard, 1830); Higman, *Slave Populations of the British Caribbean*.

13. Craton, "Changing Patterns."

14. Higman, *Slave Populations of the British Caribbean*, 74.

15. Ibid., 314–22.

16. Alexander M. Tulloch and Henry Marshall, *Statistical Reports on the Sickness, Mortality, and Invaliding Among the Troops in the West Indies* (London: War Office, 1839); George W. Roberts, "A Life Table for a West Indian Slave Population," *Population Studies* 5 (March 1952): 238–43, and *The Population of Jamaica* (Cambridge: Cambridge University Press, 1957), 165–67; Cambridge B.S.P., A. & P., 1831–32, 45:33; Craton, *In Search of the Invisible Man*, 85–99; Higman, *Slave Populations of the British Caribbean*, 333–78.

17. The actual figures for registered manumissions were 653 between 1774 and 1806 and 1,588 between 1807 and 1834, with 235 in the full three-year period from 1827 to 1830, and 339 during the thirty-one months between January 1831 and August 1834; Register of Freed Slaves, Eighteenth and Nineteenth Century, and Register of Returns of Slaves, 1822–34, Bahamas Archives, Nassau; Saunders, *Slavery in the Bahamas*, 68–76.

18. Saunders, *Slavery in the Bahamas*, 106–9, and "Slave Population of the Bahamas," 272–82.

19. Miscegenation is a difficult, as well as loaded, term. The number of persons designated as mulattos or coloreds would, of course, increase almost exponentially through the pairing of colored people as well as of free white males with black or colored women, slave or free. Saunders, "Slave Population of the Bahamas," 223–34.

20. Ibid., 196–216; Saunders, *Slavery in the Bahamas*, 94; Craton, *In Search of the Invisible Man*, 22–39; Higman, *Slave Population in Jamaica*, 68–71.

21. Map of Original Holdings, New Providence, Department of Lands and Surveys, Nassau.

22. Slave Compensation Returns, 1834, Bahamas Archives, Nassau; Saunders, *Slavery in the Bahamas*, 117–20.

23. That is, 239 out of 968 mulattos, out of 2,003 domestics, or 24.7 percent compared with 20 percent.

24. The Bahamian Slave Registration Act of 1821 veered from the 1756 act defining color gradations (among free persons) to state specifically: "All slaves removed any degree whatever from the black ancestor shall be deemed and taken to be mulattoes," whereas the most common West Indian practice, "as set out in the St. Vincent Act, and following the Trinidad Order in Council, was to list the slaves as 'Negro, Mulatto or Mustee, as the case may be, or such designation of intermediate shades of colour (if any) as are in use in these colonies.'" Higman, *Slave Population of the British Caribbean*, 20, citing B.S.P. *1823, XVIII (68)*, 5; B.S.P. *1817, XVII (338)*, 23; C.O. 295/28, 252.

25. Saunders, "Slave Population in the Bahamas," 254.

26. Higman, *Slave Population of the British Caribbean*, 307–10, 32–35. Note that the birth- and deathrate figures given by Higman are adjusted for undercounting due to deaths before registration, though if anything this points up even more clearly the disparity between the Bahamas and most of the sugar islands.

27. The Bahamas case was very similar to those of Anguilla and Barbuda, and probably Bermuda and Belize, for which the statistics are not available. Not far behind in demographic performance were the Virgin Islands and Montserrat, which had almost ceased sugar production, though the long-established and cre-olized sugar islands of Barbados, St. Kitts, and Nevis also had positive natural increases registered before the end of slavery. Ibid., 307–10.

28. A full demographic analysis of the Bermudian slaves during the registration period remains to be undertaken. Higman excluded Bermuda (along with the Cape of Good Hope, Mauritius, the Seychelles, and Ceylon) "in order to preserve the unity of the Caribbean as a geographical region and reduce the complexity of contextual variables." Ibid., 3.

29. Craton, "Changing Patterns." In our study of the Williams slaves we are partially indebted to Geoffrey P. Dunlop, "Family Patterns Among the Williams Slaves (1821–1834)" (M.A. thesis, University of Waterloo, 1978).

30. "Return showing the number of Negroes imported into this Island by Burton Williams Esq.," enclosed in Governor Woodford to Huskisson, March 7, 1828, C.O. 295/77, 33–49; R.R.S., 1821–34, Bahamas Archives; Register of Returns of Slaves, 1825–34, Public Record Office, London.

31. Evidence by Burton Williams to Trinidad Council, January 18, 1825, C.O. 295/66, 53–59.

32. Craton, "Changing Patterns," 19–21.

33. Williams slave transfers, Bahamian slave transfers, and Trinidad slaves, general, 1819–34, T. 71/501-519, Public Record Office, London; Higman, *Slave Populations of the British Caribbean*, 280–92.

34. January 18, 1825, C.O. 295/66, 53–59.

35. Ibid., 57.

36. Governor Woodford to Bathurst, April 13, 1826, C.O. 295/71, 26.

Chapter 17

1. C.O. 295/66, 55; Wills, Christopher Neely, April 15, 1807, proved September 10, 1807, Bahamas Archives.

2. Wylly, *Regulations*, 147ff., reprinted in Saunders, *Slavery in the Bahamas*, appendix 2, 228–30.

3. That is, the near equivalent of the twenty-one pints of flour, seven quarts of rice, or fifty-six pounds of potatoes (for those over ten years old) specified in the 1797 act. See above, chap. 13, p. 208.

4. Wylly to Munnings, August 31, 1818, enclosed in Munnings to Bathurst, September 9, 1818, C.O. 23/67, 147–50.

5. Enclosure in Wylly to Munnings, October 3, 1818, enclosed in Munnings to Bathurst, same date, C.O. 23/67, 165.

6. Wylly to overseer James Rutherford, August 24, 1818, C.O. 23/67, 165.

7. *Bahama Gazette*, January 24, 1821.

8. Apparently the only exceptions were Sarah, aged twenty-one, and Tom, aged nineteen, the children of Tom Deveaux, manumitted on January 1, 1826, and perhaps Tom Deveaux himself; R.R.S., 1828, Bahamas Archives.

9. R.R.S., 1822. Richard Peages (aged fifty-nine), his wife, Louisa (thirty-seven), and children Tilla (twenty-four) and Mary (nineteen) were drowned. Patrick (twenty-one) escaped and was shipped to St. Vincent in February 1823. Anthony (twenty-two) and Tom (sixteen) were left behind in Nassau, where they were later sold. R.R.S., 1825–34.

10. Ibid. All survived until emancipation, when they were aged sixty-one, fifty-four, twenty-five, twenty-two, eighteen, and seventeen respectively. Boatswain was listed as a field laborer and salt jobber, Chloe as a sick nurse and midwife, the children as field slaves and salt rakers at Long Cay.

11. Thomas Pringle, ed., *The History of Mary Prince, a West Indian Slave, Related by Herself* (London: Westley and Davis, 1831), quoted by Higman, *Slave Populations of the British Caribbean*, 227.

12. Kiple, *The Caribbean Slave*, 78–79.

13. Pringle, *Mary Prince*, 10.

14. Kiple, *The Caribbean Slave*, 76–88.

15. Ibid., 82–85.

16. Robert Montgomery Martin, *Statistics of the Colonies of the British Empire* (London: W. H. Allen, 1839), 110; Saunders, *Slavery in the Bahamas*, 21, 33; Higman, *Slave Populations of the British Caribbean*, 703.

17. *The Salt Industry of the Bahamas*, Handbook of Archives Exhibition, February 1980, Department of Archives, Nassau.

18. Michael Craton, "Hobbesian or Panglossian? The Two Extremes of Slave Conditions in the British Caribbean, 1783 to 1834," *William and Mary Quarterly*, 3d ser., 35 (April 1978): 324–56.

19. Rolle to Bathurst, March 31, 1825, C.O. 23/74, 275–76.

20. Grace to Carmichael Smyth, enclosed in Carmichael Smyth to Murray, June 29, 1830, C.O. 23/82, 355–67.

21. Kiple, *The Caribbean Slave*, 7–22.

22. Ibid., 89–103; Pringle, *Mary Prince*, 9–13.

23. Kiple, *The Caribbean Slave*, 146–48.

24. Ibid., 123–25; Higman, *Slave Populations of the British Caribbean*, 339–46.

25. C.O. 295/66, 56; Higman, *Slave Populations of the British Caribbean*, 25–34, 310, 314–22. Above, chap. 16, pp. 271–76.

26. Higman, *Slave Populations of the British Caribbean*, table 9.1, p. 310.

27. Pringle, *Mary Prince*, 11.

28. *Nassau, Bahamas, 1823–24*, 17–18, 40, 42.

29. Ibid., 44.

30. Ibid., 46. Above, chap. 15, pp. 256–57.

31. Kiple, *The Caribbean Slave*, 120–25.

32. Higman, *Slave Populations of the British Caribbean*, 22, 12, 24–25. The Berbice returns sometimes give family and relationship details, the Jamaican returns intermittent details of relationships.

33. Craton, "Changing Patterns," 1–35.

34. Barry W. Higman, "African and Creole Slave Family Patterns in Trinidad," *Journal of Family History* 3 (1978): 163–80, "Household Structure and Fertility on Jamaican Slave Plantations: A Nineteenth Century Example," *Population Studies* 27 (1973): 527–50, and "The Slave Family and Household in the British West Indies, 1800–1834," *Journal of Interdisciplinary History* 6 (1975): 261–87; Edith Clarke, *My Mother Who Fathered Me* (London: Andre Deutsch, 1957).

35. Craton, "Changing Patterns," table 1, p. 9.

36. Ibid., table 2, p. 10. This table, though, includes many older mothers whose earlier offspring had left the household and were thus missing from the record. Excluding the 251 of 479 mothers who were aged 35 or more when the census was made, the average age of the remainder at the birth of their first surviving child was 19.27 years.

37. Ibid., fig. 2, p. 7.

38. C.O. 295/67, 219; 295/71, 26; 295/78, 233–36; 23/82, 45.

39. October 20, 1788, C.O. 137/88; Craton, "Changing Patterns," 1.

40. For example, Governor Carmichael Smyth's speech to the SPCK Nassau chapter, reported in *Royal Gazette* 17: 1681, March 6, 1830.

41. *Bahama Gazette* 2:52, July 23–30, 1875.

42. Indenture, John Brown to Stephen Delancey, book 02, 159–61, Registrar General's Department, Nassau; Delancey Town plan, 1903, Department of Lands and Surveys, Nassau; *Settlements in New Providence*, Handbook of Archives Exhibition (Nassau: Department of Archives, 1982), 17.

43. Ibid.

44. Antonina Canzoneri, "Early History of Baptists in the Bahamas," *Journal of the Bahamas Historical Society* 4, no. 1 (October 1982): 9–16.

45. Pascoe, *Two Hundred Years*.

46. A. Deans Peggs, ed., *Dowson's Journal* (Nassau: Privately published, 1961); Williams, *Methodist Contribution*.

47. Craton, *History of the Bahamas*, 170–71; Riley, *Homeward Bound*, 248 n. 19.

48. Acts of 57 Geo III, c.9.

49. Pringle, *Mary Prince*, 13; Canzoneri, "History of Baptists," 11.

50. Grant to Goderich, February 10, 1824, Duplicate Correspondence 5, 1834, Bahamas Archives.

51. *Royal Gazette*, 14:1411, August 4, 1827; October 31, 1827; April 29, 1829; November 26, 1836.

52. *Bahamas Argus* 1: xvii, March 7, 1831.

53. Ibid.

54. Canzoneri, "Baptists in the Bahamas," 12.

55. Ibid., 57.

Chapter 18

1. The journal, discovered and transcribed in 1903 by Ormond McDonald, assistant resident justice in San Salvador, was published by Alfred Deans Peggs as *A Relic of Slavery: Farquharson's Journal for 1831–2* (Nassau: Deans Peggs Research Fund, 1957).

2. See also Kathy Gerace, "Three Loyalist Plantations," *Florida Anthropologist* 35, no. 4 (December 1982): 216–22; Riley, *Homeward Bound*, 215–19; Saunders, *Slavery in the Bahamas*, 109–13, 149–57.

3. Riley, *Homeward Bound*, 258 n. 5; Charles Farquharson's will, O.R.G. C4, 74–75, Office of the Registrar General, Nassau; *Royal Gazette*, May 29 and June 9, 1824.

4. *Royal Gazette*, April 4, 1835.

5. Notably the family of Alick the head driver, whose parents, Charles and Rachel, were Africans, and his wife, Eliza, whose father, Harry, certainly and mother, Mary, probably were Africans. R.R.S., 1822.

6. Ibid., 1822–34.

7. Peggs, *A Relic of Slavery*, 64.

8. Ibid., 75.

9. The value of the furniture compared with £24 for sixty gallons of rum, £674 for stock animals, and £1,384 for slaves; O.R.G. C4, 74–75; Slave Compensation Returns, 1834, Bahamas Archives, Nassau.

10. Peggs, *A Relic of Slavery*, 67; Adm 151, HMS *Blossom*, 1829–32, May 29, 1832, Public Record Office, London.

11. Partial exceptions were the whole holidays for some slaves on July 9, 1831, and March 3, 1832; Peggs, *A Relic of Slavery*, 24, 53.

12. In 1834 only thirty-one of the fifty-two Farquharson slaves were listed as field workers and eleven as domestics (with nine of the total being under six and only one reckoned too old to work). But only four of the listed domestics worked in the Great House, the remainder being employed mainly in the fields; R.R.S., July 1834, 391.

13. Peggs, *A Relic of Slavery*, 75–76.

14. Ibid., 55–57.

15. O.R.G. C4, 74–75; S.C.R., 1834, 391. The £1,384 estimated value of Farquharson's slaves was broken down as follows: twenty-one efficient field slaves, £735; ten inferior field slaves, £199; four head domestics, £180; seven inferior do-

mestics, £175; nine children under six, £90; one superannuated slave, £5. Instead of the estimated average value of about £27, Farquharson's estate in fact received an average of some £18.10s.

16. Peggs, *A Relic of Slavery*, 5, 28, 71.

17. See, for example, Joel S. Savashinsky, ed., *Strangers No More: Anthropological Studies of Cat Island, the Bahamas* (Ithaca, N.Y.: Ithaca College, 1978), 75–96.

18. Peggs, *A Relic of Slavery*, 12–15, 72.

19. Ibid., 3.

20. Ibid., 4.

21. Ibid., 6.

22. Ibid., 16–17, 44–45, 70–71, 78–79.

23. Ibid., 17. Sarah Lowther/Lauder had left San Salvador on March 5, 1831. Mrs. Dean and Mr. Vass were probably Farquharson's hosts in Nassau, and Vass may have been his agent. See n. 39 below.

24. Ibid., 44–45, 48.

25. Ibid., 38–45.

26. Ibid., 47–48.

27. Ibid., 81–82.

28. Ibid., 46.

29. But see the entry for Saturday, February 3, 1832: "The people has today to themselves in return for Sunday 5th Feby that they went to Sandy Point to bring some of the light lugage home." Ibid., 53.

30. Ibid., 30, 80.

31. Ibid., 82–84.

32. Ormond McDonald's manuscript has the note "The missing dates from Decr 9th to Feby 13th are lost by being torn out of the Journal." Ibid., 48.

33. May 14, 1831; ibid., 15.

34. Ibid., 51.

35. Apparently, the crop for 1832 was a fifth less than for 1831. February 24, 1832; ibid., 52.

36. February 20–21, 1832; ibid., 50–51.

37. Charles Farquharson, Watling's Island, March 21, 1832, O'Brien Collection, Bahamas Archives.

38. C.O. 23/68, 170–71. This, apparently, was the only occasion when the Farquharson estate came to the notice of the governor. The reputation of Sir James Carmichael Smyth as a liberal and friend of the slaves was exaggerated by the diehard Bahamian slaveowners. Governor between 1829 and 1835, he was zealous in carrying out his instructions but equally firm in suppressing any incidents of slave unrest. Of Scots extraction, Smyth (1779–1838) had been a professional military engineer who served on Wellington's staff at Waterloo. Made baronet (1821) and promoted to major-general (1826) under Wellington's patronage, he was responsible for surveys of the defenses of the West Indies, Canada, and Ireland before being appointed governor of the Bahamas. Transferred to be gov-

ernor of Guyana in 1833, he was in that colony through the troubled transition of slave emancipation before dying suddenly of a fever at age fifty-nine.

39. Peggs, *A Relic of Slavery*, 57–64. According to the R.R.S. for 1834, both Alick (aged thirty-two) and Mary Ann (nineteen) were sold in 1832 to the same Mr. Vass mentioned earlier. This was almost certainly the William Vass, J.P., sacked by Governor Carmichael Smyth along with Robert Duncombe (and John Anderson) in 1830. See below, chap. 19, p. 384.

40. Riley, *Homeward Bound*, 214–19.

Chapter 19

1. Edward Long, *History of Jamaica*, 3 vols. (London: Lowndes, 1774), 1:25; Bryan Edwards, *The History, Civil and Commercial, of the British Colonies in the West Indies*, 3 vols. (London: Stockdale, 1793), 3:36. The literature of slave resistance is now immense, but for the British West Indies, including the Bahamas, the following provide an adequate range and survey: James, *The Black Jacobins*; Herbert Aptheker, *American Negro Slave Revolts* (New York: Columbia University Press, 1943); Raymond Bauer and Alice Bauer, "Day to Day Resistance to Slavery," *Journal of Negro History* 27 (October 1942); Gerald W. Mullin, *Flight and Rebellion: Slave Resistance in Eighteenth-Century Virginia* (New York: Oxford University Press, 1972); Richard Price, ed., *Maroon Societies: Rebel Slave Communities in the Americas* (New York: Doubleday, 1973); Packwood, *Chained on the Rock*; O. Nigel Bolland, *The Formation of a Colonial Society: Belize from Conquest to Crown Colony* (Baltimore: Johns Hopkins University Press, 1977); Genovese, *From Rebellion to Revolution*; Craton, *Testing the Chains*; Hilary Beckles, *Black Rebellion in Barbados: The Struggle Against Slavery, 1627–1838* (Bridgetown, Barbados: Antilles Press, 1984), and *Natural Rebels: A Social History of Enslaved Black Women in Barbados* (New Brunswick, N.J.: Rutgers University Press, 1989); Thomas J. Davis, *A Rumor of Revolt: The "Great Negro Plot" in Colonial New York* (New York: Free Press, 1985); David Barry Gaspar, *Bondmen and Rebels: A Study of Master-Slave Relations in Antigua, with Implications for Colonial British America* (Baltimore: Johns Hopkins University Press, 1985); Robert Paquette, *Sugar Is Made with Blood: The Conspiracy of La Escalera and the Conflict Between Empires over Slavery in Cuba* (Middletown, Conn.: Wesleyan University Press, 1988); Blackburn, *Overthrow of Colonial Slavery*; Mavis Campbell, *The Maroons of Jamaica 1655–1796: A History of Resistance, Collaboration, and Betrayal* (Granby, Mass.: Bergin and Garvey, 1988); Barbara Bush, *Slave Women in Caribbean Society, 1650–1838* (London: James Currey, 1990).

2. Above, chaps. 10, 12, 13.

3. By the Slave Act of 1767, slaveowners were bound to advertise their runaways "in the usual publick places." Until the coming of the Loyalists and the printing of the first newspapers in 1784, this normally meant posting a notice at the Vendue House on Nassau's Bay Street. Unfortunately, none of these ad-

vertisements has survived. The *Bahama Gazette*, published by John Wells, first appeared on August 7, 1784, and continued until 1857. During the slavery period it was joined by the *Royal Gazette* (1804–13) and the *Bahama Argus* (1831–40), both of which carried runaway advertisements. Nearly complete runs of these newspapers still exist in the Bahamas Archives, in microfilm as well as the rather decayed original form. In the present work we are specially indebted to the work of Godwin L. Friday, as laid out in a 1984 University of Waterloo M.A. thesis, "Fifty Years of Freedom: Runaway Slaves in the Bahamas, 1784–1834."

4. *Bahama Gazette*, July 26, 1799; November 19, 1785; February 27, 1798; November 19, 1785; July 21, 1797. The whole question of slave "criminality" is, of course, problematical. If a slave was legally a chattel how could he or she, logically, commit a crime? An Afro-Caribbean proverb encapsulates this: "Massa horse, massa grass." For a Brazilian discussion, see Leila Mezan Algranti, "Criminalidade Escrava e Controle Social no Rio de Janeiro, 1810–1821," and Maria Helene Machado, "Trabalho, Compensacão e Crime: Estratégias e Contra-Estratégias," in *Estudos Econômicas*, São Paulo, special no. 18 (1988): 45–80, 81–102.

5. *Bahama Gazette*, November 3, 1814; *Royal Gazette*, January 17, 1824, and March 13, 1833.

6. *Bahama Gazette*, May 14, 1799, January 31, 1800, and May 18, 1819; *Royal Gazette*, September 17, 1808.

7. *Bahama Gazette*, October 28, 1786.

8. Craton, *Testing the Chains*, 99–158. The relatively few Africans, and the even smaller number whose ethnicity is suggested in the Bahamian advertisements, include three Angolas, three Congoes, two "Guinea born," two Fulani, and one each Senegal, Ebo, and Quaqua.

9. *Bahama Gazette*, November 21, 1800.

10. *Bahama Gazette*, July 15, 1794, and October 6, 1797.

11. *Bahama Gazette*, June 5, 1792.

12. *Bahama Gazette*, January 19, 1790, September 23, 1791, and May 27, 1800.

13. Above, chap. 13, pp. 207–8; *Bahama Gazette*, September 20, 1799.

14. *Bahama Gazette*, October 1, 1793.

15. *Bahama Gazette*, February 5, 1785.

16. *Bahama Gazette*, May 28, 1812.

17. *Royal Gazette*, January 2, 1808.

18. *Royal Gazette*, June 3, 1786; *Bahama Gazette*, September 30, 1800.

19. *Bahama Gazette*, November 21, 1789.

20. *Bahama Gazette*, February 7, 1789, and July 15, 1796. The reward offered in 1789 was fifteen dollars; that in 1796 was simply described as "handsome."

21. *Bahama Gazette*, May 10, 1791.

22. *Royal Gazette*, June 19, 1816.

23. *Bahama Gazette*, February 22, 1799, June 25, 1799, March 5, 1799, May 10, 1799, and August 26, 1800.

24. *Bahama Gazette*, January 21, 1800; *Royal Gazette*, January 20, 1821, and March 28, 1818.

25. Friday, "Fifty Years of Freedom"; *Bahama Gazette*, January 29, 1793.

26. *Bahama Gazette*, October 14, 1800, and May 14, 1817. Craton, *History of the Bahamas*, 184–85.

27. *Bahama Gazette*, January 14, 1786.

28. Craton, *Testing the Chains*, 61–96.

29. Above, chap. 12, p. 187.

30. *Bahama Gazette*, June 13, 1789, and February 27, 1798.

31. *Bahama Gazette*, August 30, 1790, and June 13, 1813.

32. *Royal Gazette*, August 6, 1817; David E. Wood, *A Guide to Selected Sources for the History of the Seminole Settlements at Red Bays, Andros, 1817–1980* (Nassau: Archives Department, 1989).

33. *Bahama Gazette*, February 23, 1796, May 11, 1796, and June 15, 1798.

34. *Bahama Gazette*, July 17, 1798, August 6, 1799, and August 20, 1799.

35. *Royal Gazette*, May 21, 1823.

36. *Royal Gazette*, August 28, 1824.

37. Neville A. Hall, "Maritime Maroons: *Grand Marronage* from the Danish West Indies," *William and Mary Quarterly*, 3d ser., 42 (October 1985): 476–98.

38. *Bahama Gazette*, May 7, 1785.

39. *Bahama Gazette*, July 18, 1789, October 24, 1789, and December 26, 1789.

40. *Bahama Gazette*, October 14, 1800; *Royal Gazette*, May 14, 1808.

41. Rebecca Scott, *Slavery and Emancipation in Cuba: The Transition to Free Labor, 1860–1899* (Princeton, N.J.: Princeton University Press, 1985).

42. *Bahama Gazette*, February 18, 1794, February 19, 1799, and June 14, 1812.

43. *Royal Gazette*, May 11, 1816; *Bahama Gazette*, September 1, 1795.

44. C.O. 23/63, 37–39.

45. *Bahama Gazette*, November 26, 1790, January 28, 1794, and February 14, 1792.

46. *Royal Gazette*, January 28, 1810, and February 14, 1810.

47. Carmichael Smyth to Goderich, August 9, 1832, C.O. 23/87, 302.

48. *Royal Gazette*, August 4, 1810, and November 7, 1810; *Bahama Gazette*, April 20, 1815.

49. *Royal Gazette*, January 11, 1804.

50. *Bahama Gazette*, June 23, 1799.

51. *Bahama Gazette*, May 11, 1800; *Royal Gazette*, June 27, 1832.

52. *Bahama Gazette*, June 24, 1800, March 2, 1792, and October 27, 1795.

53. Craton, *History of the Bahamas*, 190; Riley, *Homeward Bound*; Saunders, *Slavery in the Bahamas*, 175.

54. *Royal Gazette*, June 11, 1831.

55. *Bahama Gazette*, May 17, 1791, July 1, 1794, and May 8, 1798; *Royal Gazette*, May 11, 1807.

56. For previous treatments of the Rolle slaves, see Michael Craton, "Hobbesian or Panglossian?," "Changing Patterns," and "We Shall Not Be Moved: Pompey's Proto-Peasant Slave Revolt in Exuma Island, Bahamas, 1829–

1830," *Nieuwe West Indische Gids*, Spring 1983; Saunders, *Slavery in the Bahamas*, 184–88.

57. Craton, "Hobbesian or Panglossian?" 333.

58. Rolle to Bathurst, August 12, 1824, C.O. 23/73, 257; Rolle to Bathurst, March 31, 1825, C.O. 23/74, 275–76; Woodford to Bathurst, December 31, 1825, and April 13, 1826, C.O. 295/67, 219, 295/71, 26; Farquharson to Huskisson, October 12, 1828, C.O. 295/78, 233–38; Craton, "We Shall Not Be Moved," 25.

59. Lewis Grant (on board HMS *Barham* en route to Trinidad), December 27, 1828, C.O. 23/78, 182. See also Carmichael Smyth to Goderich, March 28, 1833, C.O. 23/88, 108–17.

60. Thompson to Taylor, November 21, 1828, C.O. 23/78, 170.

61. Listed as Seaborn (aged fifty-five), Damon and wife (fifty-three and fifty-one), March (thirty-two) and wife (name unstated and age not known), Moses (twenty-six), Fanny (eighteen), Young Jack (fifteen), and Amelia (twenty-six). R.R.S., 1828.

62. Grant to Murray, December 27, 1828, C.O. 23/78, 182; McPherson's report, December 10, 1828, C.O. 23/78, 176–78.

63. Thompson to Taylor, November 28, 1828, C.O. 23/78, 180.

64. Rolle to Murray, Great Torrington, August 22, 1829, C.O. 23/81, 275–76.

65. Carmichael Smyth to Murray, January 13, March 22, and June 9, 1830, C.O. 23/82.

66. Ibid. Carmichael Smyth's informant was a Cat Island planter called Hepburn, who feared the Rolle slaves' reputation for rebelliousness.

67. Carmichael Smyth to Murray, June 29, 1830, C.O. 23/82, 355–67.

68. McPherson report, June 29, 1830, C.O. 23/82, 364–65.

69. Grace's report, June 29, 1830, C.O. 23/82, 366–67. See also *Royal Gazette*, April 28, May 8, May 12, and June 12, 1830.

70. *Royal Gazette*, January 4 and February 1, 1832; *Bahama Argus*, March 3, 1832; Saunders, *Slavery in the Bahamas*, 188.

71. Carmichael Smyth to Goderich, August 9, 1832, C.O. 23/87, 345–50; Acting Governor Balfour to Stanley, October 1, 1833, C.O. 23/89, 152–53; Balfour to Spring-Rice, September 9, 1834, C.O. 23/91, 379–80.

72. *Bahama Argus*, January 11, 1832.

73. *Royal Gazette*, January 28, 1832.

74. *Bahama Argus*, January 11, 1832. It is interesting to speculate whether the disturbances would have been greater or less had colored and black freemen been eligible to stand for election, as they became with the passage of the act of 4 William IV, c.1 in 1833. In fact, the general election of January 1834, in which three nonwhites were elected to the Assembly, seems to have been considerably less rowdy than that of January 1832.

75. *Royal Gazette*, March 30, 1832.

76. *Bahama Argus*, April 15, 1833; *Royal Gazette*, April 24, May 18, June 1, July 29, and August 15, 1833.

77. *Bahama Argus*, February 18, 1833.

78. Balfour to Stanley, October 1, 1833, C.O. 23/89, 152–53.

79. Rolle to Spring-Rice, January 6 and 10, 1834, C.O. 23/92, 490–93.

80. Balfour to Spring-Rice, September 13, 1834, C.O. 23/91, 380a–380b.

81. Rolle to Spring-Rice, August 11, 1834, C.O. 23/92, 497.

82. For example, Craton, *History of the Bahamas*, 1st ed. (1962), 210. But see Benson McDermott, *Bahamas Handbook*, 1981, 15–16, 27–31.

Epilogue

1. West Indian Letters, September 1833–February 1835, no. 169, from Thomas Lofthouse, August 8, 1834, and no. 206, from Charles Penny, August 28, 1834, Methodist Missionary Society, London; Balfour to Spring-Rice, September 13, 1834, C.O. 23/92, 400.

2. Colebrooke to Glenelg, August 1, 1835, C.O. 23/93, 74; Duplicate Governors' Despatches, 96, Cockburn to Glenelg, August 6, 1838 (C.O. 23/108), Bahamas Archives, Nassau.

3. M.M.S., Bahamas 1838–40, from Thomas Lofthouse, Harbour Island, August 9, 1838; M.M.S., Bahamas 1838–40, from William West, Nassau, August 6, 1838.

4. Reginald Coupland, *Wilberforce: A Narrative* (Oxford: Oxford University Press, 1923), and *The British Anti-Slavery Movement* (London: Butterworth, 1933); G. R. Mellor, *British Imperial Trusteeship, 1783–1850* (London: Faber, 1951); Roger Anstey, *The Atlantic Slave Trade and British Abolition, 1760–1810* (London: Macmillan, 1975); Seymour Drescher, *Econocide: British Slavery in the Era of Abolition* (Pittsburgh: University of Pittsburgh Press, 1977); Eric Williams, *Capitalism and Slavery* (London: André Deutsch, 1944); Walvin, *Slavery and British Society*; Jack Hayward, ed., *Out of Slavery: Abolition and After* (London: Frank Cass, 1985); Stanley Engerman and Barbara Solow, eds., *Caribbean Slavery and British Capitalism: The Legacy of Eric Williams* (Cambridge: Cambridge University Press, 1987).

Index